Michael Welter

# Diode Dictionary

Michael Welter

# Diode Dictionary

Datenvergleichstabellen
comparsion tables
tables d'équivalence
tablas comparativas

# IWT Verlag GmbH
An International Thomson Publishing Company

Bonn • Albany • Belmont • Boston • Cincinnati • Detroit • London • Madrid
Melbourne • Mexico City • New York • Paris • Singapore • Tokyo

**Die Deutsche Bibliothek – CIP-Einheitsaufnahme**

Welter, Michael:
Diode dictionary: Datenvergleichstabellen / Michael Welter. –
1. Aufl. – Bonn [u.a.]: IWT-Verl., 1995
ISBN: 3-88322-541-X

ISBN 3-88322-541-X
1. Auflage 1995

Printed in Germany
© Copyright 1995 by IWT Verlag GmbH, Bonn

Herstellung: Kösel, Kempten
Umschlaggestaltung: Schiffer Graphic Design, München
Satz: Alfes Computers, Publishing & Graphics, Siegen

# Table of contents
# Inhaltsverzeichnis
# Sommaire
# Indice

# Table of contents

# Inhaltsverzeichnis

# Sommaire

# Indice

# Preface
# Vorwort
# Préface
# Prólogo

# Preface

This table book on hand was compiled using most recent datasheets and manuals provided by well recommended manufacturers. It contains an easy to handle overview of general technical data, typical and maximum ratings for more than 7000 up-to-date diodes. Additionally, information about manufacturers, general device information, case outline drawings and recommended applications are provided.

The book is meant to support the selection of individual device as well being used as a directory to find essential parameters and comparable types. Of course, it cannot replace original manufacturer datasheets. As neither all data nor all test conditions could be stated, it is recommended to consult the manufacturer's original documentation for further details when in doubt.

This first edition of the table book is compiled using device data for the 1990 to 1994 product lines of leading European, American and Japanese Manufacturers.

# Vorwort

Das vorliegende Tabellenbuch entstand auf der Basis der aktuellen Datenbücher namhafter Hersteller. Es enthält in übersichtlicher Form die wichtigsten technischen Grenz- und Kenndaten von etwa 7000 aktuellen Diodentypen. Aufgenommen wurden außerdem die Hersteller und ergänzende Informationen, die Anschlußbilder und Hinweise auf die Anwendung des Bauelementes.

Das Buch ist als Unterstützung bei der Auswahl von Dioden gedacht, außerdem als Nachschlagewerk zum schnellen Auffinden der wichtigsten Parameter und zur Ermittlung von Vergleichstypen. Natürlich kann es nicht die Datenblätter der Hersteller ersetzen. Da weder alle Daten noch die vollständigen Testbedingungen angegeben werden können, empfiehlt es sich, im Zweifelsfall auch die Unterlagen des Herstellers heranzuziehen.

Für die erste Auflage wurde zunächst das aktuelle Sortiment der Jahre 1990 bis 1994 der wichtigsten Hersteller in Europa, den USA und Japan aufgenommen.

# Préface

Le présent recueil de tables tire ses informations des plus récents catalogues de fabricants réputés. Il regroupe de manière facilement accessible les principales caractéristiques techniques d'environ sept mille types de diodes actuels. Des informations complémentaires sur les fabricants et les composants, les schémas extérieurs des boîtiers ainsi que des indications quant à l'utilisation des composants sont également intégrés au recueil.

Le recueil est soit utilisable en tant qu'aide lors du choix de diodes, soit ensuite en tant qu'ouvrage de référence dans le but de retrouver rapidement les paramètres principaux d'un type de diodes ou des types comparables. Il est bien évident qu'il ne peut en aucun cas remplacer les notices des fabricants. Dans la mesure où la totalité des caractéristiques et des conditions de test ne peuvent être indiquées ici, il est d'ailleurs vivement conseillé de se référer en cas de doute également à ces notices.

La première édition de ce recueil regroupe les produits des années 1990 à 1994 des principaux fabricants européens, américains et japonais.

# Prólogo

El presente libro de tablas de valores se realizó en base a los datos actuales de conocidos fabricantes de diodos. Los valores técnicos característicos y límites más importantes de aproximadamente 7000 diodos se listan sinópticamente. Además, se han incluido los datos de los fabricantes e informaciones adicionales, planos de conexión e indicaciones sobre la aplicación de los dispositivos electrónicos.

El libro debe tomarse como una ayuda en la elección del diodo adecuado. Como obra de consulta posibilita por una parte encontrar de forma rápida los parámetros más característicos del dispositivo, y por otra, comparar las características de los diodos entre sí. Evidentemente, no puede reemplazar las tables ofrecidas por los fabricantes de depositivos. Ya que no pueden incluirse ni la totalidad de los datos ni todas las condiciones de test, se aconseja consultar en caso de duda con las referencias directas del fabricante.

Para la primera edición se ha tenido en cuenta el surtido ofrecido por los más importantes fabricantes de Europa, Estados Unidos y Japón entre los años 1990 a 1994.

# Explanations
# Erläuterungen
# Explications
# Aclaraciones

# Explanations

## About the data tables

### General

For maximum ratings the upper maximum rating is stated. For operational ratings, either the typical Values, the minimum Value – with a preceding »>« – or the maximum Value – with preceding »<« – is stated. In case manufacturer data are given in a range of values, the average value is stated.

For some data there may be alternative parameters with different meaníng. In this case values are provided in italic letters.

If not otherwise stated, data provided in the tables is based on a suppoded ambient temperature of 25°C.

For Diode Arrays all data stated apply to the individual diodes except of the Pv (maximum power dissipation) value which applies to the device.

 ### Type

Type are generally listed in ascending alphabetical sorting order. Model lines are grouped together. Some diodes on a model line do not fit into this sorting order. These items are duplicated and can be found at in the appropriate place in the sorting order if the letter is not located at the same page (e.g. 1N754A or 1N4100).

 ### Case

Case outline drawings include the short name for the case itself and the case material being used. The following abbrevations are used for case materials:

| | |
|---|---|
| P | Plastic |
| M | Metal |
| G | Glass |
| MG | Metal/Glass |

 ### Pincode

The pincode column assigns the actual pinout to the case. Pincode tables are provided in chapter 2.

 ### Function

This Column provides information on a device's general characteristics with regard to production technology and application.

 ### Manufacturer

For details please refer to »Manufacturers list«.

 ### Note

This column provides either explanations or additional information to the individual device or device data.

For model line this column includes information about consecutive model lines. Information in this column is correlating to manufacturers abbrevations being used.

### Example

| | |
|---|---|
| Type | BZX84C11 |
| Manufacturer | SG, PH, IT, RO |
| Note | .A.BD |
| Line C | all manufacturers |
| SG, IT | no consecutive lines (indicated by ».«) |
| PH | Model line A |
| RO | Model lines B and D |

# Explanations

## Rectifier Diode Data Tables

 **Maximum reverse voltage (Vrm)**
The highest periodically applied reverse voltage. DC Voltage is stated in »()« paranthesis.

 **Maximum reverse current (Irm)**
Maximum reverse current on maximum reverse voltage.

 **Average forward current (Ifav)**
Maximum average forward current. In case this value is not provided by the manufacturer, the peak of the periodic forward current is stated in *italic letters (Ifm)*.

 **Maximum power dissipation (Pv)**
Maximum continous power dissipation. Data put in »()« refer to devices using a heatsink.

 **Forward Voltage (Vf)**
Forward voltage in continuous operation.

 **Forward current (If)**
Forward current in continuous operation. Alternatively the periodic pulse value of the forward current is stated in *italic letters (Ifp)*.

 **Junction capacitance (C0)**
Junction capacitance. Please refer to column notes for details on applied voltages.

 **Capacitance ratio (Cr)**
Junction capacitance maximum to minimum ratio for C diodes. Please refer to column notes for details on applied voltages.

 **Reverse recovery time (trr)**
Reverse recovery time or switching time, in case of switching time in *italic letters (ts)*.

## Zener Diodes & TVS Data Tables

 **Clamping voltage (Vcla)**
Maximum limiting voltage for suppressor diodes. For breakover diodes the breakover voltage in *italic letters (Vbro)*.

 **Transient peak current (Its)**
Transient peak current in breakover range.

 **Maximum zener current (Izm)**
Maximum continuous zener current.

 **Maximum dissipation power (Pv)**
Maximum continuous total power dissipation. Data put in »()« refer to devices using a heatsink.

 **Transient power dissipation (Pvts)**
Maximum transient power dissipation in breakover range.

 **Zener voltage (Vz)**
Typical zener voltage on Iz or average of the stated range of zener voltages.

 **Zener current (Iz)**
Zener current at Vz. For breakover diodes the switching current is stated in *italic letters (Is)*.

 **Differential zener resistance (rz)**
Differential zener resistance at Vz/Iz.

 **Temperature coefficient (TK)**
Maximum temperature coefficient in ppm/°C or in mV/°C.

# Explanations

## Abbreviations in the headers

| | |
|---|---|
| C0 | Junction capacitance |
| Cr | Capacitance ratio |
| If | Forward current |
| Ifav | Maximum average forward current |
| Ifm | Maximum periodic forward current |
| Ifp | Periodic peak forward current |
| Irm | Maximum reverse current |
| Is | Switching current |
| Its | Transistent peak current |
| Iz | Zener current |
| Izm | Maximum zener current |
| Pv | Maximum continuous power dissipation |
| Pvts | Maximum transient power dissipation |
| rz | Differential zener resistance |
| TK | Temperature coefficient |
| trr | Reverse recovery time |
| ts | Switching time |
| Vbro | Breakover voltage |
| Vcla | Clamping voltage |
| Vf | Forward voltage |
| Vrm | Maximum reverse voltage |
| Vz | Zener voltage |

## Abbreviations in column notes

| | |
|---|---|
| antip | Antiparallel |
| CD | Variable capacitance diode |
| comm-a | Common anode |
| comm-k | Common cathode |
| doubler | used in doubler circuits |
| F | Noise figure |
| Nd | Noise density |
| indep | Independent diodes |
| P | Preferred type |
| ser | Serial |
| Ta | Ambient temperature |
| Tc | Case temperature |
| Tj | Junction temperature |
| Vr | Applied reverse voltage |
| TVS | Suppressor diode |
| Vz | Zener voltage |
| $\delta$ | Deviation data between paired types |
| ZD | Zener diode |

## Abbreviations used in column function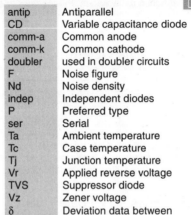

| | |
|---|---|
| Array | Diode array, multiple diodes |
| Avalanche | Avalanche Diode |
| Bidir. | Bidirectional |
| Breakover, BRO | Breakover diode |
| C Diode, CD | Capacitance diode |
| Rectifier, Rect. | Rectifier diode |
| Bridge | Rectifier bridge |
| CLMP | Clamping diode |
| HV Rectifier | High voltage rectifier |
| Network | Diode network |
| PIN Diode | PIN diode |
| Pair | Pair of diodes |
| Ref. LED | Reference LED |
| Ref. Z Diode | Reference Zener diode |
| RF Diode | High frequency diode |
| Stabistor | Forward Zener diode |
| Switch | Switching diode |
| TVS | Suppressor diode |
| Uni | General purpose or small signal diode |
| Z Diode | Zener diode |

These abbreviations may be used in conjunction, e.g.:

| | |
|---|---|
| Rect. Pair | Pair of rectifiers |
| Z Diode, TVS | Zener diode and TVS |

# Erläuterungen

## Erläuterungen zu den Datentabellen

### Allgemeine Angaben

Bei Grenzdaten sind die oberen Grenzwerte ausgewiesen. Für Betriebsdaten wird der typische Wert, der minimale Wert (mit vorangestelltem »>«-Zeichen) oder der Maximalwert (mit »<«) angegeben. Gibt der Hersteller Bereichsgrenzen an, ist der Mittelwert genannt.

Für einige Daten werden alternativ Parameter mit abweichender Bedeutung angegeben. Diese werden *kursiv* gesetzt.

Wenn nicht anders angegeben, gelten die angegebenen Daten für 25°C.

Bei Mehrfach-Dioden gelten die angegebenen Daten mit Ausnahme von Pv für jede Einzeldiode.

 **Type**
Die Typen sind in alphabetischer Reihenfolge aufgelistet. Baureihen sind zusammengefaßt. Typen einer Baureihe, deren Bezeichnungen nicht in die alphabetische Reihenfolge passen, werden noch einmal in der alphabetischen Anordnung geführt, soweit diese nicht auf der gleichen Seite plaziert ist (siehe z.B. 1N754A oder 1N4100).

 **Case**
Zeichnungsnummer des Gehäuses (Kapitel 4). In den Zeichnungen werden auch die Gehäusebezeichnung und das Gehäusematerial angegeben. Folgende Abkürzungen werden für das Gehäusematerial verwendet:

| | |
|---|---|
| P | Plastik |
| M | Metall |
| G | Glas |
| MG | Metall/Glas |

 **Pincode**
Pincode. Er kennzeichnet die tatsächliche Belegung der Pins. Die Tabellen der Pinbelegungen sind in Kapitel 2 zusammengestellt.

 **Funktion**
Allgemeine Charakterisierung eines Typs nach Technologie und Anwendung.

 **Hersteller**
Abgekürzte Herstellerbezeichnung (siehe Herstellerverzeichnis).

 **Note**
Zusätzliche oder erläuternde Angaben zum Bauelement oder zu den Daten.

Bei Baureihen: Angabe der Kennbuchstaben weiterer Reihen. Die Angaben korrelieren mit denen der Spalte Hersteller.

| Beispiel | |
|---|---|
| Typ | BZX84C11 |
| Herst | SG,PH,IT,RO |
| Note | .A.BD |
| Reihe C | alle Hersteller |
| SG, IT | keine weitere Reihe (durch den Punkt angezeigt) |
| PH | Reihe A |
| RO | Reihe B und D |

## Datentabelle Gleichrichterdioden

 **Maximale Sperrspannung (Vrm)**
Maximale periodisch anliegende Sperrspannung oder Gleichspannung (letztere in Klammern).

 **Maximaler Sperrstrom (Irm)**
Maximaler Strom in Sperrichtung bei maximaler Sperrspannung.

 **Mittlerer Durchlaßstrom (Ifav)**
Maximaler mittlerer Wert des Durchlaßstromes. Ist dieser Wert in den vorliegenden Herstellerangaben nicht verfügbar, wird in *kursiver Schrift* der Spitzenwert des periodischen Durchlaßstromes (*Ifm*) angegeben.

# Erläuterungen

**Maximale Verlustleistung (Pv)**
Maximale Dauerverlustleistung. Angaben in »()« Klammern gelten für Leistungstypen mit Kühlkörper.

**Flußspannung (Vf)**
Flußspannung für den Dauerbetrieb.

**Flußstrom (If)**
Wert des Flußstromes im Dauerbetrieb. Alternativ kann in *kursiver Schrift* der Wert des Flußstromes im periodischen Impulsbetrieb *Ifp* angegeben sein.

**Sperrschichtkapazität (C0)**
Kapazität der Sperrschicht. Zugehörige Spannungsangaben unter Note.

**Kapazitätsverhältnis (Cr)**
Verhältnis von maximaler zu minimaler Sperrschichtkapazität bei C-Dioden. Zugehörige Spannungsangaben unter Note.

**Sperrerholungszeit (trr)**
Sperrerholungszeit oder Schaltzeit *ts* (*letztere kursiv*).

## Datentabellen Z-Dioden & TVS

**Clampingspannung (Vcla)**
Maximale Begrenzerspannung bei Suppressor-Dioden. Für Breakover-Dioden erfolgt in *kursiver Schrift* die Angabe der Breakover-Spannung *(Vbro)*.

**Transienter Spitzenstrom (Its)**
Transienter Spitzenstrom im Durchbruchsbereich.

**Maximaler Zenerstrom (Izm)**
Maximaler Dauerstrom im Durchbruchsbereich.

**Dauerverlustleistung (Pv)**
Maximale Dauerverlustleistung. Angaben in Klammern »()« gelten für Leistungstypen mit Kühlkörper.

**Transiente Verlustleistung (Pvts)**
Maximale Impulsverlustleistung im Durchbruchsbereich.

**Zenerspannung (Vz)**
Typischer Wert der Zenerspannung bei Iz oder der Mittelwert des angegebenen Bereiches der Zenerspannungen.

**Zenerstrom (Iz)**
Zenerstrom im Arbeitspunkt Vz. Bei Breakover-Dioden der Switching-Strom *Is* (Angabe kursiv).

**Differentieller Zenerwiderstand (rz)**
Differentieller Zenerwiderstand bei Iz/Vz.

**Temperaturkoeffizient (TK)**
Maximaler Temperaturkoeffizient in ppm/°C oder in mV/°C.

# Erläuterungen

## Abkürzungen in den Tabellenköpfen

| | |
|---|---|
| C0 | Sperrschichtkapazität |
| Cr | Kapazitätsverhältnis |
| If | Flußstrom |
| Ifav | max. mittl. Flußstrom |
| Ifm | max. Flußstrom (periodisch) |
| Ifp | Flußstrom (periodischer Impulsbetrieb) |
| Irm | max. Sperrstrom |
| Is | Switching-Strom |
| Its | Transienter Spitzenstrom |
| Izm | max. Zenerstrom |
| Iz | Zenerstrom |
| Pv | max. Dauerverlustleistung |
| Pvts | max. Impulsverlustleistung |
| rz | diff. Zenerwiderstand |
| TK | Temperaturkoeffizient |
| trr | Sperrerholungszeit |
| ts | Schaltzeit |
| Vbro | Breakover-Spannung |
| Vcla | Clamping-Spannung |
| Vf | Flußspannung |
| Vrm | max. Sperrspannung |
| Vz | Zenerspannung |

## Abkürzungen Spalte Note

| | |
|---|---|
| antip | antiparallel |
| CD | Kapazitätsdiode |
| comm-a | gemeinsame Anode |
| comm-k | gemeinsame Katode |
| doubler | für Verdoppler-Schaltungen |
| F | Rauschzahl |
| indep | unabhängige Dioden |
| Nd | Rauschdichte |
| P | Vorzugstyp, gegebenenfalls in Klammern Angabe des Herstellers |
| ser | in Serie |
| Ta | Umgebungstemperatur |
| Tc | Gehäusetemperatur |
| Tj | Sperrschichttemperatur |
| Vr | angelegte Sperrspannung |
| TVS | Suppressor-Diode |
| Vz | Zenerspannung |
| $\delta$ | Abweichung zwischen gepaarten Typen |
| ZD | Zenerdiode |

## Abkürzungen Spalte Funktion

| | |
|---|---|
| Array | Dioden-Array, Mehrfachdiode |
| Avalanche | Avalanche Diode |
| Bidir. | Bidirektional |
| Breakover, BRO | Breakover-Diode |
| C Diode, CD | Kapazitätsdiode |
| Rectifier, Rect. | Gleichrichter |
| Bridge | Brückenanordnung |
| CLMP | Clamping-Diode |
| HV Rectifier | Hochspannungs-Gleichrichter |
| Network | Dioden-Netzwerk |
| PIN Diode | PIN-Diode |
| Pair | Diodenpaar |
| Ref. LED | Referenz-LED |
| Ref. Z Diode | Referenz-Z-Diode |
| RF Diode | Hochfrequenz-Diode |
| Stabistor | Z-Diode in Flußrichtung |
| Switch | Schaltdiode |
| TVS | Suppressor-Diode |
| Uni | Universal-, Kleinsignal-Diode |
| Z Diode | Z-Diode (Zener-Diode) |

Diese Bezeichnungen werden ebenso in Kombination, oder auch als Aufzählung zur Kennzeichnung mehrerer Funktionen verwendet:

| | |
|---|---|
| Rect. Pair | Gleichrichterpaar |
| Z Diode, TVS | Z-Diode und TVS |

# Explications

## Aide à la lecture des tables

### Généralités

Les bornes supérieures des caractéristiques sont indiquées. Pour les valeurs de fonctionnement, une valeur caractéristique, la valeur minimale (précédée du signe »>«) ou la valeur maximale (précédée du signe »<«) est indiquée. Lorsque le fabricant fournit un domaine de validité, c'est la moyenne qui est notée.

Dans certains cas, d'autres paramètres n'ayant pas la même signification sont fournis. Ils sont alors placés entre parenthèses.

Sauf indication contraire, toutes les données sont valables à une température de 25 °C.

Dans le cas des diodes multiples, toutes les données fournies, à l'exception de Pv (la puissance dissipée), sont également applicables à chaque diode prise séparément.

 **Type**
Les différents types sont rangés par ordre alphabétique. Les séries sont regroupées. Les types d'une série, dont la description devrait normalement se trouver à un autre endroit de la liste, sont également répétés à cet autre endroit (cf. 1N754A ou 1N4100).

 **Boîtier**
Numéro du schéma du boîtier (chapitre 4). Sur les schémas sont également indiqués le nom et le matériau du boîtier. Les abréviations suivantes sont utilisées pour le matériau:

| | |
|---|---|
| P | plastique |
| M | métal |
| G | verre |
| MG | métal/verre |

 **Code-Pin**
Ce code indique la destination de la patte. Une table des codes est fournie au chapitre 2.

 **Fonction**
Cette colonne donne la caractérisation générale d'un type de diode selon la technologie de production et l'utilisation.

 **Fabricant**
Cette colonne contient une abréviation du nom du fabricant. Se reporter à la table des fabricants pour connaître les correspondances.

 **Note**
Ici sont regroupées les informations complémentaires et/ou explications au sujet du composant lui-même ou de ses caractéristiques.

Dans le cas de séries, cette colonne contient une indication sur les séries suivantes. Ces informations sont corrélées avec celles de la colonne »Fabricant«.

| **Exemples** | |
|---|---|
| Type | BZX84C11 |
| Fabricant | SG, PH, IT, RO |
| Note | .A.BD |
| Série C | tous les fabricants |
| SG, IT | pas de série suivante (indiqué par un point ».«). |
| PH | série A |
| RO | séries B et D |

## Table des redresseurs

 **Tension de claquage (Vrm)**
Tension alternative ou continue maximale appliquée en polarisation inverse (tension continue entre parenthèses).

 **Courant de saturation inverse (Irm)**
Courant maximal dans le sens bloqué à la tension de claquage.

# Explications

 **Courant moyen en polarisation directe (Ifav)**
Valeur moyenne maximale du courant passant en polarisation directe. Dans le cas où cette valeur n'est pas fournie par le fabricant, la valeur maximale en polarisation directe du courant alternatif est indiquée en *italique (Ifm)*.

 **Puissance dissipée maximale (Pv)**
Puissance dissipée maximale en régime stabilisé. Les valeurs entre parenthèses sont valides pour les composants munis d'un radiateur.

 **Tension en polarisation directe (Vf)**
Tension en polarisation directe en régime stabilisé.

 **Courant en polarisation directe (If)**
Valeur du courant en polarisation directe en régime stabilisé. Parfois, la valeur du courant correspondant à un régime périodique d'impulsions est indiqué en *italique (Ifp)*.

 **Capacité de la jonction (C0)**
Valeur de la capacité de la jonction. Les tensions appliquées sont indiquées dans la colonne »Note«.

 **Rapport de capacités (Cr)**
Rapport de la capacité maximale de la jonction sur sa capacité minimale pour les diodes à capacité variable. Les tensions appliquées sont indiquées dans la colonne »Note«.

 **Temps de recouvrement inverse (trr)**
Temps de recouvrement inverse ou temps de commutation si l'indication est en *italique (ts)*.

## Tables des diodes Zener & TVS

 **Tension d'attache (clamping voltage) (Vcla)**
Limite maximale de la tension pour les diodes antiparasites. Pour les diodes »breakover«, la tension critique est indiquée en *italique (Vbro)*.

 **Courant transitoire maximal (Its)**
Courant transitoire maximal dans le domaine Zener.

 **Courant Zener maximal (Izm)**
Courant Zener maximal en régime stabilisé.

 **Puissance dissipée en régime stabilisé (Pv)**
Puissance dissipée maximale en régime stabilisé. Les valeurs entre parenthèses sont valides pour les composants munis d'un radiateur.

 **Puissance dissipée en régime transitoire (Pvts)**
Puissance dissipée maximale dans le domaine Zener en régime transitoire d'impulsions.

 **Tension Zener (Vz)**
Valeur caractéristique de la tension Zener avec un courant Iz, ou la valeur moyenne du domaine des tensions Zener.

 **Courant Zener (Iz)**
Courant Zener au point de fonctionnement Vz. Pour les diodes »breakover«, la valeur critique du courant est indiquée en *italique (Is)*.

 **Résistance Zener différentielle (rz)**
Résistance Zener différentielle, calculée selon la formule Iz/Vz.

 **Coefficient de température (TK)**
Coefficient de température maximal en ppm/°C ou en mV/°C.

# Explications

## Résumé des abréviations

| | |
|---|---|
| C0 | Capacité de la jonction |
| Cr | Rapport de capacités |
| If | Courant en polarisation directe |
| Ifav | Courant moyen en polarisation directe |
| Ifm | Courant maximal en polarisation directe |
| Ifp | Courant en polarisation directe en régime d'impulsions |
| Irm | Courant de saturation inverse |
| Is | Courant critique (diodes »breakover«) |
| Its | Courant Zener maximal |
| Iz | Courant Zener |
| Izm | Courant Zener maximal |
| Pv | Puissance dissipée maximale en régime stabilisé |
| Pvts | Puissance dissipée maximale en régime d'impulsions |
| rz | Résistance Zener différentielle |
| TK | Coefficient de température |
| Trr | Temps de recouvrement inverse |
| Ts | temps de commutation |
| Vbro | tension critique (diodes »breakover«) |
| Vcla | Tension d'attache (clamping voltage) |
| Vf | Tension en polarisation directe |
| Vrm | Tension de claquage |
| Vz | Tension Zener |

## Abréviations dans la colonne Note

| | |
|---|---|
| antip | antiparallèle |
| CD | diode à capacité variable |
| comma | anode commune |
| commk | cathode commune |
| doubler | pour les circuits doubleurs |
| F | nombre du bruit |
| Nd | densité de bruit |
| indep | diodes indépendantes |
| P | type préférentiel, auquel cas le fabricant est indiqué entre parenthèses |
| ser | en série |
| Ta | température ambiante |
| Tc | température du boîtier |
| Tj | température de la jonction |
| Vr | Tension de polarisation inverse |
| TVS | Diode antiparasites |
| Vz | Tension Zener |
| δ | Différence dans un couple de types |
| ZD | Diode Zener |

## Abréviations dans la colonne Fonction

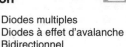

| | |
|---|---|
| Array | Diodes multiples |
| Avalanche | Diodes à effet d'avalanche |
| Bidir. | Bidirectionnel |
| Breakover, BRO | Breakover diode |
| C Diode, CD | Diode à capacité variable |
| Rectifier, Rect. | Redresseur |
| Bridge | Montage en pont |
| CLMP | Clamping diode |
| HV Rectifier | Redresseur hautes tensions |
| Network | Réseau de diodes |
| PIN Diode | Diode PIN |
| Pair | Couple de diodes |
| Ref. LED | Diode électroluminescente de référence |
| Ref. Z Diode | Diode Zener de référence |
| RF Diode | Diode à hautes fréquences |
| Stabistor | Diode Zener en polarisation directe |
| Switch | Diode interrupteur |
| TVS | Diode antiparasites |
| Uni | Diode universelle et diode en petits signaux |
| Z Diode | Diode Zener |

Ces abréviations peuvent être utilisées à plusieurs, comme par exemple:

| | |
|---|---|
| Rect. Pair | Couple de redresseurs |
| Z Diode, TVS | Diode Zener et antiparasite |

# Aclaraciones

## Aclaraciones a las tablas de valores

### Información General

Los valores límite de los dispositivos deben identificarse con sus correspondientes valores máximos. Las especificaciones para el funcionamiento nominal de los dispositivos incluyen los valores típicos, los mínimos (antecedidos por el signo »>«) y los valores máximos (antecedidos por el signo »<«). En caso que el fabricante indique un márgen de valores para un parámetro determinado, se muestra el valor medio.

Alternativamente se ofrece para algunos datos parámetros de diferente significación. En este caso, se indican entre paréntesis.

En caso de no especificarse lo contrario, los datos son válidos para una temperatura de 25°C.

Para los diodos múltiples son válidos los datos señalados, con excepción de Pv para cada diodo.

 **Tipos**

Los tipos de diodo se listan por orden alfabético. Las series de fabricación se han resumido. Los diferentes tipos de una serie de fabricación, cuya notación no pueda incluirse en el orden alfabético, se muestran adicionalmente en la disposición alfabética (p.e. 1N754A–1N4100).

 **Encapsulado**

Número de plano del encapsulado (capítulo 4). En los planos se indica la notación y el material del encapsulado. Las siguientes abreviaturas se aplican para la notación del material del encapsulado del dispositivo:

| | |
|---|---|
| P | Plástico |
| M | Metal |
| G | Vidrio |
| MG | Metal/Vidrio |

 **Código de pin**

Código de pin. El código de pin.indica la disposición efectiva de los pins. Las tablas con la disposición de los pins se encuentran resumidas en el capítulo 2.

 **Función**

Caracterización general de un tipo de dispositivo según tecnología y aplicación.

 **Fabricante**

Denominación abreviada de los fabricantes (ver índice de fabricantes).

 **Notas**

Datos aclaratorios o adicionales del dispositivo ó de sus valores.

En series de fabricación: Datos de la letra indicadora de otras series. Los datos se correlacionan con aquellos de la columna Fabricantes.

| Ejemplo | |
|---|---|
| Tipo | BZX84C11 |
| Fabricante | SG,PH,IT,RO |
| Nota | .A.BD |
| SerieC | Todos los fabricantes |
| SG, IT | ninguna otra serie (punto) |
| Serie A | PH |
| Serie B y D | RO |

## Tablas de valores Diodos rectificadores

 **Tensión inversa máxima (Vrm)**

La tensión inversa ó de corte periódica máxima que se pueda aplicar al dispositivo. En caso de ser tensión contínua, se indica entre paréntesis »()«.

 **Corriente inversa máxima (Irm)**

Indica la corriente máxima en polarización inversa al aplicar la tensión máxima de corte.

# Aclaraciones

 **Corriente media de conducción (Ifav)**
Valor máximo medio de la corriente de conducción. En caso de no encontrarse este valor entre los ofrecidos por el fabricante, se indica en *letra cursiva* el valor máximo de la corriente periódica de conducción *(Ifm)*.

 **Máxima potencia de pérdida (Pv)**
Máxima potencia de pérdida ó de disipación en régimen contínuo. Los valores entre paréntesis son válidos para tipos de dispositivos con refrigeración.

 **Tensión directa ó de flujo (Vf)**
Tensión directa ó de flujo para el régimen contínuo.

 **Corriente directa ó de flujo (If)**
Corriente directa ó de flujo en régimen contínuo. Alternativamente se puede indicar en *cursiva* el valor de la corriente directa en régimen de barrido periódico *(Ifp)*.

 **Capacidad de la zona dipolar ó de la unión (C0)**
Capacidad de la zona dipolar ó de la unión. Los datos correspondientes a las tensiones se indican bajo el punto Notas.

 **Relación de capacidades (Cr)**
Indica la relación de la capacidad máxima a la capacidad mínima de la zona dipolar en diodos C. Los datos relativos a la tensión se muestran bajo el punto Notas.

 **Tiempo de retardo (trr)**
Tiempo de retardo ó tiempo de conmutación *ts* (el último, en *cursiva*).

## Tablas de valores de diodos Z & TVS

 **Tensión clamping (Vcla)**
Tensión máxima limitadora para diodos Suppressor. Para diodos Breakover, se indican en *cursiva* los valores de la tensión de ruptura o de disrupción *(Vbro)*.

 **Máxima corriente transitoria (Its)**
Máxima corriente transitoria en la zona de avalancha.

 **Máxima corriente Zener (Izm)**
Máxima corriente en régimen contínuo en la zona de avalancha.

 **Máxima potencia de pérdida (Pv)**
Máxima potencia de pérdida ó de disipación en régimen contínuo. Los valores entre paréntesis son válidos para tipos de dispositivos con refrigeración.

 **Potencia de pérdida transitoria (Pvts)**
Máxima potencia de pérdida o de disipación en la zona de avalancha.

 **Tensión Zener (Vz)**
Valor típico de la tensión zener a la corriente Iz o el valor medio de la región indicada para la tensión Zener.

 **Corriente Zener (Iz)**
Valor de la corriente Zener a la tensión Vz. En diodos Breakover, se indica la corriente de conmutación (Switching), en *cursiva* *(Is)*.

 **Resistencia diferencial Zener (rz)**
Valor de la resistencia diferencial Zener a Iz/Vz.

 **Coeficiente de temperatura (TK)**
Coeficiente de temperatura máxima a ppm/°C o en mV/°C.

# Aclaraciones

## Resumen de las abreviaturas

| | |
|---|---|
| C0 | Capacidad de la zona dipolar |
| Cr | Relación de capacidades |
| Irm | Máxima corriente de corte |
| If | Corriente directa ó de flujo |
| Ifav | Máxima corriente directa ó de flujo media |
| Ifm | Máxima corriente directa ó deflujo en régimen periódico |
| Ifp | Corriente directa ó de flujo en régimen de barrido periódico |
| Is | Corriente de conmutactión (Switching) |
| Its | Máxima corriente transitoria |
| Iz | Corriente Zener |
| Izm | Máxima corriente Zener |
| Pv | Máxima potencia de pérdida o de disipación |
| Pvts | Máxima potencia de disipación en barrido |
| rz | Resistencia diferencial Zener |
| TK | Coeficiente de temperatura |
| trr | Tiempo de retardo |
| ts | tiempo de conmutactión |
| Vbro | tensión de ruptura o de disruptión |
| Vcla | Tensión clamping |
| Vf | Tensión directa ó de flujo |
| Vrm | Tensión máxima de corte |
| Vz | Tensión Zener |

## Abreviaturas de la columna Notas

| | |
|---|---|
| antip | antiparalelo |
| CD | diodo de capacidad |
| comm-a | ánodo común |
| comm-k | cátodo común |
| doubler | para circuítos dobladores |
| F | factor de ruido |
| Nd | densidad de ruido |
| P | tipo preferencial, indicación del fabricante entre paréntesis |
| ser | en serie |
| Ta | temperatura ambiente |
| Tc | temperatura de la carcasa |
| Tj | temperatura de la capa de conductividad unidireccional |
| Vr | tensión inversa aplicada |
| TVS | diodo Suppressor |
| Vz | tensión Zener |
| d | Diferencia entre tipos pareados |
| ZD | diodo Zener |

## Abreviaturas de la columna Función

| | |
|---|---|
| Array | diodos Array, diodos múltiples |
| Avalanche | diodos Avalancha |
| Bidir | bidireccional |
| Breakover, BRO | diodos Breakover |
| C Diode, CD | diodo de capacidad |
| Rectifier, Rect. | rectificador |
| Bridge | disposición puente |
| CLMP | diodo Clamping |
| HV Rectifier | Rectificador de alto voltaje |
| Network | diodo de red |
| PIN Diode | diode de pin |
| Pair | par de diodos |
| Ref. LED | LED de referencia |
| Ref. Z Diode | diodo Z de referencia |
| RF Diode | diodo de alta frecuencia |
| Stabistor | diodo Z en directa |
| Switch | diodo de conmutación |
| TVS | diode Suppressor |
| Uni | diodo universal de pequeña señal |
| Z Diode | diodo Z (diodo Zener) |

Estas abreviaturas pueden aplicarse también para la caracterización de varias funciones o en combinación, p.e.:

| | |
|---|---|
| Rect. Pair | par de rectificadores |
| Z Diode, TVS | diodo Z y TVS |

# Manufacturers
# Hersteller
# Fabricants
# Fabricantes

**IT** **ITT Intermetall**

D
Hans-Bunte-Str. 19
D-79108 Freiburg
Tel.: (0761) 5 17-0
Fax.: (0761) 51 71 74

F
157, rue des Blains
F-92220 Bagneux
Tel.: (01) 45 45 81 81
Fax.: (01) 45 47 83 92

GB
Rosemount House
Rosemount Avenue
West Byfleet
Surrey KT146LB
Tel.: (0932) 33 61 16
Fax.: (0932) 33 61 48

I
Viale Milanofiori, E/5
I-20090 Assago (Mi)
Tel.: (02) 8 24 70.1
Fax.: (02) 8 24 26.31

E
Sagitron
Corazón de Maria
E-28002 Madrid
Tel:. (01) 4 16-92 61
Fax.: (01) 4 16-46 09

A
ITT MULTIcomponents
Akaziengasse 42
A-1234 Wien
Tel.: (01) 69 45 17-0
Fax.: (01) 69 45 10

CH
ITT MULTIcomponents
Brandschenkenstr. 178
CH-8027 Zürich
Tel.: (01) 2 04 61 11
Fax.: (01) 2 04 64 54

B
ITT MULTIcomponents
Belgicastraat 2
B-1930 Zalventern
Tel.: (02) 7 25 35 33
Fax.: (02) 7 25 41 35

**MO** **Motorola**

D
EBV Elektronik GmbH
D-85540 Haar
Hans-Pinsel-Str. 4
Tel.: (089) 46 09 60
Fax.: (089) 46 44 88

F
Scaib
80 Rue d' Arcueil, Silic 137
F-94523 Rungis Cedex
Tel.: (01) 46 87 23 71
Fax.: (01) 46 60 55 49

GB
Arrow Electronics
St Martins Way Industrial
Estate
Cambridge Road
Bedford MK42OLF
Tel.: (0234) 3 47 21 11
Fax.: (0234) 21 46 74

I
Adelsi S.p.A
Via Novara 570
I-20153 Milano
Tel.: (02) 3 58 06 41
Fax.: (02) 3 00 29 88

E
Kontron Electronic SA
Salvatierra 4
E-28034 Madrid
Tel.: ((01) 3 58 18 35
Fax.: (01) 7 29 37 52

A
EBV Elektronik
Diefenbachstr. 35/6
A-1150 Wien
Tel.: (0222) 8 94 17 74
Fax.: (0222) 8 94 17 74

CH
Elbatex AG
Hardstr. 72
CH-5430 Wettingen
Tel.: (056) 27 51 11
Fax.: (056) 27 19 24

B
EBV Elektronik
Excelsiorlaan 35
B-1930 Zaventern
Tel.: (02) 7 20 99 36
Fax.: (02) 7 20 81 52

RU
Soninfo Joint Venture
SSR-France a/b Nb 19
RU-103220 Moskva
Tel.: (095) 3 67 07 72
Fax.: (095) 1 66 08 18

**NS** **National Semiconductor**

D
National Semiconductor
Industriestr. 10
D-82256 Fürstenfeldbruck
Tel.: (08141) 1 03-0
Fax.: (08141) 10 35 54

| | |
|---|---|
| F | Centre d' Affair. "La Boursidiére"<br>Batiment Champagne, P.90<br>Route Nationale 186<br>F-92357 La Plessis Robinson<br>Tel.: (01) 40 94 88 88<br>Fax.: (01) 40 94 88 11 |
| GB | The Marple, Kenbrey Park<br>Swindon, Wildshire SN2UT<br>Tel.: (0793) 61 41 41<br>Fax.: (0793) 69 75 22 |
| I | Strada 7-Palazzo R3-Milanofiori<br>I-20089 Rozzano (Mi)<br>Tel.: (02) 57 50 03 00<br>Fax.: (02) 57 50 04 00 |
| E | Calle Augustin de Foxa, 27 (9°D)<br>E-28036 Madrid<br>Tel.: (01) 7 33 29 58<br>Fax.: (01) 7 33 80 18 |
| NL | Natonaltional Semiconductor<br>Benelux B.V.<br>Flevolan 4<br>NL-1380 AB Weesp<br>Tel.: (02) 94 03 04 48<br>Fax.: (02) 94 03 04 30 |
| CH | National Semiconductor<br>Alte Winterhuserstr. 53<br>CH-5304 Walisellen-Zürich<br>Tel.: (01) 8 30 27 27<br>Fax.: (01) 8 30 19 00 |

## Philips

| | |
|---|---|
| PH | **Philips** |
| D | Philips Components<br>Burchardstr 19<br>D-20095 Hamburg<br>Tel.: (040) 32 96-0<br>Fax.: (040) 32 96 -213 |
| F | Philips Composants<br>117 Quai du Président Roosevelt<br>F-92134 Issy-Les-Mopoulineeaux<br>Cedex<br>Tel.: (01) 40 93 80 00<br>Fax.: (01) 40 93 86 92 |
| GB | Philips Component Ltd.<br>Mullard House, Torrington  Palace<br>London WC1E 7HD<br>Tel.: (071) 4 80 66 33<br>Fax.: (071) 4 36 21 96 |
| I | Philips S.p.A.<br>Piazza IV Novembre 3<br>I-20124 Milano<br>Tel.: (02) 67 52-1<br>Fax.: (02) 67 52 26 42 |
| E | Philips Components<br>Balmes 22<br>E-08007 Barcelona<br>Tel.: (03) 3 01 63 12<br>Fax.: (03) 3 01 42 43 |
| A | Österreichische Philips Industri<br>GmbH<br>UB Bauelemente<br>Triester Str. 64<br>A-1102 Wien<br>Tel.: (0222) 6 01 01-820 |

| | |
|---|---|
| B | N.V Philips Prof. Systems<br>Components Div.<br>80 Rue Des Deux Gares<br>B-1070 Bruxelles<br>Tel.: (02) 5 25 61 11 |
| CH | Philips A.G<br>Components Div.<br>Allmendstr. 140-142<br>CH-8027 Zürich<br>Tel.: (01) 4 88 22 11 |
| NL | Philips Component Division<br>Strat. Acc. and Internat. Sales<br>PO Box 218<br>NL-5600 MD Eindhoven<br>Fax.: 23753 |

| | |
|---|---|
| RD | **Roederstein** |
| D | Roederstein GmbH<br>Ludmillastr. 23-25<br>D-84034 Landshut<br>Tel.: (0871) 86-425<br>Fax.: (0871) 8 20 53 |

| | |
|---|---|
| RO | **Rohm** |
| D | Rohm Electronics GmbH<br>Mühlenstr. 70<br>D-41532 Korschenbroich<br>Tel.: (02161) 6 10 10<br>Fax.: (02161) 64 21 02 |

**GB**    Rohm Electronics (UK) Ltd
15 Peverel Drive , Granby
Milton Keynes, MK1 1NN
Tel.: (0908) 2 71-311
Fax.: (0908) 2 70-380

**SI**    **Siemens**

**D**    Siemens AG
Von-der-Tann-Str. 30
D-90439 Nürnberg
Tel. (0911) 6  54-0
Fax.: (0911) 6 54-46 92

**F**    Siemens S:A:
39/47 Bd. Ormano
F-93527 Saint Denis Cedex
Tel.: (1) 49 22 31 00
Fax.: (1) 49 22 39 70

**GB**    Siemens plc, Siemens House
Oldbury
Bracknell
Berkshire RG12 8FZ
Tel.: (0344) 39 60 00
Fax.: (0344) 39 66 32

**I**    Siemens S.p.A.
Div. Componenti
Via Fabio Fitzi 25/A
I-20110 Milano
Tel.: (02) 67 66-1
Fax.: (02) 67 66-43 95

**E**    Siemens S.A.
Departamento de Componentes
Orense, 2; artado 155
E-28020 Madrid
Tel.: (01) 5 55 25 00
Fax.: (01) 5 56 54 08

**A**    Siemens AG Österreich
Postfach 326
A-1131 Wien
Tel.: (01) 7 17 11-56 61
Fax.: (01) 7 17 11-59 73

**B**    Siemens S.A
Chaussée de Charleroi 116
B-1060 Bruxelles
Tel.: (02) 5 36-21 11
Fax.: (02) 5 36-24 92

**CH**    Siemens-Albis AG
Freilagerstr. 28
CH-8047 Zürich
Tel.: (01) 4 95-31 11
Fax. (01) 4 95-50 50

**SO**    **Sony**

**D**    Sony Europe
Landsberger Tsr. 428
D-81241 München
Tel.: (089) 8 29 16-0
Fax.: (089) 8 29 16-444

**J**    Sony Corporation
International Marketing Div.
4-10-18 Takanawa Minato-ku
Tokyo 108
Tel.: (03) 54 48-34 26
Fax.: (03) 54 48-74 93

**TE**    **Temic**

**D**    Temic Telefunken
Microelectronic GmbH
Theresienstr. 2
D-74072 Heilbronn
Tel.: (07131) 31 67 0
Fax.: (07131) 31 57 23 40

**F**    Temic France c/o Matra MHS
Les Quadrants
3, Avenue du centre
F-78054 St.-Quentin-en-Yvelines
Tel.: (01) 30 60 70 00
Fax.: (01) 30 64 06 93

**GB**    Temic UK Ltd.
Easthampstead Road
Bracknell
Berkshire RG12 1LX
Tel.: (0344) 48 57 57
Fax.: (0344) 42 73 71

**I**    Temic Italiana
c/o AEG Italiana
Via Stephenson 94
I-20157 Milano
Tel.: (02) 3 32 12-1
Fax.: (02) 3 32 12 -201

**E**    Temic Ibérica
c/o AEG Ibérica
Principe de Vergara, 112
E-28002 Madrid
Tel.: (01) 5 62 76 00
Fax.: (01) 5 62 75 14

# Manufacturers
# Hersteller

# Fabricants
# Fabricantes

B    Temic Benelux
Verheydenstr. 39
B-1070 Bruxelles
Tel.: (02) 5 29 62 11
Fax.: (02) 5 29 64 14

A    EBV Elektronik
Diefenbachsrtr. 35/6
A-1160 Wien
Tel.: (0222) 8 94 17 74
Fax.: (0222) 8 94 17 75

CH    Fabrimax
Distribution AG
Kirchenweg 5
CH-8032 Zürich
Tel.: (01) 3 86 86 86
Fax.: (01) 3 83 23 79

**SG**    **Thomson**

D    Bretonischer Ring
D-85630 Grasbrunn
Tel.: (089) 4 60 06-0
Fax.: (089) 4 60 54 54

F    7-avenue Gallieni-BP.93
F-94253 Gentilly Cedex
Tel.: (01) 47 40 70 70
Fax.: (01) 47 40 79 10

GB    Planar House, Parkway
Globe Park
Marlow, Bucks
Tel.: (0628) 89 08 00
Fax.: (0628) 89 02 91

I    V.le Milanofiori-Strada 4-
Palazzo A/4/A
I-20090 Milano
Tel.: (02) 8 92 13.1
Fax.: (02) 8 25 04 49

E    Calle Albacete, 5
E-28027 Madrid
Tel.: (01) 4 05 16 15
Fax.: (01) 4 03 11 34

CH    Chemin- Francois- Lehmann 18/A
CH-1218 Grand-Saconnex (Geneva)
Tel.: (022) 7 98 64 62
Fax.: (022) 7 98 48 69

**TO**    **Toshiba**

D    Düsseldorf Head Office
Hansaallee 181
D-40549 Düsseldorf
Tel.: (0211) 52 96-0
Fax.: (0211) 52 96-400

F    Toshiba Electronics France
3. Rue de Rome
F-93561 Rosny Sous Bois Cedex
Tel.: (01) 48 12 48 12
Fax.: (01) 48 94 51 15

GB    Toshiba Electronics (UK) Ltd.
Riverside Way
Camberley Surrey GU15 3YA
Tel.: (0276) 69 46 00
Fax.: (0276) 69 15 83

I    Toshiba Electronics Italiana
Palazzo Orione-Ingresso 3
I-29941 Agrate Brienzana Milano
Tel.: (039) 6 05 72 34
Fax.: (039) 6 05 72 52

E    Toshiba Electronics Espana, SA
Augustin de Foxá 27-9° A
E-28036 Madrid
Tel.: (01) 3 14 36 93
Fax.: (01) 3 14 36 10

A    Unielectromic
Heiligenstädter Str. 52
A-1190 Wien
Tel.: (0222) 3 63 65 00
Fax.: (0222) 3 69 22 73

B    Alcom Electronics NV/SA
Siegel 3
B-2550 Kortlich
Tel.: (03) 4 58 30 33
Fax.: (03) 4 58 31 26

CH    Fabrimax
Distribution AG
Kirchenweg 5
CH-8032 Zürich
Tel.: (01) 3 86 86 86
Fax.: (01) 3 83 23 79

# Chapter 1
# Kapitel 1
# Chapitre 1
# Capitulo 1

# Rectifier Diodes

- ▶ Bridge Rectifiers
- ▶ Small Signal Diodes
- ▶ RF Diodes
- ▶ Switching Diodes
- ▶ C Diodes
- ▶ PIN Diodes
- ▶ HV Rectifiers
- ▶ Avalanche Diodes
- ▶ Diode Arrays

| Type | Case | Pin-code | | | Maximum Ratings | | | | Electrical Characteristics | | | | | |
|---|---|---|---|---|---|---|---|---|---|---|---|---|---|---|
| | | | | | Vrm | Irm | Ifav / Ifm | Pv | Vf | If / Ifp | C0 | Cr | trr / ts | |
| 1B4B1 | O1 | d24 | TO | Rect. Bridge | 100 V | 400 µA | 1.5 A | | <1.2 V | 1.5 A | | | | Ir at Tj=150°C |
| 1G4B1 | O1 | d24 | TO | Rect. Bridge | 400 V | 400 µA | 1.5 A | | <1.2 V | 1.5 A | | | | Ir at Tj=150°C |
| 1J4B1 | O1 | d24 | TO | Rect. Bridge | 600 V | 400 µA | 1.5 A | | <1.2 V | 1.5 A | | | | Ir at Tj=150°C |
| 1B4B41 | N1 | d22 | TO | Rect. Bridge | 100 V | 10 µA | 1 A | | <1.2 V | 1.5 A | | | | |
| 1G4B41 | N1 | d22 | TO | Rect. Bridge | 400 V | 10 µA | 1 A | | <1.2 V | 1.5 A | | | | |
| 1J4B41 | N1 | d22 | TO | Rect. Bridge | 600 V | 10 µA | 1 A | | <1.2 V | 1.5 A | | | | |
| 1B4B42 | F16 | d23 | TO | Rect. Bridge | 100 V | 10 µA | 1 A | | <1 V | 500 mA | | | | |
| 1G4B42 | F16 | d23 | TO | Rect. Bridge | 400 V | 10 µA | 1 A | | <1 V | 500 mA | | | | |
| 1J4B42 | F16 | d23 | TO | Rect. Bridge | 600 V | 10 µA | 1 A | | <1 V | 500 mA | | | | |
| 1DL41A | A16 | a1 | TO | Rectifier | 200 V | 100 µA | 1 A | | <0.98 V | 1 A | | | <35 ns | |
| 1DL42A | A17 | a1 | TO | Rectifier | 200 V | 100 µA | 1 A | | <0.98 V | 1 A | | | <35 ns | |
| 1GH45 | A16 | a1 | TO | Rectifier | 400 V | 100 µA | 1 A | | <1.1 V | 1 A | | | <200 ns | |
| 1GH46 | A16 | a1 | TO | Rectifier | 400 V | 100 µA | 1 A | | <1.1 V | 1 A | | | <200 ns | |
| 1GU42 | A17 | a1 | TO | Rectifier | 400 V | 50 µA | 1 A | | <1.5 V | 1 A | | | <100 ns | |
| 1GWJ42 | A16 | a1 | TO | Rectifier | 40 V | 500 µA | 1 A | | <0.55 V | 1 A | 47 pF | | <35 ns | |
| 1GWJ43 | A17 | a1 | TO | Rectifier | 40 V | 500 µA | 1 A | | <0.55 V | 1 A | | | <35 ns | |
| 1JH45 | A16 | a1 | TO | Rectifier | 600 V | 100 µA | 1 A | | <1.2 V | 1 A | | | <200 ns | |
| 1JH46 | A17 | a1 | TO | Rectifier | 600 V | 100 µA | 1 A | | <1.2 V | 1 A | | | <200 ns | |
| 1JU41 | A16 | a1 | TO | Rectifier | 600 V | 100 µA | 1 A | | <2 V | 1 A | | | <100 ns | |
| 1JU42 | A17 | a1 | TO | Rectifier | 600 V | 100 µA | 1 A | | <2 V | 1 A | | | <100 ns | |
| 1N248B | E4 | a1 | SG | Rectifier | 50 V | 5 mA | 20 A | (25) W | <1.5 V | 70 A | | | | Ifav at Tc=150°C |
| 1N249B | E4 | a1 | SG | Rectifier | 100 V | 5 mA | 20 A | (25) W | <1.5 V | 70 A | | | | Ifav at Tc=150°C |
| 1N250B | E4 | a1 | SG | Rectifier | 200 V | 5 mA | 20 A | (25) W | <1.5 V | 70 A | | | | Ifav at Tc=150°C |
| 1N456 | A1 | a1 | NS | Uni | 30 V | 25 nA | | | <1 V | 40 mA | <10 pF | | | Ir at 25V |
| 1N457 | A1 | a1 | NS | Uni | 70 V | 25 nA | | | <1 V | 20 mA | <6 pF | | | Ir at 60V |
| 1N458 | A1 | a1 | NS | Uni | 150 V | 25 nA | | | <1 V | 7 mA | <6 pF | | | Ir at 125V |
| 1N459 | A1 | a1 | NS | Uni | 200 V | 25 nA | | | <1 V | 3 mA | <6 pF | | | Ir at 175V |
| 1N456A | A1 | a1 | NS | Uni | 30 V | 25 nA | | | <1 V | 100 mA | | | | Ir at 25V |
| 1N457A | A1 | a1 | NS | Uni | 70 V | 25 nA | | | <1 V | 100 mA | | | | Ir at 60V |
| 1N458A | A1 | a1 | NS | Uni | 150 V | 25 nA | | | <1 V | 100 mA | | | | Ir at 125V |
| 1N459A | A1 | a1 | NS | Uni | 200 V | 25 nA | | | <1 V | 100 mA | | | | Ir at 175V |
| 1N457JAN | A1 | a1 | NS | Uni | 70 V | 25 nA | | | <1 V | 20 mA | <6 pF | | | Ir at 60V |
| 1N458JAN | A1 | a1 | NS | Uni | 150 V | 25 nA | | | <1 V | 7 mA | <6 pF | | | Ir at 125V |
| 1N459JAN | A1 | a1 | NS | Uni | 200 V | 25 nA | | | <1 V | 3 mA | <6 pF | | | Ir at 175V |
| 1N461A | A1 | a1 | NS | Uni | 30 V | 0.5 µA | | | <1 V | 100 mA | | | | Ir at 25V |
| 1N462A | A1 | a1 | NS | Uni | 70 V | 0.5 µA | | | <1 V | 100 mA | | | | Ir at 60V |
| 1N463A | A1 | a1 | NS | Uni | 200 V | 0.5 µA | | | <1 V | 100 mA | | | | Ir at 175V |
| 1N482B | A1 | a1 | NS | Uni | 40 V | 25 nA | | | <1 V | 100 mA | | | | Ir at 36V |
| 1N483B | A1 | a1 | NS | Uni | 80 V | 25 nA | | | <1 V | 100 mA | | | | Ir at 70V |
| 1N484B | A1 | a1 | NS | Uni | 150 V | 25 nA | | | <1 V | 100 mA | | | | Ir at 130V |

| Type | Case | Pin-code | | | Maximum Ratings | | | | Electrical Characteristics | | | | | |
|---|---|---|---|---|---|---|---|---|---|---|---|---|---|---|
| | | | | | Vrm | Irm | Ifav / Ifm | Pv | Vf | If / Ifp | C0 | Cr | trr / ts | |
| 1N485B | A1 | a1 | NS | Uni | 200 V | 25 nA | | | <1 V | 100 mA | | | | Ir at 180V |
| 1N486B | A1 | a1 | NS | Uni | 250 V | 25 nA | | | <1 V | 100 mA | | | | Ir at 225V |
| 1N483BJAN | A1 | a1 | NS | Uni | 80 V | 25 nA | | | <1 V | 100 mA | | | | Ir at 70V |
| 1N485BJAN | A1 | a1 | NS | Uni | 200 V | 25 nA | | | <1 V | 100 mA | | | | Ir at 180V |
| 1N486BJAN | A1 | a1 | NS | Uni | 250 V | 25 nA | | | <1 V | 100 mA | | | | Ir at 225V |
| 1N483BJANTX | A1 | a1 | NS | Uni | 80 V | 25 nA | | | <1 V | 100 mA | | | | Ir at 70V |
| 1N485BJANTX | A1 | a1 | NS | Uni | 200 V | 25 nA | | | <1 V | 100 mA | | | | Ir at 180V |
| 1N486BJANTX | A1 | a1 | NS | Uni | 250 V | 25 nA | | | <1 V | 100 mA | | | | Ir at 225V |
| 1N625 | A1 | a1 | NS | Uni | 30 V | 1 µA | | | <1.5 V | 4 mA | | | <1 µs | Ir at 20V |
| 1N626 | A1 | a1 | NS | Uni | 50 V | 1 µA | | | <1.5 V | 4 mA | | | <1 µs | Ir at 35V |
| 1N627 | A1 | a1 | NS | Uni | 100 V | 1 µA | | | <1.5 V | 4 mA | | | <1 µs | Ir at 75V |
| 1N628 | A1 | a1 | NS | Uni | 150 V | 1 µA | | | <1.5 V | 4 mA | | | <1 µs | Ir at 125V |
| 1N629 | A1 | a1 | NS | Uni | 200 V | 1 µA | | | <1.5 V | 4 mA | | | <1 µs | Ir at 175V |
| 1N658 | A1 | a1 | NS | Uni | 120 V | 50 nA | | | <1 V | 100 mA | | | <300 ns | Ir at 50V |
| 1N659 | A1 | a1 | NS | Uni | 60 V | 5 µA | | | <1 V | 6 mA | | | <300 ns | Ir at 50V |
| 1N660 | A1 | a1 | NS | Uni | 120 V | 5 µA | | | <1 V | 6 mA | | | <300 ns | Ir at 100V |
| 1N661 | A1 | a1 | NS | Uni | 240 V | 10 µA | | | <1 V | 6 mA | | | <300 ns | Ir at 200V |
| 1N914 | A1 | a1 | IT,PH,NS | Uni | 100 V | 5 µA | 75 mA | 0.25 W | <1 V | 10 mA | <4 pF | | <4 ns | Ir at 75V |
| 1N914A | A1 | a1 | NS | Uni | 100 V | 25 µA | | | <1 V | 20 mA | | | <4 ns | Ir at 75V |
| 1N914B | A1 | a1 | NS | Uni | 100 V | 25 µA | | | <1 V | 100 mA | | | <4 ns | Ir at 75V |
| 1N914AJAN | A1 | a1 | NS | Uni | 100 V | 25 µA | | | <1 V | 20 mA | | | <4 ns | Ir at 75V |
| 1N916 | A1 | a1 | PH,NS | Uni | 100 V | 25 µA | 75 mA | 0.25 W | <1 V | 10 mA | <2 pF | | <4 ns | Ir at 75V |
| 1N916A | A1 | a1 | NS | Uni | 100 V | 25 µA | | | <1 V | 20 mA | | | <4 ns | Ir at 75V |
| 1N916B | A1 | a1 | NS | Uni | 100 V | 25 µA | | | <1 V | 30 mA | | | <4 ns | Ir at 75V |
| 1N1183 | E4 | a1 | SG | Rectifier | 50 V | 500 µA | 40 A | (44) W | <1.5 V | 110 A | | | | Ifav at Tc=140°C |
| 1N1184 | E4 | a1 | SG | Rectifier | 100 V | 500 µA | 40 A | (44) W | <1.5 V | 110 A | | | | Ifav at Tc=140°C |
| 1N1186 | E4 | a1 | SG | Rectifier | 200 V | 500 µA | 40 A | (44) W | <1.5 V | 110 A | | | | Ifav at Tc=140°C |
| 1N1187 | E4 | a1 | SG | Rectifier | 300 V | 500 µA | 40 A | (44) W | <1.5 V | 110 A | | | | Ifav at Tc=140°C |
| 1N1188 | E4 | a1 | SG | Rectifier | 400 V | 500 µA | 40 A | (44) W | <1.5 V | 110 A | | | | Ifav at Tc=140°C |
| 1N1189 | E4 | a1 | SG | Rectifier | 500 V | 500 µA | 40 A | (44) W | <1.5 V | 110 A | | | | Ifav at Tc=140°C |
| 1N1190 | E4 | a1 | SG | Rectifier | 600 V | 500 µA | 40 A | (44) W | <1.5 V | 110 A | | | | Ifav at Tc=140°C |
| 1N3766 | E4 | a1 | SG | Rectifier | 800 V | 500 µA | 40 A | (44) W | <1.5 V | 110 A | | | | Ifav at Tc=140°C |
| 1N3768 | E4 | a1 | SG | Rectifier | 1000 V | 500 µA | 40 A | (44) W | <1.5 V | 110 A | | | | Ifav at Tc=140°C |
| 1N1183A | E4 | a1 | MO | Rectifier | 50 V | 5 mA | 40 A | | <1.1 V | 100 A | | | | Ir at Tc=150°C |
| 1N1184A | E4 | a1 | MO | Rectifier | 100 V | 5 mA | 40 A | | <1.1 V | 100 A | | | | Ir at Tc=150°C |
| 1N1186A | E4 | a1 | MO | Rectifier | 200 V | 5 mA | 40 A | | <1.1 V | 100 A | | | | Ir at Tc=150°C |
| 1N1188A | E4 | a1 | MO | Rectifier | 400 V | 5 mA | 40 A | | <1.1 V | 100 A | | | | Ir at Tc=150°C |
| 1N1190A | E4 | a1 | MO | Rectifier | 600 V | 5 mA | 40 A | | <1.1 V | 100 A | | | | Ir at Tc=150°C |
| 1N1183AR | E4 | b1 | MO | Rectifier | 50 V | 5 mA | 40 A | | <1.1 V | 100 A | | | | Ir at Tc=150°C |
| 1N1184AR | E4 | b1 | MO | Rectifier | 100 V | 5 mA | 40 A | | <1.1 V | 100 A | | | | Ir at Tc=150°C |

| Type | Case | Pin-code | | | Maximum Ratings | | | | Electrical Characteristics | | | | | |
|---|---|---|---|---|---|---|---|---|---|---|---|---|---|---|
| | | | | | Vrm | Irm | Ifav / Ifm | Pv | Vf | If / Ifp | C0 | Cr | trr / ts | |
| 1N1186AR | E4 | b1 | MO | Rectifier | 200 V | 5 mA | 40 A | | <1.1 V | 100 A | | | | Ir at Tc=150°C |
| 1N1188AR | E4 | b1 | MO | Rectifier | 400 V | 5 mA | 40 A | | <1.1 V | 100 A | | | | Ir at Tc=150°C |
| 1N1190AR | E4 | b1 | MO | Rectifier | 600 V | 5 mA | 40 A | | <1.1 V | 100 A | | | | Ir at Tc=150°C |
| 1N248B | E4 | a1 | SG | Rectifier | 50 V | 5 mA | 20 A | (25) W | <1.5 V | 70 A | | | | Ifav at Tc=150°C |
| 1N249B | E4 | a1 | SG | Rectifier | 100 V | 5 mA | 20 A | (25) W | <1.5 V | 70 A | | | | Ifav at Tc=150°C |
| 1N250B | E4 | a1 | SG | Rectifier | 200 V | 5 mA | 20 A | (25) W | <1.5 V | 70 A | | | | Ifav at Tc=150°C |
| 1N1195A | E4 | a1 | SG | Rectifier | 400 V | 5 mA | 20 A | (25) W | <1.5 V | 70 A | | | | Ifav at Tc=150°C |
| 1N1196A | E4 | a1 | SG | Rectifier | 500 V | 5 mA | 20 A | (25) W | <1.5 V | 70 A | | | | Ifav at Tc=150°C |
| 1N1197A | E4 | a1 | SG | Rectifier | 500 V | 5 mA | 20 A | (25) W | <1.5 V | 70 A | | | | Ifav at Tc=150°C |
| 1N1198A | E4 | a1 | SG | Rectifier | 600 V | 5 mA | 20 A | (25) W | <1.5 V | 70 A | | | | Ifav at Tc=150°C |
| RN820 | E4 | a1 | SG | Rectifier | 800 V | 5 mA | 20 A | (25) W | <1.5 V | 70 A | | | | Ifav at Tc=150°C |
| RN1120 | E4 | a1 | SG | Rectifier | 1100 V | 5 mA | 20 A | (25) W | <1.5 V | | | | | Ifav at Tc=150°C |
| 1N1199 | E2 | a1 | MO | Rectifier | 50 V | 10 mA | 12 A | | <1.8 V | 40 A | | | | Ir at Tc=150°C |
| 1N1200 | E2 | a1 | MO | Rectifier | 100 V | 10 mA | 12 A | | <1.8 V | 40 A | | | | Ir at Tc=150°C |
| 1N1202 | E2 | a1 | MO | Rectifier | 200 V | 10 mA | 12 A | | <1.8 V | 40 A | | | | Ir at Tc=150°C |
| 1N1204 | E2 | a1 | MO | Rectifier | 400 V | 10 mA | 12 A | | <1.8 V | 40 A | | | | Ir at Tc=150°C |
| 1N1206 | E2 | a1 | MO | Rectifier | 600 V | 10 mA | 12 A | | <1.8 V | 40 A | | | | Ir at Tc=150°C |
| 1N1199A | E2 | a1 | MO | Rectifier | 50 V | 3 mA | 12 A | | <1.35 V | 40 A | | | | Ir at Tc=150°C |
| 1N1200A | E2 | a1 | MO | Rectifier | 100 V | 2.5 mA | 12 A | | <1.35 V | 40 A | | | | Ir at Tc=150°C |
| 1N1202A | E2 | a1 | MO | Rectifier | 200 V | 1 mA | 12 A | | <1.35 V | 40 A | | | | Ir at Tc=150°C |
| 1N1204A | E2 | a1 | MO | Rectifier | 400 V | 1.5 mA | 12 A | | <1.35 V | 40 A | | | | Ir at Tc=150°C |
| 1N1206A | E2 | a1 | MO | Rectifier | 600 V | 1 mA | 12 A | | <1.35 V | 40 A | | | | Ir at Tc=150°C |
| 1N1199B | E2 | a1 | MO | Rectifier | 50 V | 1 mA | 12 A | | <1.1 V | 12 A | | | 5 µs | Ir at Tc=150°C |
| 1N1200B | E2 | a1 | MO | Rectifier | 100 V | 1 mA | 12 A | | <1.1 V | 12 A | | | 5 µs | Ir at Tc=150°C |
| 1N1202B | E2 | a1 | MO | Rectifier | 200 V | 1 mA | 12 A | | <1.1 V | 12 A | | | 5 µs | Ir at Tc=150°C |
| 1N1204B | E2 | a1 | MO | Rectifier | 400 V | 1 mA | 12 A | | <1.1 V | 12 A | | | 5 µs | Ir at Tc=150°C |
| 1N1206B | E2 | a1 | MO | Rectifier | 600 V | 1 mA | 12 A | | <1.1 V | 12 A | | | 5 µs | Ir at Tc=150°C |
| 1N1199R | E2 | b1 | MO | Rectifier | 50 V | 10 mA | 12 A | | <1.8 V | 40 A | | | | Ir at Tc=150°C |
| 1N1200R | E2 | b1 | MO | Rectifier | 100 V | 10 mA | 12 A | | <1.8 V | 40 A | | | | Ir at Tc=150°C |
| 1N1202R | E2 | b1 | MO | Rectifier | 200 V | 10 mA | 12 A | | <1.8 V | 40 A | | | | Ir at Tc=150°C |
| 1N1204R | E2 | b1 | MO | Rectifier | 400 V | 10 mA | 12 A | | <1.8 V | 40 A | | | | Ir at Tc=150°C |
| 1N1206R | E2 | b1 | MO | Rectifier | 600 V | 10 mA | 12 A | | <1.8 V | 40 A | | | | Ir at Tc=150°C |
| 1N1199AR | E2 | b1 | MO | Rectifier | 50 V | 3 mA | 12 A | | <1.35 V | 40 A | | | | Ir at Tc=150°C |
| 1N1200AR | E2 | b1 | MO | Rectifier | 100 V | 2.5 mA | 12 A | | <1.35 V | 40 A | | | | Ir at Tc=150°C |
| 1N1202AR | E2 | b1 | MO | Rectifier | 200 V | 1 mA | 12 A | | <1.35 V | 40 A | | | | Ir at Tc=150°C |
| 1N1204AR | E2 | b1 | MO | Rectifier | 400 V | 1.5 mA | 12 A | | <1.35 V | 40 A | | | | Ir at Tc=150°C |
| 1N1206AR | E2 | b1 | MO | Rectifier | 600 V | 1 mA | 12 A | | <1.35 V | 40 A | | | | Ir at Tc=150°C |
| 1N1199BR | E2 | b1 | MO | Rectifier | 50 V | 1 mA | 12 A | | <1.1 V | 12 A | | | 5 µs | Ir at Tc=150°C |
| 1N1200BR | E2 | b1 | MO | Rectifier | 100 V | 1 mA | 12 A | | <1.1 V | 12 A | | | 5 µs | Ir at Tc=150°C |
| 1N1202BR | E2 | b1 | MO | Rectifier | 200 V | 1 mA | 12 A | | <1.1 V | 12 A | | | 5 µs | Ir at Tc=150°C |

39

| Type | Case | Pin-code | | | Maximum Ratings | | | | Electrical Characteristics | | | | | |
|---|---|---|---|---|---|---|---|---|---|---|---|---|---|---|
| | | | | | Vrm | Irm | Ifav / Ifm | Pv | Vf | If / Ifp | C0 | Cr | trr / ts | |
| 1N1204BR | E2 | b1 | MO | Rectifier | 400 V | 1 mA | 12 A | | <1.1 V | 12 A | | | 5 µs | Ir at Tc=150°C |
| 1N1206BR | E2 | b1 | MO | Rectifier | 600 V | 1 mA | 12 A | | <1.1 V | 12 A | | | 5 µs | Ir at Tc=150°C |
| 1N1341B | E2 | a1 | SG | Rectifier | 50 V | 500 µA | 20 A | (25) W | <1.2 V | 20 A | | | | Ifav at Tc=150°C |
| 1N1342B | E2 | a1 | SG | Rectifier | 100 V | 500 µA | 20 A | (25) W | <1.2 V | 20 A | | | | Ifav at Tc=150°C |
| 1N1344B | E2 | a1 | SG | Rectifier | 200 V | 500 µA | 20 A | (25) W | <1.2 V | 20 A | | | | Ifav at Tc=150°C |
| 1N1345B | E2 | a1 | SG | Rectifier | 300 V | 500 µA | 20 A | (25) W | <1.2 V | 20 A | | | | Ifav at Tc=150°C |
| 1N1346B | E2 | a1 | SG | Rectifier | 400 V | 500 µA | 20 A | (25) W | <1.2 V | 20 A | | | | Ifav at Tc=150°C |
| 1N1347B | E2 | a1 | SG | Rectifier | 500 V | 500 µA | 20 A | (25) W | <1.2 V | 20 A | | | | Ifav at Tc=150°C |
| 1N1348B | E2 | a1 | SG | Rectifier | 600 V | 500 µA | 20 A | (25) W | <1.2 V | 20 A | | | | Ifav at Tc=150°C |
| 1N3988B | E2 | a1 | SG | Rectifier | 800 V | 500 µA | 20 A | (25) W | <1.2 V | 20 A | | | | Ifav at Tc=150°C |
| 1N3990B | E2 | a1 | SG | Rectifier | 1000 V | 500 µA | 20 A | (25) W | <1.2 V | 20 A | | | | Ifav at Tc=150°C |
| 1N3064 | A1 | a1 | NS | Uni | 75 V | 0.1 µA | | | <1 V | 10 mA | <2 pF | | <4 ns | Ir at 50V |
| 1N3064JAN | A1 | a1 | NS | Uni | 75 V | 0.1 µA | | | <1 V | 10 mA | <2 pF | | <4 ns | Ir at 50V |
| 1N3070 | A1 | a1 | NS | Uni | 200 V | 100 µA | | | <1 V | 100 mA | <5 pF | | <50 ns | Ir at 175V |
| 1N3070JAN | A1 | a1 | NS | Uni | 200 V | 100 µA | | | <1 V | 100 mA | <5 pF | | <50 ns | Ir at 175V |
| 1N3070JANTX | A1 | a1 | NS | Uni | 200 V | 100 µA | | | <1 V | 100 mA | <5 pF | | <50 ns | Ir at 175V |
| 1N3208 | E4 | a1 | MO | Rectifier | 50 V | 1 mA | 15 A | | <1.5 V | 40 A | | | | Ir at Tc=150°C |
| 1N3209 | E4 | a1 | MO | Rectifier | 100 V | 1 mA | 15 A | | <1.5 V | 40 A | | | | Ir at Tc=150°C |
| 1N3210 | E4 | a1 | MO | Rectifier | 200 V | 1 mA | 15 A | | <1.5 V | 40 A | | | | Ir at Tc=150°C |
| 1N3211 | E4 | a1 | MO | Rectifier | 300 V | 1 mA | 15 A | | <1.5 V | 40 A | | | | Ir at Tc=150°C |
| 1N3212 | E4 | a1 | MO | Rectifier | 400 V | 1 mA | 15 A | | <1.5 V | 40 A | | | | Ir at Tc=150°C |
| 1N3208R | E4 | b1 | MO | Rectifier | 50 V | 1 mA | 15 A | | <1.5 V | 40 A | | | | Ir at Tc=150°C |
| 1N3209R | E4 | b1 | MO | Rectifier | 100 V | 1 mA | 15 A | | <1.5 V | 40 A | | | | Ir at Tc=150°C |
| 1N3210R | E4 | b1 | MO | Rectifier | 200 V | 1 mA | 15 A | | <1.5 V | 40 A | | | | Ir at Tc=150°C |
| 1N3211R | E4 | b1 | MO | Rectifier | 300 V | 1 mA | 15 A | | <1.5 V | 40 A | | | | Ir at Tc=150°C |
| 1N3212R | E4 | b1 | MO | Rectifier | 400 V | 1 mA | 15 A | | <1.5 V | 40 A | | | | Ir at Tc=150°C |
| 1N3595 | A1 | a1 | NS | Uni | 150 V | 1 µA | | | <0.8 V | 10 mA | | | | Ir at 125V |
| 1N6099 | A1 | a1 | NS | Uni | 150 V | 1 µA | | | <0.8 V | 10 mA | <8 pF | | | Ir at 125V |
| 1N3595JAN | A1 | a1 | NS | Uni | 150 V | 1 µA | | | <0.8 V | 10 mA | | | | Ir at 125V |
| 1N3595JANTX | A1 | a1 | NS | Uni | 150 V | 1 µA | | | <0.8 V | 10 mA | | | | Ir at 125V |
| 1N3595JANTXV | A1 | a1 | NS | Uni | 150 V | 1 µA | | | <0.8 V | 10 mA | | | | Ir at 125V |
| 1N3600 | A1 | a1 | NS | Uni | 75 V | 0.1 µA | | | <0.86 V | 50 mA | <2.5 pF | | <4 ns | Ir at 50V |
| 1N3600JAN | A1 | a1 | NS | Uni | 75 V | 0.1 µA | | | <0.86 V | 50 mA | <2.5 pF | | <4 ns | Ir at 50V |
| 1N3600JANTX | A1 | a1 | NS | Uni | 75 V | 0.1 µA | | | <0.86 V | 50 mA | <2.5 pF | | <4 ns | Ir at 50V |
| 1N3600JANTXV | A1 | a1 | NS | Uni | 75 V | 0.1 µA | | | <0.86 V | 50 mA | <2.5 pF | | <4 ns | Ir at 50V |
| 1N3766 | E4 | a1 | SG | Rectifier | 800 V | 500 µA | 40 A | 44 W | <1.5 V | 110 A | | | | Ifav at Tc=140°C |
| 1N3768 | E4 | a1 | SG | Rectifier | 1000 V | 500 µA | 40 A | 44 W | <1.5 V | 110 A | | | | Ifav at Tc=140°C |
| 1N3879 | E2 | a1 | SG,MO | Rectifier | 50 V | 15 µA | 6 A | (20) W | <1.4 V | 6 A | | | <200 ns | Ifav at Tc=100°C |
| 1N3880 | E2 | a1 | SG,MO | Rectifier | 100 V | 15 µA | 6 A | (20) W | <1.4 V | 6 A | | | <200 ns | Ifav at Tc=100°C |
| 1N3881 | E2 | a1 | SG,MO | Rectifier | 200 V | 15 µA | 6 A | (20) W | <1.4 V | 6 A | | | <200 ns | Ifav at Tc=100°C |

| Type | Case | Pin-code | | | Maximum Ratings | | | | Electrical Characteristics | | | | | |
|---|---|---|---|---|---|---|---|---|---|---|---|---|---|---|
| | | | | | Vrm | Irm | Ifav / Ifm | Pv | Vf | If / Ifp | C0 | Cr | trr / ts | |
| 1N3882 | E2 | a1 | SG,MO | Rectifier | 300 V | 15 µA | 6 A | (20) W | <1.4 V | 6 A | | | <200 ns | Ifav at Tc=100°C |
| 1N3883 | E2 | a1 | SG,MO | Rectifier | 400 V | 15 µA | 6 A | (20) W | <1.4 V | 6 A | | | <200 ns | Ifav at Tc=100°C |
| MR1366 | E2 | a1 | MO | Rectifier | 600 V | 15 µA | 6 A | | <1.4 V | 6 A | | | <200 ns | Ifav at Tc=100°C |
| 1N3889 | E2 | a1 | SG,MO | Rectifier | 50 V | 25 µA | 12 A | (20) W | <1.4 V | 12 A | | | <200 ns | Ifav at Tc=100°C |
| 1N3890 | E2 | a1 | SG,MO | Rectifier | 100 V | 25 µA | 12 A | (20) W | <1.4 V | 12 A | | | <200 ns | Ifav at Tc=100°C |
| 1N3891 | E2 | a1 | SG,MO | Rectifier | 200 V | 25 µA | 12 A | (20) W | <1.4 V | 12 A | | | <200 ns | Ifav at Tc=100°C |
| 1N3892 | E2 | a1 | SG,MO | Rectifier | 300 V | 25 µA | 12 A | (20) W | <1.4 V | 12 A | | | <200 ns | Ifav at Tc=100°C |
| 1N3893 | E2 | a1 | SG,MO | Rectifier | 400 V | 25 µA | 12 A | (20) W | <1.4 V | 12 A | | | <200 ns | Ifav at Tc=100°C |
| BYX62-600 | E2 | a1 | SG | Rectifier | 600 V | 25 µA | 12 A | (20) W | <1.4 V | 12 A | | | <200 ns | Ifav at Tc=100°C |
| MR1376 | E2 | a1 | MO | Rectifier | 600 V | 25 µA | 12 A | (20) W | <1.4 V | 12 A | | | <200 ns | Ifav at Tc=100°C |
| 1N3899 | E4 | a1 | SG,MO | Rectifier | 50 V | 50 µA | 20 A | (35) W | <1.4 V | 20 A | | | <200 ns | Ifav at Tc=100°C |
| 1N3900 | E4 | a1 | SG,MO | Rectifier | 100 V | 50 µA | 20 A | (35) W | <1.4 V | 20 A | | | <200 ns | Ifav at Tc=100°C |
| 1N3901 | E4 | a1 | SG,MO | Rectifier | 200 V | 50 µA | 20 A | (35) W | <1.4 V | 20 A | | | <200 ns | Ifav at Tc=100°C |
| 1N3902 | E4 | a1 | SG,MO | Rectifier | 300 V | 50 µA | 20 A | (35) W | <1.4 V | 20 A | | | <200 ns | Ifav at Tc=100°C |
| 1N3903 | E4 | a1 | SG,MO | Rectifier | 400 V | 50 µA | 20 A | (35) W | <1.4 V | 20 A | | | <200 ns | Ifav at Tc=100°C |
| BYX63-600 | E4 | a1 | SG | Rectifier | 600 V | 50 µA | 20 A | (35) W | <1.4 V | 20 A | | | <200 ns | Ifav at Tc=100°C |
| MR1386 | E4 | a1 | MO | Rectifier | 600 V | 50 µA | 20 A | | <1.4 V | 20 A | | | <200 ns | Ifav at Tc=100°C |
| 1N3909 | E4 | a1 | SG,MO | Rectifier | 50 V | 50 µA | 30 A | (50) W | <1.4 V | 30 A | | | <200 ns | Ifav at Tc=100°C |
| 1N3910 | E4 | a1 | SG,MO | Rectifier | 100 V | 50 µA | 30 A | (50) W | <1.4 V | 30 A | | | <200 ns | Ifav at Tc=100°C |
| 1N3911 | E4 | a1 | SG,MO | Rectifier | 200 V | 50 µA | 30 A | (50) W | <1.4 V | 30 A | | | <200 ns | Ifav at Tc=100°C |
| 1N3912 | E4 | a1 | SG,MO | Rectifier | 300 V | 50 µA | 30 A | (50) W | <1.4 V | 30 A | | | <200 ns | Ifav at Tc=100°C |
| 1N3913 | E4 | a1 | SG,MO | Rectifier | 400 V | 50 µA | 30 A | (50) W | <1.4 V | 30 A | | | <200 ns | Ifav at Tc=100°C |
| BYX64-600 | E4 | a1 | SG | Rectifier | 660 V | 50 µA | 30 A | (50) W | <1.4 V | 30 A | | | <200 ns | Ifav at Tc=100°C |
| MR1396 | E4 | a1 | MO | Rectifier | 600 V | 50 µA | 30 A | | <1.4 V | 30 A | | | <200 ns | Ifav at Tc=100°C |
| 1N3988 | E2 | a1 | SG | Rectifier | 800 V | | 20 A | 25 W | <1.2 V | 20 A | | | | |
| 1N3990 | E2 | a1 | SG | Rectifier | 1000 V | | 20 A | 25 W | <1.2 V | 20 A | | | | |
| 1N4001 | A3 | a1 | RD,MO | Rectifier | 50 V | 1 µA | 1 A | | 1.1 V | 1 A | | | | |
| 1N4001 | B1 | a1 | IT | Rectifier | 50 V | 1 µA | 1 A | | <1.3 V | 1 A | | | | |
| 1N4002 | A3 | a1 | RD,MO | Rectifier | 100 V | 1 µA | 1 A | | 1.1 V | 1 A | | | | |
| 1N4002 | B1 | a1 | IT | Rectifier | 100 V | 1 µA | 1 A | | <1.3 V | 1 A | | | | |
| 1N4003 | A3 | a1 | RD,MO | Rectifier | 200 V | 1 µA | 1 A | | 1.1 V | 1 A | | | | |
| 1N4003 | B1 | a1 | IT | Rectifier | 200 V | 1 µA | 1 A | | <1.3 V | 1 A | | | | |
| 1N4004 | A3 | a1 | RD,MO | Rectifier | 400 V | 1 µA | 1 A | | 1.1 V | 1 A | | | | |
| 1N4005 | A3 | a1 | RD,MO | Rectifier | 600 V | 1 µA | 1 A | | 1.2 V | 1 A | | | | |
| 1N4006 | A3 | a1 | RD,MO | Rectifier | 800 V | 1 µA | 1 A | | 1.1 V | 1 A | | | | |
| 1N4007 | A3 | a1 | RD,MO | Rectifier | 1000 V | 1 µA | 1 A | | 1.1 V | 1 A | | | | |
| 1N4007H | A3 | a1 | RD | Rectifier | 1600 V | 1 µA | 1 A | | 1.1 V | 1 A | | | | |
| 1N4007S | A3 | a1 | RD | Rectifier | 1250 V | 1 µA | 1 A | | 1.1 V | 1 A | | | | |
| 1N4001G | A4 | a1 | PH | Rectifier | 50 V | 10 µA | 1 A | | <1.1 V | 1 A | | | | |
| 1N4002G | A4 | a1 | PH | Rectifier | 100 V | 10 µA | 1 A | | <1.1 V | 1 A | | | | |

| Type | Case | Pin-code | | | Maximum Ratings | | | | Electrical Characteristics | | | | | |
|---|---|---|---|---|---|---|---|---|---|---|---|---|---|---|
| | | | | | Vrm | Irm | Ifav / Ifm | Pv | Vf | If / Ifp | C0 | Cr | trr / ts | |
| 1N4003G | A4 | a1 | PH | Rectifier | 200 V | 10 µA | 1 A | | <1.1 V | 1 A | | | | |
| 1N4004G | A4 | a1 | PH | Rectifier | 400 V | 10 µA | 1 A | | <1.1 V | 1 A | | | | |
| 1N4005G | A4 | a1 | PH | Rectifier | 600 V | 10 µA | 1 A | | <1.1 V | 1 A | | | | |
| 1N4006G | A4 | a1 | PH | Rectifier | 800 V | 10 µA | 1 A | | <1.1 V | 1 A | | | | |
| 1N4007G | A4 | a1 | PH | Rectifier | 1000 V | 10 µA | 1 A | | <1.1 V | 1 A | | | | |
| 1N4001ID | A8 | a1 | PH | Rectifier | 50 V | 10 µA | 1 A | | <1.1 V | 1 A | | | | |
| 1N4002ID | A8 | a1 | PH | Rectifier | 100 V | 10 µA | 1 A | | <1.1 V | 1 A | | | | |
| 1N4003ID | A8 | a1 | PH | Rectifier | 200 V | 10 µA | 1 A | | <1.1 V | 1 A | | | | |
| 1N4004ID | A8 | a1 | PH | Rectifier | 400 V | 10 µA | 1 A | | <1.1 V | 1 A | | | | |
| 1N4005ID | A8 | a1 | PH | Rectifier | 600 V | 10 µA | 1 A | | <1.1 V | 1 A | | | | |
| 1N4006ID | A8 | a1 | PH | Rectifier | 800 V | 10 µA | 1 A | | <1.1 V | 1 A | | | | |
| 1N4007ID | A8 | a1 | PH | Rectifier | 1000 V | 10 µA | 1 A | | <1.1 V | 1 A | | | | |
| 1N4009 | A1 | a1 | NS | Uni | 35 V | 0.1 µA | | | <1 V | 30 mA | <4 pF | | <4 ns | Ir at 25V |
| 1N4146 | A1 | a1 | NS | Uni | 100 V | 25 nA | | | <1 V | 20 mA | | | <4 ns | Ir at 20V |
| 1N4147 | A1 | a1 | NS | Uni | 100 V | 25 nA | | | <1 V | 100 mA | | | <4 ns | Ir at 20V |
| 1N4148 | A1 | a1 | RD,IT,TE,PH,NS | Uni | (75) V | 5 µA | 150 mA | 0.5 W | 1 V | 10 mA | <4 pF | | <4 ns | |
| 1N4148-1JAN | A1 | a1 | NS | Uni | 100 V | 25 nA | | | <1 V | 10 mA | <4 pF | | <4 ns | Ir at 20V |
| 1N4148-1JANTX | A1 | a1 | NS | Uni | 100 V | 25 nA | | | <1 V | 10 mA | <4 pF | | <4 ns | Ir at 20V |
| 1N4148-1JANTXV | A1 | a1 | NS | Uni | 100 V | 25 nA | | | <1 V | 10 mA | <4 pF | | <4 ns | Ir at 20V |
| 1N4148S | A2 | a1 | IT | Uni | (75) V | 5 µA | 150 mA | 0.3 W | 1 V | 10 mA | <4 pF | | <4 ns | |
| 1N4149 | A1 | a1 | TE,IT,NS | Uni | (100) V | 5 µA | 150 mA | 0.5 W | <1 V | 10 mA | | | <4 ns | |
| 1N4149S | A2 | a1 | IT | Uni | (100) V | 5 µA | 150 mA | 0.3 W | <1 V | 10 mA | | | <4 ns | |
| 1N4150 | A1 | a1 | TE,IT,PH,NS | Uni | (50) V | 0.1 µA | 200 mA | 0.5 W | <1 V | 200 mA | | | <4 ns | |
| 1N4150-1JAN | A1 | a1 | NS | Uni | 75 V | 0.1 µA | | | <1 V | 200 mA | <2.5 pF | | <4 ns | Ir at 50V |
| 1N4150-1JANTX | A1 | a1 | NS | Uni | 75 V | 0.1 µA | | | <1 V | 200 mA | <2.5 pF | | <4 ns | Ir at 50V |
| 1N4150-1JANTXV | A1 | a1 | NS | Uni | 75 V | 0.1 µA | | | <1 V | 200 mA | <2.5 pF | | <4 ns | Ir at 50V |
| 1N4151 | A1 | a1 | TE,IT,PH,NS | Uni | (50) V | 50 nA | 150 mA | 0.5 W | <1 V | 50 mA | <2 pF | | <4 ns | Ir at 50V |
| 1N4152 | A1 | a1 | IT,NS | Uni | (40) V | 50 nA | 150 mA | 0.5 W | <0.55 V | 0.1 mA | | | <2 ns | Ir at 30V |
| 1N4153 | A1 | a1 | IT,PH,NS | Uni | 75 V | 25 nA | 150 mA | 0.5 W | <0.55 V | 0.1 mA | | | <2 ns | Ir at 50V |
| 1N4154 | A1 | a1 | TE,IT,NS | Uni | (25) V | 0.1 µA | 150 mA | 0.5 W | <1 V | 30 mA | <4 pF | | <4 ns | Ir at 25V |
| 1N4154S | A2 | a1 | IT | Uni | (25) V | 0.1 µA | 150 mA | 0.3 W | <1 V | 30 mA | <4 pF | | <4 ns | Ir at 25V |
| 1N4244 | A15 | a1 | NS | Uni | 20 V | 0.1 µA | | | <1 V | 20 mA | <0.8 pF | | <0.75 ns | Ir at 10V |
| 1N4305 | A1 | a1 | NS | Uni | 75 V | 0.1 µA | | | <0.85 V | 10 mA | <2 pF | | <2 ns | Ir at 50V |
| 1N4306JAN | A15 | a1 | NS | Uni | 75 V | 50 nA | | | <1 V | 50 mA | <2 pF | | <4 ns | Ir at 50V |
| 1N4306JANTX | A15 | a1 | NS | Uni | 75 V | 50 nA | | | <1 V | 50 mA | <2 pF | | <4 ns | Ir at 50V |
| 1N4306JANTXV | A15 | a1 | NS | Uni | 75 V | 50 nA | | | <1 V | 50 mA | <2 pF | | <4 ns | Ir at 50V |
| 1N4307JAN | A15 | a1 | NS | Uni | 75 V | 50 nA | | | <1 V | 50 mA | <2 pF | | <4 ns | Ir at 50V |
| 1N4307JANTX | A15 | a1 | NS | Uni | 75 V | 50 nA | | | <1 V | 50 mA | <2 pF | | <4 ns | Ir at 50V |
| 1N4307JANTXV | A15 | a1 | NS | Uni | 75 V | 50 nA | | | <1 V | 50 mA | <2 pF | | <4 ns | Ir at 50V |
| 1N4376 | A15 | a1 | NS | Uni | 20 V | 0.1 µA | | | <0.88 V | 10 mA | <1 pF | | <750 ns | Ir at 50V |

| Type | Case | Pin-code | | | Maximum Ratings Vrm | Irm | Ifav Ifm | Pv | Electrical Characteristics Vf | If Ifp | C0 | Cr | trr ts | |
|---|---|---|---|---|---|---|---|---|---|---|---|---|---|---|
| 1N4376JAN | A15 | a1 | NS | Uni | 20 V | 0.1 µA | | | <0.88 V | 10 mA | <1 pF | | <750 ns | Ir at 50V |
| 1N4446 | A1 | a1 | TE,IT,PH,NS | Uni | (100) V | 5 µA | 150 mA | 0.5 W | <1 V | 10 mA | <4 pF | | <4 ns | Ir at 75V |
| 1N4446S | A2 | a1 | IT | Uni | (100) V | 5 µA | 150 mA | 0.3 W | <1 V | 10 mA | <4 pF | | <4 ns | Ir at 75V |
| 1N4447 | A1 | a1 | TE,IT,NS | Uni | 100 V | 5 µA | 150 mA | 0.5 W | <1 V | 20 mA | | | <4 ns | Ir at 75V |
| 1N4447S | A2 | a1 | IT | Uni | 100 V | 5 µA | 150 mA | 0.3 W | <1 V | 20 mA | | | <4 ns | Ir at 75V |
| 1N4448 | A1 | a1 | RD,TE,IT,PH,NS | Uni | (100) V | 5 µA | 150 mA | 0.5 W | <1 V | 10 mA | <4 pF | | <4 ns | Ir at 75V |
| 1N4448S | A2 | a1 | IT | Uni | (100) V | 5 µA | 150 mA | 0.3 W | <1 V | 10 mA | <4 pF | | <4 ns | Ir at 75V |
| 1N4449 | A1 | a1 | TE,IT,NS | Uni | 100 V | 5 µA | 150 mA | 0.5 W | <1 V | 30 mA | | | <8 ns | Ir at 75V |
| 1N4449S | A2 | a1 | IT | Uni | 100 V | 5 µA | 150 mA | 0.3 W | <1 V | 30 mA | | | <8 ns | Ir at 75V |
| 1N4450 | A1 | a1 | IT,NS | Uni | (40) V | 50 nA | 150 mA | 0.4 W | <0.54 V | 0.5 mA | | | <4 ns | Ir at 30V |
| 1N4451 | A1 | a1 | IT | Uni | (40) V | 50 nA | 150 mA | 0.4 W | <0.5 V | 0.3 mA | | | <10 ns | Ir at 30V |
| 1N4453 | A1 | a1 | IT | Uni | (30) V | 50 nA | 150 mA | 0.4 W | <0.55 V | 0.01 mA | | | | Ir at 20V |
| 1N4454 | A1 | a1 | IT,NS | Uni | (75) V | 100 µA | 150 mA | 0.4 W | <1 V | 10 mA | | | | Ir at 50V |
| 1N4454-1JAN | A1 | a1 | NS | Uni | 75 V | 0.1 µA | | | <1 V | 10 mA | <2 pF | | <4 ns | Ir at 50V |
| 1N4454-1JANTX | A1 | a1 | NS | Uni | 75 V | 0.1 µA | | | <1 V | 10 mA | <2 pF | | <4 ns | Ir at 50V |
| 1N4454-1JANTXV | A1 | a1 | NS | Uni | 75 V | 0.1 µA | | | <1 V | 10 mA | <2 pF | | <4 ns | Ir at 50V |
| 1N4531 | A2 | a1 | PH | Uni | 75 V | 25 nA | 200 mA | | <1 V | 10 mA | <4 pF | | <4 ns | Ir at 20V |
| 1N4532 | A2 | a1 | PH | Uni | 75 V | 0.1 µA | 200 mA | | <1 V | 10 mA | <2 pF | | <2 ns | Ir at 50V |
| 1N4719 | C3 | a1 | MO | Rectifier | 50 V | 0.5 mA | 3 A | | <1 V | 3 A | | | | Ifav at Ta=75°C |
| 1N4720 | C3 | a1 | MO | Rectifier | 100 V | 0.5 mA | 3 A | | <1 V | 3 A | | | | Ifav at Ta=75°C |
| 1N4721 | C3 | a1 | MO | Rectifier | 200 V | 0.5 mA | 3 A | | <1 V | 3 A | | | | Ifav at Ta=75°C |
| 1N4722 | C3 | a1 | MO | Rectifier | 400 V | 0.5 mA | 3 A | | <1 V | 3 A | | | | Ifav at Ta=75°C |
| 1N4723 | C3 | a1 | MO | Rectifier | 600 V | 0.5 mA | 3 A | | <1 V | 3 A | | | | Ifav at Ta=75°C |
| 1N4724 | C3 | a1 | MO | Rectifier | 800 V | 0.5 mA | 3 A | | <1 V | 3 A | | | | Ifav at Ta=75°C |
| 1N4725 | C3 | a1 | MO | Rectifier | 1000 V | 0.5 mA | 3 A | | <1 V | 3 A | | | | Ifav at Ta=75°C |
| 1N4933 | A3 | a1 | RD,MO | Rectifier | 50 V | 5 µA | 1 A | | 1.2 V | 1 A | | | 200 ns | Ifav at Ta=50°C |
| 1N4934 | A3 | a1 | RD,MO | Rectifier | 100 V | 5 µA | 1 A | | 1.2 V | 1 A | | | 200 ns | Ifav at Ta=50°C |
| 1N4935 | A3 | a1 | RD,MO | Rectifier | 200 V | 5 µA | 1 A | | 1.2 V | 1 A | | | 200 ns | Ifav at Ta=50°C |
| 1N4936 | A3 | a1 | RD,MO | Rectifier | 400 V | 5 µA | 1 A | | 1.2 V | 1 A | | | 200 ns | Ifav at Ta=50°C |
| 1N4937 | A3 | a1 | RD,MO | Rectifier | 600 V | 5 µA | 1 A | | 1.2 V | 1 A | | | 200 ns | Ifav at Ta=50°C |
| 1N4938 | A1 | a1 | NS | Uni | 200 V | 100 µA | | | <1 V | 100 mA | <5 pF | | <50 ns | Ir at 175V |
| 1N5059 | A4 | a1 | TE,PH | Rectifier | 200 V | 1 µA | 2 A | | <1 V | 1 A | | | 3 µs | |
| 1N5060 | A4 | a1 | TE,PH | Rectifier | 400 V | 1 µA | 2 A | | <1 V | 1 A | | | 3 µs | |
| 1N5061 | A4 | a1 | TE,PH | Rectifier | 600 V | 1 µA | 2 A | | <1 V | 1 A | | | 3 µs | |
| 1N5062 | A4 | a1 | TE,PH | Rectifier | 800 V | 1 µA | 2 A | | <1 V | 1 A | | | 3 µs | |
| 1N5282 | A1 | a1 | NS | Uni | 80 V | 0.1 µA | | | <0.9 V | 100 mA | <2.5 pF | | <2 ns | Ir at 55V |
| 1N5400 | B7 | a1 | RD,MO | Rectifier | 50 V | 20 µA | 3 A | | 1.2 V | 3 A | | | | |
| 1N5401 | B7 | a1 | RD,MO | Rectifier | 100 V | 20 µA | 3 A | | 1.2 V | 3 A | | | | |
| 1N5402 | B7 | a1 | RD,MO | Rectifier | 200 V | 20 µA | 3 A | | 1.2 V | 3 A | | | | |
| 1N5403 | B7 | a1 | RD | Rectifier | 300 V | 20 µA | 3 A | | 1.2 V | 3 A | | | | |

| Type | Case | Pin-code | | | Maximum Ratings | | | | Electrical Characteristics | | | | | |
|---|---|---|---|---|---|---|---|---|---|---|---|---|---|---|
| | | | | | Vrm | Irm | Ifav / Ifm | Pv | Vf | If / Ifp | C0 | Cr | trr / ts | |
| 1N5404 | B7 | a1 | RD,MO | Rectifier | 400 V | 20 µA | 3 A | | 1.2 V | 3 A | | | | |
| 1N5405 | B7 | a1 | RD | Rectifier | 500 V | 20 µA | 3 A | | 1.2 V | 3 A | | | | |
| 1N5406 | B7 | a1 | RD,MO | Rectifier | 600 V | 20 µA | 3 A | | 1.2 V | 3 A | | | | |
| 1N5407 | B7 | a1 | RD,MO | Rectifier | 800 V | 20 µA | 3 A | | 1.2 V | 3 A | | | | |
| 1N5408 | B7 | a1 | RD,MO | Rectifier | 1000 V | 20 µA | 3 A | | 1.2 V | 3 A | | | | |
| 1N5417 | A5 | a1 | TE | Rectifier | 200 V | 1 µA | 3 A | | <1.1 V | 3 A | | | <100 ns | Ifav at Ta=45°C |
| 1N5418 | A5 | a1 | TE | Rectifier | 400 V | 1 µA | 3 A | | <1.1 V | 3 A | | | <100 ns | Ifav at Ta=45°C |
| 1N5624 | A5 | a1 | TE | Rectifier | 200 V | 1 µA | 3 A | | ≤1 V | 3 A | | | <4 µs | Ifav at Ta=45°C |
| 1N5625 | A5 | a1 | TE | Rectifier | 400 V | 1 µA | 3 A | | ≤1 V | 3 A | | | <4 µs | Ifav at Ta=45°C |
| 1N5626 | A5 | a1 | TE | Rectifier | 600 V | 1 µA | 3 A | | ≤1 V | 3 A | | | <4 µs | Ifav at Ta=45°C |
| 1N5627 | A5 | a1 | TE | Rectifier | 800 V | 1 µA | 3 A | | ≤1 V | 3 A | | | <4 µs | Ifav at Ta=45°C |
| 1N5711 | A1 | a1 | SG | Uni | 70 V | | | 0.43 W | <0.41 V | 1 mA | 2 pF | | 0.1 ns | |
| 1N5712 | A1 | a1 | SG | Uni | 20 V | | | 0.43 W | <1 V | 35 mA | 1.2 pF | | 0.1 ns | |
| 1N5817 | A8 | a1 | PH | Rectifier | 20 V | 1 mA | 1 A | | <0.45 V | 1 A | 80 pF | | | |
| 1N5818 | A8 | a1 | PH | Rectifier | 30 V | 1 mA | 1 A | | <0.55 V | 1 A | 50 pF | | | |
| 1N5819 | A8 | a1 | PH | Rectifier | 40 V | 1 mA | 1 A | | <0.6 V | 1 A | 50 pF | | | |
| 1N5820 | B2 | a1 | MO | Rectifier | 20 V | 2 mA | 3 A | | <0.38 V | 1 A | | | | |
| 1N5821 | B2 | a1 | MO | Rectifier | 30 V | 2 mA | 3 A | | <0.5 V | 1 A | | | | |
| 1N5822 | B2 | a1 | MO | Rectifier | 40 V | 2 mA | 3 A | | <0.9 V | 1 A | | | | |
| 1N5820ID | A13 | a1 | PH | Rectifier | 20 V | 2 mA | 3 A | | <0.48 V | 3 A | 250 pF | | | |
| 1N5821ID | A13 | a1 | PH | Rectifier | 30 V | 2 mA | 3 A | | <0.5 V | 3 A | 175 pF | | | |
| 1N5822ID | A13 | a1 | PH | Rectifier | 40 V | 2 mA | 3 A | | <0.53 V | 3 A | 175 pF | | | |
| 1N5823 | C3 | a1 | MO | Rectifier | 20 V | 10 mA | 5 A | | 0.36 V | 5 A | | | | |
| 1N5824 | C3 | a1 | MO | Rectifier | 30 V | 10 mA | 5 A | | 0.37 V | 5 A | | | | |
| 1N5825 | C3 | a1 | MO | Rectifier | 40 V | 10 mA | 5 A | | 0.38 V | 5 A | | | | |
| MBR5825 | C3 | a1 | MO | Rectifier | 40 V | 10 mA | 5 A | | 0.38 V | 5 A | | | | |
| MBR5825H | C3 | a1 | MO | Rectifier | 40 V | 10 mA | 5 A | | 0.38 V | 5 A | | | | |
| MBR5825H1 | C3 | a1 | MO | Rectifier | 40 V | 10 mA | 5 A | | 0.38 V | 5 A | | | | |
| 1N5826 | E2 | a1 | MO | Rectifier | 20 V | 10 mA | 15 A | | 0.44 V | 15 A | | | | |
| 1N5827 | E2 | a1 | MO | Rectifier | 30 V | 10 mA | 15 A | | 0.47 V | 15 A | | | | |
| 1N5828 | E2 | a1 | MO | Rectifier | 40 V | 10 mA | 15 A | | 0.5 V | 15 A | | | | |
| 1N5829 | E2 | a1 | MO | Rectifier | 20 V | 20 mA | 25 A | | <0.44 V | 25 A | | | | |
| 1N5830 | E2 | a1 | MO | Rectifier | 30 V | 20 mA | 25 A | | <0.46 V | 25 A | | | | |
| 1N5831 | E2 | a1 | MO | Rectifier | 40 V | 20 mA | 25 A | | <0.48 V | 25 A | | | | |
| MBR5831 | E2 | a1 | MO | Rectifier | 40 V | 20 mA | 25 A | | <0.48 V | 25 A | | | | |
| MBR5831H | E2 | a1 | MO | Rectifier | 40 V | 20 mA | 25 A | | <0.48 V | 25 A | | | | |
| MBR5831H1 | E2 | a1 | MO | Rectifier | 40 V | 20 mA | 25 A | | <0.48 V | 25 A | | | | |
| 1N5832 | E4 | a1 | MO | Rectifier | 20 V | 20 mA | 40 A | | <0.52 V | 40 A | | | | |
| 1N5833 | E4 | a1 | MO | Rectifier | 30 V | 20 mA | 40 A | | <0.55 V | 40 A | | | | |
| 1N5834 | E4 | a1 | MO | Rectifier | 40 V | 20 mA | 40 A | | <0.59 V | 40 A | | | | |

| Type | Case | Pin-code | | | Vrm | Irm | Ifav / Ifm | Pv | Vf | If / Ifp | C0 | Cr | trr / ts | |
|------|------|----------|---|---|-----|-----|------------|----|----|----------|----|----|----------|---|
| 1N6095 | E2 | a1 | MO | Rectifier | 30 V | 250 mA | 25 A | | <0.89 V | 78.5 A | 6 nF | | | Ir at Tc=125°C |
| 1N6096 | E2 | a1 | MO | Rectifier | 40 V | 250 mA | 25 A | | <0.89 V | 78.5 A | 6 nF | | | Ir at Tc=125°C |
| SD41 | E2 | a1 | MO | Rectifier | 45 V | 125 mA | 30 A | | <0.55 V | 30 A | 2 nF | | | Ir at Tc=125°C |
| 1N6097 | E4 | a1 | MO | Rectifier | 30 V | 250 mA | 50 A | | <0.86 V | 60 A | 7 nF | | | Tc=115°C |
| 1N6098 | E4 | a1 | MO | Rectifier | 40 V | 250 mA | 50 A | | <0.86 V | 60 A | 7 nF | | | Tc=115°C |
| SD51 | E4 | a1 | MO | Rectifier | 45 V | 200 mA | 120 A | | <0.6 V | 60 A | 4 nF | | | Tc=90°C |
| 1N6263 | A1 | a1 | SG | Uni | 60 V | | | | <1 V | 15 mA | 2.2 pF | | 0.1 ns | |
| 1NH41 | A16 | a1 | TO | Rectifier | 1000 V | 10 µA | 1 A | | <1.3 V | 1 A | | | <400 ns | |
| 1NH42 | A17 | a1 | TO | Rectifier | 1000 V | 10 µA | 1 A | | <1.3 V | 1 A | | | <400 ns | |
| 1NU41 | B1 | a1 | TO | Rectifier | 1000 V | 100 µA | 1 A | | <3.3 V | 1 A | | | <100 ns | |
| 1Q4B42 | F16 | d23 | TO | Rect. Bridge | 1200 V | 10 µA | 1 A | | <1.2 V | 500 mA | | | | |
| 1R5BZ41 | B16 | a1 | TO | Rectifier | 100 V | 10 µA | 1.5 A | | <0.95 V | 1.5 A | | | | |
| 1R5GZ41 | B16 | a1 | TO | Rectifier | 400 V | 10 µA | 1.5 A | | <0.95 V | 1.5 A | | | | |
| 1R5DL41A | B16 | a1 | TO | Rectifier | 200 V | 100 µA | 1.5 A | | <0.98 V | 1.5 A | | | <35 ns | |
| 1R5GH45 | B16 | a1 | TO | Rectifier | 400 V | 100 µA | 1.5 A | | <1.1 V | 1.5 A | | | <35 ns | |
| 1R5GU41 | B16 | a1 | TO | Rectifier | 400 V | 50 µA | 1.5 A | | <1.2 V | 1.5 A | | | <100 ns | |
| 1R5JH45 | B16 | a1 | TO | Rectifier | 600 V | 100 µA | 1.5 A | | <1.2 V | 1.5 A | | | <200 ns | |
| 1R5JU41 | B16 | a1 | TO | Rectifier | 600 V | 100 µA | 1.5 A | | <2 V | 2 A | | | <100 ns | |
| 1R5JZ41 | B16 | a1 | TO | Rectifier | 600 V | 10 µA | 1.5 A | | <1 V | 1.5 A | | | | |
| 1R5NZ41 | B16 | a1 | TO | Rectifier | 1000 V | 10 µA | 1.5 A | | <1 V | 1.5 A | | | | |
| 1R5NH41 | B16 | a1 | TO | Rectifier | 1000 V | 10 µA | 1.5 A | | <1.3 V | 1.5 A | | | <750 ns | |
| 1R5NH45 | B16 | a1 | TO | Rectifier | 1000 V | 10 µA | 1.5 A | | <1.5 V | 1.5 A | | | <100 ns | |
| 1R5NU41 | B16 | a1 | TO | Rectifier | 1000 V | 10 µA | 1.5 A | | <3 V | 2 A | | | <100 ns | |
| 1S44 | A1 | a1 | NS | Uni | 50 V | 50 nA | | | <1 V | 10 mA | <4 pF | | <8 ns | Ir at 10V |
| 1S920 | A1 | a1 | NS | Uni | 50 V | 0.1 µA | | | <1.2 V | 100 mA | <6.5 pF | | | |
| 1S921 | A1 | a1 | NS | Uni | 100 V | 0.1 µA | | | <1.2 V | 100 mA | <6.5 pF | | | |
| 1S922 | A1 | a1 | NS | Uni | 150 V | 0.1 µA | | | <1.2 V | 100 mA | <6.5 pF | | | |
| 1S923 | A1 | a1 | NS | Uni | 200 V | 0.1 µA | | | <1.2 V | 100 mA | <6.5 pF | | | |
| 1S1832 | B1 | a1 | TO | Rectifier | 1800 V | 10 µA | 700 mA | | <2 V | 1.5 A | | | <6 µs | |
| 1S1834 | B1 | a1 | TO | Rectifier | 400 V | 10 µA | 1 A | | <1.2 V | 1.5 A | | | <1.5 µs | |
| 1S1835 | B1 | a1 | TO | Rectifier | 600 V | 10 µA | 1 A | | <1.2 V | 1.5 A | | | <1.5 µs | |
| 1S1830 | B1 | a1 | TO | Rectifier | 1000 V | 10 µA | 1 A | | <1.2 V | 1.5 A | | | | |
| 1S1885 | B1 | a1 | TO | Rectifier | 100 V | 10 µA | 1 A | | <1.2 V | 1.5 A | | | | |
| 1S1887 | B1 | a1 | TO | Rectifier | 400 V | 10 µA | 1 A | | <1.2 V | 1.5 A | | | | |
| 1S1888 | B1 | a1 | TO | Rectifier | 600 V | 10 µA | 1 A | | <1.2 V | 1.5 A | | | | |
| 1S1885A | B1 | a1 | TO | Rectifier | 100 V | 10 µA | 1.2 A | | <1 V | 5 A | | | | |
| 1S1887A | B1 | a1 | TO | Rectifier | 400 V | 10 µA | 1.2 A | | <1 V | 5 A | | | | |
| 1S1888A | B1 | a1 | TO | Rectifier | 600 V | 10 µA | 1.2 A | | <1 V | 5 A | | | | |
| 1SR154-100 | G5 | a1 | RO | Rectifier | (100) V | 10 µA | 1 A | | <1.1 V | 1.1 A | | | | |
| 1SR154-200 | G5 | a1 | RO | Rectifier | (200) V | 10 µA | 1 A | | <1.1 V | 1.1 A | | | | |

| Type | Case | Pin-code | | | Maximum Ratings | | | | Electrical Characteristics | | | | | |
|---|---|---|---|---|---|---|---|---|---|---|---|---|---|---|
| | | | | | Vrm | Irm | Ifav / Ifm | Pv | Vf | If / Ifp | C0 | Cr | trr / ts | |
| 1SR154-400 | G5 | a1 | RO | Rectifier | (400) V | 10 µA | 1 A | | <1.1 V | 1.1 A | | | | |
| 1SR154-600 | G5 | a1 | RO | Rectifier | (600) V | 10 µA | 1 A | | <1.1 V | 1.1 A | | | | |
| 1SR154-800 | G5 | a1 | RO | Rectifier | (800) V | 10 µA | 1 A | | <1.1 V | 1.1 A | | | | |
| 1SR156-100 | G5 | a1 | RO | Rectifier | (100) V | 10 µA | 800 mA | | <1.3 V | 800 mA | | | <400 ns | |
| 1SR156-200 | G5 | a1 | RO | Rectifier | (200) V | 10 µA | 800 mA | | <1.3 V | 800 mA | | | <400 ns | |
| 1SR156-400 | G5 | a1 | RO | Rectifier | (400) V | 10 µA | 800 mA | | <1.3 V | 800 mA | | | <400 ns | |
| 1SR159-200 | G5 | a1 | RO | Rectifier | (200) V | 10 µA | 1 A | | <0.98 V | | | | <50 ns | |
| 1SS154 | F1 | c3 | TO | RF Diode | (6) V | 0.5 µA | 30 mA | | 0.5 V | 10 mA | 0.8 pF | | | Ir at 5V |
| 1SS239 | G9 | a1 | TO | RF Diode | (6) V | 0.5 µA | 30 mA | | 0.47 V | 10 mA | 0.2 pF | | | Ir at 5V |
| 1SS241 | G9 | a1 | TO | RF Diode | (30) V | 0.1 µA | 100 mA | | <0.85 V | 2 mA | 0.8 pF | | | Ir at 15V |
| 1SS242 | G9 | a1 | TO | RF Diode | (5) V | 25 µA | 30 mA | | 0.25 V | 2 mA | 0.6 pF | | | Ir at 0.5V |
| 1SS268 | F1 | c5 | TO | Pair RF Diode | (30) V | 0.1 µA | 50 mA | | <0.85 V | 2 mA | 0.8 pF | | | comm-k |
| 1SS269 | F1 | c2 | TO | Pair RF Diode | (30) V | 0.1 µA | 50 mA | | <0.85 V | 2 mA | 0.8 pF | | | comm-a |
| 1SS271 | F1 | c6 | TO | Pair RF Diode | (6) V | 0.5 µA | 30 mA | | 0.5 V | 10 mA | 0.8 pF | | | ser |
| 1SS295 | F1 | c6 | TO | Pair RF Diode | (4) V | 25 µA | 30 mA | | 0.25 V | 2 mA | 0.6 pF | | | ser |
| 1SS312 | F1 | c14 | TO | RF Diode | (30) V | 0.1 µA | 50 mA | | <0.85 V | 2 mA | 0.8 pF | | | Ir at 15V |
| 1SS313 | F1 | c12 | TO | RF Diode | (30) V | 0.1 µA | 50 mA | | <0.85 V | 2 mA | 0.8 pF | | | Ir at 15V |
| 1SS314 | G6 | a1 | TO | RF Diode | (30) V | 0.1 µA | 100 mA | | <0.85 V | 2 mA | 0.7 pF | | | Ir at 15V |
| 1SS315 | G6 | a1 | TO | RF Diode | (5) V | 25 µA | 30 mA | | 0.25 V | 2 mA | 0.6 pF | | | Ir at 0.5V |
| 1SS353 | G10 | a1 | RO | Switch | (90) V | 0.5 µA | 100 mA | | <1.2 V | 100 mA | <3 pF | | <4 ns | C0 at .5V |
| 1SS354 | G10 | a1 | RO | Switch | (55) V | 0.5 µA | 100 mA | | <1.2 V | 100 mA | <3 pF | | <4 ns | C0 at .5V |
| 1SS355 | G10 | a1 | RO | Switch | (40) V | 0.5 µA | 100 mA | | <1.2 V | 100 mA | <3 pF | | <4 ns | C0 at .5V |
| 1SS356 | G10 | a1 | RO | RF Diode | (35) V | 10 nA | | | <1 V | 10 mA | <1.2 pF | | | C0 at 6V |
| 1SS364 | F1 | c5 | TO | Pair RF Diode | (30) V | 0.1 µA | 50 mA | | <0.85 V | 2 mA | 0.85 pF | | | comm-k |
| 1SV128 | F1 | c3 | TO | PIN Diode | (50) V | 0.1 µA | 50 mA | | 0.95 V | 50 mA | 0.25 pF | | 400 ns | Ir at 15V |
| 1SV153 | G9 | a1 | TO | C Diode | (30) V | 10 nA | | | | | <16.25 pF | 6.5 | | Ir at 15V |
| 1SV153A | G9 | a1 | TO | C Diode | (30) V | 10 nA | | | | | <16.25 pF | 6.5 | | Ir at 15V |
| 1SV160 | F1 | c17 | TO | C Diode | (15) V | 100 nA | | | | | <14 pF | <9.3 | | Ir at 4V |
| 1SV161 | G9 | a1 | TO | C Diode | (30) V | 10 nA | | | | | <32 pF | 10.5 | | Ir at 28V |
| 1SV172 | F1 | c6 | TO | Pair PIN | (50) V | 0.1 µA | 50 mA | | 0.95 V | 50 mA | 0.25 pF | | | ser |
| 1SV186 | G9 | a1 | TO | C Diode | (30) V | 10 nA | | | | | <4.55 pF | 5.2 | | Ir at 28V |
| 1SV204 | G9 | a1 | TO | C Diode | (30) V | 10 nA | | | | | <5.7 pF | <3.4 | | Ir at 28V |
| 1SV211 | G9 | a1 | TO | C Diode | (30) V | 10 nA | | | | | 36 pF | 12.5 | | Ir at 28V |
| 1SV212 | G9 | a1 | TO | C Diode | (15) V | 3 nA | | | | | 15 pF | 2.5 | | Vr 2..10V |
| 1SV214 | G6 | a1 | TO | C Diode | (30) V | 10 nA | | | | | <16.25 pF | 6.5 | | Ir 2..25V |
| 1SV215 | G6 | a1 | TO | C Diode | (30) V | 10 nA | | | | | <32 pF | 10.5 | | Ir 2..25V |
| 1SV216 | G6 | a1 | TO | C Diode | (30) V | 10 nA | | | | | <16 pF | <3.4 | | Ir 2..10V |
| 1SV217 | G6 | a1 | TO | C Diode | (30) V | 10 nA | | | | | 36 pF | 12.5 | | Ir 2..25V |
| 1SV223 | G6 | a1 | RO | C Diode | 30 V | 10 µA | | | | | <16 pF | <8 | | Ir 2..25V |
| 1SV224 | G9 | a1 | TO | C Diode | (30) V | 10 nA | | | | | 15 pF | 8 | | Ir 2..20V |

| Type | Case | Pin-code | | | Maximum Ratings | | | | Electrical Characteristics | | | | | |
|---|---|---|---|---|---|---|---|---|---|---|---|---|---|---|
| | | | | | Vrm | Irm | Ifav *Ifm* | Pv | Vf | If *Ifp* | C0 | Cr | trr *ts* | |
| 1SV225 | F1 | c5 | TO | Pair C Diode | (32) V | 50 nA | | | | | 19.7 pF | <2.9 | | comm-k |
| 1SV226 | G9 | a1 | TO | C Diode | (30) V | 10 nA | | | | | 45 pF | 15 | | Ir 2..25V |
| 1SV227 | G9 | a1 | TO | C Diode | (30) V | 10 nA | | | | | 30.3 pF | 10.5 | | Ir 2..25V |
| 1SV228 | F1 | c5 | TO | Pair C Diode | (15) V | 10 nA | | | | | 30.5 pF | <2.6 | | comm-k |
| 1SV229 | G6 | a1 | TO | C Diode | (15) V | 3 nA | | | | | 15 pF | <2.5 | | Vr 2..10V |
| 1SV230 | G6 | a1 | TO | C Diode | (30) V | 10 nA | | | | | 15 pF | 8 | | Ir at 2..20V |
| 1SV231 | G6 | a1 | TO | C Diode | (30) V | 10 nA | | | | | 45 pF | 15 | | Ir at 2..25V |
| 1SV232 | G6 | a1 | TO | C Diode | (30) V | 10 nA | | | | | 32 pF | 10.5 | | Ir at 2..25V |
| 1SV237 | F12 | d10 | TO | Pair PIN | (50) V | 0.1 µA | *50 mA* | | 0.95 V | 50 mA | 0.25 pF | | | indep |
| 1SV238 | G6 | a1 | TO | C Diode | (30) V | 10 nA | | | | | 35 pF | 11.5 | | Ir at 28V |
| 1SV239 | G6 | a1 | TO | C Diode | (15) V | 10 nA | | | | | 4.25 pF | 2.4 | | Vr 2..25V |
| 1SV242 | F1 | c5 | TO | Pair C Diode | (30) V | 10 nA | | | | | 39 pF | 14.5 | | comm-k |
| 1SV245 | G6 | a1 | TO | C Diode | (30) V | 10 nA | | | | | <4.55 pF | 5.7 | | Ir at 28V |
| 1SV252 | F1 | c6 | TO | Pair PIN | (50) V | 0.1 µA | *50 mA* | | 0.95 V | 50 mA | 0.25 pF | | | ser |
| 1T32-T7 | G7 | a1 | SO | C Diode | 35 V | 10 nA | | | | | 15 pF | 6.5 | | Vr 2..25V |
| 1T32-T8 | G7 | a1 | SO | C Diode | 35 V | 10 nA | | | | | 15 pF | 6.5 | | Vr 2..25V |
| 1T32A-T7 | G7 | a1 | SO | C Diode | 35 V | 10 nA | | | | | 15 pF | 6.5 | | Vr 2..25V |
| 1T32A-T8 | G7 | a1 | SO | C Diode | 35 V | 10 nA | | | | | 15 pF | 6.5 | | Vr 2..25V |
| 1T33C-T7 | G7 | a1 | SO | C Diode | 35 V | 10 nA | | | | | 38 pF | 15 | | Vr 2..25V |
| 1T33C-T8 | G7 | a1 | SO | C Diode | 35 V | 10 nA | | | | | 38 pF | 15 | | Vr 2..25V |
| 1T33-T7 | G7 | a1 | SO | C Diode | 35 V | 10 nA | | | | | 27 pF | 10 | | Vr 2..25V |
| 1T33-T8 | G7 | a1 | SO | C Diode | 35 V | 10 nA | | | | | 27 pF | 10 | | Vr 2..25V |
| 1T33A-T7 | G7 | a1 | SO | C Diode | 35 V | 10 nA | | | | | 27 pF | 10 | | Vr 2..25V |
| 1T33A-T8 | G8 | a1 | SO | C Diode | 35 V | 10 nA | | | | | 27 pF | 10 | | Vr 2..25V |
| 1T359 | G7 | a1 | SO | C Diode | 35 V | 10 nA | | | | | 29.5 pF | 6.5 | | Vr 2..25V |
| 1T360-T7 | G7 | a1 | SO | C Diode | 35 V | 10 nA | | | | | 31.3 pF | 12.5 | | Vr 2..25V |
| 1T360-T8 | G8 | a1 | SO | C Diode | 35 V | 10 nA | | | | | 31.3 pF | 12.5 | | Vr 2..25V |
| 1T362 | G6 | a1 | SO | C Diode | 35 V | 10 nA | | | | | 15 pF | 6.5 | | Vr 2..25V |
| 1T363 | G6 | a1 | SO | C Diode | 35 V | 10 nA | | | | | 38 pF | 15 | | Vr 2..25V |
| 2B4B41 | O2 | d26 | TO | Rect. Bridge | 100 V | 10 µA | 2 A | | <1.2 V | 2 A | | | | |
| 2G4B41 | O2 | d26 | TO | Rect. Bridge | 400 V | 10 µA | 2 A | | <1.2 V | 2 A | | | | |
| 2J4B41 | O2 | d26 | TO | Rect. Bridge | 600 V | 10 µA | 2 A | | <1.2 V | 2 A | | | | |
| 2GWJ2C42 | F10 | c7 | TO | Rect. Pair | 40 V | 1 mA | 2 A | | <0.55 V | 1 A | 45 pF | | | comm-k |
| 2GWJ42 | B16 | a1 | TO | Rectifier | 40 V | 0.5 mA | 2 A | | <0.55 V | 2 A | 125 pF | | <35 ns | |
| 2NH45 | B10 | a1 | TO | Rectifier | 1000 V | 100 µA | 2 A | | <1.5 V | 2 A | | | <200 ns | |
| 2NU41 | B10 | a1 | TO | Rectifier | 1000 V | 100 µA | 2 A | | <3 V | 3 A | | | <100 ns | |
| 3B4B41 | O3 | d26 | TO | Rect. Bridge | 100 V | 10 µA | 3 A | | <1.2 V | 3 A | | | | |
| 3G4B41 | O3 | d26 | TO | Rect. Bridge | 400 V | 10 µA | 3 A | | <1.2 V | 3 A | | | | |
| 3J4B41 | O3 | d26 | TO | Rect. Bridge | 600 V | 10 µA | 3 A | | <1.2 V | 3 A | | | | |
| 3BH41 | B10 | a1 | TO | Rectifier | 100 V | 10 µA | 3 A | | <1.2 V | 3 A | | | <1.5 µs | |

**3GH41 – 10B4B41**

| Type | Case | Pin-code | | | Maximum Ratings | | | | Electrical Characteristics | | | | | |
|---|---|---|---|---|---|---|---|---|---|---|---|---|---|---|
| | | | | | Vrm | Irm | Ifav / Ifm | Pv | Vf | If / Ifp | C0 | Cr | trr / ts | |
| 3GH41 | B10 | a1 | TO | Rectifier | 400 V | 10 µA | 3 A | | <1.2 V | 3 A | | | <1.5 µs | |
| 3JH41 | B10 | a1 | TO | Rectifier | 600 V | 10 µA | 3 A | | <1.2 V | 3 A | | | <1.5 µs | |
| 3BZ41 | B10 | a1 | TO | Rectifier | 100 V | 10 µA | 3 A | | <1 V | 3 A | | | | |
| 3GZ41 | B10 | a1 | TO | Rectifier | 400 V | 10 µA | 3 A | | <1 V | 3 A | | | | |
| 3JZ41 | B10 | a1 | TO | Rectifier | 600 V | 10 µA | 3 A | | <1 V | 3 A | | | | |
| 3NZ41 | B10 | a1 | TO | Rectifier | 1000 V | 10 µA | 3 A | | <1 V | 3 A | | | | |
| 3DL41A | B10 | a1 | TO | Rectifier | 200 V | 100 µA | 3 A | | <0.98 V | 3 A | | | <35 ns | |
| 3GH45 | B10 | a1 | TO | Rectifier | 400 V | 100 µA | 3 A | | <1.1 V | 3 A | | | <200 ns | |
| 3GU41 | B10 | a1 | TO | Rectifier | 400 V | 300 µA | 3 A | | <1.5 V | 3 A | | | <100 ns | |
| 3GWJ2C42 | F10 | a1 | TO | Rect. Pair | 40 V | 2 mA | 3 A | | <0.55 V | 3 A | 45 pF | | | comm-k |
| 3JH45 | B10 | a1 | TO | Rectifier | 600 V | 100 µA | 3 A | | <1.2 V | 3 A | | | <200 ns | |
| 3JU41 | B10 | a1 | TO | Rectifier | 600 V | 100 µA | 3 A | | <2 V | 3 A | | | <100 ns | |
| 3NH41 | B10 | a1 | TO | Rectifier | 1000 V | 10 µA | 3 A | | <1.3 V | 3 A | | | <400 ns | |
| 3TH41 | B10 | a1 | TO | Rectifier | 1500 V | 10 µA | 3 A | | <1.2 V | 3 A | | | <1.5 µs | |
| 4B4B41 | O4 | d26 | TO | Rect. Bridge | 100 V | 10 µA | 3 A | | <1 V | 6 A | | | | |
| 4G4B41 | O4 | d26 | TO | Rect. Bridge | 400 V | 10 µA | 3 A | | <1 V | 6 A | | | | |
| 4J4B41 | O4 | d26 | TO | Rect. Bridge | 600 V | 10 µA | 3 A | | <1 V | 6 A | | | | |
| 5DL2C41A | I4 | c7 | TO | Rect. Pair | 200 V | 10 µA | 5 A | | <0.98 V | 2.5 A | | | <35 ns | comm-k |
| 5DL2C48A | I23 | c7 | TO | Rect. Pair | 200 V | 10 µA | 5 A | | <0.98 V | 2.5 A | | | <35 ns | comm-k |
| 5FL2C48A | I23 | c7 | TO | Rect. Pair | 300 V | 10 µA | 5 A | | <1.3 V | 2.5 A | | | <35 ns | comm-k |
| 5DL2CZ47A | I22 | c7 | TO | Rect. Pair | 200 V | 10 µA | 5 A | | <0.98 V | 2.5 A | | | <35 ns | comm-k |
| 5FL2CZ47A | I22 | c7 | TO | Rect. Pair | 300 V | 10 µA | 5 A | | <1.3 V | 2.5 A | | | <35 ns | comm-k |
| 5GL2CZ47A | I22 | c7 | TO | Rect. Pair | 400 V | 50 µA | 5 A | | <1.8 V | 2.5 A | | | <35 ns | comm-k |
| 5DLZ47A | I21 | a1 | TO | Rectifier | 200 V | 10 µA | 5 A | | <0.98 V | 5 A | | | <35 ns | |
| 5GLZ47A | I21 | a1 | TO | Rectifier | 400 V | 50 µA | 5 A | | <1.8 V | 5 A | | | <35 ns | |
| 5GUZ47 | I21 | a1 | TO | Rectifier | 400 V | 100 µA | 5 A | | <1.2 V | 5 A | | | <100 ns | |
| 5GWJ2C42 | I4 | c7 | TO | Rect. Pair | 40 V | 3.5 mA | 5 A | | <0.55 V | 2.5 A | | | <35 ns | comm-k |
| 5GWJ2C48 | I23 | c7 | TO | Rect. Pair | 40 V | 3.5 mA | 5 A | | <0.55 V | 2.5 A | 125 pF | | | comm-k |
| 5GWJ2CZ47 | I22 | c7 | TO | Rect. Pair | 40 V | 3.5 mA | 5 A | | <0.55 V | 2.5 A | 125 pF | | | comm-k |
| 5JWJ2CZ47 | I22 | c7 | TO | Rect. Pair | 60 V | 3.5 mA | 5 A | | <0.58 V | 2 A | 100 pF | | | comm-k |
| 5MWJ2CZ47 | I22 | c7 | TO | Rect. Pair | 90 V | 3.5 mA | 5 A | | <0.81 V | 2 A | 72 pF | | | comm-k |
| 5GWJZ47 | I21 | a1 | TO | Rectifier | 40 V | 3.5 mA | 5 A | | <0.55 V | 5 A | 200 pF | | <35 ns | |
| 5JL2CZ47 | I22 | c7 | TO | Rect. Pair | 600 V | 50 µA | 5 A | | <2 V | 2.5 A | | | <50 ns | comm-k |
| 5JLZ47 | I21 | a1 | TO | Rectifier | 600 V | 50 µA | 5 A | | <2 V | 5 A | | | <50 ns | |
| 5JUZ47 | I21 | a1 | TO | Rectifier | 600 V | 100 µA | 5 A | | <1.5 V | 5 A | | | <100 ns | |
| 5THZ52 | J15 | a1 | TO | Rectifier | 1500 V | 50 µA | 5 A | | <1.5 V | 5 A | | | <1.5 µs | |
| 6B4B41 | O5 | d26 | TO | Rect. Bridge | 100 V | 10 µA | 3.8 A | | <1 V | 9 A | | | | |
| 6G4B41 | O5 | d26 | TO | Rect. Bridge | 400 V | 10 µA | 3.8 A | | <1 V | 9 A | | | | |
| 6J4B41 | O5 | d26 | TO | Rect. Bridge | 600 V | 10 µA | 3.8 A | | <1 V | 9 A | | | | |
| 10B4B41 | O5 | d26 | TO | Rect. Bridge | 100 V | 10 µA | 4.3 A | | <1.05 V | 15 A | | | | |

| Type | Case | Pin-code | | | Maximum Ratings | | | | Electrical Characteristics | | | | | |
|---|---|---|---|---|---|---|---|---|---|---|---|---|---|---|
| | | | | | Vrm | Irm | Ifav / Ifm | Pv | Vf | If / Ifp | C0 | Cr | trr / ts | |
| 10G4B41 | O5 | d26 | TO | Rect. Bridge | 400 V | 10 µA | 4.3 A | | <1.05 V | 15 A | | | | |
| 10J4B41 | O5 | d26 | TO | Rect. Bridge | 600 V | 10 µA | 4.3 A | | <1.05 V | 15 A | | | | |
| 10DL2C41A | I4 | c7 | TO | Rect. Pair | 200 V | 10 µA | 10 A | | <0.98 V | 5 A | | | <35 ns | comm-k |
| 10DL2C48A | I23 | c7 | TO | Rect. Pair | 200 V | 10 µA | 10 A | | <0.98 V | 5 A | | | <35 ns | comm-k |
| 10FL2C48A | I23 | c7 | TO | Rect. Pair | 300 V | 10 µA | 10 A | | <1.3 V | 5 A | | | <35 ns | comm-k |
| 10DL2CZ47A | I22 | c7 | TO | Rect. Pair | 200 V | 10 µA | 10 A | | <0.98 V | 5 A | | | <35 ns | comm-k |
| 10FL2CZ47A | I22 | c7 | TO | Rect. Pair | 300 V | 10 µA | 10 A | | <1.3 V | 5 A | | | <35 ns | comm-k |
| 10GL2CZ47A | I22 | c7 | TO | Rect. Pair | 400 V | 50 µA | 10 A | | <1.8 V | 5 A | | | <35 ns | comm-k |
| 10GWJ2C42 | I4 | c7 | TO | Rect. Pair | 40 V | 3.5 mA | 10 A | | <0.55 V | 5 A | 235 pF | | <35 ns | comm-k |
| 10GWJ2C48 | I23 | c7 | TO | Rect. Pair | 40 V | 3.5 mA | 10 A | | <0.55 V | 5 A | 235 pF | | <35 ns | comm-k |
| 10GWJ2CZ47 | I22 | c7 | TO | Rect. Pair | 40 V | 3.5 mA | 10 A | | <0.55 V | 5 A | 235 pF | | <35 ns | comm-k |
| 10JWJ2CZ47 | I22 | c7 | TO | Rect. Pair | 60 V | 3.5 mA | 10 A | | <0.58 V | 4 A | 195 pF | | <35 ns | comm-k |
| 10MWJ2CZ47 | I22 | c7 | TO | Rect. Pair | 90 V | 3.5 mA | 10 A | | <0.81 V | 4 A | 138 pF | | <35 ns | comm-k |
| 10JL2CZ47 | I22 | c7 | TO | Rect. Pair | 600 V | 50 µA | 10 A | | <2 V | 5 A | | | <50 ns | comm-k |
| 15B4B42 | O6 | d26 | TO | Rect. Bridge | 100 V | 10 µA | 4.5 A | | <1.05 V | 15 A | | | | |
| 15G4B42 | O6 | d26 | TO | Rect. Bridge | 400 V | 10 µA | 4.5 A | | <1.05 V | 15 A | | | | |
| 15J4B42 | O6 | d26 | TO | Rect. Bridge | 600 V | 10 µA | 4.5 A | | <1.05 V | 15 A | | | | |
| 16DL2C41A | J13 | c7 | TO | Rect. Pair | 200 V | 50 µA | 16 A | | <0.98 V | 8 A | | | <35 ns | comm-k |
| 16DL2CZ47A | I22 | c7 | TO | Rect. Pair | 200 V | 50 µA | 16 A | | <0.98 V | 8 A | | | <35 ns | comm-k |
| 16FL2CZ47A | I22 | c7 | TO | Rect. Pair | 300 V | 50 µA | 16 A | | <1.3 V | 8 A | | | <35 ns | comm-k |
| 16FWJ2C42 | J13 | c7 | TO | Rect. Pair | 30 V | 15 mA | 16 A | | <0.55 V | 8 A | 360 pF | | <35 ns | comm-k |
| 16GWJ2C42 | J13 | c7 | TO | Rect. Pair | 40 V | 15 mA | 16 A | | <0.55 V | 8 A | 360 pF | | <35 ns | comm-k |
| 16GWJ2CZ47 | I22 | c7 | TO | Rect. Pair | 40 V | 15 mA | 16 A | | <0.55 V | 8 A | 360 pF | | <35 ns | comm-k |
| 20DL2C41A | J13 | c7 | TO | Rect. Pair | 200 V | 50 µA | 20 A | | <0.98 V | 10 A | | | <35 ns | comm-k |
| 20FL2C41A | J13 | c7 | TO | Rect. Pair | 300 V | 50 µA | 20 A | | <1.3 V | 10 A | | | <35 ns | comm-k |
| 20GL2C41A | J13 | c7 | TO | Rect. Pair | 400 V | 50 µA | 20 A | | <1.8 V | 10 A | | | <35 ns | comm-k |
| 20DL2C48A | F9 | c7 | TO | Rect. Pair | 200 V | 50 µA | 20 A | | <0.98 V | 10 A | | | <35 ns | comm-k |
| 20FL2C48A | I23 | c7 | TO | Rect. Pair | 300 V | 50 µA | 20 A | | <1.3 V | 10 A | | | <35 ns | comm-k |
| 20DL2CZ47A | I22 | c7 | TO | Rect. Pair | 200 V | 50 µA | 20 A | | <0.98 V | 10 A | | | <35 ns | comm-k |
| 20FL2CZ47A | I22 | c7 | TO | Rect. Pair | 300 V | 50 µA | 20 A | | <1.3 V | 10 A | | | <35 ns | comm-k |
| 20DL2CZ51A | J14 | c7 | TO | Rect. Pair | 200 V | 50 µA | 20 A | | <0.98 V | 10 A | | | <35 ns | comm-k |
| 20FL2CZ51A | J14 | c7 | TO | Rect. Pair | 300 V | 50 µA | 20 A | | <1.3 V | 10 A | | | <35 ns | comm-k |
| 20JL2C41 | J13 | c7 | TO | Rect. Pair | 600 V | 50 µA | 20 A | | <2 V | 10 A | | | <50 ns | comm-k |
| 20L6P45 | N10 | e4 | TO | Rect. Bridge | 800 V | 100 µA | 20 A | | <1.2 V | 20 A | | | | |
| 25B4B42 | O6 | d26 | TO | Rect. Bridge | 100 V | 10 µA | 25 A | | <1 V | 22 A | | | | |
| 25G4B42 | O6 | d26 | TO | Rect. Bridge | 400 V | 10 µA | 25 A | | <1 V | 22 A | | | | |
| 25J4B42 | O6 | d26 | TO | Rect. Bridge | 600 V | 10 µA | 25 A | | <1 V | 22 A | | | | |
| 30GWJ2C42 | J13 | c7 | TO | Rect. Pair | 40 V | 15 mA | 30 A | | <0.55 V | 15 A | 620 pF | | <35 ns | comm-k |
| 30GWJ2C48 | I23 | c7 | TO | Rect. Pair | 40 V | 15 mA | 30 A | | <0.55 V | 15 A | 620 pF | | | comm-k |
| 30JWJ2C48 | I23 | c7 | TO | Rect. Pair | 40 V | 15 mA | 30 A | | <0.58 V | 12 A | 580 pF | | | comm-k |

| Type | Case | Pin-code | | | Maximum Ratings | | | | Electrical Characteristics | | | | | |
|------|------|----------|--|--|------|------|------------|------|------|-----------|------|------|------------|------|
| | | | | | Vrm | Irm | Ifav / Ifm | Pv | Vf | If / Ifp | C0 | Cr | trr / ts | |
| 30JL2C41 | J13 | c7 | TO | Rect. Pair | 600 V | 50 µA | 30 A | | <2 V | 15 A | | | <50 ns | comm-k |
| 30L6P45 | N10 | e4 | TO | Rect. Bridge | 800 V | 100 µA | 30 A | | <1.2 V | 30 A | | | | |
| 50G6P43 | H5 | e5 | TO | Rect. Bridge | 400 V | 5 mA | 50 A | | <1.2 V | 50 A | | | | Ir at Tj=150°C |
| 50L6P43 | H5 | e5 | TO | Rect. Bridge | 800 V | 5 mA | 50 A | | <1.2 V | 50 A | | | | Ir at Tj=150°C |
| 50Q6P43 | H5 | e5 | TO | Rect. Bridge | 1200 V | 5 mA | 50 A | | <1.2 V | 50 A | | | | Ir at Tj=150°C |
| 50U6P43 | H5 | e5 | TO | Rect. Bridge | 1600 V | 5 mA | 50 A | | <1.2 V | 50 A | | | | Ir at Tj=150°C |
| 75G6P43 | H5 | e5 | TO | Rect. Bridge | 400 V | 5 mA | 75 A | | <1.2 V | 75 A | | | | Ir at Tj=150°C |
| 75L6P43 | H5 | e5 | TO | Rect. Bridge | 800 V | 5 mA | 75 A | | <1.2 V | 75 A | | | | Ir at Tj=150°C |
| 75Q6P43 | H5 | e5 | TO | Rect. Bridge | 1200 V | 5 mA | 75 A | | <1.2 V | 75 A | | | | Ir at Tj=150°C |
| 75U6P43 | H5 | e5 | TO | Rect. Bridge | 1600 V | 5 mA | 75 A | | <1.2 V | 75 A | | | | Ir at Tj=150°C |
| 100G6P43 | H5 | e5 | TO | Rect. Bridge | 400 V | 5 mA | 100 A | | <1.2 V | 100 A | | | | Ir at Tj=150°C |
| 100L6P43 | H5 | e5 | TO | Rect. Bridge | 800 V | 5 mA | 100 A | | <1.2 V | 100 A | | | | Ir at Tj=150°C |
| 100Q6P43 | H5 | e5 | TO | Rect. Bridge | 1200 V | 5 mA | 100 A | | <1.2 V | 100 A | | | | Ir at Tj=150°C |
| 100U6P43 | H5 | e5 | TO | Rect. Bridge | 1600 V | 5 mA | 100 A | | <1.2 V | 100 A | | | | Ir at Tj=150°C |
| 110G2G43 | H4 | c20 | TO | Rect. Pair | 400 V | 20 mA | 110 A | | <1.2 V | 160 A | | | | ser |
| 110L2G43 | H4 | c20 | TO | Rect. Pair | 800 V | 20 mA | 110 A | | <1.2 V | 160 A | | | | ser |
| 110Q2G43 | H4 | c20 | TO | Rect. Pair | 1200 V | 20 mA | 110 A | | <1.2 V | 160 A | | | | ser |
| 110U2G43 | H4 | c20 | TO | Rect. Pair | 1600 V | 20 mA | 110 A | | <1.2 V | 160 A | | | | ser |
| 160G2G43 | H4 | c20 | TO | Rect. Pair | 400 V | 20 mA | 160 A | | <1.2 V | 240 A | | | | ser |
| 160L2G43 | H4 | c20 | TO | Rect. Pair | 800 V | 20 mA | 160 A | | <1.2 V | 240 A | | | | ser |
| 160Q2G43 | H4 | c20 | TO | Rect. Pair | 1200 V | 20 mA | 160 A | | <1.2 V | 240 A | | | | ser |
| 160U2G43 | H4 | c20 | TO | Rect. Pair | 1600 V | 20 mA | 160 A | | <1.2 V | 240 A | | | | ser |
| AG01 | A19 | a1 | RD | Rectifier | 400 V | 100 µA | 700 mA | | 1.8 V | 700 mA | | | 100 ns | |
| AG01A | A19 | a1 | RD | Rectifier | 600 V | 100 µA | 500 mA | | 1.8 V | 500 mA | | | 100 ns | |
| AG01Z | A19 | a1 | RD | Rectifier | 200 V | 100 µA | 700 mA | | 1.8 V | 700 mA | | | 100 ns | |
| AG01Y | A19 | a1 | RD | Rectifier | 70 V | 100 µA | 1 A | | 1.2 V | 1 A | | | 100 ns | |
| AK03 | A19 | a1 | RD | Rectifier | 30 V | 5 mA | 1 A | | 0.6 V | 1 A | | | | |
| AK04 | A19 | a1 | RD | Rectifier | 40 V | 5 mA | 1 A | | 0.6 V | 1 A | | | | |
| AK06 | A19 | a1 | RD | Rectifier | 60 V | 1 mA | 700 mA | | 0.62 V | 700 mA | | | | |
| AK09 | A19 | a1 | RD | Rectifier | 90 V | 1 mA | 700 mA | | 0.81 V | 700 mA | | | | |
| AL01Z | A19 | a1 | RD | Rectifier | 200 V | 100 µA | 1 A | | 1.05 V | 1 A | | | 50 ns | |
| B125-110-35 | O11 | d26 | RD | Rect. Bridge | 400 V | | | | | | | | | |
| B250-220-35 | O11 | d26 | RD | Rect. Bridge | 600 V | | | | | | | | | |
| B40-35-35 | O11 | d26 | RD | Rect. Bridge | 100 V | | | | | | | | | |
| B80-70-35 | O11 | d26 | RD | Rect. Bridge | 200 V | | | | | | | | | |
| B125C1500 | N2 | d21 | RD | Rect. Bridge | 300 V | | | | | | | | | 1000µ/3 Ω |
| B250C1500 | N2 | d21 | RD | Rect. Bridge | 600 V | | | | | | | | | 500µ/6 Ω |
| B380C1500 | N2 | d21 | RD | Rect. Bridge | 800 V | | | | | | | | | 250µ/8 Ω |
| B40C1500 | N2 | d21 | RD | Rect. Bridge | 100 V | | | | | | | | | 5000µ/0.7 Ω |
| B500C1500 | N2 | d21 | RD | Rect. Bridge | 1000 V | | | | | | | | | 150µ/10 Ω |

| Type | Case | Pin-code | | | Maximum Ratings | | | | Electrical Characteristics | | | | | |
|---|---|---|---|---|---|---|---|---|---|---|---|---|---|---|
| | | | | | Vrm | Irm | Ifav / Ifm | Pv | Vf | If / Ifp | C0 | Cr | trr / ts | |
| B80C1500 | N2 | d21 | RD | Rect. Bridge | 200 V | | | | | | | | | 2500µ/1.3 Ω |
| B125C3700 | N3 | d21 | RD | Rect. Bridge | 300 V | | | | | | | | | 1000µ/1.4 Ω |
| B250C3700 | N3 | d21 | RD | Rect. Bridge | 600 V | | | | | | | | | 600µ/2.8 Ω |
| B380C3700 | N3 | d21 | RD | Rect. Bridge | 1000 V | | | | | | | | | 300µ/4.2 Ω |
| B40C3700 | N3 | d21 | RD | Rect. Bridge | 100 V | | | | | | | | | 5000µ/0.6 Ω |
| B80C3700 | N3 | d21 | RD | Rect. Bridge | 200 V | | | | | | | | | 2500µ/1.2 Ω |
| B125C5000 | N3 | d21 | RD | Rect. Bridge | 300 V | | | | | | | | | 5000µ/0.6 Ω |
| B250C5000 | N3 | d21 | RD | Rect. Bridge | 600 V | | | | | | | | | 2500µ/1.2 Ω |
| B380C5000 | N3 | d21 | RD | Rect. Bridge | 900 V | | | | | | | | | 1000µ/1.8 Ω |
| B40C5000 | N3 | d21 | RD | Rect. Bridge | 100 V | | | | | | | | | 10m/0.15 Ω |
| B80C5000 | N3 | d21 | RD | Rect. Bridge | 190 V | | | | | | | | | 5000µ/0.3 Ω |
| BA128 | A1 | a1 | NS | Uni | 75 V | 0.1 µA | | | <0.79 V | 10 mA | <5 pF | | | Ir at 50V |
| BA129 | A1 | a1 | NS | Uni | 200 V | 10 µA | | | <0.83 V | 10 mA | <6 pF | | | Ir at 180V |
| BA130 | A1 | a1 | NS | Uni | 30 V | 0.1 µA | | | <1 V | 10 mA | <2 pF | | | Ir at 25V |
| BA133 | B1 | a1 | IT | Rectifier | 1300 V | 5 µA | 1 A | | <1.3 V | 2 A | | | | |
| BA157 | B1 | a1 | RD,IT | Rectifier | 400 V | 5 µA | 1 A | | <1.3 V | 1 A | 2.2 pF | | <300 ns | C0 at Vr=400V |
| BA158 | B1 | a1 | RD,IT | Rectifier | 600 V | 5 µA | 1 A | | <1.3 V | 1 A | 2 pF | | <300 ns | C0 at Vr=600V |
| BA159 | B1 | a1 | RD,IT | Rectifier | 1000 V | 5 µA | 1 A | | <1.3 V | 1 A | 1.8 pF | | <500 ns | C0 at Vr=1000V |
| BA157S | B7 | a1 | IT | Rectifier | 400 V | 5 µA | 1 A | | <1.3 V | 1 A | | | <300 ns | |
| BA158S | B7 | a1 | IT | Rectifier | 600 V | 5 µA | 1 A | | <1.3 V | 1 A | | | <300 ns | |
| BA159S | B7 | a1 | IT | Rectifier | 1000 V | 5 µA | 1 A | | <1.3 V | 1 A | | | <500 ns | |
| BA170 | A1 | a1 | IT | Uni | 20 V | 10 nA | 150 mA | 0.3 W | <1 V | 80 mA | | | 100 ns | |
| BA217 | A1 | a1 | NS | Uni | 30 V | 0.2 µA | | | <1.5 V | 50 mA | <3 pF | | <4 ns | |
| BA218 | A1 | a1 | NS | Uni | 50 V | 0.2 µA | | | <1.5 V | 50 mA | <3 pF | | <4 ns | |
| BA220 | A1 | a1 | PH | Uni | 10 V | 1.5 µA | 200 mA | | <0.95 V | 100 mA | <2.5 pF | | <4 ns | |
| BA221 | A1 | a1 | PH | Uni | 30 V | 0.2 µA | 200 mA | | <0.95 V | 100 mA | <2.5 pF | | <4 ns | |
| BA223 | A2 | a1 | PH | RF Diode | 20 V | 0.1 µA | 50 mA | | <1 V | 50 mA | <3.5 pF | | | |
| BA243 | A1 | a1 | TE | RF Diode | 20 V | | | | | | <2 pF | | | C0 at Vr=15V |
| BA244 | A1 | a1 | TE | RF Diode | 20 V | | | | | | <2 pF | | | C0 at Vr=15V |
| BA243A | A1 | a1 | TE | RF Diode | 20 V | 50 µA | | | <1 V | 100 mA | <2 pF | | | C0 at Vr=15V |
| BA244A | A1 | a1 | TE | RF Diode | 20 V | 50 µA | | | <1 V | 100 mA | <2 pF | | | C0 at Vr=15V |
| BA281 | A1 | a1 | PH | RF Diode | 50 V | 50 nA | 200 mA | | <1 V | 100 mA | <1.2 pF | | | |
| BA282 | A1 | a1 | TE,IT | RF Diode | 35 V | 50 µA | | | <1 V | 100 mA | <1.5 pF | | | C0 at Vr=1V |
| BA283 | A1 | a1 | TE,IT | RF Diode | 35 V | 50 µA | | | <1 V | 100 mA | <1.5 pF | | | C0 at Vr=1V |
| BA316 | A1 | a1 | PH | Uni | 10 V | 0.2 µA | 100 mA | | <0.85 V | 10 mA | 2 pF | | <4 ns | |
| BA317 | A1 | a1 | PH,NS | Uni | 30 V | 0.2 µA | 100 mA | | <0.85 V | 10 mA | 2 pF | | <4 ns | |
| BA318 | A1 | a1 | PH,NS | Uni | 50 V | 0.2 µA | 100 mA | | <0.85 V | 10 mA | 2 pF | | <4 ns | |
| BA423 | A2 | a1 | PH | RF Diode | 20 V | 0.1 µA | 50 mA | | <0.9 V | 50 mA | <2.5 pF | | | |
| BA423L | D2 | a1 | PH | RF Diode | 20 V | 0.1 µA | 50 mA | | <0.9 V | 50 mA | <2.5 pF | | | |
| BA479G | A1 | a1 | TE | PIN Diode | 30 V | 50 nA | 50 mA | | <1 V | 20 mA | 0.5 pF | | | C0 at Vr=0V |

| Type | Case | Pin-code | | | Maximum Ratings | | | | Electrical Characteristics | | | | | |
|---|---|---|---|---|---|---|---|---|---|---|---|---|---|---|
| | | | | | Vrm | Irm | Ifav / Ifm | Pv | Vf | If / Ifp | C0 | Cr | trr / ts | |
| BA479S | A1 | a1 | TE | PIN Diode | 30 V | 50 nA | 50 mA | | <1 V | 20 mA | 0.5 pF | | | C0 at Vr=0V |
| BA481 | A2 | a1 | PH | RF Diode | 5 V | 10 µA | 30 mA | | <0.65 V | 10 mA | <1.1 pF | | | |
| BA482 | A2 | a1 | PH | RF Diode | 35 V | 0.1 µA | 100 mA | | <1.2 V | 100 mA | 0.8 pF | | | |
| BA483 | A2 | a1 | PH | RF Diode | 35 V | 0.1 µA | 100 mA | | <1.2 V | 100 mA | 0.7 pF | | | |
| BA484 | A2 | a1 | PH | RF Diode | 35 V | 0.1 µA | 100 mA | | <1.2 V | 100 mA | 1 pF | | | |
| BA582 | G4 | a1 | PH | RF Diode | 35 V | 10 nA | 100 mA | | <1.1 V | 100 mA | <1.1 pF | | | |
| BA604 | D2 | a1 | TE | Uni | 80 V | 1 µA | 450 mA | | <1.1 V | 500 mA | | | <20 ns | Ir at 50V |
| BA679 | D2 | a1 | TE | PIN Diode | 30 V | 50 nA | 50 mA | | <1 V | 20 mA | 0.5 pF | | | C0 at Vr=0V |
| BA679S | D2 | a1 | TE | PIN Diode | 30 V | 50 nA | 50 mA | | <1 V | 20 mA | 0.5 pF | | | C0 at Vr=0V |
| BA682 | D2 | a1 | TE,IT,PH | RF Diode | 35 V | 50 µA | 100 mA | | <1 V | 100 mA | <1.5 pF | | | C0 at Vr=1V |
| BA683 | D2 | a1 | TE,IT,PH | RF Diode | 35 V | 50 µA | 100 mA | | <1 V | 100 mA | <1.5 pF | | | C0 at Vr=1V |
| BA779 | F1 | c3 | TE | PIN Diode | 30 V | 50 nA | 50 mA | | <1 V | 20 mA | 0.5 pF | | | C0 at Vr=0V |
| BA779S | F1 | c3 | TE | PIN Diode | 30 V | 50 nA | 50 mA | | <1 V | 20 mA | 0.5 pF | | | C0 at Vr=0V |
| BA779-2 | F1 | c6 | TE | Pair PIN | 30 V | 50 nA | 50 mA | | <1 V | 20 mA | 0.5 pF | | | ser |
| BA782 | G4 | a1 | IT | RF Diode | 35 V | 50 µA | | | <1 V | 100 mA | <1.5 pF | | | C0 at Vr=1V |
| BA783 | G4 | a1 | IT | RF Diode | 35 V | 50 µA | | | <1 V | 100 mA | <1.5 pF | | | C0 at Vr=1V |
| BAL74 | F1 | c10 | PH | Switch | 50 V | 0.1 µA | 250 mA | | <1 V | 50 mA | <2 pF | | <6 ns | |
| BAL99 | F1 | c10 | PH | Switch | 70 V | 1 µA | 250 mA | | <1 V | 50 mA | <1.5 pF | | <6 ns | |
| BAQ33 | D2 | a1 | TE | Uni | 30 V | 3 nA | 450 mA | | <1 V | 100 mA | | | | Ir at 30V |
| BAQ34 | D2 | a1 | TE | Uni | 70 V | 3 nA | 450 mA | | <1 V | 100 mA | | | | Ir at 60V |
| BAQ35 | D2 | a1 | TE | Uni | 140 V | 3 nA | 450 mA | | <1 V | 100 mA | | | | Ir at 125V |
| BAQ133 | -- | a1 | TE | Uni | 40 V | 3 nA | 450 mA | | <1 V | 100 mA | | | | Ir at 30V |
| BAQ134 | -- | a1 | TE | Uni | 70 V | 3 nA | 450 mA | | <1 V | 100 mA | | | | Ir at 60V |
| BAQ135 | -- | a1 | TE | Uni | 140 V | 3 nA | 450 mA | | <1 V | 100 mA | | | <50 ns | Ir at 125V |
| BAV200 | -- | a1 | TE | Uni | 60 V | 0.1 µA | 200 mA | 0.4 W | <1 V | 100 mA | | | <50 ns | Ir at 20V |
| BAV201 | -- | a1 | TE | Uni | 120 V | 0.1 µA | 200 mA | 0.4 W | <1 V | 100 mA | | | <50 ns | Ir at 100V |
| BAV202 | -- | a1 | TE | Uni | 200 V | 0.1 µA | 200 mA | 0.4 W | <1 V | 100 mA | | | <50 ns | Ir at 150V |
| BAV203 | -- | a1 | TE | Uni | 250 V | 0.1 µA | 200 mA | 0.4 W | <1 V | 100 mA | | | <50 ns | Ir at 200V |
| BAR10 | A1 | a1 | SG | Uni | 20 V | | | | <1 V | 35 mA | <1.2 pF | | 0.1 ns | |
| BAR11 | A1 | a1 | SG | Uni | 15 V | | | | <1 V | 20 mA | <1.2 pF | | 0.1 ns | |
| BAR18 | F1 | c3 | SG | RF Diode | 70 V | 0.2 µA | | | <0.41 V | 1 mA | <2 pF | | 0.1 ns | |
| BAR19 | A1 | a1 | SG | RF Diode | 4 V | | | | <0.6 V | 10 mA | 1 pF | | | |
| BAR28 | A1 | a1 | SG | RF Diode | 70 V | | | | <1 V | 15 mA | <2 pF | | 0.1 ns | |
| BAR42 | F1 | c3 | SG | Uni | 30 V | | | | 0.5 V | 50 mA | 7 pF | | <5 ns | |
| BAR43 | F1 | c3 | SG | Uni | 30 V | | | | <0.45 V | 15 mA | 7 pF | | <5 ns | |
| BAR43A | F1 | c2 | SG | Pair Uni | 30 V | | | | 0.5 V | 50 mA | 7 pF | | <5 ns | comm-a |
| BAR43C | F1 | c5 | SG | Pair Uni | 30 V | | | | 0.5 V | 50 mA | 7 pF | | <5 ns | comm-k |
| BAR43S | F1 | c5 | SG | Pair Uni | 30 V | | | | 0.5 V | 50 mA | 7 pF | | <5 ns | comm-k |
| BAS11 | A7 | a1 | PH | Avalanche | 300 V | 0.25 µA | 350 mA | | <1.1 V | 300 mA | <2.5 pF | | | |
| BAS12 | A7 | a1 | PH | Avalanche | 400 V | 0.25 µA | 350 mA | | <1.1 V | 300 mA | <2.5 pF | | | |

| Type | Case | Pin-code | (mfr) | (appl) | Vrm | Irm | Ifav / Ifm | Pv | Vf | If / Ifp | C0 | Cr | trr / ts | |
|------|------|----------|-------|--------|-----|-----|------------|-----|-----|----------|-----|-----|----------|---|
| BAS15 | A2 | a1 | PH | Uni | 50 V | 0.1 µA | 100 mA | | <0.85 V | 10 mA | <2 pF | | <4 ns | |
| BAS16 | F1 | c1 | RD,PH,NS | Switch | 70 V | 1 µA | 250 mA | | 1.25 V | 150 mA | 2 pF | | <6 ns | |
| BAS19 | F1 | c10 | PH,NS | Switch | (100) V | 100 µA | 200 mA | 0.25 W | <1 V | 100 mA | <5 pF | | 50 ns | |
| BAS20 | F1 | c10 | PH,NS | Switch | (200) V | 100 µA | 200 mA | 0.25 W | <1 V | 100 mA | <5 pF | | 50 ns | |
| BAS21 | F1 | c10 | PH,NS | Switch | (250) V | 100 µA | 200 mA | 0.25 W | <1 V | 100 mA | <5 pF | | 50 ns | |
| BAS28 | F3 | d3 | PH | Pair Switch | (75) V | 1 µA | 215 mA | | <1.25 V | 150 mA | <2 pF | | 6 ns | indep |
| BAS29 | F1 | c10 | PH,NS | Switch | (90) V | 0.1 µA | 250 mA | | <1.25 V | 400 mA | <35 pF | | 50 ns | |
| BAS30 | F1 | c6 | PH | Pair Switch | (90) V | 0.1 µA | 250 mA | | <1.25 V | 400 mA | <35 pF | | 50 ns | ser |
| BAS31 | F1 | c11 | PH,NS | Pair Switch | (90) V | 0.1 µA | 250 mA | | <1.25 V | 400 mA | <35 pF | | 50 ns | ser |
| BAS32L | D4 | a1 | PH | Switch | 75 V | 5 µA | 150 mA | | <1 V | 100 mA | <2 pF | | 4.5 ns | |
| BAS33 | A1 | a1 | TE | Uni | 40 V | 3 nA | 450 mA | | <1 V | 100 mA | | | | Ir at 30V |
| BAS34 | A1 | a1 | TE | Uni | 70 V | 3 nA | 450 mA | | <1 V | 100 mA | | | | Ir at 60V |
| BAS35 | F1 | c8 | PH,NS | Pair Switch | 90 V | 10 nA | 250 mA | | <0.9 V | 100 mA | <35 pF | | <50 ns | comm-a |
| BAS45 | A2 | a1 | PH | Switch | (125) V | 1 nA | 225 mA | | <1 V | 200 mA | <8 pF | | | |
| BAS45L | D2 | a1 | PH | Switch | (125) V | 1 nA | 225 mA | | <1 V | 200 mA | <8 pF | | | |
| BAS55 | F1 | c3 | PH | Switch | 60 V | 0.1 µA | 200 mA | | <1 V | 200 mA | <2.5 pF | | <6 ns | |
| BAS56 | F3 | d3 | PH | Pair Switch | 60 V | 0.1 µA | 200 mA | 0.25 W | <1 V | 200 mA | <2.5 pF | | <6 ns | indep |
| BAS70-04 | F1 | c6 | SG | Pair RF Diode | 70 V | 0.2 µA | | | <0.41 V | 1 mA | <2 pF | | 0.1 ns | ser |
| BAS70-05 | F1 | c5 | SG | Pair RF Diode | 70 V | 0.2 µA | | | <0.41 V | 1 mA | <2 pF | | 0.1 ns | ser |
| BAS70-06 | F1 | c2 | SG | Pair RF Diode | 70 V | 0.2 µA | | | <0.41 V | 1 mA | <2 pF | | 0.1 ns | ser |
| BAS81 | D4 | a1 | PH | Uni | (40) V | 0.2 µA | 30 mA | | <0.41 V | 1 mA | <1.6 pF | | | |
| BAS82 | D4 | a1 | PH | Uni | 50 V | -0.2 µA | 30 mA | | <0.41 V | 1 mA | <1.6 pF | | | |
| BAS83 | D4 | a1 | PH | Uni | 60 V | 0.2 µA | 30 mA | | <0.41 V | 1 mA | <1.6 pF | | | |
| BAS85 | D4 | a1 | PH | Uni | 30 V | 2.3 µA | 200 mA | | <0.4 V | 10 mA | <10 pF | | | |
| BAS86 | D4 | a1 | PH | Uni | 50 V | 5 µA | 250 mA | | <0.6 V | 1 mA | <8 pF | | | |
| BAS678 | F1 | c3 | PH | Switch | (80) V | 0.1 µA | 200 mA | 0.25 W | <1 V | 200 mA | <2 pF | | <6 ns | |
| BAT17 | F1 | c3 | SG, PH | RF Diode | (4) V | 0.25 µA | 30 mA | | <0.6 V | 10 mA | <1 pF | | | F<7dB |
| BAT17DS | F1 | c6 | SG | Pair RF Diode | 4 V | | | | <0.6 V | 10 mA | <1 pF | | | ser |
| BAT18 | F1 | c3 | PH | RF Diode | (35) V | 0.1 µA | 100 mA | | <1.2 V | 100 mA | 0.8 pF | | | |
| BAT19 | A1 | a1 | SG | RF Diode | 10 V | | | | <1 V | 20 mA | <1.2 pF | | 0.1 ns | F<6dB |
| BAT29 | A1 | a1 | SG | RF Diode | 5 V | | | | <5.5 V | 10 mA | <1 pF | | | F<7dB |
| BAT41 | A1 | a1 | SG | Uni | 100 V | | 100 mA | | <1 V | 200 mA | 2 pF | | | |
| BAT42 | A1 | a1 | SG,IT | Uni | 30 V | 0.5 µA | 50 mA | 0.2 W | <0.65 V | 50 mA | 7 pF | | <5 ns | |
| BAT43 | A1 | a1 | SG,IT | Uni | 30 V | 0.5 µA | 15 mA | 0.2 W | <0.45 V | 15 mA | 7 pF | | <5 ns | |
| BAT43W | G4 | a1 | IT | Uni | 30 V | 0.5 µA | 15 mA | 0.2 W | <0.45 V | 15 mA | 7 pF | | <5 ns | |
| BAT45 | A1 | a1 | SG | RF Diode | 15 V | 0.1 µA | 30 mA | | <1 V | 30 mA | <1.1 pF | | 0.1 ns | |
| BAT46 | A1 | a1 | SG,IT | Uni | 100 V | 5 µA | 250 mA | 0.15 W | <0.45 V | 10 mA | 10 pF | | | |
| BAT46W | G4 | a1 | IT | Uni | 100 V | 5 µA | 250 mA | 0.2 W | <0.45 V | 10 mA | 10 pF | | | |
| BAT47 | A1 | a1 | SG | Uni | 20 V | | 150 mA | 0.33 W | <0.5 V | 30 mA | 20 pF | | 10 ns | |
| BAT48 | A1 | a1 | SG | Uni | 40 V | | 150 mA | 0.33 W | <0.5 V | 50 mA | 20 pF | | 10 ns | |

| Type | Case | Pin-code | | | Maximum Ratings | | | | Electrical Characteristics | | | | | |
|---|---|---|---|---|---|---|---|---|---|---|---|---|---|---|
| | | | | | Vrm | Irm | Ifav / Ifm | Pv | Vf | If / Ifp | C0 | Cr | trr / ts | |
| BAT49 | A1 | a1 | SG | Uni | 80 V | 200 µA | 500 mA | | <0.42 V | 100 mA | 120 pF | | | |
| BAT54 | F1 | c3 | PH | Uni | (30) V | ≤2 µA | 200 mA | 0.23 W | <0.5 V | 30 mA | ≤10 pF | | ≤5 ns | |
| BAT54A | F1 | c4 | PH | Pair Uni | (30) V | <2 µA | 200 mA | | <0.4 V | 10 mA | <10 pF | | <5 ns | |
| BAT54C | F1 | c5 | PH | Pair Uni | (30) V | <2 µA | 200 mA | | <0.4 V | 10 mA | <10 pF | | <5 ns | |
| BAT54S | F1 | c6 | PH | Pair Uni | (30) V | <2 µA | 200 mA | | <0.4 V | 10 mA | <10 pF | | <5 ns | |
| BAT74 | F3 | d3 | PH | Pair Uni | (30) V | ≤2 µA | 200 mA | 0.23 W | <0.4 V | 10 mA | <10 pF | | ≤5 ns | |
| BAT81 | A2 | a1 | PH | Switch | (40) V | 0.2 µA | 30 mA | | <0.41 V | 1 mA | <1.6 pF | | | |
| BAT82 | A2 | a1 | PH | Switch | (50) V | 0.2 µA | 30 mA | | <0.41 V | 1 mA | <1.6 pF | | | |
| BAT83 | A2 | a1 | PH | Switch | (60) V | 0.2 µA | 30 mA | | <0.41 V | 1 mA | <1.6 pF | | | |
| BAT85 | A2 | a1 | PH | Switch | (30) V | 2 µA | 200 mA | | <0.4 V | 10 mA | <10 pF | | | |
| BAT86 | A2 | a1 | PH | Switch | (50) V | 5 µA | 200 mA | | <0.45 V | 1 mA | <8 pF | | <4 ns | |
| BAV10 | A1 | a1 | PH | Switch | (60) V | 0.1 µA | 300 mA | | <1 V | 100 mA | <2.5 pF | | 2 ns | |
| BAT442W | G4 | a1 | IT | Uni | 30 V | 0.5 µA | 50 mA | 0.2 W | <0.65 V | 50 mA | 7 pF | | <5 ns | |
| BAV17 | A1 | a1 | TE,IT,NS | Uni | 25 V | 0.1 µA | 200 mA | 0.4 W | <1 V | 100 mA | | | <50 ns | Ir at 20V |
| BAV18 | A1 | a1 | TE,IT,RD,PH,NS | Uni | 60 V | 0.1 µA | 200 mA | 0.4 W | <1 V | 100 mA | | | | Ir at 50V |
| BAV19 | A1 | a1 | TE,IT,RD,PH,NS | Uni | 120 V | 0.1 µA | 200 mA | 0.4 W | <1 V | 100 mA | | | | Ir at 100V |
| BAV20 | A1 | a1 | TE,IT,RD,PH,NS | Uni | 200 V | 0.1 µA | 200 mA | 0.4 W | <1 V | 150 mA | | | | Ir at 150V |
| BAV21 | A1 | a1 | TE,IT,RD,PH,NS | Uni | 250 V | 0.1 µA | 200 mA | 0.4 W | <1 V | 200 mA | | | | Ir at 200V |
| BAV17S | A2 | a1 | IT | Uni | 25 V | 0.1 µA | 200 mA | 0.3 W | <1 V | 100 mA | | | <50 ns | Ir at 20V |
| BAV18S | A2 | a1 | IT | Uni | 60 V | 0.1 µA | 200 mA | 0.3 W | <1 V | 100 mA | | | | Ir at 50V |
| BAV19S | A2 | a1 | IT | Uni | 120 V | 0.1 µA | 200 mA | 0.3 W | <1 V | 100 mA | | | | Ir at 100V |
| BAV20S | A2 | a1 | IT | Uni | 200 V | 0.1 µA | 200 mA | 0.3 W | <1 V | 150 mA | | | | Ir at 150V |
| BAV21S | A2 | a1 | IT | Uni | 250 V | 0.1 µA | 200 mA | 0.3 W | <1 V | 200 mA | | | | Ir at 200V |
| BAV23 | F1 | d3 | PH | Pair Uni | 250 V | | 200 mA | 0.3 W | <1 V | 100 mA | <2.5 pF | | <50 ns | |
| BAV23S | F1 | c4 | PH | Pair Uni | 250 V | | 200 mA | 0.3 W | <1 V | 100 mA | <2.5 pF | | <50 ns | |
| BAV45 | K4 | a1 | PH | Uni | 35 V | 10p µA | 50 mA | | <1 V | 10 mA | <1.3 pF | | <600 ns | |
| BAV70 | F1 | c5 | RD,PH,NS | Pair Switch | 70 V | 5 µA | 215 mA | | 1.25 V | 150 mA | <5 pF | | <6 ns | |
| BAV74 | F1 | c5 | PH | Pair Switch | 50 V | 0.1 µA | 250 mA | 0.3 W | <1 V | 100 mA | <2 pF | | ≤4 ns | |
| BAV99 | F1 | c6 | RD,PH,NS | Pair Switch | 70 V | 2.5 µA | 250 mA | | 1.25 V | 150 mA | <1.5 pF | | <6 ns | |
| BAV100 | D2 | a1 | TE,IT,PH | Uni | 60 V | 0.1 µA | 200 mA | 0.4 W | <1 V | 100 mA | | | <50 ns | Ir at 50V |
| BAV101 | D2 | a1 | TE,IT,PH | Uni | 120 V | 0.1 µA | 200 mA | 0.4 W | <1 V | 100 mA | | | <50 ns | Ir at 100V |
| BAV102 | D2 | a1 | TE,IT,PH | Uni | 200 V | 0.1 µA | 200 mA | 0.4 W | <1 V | 100 mA | | | <50 ns | Ir at 150V |
| BAV103 | D2 | a1 | RD,TE,PH,IT | Uni | 250 V | 0.1 µA | 200 mA | | 1 V | 100 mA | 1.5 pF | | <50 ns | |
| BAV105 | D2 | a1 | PH | Switch | (60) V | 0.1 µA | 300 mA | | <1 mA | <2.5 pF | | <6 ns | | |
| BAW24 | A1 | a1 | TE | Uni | 50 V | 0.1 µA | 600 mA | | <1.2 V | 200 mA | | | | Ir at 40V |
| BAW25 | A1 | a1 | TE | Uni | 50 V | 0.1 µA | 600 mA | | <1 V | 200 mA | | | | Ir at 40V |
| BAW26 | A1 | a1 | TE | Uni | 75 V | 0.1 µA | 600 mA | | <1.2 V | 200 mA | | | | Ir at 60V |
| BAW27 | A1 | a1 | TE | Uni | 75 V | 0.1 µA | 600 mA | | <1 V | 200 mA | | | | Ir at 60V |
| BAW56 | F1 | c7 | RD,PH,NS | Pair Switch | 70 V | 2.5 µA | 250 mA | | 1.25 V | 150 mA | <2 pF | | 6 ns | |
| BAW62 | A1 | a1 | PH | Switch | 75 V | 5 µA | 150 mA | | <1 mA | <2 pF | | <4 ns | | |

| Type | Case | Pin-code | | | Maximum Ratings | | | | Electrical Characteristics | | | | | |
|------|------|----------|---|---|---|---|---|---|---|---|---|---|---|---|
| | | | | | Vrm | Irm | Ifav / Ifm | Pv | Vf | If / Ifp | C0 | Cr | trr / ts | |
| BAW75 | A1 | a1 | TE,IT,NS | Uni | 35 V | 0.1 µA | 150 mA | 0.5 W | <1 V | 30 mA | 4 pF | | <4 ns | Ir at 25V |
| BAW76 | A1 | a1 | TE,IT,NS | Uni | 50 V | 0.1 µA | 150 mA | 0.5 W | <1 V | 100 mA | | | <24 ns | Ir at 35V |
| BAX12 | A1 | a1 | PH | Avalanche | (90) V | 0.1 µA | 400 mA | | | <1 mA | 15 pF | | <50 ns | |
| BAX13 | A1 | a1 | IT,NS | Switch | 50 V | 0.2 µA | 150 mA | 0.5 W | 1 V | 20 mA | 3 pF | | 4 ns | |
| BAX14 | A1 | a1 | PH | Uni | 40 V | 0.1 µA | 500 mA | | | <1 mA | 20 pF | | <50 ns | |
| BAX16 | A1 | a1 | IT,NS | Switch | 165 V | 0.2 µA | 200 mA | 0.4 W | 1.3 V | 100 mA | 10 pF | | 120 ns | |
| BAX17 | A1 | a1 | NS | Uni | 200 V | | | | <1.2 V | 200 mA | <10 pF | | <120 ns | |
| BAX18 | A1 | a1 | PH | Uni | (75) V | 100 µA | 400 mA | | | <1.5 mA | 20 pF | | | |
| BAX80 | A1 | a1 | PH | Uni | 150 V | 0.1 µA | 200 mA | 0.4 W | <1.07 V | 150 mA | <6 pF | | <50 ns | |
| BAY71 | A1 | a1 | NS | Uni | 50 V | 0.1 µA | | | <0.88 V | | <2 pF | | <2 ns | Ir at 35V |
| BAY72 | A1 | a1 | NS | Uni | 125 V | 100 µA | | | <0.78 V | 10 mA | <5 pF | | <50 ns | Ir at 100V |
| BAY73 | A1 | a1 | NS | Uni | 125 V | 5 µA | | | <0.8 V | 10 mA | <8 pF | | | Ir at 100V |
| BAY74 | A1 | a1 | NS | Uni | 50 V | 0.1 µA | | | <0.88 V | 50 mA | <3 pF | | <4 ns | Ir at 35V |
| BAY80 | A1 | a1 | IT,NS | Switch | 150 V | 0.1 µA | 200 mA | | <0.92 V | 50 mA | 6 pF | | 50 ns | |
| BAY82 | A15 | a1 | NS | Uni | 15 V | 0.1 µA | | | <0.94 V | 10 mA | <1 pF | | <0.7 ns | Ir at 12V |
| BAY135 | A1 | a1 | TE | Uni | 140 V | 3 nA | 450 mA | | <1 V | 100 mA | | | <50 ns | Ir at 125V |
| BB112 | K1 | a1 | PH | C Diode | 12 V | 50 nA | 50 mA | | | | <540 pF | >18 | | Vr 1..8.5V |
| BB119 | A1 | a1 | PH | C Diode | (15) V | 2 µA | 200 mA | | <0.95 V | 100 mA | <25 pF | 1.3 | | |
| BB130 | K1 | a1 | PH | C Diode | (30) V | 50 nA | 50 mA | | | | <550 pF | >23 | | Vr 1..28V |
| BB131 | G3 | a1 | PH | C Diode | (30) V | 10 nA | 20 mA | | | | <17 pF | >12 | | |
| BB132 | G3 | a1 | PH | C Diode | (30) V | 10 nA | 20 mA | | | | <75 pF | >24 | | Vr .5..28V |
| BB133 | G3 | a1 | PH | C Diode | (30) V | 10 nA | 20 mA | | | | <46 pF | >21 | | Vr .5..28V |
| BB134 | G3 | a1 | PH | C Diode | (30) V | 10 nA | 20 mA | | | | <21 pF | >12 | | Vr .5..28V |
| BB135 | G3 | a1 | PH | C Diode | (30) V | 10 nA | 20 mA | | | | <21 pF | >12 | | |
| BB204(B) | K3 | c7 | TE,PH | Pair C Diode | 30 V | | | | | | <42 pF | <2.8 | | Vr 3..30V |
| BB204(G) | K3 | c7 | TE,PH | Pair C Diode | 30 V | | | | | | <39 pF | <2.8 | | Vr 3..30V |
| BB212 | K2 | C7 | PH | Pair C Diode | (12) V | 50 nA | 100 mA | | | | <620 pF | >22.5 | | |
| BB215 | D2 | a1 | PH | C Diode | (30) V | 10 nA | 20 mA | | | | 17 pF | 8.3 | | Vr 1..28V |
| BB219 | D2 | a1 | PH | C Diode | 30 V | 10 nA | 20 mA | | | | >31 pF | >12 | | Vr 1..28V |
| BB240 | D2 | a1 | PH | C Diode | 32 V | 10 nA | 20 mA | | | | >38 pF | >14 | | Vr .5..28V |
| BB241 | D2 | a1 | PH | C Diode | 32 V | 10 nA | 20 mA | | | | >63 pF | >21 | | Vr .5..28V |
| BB249 | D2 | a1 | PH | C Diode | 30 V | 10 nA | 20 mA | | | | <46 pF | <10 | | Vr 1..28V |
| BB304 | K2 | c7 | TE | Pair C Diode | 30 V | | | | | | <47.5 pF | <1.75 | | Vr 2..8V |
| BB404A | F1 | c5 | IT | Pair C Diode | 10 V | 20 nA | | | | | <43.5 pF | <1.75 | | |
| BB404B | F1 | c5 | IT | Pair C Diode | 10 V | 20 nA | | | | | <44.5 pF | <1.75 | | |
| BB404C | F1 | c5 | IT | Pair C Diode | 10 V | 20 nA | | | | | <45.5 pF | <1.75 | | |
| BB404D | F1 | c5 | IT | Pair C Diode | 10 V | 20 nA | | | | | <46.5 pF | <1.75 | | |
| BB404E | F1 | c5 | IT | Pair C Diode | 10 V | 20 nA | | | | | <47.5 pF | <1.75 | | |
| BB405B | A2 | a1 | PH | C Diode | (30) V | 10 nA | 20 mA | | | | 11 pF | >7.6 | | Vr 1..28V |
| BB417 | A2 | a1 | PH | C Diode | (30) V | 0.1 µA | 20 mA | | | | <11 pF | >2 | | |

| Type | Case | Pin-code | | | Maximum Ratings | | | | Electrical Characteristics | | | | | |
|------|------|----------|---|---|-----|-----|----------|-----|------|--------|-----|-----|--------|---|
| | | | | | Vrm | Irm | Ifav / Ifm | Pv | Vf | If / Ifp | C0 | Cr | trr / ts | |
| BB515 | G4 | a1 | PH | C Diode | (30) V | 10 nA | 20 mA | | | | <19.5 pF | >8 | | Vr 1..28V |
| BB619 | G4 | a1 | PH | C Diode | (30) V | 10 nA | 20 mA | | | | <41 pF | 14 | | Vr 1..28V |
| BB620 | G4 | a1 | PH | C Diode | (30) V | 10 nA | 20 mA | | | | <76 pF | >19.5 | | Vr 1..28V |
| BB701 | G4 | a1 | IT | C Diode | 30 V | 10 nA | | | | | <9 pF | <9 | | |
| BB721 | G4 | a1 | IT | C Diode | 30 V | 10 nA | | | | | <16.3 pF | >8 | | |
| BB723 | G4 | a1 | IT | C Diode | 30 V | 10 nA | | | | | 20 pF | <15 | | |
| BB729 | G4 | a1 | IT | C Diode | 30 V | 10 nA | | | | | <33.1 pF | <15 | | |
| BB730 | G4 | a1 | IT | C Diode | 28 V | 30 nA | | | | | 42 pF | <16.8 | | |
| BB731 | G4 | a1 | IT | C Diode | 28 V | 30 nA | | | | | 50 pF | <25 | | |
| BB804 | F1 | c5 | TE | Pair C Diode | 20 V | | | | | | <47.5 pF | <1.75 | | Vr 2..8V |
| BB804-1 | F1 | c5 | PH | Pair C Diode | (18) V | 20 nA | 50 mA | | | | <44.5 pF | <1.75 | | yellow |
| BB804-2 | F1 | c5 | PH | Pair C Diode | (18) V | 20 nA | 50 mA | | | | <45.5 pF | <1.75 | | white |
| BB804-3 | F1 | c5 | PH | Pair C Diode | (18) V | 20 nA | 50 mA | | | | <46.5 pF | <1.75 | | green |
| BB809 | A2 | a1 | PH | C Diode | (28) V | 10 nA | 20 mA | | | | ≤46 pF | ≤10 | | Vr 1..28V |
| BB811 | G4 | a1 | PH | C Diode | (30) V | 20 nA | 30 mA | | | | ≤8.8 pF | ≤9.5 | | Vr 1..28V |
| BB814 | F1 | c5 | TE | Pair C Diode | 20 V | | | | | | <46.5 pF | <1.75 | | Vr 2..8V |
| BB824 | F1 | c5 | TE | Pair C Diode | 20 V | | | | | | <45 pF | <1.75 | | Vr 2..8V |
| BB901 | F1 | c3 | PH | C Diode | (28) V | 10 nA | 20 mA | | | | <1.05 pF | >12 | | |
| BB909A | A2 | a1 | PH | C Diode | 32 V | 10 nA | 20 mA | | | | >31 pF | ≤12 | | Vr 1..28V |
| BB909B | A2 | a1 | PH | C Diode | 32 V | 10 nA | 20 mA | | | | >33.5 pF | ≤12 | | Vr 1..28V |
| BB910 | A2 | a1 | PH | C Diode | 32 V | 10 nA | 20 mA | | | | >38 pF | >14 | | Vr .5..28V |
| BB911 | A2 | a1 | PH | C Diode | 32 V | 10 nA | 20 mA | | | | >63 pF | >21 | | Vr .5..28V |
| BBY31 | F1 | c3 | PH | C Diode | (30) V | 10 nA | 20 mA | | | | <2 pF | 8.6 | | Vr 1..28V |
| BBY39 | F1 | c5 | PH | Pair C Diode | (30) V | 10 nA | 20 mA | | | | 17.5 pF | >8 | | Vr 1..28V |
| BBY40 | F1 | c3 | PH | C Diode | (28) V | 10 nA | 20 mA | | | | <32 pF | >5 | | Vr 3..25V |
| BBY42 | F1 | c3 | PH | C Diode | (32) V | 10 nA | 20 mA | | | | <31 pF | ≤12 | | Vr 1..28V |
| BBY62 | F1 | d10 | PH | Pair C Diode | (32) V | 10 nA | 20 mA | | | | 15 pF | 8.3 | | Vr 1..28V |
| BYP20-100 | I4 | c7 | PH | Rect. Pair | 100 V | 5 µA | 5 A | | <1.0 V | 3 A | | | <30 ns | |
| BYP20-150 | I4 | c7 | PH | Rect. Pair | 150 V | 5 µA | 5 A | | <1.0 V | 3 A | | | <30 ns | |
| BYP20-50 | I4 | c7 | PH | Rect. Pair | 50 V | 5 µA | 5 A | | <1.0 V | 3 A | | | <30 ns | |
| BYP21-100 | I5 | a1 | PH | Rectifier | 100 V | 5 µA | 4 A | | <1.05 V | 8 A | | | <25 ns | |
| BYP21-150 | I5 | a1 | PH | Rectifier | 150 V | 5 µA | 4 A | | <1.05 V | 8 A | | | <25 ns | |
| BYP21-50 | I5 | a1 | PH | Rectifier | 50 V | 5 µA | 4 A | | <1.05 V | 8 A | | | <25 ns | |
| BYP21-200 | I5 | a1 | PH | Rectifier | 200 V | 5 µA | 4 A | | <1.05 V | 8 A | | | <25 ns | |
| BY229-200 | I5 | a1 | PH | Rectifier | 200 V | 400 µA | 7 A | | <1.85 V | 20 A | | | <150 ns | Ir at Tj=125°C |
| BY229-400 | I5 | a1 | PH | Rectifier | 400 V | 400 µA | 7 A | | <1.85 V | 20 A | | | <150 ns | Ir at Tj=125°C |
| BY229-600 | I5 | a1 | PH | Rectifier | 600 V | 400 µA | 7 A | | <1.85 V | 20 A | | | <150 ns | Ir at Tj=125°C |
| BY229-800 | I5 | a1 | PH | Rectifier | 800 V | 400 µA | 7 A | | <1.85 V | 20 A | | | <150 ns | Ir at Tj=125°C |
| BY229F-200 | J7 | a1 | PH | Rectifier | 200 V | 400 µA | 7 A | | <1.85 V | 20 A | 12 pF | | <150 ns | Ir at Tj=125°C |
| BY229F-400 | J7 | a1 | PH | Rectifier | 400 V | 400 µA | 7 A | | <1.85 V | 20 A | 12 pF | | <150 ns | Ir at Tj=125°C |

| Type | Case | Pin-code | | | Maximum Ratings | | | | Electrical Characteristics | | | | | |
|---|---|---|---|---|---|---|---|---|---|---|---|---|---|---|
| | | | | | Vrm | Irm | Ifav / Ifm | Pv | Vf | If / Ifp | C0 | Cr | trr / ts | |
| BY229F-600 | J7 | a1 | PH | Rectifier | 600 V | 400 µA | 7 A | | <1.85 V | 20 A | 12 pF | | <150 ns | Ir at Tj=125°C |
| BY229F-800 | J7 | a1 | PH | Rectifier | 800 V | 400 µA | 7 A | | <1.85 V | 20 A | 12 pF | | <150 ns | Ir at Tj=125°C |
| BY229-200R | I5 | b1 | PH | Rectifier | 200 V | 600 µA | 7 A | | <1.85 V | 20 A | | | <150 ns | Ir at Tj=125°C |
| BY229-400R | I5 | b1 | PH | Rectifier | 400 V | 600 µA | 7 A | | <1.85 V | 20 A | | | <150 ns | Ir at Tj=125°C |
| BY229-600R | I5 | b1 | PH | Rectifier | 600 V | 600 µA | 7 A | | <1.85 V | 20 A | | | <150 ns | Ir at Tj=125°C |
| BY229-800R | I5 | b1 | PH | Rectifier | 800 V | 600 µA | 7 A | | <1.85 V | 20 A | | | <150 ns | Ir at Tj=125°C |
| BY249-300 | I5 | a1 | PH | Rectifier | 300 V | 400 µA | 6.5 A | | <1.6 V | 20 A | | | | Ir at Tj=125°C |
| BY249-600 | I5 | a1 | PH | Rectifier | 600 V | 400 µA | 6.5 A | | <1.6 V | 20 A | | | | Ir at Tj=125°C |
| BY249F-300 | J7 | a1 | PH | Rectifier | 300 V | 400 µA | 6.5 A | | <1.6 V | 20 A | 12 pF | | | Ir at Tj=125°C |
| BY249F-600 | J7 | a1 | PH | Rectifier | 600 V | 400 µA | 6.5 A | | <1.6 V | 20 A | 12 pF | | | Ir at Tj=125°C |
| BY249-300R | I5 | b1 | PH | Rectifier | 300 V | 400 µA | 6.5 A | | <1.6 V | 20 A | | | | Ir at Tj=125°C |
| BY249-600R | I5 | b1 | PH | Rectifier | 600 V | 400 µA | 6.5 A | | <1.6 V | 20 A | | | | Ir at Tj=125°C |
| BY329-1000 | I5 | a1 | PH | Rectifier | 1000 V | 1 mA | 8 A | | <1.85 V | 20 A | 12 pF | | <150 ns | Ir at Tj=125°C |
| BY329-1200 | I5 | a1 | PH | Rectifier | 1200 V | 1 mA | 8 A | | <1.85 V | 20 A | 12 pF | | <150 ns | Ir at Tj=125°C |
| BY329-800 | I5 | a1 | PH | Rectifier | 800 V | 1 mA | 8 A | | <1.85 V | 20 A | 12 pF | | <150 ns | Ir at Tj=125°C |
| BY359-1000 | I5 | a1 | PH | Rectifier | 1000 V | 600 µA | 6.5 A | | <2.3 V | 20 A | | | <600 ns | Ir at Tj=125°C |
| BY359-1300 | I5 | a1 | PH | Rectifier | 1300 V | 600 µA | 6.5 A | | <2.3 V | 20 A | | | <600 ns | Ir at Tj=125°C |
| BY359-1500 | I5 | a1 | PH | Rectifier | 1500 V | 600 µA | 6.5 A | | <2.3 V | 20 A | | | <600 ns | Ir at Tj=100°C |
| BY203-12S | A4 | a1 | TE | Rectifier | 1200 V | 100 µA | 250 mA | | <2.4 V | 200 mA | | | <300 ns | |
| BY203-16S | A4 | a1 | TE | Rectifier | 1600 V | 100 µA | 250 mA | | <2.4 V | 200 mA | | | <300 ns | |
| BY203-20S | A4 | a1 | TE | Rectifier | 2000 V | 100 µA | 250 mA | | <2.4 V | 200 mA | | | <300 ns | |
| BY203-25S | A4 | a1 | TE | Rectifier | 2500 V | 100 µA | 250 mA | | <2.2 V | 200 mA | | | <300 ns | |
| BY214-1000 | B6 | a1 | SG | Rectifier | 1000 V | 250 µA | 6 A | 6 W | <1.2 V | 20 A | | | | Ifav at Tc=90°C |
| BY214-200 | B6 | a1 | SG | Rectifier | 200 V | 250 µA | 6 A | 6 W | <1.2 V | 20 A | | | | Ifav at Tc=90°C |
| BY214-400 | B6 | a1 | SG | Rectifier | 400 V | 250 µA | 6 A | 6 W | <1.2 V | 20 A | | | | Ifav at Tc=90°C |
| BY214-600 | B6 | a1 | SG | Rectifier | 600 V | 250 µA | 6 A | 6 W | <1.2 V | 20 A | | | | Ifav at Tc=90°C |
| BY228 | A5 | a1 | TE,PH | Rectifier | 1500 V | 5 µA | 3 A | | <1.5 V | 5 A | | | <20 µs | |
| BY228-13 | A5 | a1 | TE | Rectifier | 1000 V | 5 µA | 3 A | | <1.5 V | 5 A | | | <20 µs | |
| BY228-15 | A5 | a1 | TE | Rectifier | 1200 V | 5 µA | 3 A | | <1.5 V | 5 A | | | <20 µs | |
| BY233-200A | I1 | a1 | SG | Rectifier | 200 V | 20 µA | 20 A | (20) W | <1.5 V | 8 A | | | <150 ns | Ifav at Tc=115°C |
| BY233-400A | I1 | a1 | SG | Rectifier | 400 V | 20 µA | 20 A | (20) W | <1.5 V | 8 A | | | <150 ns | Ifav at Tc=115°C |
| BY233-600A | I1 | a1 | SG | Rectifier | 600 V | 20 µA | 20 A | (20) W | <1.5 V | 8 A | | | <150 ns | Ifav at Tc=115°C |
| BY239-200A | I1 | a1 | SG | Rectifier | 200 V | 500 µA | 10 A | (12.5) W | <1.45 V | 30 A | | | | Ifav at Tc=115°C |
| BY239-400A | I1 | a1 | SG | Rectifier | 400 V | 500 µA | 10 A | (12.5) W | <1.45 V | 30 A | | | | Ifav at Tc=115°C |
| BY239-600A | I1 | a1 | SG | Rectifier | 600 V | 500 µA | 10 A | (12.5) W | <1.45 V | 30 A | | | | Ifav at Tc=115°C |
| BY239-800A | I1 | a1 | SG | Rectifier | 800 V | 500 µA | 10 A | (12.5) W | <1.45 V | 30 A | | | | Ifav at Tc=115°C |
| BY251 | B7 | a1 | RD,IT | Rectifier | 200 V | 10 µA | 3 A | | 1.1 V | 3 A | | | | |
| BY253 | B7 | a1 | RD,IT | Rectifier | 600 V | 10 µA | 3 A | | 1.1 V | 3 A | | | | |
| BY254 | B7 | a1 | RD,IT | Rectifier | 800 V | 10 µA | 3 A | | 1.1 V | 3 A | | | | |
| BY255 | B7 | a1 | RD,IT | Rectifier | 1300 V | 10 µA | 3 A | | 1.1 V | 3 A | | | | |

| Type | Case | Pin-code | | | | Maximum Ratings | | | | Electrical Characteristics | | | | | |
|------|------|----------|---|---|---|------|------|-----------|------|------|--------|------|------|------|------|
| | | | | | | Vrm | Irm | Ifav / Ifm | Pv | Vf | If / Ifp | C0 | Cr | trr / ts | |
| BY251S | B7 | a1 | IT | Rectifier | | 200 V | 10 µA | 3 A | | 1.1 V | 3 A | | | | |
| BY252S | B7 | a1 | IT | Rectifier | | 400 V | 10 µA | 3 A | | 1.1 V | 3 A | | | | |
| BY253S | B7 | a1 | IT | Rectifier | | 600 V | 10 µA | 3 A | | 1.1 V | 3 A | | | | |
| BY254S | B7 | a1 | IT | Rectifier | | 800 V | 10 µA | 3 A | | 1.1 V | 3 A | | | | |
| BY255S | B7 | a1 | IT | Rectifier | | 1300 V | 10 µA | 3 A | | 1.1 V | 3 A | | | | |
| BY268 | A4 | a1 | TE | Rectifier | | 1400 V | 2 µA | 800 mA | | <1.25 V | 400 mA | | | <400 ns | |
| BY269 | A4 | a1 | TE | Rectifier | | 1600 V | 2 µA | 800 mA | | <1.25 V | 400 mA | | | <400 ns | |
| BY296 | B7 | a1 | RD,IT | Rectifier | | 100 V | 10 µA | 2 A | | 1.3 V | 3 A | | | <500 ns | Ifav at Ta=50°C |
| BY297 | B7 | a1 | RD,IT | Rectifier | | 200 V | 10 µA | 2 A | | 1.3 V | 3 A | | | <500 ns | Ifav at Ta=50°C |
| BY298 | B7 | a1 | RD,IT | Rectifier | | 400 V | 10 µA | 2 A | | 1.3 V | 3 A | | | <500 ns | Ifav at Ta=50°C |
| BY299 | B7 | a1 | RD,IT | Rectifier | | 800 V | 10 µA | 2 A | | 1.3 V | 3 A | | | <500 ns | Ifav at Ta=50°C |
| BY296S | B7 | a1 | IT | Rectifier | | 100 V | 10 µA | 2 A | | 1.3 V | 3 A | | | <500 ns | |
| BY297S | B7 | a1 | IT | Rectifier | | 200 V | 10 µA | 2 A | | 1.3 V | 3 A | | | <500 ns | |
| BY298S | B7 | a1 | IT | Rectifier | | 400 V | 10 µA | 2 A | | 1.3 V | 3 A | | | <500 ns | |
| BY299S | B7 | a1 | IT | Rectifier | | 800 V | 10 µA | 2 A | | 1.3 V | 3 A | | | <500 ns | |
| BY328 | A5 | a1 | PH | Rectifier | | 1300 V | | 3 A | | <1.45 V | 6 A | | | <13 µs | |
| BY359F-1500 | J7 | a1 | PH | Rectifier | | 1500 V | 600 µA | 6.5 A | | <2.3 V | 20 A | 12 pF | | <600 ns | Ir at Tj=100°C |
| BY396 | B7 | a1 | RD,IT | Rectifier | | 100 V | 10 µA | 3 A | | 1.2 V | 5 A | | | <500 ns | Ifav at Ta=50°C |
| BY397 | B7 | a1 | RD,IT | Rectifier | | 200 V | 10 µA | 3 A | | 1.2 V | 5 A | | | <500 ns | Ifav at Ta=50°C |
| BY398 | B7 | a1 | RD,IT | Rectifier | | 400 V | 10 µA | 3 A | | 1.2 V | 5 A | | | <500 ns | Ifav at Ta=50°C |
| BY399 | B7 | a1 | RD,IT | Rectifier | | 800 V | 10 µA | 3 A | | 1.2 V | 5 A | | | <500 ns | Ifav at Ta=50°C |
| BY396S | B7 | a1 | IT | Rectifier | | 100 V | 10 µA | 3 A | | 1.2 V | 5 A | | | <500 ns | |
| BY397S | B7 | a1 | IT | Rectifier | | 200 V | 10 µA | 3 A | | 1.2 V | 5 A | | | <500 ns | |
| BY398S | B7 | a1 | IT | Rectifier | | 400 V | 10 µA | 3 A | | 1.2 V | 5 A | | | <500 ns | |
| BY399S | B7 | a1 | IT | Rectifier | | 800 V | 10 µA | 3 A | | 1.2 V | 5 A | | | <500 ns | |
| BY428 | A5 | a1 | PH | Rectifier | | 1400 V | | 4 A | | <1.95 V | 4 A | | | <6 µs | |
| BY438 | A5 | a1 | PH | Rectifier | | 1200 V | | 5 A | | <1.5 V | 5 A | | | <20 µs | |
| BY448 | A4 | a1 | TE,PH | Rectifier | | 1500 V | 3 µA | 2 A | | <1.6 V | 3 mA | | | <20 µs | |
| BY458 | A4 | a1 | TE,PH | Rectifier | | 1200 V | 3 µA | 2 A | | <1.6 V | 3 mA | | | <20 µs | |
| BY500-100 | B20 | a1 | RD | Rectifier | | 100 V | 10 µA | 5 A | | 1.3 V | 5 A | | | 200 ns | Ifav at Ta=45°C |
| BY500-200 | B20 | a1 | RD | Rectifier | | 200 V | 10 µA | 5 A | | 1.3 V | 5 A | | | 200 ns | Ifav at Ta=45°C |
| BY500-400 | B20 | a1 | RD | Rectifier | | 400 V | 10 µA | 5 A | | 1.3 V | 5 A | | | 200 ns | Ifav at Ta=45°C |
| BY500-600 | B20 | a1 | RD | Rectifier | | 600 V | 10 µA | 5 A | | 1.3 V | 5 A | | | 200 ns | Ifav at Ta=45°C |
| BY500-800 | B20 | a1 | RD | Rectifier | | 800 V | 10 µA | 5 A | | 1.3 V | 5 A | | | 200 ns | Ifav at Ta=45°C |
| BY505 | A10 | a1 | PH | HV Rectifier | | 2200 V | | 85 mA | | <8.5 V | 100 mA | | | <200 ns | |
| BY527 | A4 | a1 | TE,PH | HV Rectifier | | 1250 V | 1 µA | 2 A | | <1 V | 1 A | | | 2.5 ns | |
| BY584 | A11 | a1 | PH | HV Rectifier | | 1800 V | 3 µA | 85 mA | | <8.5 V | 100 mA | | | <200 ns | |
| BY614 | A12 | a1 | PH | HV Rectifier | | 2200 V | 10 µA | 60 mA | | <6 V | 50 mA | | | <300 ns | |
| BY617 | A10 | a1 | PH | HV Rectifier | | 9 kV | 3 µA | 4 mA | | <37.5 V | 100 mA | | | <100 ns | |
| BY619 | A10 | a1 | PH | HV Rectifier | | 15 kV | 3 µA | 4 mA | | <75 V | 100 mA | | | <100 ns | |

| Type | Case | Pin-code | | | Maximum Ratings | | | | Electrical Characteristics | | | | | |
|------|------|----------|----|----|-----|-----|----------|----|-----|--------|----|----|-----|----|
| | | | | | Vrm | Irm | Ifav Ifm | Pv | Vf | If Ifp | C0 | Cr | trr ts | |
| BY620 | A10 | a1 | PH | HV Rectifier | 17 kV | 3 µA | 4 mA | | <75 V | 100 mA | | | <100 ns | |
| BY627 | A6 | a1 | PH | Rectifier | 1250 V | 1 µA | 1 A | | <1.15 V | 3 A | 50 pF | | 2.5 µs | |
| BY705 | A10 | a1 | PH | HV Rectifier | 5 kV | 3 µA | 20 mA | | <21 V | 100 mA | | | <200 ns | |
| BY706 | A10 | a1 | PH | HV Rectifier | 6 kV | 3 µA | 20 mA | | <21 V | 100 mA | | | <200 ns | |
| BY707 | A10 | a1 | PH | HV Rectifier | 10 kV | 3 µA | 4 mA | | <52 V | 100 mA | | | <200 ns | |
| BY708 | A10 | a1 | PH | HV Rectifier | 12 kV | 3 µA | 4 mA | | <52 V | 100 mA | | | <200 ns | |
| BY709 | A10 | a1 | PH | HV Rectifier | 14 kV | 3 µA | 4 mA | | <52 V | 100 mA | | | <200 ns | |
| BY710 | A10 | a1 | PH | HV Rectifier | 17 kV | 3 µA | 3 mA | | <70 V | 100 mA | | | <200 ns | |
| BY711 | A10 | a1 | PH | HV Rectifier | 19 kV | 3 µA | 4 mA | | <52 V | 100 mA | | | <200 ns | |
| BY712 | A10 | a1 | PH | HV Rectifier | 22 kV | 3 µA | 3 mA | | <76 V | 50 mA | | | <200 ns | |
| BY713 | A10 | a1 | PH | HV Rectifier | 24 kV | 3 µA | 3 mA | | <76 V | 50 mA | | | <200 ns | |
| BY714 | A10 | a1 | PH | HV Rectifier | 30 kV | 3 µA | 3 mA | | <76 V | 50 mA | | | <200 ns | |
| BY715 | A10 | a1 | PH | HV Rectifier | 5 kV | 3 µA | 20 mA | | <28 V | 100 mA | | | <100 ns | |
| BY716 | A10 | a1 | PH | HV Rectifier | 6 kV | 3 µA | 20 mA | | <28 V | 100 mA | | | <100 ns | |
| BY717 | A10 | a1 | PH | HV Rectifier | 10 kV | 3 µA | 4 mA | | <69 V | 100 mA | | | <100 ns | |
| BY718 | A10 | a1 | PH | HV Rectifier | 12 kV | 3 µA | 4 mA | | <69 V | 100 mA | | | <100 ns | |
| BY719 | A10 | a1 | PH | HV Rectifier | 14 kV | 3 µA | 4 mA | | <69 V | 100 mA | | | <100 ns | |
| BY720 | A10 | a1 | PH | HV Rectifier | 17 kV | 3 µA | 3 mA | | <92 V | 100 mA | | | <100 ns | |
| BY721 | A10 | a1 | PH | HV Rectifier | 19 kV | 3 µA | 3 mA | | <92 V | 100 mA | | | <100 ns | |
| BY722 | A10 | a1 | PH | HV Rectifier | 22 kV | 3 µA | 3 mA | | <88 V | 50 mA | | | <100 ns | |
| BY723 | A10 | a1 | PH | HV Rectifier | 24 kV | 3 µA | 3 mA | | <88 V | 50 mA | | | <100 ns | |
| BY724 | A10 | a1 | PH | HV Rectifier | 30 kV | 3 µA | 3 mA | | <88 V | 50 mA | | | <100 ns | |
| BYD11D | A7 | a1 | PH | Rectifier | 200 V | 1 µA | 500 mA | | <1.06 V | 0.5 mA | 14 pF | | | |
| BYD11G | A7 | a1 | PH | Rectifier | 400 V | 1 µA | 500 mA | | <1.06 V | 0.5 mA | 14 pF | | | |
| BYD11J | A7 | a1 | PH | Rectifier | 600 V | 1 µA | 500 mA | | <1.06 V | 0.5 mA | 14 pF | | | |
| BYD11K | A7 | a1 | PH | Rectifier | 800 V | 1 µA | 500 mA | | <1.06 V | 0.5 mA | 14 pF | | | |
| BYD11M | A7 | a1 | PH | Rectifier | 1000 V | 1 µA | 500 mA | | <1.06 V | 0.5 mA | 14 pF | | | |
| BYD13D | A8 | a1 | PH | Rectifier | 200 V | 1 µA | 1.4 A | | <1.05 V | 1 A | 21 pF | | | |
| BYD13G | A8 | a1 | PH | Rectifier | 400 V | 1 µA | 1.4 A | | <1.05 V | 1 A | 21 pF | | | |
| BYD13J | A8 | a1 | PH | Rectifier | 600 V | 1 µA | 1.4 A | | <1.05 V | 1 A | 21 pF | | | |
| BYD13K | A8 | a1 | PH | Rectifier | 800 V | 1 µA | 1.4 A | | <1.05 V | 1 A | 21 pF | | | |
| BYD13M | A8 | a1 | PH | Rectifier | 1000 V | 1 µA | 1.4 A | | <1.05 V | 1 A | 21 pF | | | |
| BYD14D | A6 | a1 | PH | Rectifier | 200 V | 1 µA | 2 A | | <1.15 V | 3 A | 50 pF | | | |
| BYD14G | A6 | a1 | PH | Rectifier | 400 V | 1 µA | 2 A | | <1.15 V | 3 A | 50 pF | | | |
| BYD14J | A6 | a1 | PH | Rectifier | 600 V | 1 µA | 2 A | | <1.15 V | 3 A | 50 pF | | | |
| BYD14K | A6 | a1 | PH | Rectifier | 800 V | 1 µA | 2 A | | <1.15 V | 3 A | 50 pF | | | |
| BYD14M | A6 | a1 | PH | Rectifier | 1000 V | 1 µA | 2 A | | <1.15 V | 3 A | 50 pF | | | |
| BYD17D | D5 | a1 | PH | Rectifier | 200 V | 1 µA | 600 mA | | <0.93 V | 1 A | 21 pF | | | |
| BYD17G | D5 | a1 | PH | Rectifier | 400 V | 1 µA | 600 mA | | <0.93 V | 1 A | 21 pF | | | |
| BYD17J | D5 | a1 | PH | Rectifier | 600 V | 1 µA | 600 mA | | <0.93 V | 1 A | 21 pF | | | |

| Type | Case | Pin-code | | | | Maximum Ratings | | | | Electrical Characteristics | | | | | |
|---|---|---|---|---|---|---|---|---|---|---|---|---|---|---|---|
| | | | | | | Vrm | Irm | Ifav / Ifm | Pv | Vf | If / Ifp | C0 | Cr | trr / ts | |
| BYD17K | D5 | a1 | PH | | Rectifier | 800 V | 1 µA | 600 mA | | <0.93 V | 1 A | 21 pF | | | |
| BYD17M | D5 | a1 | PH | | Rectifier | 1000 V | 1 µA | 600 mA | | <0.93 V | 1 A | 21 pF | | | |
| BYD31D | A7 | a1 | PH | | Rectifier | 200 V | 1 µA | 440 mA | | <1.35 V | 500 mA | | | <250 ns | |
| BYD31G | A7 | a1 | PH | | Rectifier | 400 V | 1 µA | 440 mA | | <1.35 V | 500 mA | | | <250 ns | |
| BYD31J | A7 | a1 | PH | | Rectifier | 600 V | 1 µA | 440 mA | | <1.35 V | 500 mA | | | <250 ns | |
| BYD31K | A7 | a1 | PH | | Rectifier | 800 V | 1 µA | 440 mA | | <1.35 V | 500 mA | | | <300 ns | |
| BYD31M | A7 | a1 | PH | | Rectifier | 1000 V | 1 µA | 440 mA | | <1.35 V | 500 mA | | | <300 ns | |
| BYD33D | A8 | a1 | PH | | Rectifier | 200 V | 1 µA | 700 mA | | <1.3 V | 1 A | | | <250 ns | |
| BYD33G | A8 | a1 | PH | | Rectifier | 400 V | 1 µA | 700 mA | | <1.3 V | 1 A | | | <250 ns | |
| BYD33J | A8 | a1 | PH | | Rectifier | 600 V | 1 µA | 700 mA | | <1.3 V | 1 A | | | <250 ns | |
| BYD33K | A8 | a1 | PH | | Rectifier | 800 V | 1 µA | 700 mA | | <1.3 V | 1 A | | | <300 ns | |
| BYD33M | A8 | a1 | PH | | Rectifier | 1000 V | 1 µA | 700 mA | | <1.3 V | 1 A | | | <300 ns | |
| BYD34D | A6 | a1 | PH | | Rectifier | 200 V | 1 µA | 1 A | | <1.4 V | 3 A | | | <250 ns | |
| BYD34G | A6 | a1 | PH | | Rectifier | 400 V | 1 µA | 1 A | | <1.4 V | 3 A | | | <250 ns | |
| BYD34J | A6 | a1 | PH | | Rectifier | 600 V | 1 µA | 1 A | | <1.4 V | 3 A | | | <250 ns | |
| BYD34K | A6 | a1 | PH | | Rectifier | 800 V | 1 µA | 1 A | | <1.4 V | 3 A | | | <300 ns | |
| BYD34M | A6 | a1 | PH | | Rectifier | 1000 V | 1 µA | 1 A | | <1.4 V | 3 A | | | <300 ns | |
| BYD37D | D5 | a1 | PH | | Rectifier | 200 V | 1 µA | 600 mA | | <1.3 V | 1 A | | | <250 ns | |
| BYD37G | D5 | a1 | PH | | Rectifier | 400 V | 1 µA | 600 mA | | <1.3 V | 1 A | | | <250 ns | |
| BYD37J | D5 | a1 | PH | | Rectifier | 600 V | 1 µA | 600 mA | | <1.3 V | 1 A | | | <250 ns | |
| BYD37K | D5 | a1 | PH | | Rectifier | 800 V | 1 µA | 600 mA | | <1.3 V | 1 A | | | <300 ns | |
| BYD37M | D5 | a1 | PH | | Rectifier | 1000 V | 1 µA | 600 mA | | <1.3 V | 1 A | | | <300 ns | |
| BYD43-20 | A8 | a1 | PH | | HV Rectifier | 2000 V | 5 µA | 440 mA | | <2.4 V | 1 A | 6 pF | | <300 ns | |
| BYD71A | A7 | a1 | PH | | Rectifier | 50 V | 1 µA | 560 mA | | <0.9 V | 500 mA | 6 pF | | <25 ns | |
| BYD71B | A7 | a1 | PH | | Rectifier | 100 V | 1 µA | 560 mA | | <0.9 V | 500 mA | 6 pF | | <25 ns | |
| BYD71C | A7 | a1 | PH | | Rectifier | 150 V | 1 µA | 560 mA | | <0.9 V | 500 mA | 6 pF | | <25 ns | |
| BYD71D | A7 | a1 | PH | | Rectifier | 200 V | 1 µA | 560 mA | | <1.1 V | 500 mA | 6 pF | | <50 ns | |
| BYD71E | A7 | a1 | PH | | Rectifier | 250 V | 1 µA | 540 mA | | <1.1 V | 500 mA | 6 pF | | <50 ns | |
| BYD71F | A7 | a1 | PH | | Rectifier | 300 V | 1 µA | 540 mA | | <1.1 V | 500 mA | 6 pF | | <50 ns | |
| BYD71G | A7 | a1 | PH | | Rectifier | 400 V | 1 µA | 540 mA | | <1.1 V | 500 mA | 6 pF | | <50 ns | |
| BYD73A | A8 | a1 | PH | | Rectifier | 50 V | 1 µA | 1 A | | <0.98 V | 1 A | | | <25 ns | |
| BYD73B | A8 | a1 | PH | | Rectifier | 100 V | 1 µA | 1 A | | <0.98 V | 1 A | | | <25 ns | |
| BYD73C | A8 | a1 | PH | | Rectifier | 150 V | 1 µA | 1 A | | <0.98 V | 1 A | | | <25 ns | |
| BYD73D | A8 | a1 | PH | | Rectifier | 200 V | 1 µA | 1 A | | <0.98 V | 1 A | | | <25 ns | |
| BYD73E | A8 | a1 | PH | | Rectifier | 250 V | 1 µA | 950 mA | | <1.05 V | 1 A | | | <50 ns | |
| BYD73F | A8 | a1 | PH | | Rectifier | 300 V | 1 µA | 950 mA | | <1.05 V | 1 A | | | <50 ns | |
| BYD73G | A8 | a1 | PH | | Rectifier | 400 V | 1 µA | 950 mA | | <1.05 V | 1 A | | | | |
| BYD74A | A6 | a1 | PH | | Rectifier | 50 V | 1 µA | 1.35 A | | <0.94 V | 2 A | | | <25 ns | |
| BYD74B | A6 | a1 | PH | | Rectifier | 100 V | 1 µA | 1.35 A | | <0.94 V | 2 A | | | <25 ns | |
| BYD74C | A6 | a1 | PH | | Rectifier | 150 V | 1 µA | 1.35 A | | <0.94 V | 2 A | | | <25 ns | |

| Type | Case | Pin-code | | | Maximum Ratings | | | | Electrical Characteristics | | | | | |
|---|---|---|---|---|---|---|---|---|---|---|---|---|---|---|
| | | | | | Vrm | Irm | Ifav Ifm | Pv | Vf | If Ifp | C0 | Cr | trr ts | |
| BYD74D | A6 | a1 | PH | Rectifier | 200 V | 1 μA | 1.2 A | | <1.05 V | 2 A | | | <50 ns | |
| BYD74E | A6 | a1 | PH | Rectifier | 250 V | 1 μA | 1.2 A | | <1.05 V | 2 A | | | <50 ns | |
| BYD74F | A6 | a1 | PH | Rectifier | 300 V | 1 μA | 1.2 A | | <1.05 V | 2 A | | | <50 ns | |
| BYD74G | A6 | a1 | PH | Rectifier | 400 V | 1 μA | 1.2 A | | <1.05 V | 2 A | | | <50 ns | |
| BYD77A | D5 | a1 | PH | Rectifier | 50 V | 1 μA | 850 mA | | <0.98 V | 1 A | | | <25 ns | |
| BYD77B | D5 | a1 | PH | Rectifier | 100 V | 1 μA | 850 mA | | <0.98 V | 1 A | | | <25 ns | |
| BYD77C | D5 | a1 | PH | Rectifier | 150 V | 1 μA | 850 mA | | <0.98 V | 1 A | | | <25 ns | |
| BYD77D | D5 | a1 | PH | Rectifier | 200 V | 1 μA | 850 mA | | <0.98 V | 1 A | | | <25 ns | |
| BYD77E | D5 | a1 | PH | Rectifier | 250 V | 1 μA | 800 mA | | <1.05 V | 1 A | | | <50 ns | |
| BYD77F | D5 | a1 | PH | Rectifier | 300 V | 1 μA | 800 mA | | <1.05 V | 1 A | | | <50 ns | |
| BYD77D | D5 | a1 | PH | Rectifier | 400 V | 1 μA | 800 mA | | <1.05 V | 1 A | | | <50 ns | |
| BYG10D | G5 | a1 | TE | Rectifier | 200 V | | 1.5 A | | <1.1 V | 1 mA | | | <4 μs | |
| BYG10G | G5 | a1 | TE | Rectifier | 400 V | | 1.5 A | | <1.1 V | 1 mA | | | <4 μs | |
| BYG10J | G5 | a1 | TE | Rectifier | 600 V | | 1.5 A | | <1.1 V | 1 mA | | | <4 μs | |
| BYG10K | G5 | a1 | TE | Rectifier | 800 V | | 1.5 A | | <1.1 V | 1 mA | | | <4 μs | |
| BYG10M | G5 | a1 | TE | Rectifier | 1000 V | | 1.5 A | | <1.1 V | 1 mA | | | <4 μs | |
| BYG20D | G5 | a1 | TE | Rectifier | 200 V | | 1.5 A | | <1.3 V | 1 A | | | 75 ns | |
| BYG20G | G5 | a1 | TE | Rectifier | 400 V | | 1.5 A | | <1.3 V | 1 A | | | 75 ns | |
| BYG20J | G5 | a1 | TE | Rectifier | 600 V | | 1.5 A | | <1.3 V | 1 A | | | 75 ns | |
| BYG21K | G5 | a1 | TE | Rectifier | 800 V | | 1.5 A | | <1.3 V | 1 A | | | 75 ns | |
| BYG21M | G5 | a1 | TE | Rectifier | 1000 V | | 1.5 A | | <1.3 V | 1 A | | | 75 ns | |
| BYM26A | A5 | a1 | PH | Rectifier | 200 V | 10 μA | 1 A | | <2.65 V | 2 A | | | <30 ns | |
| BYM26B | A5 | a1 | PH | Rectifier | 400 V | 10 μA | 1 A | | <2.65 V | 2 A | | | <30 ns | |
| BYM26C | A5 | a1 | PH | Rectifier | 600 V | 10 μA | 1 A | | <2.65 V | 2 A | | | <30 ns | |
| BYM26D | A5 | a1 | PH | Rectifier | 800 V | 10 μA | 1 A | | <2.65 V | 2 A | | | <75 ns | |
| BYM26E | A5 | a1 | PH | Rectifier | 1000 V | 10 μA | 1 A | | <2.65 V | 2 A | | | <75 ns | |
| BYM36A | A5 | a1 | PH | Rectifier | 200 V | 5 μA | 1.25 A | | <1.6 V | 3 A | | | <100 ns | |
| BYM36B | A5 | a1 | PH | Rectifier | 400 V | 5 μA | 1.25 A | | <1.6 V | 3 A | | | <100 ns | |
| BYM36C | A5 | a1 | PH | Rectifier | 600 V | 5 μA | 1.25 A | | <1.6 V | 3 A | | | <100 ns | |
| BYM36D | A5 | a1 | PH | Rectifier | 800 V | 5 μA | 1.2 A | | <1.78 V | 3 A | | | <150 ns | |
| BYM36E | A5 | a1 | PH | Rectifier | 1000 V | 5 μA | 1.2 A | | <1.78 V | 3 A | | | <150 ns | |
| BYM56A | A5 | a1 | PH | Rectifier | 200 V | 1 μA | 1.4 A | | <1.25 V | 5 A | 90 pF | | | |
| BYM56B | A5 | a1 | PH | Rectifier | 400 V | 1 μA | 1.4 A | | <1.25 V | 5 A | 90 pF | | | |
| BYM56C | A5 | a1 | PH | Rectifier | 600 V | 1 μA | 1.4 A | | <1.25 V | 5 A | 90 pF | | | |
| BYM56D | A5 | a1 | PH | Rectifier | 800 V | 1 μA | 1.4 A | | <1.25 V | 5 A | 90 pF | | | |
| BYM56E | A5 | a1 | PH | Rectifier | 1000 V | 1 μA | 1.4 A | | <1.25 V | 5 A | 90 pF | | | |
| BYP22-100 | I4 | c7 | PH | Rect. Pair | 100 V | 5 μA | 4 A | | <0.98 V | 8 A | | | <25 ns | |
| BYP22-150 | I4 | c7 | PH | Rect. Pair | 150 V | 5 μA | 4 A | | <0.98 V | 8 A | | | <25 ns | |
| BYP22-200 | I4 | c7 | PH | Rect. Pair | 200 V | 5 μA | 4 A | | <0.98 V | 8 A | | | <25 ns | |
| BYP22-50 | I4 | c7 | PH | Rect. Pair | 50 V | 5 μA | 4 A | | <0.98 V | 8 A | | | <25 ns | |

| Type | Case | Pin-code | | | Maximum Ratings | | | | Electrical Characteristics | | | | | |
|---|---|---|---|---|---|---|---|---|---|---|---|---|---|---|
| | | | | | Vrm | Irm | Ifav / Ifm | Pv | Vf | If / Ifp | C0 | Cr | trr / ts | |
| BYQ27-100 | I18 | c7 | PH | Rect. Pair | 100 V | 10 µA | 5 A | | <1.25 V | 10 A | | | <20 ns | |
| BYQ27-150 | I18 | c7 | PH | Rect. Pair | 150 V | 10 µA | 5 A | | <1.25 V | 10 A | | | <20 ns | |
| BYQ27-200 | I18 | c7 | PH | Rect. Pair | 200 V | 10 µA | 5 A | | <1.25 V | 10 A | | | <20 ns | |
| BYQ27-50 | I18 | c7 | PH | Rect. Pair | 50 V | 10 µA | 5 A | | <1.25 V | 10 A | | | <20 ns | |
| BYQ28-100 | I4 | c7 | PH | Rect. Pair | 100 V | 10 µA | 5 A | | <1.25 V | 10 A | | | <20 ns | |
| BYQ28-150 | I4 | c7 | PH | Rect. Pair | 150 V | 10 µA | 5 A | | <1.25 V | 10 A | | | <20 ns | |
| BYQ28-200 | I4 | c7 | PH | Rect. Pair | 200 V | 10 µA | 5 A | | <1.25 V | 10 A | | | <20 ns | |
| BYQ28-50 | I4 | c7 | PH | Rect. Pair | 50 V | 10 µA | 5 A | | <1.25 V | 10 A | | | <20 ns | |
| BYQ28F-100 | J8 | c7 | PH | Rect. Pair | 100 V | 10 µA | 5 A | | <1.25 V | 10 A | 12 pF | | <20 ns | |
| BYQ28F-150 | J8 | c7 | PH | Rect. Pair | 150 V | 10 µA | 5 A | | <1.25 V | 10 A | 12 pF | | <20 ns | |
| BYQ28F-200 | J8 | c7 | PH | Rect. Pair | 200 V | 10 µA | 5 A | | <1.25 V | 10 A | 12 pF | | <20 ns | |
| BYQ28F-50 | J8 | c7 | PH | Rect. Pair | 50 V | 10 µA | 5 A | | <1.25 V | 10 A | 12 pF | | <20 ns | |
| BYR28-500 | I4 | c7 | PH | Rect. Pair | 500 V | 25 µA | 5 A | | <2 V | 10 A | | | <80 ns | |
| BYR28-600 | I4 | c7 | PH | Rect. Pair | 600 V | 25 µA | 5 A | | <2 V | 10 A | | | <80 ns | |
| BYR28-700 | I4 | c7 | PH | Rect. Pair | 700 V | 25 µA | 5 A | | <2 V | 10 A | | | <80 ns | |
| BYR28-800 | I4 | c7 | PH | Rect. Pair | 800 V | 25 µA | 5 A | | <2 V | 10 A | | | <80 ns | |
| BYR29-500 | I5 | a1 | PH | Rectifier | 500 V | 10 µA | 8 A | | <1.75 V | 25 A | | | <75 ns | |
| BYR29-600 | I5 | a1 | PH | Rectifier | 600 V | 10 µA | 8 A | | <1.75 V | 25 A | | | <75 ns | |
| BYR29-700 | I5 | a1 | PH | Rectifier | 700 V | 10 µA | 8 A | | <1.75 V | 25 A | | | <75 ns | |
| BYR29-800 | I5 | a1 | PH | Rectifier | 800 V | 10 µA | 8 A | | <1.75 V | 25 A | | | <75 ns | |
| BYR29F-600 | J7 | a1 | PH | Rectifier | 600 V | 10 µA | 8 A | | <1.75 V | 25 A | 12 pF | | <75 ns | |
| BYR29F-700 | J7 | a1 | PH | Rectifier | 700 V | 10 µA | 8 A | | <1.75 V | 25 A | 12 pF | | <75 ns | |
| BYR29F-800 | J7 | a1 | PH | Rectifier | 800 V | 10 µA | 8 A | | <1.75 V | 25 A | 12 pF | | <75 ns | |
| BYR30-500 | E1 | a1 | PH | Rectifier | 500 V | 25 µA | 14 A | | <2 V | 50 A | | | <100 ns | |
| BYR30-600 | E1 | a1 | PH | Rectifier | 600 V | 25 µA | 14 A | | <2 V | 50 A | | | <100 ns | |
| BYR30-700 | E1 | a1 | PH | Rectifier | 700 V | 25 µA | 14 A | | <2 V | 50 A | | | <100 ns | |
| BYR30-500U | E2 | a1 | PH | Rectifier | 500 V | 25 µA | 14 A | | <2 V | 50 A | | | <100 ns | |
| BYR30-600U | E2 | a1 | PH | Rectifier | 600 V | 25 µA | 14 A | | <2 V | 50 A | | | <100 ns | |
| BYR30-700U | E2 | a1 | PH | Rectifier | 700 V | 25 µA | 14 A | | <2 V | 50 A | | | <100 ns | |
| BYR34-500 | I4 | c7 | PH | Rect. Pair | 500 V | 25 µA | 10 A | | <1.65 V | 30 A | | | <80 ns | |
| BYR34-600 | I4 | c7 | PH | Rect. Pair | 600 V | 25 µA | 10 A | | <1.65 V | 30 A | | | <80 ns | |
| BYR34-700 | I4 | c7 | PH | Rect. Pair | 700 V | 25 µA | 10 A | | <1.65 V | 30 A | | | <80 ns | |
| BYR34-800 | I4 | c7 | PH | Rect. Pair | 800 V | 25 µA | 10 A | | <1.65 V | 30 A | | | <80 ns | |
| BYR79-500 | I5 | a1 | PH | Rectifier | 500 V | 25 µA | 14 A | | <2 V | 50 A | | | <100 ns | |
| BYR79-600 | I5 | a1 | PH | Rectifier | 600 V | 25 µA | 14 A | | <2 V | 50 A | | | <100 ns | |
| BYR79-700 | I5 | a1 | PH | Rectifier | 700 V | 25 µA | 14 A | | <2 V | 50 A | | | <100 ns | |
| BYR79-800 | I5 | a1 | PH | Rectifier | 800 V | 25 µA | 14 A | | <2 V | 50 A | | | <100 ns | |
| BYT01-200 | B4 | a1 | SG | Rectifier | 200 V | 20 µA | 1 mA | 1.33 W | <1.5 V | 1 A | | | <25 ns | Ifav at Tc=70°C |
| BYT01-300 | B4 | a1 | SG | Rectifier | 300 V | 20 µA | 1 mA | 1.33 W | <1.5 V | 1 A | | | <25 ns | Ifav at Tc=70°C |
| BYT01-400 | B4 | a1 | SG | Rectifier | 400 V | 20 µA | 1 mA | 1.33 W | <1.5 V | 1 A | | | <25 ns | Ifav at Tc=70°C |

| Type | Case | Pin-code | | | Maximum Ratings | | | | Electrical Characteristics | | | | | |
|---|---|---|---|---|---|---|---|---|---|---|---|---|---|---|
| | | | | | Vrm | Irm | Ifav / Ifm | Pv | Vf | If / Ifp | C0 | Cr | trr / ts | |
| BYT03-200 | b5 | a1 | SG | Rectifier | 200 V | 20 µA | 3 mA | 4.2 W | <1.5 V | 3 A | | | <25 ns | Ifav at Tc=65°C |
| BYT03-300 | b5 | a1 | SG | Rectifier | 300 V | 20 µA | 3 mA | 4.2 W | <1.5 V | 3 A | | | <25 ns | Ifav at Tc=65°C |
| BYT03-400 | b5 | a1 | SG | Rectifier | 400 V | 20 µA | 3 mA | 4.2 W | <1.5 V | 3 A | | | <25 ns | Ifav at Tc=65°C |
| BYT08P-1000A | I1 | a1 | SG | Rectifier | 1000 V | 35 µA | 16 mA | (17) | <1.9 V | 8 A | | | <65 ns | Ifav at Tc=115°C |
| BYT08P-1000A | I3 | a1 | TE | Rectifier | 1000 V | 35 µA | 16 mA | | 1.9 V | 8 A | | | 50 ns | Ifav at Tc=115°C |
| BYT08P-200A | I1 | a1 | SG | Rectifier | 200 V | 15 µA | 16 mA | (20) W | <1.5 V | 8 A | | | <35 ns | Ifav at Tc=120°C |
| BYT08P-300A | I1 | a1 | SG | Rectifier | 300 V | 15 µA | 16 mA | (20) W | <1.5 V | 8 A | | | <35 ns | Ifav at Tc=120°C |
| BYT08P-400A | I1 | a1 | SG | Rectifier | 400 V | 15 µA | 16 mA | (20) W | <1.5 V | 8 A | | | <35 ns | Ifav at Tc=120°C |
| BYT08P-600A | I1 | a1 | SG | Rectifier | 600 V | 35 µA | 8 mA | (15) W | <1.9 V | 8 A | | | <50 ns | Ifav at Tc=115°C |
| BYT08P-600A | I3 | a1 | TE | Rectifier | 600 V | 35 µA | 8 mA | | 1.9 V | 8 A | | | 50 ns | Ifav at Tc=115°C |
| BYT08P-800A | I1 | a1 | SG | Rectifier | 800 V | 35 µA | 8 mA | (17) | <1.9 V | 8 A | | | <50 ns | Ifav at Tc=115°C |
| BYT08P-800A | I3 | a1 | TE | Rectifier | 800 V | 35 µA | 8 mA | | 1.9 V | 8 A | | | 50 ns | Ifav at Tc=115°C |
| BYT08PI-1000 | I13 | a1 | SG | Rectifier | 1000 V | 35 µA | 8 A | (17) | <1.9 V | 8 A | | | <65 ns | Ifav at Tc=80°C |
| BYT08PI-200 | I13 | a1 | SG | Rectifier | 200 V | 15 µA | 8 A | (20) | <1.5 V | 8 A | | | <35 ns | Ifav at Tc=105°C |
| BYT08PI-300 | I13 | a1 | SG | Rectifier | 300 V | 15 µA | 8 A | (20) | <1.5 V | 8 A | | | <35 ns | Ifav at Tc=105°C |
| BYT08PI-400 | I13 | a1 | SG | Rectifier | 400 V | 15 µA | 8 A | (20) | <1.5 V | 8 A | | | <35 ns | Ifav at Tc=105°C |
| BYT08PI-600 | I13 | a1 | SG | Rectifier | 600 V | 35 µA | 8 A | (17) | <1.9 V | 8 A | | | <50 ns | Ifav at Tc=80°C |
| BYT08PI-800 | I13 | a1 | SG | Rectifier | 800 V | 35 µA | 8 A | (17) | <1.9 V | 8 A | | | <50 ns | Ifav at Tc=80°C |
| BYT11-1000 | B4 | a1 | SG | Rectifier | 1000 V | 20 µA | 1 A | 1.25 W | <1.3 V | 1 A | | | <100 ns | Ifav at Tc=75°C |
| BYT11-600 | B4 | a1 | SG | Rectifier | 600 V | 20 µA | 1 A | 1.25 W | <1.3 V | 1 A | | | <100 ns | Ifav at Tc=75°C |
| BYT11-800 | B4 | a1 | SG | Rectifier | 800 V | 20 µA | 1 A | 1.25 W | <1.3 V | 1 A | | | <100 ns | Ifav at Tc=75°C |
| BYT12-1000 | E2 | a1 | SG | Rectifier | 1000 V | 50 µA | 12 A | (26) W | <1.9 V | 12 A | | | <65 ns | Ifav at Tc=85°C |
| BYT12-200 | E2 | a1 | SG | Rectifier | 200 V | 15 µA | 12 A | (20) W | <1.5 V | 12 A | | | <50 ns | Ifav at Tc=100°C |
| BYT12-300 | E2 | a1 | SG | Rectifier | 300 V | 15 µA | 12 A | (20) W | <1.5 V | 12 A | | | <50 ns | Ifav at Tc=100°C |
| BYT12-400 | E2 | a1 | SG | Rectifier | 400 V | 15 µA | 12 A | (20) W | <1.5 V | 12 A | | | <50 ns | Ifav at Tc=100°C |
| BYT12-600 | E2 | a1 | SG | Rectifier | 600 V | 50 µA | 12 A | (20) W | <1.9 V | 12 A | | | <50 ns | Ifav at Tc=100°C |
| BYT12-800 | E2 | a1 | SG | Rectifier | 800 V | 50 µA | 12 A | (20) W | <1.9 V | 12 A | | | <50 ns | Ifav at Tc=100°C |
| BYT12P-1000A | I1 | a1 | SG | Rectifier | 1000 V | 50 µA | 12 A | (25) W | <1.9 V | 12 A | | | <65 ns | Ifav at Tc=100°C |
| BYT12P-1000A | I3 | a1 | TE | Rectifier | 1000 V | 50 µA | 12 A | | 1.9 V | 12 A | | | 50 ns | Ifav at Tc=100°C |
| BYT12P-600A | I1 | a1 | SG | Rectifier | 600 V | 50 µA | 12 A | (25) W | <1.9 V | 12 A | | | <50 ns | Ifav at Tc=100°C |
| BYT12P-600A | I3 | a1 | TE | Rectifier | 600 V | 50 µA | 12 A | | 1.9 V | 12 A | | | 50 ns | Ifav at Tc=100°C |
| BYT12P-800A | I1 | a1 | SG | Rectifier | 800 V | 50 µA | 12 A | (25) W | <1.9 V | 12 A | | | <50 ns | Ifav at Tc=100°C |
| BYT12P-800A | I3 | a1 | TE | Rectifier | 800 V | 50 µA | 12 A | | 1.9 V | 12 A | | | 50 ns | Ifav at Tc=100°C |
| BYT12PI-1000 | I13 | a1 | SG | Rectifier | 1000 V | 50 µA | 12 A | (25) W | <1.9 V | 12 A | | | <65 ns | Ifav at Tc=50°C |
| BYT12PI-600 | I13 | a1 | SG | Rectifier | 600 V | 50 µA | 12 A | (25) W | <1.9 V | 12 A | | | <50 ns | Ifav at Tc=100°C |
| BYT12PI-800 | I13 | a1 | SG | Rectifier | 800 V | 50 µA | 12 A | (25) W | <1.9 V | 12 A | | | <50 ns | Ifav at Tc=100°C |
| BYT13-1000 | b5 | a1 | SG | Rectifier | 1000 V | 20 µA | 3 A | 3.75 W | <1.3 V | 3 A | | | <150 ns | Ifav at Tc=50°C |
| BYT13-600 | b5 | a1 | SG | Rectifier | 600 V | 20 µA | 3 A | 3.75 W | <1.3 V | 3 A | | | <150 ns | Ifav at Tc=50°C |
| BYT13-800 | b5 | a1 | SG | Rectifier | 800 V | 20 µA | 3 A | 3.75 W | <1.3 V | 3 A | | | <150 ns | Ifav at Tc=50°C |
| BYT16P-200A | I4 | c7 | SG | Rect. Pair | 200 V | 15 µA | 16 A | (25) W | <1.5 V | 8 A | | | <35 ns | Ifav at Tc=55°C |

| Type | Case | Pin-code | | | Vrm | Irm | Ifav Ifm | Pv | Vf | If Ifp | C0 | Cr | trr ls | |
|------|------|----------|---|---|-----|-----|----------|-----|-----|--------|----|----|--------|---|
| BYT16P-300A | I4 | c7 | SG | Rect. Pair | 300 V | 15 µA | 16 A | (25) W | <1.5 V | 8 A | | | <35 ns | Ifav at Tc=100°C |
| BYT16P-400A | I4 | c7 | SG | Rect. Pair | 400 V | 15 µA | 16 A | (25) W | <1.5 V | 8 A | | | <35 ns | Ifav at Tc=100°C |
| BYT28-300 | I4 | c7 | PH | Rect. Pair | 300 V | 10 µA | 5 A | | <1.4 V | 15 A | | | <50 ns | |
| BYT28-400 | I4 | c7 | PH | Rect. Pair | 400 V | 10 µA | 5 A | | <1.4 V | 15 A | | | <50 ns | |
| BYT28-500 | I4 | c7 | PH | Rect. Pair | 500 V | 10 µA | 5 A | | <1.4 V | 15 A | | | <50 ns | |
| BYT30-1000 | E4 | a1 | SG | Rectifier | 1000 V | 100 µA | 30 A | (62) W | <1.9 V | 30 A | | | <70 ns | Ifav at Tc=75°C |
| BYT30-200 | E4 | a1 | SG | Rectifier | 200 V | 35 µA | 30 A | (50) W | <1.5 V | 30 A | | | <50 ns | Ifav at Tc=90°C |
| BYT30-300 | E4 | a1 | SG | Rectifier | 300 V | 35 µA | 30 A | (50) W | <1.5 V | 30 A | | | <50 ns | Ifav at Tc=90°C |
| BYT30-400 | E4 | a1 | SG | Rectifier | 400 V | 35 µA | 30 A | (50) W | <1.5 V | 30 A | | | <50 ns | Ifav at Tc=90°C |
| BYT30-600 | E4 | a1 | SG | Rectifier | 600 V | 100 µA | 30 A | (62) W | <1.9 V | 30 A | | | <55 ns | Ifav at Tc=75°C |
| BYT30-800 | E4 | a1 | SG | Rectifier | 800 V | 100 µA | 30 A | (62) W | <1.9 V | 30 A | | | <55 ns | Ifav at Tc=75°C |
| BYT30P-1000 | I14 | a1 | SG | Rectifier | 1000 V | 100 µA | 30 A | (65) W | <1.9 V | 30 A | | | <70 ns | Ifav at Tc=85°C |
| BYT30P-200 | I14 | a1 | SG | Rectifier | 200 V | 35 µA | 30 A | (50) W | <1.5 V | 30 A | | | <50 ns | Ifav at Tc=100°C |
| BYT30P-300 | I14 | a1 | SG | Rectifier | 300 V | 35 µA | 30 A | (50) W | <1.5 V | 30 A | | | <50 ns | Ifav at Tc=100°C |
| BYT30P-400 | I14 | a1 | SG | Rectifier | 400 V | 35 µA | 30 A | (50) W | <1.5 V | 30 A | | | <50 ns | Ifav at Tc=100°C |
| BYT30P-600 | I14 | a1 | SG | Rectifier | 600 V | 100 µA | 30 A | (65) W | <1.9 V | 30 A | | | <55 ns | Ifav at Tc=85°C |
| BYT30P-800 | I14 | a1 | SG | Rectifier | 800 V | 100 µA | 30 A | (65) W | <1.9 V | 30 A | | | <55 ns | Ifav at Tc=85°C |
| BYT30PI-1000 | I14 | a1 | SG | Rectifier | 1000 V | 100 µA | 30 A | (60) W | <1.9 V | 30 A | | | <70 ns | Ifav at Tc=50°C |
| BYT30PI-200 | I14 | a1 | SG | Rectifier | 200 V | 35 µA | 30 A | (50) W | <1.5 V | 30 A | | | <50 ns | Ifav at Tc=60°C |
| BYT30PI-300 | I14 | a1 | SG | Rectifier | 300 V | 35 µA | 30 A | (50) W | <1.5 V | 30 A | | | <50 ns | Ifav at Tc=60°C |
| BYT30PI-400 | I14 | a1 | SG | Rectifier | 400 V | 35 µA | 30 A | (50) W | <1.5 V | 30 A | | | <50 ns | Ifav at Tc=60°C |
| BYT30PI-600 | I14 | a1 | SG | Rectifier | 600 V | 100 µA | 30 A | (62) W | <1.9 V | 30 A | | | <55 ns | Ifav at Tc=50°C |
| BYT30PI-800 | I14 | a1 | SG | Rectifier | 800 V | 100 µA | 30 A | (62) W | <1.9 V | 30 A | | | <55 ns | Ifav at Tc=50°C |
| BYT51A | A4 | a1 | TE | Rectifier | 50 V | 1 µA | 1 A | | <1.2 V | 1 mA | | | <4 µs | Ifav at Ta=55°C |
| BYT51B | A4 | a1 | TE | Rectifier | 100 V | 1 µA | 1 A | | <1.2 V | 1 mA | | | <4 µs | Ifav at Ta=55°C |
| BYT51D | A4 | a1 | TE | Rectifier | 200 V | 1 µA | 1 A | | <1.2 V | 1 mA | | | <4 µs | Ifav at Ta=55°C |
| BYT51G | A4 | a1 | TE | Rectifier | 400 V | 1 µA | 1 A | | <1.2 V | 1 mA | | | <4 µs | Ifav at Ta=55°C |
| BYT51J | A4 | a1 | TE | Rectifier | 600 V | 1 µA | 1 A | | <1.2 V | 1 mA | | | <4 µs | Ifav at Ta=55°C |
| BYT51K | A4 | a1 | TE | Rectifier | 800 V | 1 µA | 1 A | | <1.2 V | 1 mA | | | <4 µs | Ifav at Ta=55°C |
| BYT51M | A4 | a1 | TE | Rectifier | 1000 V | 1 µA | 1 A | | <1.2 V | 1 mA | | | <4 µs | Ifav at Ta=55°C |
| BYT52A | A4 | a1 | TE | Rectifier | 50 V | 5 µA | 1 A | | <1.3 V | 1 A | | | <200 ns | Ifav at Ta=45°C |
| BYT52B | A4 | a1 | TE | Rectifier | 100 V | 5 µA | 1 A | | <1.3 V | 1 A | | | <200 ns | Ifav at Ta=45°C |
| BYT52C | A4 | a1 | TE | Rectifier | 200 V | 5 µA | 1 A | | <1.3 V | 1 A | | | <200 ns | Ifav at Ta=45°C |
| BYT52D | A4 | a1 | TE | Rectifier | 200 V | 5 µA | 1 A | | <1.3 V | 1 A | | | <200 ns | Ifav at Ta=45°C |
| BYT52G | A4 | a1 | TE | Rectifier | 400 V | 5 µA | 1 A | | <1.3 V | 1 A | | | <200 ns | Ifav at Ta=45°C |
| BYT52J | A4 | a1 | TE | Rectifier | 600 V | 5 µA | 1 A | | <1.3 V | 1 A | | | <200 ns | Ifav at Ta=45°C |
| BYT52K | A4 | a1 | TE | Rectifier | 800 V | 5 µA | 1 A | | <1.3 V | 1 A | | | <200 ns | Ifav at Ta=45°C |
| BYT52M | A4 | a1 | TE | Rectifier | 1000 V | 5 µA | 1 A | | <1.3 V | 1 A | | | <200 ns | Ifav at Ta=45°C |
| BYT53A | A4 | a1 | TE | Rectifier | 50 V | 5 µA | 1.5 A | | <1.1 V | 1 A | | | <50 ns | |
| BYT53B | A4 | a1 | TE | Rectifier | 100 V | 5 µA | 1.5 A | | <1.1 V | 1 A | | | <50 ns | |

| Type | Case | Pin-code | | | Maximum Ratings | | | | Electrical Characteristics | | | | | |
| --- | --- | --- | --- | --- | --- | --- | --- | --- | --- | --- | --- | --- | --- | --- |
| | | | | | Vrm | Irm | Ifav / Ifm | Pv | Vf | If / Ifp | C0 | Cr | trr / ts | |
| BYT53C | A4 | a1 | TE | Rectifier | 150 V | 5 μA | 1.5 A | | <1.1 V | 1 A | | | <50 ns | |
| BYT53D | A4 | a1 | TE | Rectifier | 200 V | 5 μA | 1.5 A | | <1.1 V | 1 A | | | <50 ns | |
| BYT53F | A4 | a1 | TE | Rectifier | 300 V | 5 μA | 1.5 A | | <1.1 V | 1 A | | | <50 ns | |
| BYT53G | A4 | a1 | TE | Rectifier | 400 V | 5 μA | 1.5 A | | <1.1 V | 1 A | | | <50 ns | |
| BYT54A | A4 | a1 | TE | Rectifier | 50 V | 5 μA | 1.25 A | | <1.5 V | 1 A | | | <100 ns | |
| BYT54B | A4 | a1 | TE | Rectifier | 100 V | 5 μA | 1.25 A | | <1.5 V | 1 A | | | <100 ns | |
| BYT54D | A4 | a1 | TE | Rectifier | 200 V | 5 μA | 1.25 A | | <1.5 V | 1 A | | | <100 ns | |
| BYT54G | A4 | a1 | TE | Rectifier | 400 V | 5 μA | 1.25 A | | <1.5 V | 1 A | | | <100 ns | |
| BYT54J | A4 | a1 | TE | Rectifier | 600 V | 5 μA | 1.25 A | | <1.5 V | 1 A | | | <200 ns | |
| BYT54K | A4 | a1 | TE | Rectifier | 800 V | 5 μA | 1.25 A | | <1.5 V | 1 A | | | <200 ns | |
| BYT54M | A4 | a1 | TE | Rectifier | 1000 V | 5 μA | 1.25 A | | <1.5 V | 1 A | | | <200 ns | |
| BYT56A | A5 | a1 | TE | Rectifier | 50 V | 5 μA | 3 A | | <1.4 V | 3 A | | | <100 ns | |
| BYT56B | A5 | a1 | TE | Rectifier | 100 V | 5 μA | 3 A | | <1.4 V | 3 A | | | <100 ns | |
| BYT56D | A5 | a1 | TE | Rectifier | 200 V | 5 μA | 3 A | | <1.4 V | 3 A | | | <100 ns | |
| BYT56G | A5 | a1 | TE | Rectifier | 400 V | 5 μA | 3 A | | <1.4 V | 3 A | | | <100 ns | |
| BYT56J | A5 | a1 | TE | Rectifier | 600 V | 5 μA | 3 A | | <1.4 V | 3 A | | | <100 ns | |
| BYT56K | A5 | a1 | TE | Rectifier | 800 V | 5 μA | 3 A | | <1.5 V | 3 A | | | <100 ns | |
| BYT56M | A5 | a1 | TE | Rectifier | 1000 V | 5 μA | 3 A | | <1.5 V | 3 A | | | <100 ns | |
| BYT60-1000 | E4 | a1 | SG | Rectifier | 1000 V | 100 μA | 60 A | (125) W | <1.9 V | 60 A | | | <70 ns | Ifav at Tc=50°C |
| BYT60-200 | E4 | a1 | SG | Rectifier | 200 V | 60 μA | 60 A | (100) W | <1.5 V | 60 A | | | <50 ns | Ifav at Tc=80°C |
| BYT60-300 | E4 | a1 | SG | Rectifier | 300 V | 60 μA | 60 A | (100) W | <1.5 V | 60 A | | | <50 ns | Ifav at Tc=80°C |
| BYT60-400 | E4 | a1 | SG | Rectifier | 400 V | 60 μA | 60 A | (100) W | <1.5 V | 60 A | | | <50 ns | Ifav at Tc=80°C |
| BYT60-600 | E4 | a1 | SG | Rectifier | 600 V | 100 μA | 60 A | (125) W | <1.9 V | 60 A | | | <65 ns | Ifav at Tc=50°C |
| BYT60-800 | E4 | a1 | SG | Rectifier | 800 V | 100 μA | 60 A | (125) W | <1.9 V | 60 A | | | <65 ns | Ifav at Tc=50°C |
| BYT60P-200 | I14 | a1 | SG | Rectifier | 200 V | 60 μA | 60 A | (100) W | <1.5 V | 60 A | | | <50 ns | Ifav at Tc=70°C |
| BYT60P-300 | I14 | a1 | SG | Rectifier | 300 V | 60 μA | 60 A | (100) W | <1.5 V | 60 A | | | <50 ns | Ifav at Tc=70°C |
| BYT60P-400 | I14 | a1 | SG | Rectifier | 400 V | 60 μA | 60 A | (100) W | <1.5 V | 60 A | | | <50 ns | Ifav at Tc=70°C |
| BYT71-100A | I1 | a1 | SG | Rectifier | 100 V | 20 μA | 6 A | (15) W | <1.4 V | 6 A | | | <300 ns | Ifav at Tc=115°C |
| BYT71-200A | I1 | a1 | SG | Rectifier | 200 V | 20 μA | 6 A | (15) W | <1.4 V | 6 A | | | <300 ns | Ifav at Tc=115°C |
| BYT71-400A | I1 | a1 | SG | Rectifier | 400 V | 20 μA | 6 A | (15) W | <1.4 V | 6 A | | | <300 ns | Ifav at Tc=115°C |
| BYT71-600A | I1 | a1 | SG | Rectifier | 600 V | 20 μA | 6 A | (15) W | <1.4 V | 6 A | | | <300 ns | Ifav at Tc=115°C |
| BYT71-800A | I1 | a1 | SG | Rectifier | 800 V | 20 μA | 6 A | (15) W | <1.4 V | 6 A | | | <300 ns | Ifav at Tc=115°C |
| BYT77 | A5 | a1 | TE | Rectifier | 800 V | 5 μA | 3 A | | <1.2 V | 3 A | | | <250 ns | Ifav at Ta=45°C |
| BYT78 | A5 | a1 | TE | Rectifier | 1000 V | 5 μA | 3 A | | <1.2 V | 3 A | | | <250 ns | Ifav at Ta=45°C |
| BYT79-300 | I5 | a1 | PH | Rectifier | 300 V | 50 μA | 14 A | | <1.4 V | 50 A | | | <50 ns | |
| BYT79-400 | I5 | a1 | PH | Rectifier | 400 V | 50 μA | 14 A | | <1.4 V | 50 A | | | <50 ns | |
| BYT79-500 | I5 | a1 | PH | Rectifier | 500 V | 50 μA | 14 A | | <1.4 V | 50 A | | | <50 ns | |
| BYT85-1000 | I3 | a1 | TE | Rectifier | 1000 V | 10 μA | 4 A | | 1.8 V | 4 A | | | 50 ns | |
| BYT85-600 | I3 | a1 | TE | Rectifier | 600 V | 10 μA | 4 A | | 1.8 V | 4 A | | | 50 ns | |
| BYT85-800 | I3 | a1 | TE | Rectifier | 800 V | 10 μA | 4 A | | 1.8 V | 4 A | | | 50 ns | |

| Type | Case | Pin-code | (mfr) | | Maximum Ratings | | | | Electrical Characteristics | | | | | |
|---|---|---|---|---|---|---|---|---|---|---|---|---|---|---|
| | | | | | Vrm | Irm | Ifav / Ifm | Pv | Vf | If / Ifp | C0 | Cr | trr / ts | |
| BYT86-1000 | I3 | a1 | TE | Rectifier | 1000 V | 10 µA | 8 A | | 1.8 V | 8 A | | | 50 ns | |
| BYT86-600 | I3 | a1 | TE | Rectifier | 600 V | 10 µA | 8 A | | 1.8 V | 8 A | | | 50 ns | |
| BYT86-800 | I3 | a1 | TE | Rectifier | 800 V | 10 µA | 8 A | | 1.8 V | 8 A | | | 50 ns | |
| BYT87-1000 | I3 | a1 | TE | Rectifier | 1000 V | 10 µA | 15 A | | 1.8 V | 15 A | | | 50 ns | |
| BYT87-600 | I3 | a1 | TE | Rectifier | 600 V | 10 µA | 15 A | | 1.8 V | 15 A | | | 50 ns | |
| BYT87-800 | I3 | a1 | TE | Rectifier | 800 V | 10 µA | 15 A | | 1.8 V | 15 A | | | 50 ns | |
| BYT108-200 | I3 | a1 | TE | Rectifier | 200 V | 2 µA | 8 A | | 1.3 V | 8 A | | | 50 ns | |
| BYT108-400 | I3 | a1 | TE | Rectifier | 400 V | 2 µA | 8 A | | 1.3 V | 8 A | | | 50 ns | |
| BYT115-200 | I3 | a1 | TE | Rectifier | 200 V | 2 µA | 15 A | | 1.3 V | 15 A | | | 50 ns | |
| BYT115-400 | I3 | a1 | TE | Rectifier | 400 V | 2 µA | 15 A | | 1.3 V | 15 A | | | 50 ns | |
| BYT230PI-1000 | H2 | d1 | SG,PH | Rect. Pair | 1000 V | 100 µA | 30 A | (60) W | <1.9 V | 30 A | | | <70 ns | Ifav at Tc=50°C |
| BYT230PI-1200 | H2 | d1 | SG,PH | Rect. Pair | 1200 V | 100 µA | 30 A | (60) W | <1.9 V | 30 A | | | <70 ns | Ifav at Tc=55°C |
| BYT230PI-200 | H2 | d1 | SG,PH | Rect. Pair | 200 V | 35 µA | 30 A | (50) W | <1.5 V | 30 A | | | <50 ns | Ifav at Tc=60°C |
| BYT230PI-300 | H2 | d1 | SG,PH | Rect. Pair | 300 V | 35 µA | 30 A | (50) W | <1.5 V | 30 A | | | <50 ns | Ifav at Tc=60°C |
| BYT230PI-400 | H2 | d1 | SG,PH | Rect. Pair | 400 V | 35 µA | 30 A | (50) W | <1.5 V | 30 A | | | <50 ns | Ifav at Tc=60°C |
| BYT230PI-600 | H2 | d1 | SG,PH | Rect. Pair | 600 V | 100 µA | 30 A | (60) W | <1.9 V | 30 A | | | <55 ns | Ifav at Tc=50°C |
| BYT230PI-700 | H2 | d1 | PH | Rect. Pair | 700 V | 100 µA | 30 A | (60) W | <1.9 V | 30 A | | | <55 ns | Ifav at Tc=50°C |
| BYT230PI-800 | H2 | d1 | SG,PH | Rect. Pair | 800 V | 100 µA | 30 A | (60) W | <1.9 V | 30 A | | | <55 ns | Ifav at Tc=50°C |
| BYT230PIV-1000 | H3 | d1 | SG,PH | Rect. Pair | 1000 V | 100 µA | 30 A | (60) W | <1.9 V | 30 A | | | <70 ns | Ifav at Tc=50°C |
| BYT230PIV-1200 | H3 | d1 | SG,PH | Rect. Pair | 1200 V | 100 µA | 30 A | (60) W | <1.9 V | 30 A | | | <70 ns | Ifav at Tc=50°C |
| BYT230PIV-200 | H3 | d1 | SG,PH | Rect. Pair | 200 V | 35 µA | 30 A | (50) W | <1.5 V | 30 A | | | <50 ns | Ifav at Tc=60°C |
| BYT230PIV-300 | H3 | d1 | SG,PH | Rect. Pair | 300 V | 35 µA | 30 A | (50) W | <1.5 V | 30 A | | | <50 ns | Ifav at Tc=60°C |
| BYT230PIV-400 | H3 | d1 | SG,PH | Rect. Pair | 400 V | 35 µA | 30 A | (50) W | <1.5 V | 30 A | | | <50 ns | Ifav at Tc=60°C |
| BYT230PIV-600 | H3 | d1 | SG,PH | Rect. Pair | 600 V | 100 µA | 30 A | (60) W | <1.9 V | 30 A | | | <55 ns | Ifav at Tc=55°C |
| BYT230PIV-700 | H3 | d1 | PH | Rect. Pair | 700 V | 100 µA | 30 A | (60) W | <1.9 V | 30 A | | | <55 ns | Ifav at Tc=55°C |
| BYT230PIV-800 | H3 | d1 | SG,PH | Rect. Pair | 800 V | 100 µA | 30 A | (60) W | <1.9 V | 30 A | | | <55 ns | Ifav at Tc=55°C |
| BYT261PI-1000 | H2 | d2 | SG | Rect. Pair | 1000 V | 100 µA | 60 A | (130) W | <1.9 V | 60 A | | | <70 ns | Ifav at Tc=60°C |
| BYT261PI-1200 | H2 | d2 | SG | Rect. Pair | 1200 V | 100 µA | 60 A | (130) W | <1.9 V | 60 A | | | <70 ns | Ifav at Tc=60°C |
| BYT261PI-200 | H2 | d2 | SG | Rect. Pair | 200 V | 60 µA | 60 A | (100) W | <1.5 V | 60 A | | | <50 ns | Ifav at Tc=80°C |
| BYT261PI-300 | H2 | d2 | SG | Rect. Pair | 300 V | 60 µA | 60 A | (100) W | <1.5 V | 60 A | | | <50 ns | Ifav at Tc=80°C |
| BYT261PI-400 | H2 | d2 | SG | Rect. Pair | 400 V | 60 µA | 60 A | (100) W | <1.5 V | 60 A | | | <50 ns | Ifav at Tc=80°C |
| BYT261PI-600 | H2 | d2 | SG | Rect. Pair | 600 V | 100 µA | 60 A | (130) W | <1.9 V | 60 A | | | <65 ns | Ifav at Tc=60°C |
| BYT261PI-800 | H2 | d2 | SG | Rect. Pair | 800 V | 100 µA | 60 A | (130) W | <1.9 V | 60 A | | | <65 ns | Ifav at Tc=60°C |
| BYT261PIV-1000 | H3 | d2 | SG | Rect. Pair | 1000 V | 100 µA | 60 A | (130) W | <1.9 V | 60 A | | | <70 ns | Ifav at Tc=60°C |
| BYT261PIV-1200 | H3 | d2 | SG | Rect. Pair | 1200 V | 100 µA | 60 A | (130) W | <1.9 V | 60 A | | | <70 ns | Ifav at Tc=60°C |
| BYT261PIV-200 | H3 | d2 | SG | Rect. Pair | 200 V | 60 µA | 60 A | (100) W | <1.5 V | 60 A | | | <50 ns | Ifav at Tc=80°C |
| BYT261PIV-300 | H3 | d2 | SG | Rect. Pair | 300 V | 60 µA | 60 A | (100) W | <1.5 V | 60 A | | | <50 ns | Ifav at Tc=80°C |
| BYT261PIV-400 | H3 | d2 | SG | Rect. Pair | 400 V | 60 µA | 60 A | (100) W | <1.5 V | 60 A | | | <50 ns | Ifav at Tc=80°C |
| BYT261PIV-600 | H3 | d2 | SG | Rect. Pair | 600 V | 100 µA | 60 A | (130) W | <1.9 V | 60 A | | | <65 ns | Ifav at Tc=60°C |
| BYT261PIV-800 | H3 | d2 | SG | Rect. Pair | 800 V | 100 µA | 60 A | (130) W | <1.9 V | 60 A | | | <65 ns | Ifav at Tc=60°C |

| Type | Case | Pin-code | | | Maximum Ratings | | | | Electrical Characteristics | | | | | |
|---|---|---|---|---|---|---|---|---|---|---|---|---|---|---|
| | | | | | Vrm | Irm | Ifav Ifm | Pv | Vf | If Ifp | C0 | Cr | trr ts | |
| BYV10-20 | A3 | a1 | SG,PH | Uni | 20 V | 500 µA | 1 A | | <0.55 V | 1 A | 220 pF | | <30 ns | |
| BYV10-30 | A3 | a1 | SG,PH | Uni | 30 V | 500 µA | 1 A | | <0.55 V | 1 A | 220 pF | | <30 ns | |
| BYV10-40 | A3 | a1 | SG | Uni | 40 V | 500 µA | 1 A | | <0.55 V | 1 A | 220 pF | | <30 ns | |
| BYV10-60 | A3 | a1 | SG | Uni | 60 V | 500 µA | | | <0.7 V | 1 A | 150 pF | | | Ifm at Tc=60°C |
| BYV10-20A | A3 | a1 | SG | Uni | 20 V | 300 µA | | | <0.45 V | 1 A | 330 pF | | <30 ns | Ifm at Tc=60°C |
| BYV12 | A4 | a1 | TE | Rectifier | 200 V | 5 µA | 1.5 A | | <1.5 V | 1 A | | | <300 ns | |
| BYV13 | A4 | a1 | TE | Rectifier | 400 V | 5 µA | 1.5 A | | <1.5 V | 1 A | | | <300 ns | |
| BYV14 | A4 | a1 | TE | Rectifier | 600 V | 5 µA | 1.5 A | | <1.5 V | 1 A | | | <300 ns | |
| BYV15 | A4 | a1 | TE | Rectifier | 800 V | 5 µA | 1.5 A | | <1.5 V | 1 A | | | <300 ns | |
| BYV16 | A4 | a1 | TE | Rectifier | 1000 V | 5 µA | 1.5 A | | <1.5 V | 1 A | | | <300 ns | |
| BYV24-1000 | E1 | a1 | PH | Rectifier | 1000 V | 1.5 mA | 12 A | | <1.7 V | 20 A | | | <450 ns | Ir at Tj=125°C |
| BYV24-800 | E1 | a1 | PH | Rectifier | 800 V | 1.5 mA | 12 A | | <1.7 V | 20 A | | | <450 ns | Ir at Tj=125°C |
| BYV24-1000R | E1 | b1 | PH | Rectifier | 1000 V | 1.5 mA | 12 A | | <1.7 V | 20 A | | | <450 ns | Ir at Tj=125°C |
| BYV24-800R | E1 | b1 | PH | Rectifier | 800 V | 1.5 mA | 12 A | | <1.7 V | 20 A | | | <450 ns | Ir at Tj=125°C |
| BYV26A | A4 | a1 | PH | Rectifier | 200 V | 5 µA | 650 mA | | <2.5 V | 1 A | | | <30 ns | |
| BYV26B | A4 | a1 | PH | Rectifier | 400 V | 5 µA | 650 mA | | <2.5 V | 1 A | | | <30 ns | |
| BYV26C | A4 | a1 | PH | Rectifier | 600 V | 5 µA | 650 mA | | <2.5 V | 1 A | | | <30 ns | |
| BYV26D | A4 | a1 | PH | Rectifier | 800 V | 5 µA | 650 mA | | <2.5 V | 1 A | | | <75 ns | |
| BYV26E | A4 | a1 | PH | Rectifier | 1000 V | 5 µA | 650 mA | | <2.5 V | 1 A | | | <75 ns | |
| BYV27-100 | A4 | a1 | PH,TE | Rectifier | 100 V | 1 µA | 1.3 A | | <1.07 V | 3 A | | | <25 ns | |
| BYV27-150 | A4 | a1 | PH,TE | Rectifier | 150 V | 1 µA | 1.3 A | | <1.07 V | 3 A | | | <25 ns | |
| BYV27-200 | A4 | a1 | PH,TE | Rectifier | 200 V | 1 µA | 1.3 A | | <1.07 V | 3 A | | | <25 ns | |
| BYV27-50 | A4 | a1 | PH,TE | Rectifier | 50 V | 1 µA | 1.3 A | | <1.07 V | 3 A | | | <25 ns | |
| BYV28-100 | A5 | a1 | TE,PH | Rectifier | 100 V | 1 µA | 1.9 A | | <1.1 V | 5 A | | | <30 ns | |
| BYV28-150 | A5 | a1 | TE,PH | Rectifier | 150 V | 1 µA | 1.9 A | | <1.1 V | 5 A | | | <30 ns | |
| BYV28-200 | A5 | a1 | TE,PH | Rectifier | 200 V | 1 µA | 1.9 A | | <1.1 V | 5 A | | | <30 ns | |
| BYV28-50 | A5 | a1 | TE,PH | Rectifier | 50 V | 1 µA | 1.9 A | | <1.1 V | 5 A | | | <30 ns | |
| BYV29-300 | I5 | a1 | PH | Rectifier | 300 V | 10 µA | 9 A | | <1.4 V | 20 A | | | <50 ns | |
| BYV29-400 | I5 | a1 | PH | Rectifier | 400 V | 10 µA | 9 A | | <1.4 V | 20 A | | | <50 ns | |
| BYV29-500 | I5 | a1 | PH | Rectifier | 500 V | 10 µA | 9 A | | <1.4 V | 20 A | | | <50 ns | |
| BYV29F-300 | J7 | a1 | PH | Rectifier | 300 V | 10 µA | 9 A | | <1.4 V | 20 A | | | <50 ns | |
| BYV29F-400 | J7 | a1 | PH | Rectifier | 400 V | 10 µA | 9 A | | <1.4 V | 20 A | | | <50 ns | |
| BYV29F-500 | J7 | a1 | PH | Rectifier | 500 V | 10 µA | 9 A | | <1.4 V | 20 A | | | <50 ns | |
| BYV30-300 | E1 | a1 | PH | Rectifier | 300 V | 50 µA | 14 A | | <1.4 V | 50 A | | | <50 ns | |
| BYV30-400 | E1 | a1 | PH | Rectifier | 400 V | 50 µA | 14 A | | <1.4 V | 50 A | | | <50 ns | |
| BYV30-500 | E1 | a1 | PH | Rectifier | 500 V | 50 µA | 14 A | | <1.4 V | 50 A | | | <50 ns | |
| BYV30-300U | E2 | a1 | PH | Rectifier | 300 V | 50 µA | 14 A | | <1.4 V | 50 A | | | <50 ns | |
| BYV30-400U | E2 | a1 | PH | Rectifier | 400 V | 50 µA | 14 A | | <1.4 V | 50 A | | | <50 ns | |
| BYV30-500U | E2 | a1 | PH | Rectifier | 500 V | 50 µA | 14 A | | <1.4 V | 50 A | | | <50 ns | |
| BYV31-300 | E1 | a1 | PH | Rectifier | 300 V | 50 µA | 28 A | | <1.4 V | 100 A | | | <50 ns | |

| Type | Case | Pin-code | | | Maximum Ratings Vrm | Irm | Ifav Ifm | Pv | Electrical Characteristics Vf | If Ifp | C0 | Cr | trr ts | |
|------|------|----------|---|---|-----|-----|------|----|-----|------|----|----|-----|---|
| BYV31-400 | E1 | a1 | PH | Rectifier | 400 V | 50 µA | 28 A | | <1.4 V | 100 A | | | <50 ns | |
| BYV31-500 | E1 | a1 | PH | Rectifier | 500 V | 50 µA | 28 A | | <1.4 V | 100 A | | | <50 ns | |
| BYV31-300U | E2 | a1 | PH | Rectifier | 300 V | 50 µA | 28 A | | <1.4 V | 100 A | | | <50 ns | |
| BYV31-400U | E2 | a1 | PH | Rectifier | 400 V | 50 µA | 28 A | | <1.4 V | 100 A | | | <50 ns | |
| BYV31-500U | E2 | a1 | PH | Rectifier | 500 V | 50 µA | 28 A | | <1.4 V | 100 A | | | <50 ns | |
| BYV32-100 | I4 | c7 | PH | Rect. Pair | 100 V | 10 µA | 10 A | | <1.15 V | 20 A | | | <50 ns | |
| BYV32-150 | I4 | c7 | PH | Rect. Pair | 150 V | 10 µA | 10 A | | <1.15 V | 20 A | | | <50 ns | |
| BYV32-200 | I4 | c7 | PH | Rect. Pair | 200 V | 10 µA | 10 A | | <1.15 V | 20 A | | | <50 ns | |
| BYV32-50 | I4 | c7 | PH | Rect. Pair | 50 V | 10 µA | 10 A | | <1.15 V | 20 A | | | <50 ns | |
| BYV32F-100 | J8 | c7 | PH | Rect. Pair | 100 V | 10 µA | 10 A | | <1.15 V | 20 A | | | <50 ns | |
| BYV32F-150 | J8 | c7 | PH | Rect. Pair | 150 V | 10 µA | 10 A | | <1.15 V | 20 A | | | <50 ns | |
| BYV32F-200 | J8 | c7 | PH | Rect. Pair | 200 V | 10 µA | 10 A | | <1.15 V | 20 A | | | <50 ns | |
| BYV32F-50 | J8 | c7 | PH | Rect. Pair | 50 V | 10 µA | 10 A | | <1.15 V | 20 A | | | <50 ns | |
| BYV34-300 | I4 | c7 | PH | Rect. Pair | 300 V | 50 µA | 10 A | | <1.4 V | 30 A | | | <50 ns | |
| BYV34-400 | I4 | c7 | PH | Rect. Pair | 400 V | 50 µA | 10 A | | <1.4 V | 30 A | | | <50 ns | |
| BYV34-500 | I4 | c7 | PH | Rect. Pair | 500 V | 50 µA | 10 A | | <1.4 V | 30 A | | | <50 ns | |
| BYV36A | A4 | a1 | PH | Rectifier | 200 V | 5 µA | 870 mA | | <1.35 V | 1 A | | | <100 ns | |
| BYV36B | A4 | a1 | PH | Rectifier | 400 V | 5 µA | 870 mA | | <1.35 V | 1 A | | | <100 ns | |
| BYV36C | A4 | a1 | PH | Rectifier | 600 V | 5 µA | 870 mA | | <1.35 V | 1 A | | | <100 ns | |
| BYV36D | A4 | a1 | PH | Rectifier | 800 V | 5 µA | 810 mA | | <1.45 V | 1 A | | | <150 ns | |
| BYV36E | A4 | a1 | PH | Rectifier | 1000 V | 5 µA | 810 mA | | <1.45 V | 1 A | | | <150 ns | |
| BYV37 | A4 | a1 | TE | Rectifier | 800 V | 5 µA | 2 A | | <1.1 V | 3 A | | | <30 ns | |
| BYV38 | A4 | a1 | TE | Rectifier | 1000 V | 5 µA | 2 A | | <1.1 V | 3 A | | | <30 ns | |
| BYV42-100 | I4 | c7 | PH | Rect. Pair | 100 V | 100 µA | 15 A | | <1.15 V | 30 A | | | <28 ns | |
| BYV42-150 | I4 | c7 | PH | Rect. Pair | 150 V | 100 µA | 15 A | | <1.15 V | 30 A | | | <28 ns | |
| BYV42-200 | I4 | c7 | PH | Rect. Pair | 200 V | 100 µA | 15 A | | <1.15 V | 30 A | | | <28 ns | |
| BYV42-50 | I4 | c7 | PH | Rect. Pair | 50 V | 100 µA | 15 A | | <1.15 V | 30 A | | | <28 ns | |
| BYV44-300 | I4 | c7 | PH | Rect. Pair | 300 V | 50 µA | 15 A | | <1.4 V | 50 A | | | <50 ns | |
| BYV44-400 | I4 | c7 | PH | Rect. Pair | 400 V | 50 µA | 15 A | | <1.4 V | 50 A | | | <50 ns | |
| BYV44-500 | I4 | c7 | PH | Rect. Pair | 500 V | 50 µA | 15 A | | <1.4 V | 50 A | | | <50 ns | |
| BYV52-100 | I15 | c7 | SG | Rect. Pair | 100 V | 25 µA | 50 A | 46 W | <1.0 V | 30 A | | | 10 ns | Ifav at Tc=110°C |
| BYV52-150 | I15 | c7 | SG | Rect. Pair | 150 V | 25 µA | 50 A | 46 W | <1.0 V | 30 A | | | 10 ns | Ifav at Tc=110°C |
| BYV52-200 | I15 | c7 | SG | Rect. Pair | 200 V | 25 µA | 50 A | 46 W | <1.0 V | 30 A | | | 10 ns | Ifav at Tc=110°C |
| BYV52-50 | I15 | c7 | SG | Rect. Pair | 50 V | 25 µA | 50 A | 46 W | <1.0 V | 30 A | | | 10 ns | Ifav at Tc=110°C |
| BYV52PI-100 | I15 | c7 | SG | Rect. Pair | 100 V | 25 µA | 30 A | 30 W | <1.0 V | 30 A | | | 10 ns | Ifav at Tc=90°C |
| BYV52PI-150 | I15 | c7 | SG | Rect. Pair | 150 V | 25 µA | 30 A | 30 W | <1.0 V | 30 A | | | 10 ns | Ifav at Tc=90°C |
| BYV52PI-200 | I15 | c7 | SG | Rect. Pair | 200 V | 25 µA | 30 A | 30 W | <1.0 V | 30 A | | | 10 ns | Ifav at Tc=90°C |
| BYV52PI-50 | I15 | c7 | SG | Rect. Pair | 50 V | 25 µA | 30 A | 30 W | <1.0 V | 30 A | | | 10 ns | Ifav at Tc=90°C |
| BYV54-100 | H2 | d1 | SG,PH | Rect. Pair | 100 V | 50 µA | 50 A | (50) W | <1.25 V | 160 A | | | 60 ns | Ifav at Tc=90°C |
| BYV54-150 | H2 | d1 | SG,PH | Rect. Pair | 150 V | 50 µA | 50 A | (50) W | <1.25 V | 160 A | | | 60 ns | Ifav at Tc=90°C |

| Type | Case | Pin-code | | | Maximum Ratings | | | | Electrical Characteristics | | | | | |
|---|---|---|---|---|---|---|---|---|---|---|---|---|---|---|
| | | | | | Vrm | Irm | Ifav / Ifm | Pv | Vf | If / Ifp | C0 | Cr | trr / ts | |
| BYV54-200 | H2 | d1 | SG,PH | Rect. Pair | 200 V | 50 µA | 50 A | (50) W | <1.25 V | 160 A | | | 60 ns | Ifav at Tc=90°C |
| BYV54-50 | H2 | d1 | SG,PH | Rect. Pair | 50 V | 50 µA | 50 A | (50) W | <1.25 V | 160 A | | | 60 ns | Ifav at Tc=90°C |
| BYV54V-100 | H3 | d1 | SG,PH | Rect. Pair | 100 V | 50 µA | 50 A | (50) W | <1.25 V | 160 A | | | 60 ns | Ifav at Tc=90°C |
| BYV54V-150 | H3 | d1 | SG,PH | Rect. Pair | 150 V | 50 µA | 50 A | (50) W | <1.25 V | 160 A | | | 60 ns | Ifav at Tc=90°C |
| BYV54V-200 | H3 | d1 | SG,PH | Rect. Pair | 200 V | 50 µA | 50 A | (50) W | <1.25 V | 160 A | | | 60 ns | Ifav at Tc=90°C |
| BYV54V-50 | H3 | d1 | SG,PH | Rect. Pair | 50 V | 50 µA | 50 A | (50) W | <1.25 V | 160 A | | | 60 ns | Ifav at Tc=90°C |
| BYV72-100 | I17 | c7 | PH | Rect. Pair | 100 V | 25 µA | 15 A | | <1.15 V | 30 A | | | <28 ns | |
| BYV72-150 | I17 | c7 | PH | Rect. Pair | 150 V | 25 µA | 15 A | | <1.15 V | 30 A | | | <28 ns | |
| BYV72-200 | I17 | c7 | PH | Rect. Pair | 200 V | 25 µA | 15 A | | <1.15 V | 30 A | | | <28 ns | |
| BYV72-50 | I17 | c7 | PH | Rect. Pair | 50 V | 25 µA | 15 A | | <1.15 V | 30 A | | | <28 ns | |
| BYV72F-100 | J9 | c7 | PH | Rect. Pair | 100 V | 25 µA | 10 A | | <1.15 V | 30 A | | | <28 ns | |
| BYV72F-150 | J9 | c7 | PH | Rect. Pair | 150 V | 25 µA | 10 A | | <1.15 V | 30 A | | | <28 ns | |
| BYV72F-200 | J9 | c7 | PH | Rect. Pair | 200 V | 25 µA | 10 A | | <1.15 V | 30 A | | | <28 ns | |
| BYV72F-50 | J9 | c7 | PH | Rect. Pair | 50 V | 25 µA | 10 A | | <1.15 V | 30 A | | | <28 ns | |
| BYV74-300 | I17 | c7 | PH | Rect. Pair | 300 V | 50 µA | 15 A | | <1.6 V | 50 A | | | <50 ns | |
| BYV74-400 | I17 | c7 | PH | Rect. Pair | 400 V | 50 µA | 15 A | | <1.6 V | 50 A | | | <50 ns | |
| BYV74-500 | I17 | c7 | PH | Rect. Pair | 500 V | 50 µA | 15 A | | <1.6 V | 50 A | | | <50 ns | |
| BYV74F-300 | J9 | c7 | PH | Rect. Pair | 300 V | 50 µA | 10 A | | <1.6 V | 50 A | | | <50 ns | |
| BYV74F-400 | J9 | c7 | PH | Rect. Pair | 400 V | 50 µA | 10 A | | <1.6 V | 50 A | | | <50 ns | |
| BYV74F-500 | J9 | c7 | PH | Rect. Pair | 500 V | 50 µA | 10 A | | <1.6 V | 50 A | | | <50 ns | |
| BYV79-100 | I5 | a1 | PH | Rectifier | 100 V | 50 µA | 14 A | | <1.3 V | 50 A | | | <30 ns | |
| BYV79-150 | I5 | a1 | PH | Rectifier | 150 V | 50 µA | 14 A | | <1.3 V | 50 A | | | <30 ns | |
| BYV79-200 | I5 | a1 | PH | Rectifier | 200 V | 50 µA | 14 A | | <1.3 V | 50 A | | | <30 ns | |
| BYV79-50 | I5 | a1 | PH | Rectifier | 50 V | 50 µA | 14 A | | <1.3 V | 50 A | | | <30 ns | |
| BYV92-300M | E3 | a1 | PH | Rectifier | 300 V | 50 µA | 38 A | | <1.4 V | 100 A | | | <50 ns | |
| BYV92-400M | E3 | a1 | PH | Rectifier | 400 V | 50 µA | 38 A | | <1.4 V | 100 A | | | <50 ns | |
| BYV92-500M | E3 | a1 | PH | Rectifier | 500 V | 50 µA | 38 A | | <1.4 V | 100 A | | | <50 ns | |
| BYV92-300U | E4 | a1 | PH | Rectifier | 300 V | 50 µA | 38 A | | <1.4 V | 100 A | | | <50 ns | |
| BYV92-400U | E4 | a1 | PH | Rectifier | 400 V | 50 µA | 38 A | | <1.4 V | 100 A | | | <50 ns | |
| BYV92-500U | E4 | a1 | PH | Rectifier | 500 V | 50 µA | 38 A | | <1.4 V | 100 A | | | <50 ns | |
| BYV95A | A4 | a1 | PH | Rectifier | 200 V | 150 µA | 800 mA | | <1.6 V | 3 A | | | <250 ns | Ir at Tj=165°C |
| BYV95B | A4 | a1 | PH | Rectifier | 400 V | 150 µA | 800 mA | | <1.6 V | 3 A | | | <250 ns | Ir at Tj=165°C |
| BYV95C | A4 | a1 | PH | Rectifier | 600 V | 150 µA | 800 mA | | <1.6 V | 3 A | | | <250 ns | Ir at Tj=165°C |
| BYV96D | A4 | a1 | PH | Rectifier | 800 V | 150 µA | 800 mA | | <1.6 V | 3 A | | | <300 ns | Ir at Tj=165°C |
| BYV96E | A4 | a1 | PH | Rectifier | 1000 V | 150 µA | 800 mA | | <1.6 V | 3 A | | | <300 ns | Ir at Tj=165°C |
| BYW95A | A4 | a1 | PH | Rectifier | 200 V | 150 µA | 1.25 A | | <1.5 V | 5 A | | | <250 ns | Ir at Tj=165°C |
| BYW95B | A4 | a1 | PH | Rectifier | 400 V | 150 µA | 1.25 A | | <1.5 V | 5 A | | | <250 ns | Ir at Tj=165°C |
| BYW95C | A4 | a1 | PH | Rectifier | 600 V | 150 µA | 1.25 A | | <1.5 V | 5 A | | | <250 ns | Ir at Tj=165°C |
| BYW96D | A4 | a1 | PH | Rectifier | 800 V | 150 µA | 1.25 A | | <1.5 V | 5 A | | | <300 ns | Ir at Tj=165°C |
| BYW96E | A4 | a1 | PH | Rectifier | 1000 V | 150 µA | 1.25 A | | <1.5 V | 5 A | | | <300 ns | Ir at Tj=165°C |

| Type | Case | Pin-code | | | Maximum Ratings | | | | Electrical Characteristics | | | | | |
|---|---|---|---|---|---|---|---|---|---|---|---|---|---|---|
| | | | | | Vrm | Irm | Ifav / Ifm | Pv | Vf | If / Ifp | C0 | Cr | trr / ts | |
| BYV118-35 | I4 | c7 | PH | Rect. Pair | 35 V | 100 µA | 5 A | | <0.87 V | 10 A | 200 pF | | | C0 at Vr=5V |
| BYV118-40 | I4 | c7 | PH | Rect. Pair | 40 V | 100 µA | 5 A | | <0.87 V | 10 A | 200 pF | | | C0 at Vr=5V |
| BYV118-45 | I4 | c7 | PH | Rect. Pair | 45 V | 100 µA | 5 A | | <0.87 V | 10 A | 200 pF | | | C0 at Vr=5V |
| BYV118F-35 | J8 | c7 | PH | Rect. Pair | 35 V | 100 µA | 5 A | | <0.87 V | 10 A | 200 pF | | | C0 at Vr=5V |
| BYV118F-40 | J8 | c7 | PH | Rect. Pair | 40 V | 100 µA | 5 A | | <0.87 V | 10 A | 200 pF | | | C0 at Vr=5V |
| BYV118F-45 | J8 | c7 | PH | Rect. Pair | 45 V | 100 µA | 5 A | | <0.87 V | 10 A | 200 pF | | | C0 at Vr=5V |
| BYV120-35 | E2 | a1 | PH | Rectifier | 35 V | 100 µA | 15 A | | <0.85 V | 30 A | 520 pF | | | C0 at Vr=5V |
| BYV120-40 | E2 | a1 | PH | Rectifier | 40 V | 100 µA | 15 A | | <0.85 V | 30 A | 520 pF | | | C0 at Vr=5V |
| BYV120-45 | E2 | a1 | PH | Rectifier | 45 V | 100 µA | 15 A | | <0.85 V | 30 A | 520 pF | | | C0 at Vr=5V |
| BYV120-35M | E1 | a1 | PH | Rectifier | 35 V | 100 µA | 15 A | | <0.85 V | 30 A | 520 pF | | | C0 at Vr=5V |
| BYV120-40M | E1 | a1 | PH | Rectifier | 40 V | 100 µA | 15 A | | <0.85 V | 30 A | 520 pF | | | C0 at Vr=5V |
| BYV120-45M | E1 | a1 | PH | Rectifier | 45 V | 100 µA | 15 A | | <0.85 V | 30 A | 520 pF | | | C0 at Vr=5V |
| BYV121-35 | E2 | a1 | PH | Rectifier | 35 V | 100 µA | 30 A | | <0.83 V | 60 A | 1150 pF | | | C0 at Vr=5V |
| BYV121-40 | E2 | a1 | PH | Rectifier | 40 V | 100 µA | 30 A | | <0.83 V | 60 A | 1150 pF | | | C0 at Vr=5V |
| BYV121-45 | E2 | a1 | PH | Rectifier | 45 V | 100 µA | 30 A | | <0.83 V | 60 A | 1150 pF | | | C0 at Vr=5V |
| BYV121-35M | E1 | a1 | PH | Rectifier | 35 V | 100 µA | 30 A | | <0.83 V | 60 A | 1150 pF | | | C0 at Vr=5V |
| BYV121-40M | E1 | a1 | PH | Rectifier | 40 V | 100 µA | 30 A | | <0.83 V | 60 A | 1150 pF | | | C0 at Vr=5V |
| BYV121-45M | E1 | a1 | PH | Rectifier | 45 V | 100 µA | 30 A | | <0.83 V | 60 A | 1150 pF | | | C0 at Vr=5V |
| BYV133-35 | I4 | c7 | PH | Rect. Pair | 35 V | 100 µA | 10 A | | <0.94 V | 20 A | 300 pF | | | C0 at Vr=5V |
| BYV133-40 | I4 | c7 | PH | Rect. Pair | 40 V | 100 µA | 10 A | | <0.94 V | 20 A | 300 pF | | | C0 at Vr=5V |
| BYV133-45 | I4 | c7 | PH | Rect. Pair | 45 V | 100 µA | 10 A | | <0.94 V | 20 A | 300 pF | | | C0 at Vr=5V |
| BYV133F-35 | J8 | c7 | PH | Rect. Pair | 35 V | 100 µA | 10 A | | <0.94 V | 20 A | 300 pF | | | C0 at Vr=5V |
| BYV133F-40 | J8 | c7 | PH | Rect. Pair | 40 V | 100 µA | 10 A | | <0.94 V | 20 A | 300 pF | | | C0 at Vr=5V |
| BYV133F-45 | J8 | c7 | PH | Rect. Pair | 45 V | 100 µA | 10 A | | <0.94 V | 20 A | 300 pF | | | C0 at Vr=5V |
| BYV143-35 | I4 | c7 | PH | Rect. Pair | 35 V | 200 µA | 15 A | | <0.77 V | 20 A | 500 pF | | | C0 at Vr=5V |
| BYV143-40 | I4 | c7 | PH | Rect. Pair | 40 V | 200 µA | 15 A | | <0.77 V | 20 A | 500 pF | | | C0 at Vr=5V |
| BYV143-45 | I4 | c7 | PH | Rect. Pair | 45 V | 200 µA | 15 A | | <0.77 V | 20 A | 500 pF | | | C0 at Vr=5V |
| BYV143F-35 | J8 | c7 | PH | Rect. Pair | 35 V | 200 µA | 15 A | | <0.77 V | 20 A | 500 pF | | | C0 at Vr=5V |
| BYV143F-40 | J8 | c7 | PH | Rect. Pair | 40 V | 200 µA | 15 A | | <0.77 V | 20 A | 500 pF | | | C0 at Vr=5V |
| BYV143F-45 | J8 | c7 | PH | Rect. Pair | 45 V | 200 µA | 15 A | | <0.77 V | 20 A | 500 pF | | | C0 at Vr=5V |
| BYV255-150 | H2 | d2 | SG | Rect. Pair | 150 V | 100 µA | 100 A | (100) W | <1.25 V | 320 A | | | 10 ns | Ifav at Tc=110°C |
| BYV255-50 | H2 | d2 | SG | Rect. Pair | 50 V | 100 µA | 100 A | (100) W | <1.25 V | 320 A | | | 10 ns | Ifav at Tc=110°C |
| BYV255-100 | H2 | d2 | SG | Rect. Pair | 100 V | 100 µA | 100 A | (100) W | <1.25 V | 320 A | | | 10 ns | Ifav at Tc=110°C |
| BYV255-200 | H2 | d2 | SG | Rect. Pair | 200 V | 100 µA | 100 A | (100) W | <1.25 V | 320 A | | | 10 ns | Ifav at Tc=110°C |
| BYV255V-100 | H3 | d2 | SG | Rect. Pair | 100 V | 100 µA | 100 A | (100) W | <1.25 V | 320 A | | | 10 ns | Ifav at Tc=110°C |
| BYV255V-150 | H3 | d2 | SG | Rect. Pair | 150 V | 100 µA | 100 A | (100) W | <1.25 V | 320 A | | | 10 ns | Ifav at Tc=110°C |
| BYV255V-200 | H3 | d2 | SG | Rect. Pair | 200 V | 100 µA | 100 A | (100) W | <1.25 V | 320 A | | | 10 ns | Ifav at Tc=110°C |
| BYV255V-50 | H3 | d2 | SG | Rect. Pair | 50 V | 100 µA | 100 A | (100) W | <1.25 V | 320 A | | | 10 ns | Ifav at Tc=110°C |
| BYW08-100 | E4 | a1 | SG | Rectifier | 100 V | 50 µA | 80 A | (80) W | <1.05 V | 80 A | | | 60 ns | Ifav at Tc=85°C |
| BYW08-150 | E4 | a1 | SG | Rectifier | 150 V | 50 µA | 80 A | (80) W | <1.05 V | 80 A | | | 60 ns | Ifav at Tc=85°C |

| Type | Case | Pin-code | | | Vrm | Irm | Ifav *Ifm* | Pv | Vf | If *Ifp* | C0 | Cr | trr *ts* | |
|------|------|----------|---|---|-----|-----|------------|----|----|---------|----|----|---------|---|
| BYW08-200 | E4 | a1 | SG | Rectifier | 200 V | 50 µA | 80 A | (80) W | <1.05 V | *80 A* | | | 60 ns | Ifav at Tc=85°C |
| BYW08-50 | E4 | a1 | SG | Rectifier | 50 V | 50 µA | 80 A | (80) W | <1.05 V | *80 A* | | | <60 ns | Ifav at Tc=85°C |
| BYW25-1000 | E3 | a1 | PH | Rectifier | 1000 V | 7 mA | 40 A | | <2.25 V | *150 A* | | | | Ir at Tj=125°C |
| BYW25-800 | E3 | a1 | PH | Rectifier | 800 V | 7 mA | 40 A | | <2.25 V | *150 A* | | | | Ir at Tj=125°C |
| BYW25-1000R | E3 | b1 | PH | Rectifier | 1000 V | 7 mA | 40 A | | <2.25 V | *150 A* | | | | Ir at Tj=125°C |
| BYW25-800R | E3 | b1 | PH | Rectifier | 800 V | 7 mA | 40 A | | <2.25 V | *150 A* | | | | Ir at Tj=125°C |
| BYW29-100 | I5 | a1 | PH | Rectifier | 100 V | 10 µA | 8 A | | <1.3 V | *20 A* | | | <25 ns | |
| BYW29-150 | I5 | a1 | PH | Rectifier | 150 V | 10 µA | 8 A | | <1.3 V | *20 A* | | | <25 ns | |
| BYW29-200 | I5 | a1 | PH | Rectifier | 200 V | 10 µA | 8 A | | <1.3 V | *20 A* | | | <25 ns | |
| BYW29-50 | I5 | a1 | PH | Rectifier | 50 V | 10 µA | 8 A | | <1.3 V | *20 A* | | | <25 ns | |
| BYW29-100A | I1 | a1 | SG | Rectifier | 100 V | 10 µA | 8 A | (18) W | <1.3 V | *20 A* | | | <35 ns | Ifav at Tc=130°C |
| BYW29-150A | I1 | a1 | SG | Rectifier | 150 V | 10 µA | 8 A | (18) W | <1.3 V | *20 A* | | | <35 ns | Ifav at Tc=130°C |
| BYW29-200A | I1 | a1 | SG | Rectifier | 200 V | 10 µA | 8 A | (18) W | <1.3 V | *20 A* | | | <35 ns | Ifav at Tc=130°C |
| BYW29-50A | I1 | a1 | SG | Rectifier | 50 V | 10 µA | 8 A | (18) W | <1.3 V | *20 A* | | | <35 ns | Ifav at Tc=130°C |
| BYW29F-100 | J7 | a1 | PH | Rectifier | 100 V | 10 µA | 8 A | | <1.3 V | *20 A* | | | <25 ns | |
| BYW29F-150 | J7 | a1 | PH | Rectifier | 150 V | 10 µA | 8 A | | <1.3 V | *20 A* | | | <25 ns | |
| BYW29F-200 | J7 | a1 | PH | Rectifier | 200 V | 10 µA | 8 A | | <1.3 V | *20 A* | | | <25 ns | |
| BYW29F-50 | J7 | b1 | PH | Rectifier | 50 V | 10 µA | 8 A | | <1.3 V | *20 A* | | | <25 ns | |
| BYW30-100 | E1 | a1 | PH | Rectifier | 100 V | 25 µA | 14 A | | <1.3 V | *50 A* | | | <30 ns | |
| BYW30-150 | E1 | a1 | PH | Rectifier | 150 V | 25 µA | 14 A | | <1.3 V | *50 A* | | | <30 ns | |
| BYW30-200 | E1 | a1 | PH | Rectifier | 200 V | 25 µA | 14 A | | <1.3 V | *50 A* | | | <30 ns | |
| BYW30-50 | E1 | a1 | PH | Rectifier | 50 V | 25 µA | 14 A | | <1.3 V | *50 A* | | | <30 ns | |
| BYW30-50U | E2 | a1 | PH | Rectifier | 50 V | 25 µA | 14 A | | <1.3 V | *50 A* | | | <30 ns | |
| BYW30-100U | E2 | a1 | PH | Rectifier | 100 V | 25 µA | 14 A | | <1.3 V | *50 A* | | | <30 ns | |
| BYW30-150U | E2 | a1 | PH | Rectifier | 150 V | 25 µA | 14 A | | <1.3 V | *50 A* | | | <30 ns | |
| BYW30-200U | E2 | a1 | PH | Rectifier | 200 V | 25 µA | 14 A | | <1.3 V | *50 A* | | | <30 ns | |
| BYW31-100 | E1 | a1 | PH | Rectifier | 100 V | 100 µA | 28 A | | <1.3 V | *100 A* | | | <40 ns | |
| BYW31-150 | E1 | a1 | PH | Rectifier | 150 V | 100 µA | 28 A | | <1.3 V | *100 A* | | | <40 ns | |
| BYW31-200 | E1 | a1 | PH | Rectifier | 200 V | 100 µA | 28 A | | <1.3 V | *100 A* | | | <40 ns | |
| BYW31-50 | E1 | a1 | PH | Rectifier | 50 V | 100 µA | 28 A | | <1.3 V | *100 A* | | | <40 ns | |
| BYW31-50U | E2 | a1 | PH | Rectifier | 50 V | 100 µA | 28 A | | <1.3 V | *100 A* | | | <40 ns | |
| BYW31-100U | E2 | a1 | PH | Rectifier | 100 V | 100 µA | 28 A | | <1.3 V | *100 A* | | | <40 ns | |
| BYW31-150U | E2 | a1 | PH | Rectifier | 150 V | 100 µA | 28 A | | <1.3 V | *100 A* | | | <40 ns | |
| BYW31-200U | E2 | a1 | PH | Rectifier | 200 V | 100 µA | 28 A | | <1.3 V | *100 A* | | | <40 ns | |
| BYW32 | A4 | a1 | TE | Rectifier | 200 V | 5 µA | 2 A | | <1.1 V | *1 A* | | | <200 ns | |
| BYW33 | A4 | a1 | TE | Rectifier | 300 V | 5 µA | 2 A | | <1.1 V | *1 A* | | | <200 ns | |
| BYW34 | A4 | a1 | TE | Rectifier | 400 V | 5 µA | 2 A | | <1.1 V | *1 A* | | | <200 ns | |
| BYW35 | A4 | a1 | TE | Rectifier | 500 V | 5 µA | 2 A | | <1.1 V | *1 A* | | | <200 ns | |
| BYW36 | A4 | a1 | TE | Rectifier | 600 V | 5 µA | 2 A | | <1.1 V | *1 A* | | | <200 ns | |
| BYW51-100A | I4 | c7 | SG | Rect. Pair | 100 V | 15 µA | 10 A | (10) W | <0.97 V | *8 A* | | | <35 ns | Ifav at Tc=125°C |

| Type | Case | Pin-code | | | Maximum Ratings | | | | Electrical Characteristics | | | | | |
|------|------|----------|---|---|------|------|-----------|--------|-------|---------|----|----|----------|---|
| | | | | | Vrm | Irm | Ifav Ifm | Pv | Vf | If Ifp | C0 | Cr | trr ts | |
| BYW51-150A | I4 | c7 | SG | Rect. Pair | 150 V | 15 µA | 10 A | (10) W | <0.97 V | 8 A | | | <35 ns | Ifav at Tc=125°C |
| BYW51-200A | I4 | c7 | SG | Rect. Pair | 200 V | 15 µA | 10 A | (10) W | <0.97 V | 8 A | | | <35 ns | Ifav at Tc=125°C |
| BYW51-50A | I4 | c7 | SG | Rect. Pair | 50 V | 15 µA | 10 A | (10) W | <0.97 V | 8 A | | | <35 ns | Ifav at Tc=125°C |
| BYW52 | A4 | a1 | TE | Rectifier | 200 V | 1 µA | 2 A | | <1 V | 1 mA | | | <4 µs | |
| BYW53 | A4 | a1 | TE | Rectifier | 400 V | 1 µA | 2 A | | <1 V | 1 mA | | | <4 µs | |
| BYW54 | A4 | a1 | TE,PH | Rectifier | 600 V | 1 µA | 2 A | | <1 V | 1 mA | 50 pF | | <4 µs | |
| BYW55 | A4 | a1 | TE,PH | Rectifier | 800 V | 1 µA | 2 A | | <1 V | 1 mA | 50 pF | | <4 µs | |
| BYW56 | A4 | a1 | TE,PH | Rectifier | 1000 V | 1 µA | 2 A | | <1 V | 1 mA | 50 pF | | <4 µs | |
| BYW72 | A5 | a1 | TE | Rectifier | 200 V | 5 µA | 3 A | | <1.1 V | 3 A | | | <200 ns | Ifav at Ta=45°C |
| BYW73 | A5 | a1 | TE | Rectifier | 300 V | 5 µA | 3 A | | <1.1 V | 3 A | | | <200 ns | Ifav at Ta=45°C |
| BYW74 | A5 | a1 | TE | Rectifier | 400 V | 5 µA | 3 A | | <1.1 V | 3 A | | | <200 ns | Ifav at Ta=45°C |
| BYW75 | A5 | a1 | TE | Rectifier | 500 V | 5 µA | 3 A | | <1.1 V | 3 A | | | <200 ns | Ifav at Ta=45°C |
| BYW76 | A5 | a1 | TE | Rectifier | 600 V | 5 µA | 3 A | | <1.1 V | 3 A | | | <200 ns | Ifav at Ta=45°C |
| BYW77-100 | E2 | a1 | SG | Rectifier | 100 V | 25 µA | 25 A | (33) W | <1.1 V | 63 A | | | <50 ns | Ifav at Tc=115°C |
| BYW77-150 | E2 | a1 | SG | Rectifier | 150 V | 25 µA | 25 A | (33) W | <1.1 V | 63 A | | | <50 ns | Ifav at Tc=115°C |
| BYW77-200 | E2 | a1 | SG | Rectifier | 200 V | 25 µA | 25 A | (33) W | <1.1 V | 63 A | | | <50 ns | Ifav at Tc=115°C |
| BYW77-50 | E2 | a1 | SG | Rectifier | 50 V | 25 µA | 25 A | (33) W | <1.1 V | 63 A | | | <50 ns | Ifav at Tc=115°C |
| BYW77P-100 | I14 | a1 | SG | Rectifier | 100 V | 25 µA | 25 A | (25) W | <1.15 V | 63 A | | | <50 ns | Ifav at Tc=125°C |
| BYW77P-150 | I14 | a1 | SG | Rectifier | 150 V | 25 µA | 25 A | (25) W | <1.15 V | 63 A | | | <50 ns | Ifav at Tc=125°C |
| BYW77P-200 | I14 | a1 | SG | Rectifier | 200 V | 25 µA | 25 A | (25) W | <1.15 V | 63 A | | | <50 ns | Ifav at Tc=125°C |
| BYW77P-50 | I14 | a1 | SG | Rectifier | 50 V | 25 µA | 25 A | (25) W | <1.15 V | 63 A | | | <50 ns | Ifav at Tc=125°C |
| BYW77PI-100 | I14 | a1 | SG | Rectifier | 100 V | 25 µA | 25 A | (25) W | <1.15 V | 63 A | | | <50 ns | Ifav at Tc=110°C |
| BYW77PI-150 | I14 | a1 | SG | Rectifier | 150 V | 25 µA | 25 A | (25) W | <1.15 V | 63 A | | | <50 ns | Ifav at Tc=110°C |
| BYW77PI-200 | I14 | a1 | SG | Rectifier | 200 V | 25 µA | 25 A | (25) W | <1.15 V | 63 A | | | <50 ns | Ifav at Tc=110°C |
| BYW77PI-50 | I14 | a1 | SG | Rectifier | 50 V | 25 µA | 25 A | (25) W | <1.15 V | 63 A | | | <50 ns | Ifav at Tc=110°C |
| BYW78-100 | E4 | a1 | SG | Rectifier | 100 V | 50 µA | 50 A | (60) W | <1.1 V | 160 A | | | <60 ns | Ifav at Tc=100°C |
| BYW78-150 | E4 | a1 | SG | Rectifier | 150 V | 50 µA | 50 A | (60) W | <1.1 V | 160 A | | | <60 ns | Ifav at Tc=100°C |
| BYW78-200 | E4 | a1 | SG | Rectifier | 200 V | 50 µA | 50 A | (60) W | <1.1 V | 160 A | | | <60 ns | Ifav at Tc=100°C |
| BYW78-50 | E4 | a1 | SG | Rectifier | 50 V | 50 µA | 50 A | (60) W | <1.1 V | 160 A | | | <60 ns | Ifav at Tc=100°C |
| BYW80-100A | I1 | a1 | SG | Rectifier | 100 V | 10 µA | 8 A | (20) W | <1.25 V | 22 A | | | <35 ns | Ifav at Tc=125°C |
| BYW80-150A | I1 | a1 | SG | Rectifier | 150 V | 10 µA | 8 A | (20) W | <1.25 V | 22 A | | | <35 ns | Ifav at Tc=125°C |
| BYW80-200A | I1 | a1 | SG | Rectifier | 200 V | 10 µA | 8 A | (20) W | <1.25 V | 22 A | | | <35 ns | Ifav at Tc=125°C |
| BYW80-50A | I1 | a1 | SG | Rectifier | 50 V | 10 µA | 8 A | (20) W | <1.25 V | 22 A | | | <35 ns | Ifav at Tc=125°C |
| BYW80PI-100 | I13 | a1 | SG | Rectifier | 100 V | 10 µA | 8 A | (15) W | <1.25 V | 22 A | | | <35 ns | Ifav at Tc=120°C |
| BYW80PI-150 | I13 | a1 | SG | Rectifier | 150 V | 10 µA | 8 A | (15) W | <1.25 V | 22 A | | | <35 ns | Ifav at Tc=120°C |
| BYW80PI-200 | I13 | a1 | SG | Rectifier | 200 V | 10 µA | 8 A | (15) W | <1.25 V | 22 A | | | <35 ns | Ifav at Tc=120°C |
| BYW80PI-50 | I13 | a1 | SG | Rectifier | 50 V | 10 µA | 8 A | (15) W | <1.25 V | 22 A | | | <35 ns | Ifav at Tc=120°C |
| BYW81-100 | E2 | a1 | SG | Rectifier | 100 V | 10 µA | 15 A | (22) W | <1.25 V | 38 A | | | <35 ns | Ifav at Tc=120°C |
| BYW81-150 | E2 | a1 | SG | Rectifier | 150 V | 10 µA | 15 A | (22) W | <1.25 V | 38 A | | | <35 ns | Ifav at Tc=120°C |
| BYW81-200 | E2 | a1 | SG | Rectifier | 200 V | 10 µA | 15 A | (22) W | <1.25 V | 38 A | | | <35 ns | Ifav at Tc=120°C |

| Type | Case | Pin-code | | | Vrm | Irm | Ifav Ifm | Pv | Vf | If Ifp | C0 | Cr | trr ts | |
|---|---|---|---|---|---|---|---|---|---|---|---|---|---|---|
| BYW81-50 | E2 | a1 | SG | Rectifier | 50 V | 10 µA | 15 A | (22) W | <1.25 V | 38 A | | | <35 ns | Ifav at Tc=120°C |
| BYW81P-100A | I1 | a1 | SG | Rectifier | 100 V | 10 µA | 15 A | (15) W | <1.25 V | 38 A | | | <35 ns | Ifav at Tc=125°C |
| BYW81P-150A | I1 | a1 | SG | Rectifier | 150 V | 10 µA | 15 A | (15) W | <1.25 V | 38 A | | | <35 ns | Ifav at Tc=125°C |
| BYW81P-200A | I1 | a1 | SG | Rectifier | 200 V | 10 µA | 15 A | (15) W | <1.25 V | 38 A | | | <35 ns | Ifav at Tc=125°C |
| BYW81P-50A | I1 | a1 | SG | Rectifier | 50 V | 10 µA | 15 A | (15) W | <1.25 V | 38 A | | | <35 ns | Ifav at Tc=125°C |
| BYW81PI-100 | I13 | a1 | SG | Rectifier | 100 V | 15 µA | 15 A | (16) W | <1.25 V | 38 A | | | <35 ns | Ifav at Tc=100°C |
| BYW81PI-150 | I13 | a1 | SG | Rectifier | 150 V | 15 µA | 15 A | (16) W | <1.25 V | 38 A | | | <35 ns | Ifav at Tc=100°C |
| BYW81PI-200 | I13 | a1 | SG | Rectifier | 200 V | 15 µA | 15 A | (16) W | <1.25 V | 38 A | | | <35 ns | Ifav at Tc=100°C |
| BYW81PI-50 | I13 | a1 | SG | Rectifier | 50 V | 15 µA | 15 A | (16) W | <1.25 V | 38 A | | | <35 ns | Ifav at Tc=100°C |
| BYW82 | A5 | a1 | TE | Rectifier | 200 V | 1 µA | 3 A | | ≤1 V | 3 A | | | <4 µs | Ifav at Ta=45°C |
| BYW83 | A5 | a1 | TE | Rectifier | 400 V | 1 µA | 3 A | | ≤1 V | 3 A | | | <4 µs | Ifav at Ta=45°C |
| BYW84 | A5 | a1 | TE | Rectifier | 600 V | 1 µA | 3 A | | ≤1 V | 3 A | | | <4 µs | Ifav at Ta=45°C |
| BYW85 | A5 | a1 | TE | Rectifier | 800 V | 1 µA | 3 A | | ≤1 V | 3 A | | | <4 µs | Ifav at Ta=45°C |
| BYW86 | A5 | a1 | TE | Rectifier | 1000 V | 1 µA | 3 A | | ≤1 V | 3 A | | | <4 µs | Ifav at Ta=45°C |
| BYW88-100 | E2 | a1 | SG | Rectifier | 100 V | | 12 A | (12.5) W | <1.25 V | 35 A | | | | Ifav at Tc=125°C |
| BYW88-1000 | E2 | a1 | SG | Rectifier | 1000 V | | 12 A | (12.5) W | <1.25 V | 35 A | | | | Ifav at Tc=125°C |
| BYW88-200 | E2 | a1 | SG | Rectifier | 200 V | | 12 A | (12.5) W | <1.25 V | 35 A | | | | Ifav at Tc=125°C |
| BYW88-300 | E2 | a1 | SG | Rectifier | 300 V | | 12 A | (12.5) W | <1.25 V | 35 A | | | | Ifav at Tc=125°C |
| BYW88-400 | E2 | a1 | SG | Rectifier | 400 V | | 12 A | (12.5) W | <1.25 V | 35 A | | | | Ifav at Tc=125°C |
| BYW88-50 | E2 | a1 | SG | Rectifier | 50 V | | 12 A | (12.5) W | <1.25 V | 35 A | | | | Ifav at Tc=125°C |
| BYW88-500 | E2 | a1 | SG | Rectifier | 500 V | | 12 A | (12.5) W | <1.25 V | 35 A | | | | Ifav at Tc=125°C |
| BYW88-600 | E2 | a1 | SG | Rectifier | 600 V | | 12 A | (12.5) W | <1.25 V | 35 A | | | | Ifav at Tc=125°C |
| BYW88-800 | E2 | a1 | SG | Rectifier | 800 V | | 12 A | (12.5) W | <1.25 V | 35 A | | | | Ifav at Tc=125°C |
| BYW92-100 | E4 | a1 | SG,PH | Rectifier | 100 V | 50 µA | 35 A | (50) W | <1.3 V | 100 A | | | <50 ns | Ifav at Tc=115°C |
| BYW92-100 | E1 | a1 | PH | Rectifier | 100 V | 50 µA | 35 A | | <1.3 V | 100 A | | | <40 ns | Ifav at Tc=115°C |
| BYW92-150 | E4 | a1 | SG,PH | Rectifier | 150 V | 50 µA | 35 A | (50) W | <1.3 V | 100 A | | | <50 ns | Ifav at Tc=115°C |
| BYW92-150 | E1 | a1 | PH | Rectifier | 150 V | 50 µA | 35 A | | <1.3 V | 100 A | | | <40 ns | Ifav at Tc=115°C |
| BYW92-200 | E4 | a1 | SG,PH | Rectifier | 200 V | 50 µA | 35 A | (50) W | <1.3 V | 100 A | | | <50 ns | Ifav at Tc=115°C |
| BYW92-200 | E1 | a1 | PH | Rectifier | 200 V | 50 µA | 35 A | | <1.3 V | 100 A | | | <40 ns | Ifav at Tc=115°C |
| BYW92-50 | E4 | a1 | SG,PH | Rectifier | 50 V | 50 µA | 35 A | (50) W | <1.3 V | 100 A | | | <50 ns | Ifav at Tc=115°C |
| BYW92-50 | E1 | a1 | PH | Rectifier | 50 V | 50 µA | 35 A | | <1.3 V | 100 A | | | <40 ns | Ifav at Tc=115°C |
| BYW92-100U | E2 | a1 | PH | Rectifier | 100 V | 100 µA | 40 A | | <1.3 V | 100 A | | | <40 ns | |
| BYW92-150U | E2 | a1 | PH | Rectifier | 150 V | 100 µA | 40 A | | <1.3 V | 100 A | | | <40 ns | |
| BYW92-200U | E2 | a1 | PH | Rectifier | 200 V | 100 µA | 40 A | | <1.3 V | 100 A | | | <40 ns | |
| BYW92-50U | E2 | a1 | PH | Rectifier | 50 V | 100 µA | 40 A | | <1.3 V | 100 A | | | <40 ns | |
| BYW93-100 | E1 | a1 | PH | Rectifier | 100 V | 250 µA | 60 A | | <1.3 V | 150 A | | | <45 ns | |
| BYW93-150 | E1 | a1 | PH | Rectifier | 150 V | 250 µA | 60 A | | <1.3 V | 150 A | | | <45 ns | |
| BYW93-200 | E1 | a1 | PH | Rectifier | 200 V | 250 µA | 60 A | | <1.3 V | 150 A | | | <45 ns | |
| BYW93-50 | E1 | a1 | PH | Rectifier | 50 V | 250 µA | 60 A | | <1.3 V | 150 A | | | <45 ns | |
| BYW93-100U | E2 | a1 | PH | Rectifier | 100 V | 250 µA | 60 A | | <1.3 V | 150 A | | | <45 ns | |

| Type | Case | Pin-code | | | Maximum Ratings | | | | Electrical Characteristics | | | | | |
|------|------|----------|---|---|------|-----|-----------|------|------|-----------|----|----|---------|---|
| | | | | | Vrm | Irm | Ifav Ifm | Pv | Vf | If Ifp | C0 | Cr | trr ts | |
| BYW93-150U | E2 | a1 | PH | Rectifier | 150 V | 250 µA | 60 A | | <1.3 V | 150 A | | | <45 ns | |
| BYW93-200U | E2 | a1 | PH | Rectifier | 200 V | 250 µA | 60 A | | <1.3 V | 150 A | | | <45 ns | |
| BYW93-50U | E2 | a1 | PH | Rectifier | 50 V | 250 µA | 60 A | | <1.3 V | 150 A | | | <45 ns | |
| BYW98-100 | b5 | a1 | SG | Rectifier | 100 V | 10 µA | 3 A | 2.5 W | <1.1 V | 9 A | | | <35 ns | Ifav at Tc=85°C |
| BYW98-150 | b5 | a1 | SG | Rectifier | 150 V | 10 µA | 3 A | 2.5 W | <1.1 V | 9 A | | | <35 ns | Ifav at Tc=85°C |
| BYW98-200 | b5 | a1 | SG | Rectifier | 200 V | 10 µA | 3 A | 2.5 W | <1.1 V | 9 A | | | <35 ns | Ifav at Tc=85°C |
| BYW98-50 | b5 | a1 | SG | Rectifier | 50 V | 10 µA | 3 A | 2.5 W | <1.1 V | 9 A | | | <35 ns | Ifav at Tc=85°C |
| BYW99P-100 | I15 | c7 | SG | Rect. Pair | 100 V | 15 µA | 15 A | 15 W | <1.25 V | 38 A | | | <35 ns | Ifav at Tc=125°C |
| BYW99P-150 | I15 | c7 | SG | Rect. Pair | 150 V | 15 µA | 15 A | 15 W | <1.25 V | 38 A | | | <35 ns | Ifav at Tc=125°C |
| BYW99P-200 | I15 | c7 | SG | Rect. Pair | 200 V | 15 µA | 15 A | 15 W | <1.25 V | 38 A | | | <35 ns | Ifav at Tc=125°C |
| BYW99P-50 | I15 | c7 | SG | Rect. Pair | 50 V | 15 µA | 15 A | 15 W | <1.25 V | 38 A | | | <35 ns | Ifav at Tc=125°C |
| BYW99PI-100 | I15 | c7 | SG | Rect. Pair | 100 V | 15 µA | 15 A | 15 W | <1.25 V | 38 A | | | <35 ns | Ifav at Tc=110°C |
| BYW99PI-150 | I15 | c7 | SG | Rect. Pair | 150 V | 15 µA | 15 A | 15 W | <1.25 V | 38 A | | | <35 ns | Ifav at Tc=110°C |
| BYW99PI-200 | I15 | c7 | SG | Rect. Pair | 200 V | 15 µA | 15 A | 15 W | <1.25 V | 38 A | | | <35 ns | Ifav at Tc=110°C |
| BYW99PI-50 | I15 | c7 | SG | Rect. Pair | 50 V | 15 µA | 15 A | 15 W | <1.25 V | 38 A | | | <35 ns | Ifav at Tc=110°C |
| BYW100-100 | B4 | a1 | SG | Rectifier | 100 V | 10 µA | 1.5 A | 1.3 W | <1.2 V | 4.5 A | | | <35 ns | Ifav at Tc=90°C |
| BYW100-150 | B4 | a1 | SG | Rectifier | 150 V | 10 µA | 1.5 A | 1.3 W | <1.2 V | 4.5 A | | | <35 ns | Ifav at Tc=90°C |
| BYW100-200 | B4 | a1 | SG | Rectifier | 200 V | 10 µA | 1.5 A | 1.3 W | <1.2 V | 4.5 A | | | <35 ns | Ifav at Tc=90°C |
| BYW100-50 | B4 | a1 | SG | Rectifier | 50 V | 10 µA | 1.5 A | 1.3 W | <1.2 V | 4.5 A | | | <35 ns | Ifav at Tc=90°C |
| BYX25-1000 | E2 | a1 | PH | Rectifier | (1000) V | 600 µA | 20 A | | <1.8 V | 50 A | | | | Ir at Tj=125°C |
| BYX25-1200 | E2 | a1 | PH | Rectifier | (1200) V | 500 µA | 20 A | | <1.8 V | 50 A | | | | Ir at Tj=125°C |
| BYX25-1400 | E2 | a1 | PH | Rectifier | (1400) V | 500 µA | 20 A | | <1.8 V | 50 A | | | | Ir at Tj=125°C |
| BYX25-600 | E2 | a1 | PH | Rectifier | (600) V | 1 mA | 20 A | | <1.8 V | 50 A | | | | Ir at Tj=125°C |
| BYX25-800 | E2 | a1 | PH | Rectifier | (800) V | 800 µA | 20 A | | <1.8 V | 50 A | | | | Ir at Tj=125°C |
| BYX25-1000R | E2 | b1 | PH | Rectifier | (1000) V | 600 µA | 20 A | | <1.8 V | 50 A | | | | Ir at Tj=125°C |
| BYX25-1200R | E2 | b1 | PH | Rectifier | (1200) V | 500 µA | 20 A | | <1.8 V | 50 A | | | | Ir at Tj=125°C |
| BYX25-1400R | E2 | b1 | PH | Rectifier | (1400) V | 500 µA | 20 A | | <1.8 V | 50 A | | | | Ir at Tj=125°C |
| BYX25-600R | E2 | b1 | PH | Rectifier | (600) V | 1 mA | 20 A | | <1.8 V | 50 A | | | | Ir at Tj=125°C |
| BYX25-800R | E2 | b1 | PH | Rectifier | (800) V | 800 µA | 20 A | | <1.8 V | 50 A | | | | Ir at Tj=125°C |
| BYX30-200 | E2 | a1 | PH | Rectifier | (200) V | 4 mA | 14 A | | <3.2 V | 50 A | | | <200 ns | Ir at Tj=125°C |
| BYX30-300 | E2 | a1 | PH | Rectifier | (300) V | 4 mA | 14 A | | <3.2 V | 50 A | | | <200 ns | Ir at Tj=125°C |
| BYX30-400 | E2 | a1 | PH | Rectifier | (400) V | 4 mA | 14 A | | <3.2 V | 50 A | | | <200 ns | Ir at Tj=125°C |
| BYX30-500 | E2 | a1 | PH | Rectifier | (500) V | 4 mA | 14 A | | <3.2 V | 50 A | | | <200 ns | Ir at Tj=125°C |
| BYX30-600 | E2 | a1 | PH | Rectifier | (600) V | 4 mA | 14 A | | <3.2 V | 50 A | | | <200 ns | Ir at Tj=125°C |
| BYX30-200R | E2 | b1 | PH | Rectifier | (200) V | 4 mA | 14 A | | <3.2 V | 50 A | | | <200 ns | Ir at Tj=125°C |
| BYX30-300R | E2 | b1 | PH | Rectifier | (300) V | 4 mA | 14 A | | <3.2 V | 50 A | | | <200 ns | Ir at Tj=125°C |
| BYX30-400R | E2 | b1 | PH | Rectifier | (400) V | 4 mA | 14 A | | <3.2 V | 50 A | | | <200 ns | Ir at Tj=125°C |
| BYX30-500R | E2 | b1 | PH | Rectifier | (500) V | 4 mA | 14 A | | <3.2 V | 50 A | | | <200 ns | Ir at Tj=125°C |
| BYX30-600R | E2 | b1 | PH | Rectifier | (600) V | 4 mA | 14 A | | <3.2 V | 50 A | | | <200 ns | Ir at Tj=125°C |
| BYX38-1200 | E2 | a1 | PH | Rectifier | 1200 V | 200 µA | 6 A | | <1.7 V | 20 A | | | | Ir at Tj=125°C |

| Type | Case | Pin-code | | | Maximum Ratings | | | | Electrical Characteristics | | | | | |
|------|------|----------|---|---|------|------|------|------|------|------|------|------|------|------|
| | | | | | Vrm | Irm | Ifav Ifm | Pv | Vf | If Ifp | C0 | Cr | trr ts | |
| BYX38-300 | E2 | a1 | PH | Rectifier | 300 V | 200 µA | 6 A | | <1.7 V | 20 A | | | | Ir at Tj=125°C |
| BYX38-600 | E2 | a1 | PH | Rectifier | 600 V | 200 µA | 6 A | | <1.7 V | 20 A | | | | Ir at Tj=125°C |
| BYX38-1200R | E2 | b1 | PH | Rectifier | 1200 V | 200 µA | 6 A | | <1.7 V | 20 A | | | | Ir at Tj=125°C |
| BYX38-300R | E2 | b1 | PH | Rectifier | 300 V | 200 µA | 6 A | | <1.7 V | 20 A | | | | Ir at Tj=125°C |
| BYX38-600R | E2 | b1 | PH | Rectifier | 600 V | 200 µA | 6 A | | <1.7 V | 20 A | | | | Ir at Tj=125°C |
| BYX39-1000 | E2 | a1 | PH | Rectifier | (1000) V | 200 µA | 9.5 A | | <1.7 V | 20 A | | | | Ir at Tj=125°C |
| BYX39-1200 | E2 | a1 | PH | Rectifier | (1200) V | 200 µA | 9.5 A | | <1.7 V | 20 A | | | | Ir at Tj=125°C |
| BYX39-1400 | E2 | a1 | PH | Rectifier | (1400) V | 200 µA | 9.5 A | | <1.7 V | 20 A | | | | Ir at Tj=125°C |
| BYX39-600 | E2 | a1 | PH | Rectifier | (600) V | 200 µA | 9.5 A | | <1.7 V | 20 A | | | | Ir at Tj=125°C |
| BYX39-800 | E2 | a1 | PH | Rectifier | (800) V | 200 µA | 9.5 A | | <1.7 V | 20 A | | | | Ir at Tj=125°C |
| BYX39-1000R | E2 | b1 | PH | Rectifier | (1000) V | 200 µA | 9.5 A | | <1.7 V | 20 A | | | | Ir at Tj=125°C |
| BYX39-1200R | E2 | b1 | PH | Rectifier | (1200) V | 200 µA | 9.5 A | | <1.7 V | 20 A | | | | Ir at Tj=125°C |
| BYX39-1400R | E2 | b1 | PH | Rectifier | (1400) V | 200 µA | 9.5 A | | <1.7 V | 20 A | | | | Ir at Tj=125°C |
| BYX39-600R | E2 | b1 | PH | Rectifier | (600) V | 200 µA | 9.5 A | | <1.7 V | 20 A | | | | Ir at Tj=125°C |
| BYX39-800R | E2 | b1 | PH | Rectifier | (800) V | 200 µA | 9.5 A | | <1.7 V | 20 A | | | | Ir at Tj=125°C |
| BYX42-1200 | E2 | a1 | PH | Rectifier | 1200 V | 200 µA | 12 A | | <1.4 V | 15 A | | | | Ir at Tj=125°C |
| BYX42-300 | E2 | a1 | PH | Rectifier | 300 V | 200 µA | 12 A | | <1.4 V | 15 A | | | | Ir at Tj=125°C |
| BYX42-600 | E2 | a1 | PH | Rectifier | 600 V | 200 µA | 12 A | | <1.4 V | 15 A | | | | Ir at Tj=125°C |
| BYX42-1200R | E2 | b1 | PH | Rectifier | 1200 V | 200 µA | 12 A | | <1.4 V | 15 A | | | | Ir at Tj=125°C |
| BYX42-300R | E2 | b1 | PH | Rectifier | 300 V | 200 µA | 12 A | | <1.4 V | 15 A | | | | Ir at Tj=125°C |
| BYX42-600R | E2 | b1 | PH | Rectifier | 600 V | 200 µA | 12 A | | <1.4 V | 15 A | | | | Ir at Tj=125°C |
| BYX46-200 | E2 | a1 | PH | Rectifier | (200) V | 4 mA | 22 A | | <2 V | 50 A | | | <200 ns | Ir at Tj=125°C |
| BYX46-300 | E2 | a1 | PH | Rectifier | (300) V | 4 mA | 22 A | | <2 V | 50 A | | | <200 ns | Ir at Tj=125°C |
| BYX46-400 | E2 | a1 | PH | Rectifier | (400) V | 4 mA | 22 A | | <2 V | 50 A | | | <200 ns | Ir at Tj=125°C |
| BYX46-500 | E2 | a1 | PH | Rectifier | (500) V | 4 mA | 22 A | | <2 V | 50 A | | | <200 ns | Ir at Tj=125°C |
| BYX46-600 | E2 | a1 | PH | Rectifier | (600) V | 4 mA | 22 A | | <2 V | 50 A | | | <200 ns | Ir at Tj=125°C |
| BYX46-200R | E2 | b1 | PH | Rectifier | (200) V | 4 mA | 22 A | | <2 V | 50 A | | | <200 ns | Ir at Tj=125°C |
| BYX46-300R | E2 | b1 | PH | Rectifier | (300) V | 4 mA | 22 A | | <2 V | 50 A | | | <200 ns | Ir at Tj=125°C |
| BYX46-400R | E2 | b1 | PH | Rectifier | (400) V | 4 mA | 22 A | | <2 V | 50 A | | | <200 ns | Ir at Tj=125°C |
| BYX46-500R | E2 | b1 | PH | Rectifier | (500) V | 4 mA | 22 A | | <2 V | 50 A | | | <200 ns | Ir at Tj=125°C |
| BYX46-600R | E2 | b1 | PH | Rectifier | (600) V | 4 mA | 22 A | | <2 V | 50 A | | | <200 ns | Ir at Tj=125°C |
| BYX52-1200 | E4 | a1 | PH | Rectifier | 1200 V | 1.6 mA | 48 A | | <1.8 V | 150 A | | | | Ir at Tj=125°C |
| BYX52-300 | E4 | a1 | PH | Rectifier | 300 V | 1.6 mA | 48 A | | <1.8 V | 150 A | | | | Ir at Tj=125°C |
| BYX52-600 | E4 | a1 | PH | Rectifier | 600 V | 1.6 mA | 48 A | | <1.8 V | 150 A | | | | Ir at Tj=125°C |
| BYX52-1200R | E4 | b1 | PH | Rectifier | 1200 V | 1.6 mA | 48 A | | <1.8 V | 150 A | | | | Ir at Tj=125°C |
| BYX52-300R | E4 | b1 | PH | Rectifier | 300 V | 1.6 mA | 48 A | | <1.8 V | 150 A | | | | Ir at Tj=125°C |
| BYX52-600R | E4 | b1 | PH | Rectifier | 600 V | 1.6 mA | 48 A | | <1.8 V | 150 A | | | | Ir at Tj=125°C |
| BYX56-1000 | E4 | a1 | PH | Rectifier | (1000) V | 1.6 mA | 48 A | | <1.8 V | 150 A | | | | Ir at Tj=125°C |
| BYX56-1200 | E4 | a1 | PH | Rectifier | (1200) V | 1.6 mA | 48 A | | <1.8 V | 150 A | | | | Ir at Tj=125°C |
| BYX56-1400 | E4 | a1 | PH | Rectifier | (1400) V | 1.6 mA | 48 A | | <1.8 V | 150 A | | | | Ir at Tj=125°C |

**BYX56-600 – BYX96-1600U**

| Type | Case | Pin-code | | | Maximum Ratings | | | | Electrical Characteristics | | | | | |
|---|---|---|---|---|---|---|---|---|---|---|---|---|---|---|
| | | | | | Vrm | Irm | Ifav Ifm | Pv | Vf | If Ifp | C0 | Cr | trr ts | |
| BYX56-600 | E4 | a1 | PH | Rectifier | (600) V | 1.6 mA | 48 A | | <1.8 V | 150 A | | | | Ir at Tj=125°C |
| BYX56-800 | E4 | a1 | PH | Rectifier | (800) V | 1.6 mA | 48 A | | <1.8 V | 150 A | | | | Ir at Tj=125°C |
| BYX56-1000R | E4 | b1 | PH | Rectifier | (1000) V | 1.6 mA | 48 A | | <1.8 V | 150 A | | | | Ir at Tj=125°C |
| BYX56-1200R | E4 | b1 | PH | Rectifier | (1200) V | 1.6 mA | 48 A | | <1.8 V | 150 A | | | | Ir at Tj=125°C |
| BYX56-1400R | E4 | b1 | PH | Rectifier | (1400) V | 1.6 mA | 48 A | | <1.8 V | 150 A | | | | Ir at Tj=125°C |
| BYX56-600R | E4 | b1 | PH | Rectifier | (600) V | 1.6 mA | 48 A | | <1.8 V | 150 A | | | | Ir at Tj=125°C |
| BYX56-800R | E4 | b1 | PH | Rectifier | (800) V | 1.6 mA | 48 A | | <1.8 V | 150 A | | | | Ir at Tj=125°C |
| BYX61-100 | E2 | a1 | SG | Rectifier | 100 V | 3 mA | 12 A | (20) W | <1.5 V | 12 A | | | <100 ns | Ifav at Tc=100°C |
| BYX61-200 | E2 | a1 | SG | Rectifier | 200 V | 3 mA | 12 A | (20) W | <1.5 V | 12 A | | | <100 ns | Ifav at Tc=100°C |
| BYX61-300 | E2 | a1 | SG | Rectifier | 300 V | 3 mA | 12 A | (20) W | <1.5 V | 12 A | | | <100 ns | Ifav at Tc=100°C |
| BYX61-400 | E2 | a1 | SG | Rectifier | 400 V | 3 mA | 12 A | (20) W | <1.5 V | 12 A | | | <100 ns | Ifav at Tc=100°C |
| BYX61-50 | E2 | a1 | SG | Rectifier | 50 V | 3 mA | 12 A | (20) W | <1.5 V | 12 A | | | <100 ns | Ifav at Tc=100°C |
| BYX62-600 | E2 | a1 | SG | Rectifier | 600 V | 25 µA | 12 A | 20 W | <1.4 V | 12 A | | | <200 ns | Ifav at Tc=100°C |
| BYX63-600 | E2 | a1 | SG | Rectifier | 600 V | 50 µA | 20 A | 35 W | <1.4 V | 20 A | | | <200 ns | Ifav at Tc=100°C |
| BYX64-600 | E4 | a1 | SG | Rectifier | 660 V | 50 µA | 30 A | 50 W | <1.4 V | 30 A | | | <200 ns | Ifav at Tc=100°C |
| BYX65-100 | E4 | a1 | SG | Rectifier | 100 V | 10 mA | 30 A | (50) W | <1.5 V | 30 A | | | <100 ns | Ifav at Tc=100°C |
| BYX65-200 | E4 | a1 | SG | Rectifier | 200 V | 10 mA | 30 A | (50) W | <1.5 V | 30 A | | | <100 ns | Ifav at Tc=100°C |
| BYX65-300 | E4 | a1 | SG | Rectifier | 300 V | 10 mA | 30 A | (50) W | <1.5 V | 30 A | | | <100 ns | Ifav at Tc=100°C |
| BYX65-400 | E4 | a1 | SG | Rectifier | 400 V | 10 mA | 30 A | (50) W | <1.5 V | 30 A | | | <100 ns | Ifav at Tc=100°C |
| BYX65-50 | E4 | a1 | SG | Rectifier | 50 V | 10 mA | 30 A | (50) W | <1.5 V | 30 A | | | <100 ns | Ifav at Tc=100°C |
| BYX82 | A4 | a1 | TE | Rectifier | 200 V | 1 µA | 2 A | | <1 V | 1 mA | | | <4 µs | Ifav at Ta=45°C |
| BYX83 | A4 | a1 | TE | Rectifier | 400 V | 1 µA | 2 A | | <1 V | 1 mA | | | <4 µs | Ifav at Ta=45°C |
| BYX84 | A4 | a1 | TE | Rectifier | 600 V | 1 µA | 2 A | | <1 V | 1 mA | | | <4 µs | Ifav at Ta=45°C |
| BYX85 | A4 | a1 | TE | Rectifier | 800 V | 1 µA | 2 A | | <1 V | 1 mA | | | <4 µs | Ifav at Ta=45°C |
| BYX86 | A4 | a1 | TE | Rectifier | 1000 V | 1 µA | 2 A | | <1 V | 1 mA | | | <4 µs | Ifav at Ta=45°C |
| BYX90G | A9 | a1 | PH | HV Rectifier | 7.5 kV | 50 µA | 550 mA | | <14.5 V | 2 A | | | <350 ns | |
| BYX96-1200 | E1 | a1 | PH | Rectifier | 1200 V | 1 mA | 30 A | | <1.7 V | 100 A | | | | Ir at Tj=125°C |
| BYX96-1600 | E1 | a1 | PH | Rectifier | 1600 V | 1 mA | 30 A | | <1.7 V | 100 A | | | | Ir at Tj=125°C |
| BYX96-300 | E1 | a1 | PH | Rectifier | 300 V | 1 mA | 30 A | | <1.7 V | 100 A | | | | Ir at Tj=125°C |
| BYX96-600 | E1 | a1 | PH | Rectifier | 600 V | 1 mA | 30 A | | <1.7 V | 100 A | | | | Ir at Tj=125°C |
| BYX96-1200R | E1 | b1 | PH | Rectifier | 1200 V | 1 mA | 30 A | | <1.7 V | 100 A | | | | Ir at Tj=125°C |
| BYX96-1600R | E1 | b1 | PH | Rectifier | 1600 V | 1 mA | 30 A | | <1.7 V | 100 A | | | | Ir at Tj=125°C |
| BYX96-300R | E1 | b1 | PH | Rectifier | 300 V | 1 mA | 30 A | | <1.7 V | 100 A | | | | Ir at Tj=125°C |
| BYX96-600R | E1 | b1 | PH | Rectifier | 600 V | 1 mA | 30 A | | <1.7 V | 100 A | | | | Ir at Tj=125°C |
| BYX96-1200RU | E2 | b1 | PH | Rectifier | 1200 V | 1 mA | 30 A | | <1.7 V | 100 A | | | | Ir at Tj=125°C |
| BYX96-1600RU | E2 | b1 | PH | Rectifier | 1600 V | 1 mA | 30 A | | <1.7 V | 100 A | | | | Ir at Tj=125°C |
| BYX96-300RU | E2 | b1 | PH | Rectifier | 300 V | 1 mA | 30 A | | <1.7 V | 100 A | | | | Ir at Tj=125°C |
| BYX96-600RU | E2 | b1 | PH | Rectifier | 600 V | 1 mA | 30 A | | <1.7 V | 100 A | | | | Ir at Tj=125°C |
| BYX96-1200U | E2 | a1 | PH | Rectifier | 1200 V | 1 mA | 30 A | | <1.7 V | 100 A | | | | Ir at Tj=125°C |
| BYX96-1600U | E2 | a1 | PH | Rectifier | 1600 V | 1 mA | 30 A | | <1.7 V | 100 A | | | | Ir at Tj=125°C |

| Type | Case | Pin-code | | | Maximum Ratings | | | | Electrical Characteristics | | | | | |
|---|---|---|---|---|---|---|---|---|---|---|---|---|---|---|
| | | | | | Vrm | Irm | Ifav Ifm | Pv | Vf | If Ifp | C0 | Cr | trr ts | |
| BYX96-300U | E2 | a1 | PH | Rectifier | 300 V | 1 mA | 30 A | | <1.7 V | 100 A | | | | Ir at Tj=125°C |
| BYX96-600U | E2 | a1 | PH | Rectifier | 600 V | 1 mA | 30 A | | <1.7 V | 100 A | | | | Ir at Tj=125°C |
| BYX97-1200 | E3 | a1 | PH | Rectifier | 1200 V | 4 mA | 47 A | | <1.45 V | 150 A | | | | Ir at Tj=125°C |
| BYX97-1600 | E3 | a1 | PH | Rectifier | 1600 V | 4 mA | 47 A | | <1.45 V | 150 A | | | | Ir at Tj=125°C |
| BYX97-300 | E3 | a1 | PH | Rectifier | 300 V | 4 mA | 47 A | | <1.45 V | 150 A | | | | Ir at Tj=125°C |
| BYX97-600 | E3 | a1 | PH | Rectifier | 600 V | 4 mA | 47 A | | <1.45 V | 150 A | | | | Ir at Tj=125°C |
| BYX97-1200R | E3 | b1 | PH | Rectifier | 1200 V | 4 mA | 47 A | | <1.45 V | 150 A | | | | Ir at Tj=125°C |
| BYX97-1600R | E3 | b1 | PH | Rectifier | 1600 V | 4 mA | 47 A | | <1.45 V | 150 A | | | | Ir at Tj=125°C |
| BYX97-300R | E3 | b1 | PH | Rectifier | 300 V | 4 mA | 47 A | | <1.45 V | 150 A | | | | Ir at Tj=125°C |
| BYX97-600R | E3 | b1 | PH | Rectifier | 600 V | 4 mA | 47 A | | <1.45 V | 150 A | | | | Ir at Tj=125°C |
| BYX98-1200 | E2 | a1 | PH | Rectifier | 1200 V | 200 µA | 10 A | | <1.7 V | 20 A | | | | Ir at Tj=125°C |
| BYX98-300 | E2 | a1 | PH | Rectifier | 300 V | 200 µA | 10 A | | <1.7 V | 20 A | | | | Ir at Tj=125°C |
| BYX98-600 | E2 | a1 | PH | Rectifier | 600 V | 200 µA | 10 A | | <1.7 V | 20 A | | | | Ir at Tj=125°C |
| BYX98-1200R | E2 | b1 | PH | Rectifier | 1200 V | 200 µA | 10 A | | <1.7 V | 20 A | | | | Ir at Tj=125°C |
| BYX98-300R | E2 | b1 | PH | Rectifier | 300 V | 200 µA | 10 A | | <1.7 V | 20 A | | | | Ir at Tj=125°C |
| BYX98-600R | E2 | b1 | PH | Rectifier | 600 V | 200 µA | 10 A | | <1.7 V | 20 A | | | | Ir at Tj=125°C |
| BYX99-1200 | E2 | a1 | PH | Rectifier | 1200 V | 200 µA | 15 A | | <1.55 V | 50 A | | | | Ir at Tj=125°C |
| BYX99-300 | E2 | a1 | PH | Rectifier | 300 V | 200 µA | 15 A | | <1.55 V | 50 A | | | | Ir at Tj=125°C |
| BYX99-600 | E2 | a1 | PH | Rectifier | 600 V | 200 µA | 15 A | | <1.55 V | 50 A | | | | Ir at Tj=125°C |
| BYX99-1200R | E2 | b1 | PH | Rectifier | 1200 V | 200 µA | 15 A | | <1.55 V | 50 A | | | | Ir at Tj=125°C |
| BYX99-300R | E2 | b1 | PH | Rectifier | 300 V | 200 µA | 15 A | | <1.55 V | 50 A | | | | Ir at Tj=125°C |
| BYX99-600R | E2 | b1 | PH | Rectifier | 600 V | 200 µA | 15 A | | <1.55 V | 50 A | | | | Ir at Tj=125°C |
| BYX110GP | B12 | a1 | PH | HV Rectifier | 8 kV | 1 µA | 350 mA | | <14.5 V | 2 A | | | | |
| BYX120G | A14 | a1 | PH | HV Rectifier | 3 kV | 1 µA | 100 mA | | | | | | | |
| CBT33 | I11 | c7 | RD | Rect. Pair | 30 V | 10 µA | 15 A | | 0.55 V | 15 A | | | | Ifav at Tc=100°C |
| CBT34 | I11 | c7 | RD | Rect. Pair | 40 V | 10 mA | 15 A | | 0.55 V | 15 A | | | | Ifav at Tc=100°C |
| CBT33M | I11 | c7 | RD | Rect. Pair | 30 V | 20 µA | 35 A | | 0.55 V | 15 A | | | | Ifav at Tc=88°C |
| CBT34M | I11 | c7 | RD | Rect. Pair | 40 V | 20 µA | 35 A | | 0.55 V | 15 A | | | | Ifav at Tc=88°C |
| CTB23L | I4 | c7 | RD | Rect. Pair | 30 V | 5 mA | 10 A | | 0.55 V | 5 A | | | | Ifav at Ta=99°C |
| CTB24L | I6 | c7 | RD | Rect. Pair | 40 V | 5 mA | 10 A | | 0.55 V | 5 A | | | | Ifav at Ta=99°C |
| CTG21R | I6 | c8 | RD | Rect. Pair | 70 V | 500 µA | 10 A | | 1.3 V | 5 A | | | 100 ns | Ifav at Tc=92°C |
| CTG22R | I6 | c8 | RD | Rect. Pair | 200 V | 500 µA | 10 A | | 1.8 V | 5 A | | | 100 ns | Ifav at Tc=69°C |
| CTG23R | I6 | c8 | RD | Rect. Pair | 300 V | 500 µA | 10 A | | 1.8 V | 5 A | | | 100 ns | Ifav at Tc=69°C |
| CTG24R | I6 | c8 | RD | Rect. Pair | 400 V | 500 µA | 8 A | | 2 V | 5 A | | | 100 ns | Ifav at Tc=69°C |
| CTG21S | I6 | c7 | RD | Rect. Pair | 70 V | 500 µA | 10 A | | 1.3 V | 5 A | | | 100 ns | Ifav at Tc=92°C |
| CTG22S | I6 | c7 | RD | Rect. Pair | 200 V | 500 µA | 10 A | | 1.8 V | 5 A | | | 100 ns | Ifav at Tc=69°C |
| CTG23S | I6 | c7 | RD | Rect. Pair | 300 V | 500 µA | 10 A | | 1.8 V | 5 A | | | 100 ns | Ifav at Tc=69°C |
| CTG24S | I6 | c7 | RD | Rect. Pair | 400 V | 500 µA | 8 A | | 2 V | 5 A | | | 100 ns | Ifav at Tc=69°C |
| CTG31R | J11 | c8 | RD | Rect. Pair | 70 V | 1 mA | 20 A | | 1.3 V | 10 A | | | 100 ns | Ifav at Tc=92°C |
| CTG32R | J11 | c8 | RD | Rect. Pair | 200 V | 1 mA | 20 A | | 1.8 V | 10 A | | | 100 ns | Ifav at Tc=69°C |

# CTG33R – D1JS20

| Type | Case | Pin-code | | | Maximum Ratings Vrm | Irm | Ifav Ifm | Pv | Vf | If Ifp | C0 | Cr | trr ts | |
|---|---|---|---|---|---|---|---|---|---|---|---|---|---|---|
| CTG33R | J11 | c8 | RD | Rect. Pair | 300 V | 1 mA | 20 A | | 1.8 V | 10 A | | | 100 ns | Ifav at Tc=69°C |
| CTG34R | J11 | c8 | RD | Rect. Pair | 400 V | 1 mA | 16 A | | 2 V | 10 A | | | 100 ns | Ifav at Tc=69°C |
| CTG31S | J11 | c7 | RD | Rect. Pair | 70 V | 1 mA | 20 A | | 1.3 V | 10 A | | | 100 ns | Ifav at Tc=92°C |
| CTG32S | J11 | c7 | RD | Rect. Pair | 200 V | 1 mA | 20 A | | 1.8 V | 10 A | | | 100 ns | Ifav at Tc=69°C |
| CTG33S | J11 | c7 | RD | Rect. Pair | 300 V | 1 mA | 20 A | | 1.8 V | 10 A | | | 100 ns | Ifav at Tc=69°C |
| CTG34S | J11 | c7 | RD | Rect. Pair | 400 V | 1 mA | 16 A | | 2 V | 10 A | | | 100 ns | Ifav at Tc=69°C |
| CTL11R | I6 | c8 | RD | Rect. Pair | 100 V | 100 µA | 5 A | | 0.98 V | 2.5 A | | | 35 ns | Ifav at Tc=124°C |
| CTL11S | I6 | c7 | RD | Rect. Pair | 100 V | 100 µA | 5 A | | 0.98 V | 2.5 A | | | 35 ns | Ifav at Tc=124°C |
| CTL12R | I6 | c8 | RD | Rect. Pair | 200 V | 100 µA | 5 A | | 0.98 V | 2.5 A | | | 35 ns | Ifav at Tc=124°C |
| CTL12S | I6 | c7 | RD | Rect. Pair | 200 V | 100 µA | 5 A | | 0.98 V | 2.5 A | | | 35 ns | Ifav at Tc=124°C |
| CTL21R | I6 | c8 | RD | Rect. Pair | 100 V | 200 µA | 10 A | | 0.98 V | 5.5 A | | | 35 ns | Ifav at Tc=108°C |
| CTL22R | I6 | c8 | RD | Rect. Pair | 200 V | 200 µA | 10 A | | 0.98 V | 5.5 A | | | 35 ns | Ifav at Tc=108°C |
| CTL21S | I6 | c7 | RD | Rect. Pair | 100 V | 200 µA | 10 A | | 0.98 V | 5.5 A | | | 35 ns | Ifav at Tc=108°C |
| CTL22S | I6 | c7 | RD | Rect. Pair | 200 V | 200 µA | 10 A | | 0.98 V | 5.5 A | | | 35 ns | Ifav at Tc=108°C |
| CTL31R | J11 | c8 | RD | Rect. Pair | 100 V | 500 µA | 20 A | | 0.98 V | 10 A | | | 35 ns | Ifav at Tc=94°C |
| CTL32R | J11 | c8 | RD | Rect. Pair | 200 V | 500 µA | 20 A | | 0.98 V | 10 A | | | 35 ns | Ifav at Tc=94°C |
| CTL31S | J11 | c7 | RD | Rect. Pair | 100 V | 500 µA | 20 A | | 0.98 V | 10 A | | | 35 ns | Ifav at Tc=94°C |
| CTL32S | J11 | c7 | RD | Rect. Pair | 200 V | 500 µA | 20 A | | 0.98 V | 10 A | | | 35 ns | Ifav at Tc=94°C |
| CTU-G2DR | I1 | a1 | RD | Rectifier | 1350 V | 100 µA | 4 A | | 2 V | 4 A | | | | Ifav at Ta=104°C |
| CTU36R | J11 | c8 | RD | Rect. Pair | 600 V | 10 µA | 12 A | | 1.5 V | 10 A | | | 400 ns | Ifav at Tc=118°C |
| CTU36S | J11 | c7 | RD | Rect. Pair | 600 V | 10 µA | 12 A | | 1.5 V | 10 A | | | 400 ns | Ifav at Tc=118°C |
| D1CA20 | N8 | e1 | RD | Array Univers | 200 V | | 1 A | | | | | | | |
| D1CA40 | N8 | e1 | RD | Array Univers | 400 V | | 1 A | | | | | | | |
| D1CA20R | N8 | e2 | RD | Array Univers | 200 V | | 1 A | | | | | | | |
| D1CA40R | N8 | e2 | RD | Array Univers | 400 V | | 1 A | | | | | | | |
| D1CAK20 | N8 | e1 | RD | Array Univers | 200 V | | 700 mA | | | | | | 300 ns | |
| D1CAK20R | N8 | e2 | RD | Array Univers | 200 V | | 700 mA | | | | | | 300 ns | |
| D1CS20 | N7 | d8 | RD | Array Univers | 200 V | | 1 A | | | | | | | |
| D1F10 | G1 | a1 | RD | Uni | 100 V | 10 µA | 1 A | | 1.1 V | 1 A | | | | |
| D1F20 | G1 | a1 | RD | Uni | 200 V | 10 µA | 1 A | | 1.1 V | 1 A | | | | |
| D1F40 | G1 | a1 | RD | Uni | 400 V | 10 µA | 1 A | | 1.1 V | 1 A | | | | |
| D1F60 | G1 | a1 | RD | Uni | 600 V | 10 µA | 1 A | | 1.1 V | 1 A | | | | |
| D1FK20 | G1 | a1 | RD | Rectifier | 200 V | 10 µA | 800 mA | | 1.2 V | 800 mA | | | 300 ns | |
| D1FK40 | G1 | a1 | RD | Rectifier | 400 V | 10 µA | 800 mA | | 1.2 V | 800 mA | | | 300 ns | |
| D1FL20 | G1 | a1 | RD | Rectifier | 200 V | 10 µA | 1.1 A | | 0.9 V | 1.1 A | | | 35 ns | |
| D1FS4 | G1 | a1 | RD | Rectifier | 40 V | 1 mA | 1.1 A | | 0.55 V | 1 A | | | | |
| D1JA20 | P4 | h3 | RD | Array Univers | 200 V | | 1 A | | | | | | | |
| D1JA40 | P4 | h3 | RD | Array Univers | 400 V | | 1 A | | | | | | | |
| D1JAK20 | P4 | h3 | RD | Array Univers | 200 V | | 700 mA | | | | | | 300 ns | |
| D1JS20 | P3 | f3 | RD | Array Univers | 200 V | | 1 A | | | | | | | |

| Type | Case | Pin-code | | | Maximum Ratings Vrm | Irm | Ifav Ifm | Pv | Electrical Characteristics Vf | If Ifp | C0 | Cr | trr ts | |
|------|------|----------|---|---|------|-----|------|----|------|------|----|----|----|---|
| D2F10 | G15 | d7 | RD | Rectifier | 100 V | 10 µA | 1.4 A | | 1.05 V | 1.4 A | | | | |
| D2F20 | G2 | a1 | RD | Rectifier | 200 V | 10 µA | 1.4 A | | 1.05 V | 1.4 A | | | | |
| D2F40 | G2 | a1 | RD | Rectifier | 400 V | 10 µA | 1.4 A | | 1.05 V | 1.4 A | | | | |
| D2F60 | G2 | a1 | RD | Rectifier | 600 V | 10 µA | 1.4 A | | 1.05 V | 1.4 A | | | | |
| D2FK20 | G15 | a1 | RD | Rectifier | 200 V | 10 µA | 1.3 A | | 1.2 V | 1.3 A | | | | |
| D2FK40 | G15 | a1 | RD | Rectifier | 400 V | 10 µA | 1.3 A | | 1.2 V | 1.3 A | | | | |
| D2FK60 | G15 | a1 | RD | Rectifier | 200 V | 10 µA | 1.3 A | | 0.98 V | 1.6 A | | | | |
| D2FS4 | G15 | a1 | RD | Rectifier | 40 V | 1 mA | 1.6 A | | 0.55 V | 1.6 A | | | | |
| D4LA20 | J5 | a1 | RD | Rectifier | 200 V | 10 µA | 4 A | | 0.98 V | 4 A | | | | Ifav at Ta=131°C |
| D5KC20 | J3 | c7 | RD | Rect. Pair | 200 V | 10 µA | 5 A | | 1.2 V | 2.5 A | | | 300 ns | Ifav at Tc=130°C |
| D5KC20H | J3 | c7 | RD | Rect. Pair | 200 V | 10 µA | 5 A | | 1.2 V | 2.5 A | | | 100 ns | Ifav at Tc=130°C |
| D5KC40 | J3 | c7 | RD | Rect. Pair | 400 V | 10 µA | 5 A | | 1.2 V | 2.5 A | | | 300 ns | Ifav at Tc=129°C |
| D5KC20RH | J3 | c8 | RD | Rect. Pair | 200 V | 10 µA | 5 A | | 1.2 V | 2.5 A | | | 100 ns | Ifav at Tc=130°C |
| D5KC20R | J3 | c8 | RD | Rect. Pair | 200 V | 10 µA | 5 A | | 1.2 V | 2.5 A | | | 300 ns | Ifav at Tc=130°C |
| D5KC40R | J3 | c8 | RD | Rect. Pair | 400 V | 10 µA | 5 A | | 1.2 V | 2.5 A | | | 300 ns | Ifav at Tc=129°C |
| D5KD40 | J3 | c10 | RD | Rect. Pair | 400 V | 10 µA | 5 A | | 1.2 V | 2.5 A | | | 300 ns | Ifav at Tc=129°C |
| D5LC40 | J3 | c7 | RD | Rect. Pair | 400 V | 10 µA | 5 A | | 1.3 V | 2.5 A | | | 50 ns | Ifav at Tc=125°C |
| D5LCA20 | J3 | c7 | RD | Rect. Pair | 200 V | 10 µA | 5 A | | 0.98 V | 2.5 A | | | 50 ns | Ifav at Tc=133°C |
| D5S3M | J5 | a1 | RD | Rectifier | 30 V | 3.5 mA | 5 A | | 0.55 V | 3 A | | | | Ifav at Tc=115°C |
| D5S4M | J5 | a1 | RD | Rectifier | 40 V | 3.5 mA | 5 A | | 0.55 V | 5 A | | | | Ifav at Tc=110°C |
| D5S6M | J5 | a1 | RD | Rectifier | 60 V | 4.5 mA | 5 A | | 0.58 V | 5 A | 260 pF | | | Ifav at Tc=103°C |
| D5S9M | J5 | a1 | RD | Rectifier | 90 V | 3 mA | 5 A | | 0.75 V | 5 A | 185 pF | | | Ifav at Tc=101°C |
| D6K20 | J5 | a1 | RD | Rectifier | 200 V | 10 µA | 6 A | | 1.2 V | 6 A | | | | Ifav at Ta=122°C |
| D6K40 | J5 | a1 | RD | Rectifier | 400 V | 10 µA | 6 A | | 1.2 V | 6 A | | | | Ifav at Ta=123°C |
| D6K20H | J5 | a1 | RD | Rectifier | 200 V | 10 µA | 6 A | | 1.2 V | 6 A | | | | Ifav at Ta=122°C |
| D6K20HR | J5 | b1 | RD | Rectifier | 200 V | 10 µA | 6 A | | 1.2 V | 6 A | | | | Ifav at Ta=122°C |
| D6K20R | J5 | b1 | RD | Rectifier | 200 V | 10 µA | 6 A | | 1.2 V | 6 A | | | | Ifav at Ta=122°C |
| D6K40R | J5 | b1 | RD | Rectifier | 400 V | 10 µA | 6 A | | 1.2 V | 6 A | | | | Ifav at Ta=123°C |
| D8LC20U | J3 | c7 | RD | Rect. Pair | 200 V | 10 µA | 8 A | | 0.98 V | 4 A | | | 50 ns | Ifav at Tc=120°C |
| D8LC40 | J3 | c7 | RD | Rect. Pair | 400 V | 10 µA | 8 A | | 1.3 V | 4 A | | | 50 ns | Ifav at Tc=114°C |
| D8LCA20 | J6 | c7 | RD | Rect. Pair | 200 V | 10 µA | 8 A | | 0.98 V | 4 A | | | 50 ns | Ifav at Tc=122°C |
| D8LCA20R | J6 | c8 | RD | Rect. Pair | 200 V | 10 µA | 8 A | | 0.98 V | 4 A | | | 50 ns | Ifav at Tc=122°C |
| D8LDA20 | J3 | c10 | RD | Rect. Pair | 200 V | 10 µA | 8 A | | 0.98 V | 4 A | | | 50 ns | Ifav at Tc=122°C |
| D10LC40 | J3 | c7 | RD | Rect. Pair | 400 V | 10 µA | 10 A | | 1.3 V | 5 A | | | 50 ns | Ifav at Ta=100°C |
| D10LCA20 | J3 | c7 | RD | Rect. Pair | 200 V | 10 µA | 10 A | | 0.98 V | 5 A | | | 50 ns | Ifav at Ta=115°C |
| D10SC3M | J3 | c7 | RD | Rect. Pair | 30 V | 3.5 mA | 10 A | | 0.55 V | 5 A | | | | Ifav at Ta=102°C |
| D10SC4M | J3 | c7 | RD | Rect. Pair | 40 V | 3.5 mA | 10 A | | 0.55 V | 5 A | | | | Ifav at Ta=102°C |
| D10SC4MR | J3 | c8 | RD | Rect. Pair | 40 V | 3.5 mA | 10 A | | 0.55 V | 5 A | | | | Ifav at Ta=102°C |
| D10SC6M | J3 | c7 | RD | Rect. Pair | 60 V | 4.5 mA | 10 A | | 0.58 V | 5 A | | | | Ifav at Ta=92°C |
| D10SC6MR | J3 | c8 | RD | Rect. Pair | 60 V | 3.5 mA | 10 A | | 0.58 V | 5 A | | | | Ifav at Ta=92°C |

| Type | Case | Pin-code | | | Vrm | Irm | Ifav Ifm | Pv | Vf | If Ifp | C0 | Cr | trr ts | |
|------|------|----------|---|---|-----|-----|----------|----|----|--------|----|----|--------|---|
| | | | | **Maximum Ratings** | | | | | **Electrical Characteristics** | | | | | |
| D10SC9M | J3 | c7 | RD | Rect. Pair | 90 V | 3 mA | 10 A | | 0.75 V | 5 A | | | | Ifav at Ta=91°C |
| D10SD6M | J3 | c7 | RD | Rect. Pair | 60 V | 4.5 mA | 10 A | | 0.58 V | 5 A | | | | Ifav at Ta=92°C |
| DA15LCA20 | J3 | c7 | RD | Rect. Pair | 200 V | 10 µA | 15 A | | 0.98 V | 7.5 A | | | 50 ns | Ifav at Tc=105°C |
| DAN235E | F2 | c5 | RO | Pair RF Diode | (35) V | 10 nA | | 0.15 W | <1 V | 10 mA | <1.2 pF | | | C0 at 6V |
| DAN235K | F1 | c5 | RO | Pair RF Diode | (35) V | 10 nA | | 0.15 W | <1 V | 10 mA | <1.2 pF | | | C0 at 6V |
| DAN235U | F2 | c5 | RO | Pair RF Diode | (35) V | 10 nA | | 0.15 W | <1 V | 10 mA | <1.2 pF | | | C0 at 6V |
| DAN236K | F1 | c2 | RO | Pair RF Diode | (35) V | 10 nA | | 0.15 W | <1 V | 10 mA | <1.2 pF | | | C0 at 6V |
| DAN236U | F2 | c7 | RO | Pair RF Diode | (35) V | 10 nA | | 0.15 W | <1 V | 10 mA | <1.2 pF | | | C0 at 6V |
| DE3S4M | F11 | a1 | RD | Rectifier | 40 V | 3.5 mA | 3 A | | 0.55 V | 3 A | | | | Ifav at Ta=98°C |
| DE3S6M | F11 | a1 | RD | Rectifier | 60 V | | 3 A | | 0.58 V | 3 A | | | | Ifav at Ta=26°C |
| DE5LC20U | F11 | c7 | RD | Rect. Pair | 200 V | 10 µA | 5 A | | 0.98 V | 2.5 A | | | | |
| DE5LC40 | F11 | c7 | RD | Rect. Pair | 400 V | 10 µA | 5 A | | 1.3 V | 2.5 A | | | 50 ns | Ifav at Tc=125°C |
| DE5S4M | F11 | a1 | RD | Rectifier | 40 V | | 5 A | | 0.55 V | 5 A | 180 pF | | | C0 at Vr=10V |
| DE5S6M | F11 | a1 | RD | Rectifier | 60 V | | 5 A | | 0.58 V | 5 A | 260 pF | | | C0 at Vr=10V |
| DE5SC4M | F11 | c7 | RD | Rect. Pair | 40 V | 3.5 mA | 5 A | | 0.55 V | 2.5 A | | | | Ifav at Ta=80°C |
| DE5SC6M | F11 | c7 | RD | Rect. Pair | 60 V | | 5 A | | 0.58 V | 2.5 A | 150 pF | | | C0 at Vr=10V |
| ED16H1 | B21 | a1 | RD | HV Rectifier | 16 kV | 10 µA | | | 22 V | 300 mA | | | 500 ns | Ifm at Ta=50°C |
| ED24H1 | B21 | a1 | RD | HV Rectifier | 24 kV | 10 µA | | | 33 V | 300 mA | | | 500 ns | Ifm at Ta=50°C |
| ED8H1 | B21 | a1 | RD | HV Rectifier | 8 kV | 10 µA | | | 11 V | 300 mA | | | 500 ns | Ifm at Ta=50°C |
| ED16N1 | B21 | a1 | RD | HV Rectifier | 16 kV | 10 µA | 80 mA | | 22 V | 300 mA | | | | Ifav at Ta=50°C |
| ED8N1 | B21 | a1 | RD | HV Rectifier | 8 kV | 10 µA | 200 mA | | 11 V | 300 mA | | | | Ifav at Ta=50°C |
| ED100X1 | -- | a1 | RD | HV Rectifier | 100 kV | 10 µA | 100 mA | | 165 V | 100 mA | | | | Ifav at Ta=50°C |
| ED125X1 | -- | a1 | RD | HV Rectifier | 125 kV | 10 µA | 100 mA | | 210 V | 100 mA | | | | Ifav at Ta=50°C |
| ED150X1 | -- | a1 | RD | HV Rectifier | 150 kV | 10 µA | 100 mA | | 240 V | 100 mA | | | | Ifav at Ta=50°C |
| ED75X1 | -- | a1 | RD | HV Rectifier | 75 kV | 10 µA | 100 mA | | 125 V | 100 mA | | | | Ifav at Ta=50°C |
| EK03 | A18 | a1 | RD | Rectifier | 30 V | 5 mA | 1 A | | 0.55 V | 1.5 A | | | | |
| EK04 | A18 | a1 | RD | Rectifier | 40 V | 5 mA | 1 A | | 0.55 V | 1.5 A | | | | |
| EK06 | A18 | a1 | RD | Rectifier | 60 V | 1 mA | 700 mA | | 0.62 V | 1.5 A | | | | |
| EK09 | A18 | a1 | RD | Rectifier | 90 V | 1 mA | 700 mA | | 0.81 V | 1.5 A | | | | |
| EK13 | B9 | a1 | RD | Rectifier | 30 V | 5 mA | 1.5 A | | 0.55 V | 1.5 A | | | | |
| EK14 | B9 | a1 | RD | Rectifier | 40 V | 5 mA | 1.5 A | | 0.55 V | 1.5 A | | | | |
| EK16 | B9 | a1 | RD | Rectifier | 60 V | 1 mA | 1.5 A | | 0.61 V | 1.5 A | | | | |
| EK19 | B9 | a1 | RD | Rectifier | 90 V | 2 mA | 1.5 A | | 0.81 V | 1.5 A | | | | |
| EM513 | B9 | a1 | RD | Rectifier | 1600 V | 5 µA | 1 A | | <1.3 V | 2 A | | | | |
| EM516 | B9 | a1 | RD | Rectifier | 1800 V | 5 µA | 1 A | | 1.3 V | 2 A | | | | |
| ESM243-100 | E4 | a1 | SG | Rectifier | 100 V | 10 mA | 60 A | (110) W | <1.5 V | 60 A | | | <100 ns | Ifav at Tc=90°C |
| ESM243-200 | E4 | a1 | SG | Rectifier | 200 V | 10 mA | 60 A | (110) W | <1.5 V | 60 A | | | <100 ns | Ifav at Tc=90°C |
| ESM243-300 | E4 | a1 | SG | Rectifier | 300 V | 10 mA | 60 A | (110) W | <1.5 V | 60 A | | | <100 ns | Ifav at Tc=90°C |
| ESM243-400 | E4 | a1 | SG | Rectifier | 400 V | 10 mA | 60 A | (110) W | <1.5 V | 60 A | | | <100 ns | Ifav at Tc=90°C |
| ESM243-50 | E4 | a1 | SG | Rectifier | 50 V | 10 mA | 60 A | (110) W | <1.5 V | 60 A | | | <100 ns | Ifav at Tc=90°C |

| Type | Case | Pin-code | | | Maximum Ratings | | | | Electrical Characteristics | | | | | |
|------|------|----------|---|---|------|-----|----------|----------|------|--------|------|------|------|------|
| | | | | | Vrm | Irm | Ifav Ifm | Pv | Vf | If Ifp | C0 | Cr | trr ts | |
| ESM244-100 | E4 | a1 | SG | Rectifier | 100 V | 6 mA | 60 A | (110) W | <1.5 V | 60 A | | | <200 ns | Ifav at Tc=90°C |
| ESM244-200 | E4 | a1 | SG | Rectifier | 200 V | 6 mA | 60 A | (110) W | <1.5 V | 60 A | | | <200 ns | Ifav at Tc=90°C |
| ESM244-300 | E4 | a1 | SG | Rectifier | 300 V | 6 mA | 60 A | (110) W | <1.5 V | 60 A | | | <200 ns | Ifav at Tc=90°C |
| ESM244-400 | E4 | a1 | SG | Rectifier | 400 V | 6 mA | 60 A | (110) W | <1.5 V | 60 A | | | <200 ns | Ifav at Tc=90°C |
| ESM244-50 | E4 | a1 | SG | Rectifier | 50 V | 6 mA | 60 A | (110) W | <1.5 V | 60 A | | | <200 ns | Ifav at Tc=90°C |
| ESM244-500 | E4 | a1 | SG | Rectifier | 500 V | 6 mA | 60 A | (110) W | <1.5 V | 60 A | | | <200 ns | Ifav at Tc=90°C |
| ESM244-600 | E4 | a1 | SG | Rectifier | 600 V | 6 mA | 60 A | (110) W | <1.5 V | 60 A | | | <200 ns | Ifav at Tc=90°C |
| ESM765-100A | I1 | a1 | SG | Rectifier | 100 V | 20 µA | 10 A | (20) W | <1.4 V | 10 A | | | <300 ns | Ifav at Tc=100°C |
| ESM765-200A | I1 | a1 | SG | Rectifier | 200 V | 20 µA | 10 A | (20) W | <1.4 V | 10 A | | | <300 ns | Ifav at Tc=100°C |
| ESM765-400A | I1 | a1 | SG | Rectifier | 400 V | 20 µA | 10 A | (20) W | <1.4 V | 10 A | | | <300 ns | Ifav at Tc=100°C |
| ESM765-600A | I1 | a1 | SG | Rectifier | 600 V | 20 µA | 10 A | (20) W | <1.4 V | 10 A | | | <300 ns | Ifav at Tc=100°C |
| ESM765-800A | I1 | a1 | SG | Rectifier | 800 V | 20 µA | 10 A | (20) W | <1.4 V | 10 A | | | <300 ns | Ifav at Tc=100°C |
| ESM765PI-600 | I13 | a1 | SG | Rectifier | 600 V | 20 µA | 10 A | (20) W | <1.4 V | 10 A | | | <300 ns | Ifav at Tc=100°C |
| ESM765PI-800 | I13 | a1 | SG | Rectifier | 800 V | 20 µA | 10 A | (20) W | <1.4 V | 10 A | | | <300 ns | Ifav at Tc=100°C |
| FD700 | A15 | a1 | NS | Uni | 30 V | 50 nA | | | <0.88 V | 10 mA | <1 pF | | <0.7 ns | Ir at 20V |
| FD777 | A15 | a1 | NS | Uni | 15 V | 0.1 µA | | | <0.94 V | 10 mA | <1.3 pF | | <0.75 ns | Ir at 8V |
| FDH300 | A1 | a1 | NS | Uni | 150 V | 1 µA | | | <0.8 V | 10 mA | <6 pF | | | Ir at 125V |
| FDH333 | A1 | a1 | NS | Uni | 150 V | 3 µA | | | <0.94 V | 100 mA | <6 pF | | | Ir at 125V |
| FDH400 | A1 | a1 | NS | Uni | 200 V | 100 µA | | | <1.1 V | 300 mA | <2 pF | | <50 ns | Ir at 150V |
| FDH444 | A1 | a1 | NS | Uni | 150 V | 50 µA | | | <1.2 V | 300 mA | <2.5 pF | | <60 ns | Ir at 100V |
| FDH600 | A1 | a1 | NS | Uni | 75 V | 0.1 µA | | | <0.79 V | 10 mA | <2.5 pF | | <4 ns | Ir at 50V |
| FDH666 | A1 | a1 | NS | Uni | 40 V | 0.1 µA | | | <0.79 V | 10 mA | <3.5 pF | | <4 ns | Ir at 25V |
| FDH900 | A1 | a1 | NS | Uni | 45 V | 0.5 µA | | | <1 V | 100 mA | <3 pF | | <4 ns | Ir at 40V |
| FDH999 | A1 | a1 | NS | Uni | 45 V | 1 µA | | | <1 V | 10 mA | <5 pF | | <5 ns | Ir at 35V |
| FDH1000 | A1 | a1 | NS | Uni | 75 V | 5 µA | | | <1 V | 500 mA | <5 pF | | | Ir at 50V |
| FDLL300 | D2 | a1 | NS | Uni | 150 V | 1 nA | | | <1 V | 200 mA | | | | |
| FDLL600 | D2 | a1 | NS | Uni | 75 V | 100 nA | | | <1 V | 200 mA | | | <4 ns | |
| FDLL3595 | D2 | a1 | NS | Uni | 150 V | 1 nA | | | <1 V | 200 mA | | | | |
| FDLL4148 | D2 | a1 | NS | Uni | 100 V | 25 nA | | | <1 V | 10 mA | | | <4 ns | |
| FDLL4150 | D2 | a1 | NS | Uni | 75 V | 100 nA | | | <1 V | 200 mA | | | <4 ns | |
| FDLL4448 | D2 | a1 | NS | Uni | 100 V | 25 nA | | | <1 V | 100 mA | | | <4 ns | |
| FJT1100 | A15 | a1 | NS | Uni | 30 V | 10p µA | | | <1.05 V | 50 mA | <1.5 pF | | | Ir at 15V |
| FJT1101 | A15 | a1 | NS | Uni | 20 V | 15p µA | | | <1.15 V | 50 mA | <1.8 pF | | | Ir at 15V |
| FMB-G14L | FM2 | a1 | RD | Rectifier | 40 V | 5 mA | 5 A | | 0.55 V | 5 A | | | | Ifav at Tc=88°C |
| FMB-G24H | FM2 | a1 | RD | Rectifier | 40 V | 10 mA | 10 A | | 0.55 V | 10 A | | | | Ifav at Tc=88°C |
| FMB23L | J6 | c7 | RD | Rect. Pair | 30 V | 5 mA | 10 A | | 0.55 V | 10 A | | | | Ifav at Ta=99°C |
| FMB24L | J6 | c7 | RD | Rect. Pair | 40 V | 5 mA | 10 A | | 0.55 V | 10 A | | | | Ifav at Ta=99°C |
| FMB26L | J6 | c7 | RD | Rect. Pair | 60 V | 2.5 µA | 10 A | | 0.58 V | 4 A | | | | Ifav at Ta=99°C |
| FMB24H | J6 | c7 | RD | Rect. Pair | 40 V | 7.5 mA | 15 A | | 0.55 V | 7.5 A | | | | Ifav at Ta=99°C |
| FMB24M | J6 | c7 | RD | Rect. Pair | 40 V | 5 mA | 6 A | | 0.55 V | 3 A | | | | |

| Type | Case | Pin-code | | | Maximum Ratings | | | | Electrical Characteristics | | | | | |
|---|---|---|---|---|---|---|---|---|---|---|---|---|---|---|
| | | | | | Vrm | Irm | Ifav Ifm | Pv | Vf | If Ifp | C0 | Cr | trr ts | |
| FMB29L | J6 | c7 | RD | Rect. Pair | 90 V | 2.5 µA | 8 A | | 0.81 V | 4 A | | | | Ifav at Tc=100°C |
| FMB33 | J16 | c7 | RD | Rect. Pair | 30 V | 10 mA | 15 A | | 0.55 V | 7.5 A | | | | Ifav at Tc=100°C |
| FMB34 | J16 | c7 | RD | Rect. Pair | 40 V | 10 mA | 15 A | | 0.55 V | 7.5 A | | | | Ifav at Tc=100°C |
| FMB36 | J16 | c7 | RD | Rect. Pair | 60 V | 5 mA | 15 A | | 0.62 V | 7.5 A | | | | Ifav at Tc=100°C |
| FMB39 | J16 | c7 | RD | Rect. Pair | 90 V | 10 mA | 15 A | | 0.81 V | 7.5 A | | | | Ifav at Tc=100°C |
| FMB33M | J16 | c7 | RD | Rect. Pair | 30 V | 20 µA | 30 A | | 0.55 V | 15 A | | | | Ifav at Tc=88°C |
| FMB34M | J16 | c7 | RD | Rect. Pair | 40 V | 20 µA | 30 A | | 0.55 V | 15 A | | | | Ifav at Tc=88°C |
| FMB36M | J16 | c7 | RD | Rect. Pair | 60 V | 10 µA | 30 A | | 0.62 V | 15 A | | | | Ifav at Tc=88°C |
| FMB39M | J16 | c7 | RD | Rect. Pair | 90 V | 15 µA | 20 A | | 0.81 V | 10 A | | | | Ifav at Tc=88°C |
| FMG22R | J6 | c8 | RD | Rect. Pair | 200 V | 200 µA | 10 A | | 1.8 V | 5 A | | | 35 ns | Ifav at Tc=69°C |
| FMG23R | J6 | c8 | RD | Rect. Pair | 300 V | 200 µA | 10 A | | 1.8 V | 5 A | | | 35 ns | Ifav at Tc=69°C |
| FMG22S | J6 | c7 | RD | Rect. Pair | 200 V | 200 µA | 10 A | | 1.8 V | 5 A | | | 35 ns | Ifav at Tc=69°C |
| FMG23S | J6 | c7 | RD | Rect. Pair | 300 V | 200 µA | 10 A | | 1.8 V | 5 A | | | 35 ns | Ifav at Tc=69°C |
| FMG32R | J4 | c8 | RD | Rect. Pair | 200 V | 1 mA | 20 A | | 1.8 V | 10 A | | | 100 ns | Ifav at Tc=69°C |
| FMG33R | J4 | c8 | RD | Rect. Pair | 300 V | 1 mA | 20 A | | 1.8 V | 10 A | | | 100 ns | Ifav at Tc=69°C |
| FMG32S | J4 | c7 | RD | Rect. Pair | 200 V | 1 mA | 20 A | | 1.8 V | 10 A | | | 100 ns | Ifav at Tc=69°C |
| FMG33S | J4 | c7 | RD | Rect. Pair | 300 V | 1 mA | 20 A | | 1.8 V | 10 A | | | 100 ns | Ifav at Tc=69°C |
| FML-G12S | J4 | a1 | RD | Rectifier | 200 V | 250 µA | 5 A | | 0.98 V | 4 A | | | | Ifav at Ta=124°C |
| FML-G16S | J4 | a1 | RD | Rectifier | 600 V | 100 µA | 5 A | | 1.5 V | 3 A | | | | Ifav at Ta=111°C |
| FML-G22S | J4 | a1 | RD | Rectifier | 200 V | 25 µA | 10 A | | 0.98 V | 10 A | | | 50 ns | Ifav at Ta=108°C |
| FML11R | J6 | c8 | RD | Rect. Pair | 100 V | 100 µA | 5 A | | 0.98 V | 2.5 A | | | 35 ns | Ifav at Tc=124°C |
| FML12R | J6 | c8 | RD | Rect. Pair | 200 V | 100 µA | 5 A | | 0.98 V | 2.5 A | | | 35 ns | Ifav at Tc=124°C |
| FML13R | J6 | c8 | RD | Rect. Pair | 300 V | 50 µA | 5 A | | 1.3 V | 2.5 A | | | 50 ns | Ifav at Tc=122°C |
| FML14R | J6 | c8 | RD | Rect. Pair | 400 V | 50 µA | 5 A | | 1.3 V | 2.5 A | | | 50 ns | Ifav at Tc=122°C |
| FMX12R | J6 | c8 | RD | Rect. Pair | 200 V | 50 µA | 5 A | | 0.98 V | 2.5 A | | | 30 ns | Ifav at Tc=124°C |
| FML11S | J6 | c7 | RD | Rect. Pair | 100 V | 100 µA | 5 A | | 0.98 V | 2.5 A | | | 35 ns | Ifav at Tc=124°C |
| FML12S | J6 | c7 | RD | Rect. Pair | 200 V | 100 µA | 5 A | | 0.98 V | 2.5 A | | | 35 ns | Ifav at Tc=124°C |
| FML13S | J6 | c7 | RD | Rect. Pair | 300 V | 50 µA | 5 A | | 1.3 V | 2.5 A | | | 50 ns | Ifav at Tc=122°C |
| FML14S | J6 | c7 | RD | Rect. Pair | 400 V | 50 µA | 5 A | | 1.3 V | 2.5 A | | | 50 ns | Ifav at Tc=122°C |
| FMX12S | J6 | c7 | RD | Rect. Pair | 200 V | 50 µA | 5 A | | 0.98 V | 2.5 A | | | 30 ns | Ifav at Tc=125°C |
| FML21R | J6 | c8 | RD | Rect. Pair | 100 V | 200 µA | 10 A | | 0.98 V | 5 A | | | 35 ns | Ifav at Tc=108°C |
| FML22R | J6 | c8 | RD | Rect. Pair | 200 V | 200 µA | 10 A | | 0.98 V | 5 A | | | 35 ns | Ifav at Tc=108°C |
| FML23R | J6 | c8 | RD | Rect. Pair | 300 V | 50 µA | 10 A | | 1.3 V | 5 A | | | 50 ns | Ifav at Tc=108°C |
| FML24R | J6 | c8 | RD | Rect. Pair | 400 V | 50 µA | 10 A | | 1.3 V | 5 A | | | 50 ns | Ifav at Tc=108°C |
| FML21S | J6 | c7 | RD | Rect. Pair | 100 V | 200 µA | 10 A | | 0.98 V | 5 A | | | 35 ns | Ifav at Tc=108°C |
| FML22S | J6 | c7 | RD | Rect. Pair | 200 V | 200 µA | 10 A | | 0.98 V | 5 A | | | 35 ns | Ifav at Tc=108°C |
| FML23S | J6 | c7 | RD | Rect. Pair | 300 V | 50 µA | 10 A | | 1.3 V | 5 A | | | 50 ns | Ifav at Tc=91°C |
| FML24S | J6 | c7 | RD | Rect. Pair | 400 V | 50 µA | 10 A | | 1.3 V | 5 A | | | 50 ns | Ifav at Tc=91°C |
| FML31R | J4 | c8 | RD | Rect. Pair | 100 V | 500 µA | 20 A | | 0.98 V | 10 A | | | 35 ns | Ifav at Tc=94°C |
| FML32R | J4 | c8 | RD | Rect. Pair | 200 V | 500 µA | 20 A | | 0.98 V | 10 A | | | 35 ns | Ifav at Tc=94°C |

| Type | Case | Pin code | | | Maximum Ratings Vrm | Irm | Ifav Ifm | Pv | Electrical Characteristics Vf | If Ifp | C0 | Cr | trr ts | |
|------|------|----------|---|---|-----|-----|----------|----|-----|--------|----|----|--------|---|
| FML33R | J4 | c8 | RD | Rect. Pair | 300 V | 500 µA | 20 A | | 1.3 V | 10 A | | | 50 ns | Ifav at Tc=90°C |
| FML34R | J4 | c8 | RD | Rect. Pair | 400 V | 500 µA | 20 A | | 1.3 V | 10 A | | | 50 ns | Ifav at Tc=90°C |
| FML31S | J4 | c7 | RD | Rect. Pair | 100 V | 500 µA | 20 A | | 0.98 V | 10 A | | | 35 ns | Ifav at Tc=94°C |
| FML32S | J4 | c7 | RD | Rect. Pair | 200 V | 500 µA | 20 A | | 0.98 V | 10 A | | | 35 ns | Ifav at Tc=94°C |
| FML33S | J4 | c7 | RD | Rect. Pair | 300 V | 500 µA | 20 A | | 1.3 V | 10 A | | | 50 ns | Ifav at Tc=90°C |
| FML34S | J4 | c7 | RD | Rect. Pair | 400 V | 500 µA | 20 A | | 1.3 V | 10 A | | | 50 ns | Ifav at Tc=90°C |
| FMP-G3FS | J17 | a1 | RD | Rectifier | 1500 V | 50 µA | 5 A | | 1.5 V | 3 A | | | | Ifav at Ta=133°C |
| FMU11R | J6 | c8 | RD | Rect. Pair | 100 V | 50 µA | 1 A | | 2 V | 3 A | | | 400 ns | Ifav at Tc=60°C |
| FMU12R | J6 | c8 | RD | Rect. Pair | 200 V | 50 µA | 1 A | | 2 V | 3 A | | | 400 ns | Ifav at Tc=60°C |
| FMU14R | J6 | c8 | RD | Rect. Pair | 400 V | 50 µA | 1 A | | 2 V | 3 A | | | 400 ns | Ifav at Tc=60°C |
| FMU16R | J6 | c8 | RD | Rect. Pair | 600 V | 50 µA | 1 A | | 2 V | 3 A | | | 400 ns | Ifav at Tc=60°C |
| FMU11S | J6 | c7 | RD | Rect. Pair | 100 V | 50 µA | 1 A | | 2 V | 3 A | | | 400 ns | Ifav at Tc=60°C |
| FMU12S | J6 | c7 | RD | Rect. Pair | 200 V | 50 µA | 1 A | | 2 V | 3 A | | | 400 ns | Ifav at Tc=60°C |
| FMU14S | J6 | c7 | RD | Rect. Pair | 400 V | 50 µA | 1 A | | 2 V | 3 A | | | 400 ns | Ifav at Tc=60°C |
| FMU16S | J6 | c7 | RD | Rect. Pair | 600 V | 50 µA | 1 A | | 2 V | 3 A | | | 400 ns | Ifav at Tc=60°C |
| FMU21R | J6 | c8 | RD | Rect. Pair | 100 V | 50 µA | 8 A | | 2 V | 5 A | | | 400 ns | Ifav at Tc=60°C |
| FMU22R | J6 | c8 | RD | Rect. Pair | 200 V | 50 µA | 8 A | | 2 V | 5 A | | | 400 ns | Ifav at Tc=60°C |
| FMU24R | J6 | c8 | RD | Rect. Pair | 400 V | 50 µA | 8 A | | 2 V | 5 A | | | 400 ns | Ifav at Tc=60°C |
| FMU26R | J6 | c8 | RD | Rect. Pair | 600 V | 50 µA | 8 A | | 2 V | 5 A | | | 400 ns | Ifav at Tc=60°C |
| FMU21S | J6 | c8 | RD | Rect. Pair | 100 V | 50 µA | 8 A | | 2 V | 5 A | | | 400 ns | Ifav at Tc=60°C |
| FMU22S | J6 | c8 | RD | Rect. Pair | 200 V | 50 µA | 8 A | | 2 V | 5 A | | | 400 ns | Ifav at Tc=60°C |
| FMU24S | J6 | c8 | RD | Rect. Pair | 400 V | 50 µA | 8 A | | 2 V | 5 A | | | 400 ns | Ifav at Tc=60°C |
| FMU26S | J6 | c8 | RD | Rect. Pair | 600 V | 50 µA | 8 A | | 2 V | 5 A | | | 400 ns | Ifav at Tc=60°C |
| FMU36R | J11 | c8 | RD | Rect. Pair | 600 V | 10 µA | 12 A | | 1.5 V | 10 A | | | 400 ns | Ifav at Tc=118°C |
| FMU36S | J11 | c7 | RD | Rect. Pair | 600 V | 10 µA | 12 A | | 1.5 V | 10 A | | | 400 ns | Ifav at Tc=118°C |
| FMX22S | J6 | c7 | RD | Rect. Pair | 200 V | 100 µA | 10 A | | 0.98 V | 5 A | | | 30 ns | Ifav at Ta=103°C |
| FRP805 | I5 | a1 | NS | Rectifier | 50 V | 10 µA | 8 A | | <0.95 V | 8 A | | | <35 ns | |
| FRP810 | I5 | a1 | NS | Rectifier | 100 V | 10 µA | 8 A | | <0.95 V | 8 A | | | <35 ns | |
| FRP815 | I5 | a1 | NS | Rectifier | 150 V | 10 µA | 8 A | | <0.95 V | 8 A | | | <35 ns | |
| FRP820 | I5 | a1 | NS | Rectifier | 200 V | 10 µA | 8 A | | <0.95 V | 8 A | | | <35 ns | |
| FRP840 | I5 | a1 | NS | Rectifier | 400 V | 10 µA | 8 A | | <1.5 V | 8 A | | | <75 ns | |
| FRP850 | I5 | a1 | NS | Rectifier | 500 V | 10 µA | 8 A | | <1.5 V | 8 A | | | <75 ns | |
| FRP860 | I5 | a1 | NS | Rectifier | 600 V | 10 µA | 8 A | | <1.5 V | 8 A | | | <75 ns | |
| FRP1005 | I5 | a1 | NS | Rectifier | 50 V | 5 µA | 10 A | | <1 V | 10 A | | | <35 ns | |
| FRP1010 | I5 | a1 | NS | Rectifier | 100 V | 5 µA | 10 A | | <1 V | 10 A | | | <35 ns | |
| FRP1015 | I5 | a1 | NS | Rectifier | 150 V | 5 µA | 10 A | | <1 V | 10 A | | | <35 ns | |
| FRP1020 | I5 | a1 | NS | Rectifier | 200 V | 5 µA | 10 A | | <1 V | 10 A | | | <35 ns | |
| FRP1605 | I5 | a1 | NS | Rectifier | 50 V | 25 µA | 16 A | | <0.95 V | 16 A | | | <35 ns | |
| FRP1610 | I5 | a1 | NS | Rectifier | 100 V | 25 µA | 16 A | | <0.95 V | 16 A | | | <35 ns | |
| FRP1615 | I5 | a1 | NS | Rectifier | 150 V | 25 µA | 16 A | | <0.95 V | 16 A | | | <35 ns | |

| Type | Case | Pin-code | | | Maximum Ratings | | | | Electrical Characteristics | | | | | |
|---|---|---|---|---|---|---|---|---|---|---|---|---|---|---|
| | | | | | Vrm | Irm | Ifav Ifm | Pv | Vf | If Ifp | C0 | Cr | trr ts | |
| FRP1620 | I5 | a1 | NS | Rectifier | 200 V | 25 µA | 16 A | | <0.95 V | 16 A | | | <35 ns | |
| FRP1605CC | I5 | c7 | NS | Rect. Pair | 50 V | 10 µA | 8 A | | <0.95 V | 8 A | | | <35 ns | |
| FRP1610CC | I5 | c7 | NS | Rect. Pair | 100 V | 10 µA | 8 A | | <0.95 V | 8 A | | | <35 ns | |
| FRP1615CC | I5 | c7 | NS | Rect. Pair | 150 V | 10 µA | 8 A | | <0.95 V | 8 A | | | <35 ns | |
| FRP1620CC | I5 | c7 | NS | Rect. Pair | 200 V | 10 µA | 8 A | | <0.95 V | 8 A | | | <35 ns | |
| FRP1640CC | I5 | c7 | NS | Rect. Pair | 400 V | 10 µA | 8 A | | <1.5 V | 8 A | | | <75 ns | |
| FRP1650CC | I5 | c7 | NS | Rect. Pair | 500 V | 10 µA | 8 A | | <1.5 V | 8 A | | | <75 ns | |
| FRP1660CC | I5 | c7 | NS | Rect. Pair | 600 V | 10 µA | 8 A | | <1.5 V | 8 A | | | <75 ns | |
| FRP2005CC | I5 | c7 | NS | Rect. Pair | 50 V | 5 µA | 10 A | | <1 V | 10 A | | | <35 ns | |
| FRP2010CC | I5 | c7 | NS | Rect. Pair | 100 V | 5 µA | 10 A | | <1 V | 10 A | | | <35 ns | |
| FRP2015CC | I5 | c7 | NS | Rect. Pair | 150 V | 5 µA | 10 A | | <1 V | 10 A | | | <35 ns | |
| FRP2020CC | I5 | c7 | NS | Rect. Pair | 200 V | 5 µA | 10 A | | <1 V | 10 A | | | <35 ns | |
| FRP3205CC | I5 | c7 | NS | Rect. Pair | 50 V | 25 µA | 16 A | | <0.95 V | 16 A | | | <35 ns | |
| FRP3210CC | I5 | c7 | NS | Rect. Pair | 100 V | 25 µA | 16 A | | <0.95 V | 16 A | | | <35 ns | |
| FRP3215CC | I5 | c7 | NS | Rect. Pair | 150 V | 25 µA | 16 A | | <0.95 V | 16 A | | | <35 ns | |
| FRP3220CC | I5 | c7 | NS | Rect. Pair | 200 V | 25 µA | 16 A | | <0.95 V | 16 A | | | <35 ns | |
| GSC215 | I4 | c7 | RD | Rect. Pair | 150 V | 1 mA | 6 A | | 0.95 V | 3 A | | | 7 ns | Ifav at Ta=114°C |
| GSC218 | I4 | c7 | RD | Rect. Pair | 180 V | 1 mA | 6 A | | 0.95 V | 3 A | | | 7 ns | Ifav at Ta=115°C |
| GSC235 | I4 | c7 | RD | Rect. Pair | 350 V | 1 mA | 2 A | | 1.5 V | 1 A | | | 5 ns | Ifav at Ta=115°C |
| GSC315 | J11 | c7 | RD | Rect. Pair | 150 V | 3 mA | 14 A | | 0.95 V | 9 A | | | 10 ns | Ifav at Ta=80°C |
| GSC318 | J11 | c7 | RD | Rect. Pair | 180 V | 3 mA | 14 A | | 0.95 V | 9 A | | | 10 ns | Ifav at Ta=80°C |
| HD82A | N9 | j1 | RD | Array Univers | 200 V | | 600 mA | | | | | | | |
| HD84A | N9 | j1 | RD | Array Univers | 400 V | | 600 mA | | | | | | | |
| HD87A | N9 | j1 | RD | Array Univers | 1000 V | | 600 mA | | | | | | | |
| HD82K | N9 | j2 | RD | Array Univers | 200 V | | 600 mA | | | | | | | |
| HD84K | N9 | j2 | RD | Array Univers | 400 V | | 600 mA | | | | | | | |
| HD87K | N9 | j2 | RD | Array Univers | 1000 V | | 600 mA | | | | | | | |
| HDF82A | N9 | j1 | RD | Array Univers | 200 V | | 500 mA | | | | | | 300 ns | |
| HDF84A | N9 | j1 | RD | Array Univers | 400 V | | 500 mA | | | | | | 300 ns | |
| HDF82K | N9 | j2 | RD | Array Univers | 200 V | | 500 mA | | | | | | 300 ns | |
| HDF84K | N9 | j2 | RD | Array Univers | 400 V | | 500 mA | | | | | | 300 ns | |
| HVR1X-40B | B24 | a1 | RD | HV Rectifier | 9 kV | 10 µA | 350 mA | | 9 V | 350 mA | | | | Ifav at Ta=60°C |
| HVR2X062HOA | B24 | a1 | RD | HV Rectifier | 6 kV | 10 µA | | | | | | | | |
| LL42 | D2 | a1 | IT | Uni | 30 V | 0.5 µA | 60 mA | 0.2 W | <0.65 V | 50 mA | 10 pF | | <10 ns | |
| LL43 | D2 | a1 | IT | Uni | 30 V | 0.5 µA | 15 mA | 0.2 W | <0.45 V | 15 mA | 10 pF | | <10 ns | |
| LL46 | D2 | a1 | IT | Uni | 100 V | 5 µA | 250 mA | 0.2 W | <0.45 V | 10 mA | 10 pF | | <10 ns | |
| LL101A | D2 | a1 | IT,RD | Uni | 60 V | 0.2 µA | 150 mA | 0.4 W | <1 V | 15 mA | <2 pF | | <1 ns | |
| LL101B | D2 | a1 | IT,RD | Uni | 50 V | 0.2 µA | 150 mA | 0.4 W | <0.85 V | 15 mA | <2.1 pF | | <1 ns | |
| LL101C | D2 | a1 | IT,RD | Uni | 40 V | 0.2 µA | 150 mA | 0.4 W | <1 V | 15 mA | <2.2 pF | | <1 ns | |
| LL103A | D2 | a1 | IT | Uni | 40 V | 5 µA | | 0.4 W | 0.37 V | 20 mA | <50 pF | | <10 ns | |

| Type | Case | Pin-code | | | Maximum Ratings | | | | Electrical Characteristics | | | | | |
|---|---|---|---|---|---|---|---|---|---|---|---|---|---|---|
| | | | | | Vrm | Irm | Ifav Ifm | Pv | Vf | If Ifp | C0 | Cr | trr ts | |
| LL103B | D2 | a1 | IT | Uni | 30 V | 5 µA | | 0.4 W | 0.37 V | 20 mA | <50 pF | | <10 ns | |
| LL103C | D2 | a1 | IT | Uni | 20 V | 5 µA | | 0.4 W | 0.37 V | 20 mA | <50 pF | | <10 ns | |
| LL4148 | D2 | a1 | TE,IT,RD | Uni | 100 V | 25 nA | 150 mA | 0.5 W | <1 V | 10 mA | <4 pF | | <4 ns | Ir at 20V |
| LL4149 | D2 | a1 | TE,IT | Uni | 100 V | 25 nA | 150 mA | 0.5 W | <1 V | 10 mA | <4 pF | | <4 ns | Ir at 20V |
| LL4150 | D2 | a1 | TE,IT | Uni | 50 V | 0.1 µA | 200 mA | 0.5 W | <1 V | 200 mA | <4 pF | | <4 ns | Ir at 50V |
| LL4151 | D2 | a1 | TE,IT | Uni | 75 V | 50 nA | 150 mA | 0.5 W | <1 V | 50 mA | <2 pF | | <4 ns | Ir at 50V |
| LL4152 | D2 | a1 | IT | Uni | 40 V | 50 nA | 150 mA | 0.4 W | <0.55 V | 0.1 mA | <2 pF | | | Ir at 30V |
| LL4153 | D2 | a1 | IT | Uni | 75 V | 50 nA | 150 mA | 0.4 W | <0.55 V | 0.1 mA | <2 pF | | | Ir at 50V |
| LL4154 | D2 | a1 | TE,IT | Uni | 35 V | 0.1 µA | 150 mA | 0.5 W | <1 V | 30 mA | <2 pF | | <4 ns | Ir at 25V |
| LL4446 | D2 | a1 | TE,IT | Uni | 100 V | 25 nA | 150 mA | 0.5 W | <1 V | 20 mA | <4 pF | | <4 ns | Ir at 20V |
| LL4447 | D2 | a1 | TE,IT | Uni | 100 V | 25 nA | 150 mA | 0.5 W | <1 V | 20 mA | <4 pF | | <8 ns | Ir at 20V |
| LL4448 | D2 | a1 | TE,IT,RD | Uni | 100 V | 25 nA | 150 mA | 0.5 W | <1 V | 100 mA | <4 pF | | <8 ns | Ir at 20V |
| LL4449 | D2 | a1 | TE,IT | Uni | 100 V | 25 nA | 150 mA | 0.5 W | <1 V | 30 mA | <4 pF | | <8 ns | Ir at 20V |
| LL4450 | D2 | a1 | IT | Uni | 40 V | 50 nA | | 0.4 W | <0.54 V | 0.5 mA | <4 pF | | | Ir at 30V |
| LL4451 | D2 | a1 | IT | Uni | 40 V | 50 nA | | 0.4 W | <0.5 V | 0.1 mA | <10 pF | | | Ir at 30V |
| LL4453 | D2 | a1 | IT | Uni | 30 V | 50 nA | | 0.4 W | <0.55 V | 0.01 mA | | | | Ir at 20V |
| LL4454 | D2 | a1 | IT | Uni | 75 V | 0.1 µA | | 0.4 W | <1 V | 10 mA | <4 pF | | | Ir at 50V |
| LS4148 | -- | a1 | TE | Uni | 100 V | 5 µA | 150 mA | | 1 V | 10 mA | <4 pF | | <4 ns | Ir at 75V |
| LS4149 | -- | a1 | TE | Uni | 100 V | 5 µA | 150 mA | | <1 V | 10 mA | | | <4 ns | |
| LS4150 | -- | a1 | TE | Uni | 50 V | 0.1 µA | 200 mA | | <1 V | 200 mA | | | <4 ns | |
| LS4151 | -- | a1 | TE | Uni | 75 V | 50 nA | 150 mA | | <1 V | 50 mA | <2 pF | | <4 ns | Ir at 50V |
| LS4154 | -- | a1 | TE | Uni | 35 V | 5 µA | 150 mA | | <1 V | 30 mA | <4 pF | | <4 ns | Ir at 25V |
| LS4446 | -- | a1 | TE | Uni | 100 V | 5 µA | 150 mA | | <1 V | 10 mA | <4 pF | | <4 ns | Ir at 75V |
| LS4447 | -- | a1 | TE | Uni | 100 V | 5 µA | 150 mA | | <1 V | 20 mA | | | <4 ns | Ir at 75V |
| LS4448 | -- | a1 | TE | Uni | 100 V | 5 µA | 150 mA | | <1 V | 10 mA | <4 pF | | <4 ns | Ir at 75V |
| LS4449 | -- | a1 | TE | Uni | 100 V | 5 µA | 150 mA | | <1 V | 30 mA | | | <8 ns | Ir at 75V |
| LZ4001 | D1 | a1 | IT | Rectifier | 50 V | 5 µA | 1 A | | <1.75 V | 2 A | | | <300 ns | |
| LZ4002 | D1 | a1 | IT | Rectifier | 100 V | 5 µA | 1 A | | <1.75 V | 2 A | | | <300 ns | |
| LZ4003 | D1 | a1 | IT | Rectifier | 200 V | 5 µA | 1 A | | <1.75 V | 2 A | | | <300 ns | |
| MBR1100 | B1 | a1 | MO | Rectifier | 100 V | 0.5 mA | 1 A | | <0.79 V | 1 A | | | | |
| MBR150 | B1 | a1 | MO | Rectifier | 50 V | 0.5 mA | 1 A | | <0.75 V | 1 A | | | | |
| MBR160 | B1 | a1 | MO | Rectifier | 60 V | 0.5 mA | 1 A | | <0.75 V | 1 A | | | | |
| MBR170 | B1 | a1 | MO | Rectifier | 70 V | 0.5 mA | 1 A | | <0.79 V | 1 A | | | | |
| MBR180 | B1 | a1 | MO | Rectifier | 80 V | 0.5 mA | 1 A | | <0.79 V | 1 A | | | | |
| MBR190 | B1 | a1 | MO | Rectifier | 90 V | 0.5 mA | 1 A | | <0.79 V | 1 A | | | | |
| MBR3100 | B2 | a1 | MO | Rectifier | 100 V | 0.6 mA | 3 A | | <0.79 V | 1 A | | | | |
| MBR320 | B2 | a1 | MO | Rectifier | 20 V | 0.6 mA | 3 A | | <0.6 V | 1 A | | | | |
| MBR330 | B2 | a1 | MO | Rectifier | 30 V | 0.6 mA | 3 A | | <0.6 V | 1 A | | | | |
| MBR340 | B2 | a1 | MO | Rectifier | 40 V | 0.6 mA | 3 A | | <0.6 V | 1 A | | | | |
| MBR350 | B2 | a1 | MO | Rectifier | 50 V | 0.6 mA | 3 A | | <0.74 V | 1 A | | | | |

| Type | Case | Pin-code | (factory) | (rotation) | Maximum Ratings | | | | Electrical Characteristics | | | | | |
|------|------|----------|-----------|------------|-----------------|---|---|---|---------------------------|---|---|---|---|---|
| | | | | | Vrm | Irm | Ifav Ifm | Pv | Vf | If Ifp | C0 | Cr | trr ts | (notes) |
| MBR360 | B2 | a1 | MO | Rectifier | 60 V | 0.6 mA | 3 A | | <0.74 V | 1 A | | | | |
| MBR370 | B2 | a1 | MO | Rectifier | 70 V | 0.6 mA | 3 A | | <0.79 V | 1 A | | | | |
| MBR380 | B2 | a1 | MO | Rectifier | 80 V | 0.6 mA | 3 A | | <0.79 V | 1 A | | | | |
| MBR390 | B2 | a1 | MO | Rectifier | 90 V | 0.6 mA | 3 A | | <0.79 V | 1 A | | | | |
| MBR735 | I5 | a1 | MO | Rectifier | 35 V | 0.1 mA | 7.5 A | | <0.84 V | 15 A | | | | Ifav at Tc=105°C |
| MBR745 | I5 | a1 | MO | Rectifier | 45 V | 0.1 mA | 7.5 A | | <0.84 V | 15 A | | | | Ifav at Tc=105°C |
| MBR10100 | I5 | a1 | MO | Rectifier | 100 V | 0.15 mA | 10 A | | <0.95 V | 20 A | | | | |
| MBR1035 | I5 | a1 | MO | Rectifier | 35 V | 0.1 mA | 10 A | | <0.57 V | 20 A | | | | |
| MBR1045 | I5 | a1 | MO | Rectifier | 45 V | 0.1 mA | 10 A | | <0.57 V | 20 A | | | | |
| MBR1060 | I5 | a1 | MO | Rectifier | 60 V | 0.15 mA | 10 A | | <0.95 V | 20 A | | | | |
| MBR1070 | I5 | a1 | MO | Rectifier | 70 V | 0.15 mA | 10 A | | <0.95 V | 20 A | | | | |
| MBR1080 | I5 | a1 | MO | Rectifier | 80 V | 0.15 mA | 10 A | | <0.95 V | 20 A | | | | |
| MBR1090 | I5 | a1 | MO | Rectifier | 90 V | 0.15 mA | 10 A | | <0.95 V | 20 A | | | | |
| MBR1535CT | I5 | c7 | MO | Rect. Pair | 35 V | 0.1 mA | 7.5 A | | <0.84 V | 15 A | | | | |
| MBR1545CT | I5 | c7 | MO | Rect. Pair | 45 V | 0.1 mA | 7.5 A | | <0.84 V | 15 A | | | | |
| MBR1635 | I5 | a1 | MO | Rectifier | 35 V | 0.2 mA | 16 A | | <0.63 V | 16 A | | | | |
| MBR1645 | I5 | a1 | MO | Rectifier | 45 V | 0.2 mA | 16 A | | <0.63 V | 16 A | | | | |
| MBR2015CTL | I5 | c7 | MO | Rect. Pair | 15 V | 5 mA | 10 A | | <0.52 V | 10 A | | | | |
| MBR2030CTL | I5 | c7 | MO | Rect. Pair | 30 V | 5 mA | 10 A | | <0.52 V | 10 A | | | | |
| MBR20100CT | I5 | c7 | MO | Rect. Pair | 100 V | 0.1 mA | 10 A | | <0.85 V | 10 A | | | | |
| MBR2035CT | I5 | c7 | MO | Rect. Pair | 35 V | 0.1 mA | 20 A | | <0.84 V | 20 A | | | | |
| MBR2045CT | I5 | c7 | MO | Rect. Pair | 45 V | 0.1 mA | 20 A | | <0.84 V | 20 A | | | | |
| MBR2060CT | I5 | c7 | MO | Rect. Pair | 60 V | 0.1 mA | 10 A | | <0.85 V | 10 A | | | | |
| MBR2080CT | I5 | c7 | MO | Rect. Pair | 80 V | 0.1 mA | 10 A | | <0.85 V | 10 A | | | | |
| MBR2090CT | I5 | c7 | MO | Rect. Pair | 90 V | 0.1 mA | 10 A | | <0.85 V | 10 A | | | | |
| MBR2535CT | I5 | c7 | MO | Rect. Pair | 35 V | 0.2 mA | 30 A | | <0.82 V | 30 A | | | | Ifav at Tc=130°C |
| MBR2545CT | I5 | c7 | MO | Rect. Pair | 45 V | 0.2 mA | 30 A | | <0.82 V | 30 A | | | | Ifav at Tc=130°C |
| MBR2535CTL | I5 | c7 | MO | Rect. Pair | 35 V | 5 mA | 12.5 A | | <0.47 V | 12.5 A | | | | |
| MBR3020CT | L1 | c5 | MO | Rect. Pair | 20 V | 1 mA | 15 A | | <0.76 V | 30 A | 2 nF | | | |
| MBR3035CT | L1 | c5 | MO | Rect. Pair | 35 V | 1 mA | 15 A | | <0.76 V | 30 A | 2 nF | | | |
| MBR3045CT | L1 | c5 | MO | Rect. Pair | 45 V | 1 mA | 15 A | | <0.76 V | 30 A | 2 nF | | | |
| SD241 | L1 | c5 | MO | Rect. Pair | 45 V | | 15 A | | <0.6 V | 20 A | 2 nF | | | |
| MBR3035PT | I16 | c7 | MO | Rect. Pair | 35 V | 1 mA | 15 A | | <0.76 V | 30 A | | | | Ifav at Tc=105°C |
| MBR3045PT | I16 | c7 | MO | Rect. Pair | 45 V | 1 mA | 15 A | | <0.76 V | 30 A | | | | Ifav at Tc=105°C |
| MBR3035WT | J10 | c7 | MO | Rect. Pair | 35 V | 1 mA | 15 A | | <0.76 V | 30 A | | | | Ifav at Tc=105°C |
| MBR3045WT | J10 | c7 | MO | Rect. Pair | 45 V | 1 mA | 15 A | | <0.76 V | 30 A | | | | Ifav at Tc=105°C |
| MBR3520 | E2 | a1 | MO | Rectifier | 20 V | 0.1 mA | 35 A | | <0.55 V | 35 A | 3 nF | | | Ifav at Tc=110°C |
| MBR3535 | E2 | a1 | MO | Rectifier | 35 V | 0.1 mA | 35 A | | <0.55 V | 35 A | 3 nF | | | Ifav at Tc=110°C |
| MBR3545 | E2 | a1 | MO | Rectifier | 35 V | 0.3 mA | 35 A | | <0.63 V | 35 A | 3.7 nF | | | Ifav at Tc=110°C |
| MBR3545H | E2 | a1 | MO | Rectifier | 35 V | 0.3 mA | 35 A | | <0.63 V | 35 A | 3.7 nF | | | Ifav at Tc=110°C |

**MBR3545H1 – MBR30045CT**

| Type | Case | Pin-code | | | Vrm | Irm | Ifav Ifm | Pv | Vf | If Ifp | C0 | Cr | trr ts | |
|------|------|----------|--|--|-----|-----|----------|-----|-----|--------|-----|-----|--------|--|
| MBR3545H1 | E2 | a1 | MO | Rectifier | 35 V | 0.3 mA | 35 A | | <0.63 V | 35 A | 3.7 nF | | | Ifav at Tc=110°C |
| MBR4045PT | I16 | c7 | MO | Rect. Pair | 45 V | 1 mA | 20 A | | <0.7 V | 20 A | | | | Ifav at Tc=125°C |
| MBR4045WT | J10 | c7 | MO | Rect. Pair | 45 V | 1 mA | 20 A | | <0.7 V | 20 A | | | | Ifav at Tc=125°C |
| MBR5025L | I19 | a1 | MO | Rectifier | 25 V | 0.5 mA | 50 A | | <0.54 V | 30 A | | | | Ifav at Tc=125°C |
| MBR5825H | C3 | a1 | MO | Rectifier | 40 V | 10 mA | 5 A | | 0.38 V | 5 A | | | | |
| MBR5825H1 | C3 | a1 | MO | Rectifier | 40 V | 10 mA | 5 A | | 0.38 V | 5 A | | | | |
| MBR5831H | E2 | a1 | MO | Rectifier | 40 V | 20 mA | 25 A | | <0.48 V | 25 A | | | | |
| MBR5831H1 | E2 | a1 | MO | Rectifier | 40 V | 20 mA | 25 A | | <0.48 V | 25 A | | | | |
| MBR6015L | E4 | a1 | MO | Rectifier | 15 V | 0.5 mA | 60 A | | <0.42 V | 30 A | | | | Ifav at Tc=120°C |
| MBR6020L | E4 | a1 | MO | Rectifier | 20 V | 0.5 mA | 60 A | | <0.42 V | 30 A | | | | Ifav at Tc=120°C |
| MBR6025L | E4 | a1 | MO | Rectifier | 25 V | 0.5 mA | 60 A | | <0.42 V | 30 A | | | | Ifav at Tc=120°C |
| MBR6030L | E4 | a1 | MO | Rectifier | 30 V | 0.5 mA | 60 A | | <0.42 V | 30 A | | | | Ifav at Tc=120°C |
| MBR6035 | E4 | a1 | MO | Rectifier | 35 V | 0.1 mA | 60 A | | <0.65 V | 60 A | 3 nF | | | Ifav at Tc=100°C |
| MBR6035B | E4 | a1 | MO | Rectifier | 35 V | 0.1 mA | 60 A | | <0.65 V | 60 A | 3 nF | | | Ifav at Tc=100°C |
| MBR6045 | E4 | a1 | MO | Rectifier | 45 V | 0.3 mA | 60 A | | <0.65 V | 60 A | 3.7 nF | | | Ifav at Tc=100°C |
| MBR6045B | E4 | a1 | MO | Rectifier | 45 V | 0.3 mA | 60 A | | <0.65 V | 60 A | 3.7 nF | | | Ifav at Tc=100°C |
| MBR6045H | E4 | a1 | MO | Rectifier | 45 V | 0.3 mA | 60 A | | <0.65 V | 60 A | 3.7 nF | | | Ifav at Tc=100°C |
| MBR6045H1 | E4 | a1 | MO | Rectifier | 45 V | 0.3 mA | 60 A | | <0.65 V | 60 A | 3.7 nF | | | Ifav at Tc=100°C |
| MBR6045WT | J10 | c7 | MO | Rect. Pair | 45 V | 1 mA | 30 A | | <0.62 V | 30 A | 3.7 nF | | | Ifav at Tc=90°C |
| MBR6535 | E4 | a1 | MO | Rectifier | 35 V | 70 µA | 65 A | | <0.78 V | 65 A | 3.7 nF | | | Ifav at Tc=120°C |
| MBR6545 | E4 | a1 | MO | Rectifier | 45 V | 70 µA | 65 A | | <0.78 V | 65 A | 3.7 nF | | | Ifav at Tc=120°C |
| MBR7545 | E4 | a1 | MO | Rectifier | 45 V | 150 mA | 75 A | | <0.6 V | 65 A | 4 nF | | | Ir at Tc=125°C |
| MBR7535 | E4 | a1 | MO | Rectifier | 35 V | 150 mA | 75 A | | <0.6 V | 60 A | 4 nF | | | Ir at Tc=125°C |
| MBR8035 | E4 | a1 | MO | Rectifier | 35 V | 1 mA | 80 A | | <0.72 V | 80 A | 5 nF | | | Ifav at Tc=120°C |
| MBR8045 | E4 | a1 | MO | Rectifier | 45 V | 1 mA | 80 A | | <0.72 V | 80 A | 5 nF | | | Ifav at Tc=120°C |
| MBR12035CT | H1 | c5 | MO | Rect. Pair | 35 V | 0.25 mA | 60 A | | <0.59 V | 60 A | | | | Ifav at Tc=140°C |
| MBR12045CT | E4 | a1 | MO | Rect. Pair | 45 V | 0.25 mA | 60 A | | <0.59 V | 60 A | | | | Ifav at Tc=140°C |
| MBR12050CT | E4 | a1 | MO | Rect. Pair | 50 V | 0.25 mA | 60 A | | <0.59 V | 60 A | | | | Ifav at Tc=140°C |
| MBR12060CT | E4 | a1 | MO | Rect. Pair | 60 V | 0.25 mA | 60 A | | <0.59 V | 60 A | | | | Ifav at Tc=140°C |
| MBR20015CTL | H1 | c5 | MO | Rect. Pair | 15 V | 5 mA | 100 A | | <0.46 V | 100 A | | | | Ifav at Tc=140°C |
| MBR20020CTL | H1 | c5 | MO | Rect. Pair | 20 V | 5 mA | 100 A | | <0.46 V | 100 A | | | | Ifav at Tc=140°C |
| MBR20025CTL | H1 | c5 | MO | Rect. Pair | 25 V | 5 mA | 100 A | | <0.46 V | 100 A | | | | Ifav at Tc=140°C |
| MBR20030CTL | H1 | c5 | MO | Rect. Pair | 30 V | 5 mA | 100 A | | <0.46 V | 100 A | | | | Ifav at Tc=140°C |
| MBR20035CT | H1 | c5 | MO | Rect. Pair | 35 V | 0.5 mA | 100 A | | <0.8 V | 100 A | | | | Ifav at Tc=140°C |
| MBR20045CT | H1 | c5 | MO | Rect. Pair | 45 V | 0.5 mA | 100 A | | <0.8 V | 100 A | | | | Ifav at Tc=140°C |
| MBR20050CT | H1 | c5 | MO | Rect. Pair | 50 V | 0.5 mA | 100 A | | <0.8 V | 100 A | | | | Ifav at Tc=140°C |
| MBR20060CT | H1 | c5 | MO | Rect. Pair | 60 V | 0.5 mA | 100 A | | <0.8 V | 100 A | | | | Ifav at Tc=140°C |
| MBR20200CT | I5 | c7 | MO | Rect. Pair | 200 V | 1 mA | 10 A | | <0.9 V | 10 A | 500 pF | | | Ifav at Tc=125°C |
| MBR30035CT | H1 | c5 | MO | Rect. Pair | 35 V | 0.8 mA | 150 A | | <0.74 V | 150 A | | | | Ifav at Tc=140°C |
| MBR30045CT | H1 | c5 | MO | Rect. Pair | 45 V | 0.8 mA | 150 A | | <0.74 V | 150 A | | | | Ifav at Tc=140°C |

MBR30050CT – MMBD1402

| Type | Case | Pin-code | | | Vrm | Irm | Ifav Ifm | Pv | Vf | If Ifp | C0 | Cr | trr ts | |
|---|---|---|---|---|---|---|---|---|---|---|---|---|---|---|
| MBR30050CT | H1 | c5 | MO | Rect. Pair | 50 V | 0.8 mA | 150 A | | <0.74 V | 150 A | | | | Ifav at Tc=140°C |
| MBR30060CT | H1 | c5 | MO | Rect. Pair | 60 V | 0.8 mA | 150 A | | <0.74 V | 150 A | | | | Ifav at Tc=140°C |
| MBR60035CTL | H1 | c5 | MO | Rect. Pair | 40 V | 10 mA | 300 A | | <0.57 V | 300 A | | | | Ifav at Tc=100°C |
| MBRB1545CT | F9 | c5 | MO | Rect. Pair | 45 V | 0.1 mA | 7.5 A | | <0.84 V | 15 A | | | | Ifav at Tc=105°C |
| MBRB2060CT | F9 | c5 | MO | Rect. Pair | 60 V | 0.15 mA | 10 A | | <0.95 V | 20 A | | | | Ifav at Tc=110°C |
| MBRB2515L | F9 | c14 | MO | Rectifier | 15 V | 15 mA | 25 A | | <0.45 V | 25 A | | | | Ifav at Tc=100°C |
| MBRB2535CTL | F9 | c5 | MO | Rect. Pair | 40 V | 10 mA | 12.5 A | | <0.55 V | 25 A | | | | Ifav at Tc=110°C |
| MBRB2545CT | F9 | c5 | MO | Rect. Pair | 45 V | 0.2 mA | 15 A | | <0.82 V | 30 A | | | | Ifav at Tc=130°C |
| MBRB20100CT | F9 | c5 | MO | Rect. Pair | 100 V | 0.15 mA | 10 A | | <0.85 V | 10 A | | | | Ifav at Tc=110°C |
| MBRD320 | F11 | c14 | MO | Rectifier | 20 V | 0.2 mA | 3 A | | <0.6 V | 3 A | | | | Ifav at Tc=125°C |
| MBRD330 | F11 | c14 | MO | Rectifier | 30 V | 0.2 mA | 3 A | | <0.6 V | 3 A | | | | Ifav at Tc=125°C |
| MBRD340 | F11 | c14 | MO | Rectifier | 40 V | 0.2 mA | 3 A | | <0.6 V | 3 A | | | | Ifav at Tc=125°C |
| MBRD350 | F11 | c14 | MO | Rectifier | 50 V | 0.2 mA | 3 A | | <0.6 V | 3 A | | | | Ifav at Tc=125°C |
| MBRD360 | F11 | c14 | MO | Rectifier | 60 V | 0.2 mA | 3 A | | <0.6 V | 3 A | | | | Ifav at Tc=125°C |
| MBRD620CT | F11 | c5 | MO | Rect. Pair | 20 V | 0.2 mA | 3 A | | <0.7 V | 3 A | | | | Ifav at Tc=130°C |
| MBRD630CT | F11 | c5 | MO | Rect. Pair | 30 V | 0.2 mA | 3 A | | <0.7 V | 3 A | | | | Ifav at Tc=130°C |
| MBRD640CT | F11 | c5 | MO | Rect. Pair | 40 V | 0.2 mA | 3 A | | <0.7 V | 3 A | | | | Ifav at Tc=130°C |
| MBRD650CT | F11 | c5 | MO | Rect. Pair | 50 V | 0.2 mA | 3 A | | <0.7 V | 3 A | | | | Ifav at Tc=130°C |
| MBRD660CT | F11 | c5 | MO | Rect. Pair | 60 V | 0.2 mA | 3 A | | <0.7 V | 3 A | | | | Ifav at Tc=130°C |
| MBRF2535CT | J12 | c7 | MO | Rect. Pair | 35 V | 0.2 mA | 12.5 A | | <0.7 V | 12.5 A | | | | Ifav at Tc=125°C |
| MBRF2545CT | J12 | c7 | MO | Rect. Pair | 45 V | 0.2 mA | 12.5 A | | <0.7 V | 12.5 A | | | | Ifav at Tc=125°C |
| MBRS130LT3 | G1 | a1 | MO | Rectifier | 30 V | 1 mA | 2 A | | <0.45 V | 2 A | | | | Ifav at Tc=110°C |
| MBRS140LT3 | G1 | a1 | MO | Rectifier | 40 V | 1 mA | 1 A | | <0.6 V | 1 A | | | | Ifav at Tc=115°C |
| MBRS340T3 | G2 | a1 | MO | Rectifier | 40 V | 2 mA | 3 A | | <0.52 V | 3 A | | | | Ifav at Tc=100°C |
| MBRS1100T3 | G1 | a1 | MO | Rectifier | 100 V | 0.5 mA | 1 A | | <0.75 V | 1 A | | | | Ifav at Tc=120°C |
| MD10H1 | B23 | a1 | RD | HV Rectifier | 10 kV | 5 µA | 15 mA | | 18 V | 15 mA | | | 500 ns | Ifav at Ta=50°C |
| MD12H1 | B23 | a1 | RD | HV Rectifier | 12 kV | 5 µA | 12 mA | | 21 V | 12 mA | | | 500 ns | Ifav at Ta=50°C |
| MD15H1 | B23 | a1 | RD | HV Rectifier | 15 kV | 10 µA | 10 mA | | 27 V | 10 mA | | | 500 ns | Ifav at Ta=50°C |
| MD20H1 | B23 | a1 | RD | HV Rectifier | 20 kV | 5 µA | 10 mA | | 36 V | 10 mA | | | 500 ns | Ifav at Ta=50°C |
| MD22H1 | B23 | a1 | RD | HV Rectifier | 22 kV | 5 µA | 10 mA | | 36 V | 10 mA | | | 500 ns | Ifav at Ta=50°C |
| MD3H1 | B21 | a1 | RD | HV Rectifier | 3 kV | 5 µA | 50 mA | | 7 V | 50 mA | | | 500 ns | Ifav at Ta=50°C |
| MD6H1 | B23 | a1 | RD | HV Rectifier | 6 kV | 5 µA | 30 mA | | 12 V | 30 mA | | | 500 ns | Ifav at Ta=50°C |
| MD36N4 | B22 | a1 | RD | HV Rectifier | 36 kV | 5 µA | 400 mA | | 38 V | 400 mA | | | | Ifav at Ta=50°C |
| MMBD1201 | F1 | c3 | NS | Uni | 100 V | 25 nA | | | <1 V | 200 mA | | | <50 ns | |
| MMBD1202 | F1 | c17 | NS | Uni | 100 V | 25 nA | | | <1 V | 200 mA | | | <50 ns | |
| MMBD1203 | F1 | c8 | NS | Pair Switch | 100 V | 25 nA | | | <1 V | 200 mA | | | <50 ns | |
| MMBD1204 | F1 | c5 | NS | Pair Switch | 100 V | 25 nA | | | <1 V | 200 mA | | | <50 ns | |
| MMBD1205 | F1 | c7 | NS | Pair Switch | 100 V | 25 nA | | | <1 V | 200 mA | | | <50 ns | |
| MMBD1401 | F1 | c3 | NS | Uni | 200 V | 100 nA | | | <1 V | 200 mA | | | <50 ns | |
| MMBD1402 | F1 | c17 | NS | Uni | 200 V | 100 nA | | | <1 V | 200 mA | | | <50 ns | |

| Type | Case | Pin-code | | | Vrm | Irm | Ifav Ifm | Pv | Vf | If Ifp | C0 | Cr | trr ts | |
|---|---|---|---|---|---|---|---|---|---|---|---|---|---|---|
| | | | | **Maximum Ratings** | | | | | **Electrical Characteristics** | | | | | |
| MMBD1403 | F1 | c8 | NS | Pair Switch | 200 V | 100 nA | | | <1 V | 200 mA | | | <50 ns | |
| MMBD1404 | F1 | c5 | NS | Pair Switch | 200 V | 100 nA | | | <1 V | 200 mA | | | <50 ns | |
| MMBD1405 | F1 | c7 | NS | Pair Switch | 200 V | 100 nA | | | <1 V | 200 mA | | | <50 ns | |
| MMBD1501A | F1 | c3 | NS | Uni | 200 V | 1 nA | | | <1.1 V | 200 mA | | | <50 ns | |
| MMBD1502A | F1 | c17 | NS | Uni | 200 V | 1 nA | | | <1.1 V | 200 mA | | | <50 ns | |
| MMBD1503A | F1 | c8 | NS | Pair Switch | 200 V | 1 nA | | | <1.1 V | 200 mA | | | <50 ns | |
| MMBD1504A | F1 | c5 | NS | Pair Switch | 200 V | 1 nA | | | <1.1 V | 200 mA | | | <50 ns | |
| MMBD1505A | F1 | c7 | NS | Pair Switch | 200 V | 1 nA | | | <1.1 V | 200 mA | | | <50 ns | |
| MMBD1701 | F1 | c3 | NS | Uni | 30 V | 50 nA | | | <1.1 V | 50 mA | | | <50 ns | |
| MMBD1702 | F1 | c17 | NS | Uni | 30 V | 50 nA | | | <1.1 V | 50 mA | | | <50 ns | |
| MMBD1703 | F1 | c8 | NS | Pair Switch | 30 V | 50 nA | | | <1.1 V | 50 mA | | | <50 ns | |
| MMBD1704 | F1 | c5 | NS | Pair Switch | 30 V | 50 nA | | | <1.1 V | 50 mA | | | <50 ns | |
| MMBD1705 | F1 | c7 | NS | Pair Switch | 30 V | 50 nA | | | <1.1 V | 50 mA | | | <50 ns | |
| MR750 | B15 | a1 | MO | Rectifier | 50 V | 25 µA | 6 A | | <0.9 V | 6 A | | | | |
| MR751 | B15 | a1 | MO | Rectifier | 100 V | 25 µA | 6 A | | <0.9 V | 6 A | | | | |
| MR752 | B15 | a1 | MO | Rectifier | 200 V | 25 µA | 6 A | | <0.9 V | 6 A | | | | |
| MR754 | B15 | a1 | MO | Rectifier | 400 V | 25 µA | 6 A | | <0.9 V | 6 A | | | | |
| MR756 | B15 | a1 | MO | Rectifier | 600 V | 25 µA | 6 A | | <0.9 V | 6 A | | | | |
| MR758 | B15 | a1 | MO | Rectifier | 800 V | 25 µA | 6 A | | <0.9 V | 6 A | | | | |
| MR760 | B15 | a1 | MO | Rectifier | 1000 V | 25 µA | 6 A | | <0.9 V | 6 A | | | | |
| MR820 | B15 | a1 | MO | Rectifier | 50 V | 25 µA | 5 A | | <1.1 V | 5 A | | | <200 ns | |
| MR821 | B15 | a1 | MO | Rectifier | 100 V | 25 µA | 5 A | | <1.1 V | 5 A | | | <200 ns | |
| MR822 | B15 | a1 | MO | Rectifier | 200 V | 25 µA | 5 A | | <1.1 V | 5 A | | | <200 ns | |
| MR824 | B15 | a1 | MO | Rectifier | 400 V | 25 µA | 5 A | | <1.1 V | 5 A | | | <200 ns | |
| MR826 | B15 | a1 | MO | Rectifier | 600 V | 25 µA | 5 A | | <1.1 V | 5 A | | | <200 ns | |
| MR830 | C3 | a1 | MO | Rectifier | 50 V | 0.5 mA | 3 A | | <1.1 V | 3 A | | | <200 ns | |
| MR831 | C3 | a1 | MO | Rectifier | 100 V | 0.5 mA | 3 A | | <1.1 V | 3 A | | | <200 ns | |
| MR832 | C3 | a1 | MO | Rectifier | 200 V | 0.5 mA | 3 A | | <1.1 V | 3 A | | | <200 ns | |
| MR834 | C3 | a1 | MO | Rectifier | 400 V | 0.5 mA | 3 A | | <1.1 V | 3 A | | | <200 ns | |
| MR836 | C3 | a1 | MO | Rectifier | 600 V | 0.5 mA | 3 A | | <1.1 V | 3 A | | | <200 ns | |
| MR850 | B2 | a1 | MO | Rectifier | 50 V | 10 µA | 3 A | | <1.25 V | 3 A | | | <200 ns | |
| MR851 | B2 | a1 | MO | Rectifier | 100 V | 10 µA | 3 A | | <1.25 V | 3 A | | | <200 ns | |
| MR852 | B2 | a1 | MO | Rectifier | 200 V | 10 µA | 3 A | | <1.25 V | 3 A | | | <200 ns | |
| MR854 | B2 | a1 | MO | Rectifier | 400 V | 10 µA | 3 A | | <1.25 V | 3 A | | | <200 ns | |
| MR856 | B2 | a1 | MO | Rectifier | 600 V | 10 µA | 3 A | | <1.25 V | 3 A | | | <200 ns | |
| MR1120 | E2 | a1 | MO | Rectifier | 50 V | 0.5 mA | 12 A | | <1 V | 12 A | | | | Ifav at Tc=150°C |
| MR1121 | E2 | a1 | MO | Rectifier | 100 V | 0.5 mA | 12 A | | <1 V | 12 A | | | | Ifav at Tc=150°C |
| MR1122 | E2 | a1 | MO | Rectifier | 200 V | 0.5 mA | 12 A | | <1 V | 12 A | | | | Ifav at Tc=150°C |
| MR1123 | E2 | a1 | MO | Rectifier | 300 V | 0.5 mA | 12 A | | <1 V | 12 A | | | | Ifav at Tc=150°C |
| MR1124 | E2 | a1 | MO | Rectifier | 400 V | 0.5 mA | 12 A | | <1 V | 12 A | | | | Ifav at Tc=150°C |

| Type | Case | Pin-code | | | Maximum Ratings Vrm | Irm | Ifav Ifm | Pv | Electrical Characteristics Vf | If Ifp | C0 | Cr | trr ts | |
|------|------|----------|---|---|---|---|---|---|---|---|---|---|---|---|
| MR1125 | E2 | a1 | MO | Rectifier | 500 V | 0.5 mA | 12 A | | <1 V | 12 A | | | | Ifav at Tc=150°C |
| MR1126 | E2 | a1 | MO | Rectifier | 600 V | 0.5 mA | 12 A | | <1 V | 12 A | | | | Ifav at Tc=150°C |
| MR1128 | E2 | a1 | MO | Rectifier | 800 V | 0.5 mA | 12 A | | <1 V | 12 A | | | | Ifav at Tc=150°C |
| MR1130 | E2 | a1 | MO | Rectifier | 1000 V | 0.5 mA | 12 A | | <1 V | 12 A | | | | Ifav at Tc=150°C |
| MR1366 | E2 | a1 | MO | Rectifier | 600 V | 15 µA | 6 A | | <1.4 V | 6 A | | | <200 ns | Ifav at Tc=100°C |
| MR1376 | E2 | a1 | MO | Rectifier | 600 V | 25 µA | 12 A | (20) W | <1.4 V | 12 A | | | <200 ns | Ifav at Tc=100°C |
| MR1386 | E4 | a1 | MO | Rectifier | 600 V | 50 µA | 20 A | | <1.4 V | 20 A | | | <200 ns | Ifav at Tc=100°C |
| MR1396 | E4 | a1 | MO | Rectifier | 600 V | 50 µA | 30 A | | <1.4 V | 30 A | | | <200 ns | Ifav at Tc=100°C |
| MR2000 | E2 | a1 | MO | Rectifier | 50 V | 100 µA | 20 A | | <1.1 V | 63 A | | | | Ifav at Tc=150°C |
| MR2001 | E2 | a1 | MO | Rectifier | 100 V | 100 µA | 20 A | | <1.1 V | 63 A | | | | Ifav at Tc=150°C |
| MR2002 | E2 | a1 | MO | Rectifier | 200 V | 100 µA | 20 A | | <1.1 V | 63 A | | | | Ifav at Tc=150°C |
| MR2004 | E2 | a1 | MO | Rectifier | 400 V | 100 µA | 20 A | | <1.1 V | 63 A | | | | Ifav at Tc=150°C |
| MR2006 | E2 | a1 | MO | Rectifier | 600 V | 100 µA | 20 A | | <1.1 V | 63 A | | | | Ifav at Tc=150°C |
| MR2008 | E2 | a1 | MO | Rectifier | 800 V | 100 µA | 20 A | | <1.1 V | 63 A | | | | Ifav at Tc=150°C |
| MR2010 | E2 | a1 | MO | Rectifier | 1000 V | 100 µA | 20 A | | <1.1 V | 63 A | | | | Ifav at Tc=150°C |
| MR2400 | I20 | a1 | MO | Rectifier | 50 V | 25 µA | 24 A | | <1.18 V | 75.4 A | | | | Ifav at Tc=150°C |
| MR2401 | I20 | a1 | MO | Rectifier | 100 V | 25 µA | 24 A | | <1.18 V | 75.4 A | | | | Ifav at Tc=150°C |
| MR2402 | I20 | a1 | MO | Rectifier | 200 V | 25 µA | 24 A | | <1.18 V | 75.4 A | | | | Ifav at Tc=150°C |
| MR2404 | I20 | a1 | MO | Rectifier | 400 V | 25 µA | 24 A | | <1.18 V | 75.4 A | | | | Ifav at Tc=150°C |
| MR2406 | I20 | a1 | MO | Rectifier | 600 V | 25 µA | 24 A | | <1.18 V | 75.4 A | | | | Ifav at Tc=150°C |
| MR2400F | I20 | a1 | MO | Rectifier | 50 V | 25 µA | 24 A | | <1.29 V | 75 A | | | | Ifav at Tc=150°C |
| MR2401F | I20 | a1 | MO | Rectifier | 100 V | 25 µA | 24 A | | <1.29 V | 75 A | | | | Ifav at Tc=150°C |
| MR2402F | I20 | a1 | MO | Rectifier | 200 V | 25 µA | 24 A | | <1.29 V | 75 A | | | | Ifav at Tc=150°C |
| MR2404F | I20 | a1 | MO | Rectifier | 400 V | 25 µA | 24 A | | <1.29 V | 75 A | | | | Ifav at Tc=150°C |
| MR2406F | I20 | a1 | MO | Rectifier | 600 V | 25 µA | 24 A | | <1.29 V | 75 A | | | | Ifav at Tc=150°C |
| MR2500 | B14 | a1 | MO | Rectifier | 50 V | 100 µA | 25 A | | <1.18 V | 78.5 A | | | | Ifav at Tc=150°C |
| MR2501 | B14 | a1 | MO | Rectifier | 100 V | 100 µA | 25 A | | <1.18 V | 78.5 A | | | | Ifav at Tc=150°C |
| MR2502 | B14 | a1 | MO | Rectifier | 200 V | 100 µA | 25 A | | <1.18 V | 78.5 A | | | | Ifav at Tc=150°C |
| MR2504 | B14 | a1 | MO | Rectifier | 400 V | 100 µA | 25 A | | <1.18 V | 78.5 A | | | | Ifav at Tc=150°C |
| MR2506 | B14 | a1 | MO | Rectifier | 600 V | 100 µA | 25 A | | <1.18 V | 78.5 A | | | | Ifav at Tc=150°C |
| MR2508 | B14 | a1 | MO | Rectifier | 800 V | 100 µA | 25 A | | <1.18 V | 78.5 A | | | | Ifav at Tc=150°C |
| MR2510 | B14 | a1 | MO | Rectifier | 1000 V | 100 µA | 25 A | | <1.18 V | 78.5 A | | | | Ifav at Tc=150°C |
| MR4422CT | L1 | c5 | MO | Rect. Pair | 100 V | 1 mA | 15 A | | <1.2 V | 15 A | | | | Ifav at Tc=125°C |
| MR4422CTR | L1 | c5 | MO | Rect. Pair | 100 V | 1 mA | 15 A | | <1.2 V | 15 A | | | | Ifav at Tc=125°C |
| MR10120E | I5 | a1 | MO | Rectifier | 1200 V | 50 µA | 10 A | | <1.5 V | 6.5 A | | | <175 ns | Ifav at Tc=125°C |
| MR10150E | I5 | a1 | MO | Rectifier | 1500 V | 100 µA | 10 A | | <1.5 V | 6.5 A | | | <175 ns | Ifav at Tc=125°C |
| MUR105 | B1 | a1 | MO | Rectifier | 50 V | 50 µA | 1 A | | <0.87 V | 1 A | | | <35 ns | Ifav at Ta=130°C |
| MUR110 | B1 | a1 | MO | Rectifier | 100 V | 50 µA | 1 A | | <0.87 V | 1 A | | | <35 ns | Ifav at Ta=130°C |
| MUR115 | B1 | a1 | MO | Rectifier | 150 V | 50 µA | 1 A | | <0.87 V | 1 A | | | <35 ns | Ifav at Ta=130°C |
| MUR120 | B1 | a1 | MO | Rectifier | 200 V | 50 µA | 1 A | | <0.87 V | 1 A | | | <35 ns | Ifav at Ta=130°C |

| Type | Case | Pin-code | | | Maximum Ratings | | | | Electrical Characteristics | | | | | |
|------|------|----------|---|---|-----------------|---|---|---|----------------------------|---|---|---|---|---|
| | | | | | Vrm | Irm | Ifav Ifm | Pv | Vf | If Ifp | C0 | Cr | trr ts | |
| MUR130 | B1 | a1 | MO | Rectifier | 300 V | 150 µA | 1 A | | <1.25 V | 1 A | | | <75 ns | Ifav at Ta=120°C |
| MUR140 | B1 | a1 | MO | Rectifier | 400 V | 150 µA | 1 A | | <1.25 V | 1 A | | | <75 ns | Ifav at Ta=120°C |
| MUR150 | B1 | a1 | MO | Rectifier | 500 V | 150 µA | 1 A | | <1.25 V | 1 A | | | <75 ns | Ifav at Ta=120°C |
| MUR160 | B1 | a1 | MO | Rectifier | 600 V | 150 µA | 1 A | | <1.25 V | 1 A | | | <75 ns | Ifav at Ta=120°C |
| MUR1100E | B1 | a1 | MO | Rectifier | 1000 V | 10 µA | 1 A | | <1.75 V | 1 A | | | <75 ns | Ifav at Ta=95°C |
| MUR170E | B1 | a1 | MO | Rectifier | 700 V | 10 µA | 1 A | | <1.75 V | 1 A | | | <75 ns | Ifav at Ta=95°C |
| MUR180E | B1 | a1 | MO | Rectifier | 800 V | 10 µA | 1 A | | <1.75 V | 1 A | | | <75 ns | Ifav at Ta=95°C |
| MUR190E | B1 | a1 | MO | Rectifier | 900 V | 10 µA | 1 A | | <1.75 V | 1 A | | | <75 ns | Ifav at Ta=95°C |
| MUR405 | B13 | a1 | MO | Rectifier | 50 V | 10 µA | 4 A | | <0.89 V | 4 A | | | <35 ns | Ifav at Ta=80°C |
| MUR410 | B13 | a1 | MO | Rectifier | 100 V | 10 µA | 4 A | | <0.89 V | 4 A | | | <35 ns | Ifav at Ta=80°C |
| MUR415 | B13 | a1 | MO | Rectifier | 150 V | 10 µA | 4 A | | <0.89 V | 4 A | | | <35 ns | Ifav at Ta=80°C |
| MUR420 | B13 | a1 | MO | Rectifier | 200 V | 10 µA | 4 A | | <0.89 V | 4 A | | | <35 ns | Ifav at Ta=80°C |
| MUR430 | B13 | a1 | MO | Rectifier | 300 V | 10 µA | 4 A | | <1.28 V | 4 A | | | <75 ns | Ifav at Ta=40°C |
| MUR440 | B13 | a1 | MO | Rectifier | 400 V | 10 µA | 4 A | | <1.28 V | 4 A | | | <75 ns | Ifav at Ta=40°C |
| MUR450 | B13 | a1 | MO | Rectifier | 500 V | 10 µA | 4 A | | <1.28 V | 4 A | | | <75 ns | Ifav at Ta=40°C |
| MUR460 | B13 | a1 | MO | Rectifier | 600 V | 10 µA | 4 A | | <1.28 V | 4 A | | | <75 ns | Ifav at Ta=40°C |
| MUR4100E | B2 | a1 | MO | Rectifier | 1000 V | 25 µA | 4 A | | <1.85 V | 4 A | | | <75 ns | Ifav at Ta=35°C |
| MUR470E | B2 | a1 | MO | Rectifier | 700 V | 25 µA | 4 A | | <1.85 V | 4 A | | | <75 ns | Ifav at Ta=35°C |
| MUR480E | B2 | a1 | MO | Rectifier | 800 V | 25 µA | 4 A | | <1.85 V | 4 A | | | <75 ns | Ifav at Ta=35°C |
| MUR490E | B2 | a1 | MO | Rectifier | 900 V | 25 µA | 4 A | | <1.85 V | 4 A | | | <75 ns | Ifav at Ta=35°C |
| MUR605CT | I5 | c7 | MO | Rect. Pair | 50 V | 5 µA | 3 A | | <0.97 V | 3 A | | | <35 ns | Ifav at Tc=130°C |
| MUR610CT | I5 | c7 | MO | Rect. Pair | 100 V | 5 µA | 3 A | | <0.97 V | 3 A | | | <35 ns | Ifav at Tc=130°C |
| MUR615CT | I5 | c7 | MO | Rect. Pair | 150 V | 5 µA | 3 A | | <0.97 V | 3 A | | | <35 ns | Ifav at Tc=130°C |
| MUR620CT | I5 | c7 | MO | Rect. Pair | 200 V | 5 µA | 3 A | | <0.97 V | 3 A | | | <35 ns | Ifav at Tc=130°C |
| MUR805 | I5 | a1 | MO | Rectifier | 50 V | 10 µA | 8 A | | <0.97 V | 8 A | | | <35 ns | Ifav at Tc=150°C |
| MUR810 | I5 | a1 | MO | Rectifier | 100 V | 10 µA | 8 A | | <0.97 V | 8 A | | | <35 ns | Ifav at Tc=150°C |
| MUR815 | I5 | a1 | MO | Rectifier | 150 V | 10 µA | 8 A | | <0.97 V | 8 A | | | <35 ns | Ifav at Tc=150°C |
| MUR820 | I5 | a1 | MO | Rectifier | 200 V | 10 µA | 8 A | | <0.97 V | 8 A | | | <35 ns | Ifav at Tc=150°C |
| MUR830 | I5 | a1 | MO | Rectifier | 300 V | 10 µA | 8 A | | <1.3 V | 8 A | | | <60 ns | Ifav at Tc=150°C |
| MUR840 | I5 | a1 | MO | Rectifier | 400 V | 10 µA | 8 A | | <1.3 V | 8 A | | | <60 ns | Ifav at Tc=150°C |
| MUR850 | I5 | a1 | MO | Rectifier | 500 V | 10 µA | 8 A | | <1.5 V | 8 A | | | <60 ns | Ifav at Tc=150°C |
| MUR860 | I5 | a1 | MO | Rectifier | 600 V | 10 µA | 8 A | | <1.5 V | 8 A | | | <60 ns | Ifav at Tc=150°C |
| MUR8100E | I5 | a1 | MO | Rectifier | 1000 V | 25 µA | 8 A | | <1.8 V | 8 A | | | <100 ns | Ifav at Tc=150°C |
| MUR870E | I5 | a1 | MO | Rectifier | 700 V | 25 µA | 8 A | | <1.8 V | 8 A | | | <100 ns | Ifav at Tc=150°C |
| MUR880E | I5 | a1 | MO | Rectifier | 800 V | 25 µA | 8 A | | <1.8 V | 8 A | | | <100 ns | Ifav at Tc=150°C |
| MUR890E | I5 | a1 | MO | Rectifier | 900 V | 25 µA | 8 A | | <1.8 V | 8 A | | | <100 ns | Ifav at Tc=150°C |
| MUR1505 | I5 | a1 | MO | Rectifier | 50 V | 10 µA | 15 A | | <1.05 V | 15 A | | | <35 ns | Ifav at Tc=150°C |
| MUR1510 | I5 | a1 | MO | Rectifier | 100 V | 10 µA | 15 A | | <1.05 V | 15 A | | | <35 ns | Ifav at Tc=150°C |
| MUR1515 | I5 | a1 | MO | Rectifier | 150 V | 10 µA | 15 A | | <1.05 V | 15 A | | | <35 ns | Ifav at Tc=150°C |
| MUR1520 | I5 | a1 | MO | Rectifier | 200 V | 10 µA | 15 A | | <1.05 V | 15 A | | | <35 ns | Ifav at Tc=150°C |

| Type | Case | Pin-code | | | Maximum Ratings | | | | Electrical Characteristics | | | | | |
|---|---|---|---|---|---|---|---|---|---|---|---|---|---|---|
| | | | | | Vrm | Irm | Ifav Ifm | Pv | Vf | If Ifp | C0 | Cr | trr ts | |
| MUR1530 | I5 | a1 | MO | Rectifier | 300 V | 10 µA | 15 A | | <1.25 V | 15 A | | | <60 ns | Ifav at Tc=145°C |
| MUR1540 | I5 | a1 | MO | Rectifier | 400 V | 10 µA | 15 A | | <1.25 V | 15 A | | | <60 ns | Ifav at Tc=145°C |
| MUR1550 | I5 | a1 | MO | Rectifier | 500 V | 10 µA | 15 A | | <1.50 V | 15 A | | | <60 ns | Ifav at Tc=145°C |
| MUR1560 | I5 | a1 | MO | Rectifier | 600 V | 10 µA | 15 A | | <1.50 V | 15 A | | | <60 ns | Ifav at Tc=145°C |
| MUR1605CT | I5 | c7 | MO | Rect. Pair | 50 V | 5 µA | 8 A | | <0.97 V | 8 A | | | <35 ns | Ifav at Tc=150°C |
| MUR1610CT | I5 | c7 | MO | Rect. Pair | 100 V | 5 µA | 8 A | | <0.97 V | 8 A | | | <35 ns | Ifav at Tc=150°C |
| MUR1615CT | I5 | c7 | MO | Rect. Pair | 150 V | 5 µA | 8 A | | <0.97 V | 8 A | | | <35 ns | Ifav at Tc=150°C |
| MUR1620CT | I5 | c7 | MO | Rect. Pair | 200 V | 5 µA | 8 A | | <0.97 V | 8 A | | | <35 ns | Ifav at Tc=150°C |
| MUR1630CT | I5 | c7 | MO | Rect. Pair | 300 V | 10 µA | 8 A | | <1.3 V | 8 A | | | <60 ns | Ifav at Tc=150°C |
| MUR1640CT | I5 | c7 | MO | Rect. Pair | 400 V | 10 µA | 8 A | | <1.3 V | 8 A | | | <60 ns | Ifav at Tc=150°C |
| MUR1650CT | I5 | c7 | MO | Rect. Pair | 500 V | 10 µA | 8 A | | <1.3 V | 8 A | | | <60 ns | Ifav at Tc=150°C |
| MUR1660CT | I5 | c7 | MO | Rect. Pair | 600 V | 10 µA | 8 A | | <1.3 V | 8 A | | | <60 ns | Ifav at Tc=150°C |
| MUR1605CTR | I5 | c7 | MO | Rect. Pair | 50 V | 10 µA | 8 A | | <1.1 V | 8 A | | | <85 ns | Ifav at Tc=160°C |
| MUR1610CTR | I5 | c7 | MO | Rect. Pair | 100 V | 10 µA | 8 A | | <1.1 V | 8 A | | | <85 ns | Ifav at Tc=160°C |
| MUR1615CTR | I5 | c7 | MO | Rect. Pair | 150 V | 10 µA | 8 A | | <1.1 V | 8 A | | | <85 ns | Ifav at Tc=160°C |
| MUR1620CTR | I5 | c7 | MO | Rect. Pair | 200 V | 10 µA | 8 A | | <1.1 V | 8 A | | | <85 ns | Ifav at Tc=160°C |
| MUR2505 | E2 | a1 | MO | Rectifier | 50 V | 10 µA | 25 A | | <0.95 V | 25 A | | | <50 ns | Ifav at Tc=145°C |
| MUR2510 | E2 | a1 | MO | Rectifier | 100 V | 10 µA | 25 A | | <0.95 V | 25 A | | | <50 ns | Ifav at Tc=145°C |
| MUR2515 | E2 | a1 | MO | Rectifier | 150 V | 10 µA | 25 A | | <0.95 V | 25 A | | | <50 ns | Ifav at Tc=145°C |
| MUR2520 | E2 | a1 | MO | Rectifier | 200 V | 10 µA | 25 A | | <0.95 V | 25 A | | | <50 ns | Ifav at Tc=145°C |
| MUR3005PT | I16 | c7 | MO | Rect. Pair | 50 V | 10 µA | 14 A | | <1.05 V | 15 A | | | <35 ns | Ifav at Tc=150°C |
| MUR3010PT | I16 | c7 | MO | Rect. Pair | 100 V | 10 µA | 14 A | | <1.05 V | 15 A | | | <35 ns | Ifav at Tc=150°C |
| MUR3015PT | I16 | c7 | MO | Rect. Pair | 150 V | 10 µA | 14 A | | <1.05 V | 15 A | | | <35 ns | Ifav at Tc=150°C |
| MUR3020PT | I16 | c7 | MO | Rect. Pair | 200 V | 10 µA | 14 A | | <1.05 V | 15 A | | | <35 ns | Ifav at Tc=150°C |
| MUR3030PT | I16 | c7 | MO | Rect. Pair | 300 V | 10 µA | 14 A | | <1.25 V | 15 A | | | <60 ns | Ifav at Tc=150°C |
| MUR3040PT | I16 | c7 | MO | Rect. Pair | 400 V | 10 µA | 14 A | | <1.25 V | 15 A | | | <60 ns | Ifav at Tc=145°C |
| MUR3050PT | I16 | c7 | MO | Rect. Pair | 500 V | 10 µA | 14 A | | <1.5 V | 15 A | | | <60 ns | Ifav at Tc=145°C |
| MUR3060PT | I16 | c7 | MO | Rect. Pair | 600 V | 10 µA | 14 A | | <1.5 V | 15 A | | | <60 ns | Ifav at Tc=145°C |
| MUR3020 | I19 | a1 | MO | Rectifier | 200 V | 35 µA | 30 A | | <1.5 V | 30 A | | | <100 ns | Ifav at Tc=70°C |
| MUR3030 | I19 | a1 | MO | Rectifier | 300 V | 35 µA | 30 A | | <1.5 V | 30 A | | | <100 ns | Ifav at Tc=70°C |
| MUR3040 | I19 | a1 | MO | Rectifier | 400 V | 35 µA | 30 A | | <1.5 V | 30 A | | | <100 ns | Ifav at Tc=70°C |
| MUR3020WT | J10 | c7 | MO | Rect. Pair | 200 V | 10 µA | 15 A | | <1.05 V | 15 A | | | <35 ns | Ifav at Tc=145°C |
| MUR3040WT | J10 | c7 | MO | Rect. Pair | 400 V | 10 µA | 15 A | | <1.25 V | 15 A | | | <60 ns | Ifav at Tc=145°C |
| MUR3060WT | J10 | c7 | MO | Rect. Pair | 600 V | 10 µA | 15 A | | <1.7 V | 15 A | | | <60 ns | Ifav at Tc=145°C |
| MUR5005 | E4 | a1 | MO | Rectifier | 50 V | 10 µA | 50 A | | <1.15 V | 50 A | | | <50 ns | Ifav at Tc=125°C |
| MUR5010 | E4 | a1 | MO | Rectifier | 100 V | 10 µA | 50 A | | <1.15 V | 50 A | | | <50 ns | Ifav at Tc=125°C |
| MUR5015 | E4 | a1 | MO | Rectifier | 150 V | 10 µA | 50 A | | <1.15 V | 50 A | | | <50 ns | Ifav at Tc=125°C |
| MUR5020 | E4 | a1 | MO | Rectifier | 200 V | 10 µA | 50 A | | <1.15 V | 50 A | | | <50 ns | Ifav at Tc=125°C |
| MUR5150E | I5 | a1 | MO | Rectifier | 1500 V | 50 µA | 5 A | | <2 V | 2 A | | | <175 ns | Ifav at Tc=100°C |
| MUR6020 | I19 | a1 | MO | Rectifier | 200 V | 60 µA | 60 A | | <1.5 V | 60 A | | | <100 ns | Ifav at Tc=150°C |

| Type | Case | Pin-code | | | Maximum Ratings Vrm | Irm | Ifav Ifm | Pv | Electrical Characteristics Vf | If Ifp | C0 | Cr | trr ts | |
|---|---|---|---|---|---|---|---|---|---|---|---|---|---|---|
| MUR6030 | I19 | a1 | MO | Rectifier | 300 V | 60 µA | 60 A | | <1.5 V | 60 A | | | <100 ns | Ifav at Tc=150°C |
| MUR6040 | I19 | a1 | MO | Rectifier | 400 V | 60 µA | 60 A | | <1.5 V | 60 A | | | <100 ns | Ifav at Tc=150°C |
| MUR7005 | E4 | a1 | MO | Rectifier | 50 V | 25 µA | 70 A | | <0.97 V | 70 A | | | <60 ns | Ifav at Tc=125°C |
| MUR7010 | E4 | a1 | MO | Rectifier | 100 V | 25 µA | 70 A | | <0.97 V | 70 A | | | <60 ns | Ifav at Tc=125°C |
| MUR7015 | E4 | a1 | MO | Rectifier | 150 V | 25 µA | 70 A | | <0.97 V | 70 A | | | <60 ns | Ifav at Tc=125°C |
| MUR7020 | E4 | a1 | MO | Rectifier | 200 V | 25 µA | 70 A | | <0.97 V | 70 A | | | <60 ns | Ifav at Tc=125°C |
| MUR10005CT | H1 | c5 | MO | Rect. Pair | 50 V | 25 µA | 50 A | | <1.1 V | 50 A | | | <50 ns | Ifav at Tc=140°C |
| MUR10010CT | H1 | c5 | MO | Rect. Pair | 100 V | 25 µA | 50 A | | <1.1 V | 50 A | | | <50 ns | Ifav at Tc=140°C |
| MUR10015CT | H1 | c5 | MO | Rect. Pair | 150 V | 25 µA | 50 A | | <1.1 V | 50 A | | | <50 ns | Ifav at Tc=140°C |
| MUR10020CT | H1 | c5 | MO | Rect. Pair | 200 V | 25 µA | 50 A | | <1.1 V | 50 A | | | <50 ns | Ifav at Tc=140°C |
| MUR10120E | I5 | a1 | MO | Rectifier | 1200 V | 100 µA | 10 A | | <2.2 V | 6.5 A | | | <175 ns | Ifav at Tc=125°C |
| MUR10150E | I5 | a1 | MO | Rectifier | 1500 V | 100 µA | 10 A | | <2.2 V | 6.5 A | | | <175 ns | Ifav at Tc=125°C |
| MUR20005CT | H1 | c5 | MO | Rect. Pair | 50 V | 50 µA | 100 A | | <1.25 V | 100 A | | | <50 ns | Ifav at Tc=95°C |
| MUR20010CT | H1 | c5 | MO | Rect. Pair | 100 V | 50 µA | 100 A | | <1.25 V | 100 A | | | <50 ns | Ifav at Tc=95°C |
| MUR20015CT | H1 | c5 | MO | Rect. Pair | 150 V | 50 µA | 100 A | | <1.25 V | 100 A | | | <50 ns | Ifav at Tc=95°C |
| MUR20020CT | H1 | c5 | MO | Rect. Pair | 200 V | 50 µA | 100 A | | <1.25 V | 100 A | | | <50 ns | Ifav at Tc=95°C |
| MUR20030CT | H1 | c5 | MO | Rect. Pair | 300 V | 50 µA | 100 A | | <1.35 V | 100 A | | | <75 ns | Ifav at Tc=95°C |
| MUR20040CT | H1 | c5 | MO | Rect. Pair | 400 V | 50 µA | 100 A | | <1.35 V | 100 A | | | <75 ns | Ifav at Tc=95°C |
| MURD305 | F11 | c14 | MO | Rectifier | 50 V | 5 µA | 3 A | | <0.95 V | 3 A | | | <35 ns | Ifav at Tc=158°C |
| MURD310 | F11 | c14 | MO | Rectifier | 100 V | 5 µA | 3 A | | <0.95 V | 3 A | | | <35 ns | Ifav at Tc=158°C |
| MURD315 | F11 | c14 | MO | Rectifier | 150 V | 5 µA | 3 A | | <0.95 V | 3 A | | | <35 ns | Ifav at Tc=158°C |
| MURD320 | F11 | c14 | MO | Rectifier | 200 V | 5 µA | 3 A | | <0.95 V | 3 A | | | <35 ns | Ifav at Tc=158°C |
| MURD605CT | F11 | c5 | MO | Rect. Pair | 50 V | 5 µA | 3 A | | <1 V | 3 A | | | <35 ns | Ifav at Tc=145°C |
| MURD610CT | F11 | c5 | MO | Rect. Pair | 100 V | 5 µA | 3 A | | <1 V | 3 A | | | <35 ns | Ifav at Tc=145°C |
| MURD615CT | F11 | c5 | MO | Rect. Pair | 150 V | 5 µA | 3 A | | <1 V | 3 A | | | <35 ns | Ifav at Tc=145°C |
| MURD620CT | F11 | c5 | MO | Rect. Pair | 200 V | 5 µA | 3 A | | <1 V | 3 A | | | <35 ns | Ifav at Tc=145°C |
| MURH840CT | I5 | c7 | MO | Rect. Pair | 400 V | 10 µA | 4 A | | <2.2 V | 4 A | | | <28 ns | Ifav at Tc=120°C |
| MURH860CT | I5 | c7 | MO | Rect. Pair | 600 V | 10 µA | 4 A | | <2.5 V | 4 A | | | <35 ns | Ifav at Tc=120°C |
| MURHB840CT | F9 | c5 | MO | Rect. Pair | 400 V | 10 µA | 4 A | | <2 V | 4 A | | | <28 ns | Ifav at Tc=120°C |
| MURS120T3 | G1 | a1 | MO | Rectifier | 200 V | 5 µA | 1 A | | <0.87 V | 1 A | | | <35 ns | Ifav at Tc=155°C |
| MURS160T3 | G1 | a1 | MO | Rectifier | 600 V | 5 µA | 1 A | | <1.05 V | 1 A | | | <50 ns | Ifav at Tc=155°C |
| MURS320T3 | G2 | a1 | MO | Rectifier | 200 V | 5 µA | 3 A | | <0.87 V | 3 A | | | <35 ns | Ifav at Tc=140°C |
| MURS360T3 | G2 | a1 | MO | Rectifier | 600 V | 5 µA | 3 A | | <1.05 V | 3 A | | | <50 ns | Ifav at Tc=140°C |
| O5B4B48 | F14 | d23 | TO | Rect. Bridge | 100 V | 10 µA | 500 mA | | <1 V | 400 mA | | | | |
| O5G4B48 | F14 | d23 | TO | Rect. Bridge | 400 V | 10 µA | 500 mA | | <1 V | 400 mA | | | | |
| O5J4B48 | F14 | d23 | TO | Rect. Bridge | 600 V | 10 µA | 500 mA | | <1 V | 400 mA | | | | |
| O5GU4B48 | F14 | d23 | TO | Rect. Bridge | 400 V | 100 µA | 500 mA | | <0.65 V | 20 mA | | | | |
| O5NH45 | A16 | a1 | TO | Rectifier | 1000 V | 100 µA | 500 mA | | <1.5 V | 500 mA | | | <200 ns | |
| O5NH46 | A17 | a1 | TO | Rectifier | 1000 V | 100 µA | 500 mA | | <1.5 V | 500 mA | | | <200 ns | |
| O5NU41 | A16 | a1 | TO | Rectifier | 1000 V | 100 µA | 500 mA | | <3 V | 500 mA | | | <100 ns | |

| Type | Case | Pin-code | | | Maximum Ratings | | | | Electrical Characteristics | | | | | |
|---|---|---|---|---|---|---|---|---|---|---|---|---|---|---|
| | | | | | Vrm | Irm | Ifav Ifm | Pv | Vf | If Ifp | C0 | Cr | trr ts | |
| O5NU42 | A17 | a1 | TO | Rectifier | 1000 V | 100 µA | 500 mA | | <3 V | 500 mA | | | <100 ns | |
| OR8GU41 | A3 | a1 | TO | Rectifier | 400 V | 50 µA | 800 mA | | <1.5 V | 1 A | | | <100 ns | |
| P600A | B6 | a1 | RD | Rectifier | 50 V | 25 µA | 6 A | | 0.9 V | 6 A | | | | |
| P600B | B6 | a1 | RD | Rectifier | 100 V | 25 µA | 6 A | | 0.9 V | 6 A | | | | |
| P600D | B6 | a1 | RD | Rectifier | 200 V | 25 µA | 6 A | | 0.9 V | 6 A | | | | |
| P600G | B6 | a1 | RD | Rectifier | 400 V | 25 µA | 6 A | | 0.9 V | 6 A | | | | |
| P600J | B6 | a1 | RD | Rectifier | 600 V | 25 µA | 6 A | | 0.9 V | 6 A | | | | |
| P600K | B6 | a1 | RD | Rectifier | 800 V | 25 µA | 6 A | | 0.9 V | 6 A | | | | |
| PBYR635CT | I18 | c7 | PH | Rect. Pair | 35 V | 100 µA | 5 A | | <0.87 V | 10 A | 200 pF | | | |
| PBYR640CT | I18 | c7 | PH | Rect. Pair | 40 V | 100 µA | 5 A | | <0.87 V | 10 A | 200 pF | | | |
| PBYR645CT | I18 | c7 | PH | Rect. Pair | 45 V | 100 µA | 5 A | | <0.87 V | 10 A | 200 pF | | | |
| PBYR735 | I5 | a1 | PH | Rectifier | 35 V | 100 µA | 7.5 A | | <0.84 V | 15 A | | | | |
| PBYR740 | I5 | a1 | PH | Rectifier | 40 V | 100 µA | 7.5 A | | <0.84 V | 15 A | | | | |
| PBYR745 | I5 | a1 | PH | Rectifier | 45 V | 100 µA | 7.5 A | | <0.84 V | 15 A | | | | |
| PBYR735F | J7 | a1 | PH | Rectifier | 35 V | 100 µA | 7.5 A | | <0.84 V | 15 A | | | | |
| PBYR740F | J7 | a1 | PH | Rectifier | 40 V | 100 µA | 7.5 A | | <0.84 V | 15 A | | | | |
| PBYR745F | J7 | a1 | PH | Rectifier | 45 V | 100 µA | 7.5 A | | <0.84 V | 15 A | | | | |
| PBYR1035 | I5 | a1 | PH | Rectifier | 35 V | 100 µA | 10 A | | <0.84 V | 20 A | | | | |
| PBYR1040 | I5 | a1 | PH | Rectifier | 40 V | 100 µA | 10 A | | <0.84 V | 20 A | | | | |
| PBYR1045 | I5 | a1 | PH | Rectifier | 45 V | 100 µA | 10 A | | <0.84 V | 20 A | | | | |
| PBYR1035F | J7 | a1 | PH | Rectifier | 35 V | 100 µA | 10 A | | <0.84 V | 20 A | | | | |
| PBYR1040F | J7 | a1 | PH | Rectifier | 40 V | 100 µA | 10 A | | <0.84 V | 20 A | | | | |
| PBYR1045F | J7 | a1 | PH | Rectifier | 45 V | 100 µA | 10 A | | <0.84 V | 20 A | | | | |
| PBYR1535CT | I4 | c7 | PH | Rect. Pair | 35 V | 100 µA | 7.5 A | | <0.84 V | 15 A | | | | |
| PBYR1540CT | I4 | c7 | PH | Rect. Pair | 40 V | 100 µA | 7.5 A | | <0.84 V | 15 A | | | | |
| PBYR1545CT | I4 | c7 | PH | Rect. Pair | 45 V | 100 µA | 7.5 A | | <0.84 V | 15 A | | | | |
| PBYR1535CTF | J8 | c7 | PH | Rect. Pair | 35 V | 100 µA | 7.5 A | | <0.84 V | 15 A | | | | |
| PBYR1540CTF | J8 | c7 | PH | Rect. Pair | 40 V | 100 µA | 7.5 A | | <0.84 V | 15 A | | | | |
| PBYR1545CTF | J8 | c7 | PH | Rect. Pair | 45 V | 100 µA | 7.5 A | | <0.84 V | 15 A | | | | |
| PBYR1635 | I5 | a1 | PH | Rectifier | 35 V | 100 µA | 16 A | | <0.63 V | 16 A | | | | |
| PBYR1640 | I5 | a1 | PH | Rectifier | 40 V | 100 µA | 16 A | | <0.63 V | 16 A | | | | |
| PBYR1645 | I5 | a1 | PH | Rectifier | 45 V | 100 µA | 16 A | | <0.63 V | 16 A | | | | |
| PBYR1635F | I5 | a1 | PH | Rectifier | 35 V | 100 µA | 16 A | | <0.63 V | 16 A | | | | |
| PBYR1640F | I5 | a1 | PH | Rectifier | 40 V | 100 µA | 16 A | | <0.63 V | 16 A | | | | |
| PBYR1645F | I5 | a1 | PH | Rectifier | 45 V | 100 µA | 16 A | | <0.63 V | 16 A | | | | |
| PBYR2035CT | I4 | c7 | PH | Rect. Pair | 35 V | 100 µA | 10 A | | <0.84 V | 20 A | | | | |
| PBYR2040CT | I4 | c7 | PH | Rect. Pair | 40 V | 100 µA | 10 A | | <0.84 V | 20 A | | | | |
| PBYR2045CT | I4 | c7 | PH | Rect. Pair | 45 V | 100 µA | 10 A | | <0.84 V | 20 A | | | | |
| PBYR2035CTF | J8 | c7 | PH | Rect. Pair | 35 V | 100 µA | 10 A | | <0.84 V | 20 A | | | | |
| PBYR2040CTF | J8 | c7 | PH | Rect. Pair | 40 V | 100 µA | 10 A | | <0.84 V | 20 A | | | | |

| Type | Case | Pin-code | | | Maximum Ratings | | | | Electrical Characteristics | | | | | |
|---|---|---|---|---|---|---|---|---|---|---|---|---|---|---|
| | | | | | Vrm | Irm | Ifav Ifm | Pv | Vf | If Ifp | C0 | Cr | trr ts | |
| PBYR2045CTF | J8 | c7 | PH | Rect. Pair | 45 V | 100 μA | 10 A | | <0.84 V | 20 A | | | | |
| PBYR2535CT | I4 | c7 | PH | Rect. Pair | 35 V | 200 μA | 15 A | | <0.82 V | 30 A | | | | |
| PBYR2540CT | I4 | c7 | PH | Rect. Pair | 40 V | 200 μA | 15 A | | <0.82 V | 30 A | | | | |
| PBYR2545CT | I4 | c7 | PH | Rect. Pair | 45 V | 200 μA | 15 A | | <0.82 V | 30 A | | | | |
| PBYR2535CTF | J8 | c7 | PH | Rect. Pair | 35 V | 200 μA | 15 A | | <0.82 V | 30 A | | | | |
| PBYR2540CTF | J8 | c7 | PH | Rect. Pair | 40 V | 200 μA | 15 A | | <0.82 V | 30 A | | | | |
| PBYR2545CTF | J8 | c7 | PH | Rect. Pair | 45 V | 200 μA | 15 A | | <0.82 V | 30 A | | | | |
| PBYR3035PT | I17 | c7 | PH | Rect. Pair | 35 V | 1 mA | 15 A | | <0.76 V | 30 A | | | | |
| PBYR3040PT | I17 | c7 | PH | Rect. Pair | 40 V | 1 mA | 15 A | | <0.76 V | 30 A | | | | |
| PBYR3045PT | I17 | c7 | PH | Rect. Pair | 45 V | 1 mA | 15 A | | <0.76 V | 30 A | | | | |
| PBYR12035T | H2 | d2 | PH | Rect. Pair | 35 V | 2 μA | 60 A | | <0.96 V | 120 A | 2100 pF | | | |
| PBYR12040T | H2 | d2 | PH | Rect. Pair | 40 V | 2 mA | 60 A | | <0.96 V | 120 A | 2100 pF | | | |
| PBYR12045T | H2 | d2 | PH | Rect. Pair | 45 V | 2 mA | 60 A | | <0.96 V | 120 A | 2100 pF | | | |
| PBYR12035TV | H3 | d2 | PH | Rect. Pair | 35 V | 2 mA | 60 A | | <0.96 V | 120 A | 2100 pF | | | |
| PBYR12040TV | H3 | d2 | PH | Rect. Pair | 40 V | 2 mA | 60 A | | <0.96 V | 120 A | 2100 pF | | | |
| PBYR12045TV | H3 | d2 | PH | Rect. Pair | 45 V | 2 mA | 60 A | | <0.96 V | 120 A | 2100 pF | | | |
| PBYR16035T | H2 | d2 | PH | Rect. Pair | 35 V | 2 mA | 80 A | | <1 V | 160 A | 2500 pF | | | |
| PBYR16040T | H2 | d2 | PH | Rect. Pair | 40 V | 2 mA | 80 A | | <1 V | 160 A | 2500 pF | | | |
| PBYR16045T | H2 | d2 | PH | Rect. Pair | 45 V | 2 mA | 80 A | | <1 V | 160 A | 2500 pF | | | |
| PBYR16035TV | H3 | d2 | PH | Rect. Pair | 35 V | 2 mA | 80 A | | <1 V | 160 A | 2500 pF | | | |
| PBYR16040TV | H3 | d2 | PH | Rect. Pair | 40 V | 2 mA | 80 A | | <1 V | 160 A | 2500 pF | | | |
| PBYR16045TV | H3 | d2 | PH | Rect. Pair | 45 V | 2 mA | 80 A | | <1 V | 160 A | 2500 pF | | | |
| PBYR30035CT | H1 | c5 | PH | Rect. Pair | 35 V | 4 mA | 150 A | | <0.72 V | 150 A | | | | |
| PBYR30040CT | H1 | c5 | PH | Rect. Pair | 40 V | 4 mA | 150 A | | <0.72 V | 150 A | | | | |
| PBYR30045CT | H1 | c5 | PH | Rect. Pair | 45 V | 4 mA | 150 A | | <0.72 V | 150 A | | | | |
| PBYR40035CT | H1 | c5 | PH | Rect. Pair | 35 V | 4 mA | 200 A | | <0.69 V | 200 A | | | | |
| PBYR40040CT | H1 | c5 | PH | Rect. Pair | 40 V | 4 mA | 200 A | | <0.69 V | 200 A | | | | |
| PBYR40045CT | H1 | c5 | PH | Rect. Pair | 45 V | 4 mA | 200 A | | <0.69 V | 200 A | | | | |
| PFR305 | b5 | a1 | SG | Rectifier | 50 V | 10 μA | 3 A | 3 W | <1.0 V | 1 A | | | <50 ns | Ifav at Tc=90°C |
| PFR310 | b5 | a1 | SG | Rectifier | 100 V | 10 μA | 3 A | 3 W | <1.0 V | 1 A | | | <50 ns | Ifav at Tc=90°C |
| PFR850 | b5 | a1 | SG | Rectifier | 50 V | 10 μA | 3 A | 3.5 W | <1.25 V | 3 A | | | <150 ns | Ifav at Tc=90°C |
| PFR851 | b5 | a1 | SG | Rectifier | 100 V | 10 μA | 3 A | 3.5 W | <1.25 V | 3 A | | | <150 ns | Ifav at Tc=90°C |
| PFR852 | b5 | a1 | SG | Rectifier | 200 V | 10 μA | 3 A | 3.5 W | <1.25 V | 3 A | | | <150 ns | Ifav at Tc=90°C |
| PFR854 | b5 | a1 | SG | Rectifier | 400 V | 10 μA | 3 A | 3.5 W | <1.25 V | 3 A | | | <150 ns | Ifav at Tc=90°C |
| PFR856 | b5 | a1 | SG | Rectifier | 600 V | 10 μA | 3 A | 3.5 W | <1.25 V | 3 A | | | <200 ns | Ifav at Tc=90°C |
| PLQ1 | B4 | a1 | SG | Rectifier | 100 V | 10 μA | 1 A | 1.7 W | <1.1 V | 1 A | | | <50 ns | |
| PLQ08 | B4 | a1 | SG | Rectifier | 80 V | 10 μA | 1 A | 1.7 W | <1.1 V | 1 A | | | <50 ns | |
| PMBD914 | F1 | c3 | PH | Switch | (70) V | 5 μA | 200 mA | 0.3 W | <1 V | 10 mA | <4 pF | | <4 ns | |
| PMBD2835 | F1 | c8 | PH | Switch | (35) V | 0.1 μA | 100 mA | 0.3 W | <1 V | 50 mA | <4 pF | | <6 ns | Ir at 30V |
| PMBD2836 | F1 | c8 | PH | Switch | (75) V | 0.1 μA | 100 mA | 0.3 W | <1 V | 50 mA | <4 pF | | <6 ns | Ir at 50V |

| Type | Case | Pin-code | | | Maximum Ratings | | | | Electrical Characteristics | | | | | |
|---|---|---|---|---|---|---|---|---|---|---|---|---|---|---|
| | | | | | Vrm | Irm | Ifav Ifm | Pv | Vf | If Ifp | C0 | Cr | trr ts | |
| PMBD2837 | F1 | c5 | PH | Pair Switch | 35 V | 0.1 µA | 150 mA | 0.3 W | <1 V | 50 mA | <4 pF | | <6 ns | Ir at 30V |
| PMBD2838 | F1 | c5 | PH | Pair Switch | 75 V | 0.1 µA | 150 mA | 0.3 W | <1 V | 50 mA | <4 pF | | <6 ns | Ir at 50V |
| PMBD6050 | F1 | c3 | PH | Switch | (70) V | 0.1 µA | 200 mA | 0.3 W | <1.1 V | 100 mA | <2.5 pF | | <4 ns | Ir at 50V |
| PMBD6100 | F1 | c5 | PH | Pair Switch | (70) V | 0.1 µA | 200 mA | 0.3 W | <1.1 V | 100 mA | <2.5 pF | | <6 ns | Ir at 50V |
| PMBD7000 | F1 | c6 | PH | Pair Switch | (100) V | 0.5 µA | 200 mA | 0.3 W | <1.1 V | 100 mA | <1.5 pF | | <4 ns | |
| PMLL4148 | D4 | a1 | PH | Uni | 75 V | 25 nA | 150 mA | 0.5 W | <1 V | 10 mA | <4 pF | | <4 ns | Ir at 20V |
| PMLL4446 | D4 | a1 | PH | Switch | 75 V | 25 nA | 150 mA | 0.5 W | <1 V | 20 mA | <4 pF | | <4 ns | Ir at 20V |
| PMLL4448 | D4 | a1 | PH | Uni | 75 V | 25 nA | 150 mA | 0.5 W | <1 V | 100 mA | <4 pF | | <4 ns | Ir at 20V |
| PMLL4150 | D4 | a1 | PH | Uni | (50) V | 50 nA | 300 mA | 0.5 W | <0.92 V | 100 mA | <2.5 pF | | <4 ns | |
| PMLL4151 | D4 | a1 | PH | Switch | (50) V | 50 nA | 200 mA | 0.5 W | <1 V | 50 mA | <2 pF | | <4 ns | |
| PMLL4153 | D4 | a1 | PH | Switch | (50) V | 50 nA | 200 mA | 0.5 W | <0.88 V | 20 mA | <2 pF | | <2 ns | |
| PRLL4001 | D4 | a1 | PH | Uni | (50) V | 10 µA | 1.6 A | | <1.1 V | 1 A | | | | |
| PRLL4002 | D4 | a1 | PH | Uni | (100) V | 10 µA | 1.6 A | | <1.1 V | 1 A | | | | |
| PRLL5817 | D4 | a1 | PH | Uni | 20 V | 1 mA | 1 A | | <0.45 V | 1 A | 70 pF | | | |
| PRLL5818 | D4 | a1 | PH | Uni | 30 V | 1 mA | 1 A | | <0.55 V | 1 A | 50 pF | | | |
| PRLL5819 | D4 | a1 | PH | Uni | 40 V | 1 mA | 1 A | | <0.6 V | 1 A | 50 pF | | | |
| R711XPT | I16 | c7 | MO | Rect. Pair | 100 V | 15 µA | 15 A | | <1.3 V | 15 A | | | <100 ns | Ifav at Tc=100°C |
| R712XPT | I16 | c7 | MO | Rect. Pair | 200 V | 15 µA | 15 A | | <1.3 V | 15 A | | | <100 ns | Ifav at Tc=100°C |
| R714XPT | I16 | c7 | MO | Rect. Pair | 400 V | 15 µA | 15 A | | <1.3 V | 15 A | | | <100 ns | Ifav at Tc=100°C |
| RB031B-40 | F10 | c13 | RO | Rectifier | 40 V | 2 mA | 3 A | | <0.55 V | 3 A | | | | |
| RB035B-20 | F10 | c7 | RO | Rect. Pair | 20 V | 2 mA | 4 A | | <0.55 V | 2 A | | | | |
| RB110C | F6 | c1 | RO | Rectifier | 40 V | 80 µA | 1 A | | <0.6 V | 1 A | | | | Ir at 25V |
| RB160L-40 | G5 | a1 | RO | Rectifier | 40 V | 1 mA | 1 A | | <0.55 V | 1 A | | | | |
| RB400D | F1 | c3 | RO | Rectifier | 20 V | 30 µA | 500 mA | | <0.55 V | 500 mA | | | | Ir at 10V |
| RB401D | F1 | c3 | RO | Rectifier | 40 V | 70 µA | 500 mA | | <0.5 V | 500 mA | | | | Ir at 20V |
| RB411D | F1 | c3 | RO | Rectifier | 20 V | 30 µA | 500 mA | | <0.5 V | 500 mA | | | | Ir at 10V |
| RB420D | F1 | c3 | RO | Rectifier | 25 V | 1 µA | 100 mA | | <0.45 V | 10 mA | | | | Ir at 10V |
| RB421D | F1 | c3 | RO | Rectifier | 20 V | 30 µA | 100 mA | | <0.55 V | 100 mA | | | | Ir at 10V |
| RB425D | F1 | c5 | RO | Rect. Pair | 20 V | 30 µA | 100 mA | | <0.55 V | 100 mA | | | | Ir at 10V |
| RB435C | F6 | c7 | RO | Rect. Pair | 20 V | 30 µA | 500 mA | | <0.55 V | 500 mA | | | | Ir at 10V |
| RB450F | F2 | c3 | RO | Rectifier | 25 V | 1 µA | 100 mA | | <0.45 V | 10 mA | | | | Ir at 10V |
| RB451F | F2 | c3 | RO | Rectifier | 25 V | 30 µA | 100 mA | | <0.45 V | 100 mA | | | | Ir at 10V |
| RB471E | F4 | e3 | RO | Rect. Pair | 20 V | 30 µA | 100 mA | | <0.55 V | 100 mA | | | | Ir at 10V |
| RB500H | G6 | a1 | RO | Rectifier | 25 V | 1 µA | 100 mA | | <0.45 V | 10 mA | | | | Ir at 10V |
| RB501H | G6 | a1 | RO | Rectifier | 25 V | 30 µA | 100 mA | | <0.45 V | 100 mA | | | | Ir at 10V |
| RB705D | F1 | c5 | RO | Pair Uni | (20) V | 1 µA | 30 mA | | <0.37 V | 1 mA | <2 pF | | | Ir at 10V |
| RB715F | F2 | c5 | RO | Pair Uni | (20) V | 1 µA | 30 mA | | <0.37 V | 1 mA | <2 pF | | | Ir at 10V |
| RB717F | F2 | c14 | RO | Pair Uni | (20) V | 1 µA | 30 mA | | <0.37 V | 1 mA | <2 pF | | | Ir at 10V |
| RB731U | F5 | f3 | RO | Array Univers | (20) V | 1 µA | 30 mA | | <0.37 V | 1 mA | <2 pF | | | Ir at 10V |
| RB751H | G6 | a1 | RO | Uni | (20) V | 1 µA | 30 mA | | <0.37 V | 1 mA | <2 pF | | | Ir at 10V |

| Type | Case | Pin-code | | | Vrm | Irm | Ifav Ifm | Pv | Vf | If Ifp | C0 | Cr | trr ts | |
|---|---|---|---|---|---|---|---|---|---|---|---|---|---|---|
| | | | | | **Maximum Ratings** | | | | **Electrical Characteristics** | | | | | |
| RB751H-40 | G6 | a1 | RO | Uni | (40) V | 0.5 µA | 30 mA | | <0.37 V | 1 mA | <2 pF | | | Ir at 30V |
| RBV406B | N5 | d22 | RD | Rect. Bridge | 60 V | | | | | | | | | |
| RBV408 | N4 | d22 | RD | Rect. Bridge | 800 V | | | | | | | | | |
| RBV608 | N4 | d22 | RD | Rect. Bridge | 800 V | | | | | | | | | |
| RG4 | B10 | a1 | RD | Rectifier | 400 V | 500 µA | 3 A | | 1.7 V | 3 A | | | 100 ns | |
| RG4A | B10 | a1 | RD | Rectifier | 600 V | 500 µA | 3 A | | 2 V | 2 A | | | 100 ns | |
| RG4C | B10 | a1 | RD | Rectifier | 1000 V | 500 µA | 2 A | | 3 V | 2 A | | | 100 ns | |
| RG4Y | B10 | a1 | RD | Rectifier | 70 V | 1 mA | 3.5 A | | 1.3 V | 3.5 A | | | 100 ns | |
| RG4Z | B10 | a1 | RD | Rectifier | 200 V | 1 mA | 3 A | | 1.7 V | 3 A | | | 100 ns | |
| RK43 | B10 | a1 | RD | Rectifier | 30 V | 5 mA | 3 A | | 0.55 V | 3 A | | | | Ifav at Ta=52°C |
| RK44 | B10 | a1 | RD | Rectifier | 40 V | 5 mA | 3 A | | 0.55 V | 3 A | | | | Ifav at Ta=52°C |
| RK46 | B10 | a1 | RD | Rectifier | 60 V | 3 mA | 3.5 A | | 0.62 V | 3.5 A | | | | Ifav at Ta=52°C |
| RK49 | B10 | a1 | RD | Rectifier | 90 V | 5 mA | 3.5 A | | 0.81 V | 3.5 A | | | | Ifav at Ta=52°C |
| RL4A | B10 | a1 | RD | Rectifier | 600 V | 50 µA | 3 A | | 1.5 V | 3 A | | | 500 ns | |
| RLR4001 | D1 | a1 | RO | Rectifier | (50) V | 10 µA | 800 mA | | <1 V | 800 mA | | | | |
| RLR4002 | D1 | a1 | RO | Rectifier | (100) V | 10 µA | 800 mA | | <1 V | 800 mA | | | | |
| RLR4003 | D1 | a1 | RO | Rectifier | (200) V | 10 µA | 800 mA | | <1 V | 800 mA | | | | |
| RLR4004 | D1 | a1 | RO | Rectifier | (400) V | 10 µA | 800 mA | | <1 V | 800 mA | | | | |
| RLS-71 | D2 | a1 | RO | Switch | (80) V | 0.5 µA | 130 mA | | <1.2 V | 100 mA | <3 pF | | <4 ns | C0 at 0.5V |
| RLS-72 | D2 | a1 | RO | Switch | (55) V | 0.5 µA | 120 mA | | <1.2 V | 100 mA | <3 pF | | <4 ns | C0 at 0.5V |
| RLS-73 | D2 | a1 | RO | Switch | (40) V | 0.5 µA | 110 mA | | <1.2 V | 100 mA | <3 pF | | <4 ns | C0 at 0.5V |
| RLS-92 | D2 | a1 | RO | Switch | (65) V | 0.5 µA | 200 mA | | <1 V | 100 mA | <3 pF | | <2 ns | |
| RLS-93 | D2 | a1 | RO | Switch | (55) V | 0.5 µA | 200 mA | | <1 V | 100 mA | <3 pF | | <2 ns | |
| RLS-94 | D2 | a1 | RO | Switch | (40) V | 0.5 µA | 200 mA | | <1 V | 100 mA | <3 pF | | <2 ns | |
| RLS135 | D2 | a1 | RO | RF Diode | (35) V | 100 µA | 100 mA | 0.15 W | <1 V | 10 mA | <1.5 pF | | | C0 at 10V |
| RLS139 | D2 | a1 | RO | Switch | (90) V | 0.5 µA | 130 mA | | <1.2 V | 100 mA | <5 pF | | <50 ns | C0 at 0.5V |
| RLS140 | D2 | a1 | RO | Switch | (55) V | 0.5 µA | 120 mA | | <1.2 V | 100 mA | <5 pF | | <50 ns | C0 at 0.5V |
| RLS141 | D2 | a1 | RO | Switch | (40) V | 0.5 µA | 110 mA | | <1.2 V | 100 mA | <5 pF | | <50 ns | C0 at 0.5V |
| RLS245 | D2 | a1 | RO | Switch | (220) V | 10 µA | 200 mA | | <1.5 V | 200 mA | <3 pF | | <75 ns | |
| RLS4148 | D2 | a1 | RO | Uni | (75) V | 5 µA | 200 mA | | <1 V | 10 mA | <4 pF | | <4 ns | |
| RLS4149 | D2 | a1 | RO | Switch | (75) V | 5 µA | 200 mA | | <1 V | 10 mA | <2 pF | | <4 ns | |
| RLS4150 | D2 | a1 | RO | Uni | (50) V | 0.1 µA | 250 mA | | <0.74 V | 10 mA | <2,5 pF | | <4 ns | |
| RLS4151 | D2 | a1 | RO | Switch | (50) V | 50 nA | 200 mA | | <1 V | 50 mA | <2 pF | | <2 ns | |
| RLS4152 | D2 | a1 | RO | Switch | (30) V | 50 nA | 200 mA | | <0.81 V | 10 mA | <2 pF | | <2 ns | |
| RLS4153 | D2 | a1 | RO | Switch | (50) V | 50 nA | 200 mA | | <0.81 V | 10 mA | <2 pF | | <2 ns | |
| RLS4154 | D2 | a1 | RO | Switch | (25) V | 0.1 µA | 200 mA | | <1 V | 30 mA | <4 pF | | <2 ns | |
| RLS4446 | D2 | a1 | RO | Switch | (75) V | 5 µA | 200 mA | | <1 V | 20 mA | <4 pF | | <4 ns | |
| RLS4447 | D2 | a1 | RO | Switch | (75) V | 5 µA | 200 mA | | <1 V | 20 mA | <2 pF | | <4 ns | |
| RLS4448 | D2 | a1 | RO | Uni | (75) V | 5 µA | 200 mA | | <1 V | 100 mA | <4 pF | | <4 ns | |
| RLS4449 | D2 | a1 | RO | Switch | (75) V | 5 µA | 200 mA | | <1 V | 30 mA | <2 pF | | <4 ns | |

| Type | Case | Pin-code | | | Maximum Ratings | | | | Electrical Characteristics | | | | | |
|---|---|---|---|---|---|---|---|---|---|---|---|---|---|---|
| | | | | | Vrm | Irm | Ifav Ifm | Pv | Vf | If Ifp | C0 | Cr | trr ts | |
| RLS4450 | D2 | a1 | RO | Switch | (30) V | 50 nA | 250 mA | | <0.72 V | 10 mA | <4 pF | | <4 ns | |
| RLS4454 | D2 | a1 | RO | Switch | (50) V | 0.1 µA | 250 mA | | <1 V | 10 mA | <2 pF | | <2 ns | |
| RLS4606 | D2 | a1 | RO | Switch | (70) V | 0.1 µA | 250 mA | | <0.77 V | 10 mA | <2.5 pF | | <4 ns | |
| RN711H | G6 | a1 | RO | PIN Diode | 50 V | 100 µA | 50 mA | 0.1 W | | <1 mA | <0.4 pF | | | C0 at 35V |
| RN719D | F1 | c6 | RO | Pair PIN | 50 V | 100 µA | 50 mA | 0.1 W | | <1 mA | <0.4 pF | | | C0 at 35V |
| RN719F | F2 | a1 | RO | Pair PIN | 50 V | 100 µA | 50 mA | 0.1 W | | <1 mA | <0.4 pF | | | C0 at 35V |
| RN820 | E4 | a1 | SG | Rectifier | 800 V | 5 mA | 20 A | (25) W | <1.5 V | 70 A | | | | Ifav at Tc=150°C |
| RN1120 | E4 | a1 | SG | Rectifier | 1100 V | | 20 A | 25 W | <1.5 V | 70 A | | | | |
| RU4 | B10 | a1 | RD | Rectifier | 400 V | 10 µA | 3 A | | 1.5 V | 3 A | | | 400 ns | |
| RU4A | B10 | a1 | RD | Rectifier | 600 V | 10 µA | 3 A | | 1.5 V | 5 A | | | 400 ns | |
| RU4B | B10 | a1 | RD | Rectifier | 800 V | 10 µA | 3 A | | 1.6 V | 3 A | | | 400 ns | |
| RU4C | B10 | a1 | RD | Rectifier | 1000 V | 50 µA | 2.5 A | | 1.6 V | 3 A | | | 400 ns | |
| RU4DS | B10 | a1 | RD | Rectifier | 1300 V | 60 µA | 2.5 A | | 1.8 V | 3 A | | | 400 ns | |
| RU4Y | B10 | a1 | RD | Rectifier | 150 V | 10 µA | 3.5 A | | 1.3 V | 3.5 A | | | 400 ns | |
| RU4Z | B10 | a1 | RD | Rectifier | 250 V | 10 µA | 3.5 A | | 1.3 V | 3.5 A | | | 400 ns | |
| RVB1506 | N4 | d22 | RD | Rect. Bridge | 600 V | | | | | | | | | |
| RVB2506 | N4 | d22 | RD | Rect. Bridge | 600 V | | | | | | | | | |
| S1NB10 | F16 | d23 | RD | Rect. Bridge | 100 V | | | | | | | | | |
| S1NB20 | F16 | d23 | RD | Rect. Bridge | 200 V | | | | | | | | | |
| S1NB40 | F16 | d23 | RD | Rect. Bridge | 400 V | | | | | | | | | |
| S1NB60 | F16 | d23 | RD | Rect. Bridge | 600 V | | | | | | | | | |
| S1WB10 | P1 | d20 | RD | Rect. Bridge | 100 V | | | | | | | | | |
| S1WB20 | P1 | d20 | RD | Rect. Bridge | 200 V | | | | | | | | | |
| S1WB40 | P1 | d20 | RD | Rect. Bridge | 400 V | | | | | | | | | |
| S1WB60 | P1 | d20 | RD | Rect. Bridge | 600 V | | | | | | | | | |
| S1YAK20 | P2 | d10 | RD | Pair Uni | 200 V | | 350 mA | | | | | | 300 ns | |
| S1YB10 | P2 | d20 | RD | Rect. Bridge | 100 V | | | | | | | | | 3500µ/1Ω |
| S1YB20 | P2 | d20 | RD | Rect. Bridge | 200 V | | | | | | | | | 1200µ/2Ω |
| S1YB40 | P2 | d20 | RD | Rect. Bridge | 400 V | | | | | | | | | 500µ/4Ω |
| S1YB60 | P2 | d20 | RD | Rect. Bridge | 600 V | | | | | | | | | 350µ/6Ω |
| S1ZA10 | F15 | d7 | RD | Uni | 100 V | 10 µA | 1.1 A | | 1.1 V | 0.9 A | | | | |
| S1ZA20 | F15 | d7 | RD | Uni | 200 V | 10 µA | 1.1 A | | 1.1 V | 0.9 A | | | | |
| S1ZA40 | F15 | d7 | RD | Uni | 400 V | 10 µA | 1.1 A | | 1.1 V | 0.9 A | | | | |
| S1ZA60 | F15 | d7 | RD | Uni | 600 V | 10 µA | 1.1 A | | 1.1 V | 0.9 A | | | | |
| S1ZAK20 | F15 | d7 | RD | Rectifier | 200 V | 10 µA | 700 mA | | 1.2 V | 700 mA | | | 300 ns | |
| S1ZAK40 | F15 | d7 | RD | Rectifier | 400 V | 10 µA | 700 mA | | 1.2 V | 700 mA | | | 300 ns | |
| S1ZAL20 | F15 | a1 | RD | Rectifier | 200 V | 10 µA | 1.2 A | | 0.98 V | 1.2 A | | | | |
| S1ZAS4 | F15 | a1 | RD | Rectifier | 40 V | 1 mA | 1.1 A | | 0.55 V | 1.1 A | | | | |
| S1ZB10 | F15 | d20 | RD | Rect. Bridge | 100 V | | | | | | | | | 3500µ/1Ω |
| S1ZB20 | F15 | d20 | RD | Rect. Bridge | 200 V | | | | | | | | | 1200µ/2Ω |

| Type | Case | Pin-code | | | Maximum Ratings | | | | Electrical Characteristics | | | | | |
|---|---|---|---|---|---|---|---|---|---|---|---|---|---|---|
| | | | | | Vrm | Irm | Ifav Ifm | Pv | Vf | If Ifp | C0 | Cr | trr ts | |
| S1ZB40 | F15 | d20 | RD | Rect. Bridge | 400 V | | | | | | | | | 500μ/4Ω |
| S1ZB60 | F15 | d20 | RD | Rect. Bridge | 600 V | | | | | | | | | 350μ/6Ω |
| S3S3M | B19 | a1 | RD | Rectifier | 30 V | 5 mA | 3 A | | 0.55 V | 1 A | | | | Ifav at Ta=40°C |
| S3S4M | B19 | a1 | RD | Rectifier | 40 V | 5 mA | 3 A | | 0.55 V | 1 A | | | | Ifav at Ta=40°C |
| S3S6M | B19 | a1 | RD | Rectifier | 60 V | 2.5 mA | 3 A | | 0.58 V | 3 A | | | | Ifav at Ta=25°C |
| S4VB10 | O4 | d26 | RD | Rect. Bridge | 100 V | | | | | | | | | 5000μ/1.4Ω |
| S4VB20 | O4 | d26 | RD | Rect. Bridge | 200 V | | | | | | | | | 5000μ/3.4Ω |
| S4VB40 | O4 | d26 | RD | Rect. Bridge | 400 V | | | | | | | | | 3000μ/7Ω |
| S4VB60 | O4 | d26 | RD | Rect. Bridge | 600 V | | | | | | | | | 1000μ/8Ω |
| S5KC40 | I6 | c7 | RD | Rect. Pair | 400 V | 10 μA | 5 A | | 1.2 V | 2.5 A | | | 300 ns | Ifav at Tc=134°C |
| S5KC40R | I6 | c8 | RD | Rect. Pair | 400 V | 10 μA | 5 A | | 1.2 V | 2.5 A | | | 300 ns | Ifav at Tc=134°C |
| S5KD20 | I6 | c10 | RD | Rect. Pair | 200 V | 10 μA | 5 A | | 1.2 V | 2.5 A | | | 300 ns | Ifav at Tc=135°C |
| S5KD20H | I6 | c10 | RD | Rect. Pair | 400 V | 10 μA | 5 A | | 1.2 V | 2.5 A | | | 100 ns | Ifav at Tc=135°C |
| S5KD40 | I6 | c10 | RD | Rect. Pair | 400 V | 10 μA | 5 A | | 1.2 V | 2.5 A | | | 300 ns | Ifav at Tc=135°C |
| S5S3M | I2 | a1 | RD | Rectifier | 30 V | 5 mA | 5 A | | 0.55 V | 5 A | | | | Ifav at Tc=111°C |
| S5S4M | I2 | a1 | RD | Rectifier | 40 V | 5 mA | 5 A | | 0.55 V | 5 A | | | | Ifav at Tc=111°C |
| S5VB10 | O5 | d26 | RD | Rect. Bridge | 100 V | | | | | | | | | 5000μ/1.4Ω |
| S5VB20 | O5 | d26 | RD | Rect. Bridge | 200 V | | | | | | | | | 5000μ/3.6Ω |
| S5VB40 | O5 | d26 | RD | Rect. Bridge | 400 V | | | | | | | | | 3000μ/7Ω |
| S5VB60 | O5 | d26 | RD | Rect. Bridge | 600 V | | | | | | | | | 1000μ/8Ω |
| S6K20 | I2 | a1 | RD | Rectifier | 200 V | 10 μA | 6 A | | 1.2 V | 2.5 A | | | | Ifav at Ta=134°C |
| S6K40 | I2 | a1 | RD | Rectifier | 400 V | 10 μA | 6 A | | 1.2 V | 3.5 A | | | | Ifav at Ta=131°C |
| S6K20H | I2 | a1 | RD | Rectifier | 200 V | 10 μA | 6 A | | 1.2 V | 2.5 A | | | | Ifav at Ta=134°C |
| S6K20HR | I2 | b1 | RD | Rectifier | 200 V | 10 μA | 6 A | | 1.2 V | 2.5 A | | | | Ifav at Ta=134°C |
| S6K20R | I2 | b1 | RD | Rectifier | 200 V | 10 μA | 6 A | | 1.2 V | 2.5 A | | | | Ifav at Ta=134°C |
| S6K40R | I2 | b1 | RD | Rectifier | 400 V | 10 μA | 6 A | | 1.2 V | 3.5 A | | | | Ifav at Ta=131°C |
| S10SC3M | I6 | c7 | RD | Rect. Pair | 30 V | 5 mA | 10 A | | 0.55 V | 5 A | | | | Ifav at Tc=104°C |
| S10SC3MR | I6 | c8 | RD | Rect. Pair | 30 V | 5 mA | 10 A | | 0.55 V | 5 A | | | | Ifav at Tc=104°C |
| S10SC4M | I6 | c7 | RD | Rect. Pair | 40 V | 5 mA | 10 A | | 0.55 V | 5 A | | | | Ifav at Tc=104°C |
| S10SC4MR | I6 | c8 | RD | Rect. Pair | 40 V | 5 mA | 10 A | | 0.55 V | 5 A | | | | Ifav at Tc=104°C |
| S10VB10 | O8 | d26 | RD | Rect. Bridge | 100 V | | | | | | | | | 5000μ/1.4Ω |
| S10VB20 | O8 | d26 | RD | Rect. Bridge | 200 V | | | | | | | | | 5000μ/3.6Ω |
| S10VB40 | O8 | d26 | RD | Rect. Bridge | 400 V | | | | | | | | | 3000μ/7Ω |
| S10VB60 | O8 | d26 | RD | Rect. Bridge | 600 V | | | | | | | | | 1000μ/8Ω |
| S12KC20 | J4 | c7 | RD | Rect. Pair | 200 V | 10 μA | 12 A | | 1.2 V | 6 A | | | 300 ns | Ifav at Tc=131°C |
| S12KC20H | J4 | c7 | RD | Rect. Pair | 200 V | 10 μA | 12 A | | 1.2 V | 6 A | | | 100 ns | Ifav at Tc=131°C |
| S12KC40 | J4 | c7 | RD | Rect. Pair | 400 V | 10 μA | 12 A | | 1.3 V | 6 A | | | 300 ns | Ifav at Tc=132°C |
| S15SCA4M | I6 | c7 | RD | Rect. Pair | 40 V | 5 mA | 15 A | | 0.55 V | 7.5 A | | | | Ifav at Ta=106°C |
| S15VB10 | O6 | d26 | RD | Rect. Bridge | 100 V | | | | | | | | | 10m/0.5Ω |
| S15VB20 | O6 | d26 | RD | Rect. Bridge | 200 V | | | | | | | | | 10m/1.4Ω |

| Type | Case | Pin-code | | | Maximum Ratings | | | | Electrical Characteristics | | | | | |
|---|---|---|---|---|---|---|---|---|---|---|---|---|---|---|
| | | | | | Vrm | Irm | Ifav Ifm | Pv | Vf | If Ifp | C0 | Cr | trr ts | |
| S15VB40 | O6 | d26 | RD | Rect. Bridge | 400 V | | | | | | | | | 10m/5Ω |
| S15VB60 | O6 | d26 | RD | Rect. Bridge | 600 V | | | | | | | | | 2000/4Ω |
| S15WB10 | O9 | d26 | RD | Rect. Bridge | 100 V | | | | | | | | | |
| S15WB20 | O9 | d26 | RD | Rect. Bridge | 200 V | | | | | | | | | |
| S15WB40 | O9 | d26 | RD | Rect. Bridge | 400 V | | | | | | | | | |
| S15WB60 | O9 | d26 | RD | Rect. Bridge | 600 V | | | | | | | | | |
| S20SC4M | J11 | c7 | RD | Rect. Pair | 40 V | 5 mA | 20 A | | 0.55 V | 10 A | | | | Ifav at Ta=104°C |
| S20SC9M | J11 | c7 | RD | Rect. Pair | 90 V | 10 mA | 20 A | | 0.75 V | 10 A | | | | Ifav at Ta=103°C |
| S20WB20 | O10 | d26 | RD | Rect. Bridge | 200 V | | | | | | | | | |
| S20WB40 | O10 | d26 | RD | Rect. Bridge | 400 V | | | | | | | | | |
| S20WB60 | O10 | d26 | RD | Rect. Bridge | 600 V | | | | | | | | | |
| S20WB10 | O10 | d26 | RD | Rect. Bridge | 100 V | | | | | | | | | |
| S24LCA20 | J11 | c7 | RD | Rect. Pair | 200 V | 10 µA | 24 A | | 1.2 V | 12 A | | | 50 ns | Ifav at Tc=120°C |
| S25VB10 | O7 | d26 | RD | Rect. Bridge | 100 V | | | | | | | | | 20m/0.05Ω |
| S25VB20 | O7 | d26 | RD | Rect. Bridge | 200 V | | | | | | | | | 20m/0.27Ω |
| S25VB40 | O7 | d26 | RD | Rect. Bridge | 400 V | | | | | | | | | 20m/1Ω |
| S25VB60 | O7 | d26 | RD | Rect. Bridge | 600 V | | | | | | | | | 20m/3Ω |
| S30SC3M | J11 | c7 | RD | Rect. Pair | 30 V | 20 µA | 30 A | | 0.55 V | 15 A | | | | Ifav at Tc=102°C |
| S30SC4M | J11 | c7 | RD | Rect. Pair | 40 V | 20 µA | 30 A | | 0.55 V | 15 A | | | | Ifav at Tc=102°C |
| S60SC4M | J11 | c7 | RD | Rect. Pair | 40 V | 25 µA | 60 A | | 0.55 V | 30 A | | | | Ifav at Tc=102°C |
| S5277B | A3 | a1 | TO | Rectifier | 100 V | 10 µA | 1 A | | <1.2 V | 1 A | | | | |
| S5277G | A3 | a1 | TO | Rectifier | 400 V | 10 µA | 1 A | | <1.2 V | 1 A | | | | |
| S5277J | A3 | a1 | TO | Rectifier | 600 V | 10 µA | 1 A | | <1.2 V | 1 A | | | | |
| S5277N | A3 | a1 | TO | Rectifier | 1000 V | 10 µA | 1 A | | <1.2 V | 1 A | | | | |
| S5295B | A3 | a1 | TO | Rectifier | 100 V | 10 µA | 500 mA | | <1.5 V | 1 A | | | <1.5 µs | |
| S5295G | A3 | a1 | TO | Rectifier | 400 V | 10 µA | 500 mA | | <1.5 V | 1 A | | | <1.5 µs | |
| S5295J | A3 | a1 | TO | Rectifier | 600 V | 10 µA | 500 mA | | <1.5 V | 1 A | | | <1.5 µs | |
| S5566B | A16 | a1 | TO | Rectifier | 100 V | 10 µA | 1 A | | <1.2 V | 1 A | | | <1.5 µs | |
| S5566G | A16 | a1 | TO | Rectifier | 400 V | 10 µA | 1 A | | <1.2 V | 1 A | | | <1.5 µs | |
| S5566J | A16 | a1 | TO | Rectifier | 600 V | 10 µA | 1 A | | <1.2 V | 1 A | | | <1.5 µs | |
| S5566N | A16 | a1 | TO | Rectifier | 1000 V | 10 µA | 1 A | | <1.2 V | 1 A | | | <1.5 µs | |
| S5688B | A17 | a1 | TO | Rectifier | 100 V | 10 µA | 1 A | | <1.2 V | 1 A | | | <1.5 µs | |
| S5688G | A17 | a1 | TO | Rectifier | 400 V | 10 µA | 1 A | | <1.2 V | 1 A | | | <1.5 µs | |
| S5688J | A17 | a1 | TO | Rectifier | 600 V | 10 µA | 1 A | | <1.2 V | 1 A | | | <1.5 µs | |
| S5688N | A17 | a1 | TO | Rectifier | 1000 V | 10 µA | 1 A | | <1.2 V | 1 A | | | <1.5 µs | |
| SD41 | E2 | a1 | MO | Rectifier | 45 V | 125 mA | 30 A | | <0.55 V | 30 A | 2 nF | | | Ir at Tc=125°C |
| SD51 | E4 | a1 | MO | Rectifier | 45 V | 200 mA | 120 A | | <0.6 V | 60 A | 4 nF | | | Tc=90°C |
| SD101A | A1 | a1 | IT,RD | Uni | 60 V | 0.2 µA | 150 mA | 0.4 W | <1 V | 15 mA | | <2 pF | <1 ns | |
| SD101B | A1 | a1 | IT,RD | Uni | 50 V | 0.2 µA | 150 mA | 0.4 W | <0.95 V | 15 mA | | <2.1 pF | <1 ns | |
| SD101C | A1 | a1 | IT,RD | Uni | 40 V | 0.2 µA | 150 mA | 0.4 W | <0.9 V | 15 mA | | <2.2 pF | <1 ns | |

S15VB40 – SD101C

| Type | Case | Pin-code | | | Maximum Ratings | | | | Electrical Characteristics | | | | | |
|------|------|----------|---|---|-----|-----|---------|------|------|--------|----|----|-----|---|
| | | | | | Vrm | Irm | Ifav Ifm | Pv | Vf | If Ifp | C0 | Cr | trr ts | |
| SD101AW | G4 | a1 | IT | Uni | 60 V | 0.2 µA | 150 mA | 0.4 W | <1 V | 15 mA | <2 pF | | <1 ns | |
| SD101BW | G4 | a1 | IT | Uni | 50 V | 0.2 µA | 150 mA | 0.4 W | <0.95 V | 15 mA | <2.1 pF | | <1 ns | |
| SD101CW | G4 | a1 | IT | Uni | 40 V | 0.2 µA | 150 mA | 0.4 W | <0.9 V | 15 mA | <2.2 pF | | <1 ns | |
| SD103A | A1 | a1 | IT | Uni | 40 V | 5 µA | 200 mA | 0.4 W | <0.37 V | 20 mA | <50 pF | | <10 ns | |
| SD103B | A1 | a1 | IT | Uni | 30 V | 5 µA | 200 mA | 0.4 W | <0.37 V | 20 mA | <50 pF | | <10 ns | |
| SD103C | A1 | a1 | IT | Uni | 20 V | 5 µA | 200 mA | 0.4 W | <0.37 V | 20 mA | <50 pF | | <10 ns | |
| SD103AW | G4 | a1 | IT | Uni | 40 V | 5 µA | 200 mA | 0.4 W | <0.37 V | 20 mA | <50 pF | | <10 ns | |
| SD103BW | G4 | a1 | IT | Uni | 30 V | 5 µA | 200 mA | 0.4 W | <0.37 V | 20 mA | <50 pF | | <10 ns | |
| SD103CW | G4 | a1 | IT | Uni | 20 V | 5 µA | 200 mA | 0.4 W | <0.37 V | 20 mA | <50 pF | | <10 ns | |
| SD241 | L1 | c5 | MO | Rect. Pair | 45 V | | 15 A | | <0.6 V | 20 A | 2 nF | | | |
| SGS5R05 | I10 | a1 | SG | Rectifier | 50 V | | 8 A | (50) W | 1 V | 8 A | | | <35 ns | Ifav at Tc=70°C |
| SGS5R10 | I10 | a1 | SG | Rectifier | 100 V | 10 µA | 8 A | (50) W | 1 V | 8 A | | | <35 ns | Ifav at Tc=70°C |
| SGS5R15 | I10 | a1 | SG | Rectifier | 150 V | 10 µA | 8 A | (50) W | 1 V | 8 A | | | <35 ns | Ifav at Tc=70°C |
| SGS5R20 | I10 | a1 | SG | Rectifier | 200 V | 10 µA | 8 A | (50) W | 1 V | 8 A | | | <35 ns | Ifav at Tc=70°C |
| SGS16DR05 | I5 | c7 | SG | Rect. Pair | 50 V | 10 µA | 8 A | (70) W | 1 V | 8 A | | | <35 ns | Ifav at Tc=70°C |
| SGS16DR10 | I5 | c7 | SG | Rect. Pair | 100 V | 10 µA | 8 A | (70) W | 1 V | 8 A | | | <35 ns | Ifav at Tc=70°C |
| SGS16DR15 | I5 | c7 | SG | Rect. Pair | 150 V | 10 µA | 8 A | (70) W | 1 V | 8 A | | | <35 ns | Ifav at Tc=70°C |
| SGS16DR20 | I5 | c7 | SG | Rect. Pair | 200 V | 10 µA | 8 A | (70) W | 1 V | 8 A | | | <35 ns | Ifav at Tc=70°C |
| SGS20R05 | I5 | a1 | SG | Rectifier | 50 V | 40 µA | 20 A | (60) W | 1 V | 20 A | | | <35 ns | Ifav at Tc=70°C |
| SGS20R10 | I5 | a1 | SG | Rectifier | 100 V | 40 µA | 20 A | (60) W | 1 V | 20 A | | | <35 ns | Ifav at Tc=70°C |
| SGS20R15 | I5 | a1 | SG | Rectifier | 150 V | 40 µA | 20 A | (60) W | 1 V | 20 A | | | <35 ns | Ifav at Tc=70°C |
| SGS20R20 | I5 | a1 | SG | Rectifier | 200 V | 40 µA | 20 A | (60) W | 1 V | 20 A | | | <35 ns | Ifav at Tc=70°C |
| SGS35R120 | I5 | a1 | SG | Rectifier | 1200 V | 40 µA | 35 A | (90) W | 1 V | 35 A | | | <35 ns | Ifav at Tc=70°C |
| SGS45R80 | I5 | a1 | SG | Rectifier | 800 V | 100 µA | 45 A | (90) W | 1 V | 45 A | | | <35 ns | Ifav at Tc=70°C |
| SGS60R40 | I5 | a1 | SG | Rectifier | 400 V | 100 µA | 60 A | (90) W | 1 V | 60 A | | | <35 ns | Ifav at Tc=70°C |
| SHV10 | A23 | a1 | RD | HV Rectifier | 10 kV | 3 µA | 2 mA | | 40 V | 10 mA | <0.6 pF | | 180 ns | Ifav at Ta=110°C |
| SHV12 | A23 | a1 | RD | HV Rectifier | 12 kV | 3 µA | 2 mA | | 45 V | 10 mA | <0.6 pF | | 180 ns | Ifav at Ta=110°C |
| SHV14 | A23 | a1 | RD | HV Rectifier | 14 kV | 3 µA | 2 mA | | 55 V | 10 mA | <0.6 pF | | 180 ns | Ifav at Ta=110°C |
| SHV16 | A23 | a1 | RD | HV Rectifier | 16 kV | 3 µA | 2 mA | | 60 V | 10 mA | <0.6 pF | | 180 ns | Ifav at Ta=110°C |
| SHV16S | A23 | a1 | RD | HV Rectifier | 16 kV | 3 µA | 2 mA | | 60 V | 10 mA | <0.6 pF | | 180 ns | Ifav at Ta=110°C |
| SHV02 | A20 | a1 | RD | HV Rectifier | 2 kV | 3 µA | 2 mA | | 16 V | 10 mA | <1 pF | | 180 ns | Ifav at Ta=110°C |
| SHV20 | A23 | a1 | RD | HV Rectifier | 20 kV | 3 µA | 2 mA | | 75 V | 10 mA | <0.6 pF | | 180 ns | Ifav at Ta=110°C |
| SHV24 | A23 | a1 | RD | HV Rectifier | 24 kV | 3 µA | 2 mA | | 75 V | 10 mA | <0.6 pF | | 180 ns | Ifav at Ta=110°C |
| SHV03 | A21 | a1 | RD | HV Rectifier | 3 kV | 3 µA | 2 mA | | 16 V | 10 mA | <1 pF | | 180 ns | Ifav at Ta=110°C |
| SHV06 | A22 | a1 | RD | HV Rectifier | 6 kV | 3 µA | 2 mA | | 26 V | 10 mA | <1 pF | | 180 ns | Ifav at Ta=110°C |
| SHV06N | A21 | a1 | RD | HV Rectifier | 6 kV | 3 µA | 2 mA | | 26 V | 10 mA | <1 pF | | 180 ns | Ifav at Ta=110°C |
| SHV08 | A22 | a1 | RD | HV Rectifier | 8 kV | 3 µA | 2 mA | | 36 V | 10 mA | <1 pF | | 180 ns | Ifav at Ta=110°C |
| SHV08N | A21 | a1 | RD | HV Rectifier | 8 kV | 3 µA | 2 mA | | 36 V | 10 mA | <1 pF | | 180 ns | Ifav at Ta=110°C |
| SHV10UK | A23 | a1 | RD | HV Rectifier | 10 kV | 3 µA | 2 mA | | 60 V | 10 mA | | | 150 ns | Ifav at Ta=110°C |
| SHV12UK | A23 | a1 | RD | HV Rectifier | 12 kV | 3 µA | 2 mA | | 68 V | 10 mA | | | 150 ns | Ifav at Ta=110°C |

| Type | Case | Pin-code | | | Maximum Ratings Vrm | Irm | Ifav Ifm | Pv | Electrical Characteristics Vf | If Ifp | C0 | Cr | trr ts | |
|------|------|----------|---|---|------|-----|-----------|-----|------|--------|-----|-----|--------|---|
| SHV16UK | A23 | a1 | RD | HV Rectifier | 16 kV | 3 µA | 2 mA | | 90 V | 10 mA | 0.6 pF | | 150 ns | Ifav at Ta=110°C |
| SHV06UNK | A21 | a1 | RD | HV Rectifier | 6 kV | 3 µA | 2 mA | | 26 V | 10 mA | 1 pF | | 180 ns | Ifav at Ta=110°C |
| SHV08UNK | A21 | a1 | RD | HV Rectifier | 8 kV | 3 µA | 2 mA | | 36 V | 10 mA | 1 pF | | 180 ns | Ifav at Ta=110°C |
| SHV08X | A23 | a1 | RD | HV Rectifier | 8 kV | 3 µA | 2 mA | | 60 V | 10 mA | | | 150 ns | Ifav at Ta=110°C |
| SLA1008 | N6 | k3 | RD | Array Univers | 120 V | | 2.5 A | | | | | | 100 ns | |
| SLA1012 | N6 | -- | RD | Array Network | 120 V | | 2 A | | | | | | 100 ns | |
| SMBYT01-200 | G1 | a1 | SG | Rectifier | 200 V | 20 µA | 1 A | | <1.5 V | 1 A | | | <25 ns | Ifav at Tc=110°C |
| SMBYT01-300 | G1 | a1 | SG | Rectifier | 300 V | 20 µA | 1 A | | <1.5 V | 1 A | | | <25 ns | Ifav at Tc=110°C |
| SMBYT01-400 | G1 | a1 | SG | Rectifier | 400 V | 20 µA | 1 A | | <1.5 V | 1 A | | | <25 ns | Ifav at Tc=110°C |
| SMBYT03-200 | G2 | a1 | SG | Rectifier | 200 V | 20 µA | 3 A | | <1.5 V | 3 A | | | <25 ns | Ifav at Tc=55°C |
| SMBYT03-300 | G2 | a1 | SG | Rectifier | 300 V | 20 µA | 3 A | | <1.5 V | 3 A | | | <25 ns | Ifav at Tc=55°C |
| SMBYT03-400 | G2 | a1 | SG | Rectifier | 400 V | 20 µA | 3 A | | <1.5 V | 3 A | | | <25 ns | Ifav at Tc=55°C |
| SMBYW02-100 | G1 | a1 | SG | Rectifier | 100 V | 20 µA | 2 A | | <1.25 V | 6 A | | | <35 ns | Ifav at Tc=100°C |
| SMBYW02-150 | G1 | a1 | SG | Rectifier | 150 V | 20 µA | 2 A | | <1.25 V | 6 A | | | <35 ns | Ifav at Tc=100°C |
| SMBYW02-200 | G1 | a1 | SG | Rectifier | 200 V | 20 µA | 2 A | | <1.25 V | 6 A | | | <35 ns | Ifav at Tc=100°C |
| SMBYW02-50 | G1 | a1 | SG | Rectifier | 50 V | 20 µA | 2 A | | <1.25 V | 6 A | | | <35 ns | Ifav at Tc=100°C |
| SMBYW04-100 | G2 | a1 | SG | Rectifier | 100 V | 20 µA | 4 A | | <1.25 V | 12 A | | | <35 ns | Ifav at Tc=70°C |
| SMBYW04-150 | G2 | a1 | SG | Rectifier | 150 V | 20 µA | 4 A | | <1.25 V | 12 A | | | <35 ns | Ifav at Tc=70°C |
| SMBYW04-200 | G2 | a1 | SG | Rectifier | 200 V | 20 µA | 4 A | | <1.25 V | 12 A | | | <35 ns | Ifav at Tc=70°C |
| SMBYW04-50 | G2 | a1 | SG | Rectifier | 50 V | 20 µA | 4 A | | <1.25 V | 12 A | | | <35 ns | Ifav at Tc=70°C |
| SRK12ZB | B25 | a1 | RD | HV Rectifier | 9 kV | 10 µA | 350 mA | | 9 V | 450 mA | | | | Ifav at Ta=60°C |
| SRT-2W6 | B25 | a1 | RD | HV Rectifier | 6 kV | 10 µA | | | | | | | | |
| SRT-2W6H | B25 | a1 | RD | HV Rectifier | 6 kV | 10 µA | | | | | | | | |
| SRT-3HP | -- | a1 | RD | HV Rectifier | 2.5 kV | 10 µA | 350 mA | | 8 V | 350 mA | | | 350 ns | Ifav at Ta=100°C |
| SRT-4HP | -- | a1 | RD | HV Rectifier | 4 kV | 10 µA | 350 mA | | 10 V | 350 mA | | | 350 ns | Ifav at Ta=97°C |
| STPS3035CP | I16 | c7 | SG | Rect. Pair | 35 V | 200 µA | 15 A | | <0.84 V | 30 A | | | | |
| STPS3045CP | I16 | c7 | SG | Rect. Pair | 45 V | 200 µA | 15 A | | <0.84 V | 30 A | | | | |
| STPS3035CPI | I15 | c7 | SG | Rect. Pair | 35 V | 200 µA | 15 A | | <0.84 V | 30 A | | | | |
| STPS3045CPI | I15 | c7 | SG | Rect. Pair | 45 V | 200 µA | 15 A | | <0.84 V | 30 A | | | | |
| STPS3035CT | I12 | c7 | SG | Rect. Pair | 35 V | 200 µA | 15 A | | <0.84 V | 30 A | | | | |
| STPS3045CT | I12 | c7 | SG | Rect. Pair | 45 V | 200 µA | 15 A | | <0.84 V | 30 A | | | | |
| STPS120E | F8 | d4 | SG | Rectifier | 20 V | 500 µA | 1 A | | <0.81 V | 2 A | | | | |
| STPS130E | F8 | d4 | SG | Rectifier | 30 V | 500 µA | 1 A | | <0.81 V | 2 A | | | | |
| STPS140E | F8 | d4 | SG | Rectifier | 40 V | 500 µA | 1 A | | <0.81 V | 2 A | | | | |
| STPS160E | F8 | d4 | SG | Rectifier | 40 V | 500 µA | 1 A | | <0.91 V | 2 A | | | | |
| STPS220CE | F8 | d5 | SG | Rect. Pair | 20 V | 500 µA | 1 A | | <0.91 V | 2 A | | | | |
| STPS230CE | F8 | d5 | SG | Rect. Pair | 30 V | 500 µA | 1 A | | <0.91 V | 2 A | | | | |
| STPS240CE | F8 | d5 | SG | Rect. Pair | 40 V | 500 µA | 1 A | | <0.91 V | 2 A | | | | |
| STPS260CE | F8 | d5 | SG | Rect. Pair | 60 V | 500 µA | 1 A | | <0.91 V | 2 A | | | | |
| STPS320S | G2 | a1 | SG | Rectifier | 20 V | 100 µA | 3 A | | <0.84 V | 6 A | | | | |

| Type | Case | Pin-code | | | Maximum Ratings | | | | Electrical Characteristics | | | | | |
|---|---|---|---|---|---|---|---|---|---|---|---|---|---|---|
| | | | | | Vrm | Irm | Ifav Ifm | Pv | Vf | If Ifp | C0 | Cr | trr ts | |
| STPS330S | G2 | a1 | SG | Rectifier | 30 V | 100 µA | 3 A | | <0.84 V | 6 A | | | | |
| STPS340S | G2 | a1 | SG | Rectifier | 40 V | 100 µA | 3 A | | <0.84 V | 6 A | | | | |
| STPS320U | G1 | a1 | SG | Rectifier | 20 V | 100 µA | 3 A | | <0.84 V | 6 A | | | | |
| STPS330U | G1 | a1 | SG | Rectifier | 30 V | 100 µA | 3 A | | <0.84 V | 6 A | | | | |
| STPS340U | G1 | a1 | SG | Rectifier | 40 V | 100 µA | 3 A | | <0.84 V | 6 A | | | | |
| STPS620CF | J1 | c7 | SG | Rect. Pair | 20 V | 100 µA | 10 A | | <0.84 V | 6 A | | | | |
| STPS630CF | J1 | c7 | SG | Rect. Pair | 30 V | 100 µA | 10 A | | <0.84 V | 6 A | | | | |
| STPS640CF | J1 | c7 | SG | Rect. Pair | 40 V | 100 µA | 10 A | | <0.84 V | 6 A | | | | |
| STPS620CT | I12 | c7 | SG | Rect. Pair | 20 V | 100 µA | 10 A | | <0.84 V | 6 A | | | | |
| STPS630CT | I12 | c7 | SG | Rect. Pair | 30 V | 100 µA | 10 A | | <0.84 V | 6 A | | | | |
| STPS640CT | I12 | c7 | SG | Rect. Pair | 40 V | 100 µA | 10 A | | <0.84 V | 6 A | | | | |
| STPS735D | I5 | a1 | SG | Rectifier | 35 V | 100 µA | 7.5 A | | <0.84 V | 15 A | | | | |
| STPS745D | I5 | a1 | SG | Rectifier | 45 V | 100 µA | 7.5 A | | <0.84 V | 15 A | | | | |
| STPS735F | J2 | a1 | SG | Rectifier | 35 V | 100 µA | 7.5 A | | <0.84 V | 15 A | | | | |
| STPS745F | J2 | a1 | SG | Rectifier | 45 V | 100 µA | 7.5 A | | <0.84 V | 15 A | | | | |
| STPS1035D | I5 | a1 | SG | Rectifier | 35 V | 100 µA | 10 A | | <0.84 V | 20 A | | | | |
| STPS1045D | I5 | a1 | SG | Rectifier | 45 V | 100 µA | 10 A | | <0.84 V | 20 A | | | | |
| STPS1035F | J2 | a1 | SG | Rectifier | 35 V | 100 µA | 10 A | | <0.84 V | 20 A | | | | |
| STPS1045F | J2 | a1 | SG | Rectifier | 45 V | 100 µA | 10 A | | <0.84 V | 20 A | | | | |
| STPS1535CF | J1 | a1 | SG | Rectifier | 35 V | 100 µA | 7.5 A | | <0.84 V | 15 A | | | | |
| STPS1545CF | J1 | a1 | SG | Rectifier | 45 V | 100 µA | 7.5 A | | <0.84 V | 15 A | | | | |
| STPS1535CT | I12 | c7 | SG | Rectifier | 35 V | 100 µA | 7.5 A | | <0.84 V | 15 A | | | | |
| STPS1545CT | I12 | c7 | SG | Rectifier | 45 V | 100 µA | 7.5 mA | | <0.84 V | 15 A | | | | |
| STPS1535D | I5 | a1 | SG | Rectifier | 35 V | 200 µA | 15 A | | <0.84 V | 30 A | | | | |
| STPS1545D | I5 | a1 | SG | Rectifier | 45 V | 200 µA | 15 A | | <0.84 V | 30 A | | | | |
| STPS1535F | J2 | a1 | SG | Rectifier | 35 V | 200 µA | 15 A | | <0.84 V | 30 A | | | | |
| STPS1545F | J2 | a1 | SG | Rectifier | 45 V | 200 µA | 15 A | | <0.84 V | 30 A | | | | |
| STPS2035CF | J1 | a1 | SG | Rect. Pair | 35 V | 100 µA | 10 A | | <0.84 V | 20 A | | | | |
| STPS2045CF | J1 | a1 | SG | Rect. Pair | 45 V | 100 µA | 10 A | | <0.84 V | 20 A | | | | |
| STPS2035CT | I12 | c7 | SG | Rect. Pair | 35 V | 100 µA | 10 A | | <0.84 V | 20 A | | | | |
| STPS2045CT | I12 | c7 | SG | Rect. Pair | 45 V | 100 µA | 10 A | | <0.84 V | 20 A | | | | |
| STPS6035CP | I16 | c7 | SG | Rect. Pair | 35 V | 500 µA | 30 A | | <0.84 V | 60 A | | | | |
| STPS6045CP | I16 | c7 | SG | Rect. Pair | 45 V | 500 µA | 30 A | | <0.84 V | 60 A | | | | |
| STPS6035CPI | I15 | c7 | SG | Rect. Pair | 35 V | 500 µA | 30 A | | <0.84 V | 60 A | | | | |
| STPS6045CPI | I15 | c7 | SG | Rect. Pair | 45 V | 500 µA | 30 A | | <0.84 V | 60 A | | | | |
| STPS12035T | H3 | d6 | SG | Rect. Pair | 35 V | 1 mA | 60 A | | <0.91 V | 120 A | | | | |
| STPS12045T | H3 | d6 | SG | Rect. Pair | 45 V | 1 mA | 60 A | | <0.91 V | 120 A | | | | |
| STPS12035TV | H2 | d6 | SG | Rect. Pair | 35 V | 1 mA | 60 A | | <0.91 V | 120 A | | | | |
| STPS12045TV | H2 | d6 | SG | Rect. Pair | 45 V | 1 mA | 60 A | | <0.91 V | 120 A | | | | |
| STPS16035T | H3 | d6 | SG | Rect. Pair | 35 V | 1 mA | 80 A | | <0.95 V | 160 A | | | | |

| | | | | | Maximum Ratings | | | | Electrical Characteristics | | | | | |
|---|---|---|---|---|---|---|---|---|---|---|---|---|---|---|
| **Type** | Case | Pin-code | | | Vrm | Irm | Ifav Ifm | Pv | Vf | If Ifp | C0 | Cr | trr ts | |
| STPS16045T | H3 | d6 | SG | Rect. Pair | 45 V | 1 mA | 80 A | | <0.95 V | 160 A | | | | |
| STPS16035TV | H2 | d6 | SG | Rect. Pair | 35 V | 1 mA | 80 A | | <0.95 V | 160 A | | | | |
| STPS16045TV | H2 | d6 | SG | Rect. Pair | 45 V | 1 mA | 80 A | | <0.95 V | 160 A | | | | |
| STPS24035T | H3 | d6 | SG | Rect. Pair | 35 V | 2 mA | 120 A | | <0.91 V | 240 A | | | | |
| STPS24045T | H3 | d6 | SG | Rect. Pair | 45 V | 2 mA | 120 A | | <0.91 V | 240 A | | | | |
| STPS24035TV | H2 | d6 | SG | Rect. Pair | 35 V | 2 mA | 120 A | | <0.91 V | 240 A | | | | |
| STPS24045TV | H2 | d6 | SG | Rect. Pair | 45 V | 2 mA | 120 A | | <0.91 V | 240 A | | | | |
| TFR1N | A3 | a1 | TO | Rectifier | 1000 V | 10 µA | 500 mA | | <1.3 V | 500 mA | | | <10 µs | |
| TFR1T | A3 | a1 | TO | Rectifier | 1500 V | 10 µA | 500 mA | | <1.3 V | 500 mA | | | <10 µs | |
| TFR2N | A3 | a1 | TO | Rectifier | 1000 V | 10 µA | 500 mA | | <1.5 V | 500 mA | | | <4 µs | |
| TFR2T | A3 | a1 | TO | Rectifier | 1500 V | 10 µA | 500 mA | | <1.5 V | 500 mA | | | <4 µs | |
| TFR3N | A3 | a1 | TO | Rectifier | 1000 V | 5 µA | 200 mA | | <1.5 V | 100 mA | | | <1.5 µs | |
| TFR3T | A3 | a1 | TO | Rectifier | 1500 V | 5 µA | 200 mA | | <1.5 V | 100 mA | | | <1.5 µs | |
| TFR4N | A3 | a1 | TO | Rectifier | 1000 V | 10 µA | 300 mA | | <1.5 V | 500 mA | | | <4 µs | |
| TFR4T | A3 | a1 | TO | Rectifier | 1500 V | 10 µA | 300 mA | | <1.5 V | 500 mA | | | <4 µs | |
| TMBYV10-20 | D1 | a1 | SG | Switch | 20 V | 500 µA | 1 A | | <0.55 V | 1 mA | 220 pF | | | |
| TMBYV10-30 | D1 | a1 | SG | Switch | 30 V | 500 µA | 1 A | | <0.55 V | 1 mA | 220 pF | | | |
| TMBYV10-40 | D1 | a1 | SG | Switch | 40 V | 500 µA | 1 A | | <0.55 V | 1 mA | 220 pF | | | |
| TMBYV10-60 | D1 | a1 | SG | Switch | 60 V | 500 µA | 1 A | | <0.7 V | 1 mA | 150 pF | | | |
| TMBYV10-20A | D1 | a1 | SG | Switch | 20 V | 300 µA | 1 A | | <0.45 V | 1 mA | 330 pF | | | |
| TMM5711 | D2 | a1 | SG | RF Diode | 70 V | | 15 mA | 0.43 W | <0.41 V | 1 mA | <2 pF | | 0.1 ns | |
| TMM5712 | D2 | a1 | SG | RF Diode | 20 V | | 35 mA | 0.43 W | <0.41 V | 1 mA | <1.2 pF | | 0.1 ns | |
| TMM6263 | D2 | a1 | SG | RF Diode | 60 V | | 15 mA | | <0.41 V | 1 mA | <2.2 pF | | 0.1 ns | |
| TMMBAR10 | D2 | a1 | SG | RF Diode | 20 V | | 35 mA | | <0.41 V | 1 mA | <1.2 pF | | 0.1 ns | |
| TMMBAR11 | D2 | a1 | SG | RF Diode | 15 V | | 20 mA | | <0.41 V | 1 mA | <1.2 pF | | 0.1 ns | |
| TMMBAR19 | D2 | a1 | SG | RF Diode | 4 V | 0.25 µA | 30 mA | | <0.60 V | 10 mA | | | | F=6dB |
| TMMBAR28 | D2 | a1 | SG | RF Diode | 70 V | 0.2 µA | 15 mA | | <0.41 V | 1 mA | | | 0.1 ns | F=6dB |
| TMMBAT19 | D2 | a1 | SG | RF Diode | 10 V | | 30 mA | | <0.4 V | 1 mA | <1.2 pF | | | F=6dB |
| TMMBAT29 | D2 | a1 | SG | RF Diode | 5 V | | 30 mA | | <0.55 V | 10 mA | <1 pF | | | F=6dB |
| TMMBAT41 | D2 | a1 | SG | Uni | 100 V | | 100 mA | | 0.4 V | 1 mA | 2 pF | | | |
| TMMBAT42 | D2 | a1 | SG | Uni | 30 V | | 200 mA | 0.2 W | <0.65 V | 50 mA | 7 pF | | 10 ns | |
| TMMBAT43 | D2 | a1 | SG | Uni | 30 V | | 200 mA | 0.2 W | <0.45 V | 15 mA | 7 pF | | 10 ns | |
| TMMBAT45 | D2 | a1 | SG | Uni | 15 V | | 30 mA | | <0.5 V | 10 mA | <1.1 pF | | 0.1 ns | F=6dB |
| TMMBAT46 | D2 | a1 | SG | Uni | 100 V | | 150 mA | 0.15 W | <0.45 V | 10 mA | 10 pF | | | |
| TMMBAT47 | D2 | a1 | SG | Uni | 20 V | | 350 mA | 0.33 W | <0.8 V | 150 mA | 20 pF | | 10 ns | |
| TMMBAT48 | D2 | a1 | SG | Uni | 40 V | | 350 mA | 0.33 W | <0.75 V | 150 mA | 20 pF | | 10 ns | |
| TMMBAT49 | D2 | a1 | SG | Uni | 80 V | 200 µA | 500 mA | | <0.42 V | 100 mA | 120 pF | | | |
| TVR1B | A3 | a1 | TO | Rectifier | 100 V | 10 µA | 500 mA | | <1.2 V | 500 mA | | | <20 µs | |
| TVR1G | A3 | a1 | TO | Rectifier | 400 V | 10 µA | 500 mA | | <1.2 V | 500 mA | | | <20 µs | |
| TVR1J | A3 | a1 | TO | Rectifier | 600 V | 10 µA | 500 mA | | <1.2 V | 500 mA | | | <20 µs | |

| Type | Case | Pin-code | | | Maximum Ratings | | | | Electrical Characteristics | | | | | |
|---|---|---|---|---|---|---|---|---|---|---|---|---|---|---|
| | | | | | Vrm | Irm | Ifav Ifm | Pv | Vf | If Ifp | C0 | Cr | trr ts | |
| TVR2B | A3 | a1 | TO | Rectifier | 100 V | 10 µA | 500 mA | | <1.4 V | 1 A | | | <20 µs | |
| TVR2G | A3 | a1 | TO | Rectifier | 400 V | 10 µA | 500 mA | | <1.4 V | 1 A | | | <20 µs | |
| TVR2J | A3 | a1 | TO | Rectifier | 600 V | 10 µA | 500 mA | | <1.4 V | 1 A | | | <20 µs | |
| TVR4J | B16 | a1 | TO | Rectifier | 600 V | 10 µA | 1.2 A | | <1.2 V | 5 A | | | <20 µs | |
| TVR4N | B16 | a1 | TO | Rectifier | 1000 V | 10 µA | 1.2 A | | <1.2 V | 5 A | | | <20 µs | |
| TVR5B | A17 | a1 | TO | Rectifier | 100 V | 10 µA | 500 mA | | <1.2 V | 500 mA | | | <500 ns | |
| TVR5G | A17 | a1 | TO | Rectifier | 400 V | 10 µA | 500 mA | | <1.2 V | 500 mA | | | <500 ns | |
| TVR5J | A17 | a1 | TO | Rectifier | 600 V | 10 µA | 500 mA | | <1.2 V | 500 mA | | | <500 ns | |
| U1B4B42 | F13 | d23 | TO | Rect. Bridge | 100 V | 10 µA | 1 A | | <1 V | 500 mA | | | | |
| U1G4B42 | F13 | d23 | TO | Rect. Bridge | 400 V | 10 µA | 1 A | | <1 V | 500 mA | | | | |
| U1J4B42 | F13 | d23 | TO | Rect. Bridge | 600 V | 10 µA | 1 A | | <1 V | 500 mA | | | | |
| U1BC44 | G5 | a1 | TO | Rectifier | 100 V | 10 µA | 900 mA | | <1.2 V | 1 A | | | | |
| U1GC44 | G5 | a1 | TO | Rectifier | 400 V | 10 µA | 900 mA | | <1.2 V | 1 A | | | | |
| U1JC44 | G5 | a1 | TO | Rectifier | 600 V | 10 µA | 900 mA | | <1.2 V | 1 A | | | | |
| U1DL44A | G5 | a1 | TO | Rectifier | 200 V | 10 µA | 1 A | | <0.98 V | 1 A | | | <35 ns | |
| U1DL49 | F6 | c1 | TO | Rectifier | 200 V | 10 µA | 1 A | | <0.98 V | 1 A | | | <60 ns | |
| U1GU44 | F6 | c1 | TO | Rectifier | 400 V | 50 µA | 1 A | | <1.5 V | 1 A | | | <100 ns | |
| U1GWJ2C49 | F6 | c7 | TO | Rect. Pair | 40 V | 500 µA | 1 A | | <0.55 V | 500 mA | 25 pF | | | |
| U1GWJ44 | G5 | a1 | TO | Rectifier | 40 V | 500 µA | 1 A | | <0.55 V | 1 A | 47 pF | | <35 ns | |
| U1GWJ49 | F6 | c1 | TO | Rectifier | 40 V | 500 µA | 1 A | | <0.55 V | 1 A | 50 pF | | <35 ns | |
| U1JU41 | G5 | a1 | TO | Rectifier | 600 V | 100 µA | 1 A | | <2 V | 1 A | | | <100 ns | |
| U1Q4B42 | F13 | d23 | TO | Rect. Bridge | 1200 V | 10 µA | 1 A | | <1.2 V | 500 mA | | | | |
| U2GWJ2C42 | F10 | c7 | TO | Rect. Pair | 40 V | 1 mA | 2 A | | <0.55 V | 1 A | 45 pF | | | |
| U3GWJ2C42 | F10 | a1 | TO | Rect. Pair | 40 V | 2 mA | 3 A | | <0.55 V | 3 A | 45 pF | | | comm-k |
| U3GWJ42 | B10 | a1 | TO | Rectifier | 40 V | 3 mA | 3 A | | <0.55 V | 3 A | 132 pF | | <35 ns | |
| U05B4B48 | F15 | d23 | TO | Rect. Bridge | 100 V | 10 µA | 500 mA | | <1 V | 400 mA | | | | |
| U05G4B48 | F15 | d23 | TO | Rect. Bridge | 400 V | 10 µA | 500 mA | | <1 V | 400 mA | | | | |
| U05J4B48 | F15 | d23 | TO | Rect. Bridge | 600 V | 10 µA | 500 mA | | <1 V | 400 mA | | | | |
| U5DL2C48A | F9 | c7 | TO | Rect. Pair | 200 V | 10 µA | 5 A | | <0.98 V | 2.5 A | | | <35 ns | |
| U5FL2C48A | F9 | c7 | TO | Rect. Pair | 200 V | 10 µA | 5 A | | <1.3 V | 2.5 A | | | <35 ns | |
| U05GH44 | G5 | a1 | TO | Rectifier | 400 V | 10 µA | 500 mA | | <1.2 V | 500 mA | | | <1.5 µs | |
| U05JH44 | G5 | a1 | TO | Rectifier | 600 V | 10 µA | 500 mA | | <1.2 V | 500 mA | | | <1.5 µs | |
| U05GU4B48 | F15 | d23 | TO | Rect. Bridge | 400 V | 100 µA | 500 mA | | <0.65 V | 20 mA | | | | |
| U5GWJ2C48 | F9 | c7 | TO | Rect. Pair | 40 V | 3.5 mA | 5 A | | <0.55 V | 2.5 A | 125 pF | | | |
| U05NH44 | G5 | a1 | TO | Rectifier | 1000 V | 10 µA | 500 mA | | <1.5 V | 500 mA | | | <4 µs | |
| U05TH44 | G5 | a1 | TO | Rectifier | 1500 V | 10 µA | 500 mA | | <1.5 V | 500 mA | | | <4 µs | |
| U05NU44 | G5 | a1 | TO | Rectifier | 1000 V | 100 µA | 500 mA | | <3 V | 500 mA | | | <100 ns | |
| U10DL2C48A | I23 | c7 | TO | Rect. Pair | 200 V | 10 µA | 10 A | | <0.98 V | 5 A | | | <35 ns | |
| U10FL2C48A | I23 | c7 | TO | Rect. Pair | 300 V | 10 µA | 10 A | | <1.3 V | 5 A | | | <35 ns | |
| U10GWJ2C48 | F9 | c7 | TO | Rect. Pair | 40 V | 3.5 mA | 10 A | | <0.55 V | 5 A | 235 pF | | <35 ns | comm-k |

| Type | Case | Pin-code | | | Maximum Ratings | | | | Electrical Characteristics | | | | | |
|------|------|----------|---|---|-----|-----|-----|-----|-----|-----|-----|-----|-----|-----|
| | | | | | Vrm | Irm | Ifav Ifm | Pv | Vf | If Ifp | C0 | Cr | trr *ts* | |
| U20DL2C48A | F9 | c7 | TO | Rect. Pair | 200 V | 50 µA | 20 A | | <0.98 V | 10 A | | | <35 ns | |
| U20FL2C48A | F9 | c7 | TO | Rect. Pair | 300 V | 50 µA | 20 A | | <1.3 V | 10 A | | | <35 ns | |
| U30GWJ2C48 | F9 | c7 | TO | Rect. Pair | 40 V | 15 mA | 30 A | | <0.55 V | 15 A | 620 pF | | | |
| U30JWJ2C48 | F9 | c7 | TO | Rect. Pair | 60 V | 15 mA | 30 A | | <0.58 V | 15 A | 620 pF | | | |
| UX-A1B | B24 | a1 | RD | HV Rectifier | 4 kV | 2 µA | 250 mA | | 10 V | 350 mA | | | 180 ns | Ifav at Tc=110°C |
| UX-FOB | B24 | a1 | RD | HV Rectifier | 8 kV | 10 µA | 350 mA | | 4 V | 350 mA | | | 18 ns | Ifav at Ta=100°C |

# Z Diodes & TVS

- ▶ Suppressor Diodes
- ▶ Stabistor Diodes
- ▶ Reference LEDs
- ▶ Bidirectional Z Diodes
- ▶ Bidirectional Suppressor Diodes
- ▶ Breakover Diodes
- ▶ Reference Z Diodes

| Type | Case | Pin-code | | | Maximum Ratings | | | | Electrical Characteristics | | | | |
|---|---|---|---|---|---|---|---|---|---|---|---|---|---|
| | | | | | Vcla Vbro | Its | Izm | Pv | Pvts | Vz | Iz Is | rz | TK | |
| 1N746A | A1 | a1 | MO,NS | Z Diode | | | 110 mA | 0.5 W | | 3.3 V | 20 mA | <28Ω | | CD |
| 1N747A | A1 | a1 | MO,NS | Z Diode | | | 100 mA | 0.5 W | | 3.6 V | 20 mA | <24Ω | | CD |
| 1N748A | A1 | a1 | MO,NS | Z Diode | | | 95 mA | 0.5 W | | 3.9 V | 20 mA | <23Ω | | CD |
| 1N749A | A1 | a1 | MO,NS | Z Diode | | | 85 mA | 0.5 W | | 4.3 V | 20 mA | <22Ω | | CD |
| 1N750A | A1 | a1 | MO,NS | Z Diode | | | 75 mA | 0.5 W | | 4.7 V | 20 mA | <19Ω | | CD |
| 1N751A | A1 | a1 | MO,NS | Z Diode | | | 70 mA | 0.5 W | | 5.1 V | 20 mA | <17Ω | | CD |
| 1N752A | A1 | a1 | MO,NS | Z Diode | | | 65 mA | 0.5 W | | 5.6 V | 20 mA | <11Ω | | CD |
| 1N753A | A1 | a1 | MO,NS | Z Diode | | | 60 mA | 0.5 W | | 6.2 V | 20 mA | <7Ω | | CD |
| 1N754A | A1 | a1 | MO,NS | Z Diode | | | 55 mA | 0.5 W | | 6.8 V | 20 mA | <5Ω | | CD |
| 1N755A | A1 | a1 | MO,NS | Z Diode | | | 50 mA | 0.5 W | | 7.5 V | 20 mA | <6Ω | | CD |
| 1N756A | A1 | a1 | MO,NS | Z Diode | | | 45 mA | 0.5 W | | 8.2 V | 20 mA | <8Ω | | CD |
| 1N757A | A1 | a1 | MO,NS | Z Diode | | | 40 mA | 0.5 W | | 9.1 V | 20 mA | <10Ω | | CD |
| 1N758A | A1 | a1 | MO,NS | Z Diode | | | 35 mA | 0.5 W | | 10 V | 20 mA | <17Ω | | CD |
| 1N759A | A1 | a1 | MO,NS | Z Diode | | | 30 mA | 0.5 W | | 12 V | 20 mA | <17Ω | | CD |
| 1N821 | A1 | a1 | SG | Ref. Z Diode | | | 50 mA | 0.4 W | | 6.2 V | 7.5 mA | <15Ω | 100·10^6/°C | |
| 1N823 | A1 | a1 | SG | Ref. Z Diode | | | | 0.4 W | | 6.2 V | 7.5 mA | <15Ω | 50·10^6/°C | |
| 1N825 | A1 | a1 | SG | Ref. Z Diode | | | | 0.4 W | | 6.2 V | 7.5 mA | <15Ω | 20·10^6/°C | |
| 1N827 | A1 | a1 | SG | Ref. Z Diode | | | | 0.4 W | | 6.2 V | 7.5 mA | <15Ω | 10·10^6/°C | |
| 1N829 | A1 | a1 | SG | Ref. Z Diode | | | | 0.4 W | | 6.2 V | 7.5 mA | <15Ω | 5·10^6/°C | |
| 1N821 | A2 | a1 | PH | Ref. Z Diode | | | 50 mA | 0.4 W | | 6.2 V | 7.5 mA | 15Ω | 100·10^6/°C | |
| 1N823 | A2 | a1 | PH | Ref. Z Diode | | | 50 mA | 0.4 W | | 6.2 V | 7.5 mA | 15Ω | 50·10^6/°C | |
| 1N825 | A2 | a1 | PH | Ref. Z Diode | | | 50 mA | 0.4 W | | 6.2 V | 7.5 mA | 15Ω | 20·10^6/°C | |
| 1N827 | A2 | a1 | PH | Ref. Z Diode | | | 50 mA | 0.4 W | | 6.2 V | 7.5 mA | 15Ω | 10·10^6/°C | |
| 1N829 | A2 | a1 | PH | Ref. Z Diode | | | 50 mA | 0.4 W | | 6.2 V | 7.5 mA | 15Ω | 5·10^6/°C | |
| s1N821A | A1 | a1 | SG | Ref. Z Diode | | | | 0.4 W | | 6.2 V | 7.5 mA | <10Ω | 100·10^6/°C | |
| 1N823A | A1 | a1 | SG | Ref. Z Diode | | | | 0.4 W | | 6.2 V | 7.5 mA | <10Ω | 50·10^6/°C | |
| 1N825A | A1 | a1 | SG | Ref. Z Diode | | | | 0.4 W | | 6.2 V | 7.5 mA | <10Ω | 20·10^6/°C | |
| 1N827A | A1 | a1 | SG | Ref. Z Diode | | | | 0.4 W | | 6.2 V | 7.5 mA | <10Ω | 10·10^6/°C | |
| 1N829A | A1 | a1 | SG | Ref. Z Diode | | | | 0.4 W | | 6.2 V | 7.5 mA | <10Ω | 5·10^6/°C | |
| 1N821A | A2 | a1 | PH | Ref. Z Diode | | | 50 mA | 0.4 W | | 6.2 V | 7.5 mA | 10Ω | 100·10^6/°C | |
| 1N823A | A2 | a1 | PH | Ref. Z Diode | | | 50 mA | 0.4 W | | 6.2 V | 7.5 mA | 10Ω | 50·10^6/°C | |
| 1N825A | A2 | a1 | PH | Ref. Z Diode | | | 50 mA | 0.4 W | | 6.2 V | 7.5 mA | 10Ω | 20·10^6/°C | |
| 1N827A | A2 | a1 | PH | Ref. Z Diode | | | 50 mA | 0.4 W | | 6.2 V | 7.5 mA | 10Ω | 10·10^6/°C | |
| 1N829A | A2 | a1 | PH | Ref. Z Diode | | | 50 mA | 0.4 W | | 6.2 V | 7.5 mA | 10Ω | 5·10^6/°C | |
| 1N935 | A1 | a1 | SG | Ref. Z Diode | | | | 0.5 W | | 9.0 V | 7.5 mA | <20Ω | 100·10^6/°C | |
| 1N936 | A1 | a1 | SG | Ref. Z Diode | | | | 0.5 W | | 9.0 V | 7.5 mA | <20Ω | 50·10^6/°C | |
| 1N937 | A1 | a1 | SG | Ref. Z Diode | | | | 0.5 W | | 9.0 V | 7.5 mA | <20Ω | 20·10^6/°C | |
| 1N938 | A1 | a1 | SG | Ref. Z Diode | | | | 0.5 W | | 9.0 V | 7.5 mA | <20Ω | 10·10^6/°C | |
| 1N939 | A1 | a1 | SG | Ref. Z Diode | | | | 0.5 W | | 9.0 V | 7.5 mA | <20Ω | 5·10^6/°C | |
| 1N936A | A1 | a1 | SG | Ref. Z Diode | | | | 0.5 W | | 9.0 V | 7.5 mA | <20Ω | 50·10^6/°C | |

| Type | Case | Pin-code | | | $V_{cla}$ $V_{bro}$ | $I_{ts}$ | $I_{zm}$ | $P_v$ | $P_{vts}$ | $V_z$ | $I_z$ $I_s$ | $r_z$ | TK | |
|------|------|----------|---|---|------|-----|-----|----|------|----|------|----|----|---|
| | | | | | **Maximum Ratings** | | | | | **Electrical Characteristics** | | | | |
| 1N937A | A1 | a1 | SG | Ref. Z Diode | | | | 0.5 W | | 9.0 V | 7.5 mA | <20 Ω | $20 \cdot 10^6$/°C | |
| 1N938A | A1 | a1 | SG | Ref. Z Diode | | | | 0.5 W | | 9.0 V | 7.5 mA | <20 Ω | $10 \cdot 10^6$/°C | |
| 1N939A | A1 | a1 | SG | Ref. Z Diode | | | | 0.5 W | | 9.0 V | 7.5 mA | <20 Ω | $5 \cdot 10^6$/°C | |
| 1N935A | A1 | a1 | SG | Ref. Z Diode | | | | 0.5 W | | 9.0 V | 7.5 mA | <20 Ω | $100 \cdot 10^6$/°C | |
| 1N935B | A1 | a1 | SG | Ref. Z Diode | | | | 0.5 W | | 9.0 V | 7.5 mA | <20 Ω | $100 \cdot 10^6$/°C | |
| 1N936B | A1 | a1 | SG | Ref. Z Diode | | | | 0.5 W | | 9.0 V | 7.5 mA | <20 Ω | $50 \cdot 10^6$/°C | |
| 1N937B | A1 | a1 | SG | Ref. Z Diode | | | | 0.5 W | | 9.0 V | 7.5 mA | <20 Ω | $20 \cdot 10^6$/°C | |
| 1N938B | A1 | a1 | SG | Ref. Z Diode | | | | 0.5 W | | 9.0 V | 7.5 mA | <20 Ω | $10 \cdot 10^6$/°C | |
| 1N939B | A1 | a1 | SG | Ref. Z Diode | | | | 0.5 W | | 9.0 V | 7.5 mA | <20 Ω | $5 \cdot 10^6$/°C | |
| 1N957B | A1 | a1 | MO,NS | Z Diode | | | 220 mA | 0.5 W | | 6.8 V | 18.5 mA | 4.5 Ω | | ACD |
| 1N958B | A1 | a1 | MO,NS | Z Diode | | | 200 mA | 0.5 W | | 7.5 V | 16.5 mA | 5.5 Ω | | ACD |
| 1N959B | A1 | a1 | MO,NS | Z Diode | | | 180 mA | 0.5 W | | 8.2 V | 15 mA | 6.5 Ω | | ACD |
| 1N960B | A1 | a1 | MO,NS | Z Diode | | | 165 mA | 0.5 W | | 9.1 V | 14 mA | 7.5 Ω | | ACD |
| 1N961B | A1 | a1 | MO,NS | Z Diode | | | 145 mA | 0.5 W | | 10 V | 12.5 mA | 8.5 Ω | | ACD |
| 1N962B | A1 | a1 | MO,NS | Z Diode | | | 135 mA | 0.5 W | | 11 V | 11.5 mA | 9.5 Ω | | ACD |
| 1N963B | A1 | a1 | MO,NS | Z Diode | | | 120 mA | 0.5 W | | 12 V | 10.5 mA | 11.5 Ω | | ACD |
| 1N964B | A1 | a1 | MO,NS | Z Diode | | | 110 mA | 0.5 W | | 13 V | 9.5 mA | 13 Ω | | ACD |
| 1N965B | A1 | a1 | MO,NS | Z Diode | | | 98 mA | 0.5 W | | 15 V | 8.5 mA | 16 Ω | | ACD |
| 1N966B | A1 | a1 | MO,NS | Z Diode | | | 90 mA | 0.5 W | | 16 V | 7.8 mA | 17 Ω | | ACD |
| 1N967B | A1 | a1 | MO,NS | Z Diode | | | 80 mA | 0.5 W | | 18 V | 7 mA | 21 Ω | | ACD |
| 1N968B | A1 | a1 | MO,NS | Z Diode | | | 72 mA | 0.5 W | | 20 V | 6.2 mA | 25 Ω | | ACD |
| 1N969B | A1 | a1 | MO,NS | Z Diode | | | 66 mA | 0.5 W | | 22 V | 5.6 mA | 29 Ω | | ACD |
| 1N970B | A1 | a1 | MO,NS | Z Diode | | | 60 mA | 0.5 W | | 24 V | 5.2 mA | 33 Ω | | ACD |
| 1N971B | A1 | a1 | MO,NS | Z Diode | | | 53 mA | 0.5 W | | 27 V | 4.6 mA | 41 Ω | | ACD |
| 1N972B | A1 | a1 | MO,NS | Z Diode | | | 48 mA | 0.5 W | | 30 V | 4.2 mA | 49 Ω | | ACD |
| 1N973B | A1 | a1 | MO,NS | Z Diode | | | 44 mA | 0.5 W | | 33 V | 3.8 mA | 58 Ω | | ACD |
| 1N974B | A1 | a1 | MO | Z Diode | | | 40 mA | 0.5 W | | 36 V | 3.4 mA | 70 Ω | | ACD |
| 1N975B | A1 | a1 | MO | Z Diode | | | 37 mA | 0.5 W | | 39 V | 3.2 mA | 80 Ω | | ACD |
| 1N976B | A1 | a1 | MO | Z Diode | | | 33 mA | 0.5 W | | 43 V | 3 mA | 93 Ω | | ACD |
| 1N977B | A1 | a1 | MO | Z Diode | | | 30 mA | 0.5 W | | 47 V | 2.7 mA | 105 Ω | | ACD |
| 1N978B | A1 | a1 | MO | Z Diode | | | 27 mA | 0.5 W | | 51 V | 2.5 mA | 125 Ω | | ACD |
| 1N979B | A1 | a1 | MO | Z Diode | | | 25 mA | 0.5 W | | 56 V | 2.2 mA | 150 Ω | | ACD |
| 1N980B | A1 | a1 | MO | Z Diode | | | 21 mA | 0.5 W | | 62 V | 2 mA | 185 Ω | | ACD |
| 1N981B | A1 | a1 | MO | Z Diode | | | 20 mA | 0.5 W | | 68 V | 1.8 mA | 230 Ω | | ACD |
| 1N982B | A1 | a1 | MO | Z Diode | | | 18 mA | 0.5 W | | 75 V | 1.7 mA | 270 Ω | | ACD |
| 1N983B | A1 | a1 | MO | Z Diode | | | 16 mA | 0.5 W | | 82 V | 1.5 mA | 330 Ω | | ACD |
| 1N984B | A1 | a1 | MO | Z Diode | | | 15 mA | 0.5 W | | 91 V | 1.4 mA | 400 Ω | | ACD |
| 1N985B | A1 | a1 | MO | Z Diode | | | 13 mA | 0.5 W | | 100 V | 1.3 mA | 500 Ω | | ACD |
| 1N986B | A1 | a1 | MO | Z Diode | | | 12 mA | 0.5 W | | 110 V | 1.1 mA | 750 Ω | | ACD |
| 1N987B | A1 | a1 | MO | Z Diode | | | 11 mA | 0.5 W | | 120 V | 1 mA | 900 Ω | | ACD |

| Type | Case | Pin-code | | | Vcla Vbro | Its | Izm | Pv | Pvts | Vz | Iz Is | rz | TK | |
|------|------|----------|---|---|-----------|-----|-----|-----|------|-----|-------|-----|----|---|
| | | | | | | **Maximum Ratings** | | | | **Electrical Characteristics** | | | | |
| 1N988B | A1 | a1 | MO | Z Diode | | | 10 mA | 0.5 W | | 130 V | 0.95 mA | 1100 Ω | | ACD |
| 1N989B | A1 | a1 | MO | Z Diode | | | 9 mA | 0.5 W | | 150 V | 0.85 mA | 1500 Ω | | ACD |
| 1N990B | A1 | a1 | MO | Z Diode | | | 8.6 mA | 0.5 W | | 160 V | 0.8 mA | 1700 Ω | | ACD |
| 1N991B | A1 | a1 | MO | Z Diode | | | 8 mA | 0.5 W | | 180 V | 0.68 mA | 2200 Ω | | ACD |
| 1N992B | A1 | a1 | MO | Z Diode | | | 7.5 mA | 0.5 W | | 200 V | 0.65 mA | 2500 Ω | | ACD |
| 1N3016B | C1 | b1 | SG | Z Diode | | | 140 mA | 1 W | | 6.8 V | 37 mA | <3.5 Ω | $400 \cdot 10^6/°C$ | P |
| 1N3017B | C1 | b1 | SG | Z Diode | | | 130 mA | 1 W | | 7.5 V | 34 mA | <4 Ω | $450 \cdot 10^6/°C$ | |
| 1N3018B | C1 | b1 | SG | Z Diode | | | 110 mA | 1 W | | 8.2 V | 31 mA | <4.5 Ω | $480 \cdot 10^6/°C$ | |
| 1N3019B | C1 | b1 | SG | Z Diode | | | 100 mA | 1 W | | 9.1 V | 28 mA | <5 Ω | $510 \cdot 10^6/°C$ | |
| 1N3020B | C1 | b1 | SG | Z Diode | | | 94 mA | 1 W | | 10 V | 25 mA | <7 Ω | $550 \cdot 10^6/°C$ | P |
| 1N3021B | C1 | b1 | SG | Z Diode | | | 86 mA | 1 W | | 11 V | 23 mA | <8 Ω | $600 \cdot 10^6/°C$ | |
| 1N3022B | C1 | b1 | SG | Z Diode | | | 79 mA | 1 W | | 12 V | 21 mA | <9 Ω | $650 \cdot 10^6/°C$ | P |
| 1N3023B | C1 | b1 | SG | Z Diode | | | 71 mA | 1 W | | 13 V | 19 mA | <10 Ω | $650 \cdot 10^6/°C$ | |
| 1N3024B | C1 | b1 | SG | Z Diode | | | 64 mA | 1 W | | 15 V | 17 mA | <14 Ω | $700 \cdot 10^6/°C$ | |
| 1N3025B | C1 | b1 | SG | Z Diode | | | 59 mA | 1 W | | 16 V | 15.5 mA | <16 Ω | $700 \cdot 10^6/°C$ | |
| 1N3026B | C1 | b1 | SG | Z Diode | | | 52 mA | 1 W | | 18 V | 14 mA | <20 Ω | $750 \cdot 10^6/°C$ | |
| 1N3027B | C1 | b1 | SG | Z Diode | | | 47 mA | 1 W | | 20 V | 12.5 mA | <22 Ω | $750 \cdot 10^6/°C$ | |
| 1N3028B | C1 | b1 | SG | Z Diode | | | 43 mA | 1 W | | 22 V | 11.5 mA | <23 Ω | $900 \cdot 10^6/°C$ | |
| 1N3029B | C1 | b1 | SG | Z Diode | | | 39 mA | 1 W | | 24 V | 10.5 mA | <25 Ω | $800 \cdot 10^6/°C$ | P |
| 1N3030B | C1 | b1 | SG | Z Diode | | | 35 mA | 1 W | | 27 V | 9.5 mA | <35 Ω | $850 \cdot 10^6/°C$ | |
| 1N3031B | C1 | b1 | SG | Z Diode | | | 31 mA | 1 W | | 30 V | 8.5 mA | <40 Ω | $850 \cdot 10^6/°C$ | |
| 1N3032B | C1 | b1 | SG | Z Diode | | | 29 mA | 1 W | | 33 V | 7.5 mA | <45 Ω | $850 \cdot 10^6/°C$ | |
| 1N3033B | C1 | b1 | SG | Z Diode | | | 26 mA | 1 W | | 36 V | 7 mA | <50 Ω | $850 \cdot 10^6/°C$ | |
| 1N3034B | C1 | b1 | SG | Z Diode | | | 24 mA | 1 W | | 36 V | 6.5 mA | <60 Ω | $900 \cdot 10^6/°C$ | |
| 1N3035B | C1 | b1 | SG | Z Diode | | | 22 mA | 1 W | | 43 V | 6 mA | <70 Ω | $900 \cdot 10^6/°C$ | |
| 1N3036B | C1 | b1 | SG | Z Diode | | | 20 mA | 1 W | | 47 V | 5.5 mA | <80 Ω | $900 \cdot 10^6/°C$ | |
| 1N3037B | C1 | b1 | SG | Z Diode | | | 19 mA | 1 W | | 51 V | 5 mA | <95 Ω | $900 \cdot 10^6/°C$ | |
| 1N3038B | C1 | b1 | SG | Z Diode | | | 17 mA | 1 W | | 56 V | 4.5 mA | <110 Ω | $900 \cdot 10^6/°C$ | |
| 1N3039B | C1 | b1 | SG | Z Diode | | | 15 mA | 1 W | | 62 V | 4 mA | <125 Ω | $900 \cdot 10^6/°C$ | |
| 1N3040B | C1 | b1 | SG | Z Diode | | | 14 mA | 1 W | | 68 V | 3.7 mA | <150 Ω | $900 \cdot 10^6/°C$ | |
| 1N3041B | C1 | b1 | SG | Z Diode | | | 13 mA | 1 W | | 75 V | 3.3 mA | <175 Ω | $900 \cdot 10^6/°C$ | |
| 1N3042B | C1 | b1 | SG | Z Diode | | | 12 mA | 1 W | | 82 V | 3 mA | <200 Ω | $900 \cdot 10^6/°C$ | |
| 1N3043B | C1 | b1 | SG | Z Diode | | | 10 mA | 1 W | | 91 V | 2.8 mA | <250 Ω | $900 \cdot 10^6/°C$ | |
| 1N3044B | C1 | b1 | SG | Z Diode | | | 9 mA | 1 W | | 100 V | 2.5 mA | <350 Ω | $900 \cdot 10^6/°C$ | |
| 1N3045B | C1 | b1 | SG | Z Diode | | | 9 mA | 1 W | | 110 V | 2.3 mA | <450 Ω | $950 \cdot 10^6/°C$ | |
| 1N3046B | C1 | b1 | SG | Z Diode | | | 8 mA | 1 W | | 120 V | 2 mA | <550 Ω | $950 \cdot 10^6/°C$ | |
| 1N3047B | C1 | b1 | SG | Z Diode | | | 7 mA | 1 W | | 130 V | 1.9 mA | <700 Ω | $950 \cdot 10^6/°C$ | |
| 1N3048B | C1 | b1 | SG | Z Diode | | | 6 mA | 1 W | | 150 V | 1.7 mA | <1000 Ω | $950 \cdot 10^6/°C$ | |
| 1N3049B | C1 | b1 | SG | Z Diode | | | 6 mA | 1 W | | 160 V | 1.6 mA | <1100 Ω | $950 \cdot 10^6/°C$ | |
| 1N3050B | C1 | b1 | SG | Z Diode | | | 5 mA | 1 W | | 180 V | 1.4 mA | <1200 Ω | $950 \cdot 10^6/°C$ | |

| Type | Case | Pin-code | | | Vcla Vbro | Its | Izm | Pv | Pvts | Vz | Iz Is | rz | TK | |
|------|------|------|------|------|------|------|------|------|------|------|------|------|------|------|
| | | | | | | | | **Maximum Ratings** | | | | **Electrical Characteristics** | | |
| 1N3051B | C1 | b1 | SG | Z Diode | | | 5 mA | 1 W | | 200 V | 1.2 mA | <1500 Ω | 1000·10$^6$/°C | |
| 1N3154 | A1 | a1 | SG | Ref. Z Diode | | | | 0.4 W | | 8.4 V | 10 mA | <15 Ω | 100·10$^6$/°C | |
| 1N3155 | A1 | a1 | SG | Ref. Z Diode | | | | 0.4 W | | 8.4 V | 10 mA | <15 Ω | 50·10$^6$/°C | |
| 1N3156 | A1 | a1 | SG | Ref. Z Diode | | | | 0.4 W | | 8.4 V | 10 mA | <15 Ω | 20·10$^6$/°C | |
| 1N3157 | A1 | a1 | SG | Ref. Z Diode | | | | 0.4 W | | 8.4 V | 10 mA | <15 Ω | 10·10$^6$/°C | |
| 1N3155A | A1 | a1 | SG | Ref. Z Diode | | | | 0.4 W | | 8.4 V | 10 mA | <15 Ω | 50·10$^6$/°C | |
| 1N3154A | A1 | a1 | SG | Ref. Z Diode | | | | 0.4 W | | 8.4 V | 10 mA | <15 Ω | 100·10$^6$/°C | |
| 1N3156A | A1 | a1 | SG | Ref. Z Diode | | | | 0.4 W | | 8.4 V | 10 mA | <15 Ω | 20·10$^6$/°C | |
| 1N3157A | A1 | a1 | SG | Ref. Z Diode | | | | 0.4 W | | 8.4 V | 10 mA | <15 Ω | 10·10$^6$/°C | |
| 1N4099 | A1 | a1 | SG | Z Diode | | | 35 mA | 0.25 W | | 6.8 V | 0.25 mA | 200 Ω | | |
| 1N4100 | A1 | a1 | SG | Z Diode | | | 32 mA | 0.25 W | | 7.5 V | 0.25 mA | 200 Ω | | |
| 1N4101 | A1 | a1 | SG | Z Diode | | | 29 mA | 0.25 W | | 8.2 V | 0.25 mA | 200 Ω | | |
| 1N4102 | A1 | a1 | SG | Z Diode | | | 27 mA | 0.25 W | | 8.7 V | 0.25 mA | 200 Ω | | |
| 1N4103 | A1 | a1 | SG | Z Diode | | | 26 mA | 0.25 W | | 9.1 V | 0.25 mA | 200 Ω | | |
| 1N4104 | A1 | a1 | SG | Z Diode | | | 25 mA | 0.25 W | | 10 V | 0.25 mA | 200 Ω | | |
| 1N4105 | A1 | a1 | SG | Z Diode | | | 22 mA | 0.25 W | | 11 V | 0.25 mA | 200 Ω | | |
| 1N4106 | A1 | a1 | SG | Z Diode | | | 20 mA | 0.25 W | | 12 V | 0.25 mA | 200 Ω | | |
| 1N4107 | A1 | a1 | SG | Z Diode | | | 19 mA | 0.25 W | | 13 V | 0.25 mA | 200 Ω | | |
| 1N4108 | A1 | a1 | SG | Z Diode | | | 18 mA | 0.25 W | | 14 V | 0.25 mA | 200 Ω | | |
| 1N4109 | A1 | a1 | SG | Z Diode | | | 16 mA | 0.25 W | | 15 V | 0.25 mA | 100 Ω | | |
| 1N4110 | A1 | a1 | SG | Z Diode | | | 15 mA | 0.25 W | | 16 V | 0.25 mA | 100 Ω | | |
| 1N4111 | A1 | a1 | SG | Z Diode | | | 15 mA | 0.25 W | | 17 V | 0.25 mA | 100 Ω | | |
| 1N4112 | A1 | a1 | SG | Z Diode | | | 13 mA | 0.25 W | | 18 V | 0.25 mA | 100 Ω | | |
| 1N4113 | A1 | a1 | SG | Z Diode | | | 13 mA | 0.25 W | | 19 V | 0.25 mA | 150 Ω | | |
| 1N4114 | A1 | a1 | SG | Z Diode | | | 12 mA | 0.25 W | | 20 V | 0.25 mA | 150 Ω | | |
| 1N4115 | A1 | a1 | SG | Z Diode | | | 11 mA | 0.25 W | | 22 V | 0.25 mA | 150 Ω | | |
| 1N4116 | A1 | a1 | SG | Z Diode | | | 10 mA | 0.25 W | | 24 V | 0.25 mA | 150 Ω | | |
| 1N4117 | A1 | a1 | SG | Z Diode | | | 10 mA | 0.25 W | | 25 V | 0.25 mA | 150 Ω | | |
| 1N4118 | A1 | a1 | SG | Z Diode | | | 9 mA | 0.25 W | | 27 V | 0.25 mA | 150 Ω | | |
| 1N4187B | A3 | a1 | SG | Z Diode | | | 9 mA | 1 W | | 110 V | 2.3 mA | 450 Ω | 1000·10$^6$/°C | |
| 1N4188B | A3 | a1 | SG | Z Diode | | | 8 mA | 1 W | | 120 V | 2 mA | 550 Ω | 1000·10$^6$/°C | |
| 1N4189B | A3 | a1 | SG | Z Diode | | | 7 mA | 1 W | | 130 V | 1.9 mA | 700 Ω | 1000·10$^6$/°C | |
| 1N4190B | A3 | a1 | SG | Z Diode | | | 6 mA | 1 W | | 150 V | 1.7 mA | 1000 Ω | 1000·10$^6$/°C | |
| 1N4191B | A3 | a1 | SG | Z Diode | | | 6 mA | 1 W | | 170 V | 1.6 mA | 1100 Ω | 1000·10$^6$/°C | |
| 1N4192B | A3 | a1 | SG | Z Diode | | | 5 mA | 1 W | | 180 V | 1.4 mA | 1200 Ω | 1000·10$^6$/°C | |
| 1N4193B | A3 | a1 | SG | Z Diode | | | 5 mA | 1 W | | 200 V | 1.2 mA | 1500 Ω | 1000·10$^6$/°C | |
| 1N4370A | A1 | a1 | MO | Z Diode | | | 150 mA | 0.5 W | | 2.4 V | 20 mA | <30 Ω | | CD |
| 1N4371A | A1 | a1 | MO | Z Diode | | | 135 mA | 0.5 W | | 2.7 V | 20 mA | <30 Ω | | CD |
| 1N4372A | A1 | a1 | MO | Z Diode | | | 120 mA | 0.5 W | | 3.0 V | 20 mA | <29 Ω | | CD |
| 1N746A | A1 | a1 | MO,NS | Z Diode | | | 110 mA | 0.5 W | | 3.3 V | 20 mA | <28 Ω | | CD |

| Type | Case | Pin-code | (mfr) | (type) | Vcla Vbro | Its | Izm | Pv | Pvts | Vz | Iz / Is | rz | TK | (doc) |
|------|------|------|------|------|------|------|------|------|------|------|------|------|------|------|
| | | | | | | | Maximum Ratings | | | | Electrical Characteristics | | | |
| 1N747A | A1 | a1 | MO,NS | Z Diode | | | 100 mA | 0.5 W | | 3.6 V | 20 mA | <24 Ω | | CD |
| 1N748A | A1 | a1 | MO,NS | Z Diode | | | 95 mA | 0.5 W | | 3.9 V | 20 mA | <23 Ω | | CD |
| 1N749A | A1 | a1 | MO,NS | Z Diode | | | 85 mA | 0.5 W | | 4.3 V | 20 mA | <22 Ω | | CD |
| 1N750A | A1 | a1 | MO,NS | Z Diode | | | 75 mA | 0.5 W | | 4.7 V | 20 mA | <19 Ω | | CD |
| 1N751A | A1 | a1 | MO,NS | Z Diode | | | 70 mA | 0.5 W | | 5.1 V | 20 mA | <17 Ω | | CD |
| 1N752A | A1 | a1 | MO,NS | Z Diode | | | 65 mA | 0.5 W | | 5.6 V | 20 mA | <11 Ω | | CD |
| 1N753A | A1 | a1 | MO,NS | Z Diode | | | 60 mA | 0.5 W | | 6.2 V | 20 mA | <7 Ω | | CD |
| 1N754A | A1 | a1 | MO,NS | Z Diode | | | 55 mA | 0.5 W | | 6.8 V | 20 mA | <5 Ω | | CD |
| 1N755A | A1 | a1 | MO,NS | Z Diode | | | 50 mA | 0.5 W | | 7.5 V | 20 mA | <6 Ω | | CD |
| 1N756A | A1 | a1 | MO,NS | Z Diode | | | 45 mA | 0.5 W | | 8.2 V | 20 mA | <8 Ω | | CD |
| 1N757A | A1 | a1 | MO,NS | Z Diode | | | 40 mA | 0.5 W | | 9.1 V | 20 mA | <10 Ω | | CD |
| 1N758A | A1 | a1 | MO,NS | Z Diode | | | 35 mA | 0.5 W | | 10 V | 20 mA | <17 Ω | | CD |
| 1N759A | A1 | a1 | MO,NS | Z Diode | | | 30 mA | 0.5 W | | 12 V | 20 mA | <17 Ω | | CD |
| 1N957B | A1 | a1 | MO,NS | Z Diode | | | 220 mA | 0.5 W | | 6.8 V | 18.5 mA | 4.5 Ω | | ACD |
| 1N958B | A1 | a1 | MO,NS | Z Diode | | | 200 mA | 0.5 W | | 7.5 V | 16.5 mA | 5.5 Ω | | ACD |
| 1N959B | A1 | a1 | MO,NS | Z Diode | | | 180 mA | 0.5 W | | 8.2 V | 15 mA | 6.5 Ω | | ACD |
| 1N960B | A1 | a1 | MO,NS | Z Diode | | | 165 mA | 0.5 W | | 9.1 V | 14 mA | 7.5 Ω | | ACD |
| 1N961B | A1 | a1 | MO,NS | Z Diode | | | 145 mA | 0.5 W | | 10 V | 12.5 mA | 8.5 Ω | | ACD |
| 1N962B | A1 | a1 | MO,NS | Z Diode | | | 135 mA | 0.5 W | | 11 V | 11.5 mA | 9.5 Ω | | ACD |
| 1N963B | A1 | a1 | MO,NS | Z Diode | | | 120 mA | 0.5 W | | 12 V | 10.5 mA | 11.5 Ω | | ACD |
| 1N964B | A1 | a1 | MO,NS | Z Diode | | | 110 mA | 0.5 W | | 13 V | 9.5 mA | 13 Ω | | ACD |
| 1N965B | A1 | a1 | MO,NS | Z Diode | | | 98 mA | 0.5 W | | 15 V | 8.5 mA | 16 Ω | | ACD |
| 1N966B | A1 | a1 | MO,NS | Z Diode | | | 90 mA | 0.5 W | | 16 V | 7.8 mA | 17 Ω | | ACD |
| 1N967B | A1 | a1 | MO,NS | Z Diode | | | 80 mA | 0.5 W | | 18 V | 7 mA | 21 Ω | | ACD |
| 1N968B | A1 | a1 | MO,NS | Z Diode | | | 72 mA | 0.5 W | | 20 V | 6.2 mA | 25 Ω | | ACD |
| 1N969B | A1 | a1 | MO,NS | Z Diode | | | 66 mA | 0.5 W | | 22 V | 5.6 mA | 29 Ω | | ACD |
| 1N970B | A1 | a1 | MO,NS | Z Diode | | | 60 mA | 0.5 W | | 24 V | 5.2 mA | 33 Ω | | ACD |
| 1N971B | A1 | a1 | MO,NS | Z Diode | | | 53 mA | 0.5 W | | 27 V | 4.6 mA | 41 Ω | | ACD |
| 1N972B | A1 | a1 | MO,NS | Z Diode | | | 48 mA | 0.5 W | | 30 V | 4.2 mA | 49 Ω | | ACD |
| 1N973B | A1 | a1 | MO,NS | Z Diode | | | 44 mA | 0.5 W | | 33 V | 3.8 mA | 58 Ω | | ACD |
| 1N974B | A1 | a1 | MO | Z Diode | | | 40 mA | 0.5 W | | 36 V | 3.4 mA | 70 Ω | | ACD |
| 1N975B | A1 | a1 | MO | Z Diode | | | 37 mA | 0.5 W | | 39 V | 3.2 mA | 80 Ω | | ACD |
| 1N976B | A1 | a1 | MO | Z Diode | | | 33 mA | 0.5 W | | 43 V | 3 mA | 93 Ω | | ACD |
| 1N977B | A1 | a1 | MO | Z Diode | | | 30 mA | 0.5 W | | 47 V | 2.7 mA | 105 Ω | | ACD |
| 1N978B | A1 | a1 | MO | Z Diode | | | 27 mA | 0.5 W | | 51 V | 2.5 mA | 125 Ω | | ACD |
| 1N979B | A1 | a1 | MO | Z Diode | | | 25 mA | 0.5 W | | 56 V | 2.2 mA | 150 Ω | | ACD |
| 1N980B | A1 | a1 | MO | Z Diode | | | 21 mA | 0.5 W | | 62 V | 2 mA | 185 Ω | | ACD |
| 1N981B | A1 | a1 | MO | Z Diode | | | 20 mA | 0.5 W | | 68 V | 1.8 mA | 230 Ω | | ACD |
| 1N982B | A1 | a1 | MO | Z Diode | | | 18 mA | 0.5 W | | 75 V | 1.7 mA | 270 Ω | | ACD |
| 1N983B | A1 | a1 | MO | Z Diode | | | 16 mA | 0.5 W | | 82 V | 1.5 mA | 330 Ω | | ACD |

| Type | Case | Pin-code | | | Vcla Vbro | Its | Izm | Pv | Pvts | Vz | Iz Is | rz | TK | |
|------|------|----------|---|---|-----------|-----|-----|-----|------|-----|-------|-----|-----|---|
| | | | | | **Maximum Ratings** | | | | | **Electrical Characteristics** | | | | |
| 1N984B | A1 | a1 | MO | Z Diode | | | 15 mA | 0.5 W | | 91 V | 1.4 mA | 400 Ω | | ACD |
| 1N985B | A1 | a1 | MO | Z Diode | | | 13 mA | 0.5 W | | 100 V | 1.3 mA | 500 Ω | | ACD |
| 1N986B | A1 | a1 | MO | Z Diode | | | 12 mA | 0.5 W | | 110 V | 1.1 mA | 750 Ω | | ACD |
| 1N987B | A1 | a1 | MO | Z Diode | | | 11 mA | 0.5 W | | 120 V | 1 mA | 900 Ω | | ACD |
| 1N988B | A1 | a1 | MO | Z Diode | | | 10 mA | 0.5 W | | 130 V | 0.95 mA | 1100 Ω | | ACD |
| 1N989B | A1 | a1 | MO | Z Diode | | | 9 mA | 0.5 W | | 150 V | 0.85 mA | 1500 Ω | | ACD |
| 1N990B | A1 | a1 | MO | Z Diode | | | 8.6 mA | 0.5 W | | 160 V | 0.8 mA | 1700 Ω | | ACD |
| 1N991B | A1 | a1 | MO | Z Diode | | | 8 mA | 0.5 W | | 180 V | 0.68 mA | 2200 Ω | | ACD |
| 1N992B | A1 | a1 | MO | Z Diode | | | 7.5 mA | 0.5 W | | 200 V | 0.65 mA | 2500 Ω | | ACD |
| 1N4565 | A1 | a1 | SG | Ref. Z Diode | | | | 0.4 W | | 6.4 V | 0.5 mA | <200 Ω | $100 \cdot 10^6/°C$ | |
| 1N4566 | A1 | a1 | SG | Ref. Z Diode | | | | 0.4 W | | 6.4 V | 0.5 mA | <200 Ω | $50 \cdot 10^6/°C$ | |
| 1N4567 | A1 | a1 | SG | Ref. Z Diode | | | | 0.4 W | | 6.4 V | 0.5 mA | <200 Ω | $20 \cdot 10^6/°C$ | |
| 1N4568 | A1 | a1 | SG | Ref. Z Diode | | | | 0.4 W | | 6.4 V | 0.5 mA | <200 Ω | $10 \cdot 10^6/°C$ | |
| 1N4569 | A1 | a1 | SG | Ref. Z Diode | | | | 0.4 W | | 6.4 V | 0.5 mA | <200 Ω | $5 \cdot 10^6/°C$ | |
| 1N4565A | A1 | a1 | SG | Ref. Z Diode | | | | 0.4 W | | 6.4 V | 0.5 mA | <200 Ω | $100 \cdot 10^6/°C$ | |
| 1N4566A | A1 | a1 | SG | Ref. Z Diode | | | | 0.4 W | | 6.4 V | 0.5 mA | <200 Ω | $50 \cdot 10^6/°C$ | |
| 1N4567A | A1 | a1 | SG | Ref. Z Diode | | | | 0.4 W | | 6.4 V | 0.5 mA | <200 Ω | $20 \cdot 10^6/°C$ | |
| 1N4568A | A1 | a1 | SG | Ref. Z Diode | | | | 0.4 W | | 6.4 V | 0.5 mA | <200 Ω | $10 \cdot 10^6/°C$ | |
| 1N4569A | A1 | a1 | SG | Ref. Z Diode | | | | 0.4 W | | 6.4 V | 0.5 mA | <200 Ω | $5 \cdot 10^6/°C$ | |
| 1N4570 | A1 | a1 | SG | Ref. Z Diode | | | | 0.4 W | | 6.4 V | 1 mA | <100 Ω | $100 \cdot 10^6/°C$ | |
| 1N4571 | A1 | a1 | SG | Ref. Z Diode | | | | 0.4 W | | 6.4 V | 1 mA | <100 Ω | $50 \cdot 10^6/°C$ | |
| 1N4572 | A1 | a1 | SG | Ref. Z Diode | | | | 0.4 W | | 6.4 V | 1 mA | <100 Ω | $20 \cdot 10^6/°C$ | |
| 1N4573 | A1 | a1 | SG | Ref. Z Diode | | | | 0.4 W | | 6.4 V | 1 mA | <100 Ω | $10 \cdot 10^6/°C$ | |
| 1N4574 | A1 | a1 | SG | Ref. Z Diode | | | | 0.4 W | | 6.4 V | 1 mA | <100 Ω | $5 \cdot 10^6/°C$ | |
| 1N4570A | A1 | a1 | SG | Ref. Z Diode | | | | 0.4 W | | 6.4 V | 1 mA | <100 Ω | $100 \cdot 10^6/°C$ | |
| 1N4571A | A1 | a1 | SG | Ref. Z Diode | | | | 0.4 W | | 6.4 V | 1 mA | <100 Ω | $50 \cdot 10^6/°C$ | |
| 1N4572A | A1 | a1 | SG | Ref. Z Diode | | | | 0.4 W | | 6.4 V | 1 mA | <100 Ω | $20 \cdot 10^6/°C$ | |
| 1N4573A | A1 | a1 | SG | Ref. Z Diode | | | | 0.4 W | | 6.4 V | 1 mA | <100 Ω | $10 \cdot 10^6/°C$ | |
| 1N4574A | A1 | a1 | SG | Ref. Z Diode | | | | 0.4 W | | 6.4 V | 1 mA | <100 Ω | $5 \cdot 10^6/°C$ | |
| 1N4575 | A1 | a1 | SG | Ref. Z Diode | | | | 0.4 W | | 6.4 V | 2 mA | <50 Ω | $100 \cdot 10^6/°C$ | |
| 1N4576 | A1 | a1 | SG | Ref. Z Diode | | | | 0.4 W | | 6.4 V | 2 mA | <50 Ω | $50 \cdot 10^6/°C$ | |
| 1N4577 | A1 | a1 | SG | Ref. Z Diode | | | | 0.4 W | | 6.4 V | 2 mA | <50 Ω | $20 \cdot 10^6/°C$ | |
| 1N4578 | A1 | a1 | SG | Ref. Z Diode | | | | 0.4 W | | 6.4 V | 2 mA | <50 Ω | $10 \cdot 10^6/°C$ | |
| 1N4579 | A1 | a1 | SG | Ref. Z Diode | | | | 0.4 W | | 6.4 V | 2 mA | <50 Ω | $5 \cdot 10^6/°C$ | |
| 1N4575A | A1 | a1 | SG | Ref. Z Diode | | | | 0.4 W | | 6.4 V | 2 mA | <50 Ω | $100 \cdot 10^6/°C$ | |
| 1N4576A | A1 | a1 | SG | Ref. Z Diode | | | | 0.4 W | | 6.4 V | 2 mA | <50 Ω | $50 \cdot 10^6/°C$ | |
| 1N4577A | A1 | a1 | SG | Ref. Z Diode | | | | 0.4 W | | 6.4 V | 2 mA | <50 Ω | $20 \cdot 10^6/°C$ | |
| 1N4578A | A1 | a1 | SG | Ref. Z Diode | | | | 0.4 W | | 6.4 V | 2 mA | <50 Ω | $10 \cdot 10^6/°C$ | |
| 1N4579A | A1 | a1 | SG | Ref. Z Diode | | | | 0.4 W | | 6.4 V | 2 mA | <50 Ω | $5 \cdot 10^6/°C$ | |
| 1N4580 | A1 | a1 | SG | Ref. Z Diode | | | | 0.4 W | | 6.4 V | 4 mA | <25 Ω | $100 \cdot 10^6/°C$ | |

**1N4581 – 1N4115**

| Type | Case | Pin-code | | | Vcla Vbro | Its | Izm | Pv | Pvts | Vz | Iz Is | rz | TK | |
|------|------|----------|--|--|-----------|-----|-----|-----|------|-----|-------|----|----|--|
| | | | | | **Maximum Ratings** | | | | | **Electrical Characteristics** | | | | |
| 1N4581 | A1 | a1 | SG | Ref. Z Diode | | | | 0.4 W | | 6.4 V | 4 mA | <25Ω | 50·10⁶/°C | |
| 1N4582 | A1 | a1 | SG | Ref. Z Diode | | | | 0.4 W | | 6.4 V | 4 mA | <25Ω | 20·10⁶/°C | |
| 1N4583 | A1 | a1 | SG | Ref. Z Diode | | | | 0.4 W | | 6.4 V | 4 mA | <25Ω | 10·10⁶/°C | |
| 1N4584 | A1 | a1 | SG | Ref. Z Diode | | | | 0.4 W | | 6.4 V | 4 mA | <25Ω | 5·10⁶/°C | |
| 1N4580A | A1 | a1 | SG | Ref. Z Diode | | | | 0.4 W | | 6.4 V | 4 mA | <25Ω | 100·10⁶/°C | |
| 1N4581A | A1 | a1 | SG | Ref. Z Diode | | | | 0.4 W | | 6.4 V | 4 mA | <25Ω | 50·10⁶/°C | |
| 1N4582A | A1 | a1 | SG | Ref. Z Diode | | | | 0.4 W | | 6.4 V | 4 mA | <25Ω | 20·10⁶/°C | |
| 1N4583A | A1 | a1 | SG | Ref. Z Diode | | | | 0.4 W | | 6.4 V | 4 mA | <25Ω | 10·10⁶/°C | |
| 1N4584A | A1 | a1 | SG | Ref. Z Diode | | | | 0.4 W | | 6.4 V | 4 mA | <25Ω | 5·10⁶/°C | |
| 1N4614 | A1 | a1 | SG | Z Diode | | | 120 mA | 0.25 W | | 1.8 V | 0.25 mA | <1200Ω | | |
| 1N4615 | A1 | a1 | SG | Z Diode | | | 110 mA | 0.25 W | | 2.0 V | 0.25 mA | <1250Ω | | |
| 1N4616 | A1 | a1 | SG | Z Diode | | | 100 mA | 0.25 W | | 2.2 V | 0.25 mA | <1300Ω | | P |
| 1N4617 | A1 | a1 | SG | Z Diode | | | 95 mA | 0.25 W | | 2.4 V | 0.25 mA | <1400Ω | | |
| 1N4618 | A1 | a1 | SG | Z Diode | | | 90 mA | 0.25 W | | 2.7 V | 0.25 mA | <1500Ω | | |
| 1N4619 | A1 | a1 | SG | Z Diode | | | 85 mA | 0.25 W | | 3.0 V | 0.25 mA | <1600Ω | | |
| 1N4620 | A1 | a1 | SG | Z Diode | | | 80 mA | 0.25 W | | 3.3 V | 0.25 mA | <1650Ω | | P |
| 1N4621 | A1 | a1 | SG | Z Diode | | | 75 mA | 0.25 W | | 3.6 V | 0.25 mA | <1700Ω | | P |
| 1N4622 | A1 | a1 | SG | Z Diode | | | 70 mA | 0.25 W | | 3.9 V | 0.25 mA | <1650Ω | | P |
| 1N4623 | A1 | a1 | SG | Z Diode | | | 65 mA | 0.25 W | | 4.3 V | 0.25 mA | <1600Ω | | P |
| 1N4624 | A1 | a1 | SG | Z Diode | | | 60 mA | 0.25 W | | 4.7 V | 0.25 mA | <1550Ω | | P |
| 1N4625 | A1 | a1 | SG | Z Diode | | | 55 mA | 0.25 W | | 5.1 V | 0.25 mA | <1500Ω | | P |
| 1N4626 | A1 | a1 | SG | Z Diode | | | 50 mA | 0.25 W | | 5.6 V | 0.25 mA | <1400Ω | | |
| 1N4627 | A1 | a1 | SG | Z Diode | | | 45 mA | 0.25 W | | 6.2 V | 0.25 mA | <1200Ω | | |
| 1N4099 | A1 | a1 | SG | Z Diode | | | 35 mA | 0.25 W | | 6.8 V | 0.25 mA | <200Ω | | |
| 1N4100 | A1 | a1 | SG | Z Diode | | | 32 mA | 0.25 W | | 7.5 V | 0.25 mA | <200Ω | | |
| 1N4101 | A1 | a1 | SG | Z Diode | | | 29 mA | 0.25 W | | 8.2 V | 0.25 mA | <200Ω | | |
| 1N4102 | A1 | a1 | SG | Z Diode | | | 27 mA | 0.25 W | | 8.7 V | 0.25 mA | <200Ω | | |
| 1N4103 | A1 | a1 | SG | Z Diode | | | 26 mA | 0.25 W | | 9.1 V | 0.25 mA | <200Ω | | |
| 1N4104 | A1 | a1 | SG | Z Diode | | | 25 mA | 0.25 W | | 10 V | 0.25 mA | <200Ω | | |
| 1N4105 | A1 | a1 | SG | Z Diode | | | 22 mA | 0.25 W | | 11 V | 0.25 mA | <200Ω | | |
| 1N4106 | A1 | a1 | SG | Z Diode | | | 20 mA | 0.25 W | | 12 V | 0.25 mA | <200Ω | | |
| 1N4107 | A1 | a1 | SG | Z Diode | | | 19 mA | 0.25 W | | 13 V | 0.25 mA | <200Ω | | |
| 1N4108 | A1 | a1 | SG | Z Diode | | | 18 mA | 0.25 W | | 14 V | 0.25 mA | <200Ω | | |
| 1N4109 | A1 | a1 | SG | Z Diode | | | 16 mA | 0.25 W | | 15 V | 0.25 mA | <100Ω | | |
| 1N4110 | A1 | a1 | SG | Z Diode | | | 15 mA | 0.25 W | | 16 V | 0.25 mA | <100Ω | | |
| 1N4111 | A1 | a1 | SG | Z Diode | | | 15 mA | 0.25 W | | 17 V | 0.25 mA | <100Ω | | |
| 1N4112 | A1 | a1 | SG | Z Diode | | | 13 mA | 0.25 W | | 18 V | 0.25 mA | <100Ω | | |
| 1N4113 | A1 | a1 | SG | Z Diode | | | 13 mA | 0.25 W | | 19 V | 0.25 mA | <150Ω | | |
| 1N4114 | A1 | a1 | SG | Z Diode | | | 12 mA | 0.25 W | | 20 V | 0.25 mA | <150Ω | | |
| 1N4115 | A1 | a1 | SG | Z Diode | | | 11 mA | 0.25 W | | 22 V | 0.25 mA | <150Ω | | |

| Type | Case | Pin-code | | | Vcla Vbro | Its | Izm | Pv | Pvts | Vz | Iz Is | rz | TK | |
|------|------|----------|---|---|-----------|-----|-----|-----|------|------|------|------|------|---|
| | | | | | | | **Maximum Ratings** | | | | **Electrical Characteristics** | | | |
| 1N4116 | A1 | a1 | SG | Z Diode | | | 10 mA | 0.25 W | | 24 V | 0.25 mA | <150 Ω | | |
| 1N4117 | A1 | a1 | SG | Z Diode | | | 10 mA | 0.25 W | | 25 V | 0.25 mA | <150 Ω | | |
| 1N4118 | A1 | a1 | SG | Z Diode | | | 9 mA | 0.25 W | | 27 V | 0.25 mA | <150 Ω | | |
| 1N4678 | A1 | a1 | MO | Z Diode | | | 120 mA | 0.5 W | | 1.8 V | 50 µA | (.7) Ω | | |
| 1N4679 | A1 | a1 | MO | Z Diode | | | 110 mA | 0.5 W | | 2.0 V | 50 µA | (.7) Ω | | |
| 1N4680 | A1 | a1 | MO | Z Diode | | | 100 mA | 0.5 W | | 2.2 V | 50 µA | (.75) Ω | | |
| 1N4681 | A1 | a1 | MO | Z Diode | | | 95 mA | 0.5 W | | 2.4 V | 50 µA | (.8) Ω | | |
| 1N4682 | A1 | a1 | MO | Z Diode | | | 90 mA | 0.5 W | | 2.7 V | 50 µA | (.85) Ω | | |
| 1N4683 | A1 | a1 | MO | Z Diode | | | 85 mA | 0.5 W | | 3.0 V | 50 µA | (.9) Ω | | |
| 1N4684 | A1 | a1 | MO | Z Diode | | | 80 mA | 0.5 W | | 3.3 V | 50 µA | (.95) Ω | | |
| 1N4685 | A1 | a1 | MO | Z Diode | | | 75 mA | 0.5 W | | 3.6 V | 50 µA | (.95) Ω | | |
| 1N4686 | A1 | a1 | MO | Z Diode | | | 70 mA | 0.5 W | | 3.9 V | 50 µA | (.97) Ω | | |
| 1N4687 | A1 | a1 | MO | Z Diode | | | 65 mA | 0.5 W | | 4.3 V | 50 µA | (.99) Ω | | |
| 1N4688 | A1 | a1 | MO | Z Diode | | | 60 mA | 0.5 W | | 4.7 V | 50 µA | (.99) Ω | | |
| 1N4689 | A1 | a1 | MO | Z Diode | | | 55 mA | 0.5 W | | 5.1 V | 50 µA | (.97) Ω | | |
| 1N4690 | A1 | a1 | MO | Z Diode | | | 50 mA | 0.5 W | | 5.6 V | 50 µA | (.96) Ω | | |
| 1N4691 | A1 | a1 | MO | Z Diode | | | 45 mA | 0.5 W | | 6.2 V | 50 µA | (.95) Ω | | |
| 1N4692 | A1 | a1 | MO | Z Diode | | | 35 mA | 0.5 W | | 6.8 V | 50 µA | (.9) Ω | | |
| 1N4693 | A1 | a1 | MO | Z Diode | | | 31.8 mA | 0.5 W | | 7.5 V | 50 µA | (.75) Ω | | |
| 1N4694 | A1 | a1 | MO | Z Diode | | | 29 mA | 0.5 W | | 8.2 V | 50 µA | (.5) Ω | | |
| 1N4695 | A1 | a1 | MO | Z Diode | | | 27.4 mA | 0.5 W | | 8.7 V | 50 µA | (.1) Ω | | |
| 1N4696 | A1 | a1 | MO | Z Diode | | | 26.2 mA | 0.5 W | | 9.1 V | 50 µA | (.08) Ω | | |
| 1N4697 | A1 | a1 | MO | Z Diode | | | 24.8 mA | 0.5 W | | 10 V | 50 µA | (.1) Ω | | |
| 1N4698 | A1 | a1 | MO | Z Diode | | | 21.6 mA | 0.5 W | | 11 V | 50 µA | (.11) Ω | | |
| 1N4699 | A1 | a1 | MO | Z Diode | | | 20.4 mA | 0.5 W | | 12 V | 50 µA | (.12) Ω | | |
| 1N4700 | A1 | a1 | MO | Z Diode | | | 19 mA | 0.5 W | | 13 V | 50 µA | (.13) Ω | | |
| 1N4701 | A1 | a1 | MO | Z Diode | | | 17.5 mA | 0.5 W | | 14 V | 50 µA | (.14) Ω | | |
| 1N4702 | A1 | a1 | MO | Z Diode | | | 16.3 mA | 0.5 W | | 15 V | 50 µA | (.15) Ω | | |
| 1N4703 | A1 | a1 | MO | Z Diode | | | 15.4 mA | 0.5 W | | 16 V | 50 µA | (.16) Ω | | |
| 1N4704 | A1 | a1 | MO | Z Diode | | | 14.5 mA | 0.5 W | | 17 V | 50 µA | (.17) Ω | | |
| 1N4705 | A1 | a1 | MO | Z Diode | | | 13.2 mA | 0.5 W | | 18 V | 50 µA | (.18) Ω | | |
| 1N4706 | A1 | a1 | MO | Z Diode | | | 12.5 mA | 0.5 W | | 19 V | 50 µA | (.19) Ω | | |
| 1N4707 | A1 | a1 | MO | Z Diode | | | 11.9 mA | 0.5 W | | 20 V | 50 µA | (.2) Ω | | |
| 1N4708 | A1 | a1 | MO | Z Diode | | | 10.8 mA | 0.5 W | | 22 V | 50 µA | (.22) Ω | | |
| 1N4709 | A1 | a1 | MO | Z Diode | | | 9.9 mA | 0.5 W | | 24 V | 50 µA | (.24) Ω | | |
| 1N4710 | A1 | a1 | MO | Z Diode | | | 9.5 mA | 0.5 W | | 25 V | 50 µA | (.25) Ω | | |
| 1N4711 | A1 | a1 | MO | Z Diode | | | 8.8 mA | 0.5 W | | 27 V | 50 µA | (.27) Ω | | |
| 1N4712 | A1 | a1 | MO | Z Diode | | | 8.5 mA | 0.5 W | | 28 V | 50 µA | (.28) Ω | | |
| 1N4713 | A1 | a1 | MO | Z Diode | | | 7.9 mA | 0.5 W | | 30 V | 50 µA | (.3) Ω | | |
| 1N4714 | A1 | a1 | MO | Z Diode | | | 7.2 mA | 0.5 W | | 33 V | 50 µA | (.33) Ω | | |

| Type | Case | Pin-code | (mfr) | | Vcla Vbro | Its | Izm | Pv | Pvts | Vz | Iz / Is | rz | TK | |
|---|---|---|---|---|---|---|---|---|---|---|---|---|---|---|
| 1N4715 | A1 | a1 | MO | Z Diode | | | 6.6 mA | 0.5 W | | 36 V | 50 µA | (.36) Ω | | |
| 1N4716 | A1 | a1 | MO | Z Diode | | | 6.1 mA | 0.5 W | | 39 V | 50 µA | (.39) Ω | | |
| 1N4717 | A1 | a1 | MO | Z Diode | | | 5.5 mA | 0.5 W | | 43 V | 50 µA | (.43) Ω | | |
| 1N4728A | A3 | a1 | SG,TE,PH,MO,NS | Z Diode | | | 276 mA | 1 W | | 3.3 V | 76 mA | <10 Ω | -600·10⁶/°C | P (SG) |
| 1N4729A | A3 | a1 | SG,TE,IT,PH,MO | Z Diode | | | 252 mA | 1 W | | 3.6 V | 69 mA | <10 Ω | -600·10⁶/°C | |
| 1N4730A | A3 | a1 | SG,TE,IT,PH,MO | Z Diode | | | 234 mA | 1 W | | 3.9 V | 64 mA | <9 Ω | -500·10⁶/°C | P (SG) |
| 1N4731A | A3 | a1 | SG,TE,IT,PH,MO | Z Diode | | | 217 mA | 1 W | | 4.3 V | 58 mA | <9 Ω | -300·10⁶/°C | |
| 1N4732A | A3 | a1 | SG,TE,IT,PH,MO | Z Diode | | | 193 mA | 1 W | | 4.7 V | 53 mA | <8 Ω | -100·10⁶/°C | P (SG) |
| 1N4733A | A3 | a1 | SG,TE,IT,PH,MO | Z Diode | | | 178 mA | 1 W | | 5.1 V | 49 mA | <7 Ω | 100·10⁶/°C | P (SG) |
| 1N4734A | A3 | a1 | SG,TE,IT,PH,MO | Z Diode | | | 162 mA | 1 W | | 5.6 V | 45 mA | <5 Ω | 300·10⁶/°C | P (SG) |
| 1N4735A | A3 | a1 | SG,TE,IT,PH,MO | Z Diode | | | 146 mA | 1 W | | 6.2 V | 41 mA | <2 Ω | 400·10⁶/°C | P (SG) |
| 1N4736A | A3 | a1 | SG,TE,IT,PH,MO | Z Diode | | | 133 mA | 1 W | | 6.8 V | 37 mA | <3.5 Ω | 500·10⁶/°C | P (SG) |
| 1N4737A | A3 | a1 | SG,TE,IT,PH,MO | Z Diode | | | 121 mA | 1 W | | 7.5 V | 34 mA | <4 Ω | 500·10⁶/°C | |
| 1N4738A | A3 | a1 | SG,TE,IT,PH,MO | Z Diode | | | 110 mA | 1 W | | 8.2 V | 31 mA | <4.5 Ω | 600·10⁶/°C | |
| 1N4739A | A3 | a1 | SG,TE,IT,PH,MO | Z Diode | | | 100 mA | 1 W | | 9.1 V | 28 mA | <5 Ω | 600·10⁶/°C | |
| 1N4740A | A3 | a1 | SG,TE,IT,PH,MO | Z Diode | | | 91 mA | 1 W | | 10 V | 25 mA | <7 Ω | 700·10⁶/°C | P (SG) |
| 1N4741A | A3 | a1 | SG,TE,IT,PH,MO | Z Diode | | | 83 mA | 1 W | | 11 V | 23 mA | <8 Ω | 700·10⁶/°C | |
| 1N4742A | A3 | a1 | SG,TE,IT,PH,MO | Z Diode | | | 76 mA | 1 W | | 12 V | 21 mA | <9 Ω | 700·10⁶/°C | P (SG) |
| 1N4743A | A3 | a1 | SG,TE,IT,PH,MO | Z Diode | | | 69 mA | 1 W | | 13 V | 19 mA | <10 Ω | 700·10⁶/°C | |
| 1N4744A | A3 | a1 | SG,TE,IT,PH,MO | Z Diode | | | 61 mA | 1 W | | 15 V | 17 mA | <14 Ω | 800·10⁶/°C | P (SG) |
| 1N4745A | A3 | a1 | SG,TE,IT,PH,MO | Z Diode | | | 57 mA | 1 W | | 16 V | 15.5 mA | <16 Ω | 800·10⁶/°C | P (SG) |
| 1N4746A | A3 | a1 | SG,TE,IT,PH,MO | Z Diode | | | 50 mA | 1 W | | 18 V | 14 mA | <20 Ω | 800·10⁶/°C | P (SG) |
| 1N4747A | A3 | a1 | SG,TE,IT,PH,MO | Z Diode | | | 45 mA | 1 W | | 20 V | 12.5 mA | <22 Ω | 800·10⁶/°C | P (SG) |
| 1N4748A | A3 | a1 | SG,TE,IT,PH,MO | Z Diode | | | 41 mA | 1 W | | 22 V | 11.5 mA | <23 Ω | 800·10⁶/°C | P (SG) |
| 1N4749A | A3 | a1 | SG,TE,IT,PH,MO | Z Diode | | | 38 mA | 1 W | | 24 V | 10.5 mA | <25 Ω | 800·10⁶/°C | P (SG) |
| 1N4750A | A3 | a1 | SG,TE,IT,MO,NS | Z Diode | | | 34 mA | 1 W | | 27 V | 9.5 mA | <35 Ω | 900·10⁶/°C | P (SG) |
| 1N4751A | A3 | a1 | SG,TE,IT,MO,NS | Z Diode | | | 30 mA | 1 W | | 30 V | 8.5 mA | <40 Ω | 900·10⁶/°C | P (SG) |
| 1N4752A | A3 | a1 | SG,TE,IT,MO,NS | Z Diode | | | 27 mA | 1 W | | 33 V | 7.5 mA | <45 Ω | 900·10⁶/°C | P (SG) |
| 1N4753A | A3 | a1 | SG,TE,IT,MO | Z Diode | | | 25 mA | 1 W | | 36 V | 7 mA | <50 Ω | 900·10⁶/°C | P (SG) |
| 1N4754A | A3 | a1 | SG,TE,IT,MO | Z Diode | | | 23 mA | 1 W | | 39 V | 6.5 mA | <60 Ω | 900·10⁶/°C | |
| 1N4755A | A3 | a1 | SG,TE,IT,MO | Z Diode | | | 22 mA | 1 W | | 43 V | 6 mA | <70 Ω | 900·10⁶/°C | |
| 1N4756A | A3 | a1 | SG,TE,IT,MO | Z Diode | | | 19 mA | 1 W | | 47 V | 5.5 mA | <80 Ω | 900·10⁶/°C | |
| 1N4757A | A3 | a1 | SG,TE,IT,MO | Z Diode | | | 18 mA | 1 W | | 51 V | 5 mA | <95 Ω | 900·10⁶/°C | |
| 1N4758A | A3 | a1 | SG,TE,IT,MO | Z Diode | | | 16 mA | 1 W | | 56 V | 4.5 mA | <110 Ω | 900·10⁶/°C | |
| 1N4759A | A3 | a1 | SG,TE,IT,MO | Z Diode | | | 14 mA | 1 W | | 62 V | 4 mA | <125 Ω | 900·10⁶/°C | P (SG) |
| 1N4760A | A3 | a1 | SG,TE,IT,MO | Z Diode | | | 13 mA | 1 W | | 68 V | 3.7 mA | <150 Ω | 900·10⁶/°C | |
| 1N4761A | A3 | a1 | SG,TE,IT,MO | Z Diode | | | 12 mA | 1 W | | 75 V | 3.3 mA | <175 Ω | 900·10⁶/°C | |
| 1N4762A | A3 | a1 | SG,IT,MO | Z Diode | | | 11 mA | 1 W | | 82 V | 3 mA | <200 Ω | 900·10⁶/°C | |
| 1N4763A | A3 | a1 | SG,IT,MO | Z Diode | | | 10 mA | 1 W | | 91 V | 2.8 mA | <250 Ω | 900·10⁶/°C | |
| 1N4764A | A3 | a1 | SG,IT,MO | Z Diode | | | 9 mA | 1 W | | 100 V | 2.5 mA | <350 Ω | 900·10⁶/°C | |

| Type | Case | Pin-code | | | Maximum Ratings | | | | | Electrical Characteristics | | | | |
|------|------|----------|---|---|---|---|---|---|---|---|---|---|---|---|
| | | | | | Vcla Vbro | Its | Izm | Pv | Pvts | Vz | Iz / Is | rz | TK | |
| 1N4187B | A3 | a1 | SG | Z Diode | | | 9 mA | 1 W | | 110 V | 2.3 mA | $<450\,\Omega$ | $1000 \cdot 10^6/°C$ | |
| 1N4188B | A3 | a1 | SG | Z Diode | | | 8 mA | 1 W | | 120 V | 2 mA | $<550\,\Omega$ | $1000 \cdot 10^6/°C$ | |
| 1N4189B | A3 | a1 | SG | Z Diode | | | 7 mA | 1 W | | 130 V | 1.9 mA | $<700\,\Omega$ | $1000 \cdot 10^6/°C$ | |
| 1N4190B | A3 | a1 | SG | Z Diode | | | 6 mA | 1 W | | 150 V | 1.7 mA | $<1000\,\Omega$ | $1000 \cdot 10^6/°C$ | |
| 1N4191B | A3 | a1 | SG | Z Diode | | | 6 mA | 1 W | | 170 V | 1.6 mA | $<1100\,\Omega$ | $1000 \cdot 10^6/°C$ | |
| 1N4192B | A3 | a1 | SG | Z Diode | | | 5 mA | 1 W | | 180 V | 1.4 mA | $<1200\,\Omega$ | $1000 \cdot 10^6/°C$ | |
| 1N4193B | A3 | a1 | SG | Z Diode | | | 5 mA | 1 W | | 200 V | 1.2 mA | $<1500\,\Omega$ | $1000 \cdot 10^6/°C$ | |
| 1N4765 | A1 | a1 | SG | Ref. Z Diode | | | | 0.4 W | | 9.1 V | 0.5 mA | $<350\,\Omega$ | $100 \cdot 10^6/°C$ | |
| 1N4766 | A1 | a1 | SG | Ref. Z Diode | | | | 0.4 W | | 9.1 V | 0.5 mA | $<350\,\Omega$ | $50 \cdot 10^6/°C$ | |
| 1N4767 | A1 | a1 | SG | Ref. Z Diode | | | | 0.4 W | | 9.1 V | 0.5 mA | $<350\,\Omega$ | $20 \cdot 10^6/°C$ | |
| 1N4768 | A1 | a1 | SG | Ref. Z Diode | | | | 0.4 W | | 9.1 V | 0.5 mA | $<350\,\Omega$ | $10 \cdot 10^6/°C$ | |
| 1N4769 | A1 | a1 | SG | Ref. Z Diode | | | | 0.4 W | | 9.1 V | 0.5 mA | $<350\,\Omega$ | $5 \cdot 10^6/°C$ | |
| 1N4765A | A1 | a1 | SG | Ref. Z Diode | | | | 0.4 W | | 9.1 V | 0.5 mA | $<350\,\Omega$ | $100 \cdot 10^6/°C$ | |
| 1N4766A | A1 | a1 | SG | Ref. Z Diode | | | | 0.4 W | | 9.1 V | 0.5 mA | $<350\,\Omega$ | $50 \cdot 10^6/°C$ | |
| 1N4767A | A1 | a1 | SG | Ref. Z Diode | | | | 0.4 W | | 9.1 V | 0.5 mA | $<350\,\Omega$ | $20 \cdot 10^6/°C$ | |
| 1N4768A | A1 | a1 | SG | Ref. Z Diode | | | | 0.4 W | | 9.1 V | 0.5 mA | $<350\,\Omega$ | $10 \cdot 10^6/°C$ | |
| 1N4769A | A1 | a1 | SG | Ref. Z Diode | | | | 0.4 W | | 9.1 V | 0.5 mA | $<350\,\Omega$ | $5 \cdot 10^6/°C$ | |
| 1N4770 | A1 | a1 | SG | Ref. Z Diode | | | | 0.4 W | | 9.1 V | 1 mA | $<200\,\Omega$ | $100 \cdot 10^6/°C$ | |
| 1N4771 | A1 | a1 | SG | Ref. Z Diode | | | | 0.4 W | | 9.1 V | 1 mA | $<200\,\Omega$ | $50 \cdot 10^6/°C$ | |
| 1N4772 | A1 | a1 | SG | Ref. Z Diode | | | | 0.4 W | | 9.1 V | 1 mA | $<200\,\Omega$ | $20 \cdot 10^6/°C$ | |
| 1N4773 | A1 | a1 | SG | Ref. Z Diode | | | | 0.4 W | | 9.1 V | 1 mA | $<200\,\Omega$ | $10 \cdot 10^6/°C$ | |
| 1N4774 | A1 | a1 | SG | Ref. Z Diode | | | | 0.4 W | | 9.1 V | 1 mA | $<200\,\Omega$ | $5 \cdot 10^6/°C$ | |
| 1N4770A | A1 | a1 | SG | Ref. Z Diode | | | | 0.4 W | | 9.1 V | 1 mA | $<200\,\Omega$ | $100 \cdot 10^6/°C$ | |
| 1N4771A | A1 | a1 | SG | Ref. Z Diode | | | | 0.4 W | | 9.1 V | 1 mA | $<200\,\Omega$ | $50 \cdot 10^6/°C$ | |
| 1N4772A | A1 | a1 | SG | Ref. Z Diode | | | | 0.4 W | | 9.1 V | 1 mA | $<200\,\Omega$ | $20 \cdot 10^6/°C$ | |
| 1N4773A | A1 | a1 | SG | Ref. Z Diode | | | | 0.4 W | | 9.1 V | 1 mA | $<200\,\Omega$ | $10 \cdot 10^6/°C$ | |
| 1N4774A | A1 | a1 | SG | Ref. Z Diode | | | | 0.4 W | | 9.1 V | 1 mA | $<200\,\Omega$ | $5 \cdot 10^6/°C$ | |
| 1N4775 | A1 | a1 | SG | Ref. Z Diode | | | | 0.4 W | | 8.5 V | 0.5 mA | $<200\,\Omega$ | $100 \cdot 10^6/°C$ | |
| 1N4776 | A1 | a1 | SG | Ref. Z Diode | | | | 0.4 W | | 8.5 V | 0.5 mA | $<200\,\Omega$ | $50 \cdot 10^6/°C$ | |
| 1N4777 | A1 | a1 | SG | Ref. Z Diode | | | | 0.4 W | | 8.5 V | 0.5 mA | $<200\,\Omega$ | $20 \cdot 10^6/°C$ | |
| 1N4778 | A1 | a1 | SG | Ref. Z Diode | | | | 0.4 W | | 8.5 V | 0.5 mA | $<200\,\Omega$ | $10 \cdot 10^6/°C$ | |
| 1N4779 | A1 | a1 | SG | Ref. Z Diode | | | | 0.4 W | | 8.5 V | 0.5 mA | $<200\,\Omega$ | $5 \cdot 10^6/°C$ | |
| 1N4775A | A1 | a1 | SG | Ref. Z Diode | | | | 0.4 W | | 8.5 V | 0.5 mA | $<200\,\Omega$ | $100 \cdot 10^6/°C$ | |
| 1N4776A | A1 | a1 | SG | Ref. Z Diode | | | | 0.4 W | | 8.5 V | 0.5 mA | $<200\,\Omega$ | $50 \cdot 10^6/°C$ | |
| 1N4777A | A1 | a1 | SG | Ref. Z Diode | | | | 0.4 W | | 8.5 V | 0.5 mA | $<200\,\Omega$ | $20 \cdot 10^6/°C$ | |
| 1N4778A | A1 | a1 | SG | Ref. Z Diode | | | | 0.4 W | | 8.5 V | 0.5 mA | $<200\,\Omega$ | $10 \cdot 10^6/°C$ | |
| 1N4779A | A1 | a1 | SG | Ref. Z Diode | | | | 0.4 W | | 8.5 V | 0.5 mA | $<100\,\Omega$ | $5 \cdot 10^6/°C$ | |
| 1N5135B | A3 | a1 | SG | Z Diode | | 146 mA | | 1 W | | 6.2 V | 41 mA | $2\,\Omega$ | $400 \cdot 10^6/°C$ | |
| 1N5135C | A3 | a1 | SG | Z Diode | | 146 mA | | 1 W | | 6.2 V | 41 mA | $2\,\Omega$ | $400 \cdot 10^6/°C$ | |
| 1N5135D | A3 | a1 | SG | Z Diode | | 146 mA | | 1 W | | 6.2 V | 41 mA | $2\,\Omega$ | $400 \cdot 10^6/°C$ | |

**1N5221B – 1N5260B**

| Type | Case | Pin-code | | | Maximum Ratings | | | | | Electrical Characteristics | | | | |
|------|------|----------|---|---|---|---|---|---|---|---|---|---|---|---|
| | | | | | Vcla Vbro | Its | Izm | Pv | Pvts | Vz | Iz Is | rz | TK | |
| 1N5221B | A1 | a1 | SG,TE,MO | Z Diode | | | 191 mA | 0.5 W | | 2.4 V | 20 mA | $<30\Omega$ | $-850 \cdot 10^6/°C$ | |
| 1N5222B | A1 | a1 | SG,TE,MO | Z Diode | | | 182 mA | 0.5 W | | 2.5 V | 20 mA | $<30\Omega$ | $-850 \cdot 10^6/°C$ | |
| 1N5223B | A1 | a1 | SG,TE,MO | Z Diode | | | 168 mA | 0.5 W | | 2.7 V | 20 mA | $<30\Omega$ | $-800 \cdot 10^6/°C$ | |
| 1N5224B | A1 | a1 | SG,TE,MO | Z Diode | | | 162 mA | 0.5 W | | 2.8 V | 20 mA | $<30\Omega$ | $-800 \cdot 10^6/°C$ | |
| 1N5225B | A1 | a1 | SG,TE,IT,PH,MO | Z Diode | | | 151 mA | 0.5 W | | 3.0 V | 20 mA | $<29\Omega$ | $-750 \cdot 10^6/°C$ | |
| 1N5226B | A1 | a1 | SG,TE,IT,PH,MO | Z Diode | | | 138 mA | 0.5 W | | 3.3 V | 20 mA | $<28\Omega$ | $-700 \cdot 10^6/°C$ | |
| 1N5227B | A1 | a1 | SG,TE,IT,PH,MO | Z Diode | | | 126 mA | 0.5 W | | 3.6 V | 20 mA | $<24\Omega$ | $-650 \cdot 10^6/°C$ | |
| 1N5228B | A1 | a1 | SG,TE,IT,PH,MO | Z Diode | | | 115 mA | 0.5 W | | 3.9 V | 20 mA | $<23\Omega$ | $-600 \cdot 10^6/°C$ | P (SG) |
| 1N5229B | A1 | a1 | SG,TE,IT,PH,MO | Z Diode | | | 106 mA | 0.5 W | | 4.3 V | 20 mA | $<22\Omega$ | $550 \cdot 10^6/°C$ | |
| 1N5230B | A1 | a1 | SG,TE,IT,PH,MO | Z Diode | | | 97 mA | 0.5 W | | 4.7 V | 20 mA | $<19\Omega$ | $300 \cdot 10^6/°C$ | P (SG) |
| 1N5231B | A1 | a1 | SG,TE,IT,PH,MO | Z Diode | | | 89 mA | 0.5 W | | 5.1 V | 20 mA | $<17\Omega$ | $300 \cdot 10^6/°C$ | P (SG) |
| 1N5232B | A1 | a1 | SG,TE,IT,PH,MO | Z Diode | | | 81 mA | 0.5 W | | 5,6 V | 20 mA | $<11\Omega$ | $380 \cdot 10^6/°C$ | |
| 1N5233B | A1 | a1 | SG,TE,IT,PH,MO | Z Diode | | | 76 mA | 0.5 W | | 6.0 V | 20 mA | $<7\Omega$ | $380 \cdot 10^6/°C$ | |
| 1N5234B | A1 | a1 | SG,TE,IT,PH,MO | Z Diode | | | 73 mA | 0.5 W | | 6.2 V | 20 mA | $<7\Omega$ | $450 \cdot 10^6/°C$ | P (SG) |
| 1N5235B | A1 | a1 | SG,TE,IT,PH,MO | Z Diode | | | 67 mA | 0.5 W | | 6.8 V | 20 mA | $<5\Omega$ | $500 \cdot 10^6/°C$ | P (SG) |
| 1N5236B | A1 | a1 | SG,TE,IT,PH,MO | Z Diode | | | 61 mA | 0.5 W | | 7.0 V | 20 mA | $<6\Omega$ | $580 \cdot 10^6/°C$ | P (SG) |
| 1N5237B | A1 | a1 | SG,TE,IT,PH,MO | Z Diode | | | 55 mA | 0.5 W | | 8.2 V | 20 mA | $<8\Omega$ | $620 \cdot 10^6/°C$ | |
| 1N5238B | A1 | a1 | SG,TE,IT,PH,MO | Z Diode | | | 52 mA | 0.5 W | | 8.7 V | 20 mA | $<8\Omega$ | $650 \cdot 10^6/°C$ | |
| 1N5239B | A1 | a1 | SG,TE,IT,PH,MO | Z Diode | | | 50 mA | 0.5 W | | 9.1 V | 20 mA | $<10\Omega$ | $680 \cdot 10^6/°C$ | P (SG) |
| 1N5240B | A1 | a1 | SG,TE,IT,PH,MO | Z Diode | | | 45 mA | 0.5 W | | 10 V | 20 mA | $<17\Omega$ | $750 \cdot 10^6/°C$ | P (SG) |
| 1N5241B | A1 | a1 | SG,TE,IT,PH,MO | Z Diode | | | 41 mA | 0.5 W | | 11 V | 20 mA | $<22\Omega$ | $760 \cdot 10^6/°C$ | |
| 1N5242B | A1 | a1 | SG,TE,IT,PH,MO | Z Diode | | | 38 mA | 0.5 W | | 12 V | 20 mA | $<30\Omega$ | $770 \cdot 10^6/°C$ | P (SG) |
| 1N5243B | A1 | a1 | SG,TE,IT,PH,MO | Z Diode | | | 35 mA | 0.5 W | | 13 V | 9.5 mA | $<13\Omega$ | $790 \cdot 10^6/°C$ | P (SG) |
| 1N5244B | A1 | a1 | SG,TE,IT,PH,MO | Z Diode | | | 32 mA | 0.5 W | | 14 V | 9.0 mA | $<15\Omega$ | $820 \cdot 10^6/°C$ | P (SG) |
| 1N5245B | A1 | a1 | SG,TE,IT,PH,MO | Z Diode | | | 30 mA | 0.5 W | | 15 V | 8.5 mA | $<16\Omega$ | $820 \cdot 10^6/°C$ | P (SG) |
| 1N5246B | A1 | a1 | SG,TE,IT,PH,MO | Z Diode | | | 28 mA | 0.5 W | | 16 V | 7.8 mA | $<17\Omega$ | $830 \cdot 10^6/°C$ | P (SG) |
| 1N5247B | A1 | a1 | SG,TE,IT,PH,MO | Z Diode | | | 27 mA | 0.5 W | | 17 V | 7.4 mA | $<19\Omega$ | $840 \cdot 10^6/°C$ | |
| 1N5248B | A1 | a1 | SG,TE,IT,PH,MO | Z Diode | | | 25 mA | 0.5 W | | 18 V | 7.0 mA | $<21\Omega$ | $850 \cdot 10^6/°C$ | P (SG) |
| 1N5249B | A1 | a1 | SG,TE,IT,PH,MO | Z Diode | | | 24 mA | 0.5 W | | 19 V | 6.6 mA | $<23\Omega$ | $860 \cdot 10^6/°C$ | |
| 1N5250B | A1 | a1 | SG,TE,IT,PH,MO | Z Diode | | | 23 mA | 0.5 W | | 20 V | 6.2 mA | $<25\Omega$ | $860 \cdot 10^6/°C$ | |
| 1N5251B | A1 | a1 | SG,TE,IT,PH,MO | Z Diode | | | 21 mA | 0.5 W | | 22 V | 5.6 mA | $<29\Omega$ | $870 \cdot 10^6/°C$ | P (SG) |
| 1N5252B | A1 | a1 | SG,TE,IT,PH,MO | Z Diode | | | 19 mA | 0.5 W | | 24 V | 5.2 mA | $<33\Omega$ | $880 \cdot 10^6/°C$ | P (SG) |
| 1N5253B | A1 | a1 | SG,TE,IT,PH,MO | Z Diode | | | 18 mA | 0.5 W | | 25 V | 5.0 mA | $<35\Omega$ | $890 \cdot 10^6/°C$ | |
| 1N5254B | A1 | a1 | SG,TE,IT,PH,MO | Z Diode | | | 17 mA | 0.5 W | | 27 V | 4.6 mA | $<41\Omega$ | $900 \cdot 10^6/°C$ | |
| 1N5255B | A1 | a1 | SG,TE,IT,PH,MO | Z Diode | | | 16 mA | 0.5 W | | 28 V | 4.5 mA | $<44\Omega$ | $910 \cdot 10^6/°C$ | |
| 1N5256B | A1 | a1 | SG,TE,IT,PH,MO | Z Diode | | | 15 mA | 0.5 W | | 30 V | 4.2 mA | $<49\Omega$ | $910 \cdot 10^6/°C$ | |
| 1N5257B | A1 | a1 | SG,TE,IT,PH,MO | Z Diode | | | 14 mA | 0.5 W | | 33 V | 3.8 mA | $<58\Omega$ | $920 \cdot 10^6/°C$ | |
| 1N5258B | A1 | a1 | SG,TE,IT,PH,MO | Z Diode | | | 13 mA | 0.5 W | | 36 V | 3.4 mA | $<70\Omega$ | $930 \cdot 10^6/°C$ | |
| 1N5259B | A1 | a1 | SG,TE,IT,PH,MO | Z Diode | | | 12 mA | 0.5 W | | 39 V | 3.2 mA | $<80\Omega$ | $940 \cdot 10^6/°C$ | |
| 1N5260B | A1 | a1 | SG,TE,IT,PH,MO | Z Diode | | | 11 mA | 0.5 W | | 43 V | 3.0 mA | $<93\Omega$ | $950 \cdot 10^6/°C$ | |

| Type | Case | Pin-code | | | Maximum Ratings | | | | | Electrical Characteristics | | | | |
|---|---|---|---|---|---|---|---|---|---|---|---|---|---|---|
| | | | | | Vcla Vbro | Its | Izm | Pv | Pvts | Vz | Iz Is | rz | TK | |
| 1N5261B | A1 | a1 | SG,TE,IT,PH,MO | Z Diode | | | 10 mA | 0.5 W | | 47 V | 2.7 mA | <105Ω | 950·10$^6$/°C | |
| 1N5262B | A1 | a1 | SG,TE,IT,PH,MO | Z Diode | | | 9 mA | 0.5 W | | 51 V | 2.5 mA | <125Ω | 960·10$^6$/°C | |
| 1N5263B | A1 | a1 | SG,TE,PH,MO | Z Diode | | | 8 mA | 0.5 W | | 56 V | 2.3 mA | <150Ω | 960·10$^6$/°C | |
| 1N5264B | A1 | a1 | SG,TE,PH,MO | Z Diode | | | 8 mA | 0.5 W | | 60 V | 2.1 mA | <170Ω | 970·10$^6$/°C | |
| 1N5265B | A1 | a1 | SG,TE,PH,MO | Z Diode | | | 7 mA | 0.5 W | | 62 V | 2.0 mA | <185Ω | 970·10$^6$/°C | |
| 1N5266B | A1 | a1 | SG,TE,PH,MO | Z Diode | | | 7 mA | 0.5 W | | 68 V | 1.8 mA | <230Ω | 970·10$^6$/°C | |
| 1N5267B | A1 | a1 | SG,TE,PH,MO | Z Diode | | | 6 mA | 0.5 W | | 75 V | 1.7 mA | <270Ω | 980·10$^6$/°C | |
| 1N5268B | A1 | a1 | SG,MO | Z Diode | | | 6 mA | 0.5 W | | 82 V | 1.5 mA | <330Ω | 980·10$^6$/°C | |
| 1N5269B | A1 | a1 | SG,MO | Z Diode | | | 5 mA | 0.5 W | | 87 V | 1.4 mA | <370Ω | 990·10$^6$/°C | |
| 1N5270B | A1 | a1 | SG,MO | Z Diode | | | 5 mA | 0.5 W | | 91 V | 1.4 mA | <400Ω | 990·10$^6$/°C | |
| 1N5271B | A1 | a1 | SG,MO | Z Diode | | | 5 mA | 0.5 W | | 100 V | 1.3 mA | <500Ω | 1100·10$^6$/°C | |
| 1N5272B | A1 | a1 | SG,MO | Z Diode | | | 4 mA | 0.5 W | | 110 V | 1.1 mA | <750Ω | 1100·10$^6$/°C | |
| 1N5273B | A1 | a1 | SG,MO | Z Diode | | | 4 mA | 0.5 W | | 120 V | 1.0 mA | <900Ω | 1100·10$^6$/°C | |
| 1N5274B | A1 | a1 | SG,MO | Z Diode | | | 4 mA | 0.5 W | | 130 V | 0.95 mA | <1100Ω | 1100·10$^6$/°C | |
| 1N5275B | A1 | a1 | SG,MO | Z Diode | | | 3 mA | 0.5 W | | 140 V | 0.9 mA | <1300Ω | 1100·10$^6$/°C | |
| 1N5276B | A1 | a1 | SG,MO | Z Diode | | | 3 mA | 0.5 W | | 150 V | 0.85 mA | <1500Ω | 1100·10$^6$/°C | |
| 1N5277B | A1 | a1 | SG,MO | Z Diode | | | 3 mA | 0.5 W | | 160 V | 0.8 mA | <1700Ω | 1100·10$^6$/°C | |
| 1N5278B | A1 | a1 | SG,MO | Z Diode | | | 3 mA | 0.5 W | | 170 V | 0.74 mA | <1900Ω | 1100·10$^6$/°C | |
| 1N5279B | A1 | a1 | SG,MO | Z Diode | | | 3 mA | 0.5 W | | 180 V | 0.68 mA | <2200Ω | 1100·10$^6$/°C | |
| 1N5280B | A1 | a1 | SG,MO | Z Diode | | | 2 mA | 0.5 W | | 190 V | 0.66 mA | <2400Ω | 1100·10$^6$/°C | |
| 1N5281B | A1 | a1 | SG,MO | Z Diode | | | 2 mA | 0.5 W | | 200 V | 0.65 mA | <2500Ω | 1100·10$^6$/°C | |
| 1N5228SB | A2 | a1 | IT | Z Diode | | | 69 mA | 0.3 W | | 3.9 V | 20 mA | <23Ω | -600·10$^6$/°C | |
| 1N5229SB | A2 | a1 | IT | Z Diode | | | 63 mA | 0.3 W | | 4.3 V | 20 mA | <22Ω | 550·10$^6$/°C | |
| 1N5230SB | A2 | a1 | IT | Z Diode | | | 58 mA | 0.3 W | | 4.7 V | 20 mA | <19Ω | 300·10$^6$/°C | |
| 1N5231SB | A2 | a1 | IT | Z Diode | | | 53 mA | 0.3 W | | 5.1 V | 20 mA | <17Ω | 300·10$^6$/°C | |
| 1N5232SB | A2 | a1 | IT | Z Diode | | | 48 mA | 0.3 W | | 5.6 V | 20 mA | <11Ω | 380·10$^6$/°C | |
| 1N5233SB | A2 | a1 | IT | Z Diode | | | 45 mA | 0.3 W | | 6.0 V | 20 mA | <7Ω | 380·10$^6$/°C | |
| 1N5234SB | A2 | a1 | IT | Z Diode | | | 43 mA | 0.3 W | | 6.2 V | 20 mA | <7Ω | 450·10$^6$/°C | |
| 1N5235SB | A2 | a1 | IT | Z Diode | | | 40 mA | 0.3 W | | 6.8 V | 20 mA | <5Ω | 500·10$^6$/°C | |
| 1N5236SB | A2 | a1 | IT | Z Diode | | | 36 mA | 0.3 W | | 7.0 V | 20 mA | <6Ω | 580·10$^6$/°C | |
| 1N5237SB | A2 | a1 | IT | Z Diode | | | 33 mA | 0.3 W | | 8.2 V | 20 mA | <8Ω | 620·10$^6$/°C | |
| 1N5238SB | A2 | a1 | IT | Z Diode | | | 31 mA | 0.3 W | | 8.7 V | 20 mA | <8Ω | 650·10$^6$/°C | |
| 1N5239SB | A2 | a1 | IT | Z Diode | | | 30 mA | 0.3 W | | 9.1 V | 20 mA | <10Ω | 680·10$^6$/°C | |
| 1N5240SB | A2 | a1 | IT | Z Diode | | | 27 mA | 0.3 W | | 10 V | 20 mA | <17Ω | 750·10$^6$/°C | |
| 1N5241SB | A2 | a1 | IT | Z Diode | | | 24 mA | 0.3 W | | 11 V | 20 mA | <22Ω | 760·10$^6$/°C | |
| 1N5242SB | A2 | a1 | IT | Z Diode | | | 22 mA | 0.3 W | | 12 V | 20 mA | <30Ω | 770·10$^6$/°C | |
| 1N5243SB | A2 | a1 | IT | Z Diode | | | 21 mA | 0.3 W | | 13 V | 9.5 mA | <13Ω | 790·10$^6$/°C | |
| 1N5244SB | A2 | a1 | IT | Z Diode | | | 19 mA | 0.3 W | | 14 V | 9.0 mA | <15Ω | 820·10$^6$/°C | |
| 1N5245SB | A2 | a1 | IT | Z Diode | | | 18 mA | 0.3 W | | 15 V | 8.5 mA | <16Ω | 820·10$^6$/°C | |
| 1N5246SB | A2 | a1 | IT | Z Diode | | | 17 mA | 0.3 W | | 16 V | 7.8 mA | <17Ω | 830·10$^6$/°C | |

| Type | Case | Pin-code | | | Maximum Ratings | | | | | Electrical Characteristics | | | | |
|---|---|---|---|---|---|---|---|---|---|---|---|---|---|---|
| | | | | | Vcla Vbro | Its | Izm | Pv | Pvts | Vz | Iz Is | rz | TK | |
| 1N5247SB | A2 | a1 | IT | Z Diode | | | 16 mA | 0.3 W | | 17 V | 7.4 mA | <19Ω | 840·10⁶/°C | |
| 1N5248SB | A2 | a1 | IT | Z Diode | | | 15 mA | 0.3 W | | 18 V | 7.0 mA | <21Ω | 850·10⁶/°C | |
| 1N5249SB | A2 | a1 | IT | Z Diode | | | 14 mA | 0.3 W | | 19 V | 6.6 mA | <23Ω | 860·10⁶/°C | |
| 1N5250SB | A2 | a1 | IT | Z Diode | | | 13 mA | 0.3 W | | 20 V | 6.2 mA | <25Ω | 860·10⁶/°C | |
| 1N5251SB | A2 | a1 | IT | Z Diode | | | 12 mA | 0.3 W | | 22 V | 5.6 mA | <29Ω | 870·10⁶/°C | |
| 1N5252SB | A2 | a1 | IT | Z Diode | | | 11.4 mA | 0.3 W | | 24 V | 5.2 mA | <33Ω | 880·10⁶/°C | |
| 1N5253SB | A2 | a1 | IT | Z Diode | | | 10.9 mA | 0.3 W | | 25 V | 5.0 mA | <37Ω | 890·10⁶/°C | |
| 1N5254SB | A2 | a1 | IT | Z Diode | | | 10 mA | 0.3 W | | 27 V | 4.6 mA | <41Ω | 900·10⁶/°C | |
| 1N5255SB | A2 | a1 | IT | Z Diode | | | 9.7 mA | 0.3 W | | 28 V | 4.5 mA | <44Ω | 910·10⁶/°C | |
| 1N5256SB | A2 | a1 | IT | Z Diode | | | 9 mA | 0.3 W | | 30 V | 4.2 mA | <49Ω | 910·10⁶/°C | |
| 1N5257SB | A2 | a1 | IT | Z Diode | | | 8.2 mA | 0.3 W | | 33 V | 3.8 mA | <58Ω | 920·10⁶/°C | |
| 1N5258SB | A2 | a1 | IT | Z Diode | | | 7.5 mA | 0.3 W | | 36 V | 3.4 mA | <70Ω | 930·10⁶/°C | |
| 1N5259SB | A2 | a1 | IT | Z Diode | | | 6.9 mA | 0.3 W | | 39 V | 3.2 mA | <80Ω | 940·10⁶/°C | |
| 1N5260SB | A2 | a1 | IT | Z Diode | | | 6.3 mA | 0.3 W | | 43 V | 3.0 mA | <93Ω | 950·10⁶/°C | |
| 1N5261SB | A2 | a1 | IT | Z Diode | | | 5.8 mA | 0.3 W | | 47 V | 2.7 mA | <105Ω | 950·10⁶/°C | |
| 1N5262SB | A2 | a1 | IT | Z Diode | | | 5.3 mA | 0.3 W | | 51 V | 2.5 mA | <125Ω | 960·10⁶/°C | |
| 1N5225 | A1 | a1 | IT | Z Diode | | | 151 mA | 0.5 W | | 3.0 V | 20 mA | <29Ω | -750·10⁶/°C | Vz ±20% |
| 1N5226 | A1 | a1 | IT | Z Diode | | | 138 mA | 0.5 W | | 3.3 V | 20 mA | <28Ω | -700·10⁶/°C | Vz ±20% |
| 1N5227 | A1 | a1 | IT | Z Diode | | | 126 mA | 0.5 W | | 3.6 V | 20 mA | <24Ω | -650·10⁶/°C | Vz ±20% |
| 1N5228 | A1 | a1 | IT | Z Diode | | | 115 mA | 0.5 W | | 3.9 V | 20 mA | <23Ω | -600·10⁶/°C | Vz ±20% |
| 1N5229 | A1 | a1 | IT | Z Diode | | | 106 mA | 0.5 W | | 4.3 V | 20 mA | <22Ω | 550·10⁶/°C | Vz ±20% |
| 1N5230 | A1 | a1 | IT | Z Diode | | | 97 mA | 0.5 W | | 4.7 V | 20 mA | <19Ω | 300·10⁶/°C | Vz ±20% |
| 1N5231 | A1 | a1 | IT | Z Diode | | | 89 mA | 0.5 W | | 5.1 V | 20 mA | <17Ω | 300·10⁶/°C | Vz ±20% |
| 1N5232 | A1 | a1 | IT | Z Diode | | | 81 mA | 0.5 W | | 5,6 V | 20 mA | <11Ω | 380·10⁶/°C | Vz ±20% |
| 1N5233 | A1 | a1 | IT | Z Diode | | | 76 mA | 0.5 W | | 6.0 V | 20 mA | <7Ω | 380·10⁶/°C | Vz ±20% |
| 1N5234 | A1 | a1 | IT | Z Diode | | | 73 mA | 0.5 W | | 6.2 V | 20 mA | <7Ω | 450·10⁶/°C | Vz ±20% |
| 1N5235 | A1 | a1 | IT | Z Diode | | | 67 mA | 0.5 W | | 6.8 V | 20 mA | <5Ω | 500·10⁶/°C | Vz ±20% |
| 1N5236 | A1 | a1 | IT | Z Diode | | | 61 mA | 0.5 W | | 7.0 V | 20 mA | <6Ω | 580·10⁶/°C | Vz ±20% |
| 1N5237 | A1 | a1 | IT | Z Diode | | | 55 mA | 0.5 W | | 8.2 V | 20 mA | <8Ω | 620·10⁶/°C | Vz ±20% |
| 1N5238 | A1 | a1 | IT | Z Diode | | | 52 mA | 0.5 W | | 8.7 V | 20 mA | <8Ω | 650·10⁶/°C | Vz ±20% |
| 1N5239 | A1 | a1 | IT | Z Diode | | | 50 mA | 0.5 W | | 9.1 V | 20 mA | <10Ω | 680·10⁶/°C | Vz ±20% |
| 1N5240 | A1 | a1 | IT | Z Diode | | | 45 mA | 0.5 W | | 10 V | 20 mA | <17Ω | 750·10⁶/°C | Vz ±20% |
| 1N5241 | A1 | a1 | IT | Z Diode | | | 41 mA | 0.5 W | | 11 V | 20 mA | <22Ω | 760·10⁶/°C | Vz ±20% |
| 1N5242 | A1 | a1 | IT | Z Diode | | | 38 mA | 0.5 W | | 12 V | 20 mA | <30Ω | 770·10⁶/°C | Vz ±20% |
| 1N5243 | A1 | a1 | IT | Z Diode | | | 35 mA | 0.5 W | | 13 V | 9.5 mA | <13Ω | 790·10⁶/°C | Vz ±20% |
| 1N5244 | A1 | a1 | IT | Z Diode | | | 32 mA | 0.5 W | | 14 V | 9.0 mA | <15Ω | 820·10⁶/°C | Vz ±20% |
| 1N5245 | A1 | a1 | IT | Z Diode | | | 30 mA | 0.5 W | | 15 V | 8.5 mA | <16Ω | 820·10⁶/°C | Vz ±20% |
| 1N5246 | A1 | a1 | IT | Z Diode | | | 28 mA | 0.5 W | | 16 V | 7.8 mA | <17Ω | 830·10⁶/°C | Vz ±20% |
| 1N5247 | A1 | a1 | IT | Z Diode | | | 27 mA | 0.5 W | | 17 V | 7.4 mA | <19Ω | 840·10⁶/°C | Vz ±20% |
| 1N5248 | A1 | a1 | IT | Z Diode | | | 25 mA | 0.5 W | | 18 V | 7.0 mA | <21Ω | 850·10⁶/°C | Vz ±20% |

| Type | Case | Pin-code | | | Vcla Vbro | Maximum Ratings Its | Izm | Pv | Pvts | Electrical Characteristics Vz | Iz Is | rz | TK | |
|------|------|----------|---|---|-----------|-----|-----|-----|------|-----|-----|-----|-----|---|
| 1N5249 | A1 | a1 | IT | Z Diode | | | 24 mA | 0.5 W | | 19 V | 6.6 mA | <23 Ω | 860·10⁶/°C | Vz ±20% |
| 1N5250 | A1 | a1 | IT | Z Diode | | | 23 mA | 0.5 W | | 20 V | 6.2 mA | <25 Ω | 860·10⁶/°C | Vz ±20% |
| 1N5251 | A1 | a1 | IT | Z Diode | | | 21 mA | 0.5 W | | 22 V | 5.6 mA | <29 Ω | 870·10⁶/°C | Vz ±20% |
| 1N5252 | A1 | a1 | IT | Z Diode | | | 19 mA | 0.5 W | | 24 V | 5.2 mA | <33 Ω | 880·10⁶/°C | Vz ±20% |
| 1N5253 | A1 | a1 | IT | Z Diode | | | 18 mA | 0.5 W | | 25 V | 5.0 mA | <35 Ω | 890·10⁶/°C | Vz ±20% |
| 1N5254 | A1 | a1 | IT | Z Diode | | | 17 mA | 0.5 W | | 27 V | 4.6 mA | <41 Ω | 900·10⁶/°C | Vz ±20% |
| 1N5255 | A1 | a1 | IT | Z Diode | | | 16 mA | 0.5 W | | 28 V | 4.5 mA | <44 Ω | 910·10⁶/°C | Vz ±20% |
| 1N5256 | A1 | a1 | IT | Z Diode | | | 15 mA | 0.5 W | | 30 V | 4.2 mA | <49 Ω | 910·10⁶/°C | Vz ±20% |
| 1N5257 | A1 | a1 | IT | Z Diode | | | 14 mA | 0.5 W | | 33 V | 3.8 mA | <58 Ω | 920·10⁶/°C | Vz ±20% |
| 1N5258 | A1 | a1 | IT | Z Diode | | | 13 mA | 0.5 W | | 36 V | 3.4 mA | <70 Ω | 930·10⁶/°C | Vz ±20% |
| 1N5259 | A1 | a1 | IT | Z Diode | | | 12 mA | 0.5 W | | 39 V | 3.2 mA | <80 Ω | 940·10⁶/°C | Vz ±20% |
| 1N5260 | A1 | a1 | IT | Z Diode | | | 11 mA | 0.5 W | | 43 V | 3.0 mA | <93 Ω | 950·10⁶/°C | Vz ±20% |
| 1N5261 | A1 | a1 | IT | Z Diode | | | 10 mA | 0.5 W | | 47 V | 2.7 mA | <105 Ω | 950·10⁶/°C | Vz ±20% |
| 1N5262 | A1 | a1 | IT | Z Diode | | | 9 mA | 0.5 W | | 51 V | 2.5 mA | <125 Ω | 960·10⁶/°C | Vz ±20% |
| 1N5225S | A2 | a1 | IT | Z Diode | | | 91 mA | 0.5 W | | 3.0 V | 20 mA | <29 Ω | -750·10⁶/°C | Vz ±20% |
| 1N5226S | A2 | a1 | IT | Z Diode | | | 82 mA | 0.5 W | | 3.3 V | 20 mA | <28 Ω | -700·10⁶/°C | Vz ±20% |
| 1N5227S | A2 | a1 | IT | Z Diode | | | 75 mA | 0.5 W | | 3.6 V | 20 mA | <24 Ω | -650·10⁶/°C | Vz ±20% |
| 1N5228S | A2 | a1 | IT | Z Diode | | | 69 mA | 0.5 W | | 3.9 V | 20 mA | <23 Ω | -600·10⁶/°C | Vz ±20% |
| 1N5229S | A2 | a1 | IT | Z Diode | | | 63 mA | 0.5 W | | 4.3 V | 20 mA | <22 Ω | 550·10⁶/°C | Vz ±20% |
| 1N5230S | A2 | a1 | IT | Z Diode | | | 58 mA | 0.5 W | | 4.7 V | 20 mA | <19 Ω | 300·10⁶/°C | Vz ±20% |
| 1N5231S | A2 | a1 | IT | Z Diode | | | 53 mA | 0.5 W | | 5.1 V | 20 mA | <17 Ω | 300·10⁶/°C | Vz ±20% |
| 1N5232S | A2 | a1 | IT | Z Diode | | | 48 mA | 0.5 W | | 5.6 V | 20 mA | <11 Ω | 380·10⁶/°C | Vz ±20% |
| 1N5233S | A2 | a1 | IT | Z Diode | | | 45 mA | 0.5 W | | 6.0 V | 20 mA | <7 Ω | 380·10⁶/°C | Vz ±20% |
| 1N5234S | A2 | a1 | IT | Z Diode | | | 43 mA | 0.5 W | | 6.2 V | 20 mA | <7 Ω | 450·10⁶/°C | Vz ±20% |
| 1N5235S | A2 | a1 | IT | Z Diode | | | 40 mA | 0.5 W | | 6.8 V | 20 mA | <5 Ω | 500·10⁶/°C | Vz ±20% |
| 1N5236S | A2 | a1 | IT | Z Diode | | | 36 mA | 0.5 W | | 7.0 V | 20 mA | <6 Ω | 580·10⁶/°C | |
| 1N5237S | A2 | a1 | IT | Z Diode | | | 33 mA | 0.5 W | | 8.2 V | 20 mA | <8 Ω | 620·10⁶/°C | Vz ±20% |
| 1N5238S | A2 | a1 | IT | Z Diode | | | 31 mA | 0.5 W | | 8.7 V | 20 mA | <8 Ω | 650·10⁶/°C | Vz ±20% |
| 1N5239S | A2 | a1 | IT | Z Diode | | | 30 mA | 0.5 W | | 9.1 V | 20 mA | <10 Ω | 680·10⁶/°C | Vz ±20% |
| 1N5240S | A2 | a1 | IT | Z Diode | | | 27 mA | 0.5 W | | 10 V | 20 mA | <17 Ω | 750·10⁶/°C | Vz ±20% |
| 1N5241S | A2 | a1 | IT | Z Diode | | | 24 mA | 0.5 W | | 11 V | 20 mA | <22 Ω | 760·10⁶/°C | Vz ±20% |
| 1N5242S | A2 | a1 | IT | Z Diode | | | 22 mA | 0.5 W | | 12 V | 20 mA | <30 Ω | 770·10⁶/°C | Vz ±20% |
| 1N5243S | A2 | a1 | IT | Z Diode | | | 21 mA | 0.5 W | | 13 V | 9.5 mA | <13 Ω | 790·10⁶/°C | Vz ±20% |
| 1N5244S | A2 | a1 | IT | Z Diode | | | 19 mA | 0.5 W | | 14 V | 9.0 mA | <15 Ω | 820·10⁶/°C | Vz ±20% |
| 1N5245S | A2 | a1 | IT | Z Diode | | | 18 mA | 0.5 W | | 15 V | 8.5 mA | <16 Ω | 820·10⁶/°C | Vz ±20% |
| 1N5246S | A2 | a1 | IT | Z Diode | | | 17 mA | 0.5 W | | 16 V | 7.8 mA | <17 Ω | 830·10⁶/°C | |
| 1N5247S | A2 | a1 | IT | Z Diode | | | 16 mA | 0.5 W | | 17 V | 7.4 mA | <19 Ω | 840·10⁶/°C | |
| 1N5248S | A2 | a1 | IT | Z Diode | | | 15 mA | 0.5 W | | 18 V | 7.0 mA | <21 Ω | 850·10⁶/°C | |
| 1N5249S | A2 | a1 | IT | Z Diode | | | 14 mA | 0.5 W | | 19 V | 6.6 mA | <23 Ω | 860·10⁶/°C | |
| 1N5250S | A2 | a1 | IT | Z Diode | | | 13 mA | 0.5 W | | 20 V | 6.2 mA | <25 Ω | 860·10⁶/°C | |

| Type | Case | Pin-code | | | Maximum Ratings | | | | | Electrical Characteristics | | | | |
|---|---|---|---|---|---|---|---|---|---|---|---|---|---|---|
| | | | | | Vcla Vbro | Its | Izm | Pv | Pvts | Vz | Iz Is | rz | TK | |
| 1N5251S | A2 | a1 | IT | Z Diode | | | 12 mA | 0.5 W | | 22 V | 5.6 mA | <29Ω | 870·10⁶/°C | |
| 1N5252S | A2 | a1 | IT | Z Diode | | | 11.4 mA | 0.5 W | | 24 V | 5.2 mA | <33Ω | 880·10⁶/°C | |
| 1N5253S | A2 | a1 | IT | Z Diode | | | 10.9 mA | 0.5 W | | 25 V | 5.0 mA | <35Ω | 890·10⁶/°C | |
| 1N5254S | A2 | a1 | IT | Z Diode | | | 10 mA | 0.5 W | | 27 V | 4.6 mA | <41Ω | 900·10⁶/°C | |
| 1N5255S | A2 | a1 | IT | Z Diode | | | 9.7 mA | 0.5 W | | 28 V | 4.5 mA | <44Ω | 910·10⁶/°C | |
| 1N5256S | A2 | a1 | IT | Z Diode | | | 9 mA | 0.5 W | | 30 V | 4.2 mA | <49Ω | 910·10⁶/°C | |
| 1N5257S | A2 | a1 | IT | Z Diode | | | 8.2 mA | 0.5 W | | 33 V | 3.8 mA | <58Ω | 920·10⁶/°C | |
| 1N5258S | A2 | a1 | IT | Z Diode | | | 7.5 mA | 0.5 W | | 36 V | 3.4 mA | <70Ω | 930·10⁶/°C | |
| 1N5259S | A2 | a1 | IT | Z Diode | | | 6.9 mA | 0.5 W | | 39 V | 3.2 mA | <80Ω | 940·10⁶/°C | |
| 1N5260S | A2 | a1 | IT | Z Diode | | | 6.3 mA | 0.5 W | | 43 V | 3.0 mA | <93Ω | 950·10⁶/°C | |
| 1N5261S | A2 | a1 | IT | Z Diode | | | 5.8 mA | 0.5 W | | 47 V | 2.7 mA | <105Ω | 950·10⁶/°C | |
| 1N5262S | A2 | a1 | IT | Z Diode | | | 5.3 mA | 0.5 W | | 51 V | 2.5 mA | <125Ω | 960·10⁶/°C | |
| 1N5230SA | A2 | a1 | IT | Z Diode | | | 58 mA | 0.5 W | | 4.7 V | 20 mA | <19Ω | 300·10⁶/°C | |
| 1N5231SA | A2 | a1 | IT | Z Diode | | | 53 mA | 0.5 W | | 5.1 V | 20 mA | <17Ω | 300·10⁶/°C | |
| 1N5232SA | A2 | a1 | IT | Z Diode | | | 48 mA | 0.5 W | | 5.6 V | 20 mA | <11Ω | 380·10⁶/°C | |
| 1N5233SA | A2 | a1 | IT | Z Diode | | | 45 mA | 0.5 W | | 6.0 V | 20 mA | <7Ω | 380·10⁶/°C | |
| 1N5234SA | A2 | a1 | IT | Z Diode | | | 43 mA | 0.5 W | | 6.2 V | 20 mA | <7Ω | 450·10⁶/°C | |
| 1N5235SA | A2 | a1 | IT | Z Diode | | | 40 mA | 0.5 W | | 6.8 V | 20 mA | <5Ω | 500·10⁶/°C | |
| 1N5236SA | A2 | a1 | IT | Z Diode | | | 36 mA | 0.5 W | | 7.0 V | 20 mA | <6Ω | 580·10⁶/°C | |
| 1N5333B | B3 | a1 | SG,MO | Z Diode | | | 1440 mA | 5 W | 180 W | 3.3 V | 380 mA | <3Ω | -600·10⁶/°C | .A |
| 1N5334B | B3 | a1 | SG,MO | Z Diode | | | 1320 mA | 5 W | 180 W | 3.6 V | 350 mA | <2.5Ω | -550·10⁶/°C | .A |
| 1N5335B | B3 | a1 | SG,MO | Z Diode | | | 1220 mA | 5 W | 180 W | 3.9 V | 320 mA | <2Ω | -500·10⁶/°C | .A |
| 1N5336B | B3 | a1 | SG,MO | Z Diode | | | 1100 mA | 5 W | 180 W | 4.3 V | 290 mA | <2Ω | -400·10⁶/°C | .A |
| 1N5337B | B3 | a1 | SG,MO | Z Diode | | | 1010 mA | 5 W | 180 W | 4.7 V | 260 mA | <2Ω | -200·10⁶/°C | .A |
| 1N5338B | B3 | a1 | SG,MO | Z Diode | | | 930 mA | 5 W | 180 W | 5.1 V | 240 mA | <1.5Ω | 100·10⁶/°C | .A |
| 1N5339B | B3 | a1 | SG,MO | Z Diode | | | 865 mA | 5 W | 180 W | 5.6 V | 220 mA | <1Ω | 250·10⁶/°C | .A |
| 1N5340B | B3 | a1 | SG,MO | Z Diode | | | 790 mA | 5 W | 180 W | 6.0 V | 200 mA | <1Ω | 280·10⁶/°C | .A |
| 1N5341B | B3 | a1 | SG,MO | Z Diode | | | 765 mA | 5 W | 180 W | 6.2 V | 200 mA | <1Ω | 320·10⁶/°C | .A |
| 1N5342B | B3 | a1 | SG,MO | Z Diode | | | 700 mA | 5 W | 180 W | 6.8 V | 175 mA | <1Ω | 400·10⁶/°C | .A |
| 1N5343B | B3 | a1 | SG,MO | Z Diode | | | 630 mA | 5 W | 180 W | 7.5 V | 175 mA | <1.5Ω | 450·10⁶/°C | .A |
| 1N5344B | B3 | a1 | SG,MO | Z Diode | | | 580 mA | 5 W | 180 W | 8.2 V | 150 mA | <1.5Ω | 480·10⁶/°C | .A |
| 1N5345B | B3 | a1 | SG,MO | Z Diode | | | 545 mA | 5 W | 180 W | 8.7 V | 150 mA | <2Ω | 490·10⁶/°C | .A |
| 1N5346B | B3 | a1 | SG,MO | Z Diode | | | 520 mA | 5 W | 180 W | 9.1 V | 150 mA | <2Ω | 510·10⁶/°C | .A |
| 1N5347B | B3 | a1 | SG,MO | Z Diode | | | 475 mA | 5 W | 180 W | 10 V | 125 mA | <2Ω | 550·10⁶/°C | .A |
| 1N5348B | B3 | a1 | SG,MO | Z Diode | | | 430 mA | 5 W | 180 W | 11 V | 125 mA | <2.5Ω | 600·10⁶/°C | .A |
| 1N5349B | B3 | a1 | SG,MO | Z Diode | | | 395 mA | 5 W | 180 W | 12 V | 100 mA | <2.5Ω | 650·10⁶/°C | .A |
| 1N5350B | B3 | a1 | SG,MO | Z Diode | | | 365 mA | 5 W | 180 W | 13 V | 100 mA | <2.5Ω | 650·10⁶/°C | .A |
| 1N5351B | B3 | a1 | SG,MO | Z Diode | | | 340 mA | 5 W | 180 W | 14 V | 100 mA | <2.5Ω | 700·10⁶/°C | .A |
| 1N5352B | B3 | a1 | SG,MO | Z Diode | | | 315 mA | 5 W | 180 W | 15 V | 75 mA | <2.5Ω | 700·10⁶/°C | .A |
| 1N5353B | B3 | a1 | SG,MO | Z Diode | | | 295 mA | 5 W | 180 W | 16 V | 75 mA | <2.5Ω | 700·10⁶/°C | .A |

| Type | Case | Pin-code | | | | Maximum Ratings | | | | Electrical Characteristics | | | | |
|------|------|------|---|---|---|---|---|---|---|---|---|---|---|---|
| | | | | | Vcla Vbro | Its | Izm | Pv | Pvts | Vz | Iz Is | rz | TK | |
| 1N5354B | B3 | a1 | SG,MO | Z Diode | | | 280 mA | 5 W | 180 W | 17 V | 70 mA | <2.5Ω | 700·10^6/°C | .A |
| 1N5355B | B3 | a1 | SG,MO | Z Diode | | | 264 mA | 5 W | 180 W | 18 V | 65 mA | <2.5Ω | 750·10^6/°C | .A |
| 1N5356B | B3 | a1 | SG,MO | Z Diode | | | 250 mA | 5 W | 180 W | 19 V | 65 mA | <3Ω | 750·10^6/°C | .A |
| 1N5357B | B3 | a1 | SG,MO | Z Diode | | | 237 mA | 5 W | 180 W | 20 V | 65 mA | <3Ω | 750·10^6/°C | .A |
| 1N5358B | B3 | a1 | SG,MO | Z Diode | | | 216 mA | 5 W | 180 W | 22 V | 50 mA | <3.5Ω | 800·10^6/°C | .A |
| 1N5359B | B3 | a1 | SG,MO | Z Diode | | | 198 mA | 5 W | 180 W | 24 V | 50 mA | <3.5Ω | 800·10^6/°C | .A |
| 1N5360B | B3 | a1 | SG,MO | Z Diode | | | 190 mA | 5 W | 180 W | 25 V | 50 mA | <4Ω | 800·10^6/°C | .A |
| 1N5361B | B3 | a1 | SG,MO | Z Diode | | | 176 mA | 5 W | 180 W | 27 V | 50 mA | <5Ω | 850·10^6/°C | .A |
| 1N5362B | B3 | a1 | SG,MO | Z Diode | | | 170 mA | 5 W | 180 W | 28 V | 50 mA | <6Ω | 850·10^6/°C | .A |
| 1N5363B | B3 | a1 | SG,MO | Z Diode | | | 158 mA | 5 W | 180 W | 30 V | 40 mA | <8Ω | 850·10^6/°C | .A |
| 1N5364B | B3 | a1 | SG,MO | Z Diode | | | 144 mA | 5 W | 180 W | 33 V | 40 mA | <10Ω | 850·10^6/°C | .A |
| 1N5365B | B3 | a1 | SG,MO | Z Diode | | | 132 mA | 5 W | 180 W | 36 V | 30 mA | <11Ω | 900·10^6/°C | .A |
| 1N5366B | B3 | a1 | SG,MO | Z Diode | | | 122 mA | 5 W | 180 W | 39 V | 30 mA | <14Ω | 900·10^6/°C | .A |
| 1N5367B | B3 | a1 | SG,MO | Z Diode | | | 110 mA | 5 W | 180 W | 43 V | 30 mA | <20Ω | 900·10^6/°C | .A |
| 1N5368B | B3 | a1 | SG,MO | Z Diode | | | 100 mA | 5 W | 180 W | 47 V | 25 mA | <25Ω | 900·10^6/°C | .A |
| 1N5369B | B3 | a1 | SG,MO | Z Diode | | | 93 mA | 5 W | 180 W | 51 V | 25 mA | <27Ω | 900·10^6/°C | .A |
| 1N5370B | B3 | a1 | SG,MO | Z Diode | | | 86 mA | 5 W | 180 W | 56 V | 20 mA | <35Ω | 900·10^6/°C | .A |
| 1N5371B | B3 | a1 | SG,MO | Z Diode | | | 79 mA | 5 W | 180 W | 60 V | 20 mA | <40Ω | 900·10^6/°C | .A |
| 1N5372B | B3 | a1 | SG,MO | Z Diode | | | 76 mA | 5 W | 180 W | 62 V | 20 mA | <42Ω | 900·10^6/°C | .A |
| 1N5373B | B3 | a1 | SG,MO | Z Diode | | | 70 mA | 5 W | 180 W | 68 V | 20 mA | <44Ω | 900·10^6/°C | .A |
| 1N5374B | B3 | a1 | SG,MO | Z Diode | | | 63 mA | 5 W | 180 W | 75 V | 20 mA | <45Ω | 900·10^6/°C | .A |
| 1N5375B | B3 | a1 | SG,MO | Z Diode | | | 58 mA | 5 W | 180 W | 82 V | 15 mA | <65Ω | 900·10^6/°C | .A |
| 1N5376B | B3 | a1 | SG,MO | Z Diode | | | 55 mA | 5 W | 180 W | 87 V | 15 mA | <75Ω | 900·10^6/°C | .A |
| 1N5377B | B3 | a1 | SG,MO | Z Diode | | | 53 mA | 5 W | 180 W | 91 V | 15 mA | <75Ω | 900·10^6/°C | .A |
| 1N5378B | B3 | a1 | SG,MO | Z Diode | | | 48 mA | 5 W | 180 W | 100 V | 12 mA | <90Ω | 950·10^6/°C | .A |
| 1N5379B | B3 | a1 | SG,MO | Z Diode | | | 43 mA | 5 W | 180 W | 110 V | 12 mA | <125Ω | 950·10^6/°C | .A |
| 1N5380B | B3 | a1 | SG,MO | Z Diode | | | 40 mA | 5 W | 180 W | 120 V | 10 mA | <170Ω | 950·10^6/°C | .A |
| 1N5381B | B3 | a1 | SG,MO | Z Diode | | | 37 mA | 5 W | 180 W | 130 V | 10 mA | <190Ω | 950·10^6/°C | .A |
| 1N5382B | B3 | a1 | SG,MO | Z Diode | | | 34 mA | 5 W | 180 W | 140 V | 8 mA | <230Ω | 950·10^6/°C | .A |
| 1N5383B | B3 | a1 | SG,MO | Z Diode | | | 32 mA | 5 W | 180 W | 150 V | 8 mA | <330Ω | 950·10^6/°C | .A |
| 1N5384B | B3 | a1 | SG,MO | Z Diode | | | 29 mA | 5 W | 180 W | 160 V | 8 mA | <350Ω | 950·10^6/°C | .A |
| 1N5385B | B3 | a1 | SG,MO | Z Diode | | | 28 mA | 5 W | 180 W | 170 V | 8 mA | <380Ω | 950·10^6/°C | .A |
| 1N5386B | B3 | a1 | SG,MO | Z Diode | | | 26 mA | 5 W | 180 W | 180 V | 5 mA | <430Ω | 950·10^6/°C | .A |
| 1N5387B | B3 | a1 | SG,MO | Z Diode | | | 25 mA | 5 W | 180 W | 190 V | 5 mA | <450Ω | 950·10^6/°C | .A |
| 1N5388B | B3 | a1 | SG,MO | Z Diode | | | 24 mA | 5 W | 180 W | 200 V | 5 mA | <480Ω | 1000·10^6/°C | .A |
| 1N5913B | A3 | a1 | MO | Z Diode | | | 454 mA | 1.5 W | | 3.3 V | 113.6 mA | <10Ω | | A |
| 1N5914B | A3 | a1 | MO | Z Diode | | | 416 mA | 1.5 W | | 3.6 V | 104.2 mA | <9Ω | | A |
| 1N5915B | A3 | a1 | MO | Z Diode | | | 384 mA | 1.5 W | | 3.9 V | 96.1 mA | <7.5Ω | | A |
| 1N5916B | A3 | a1 | MO | Z Diode | | | 348 mA | 1.5 W | | 4.3 V | 87.2 mA | <6Ω | | A |
| 1N5917B | A3 | a1 | MO | Z Diode | | | 319 mA | 1.5 W | | 4.7 V | 79.8 mA | <5Ω | | A |

| Type | Case | Pin-code | | | Maximum Ratings | | | | | Electrical Characteristics | | | | |
|---|---|---|---|---|---|---|---|---|---|---|---|---|---|---|
| | | | | | Vcla Vbro | Its | Izm | Pv | Pvts | Vz | Iz / Is | rz | TK | |
| 1N5918B | A3 | a1 | MO | Z Diode | | | 294 mA | 1.5 W | | 5.1 V | 73.5 mA | <4 Ω | | A |
| 1N5919B | A3 | a1 | MO | Z Diode | | | 267 mA | 1.5 W | | 5.6 V | 66.9 mA | <2 Ω | | A |
| 1N5920B | A3 | a1 | MO | Z Diode | | | 241 mA | 1.5 W | | 6.2 V | 60.5 mA | <2 Ω | | A |
| 1N5921B | A3 | a1 | MO | Z Diode | | | 220 mA | 1.5 W | | 6.8 V | 55.1 mA | <2.5 Ω | | A |
| 1N5922B | A3 | a1 | MO | Z Diode | | | 200 mA | 1.5 W | | 7.5 V | 50 mA | <3 Ω | | A |
| 1N5923B | A3 | a1 | MO | Z Diode | | | 182 mA | 1.5 W | | 8.2 V | 45.7 mA | <3.5 Ω | | A |
| 1N5924B | A3 | a1 | MO | Z Diode | | | 164 mA | 1.5 W | | 9.1 V | 41.2 mA | <4 Ω | | A |
| 1N5925B | A3 | a1 | MO | Z Diode | | | 150 mA | 1.5 W | | 10 V | 37.5 mA | <4.5 Ω | | A |
| 1N5926B | A3 | a1 | MO | Z Diode | | | 136 mA | 1.5 W | | 11 V | 34.1 mA | <5.5 Ω | | A |
| 1N5927B | A3 | a1 | MO | Z Diode | | | 125 mA | 1.5 W | | 12 V | 31.2 mA | <6.5 Ω | | A |
| 1N5928B | A3 | a1 | MO | Z Diode | | | 115 mA | 1.5 W | | 13 V | 28.8 mA | <7 Ω | | A |
| 1N5929B | A3 | a1 | MO | Z Diode | | | 100 mA | 1.5 W | | 15 V | 25 mA | <9 Ω | | A |
| 1N5930B | A3 | a1 | MO | Z Diode | | | 93 mA | 1.5 W | | 16 V | 23.4 mA | <10 Ω | | A |
| 1N5931B | A3 | a1 | MO | Z Diode | | | 83 mA | 1.5 W | | 18 V | 20.8 mA | <12 Ω | | A |
| 1N5932B | A3 | a1 | MO | Z Diode | | | 75 mA | 1.5 W | | 20 V | 18.7 mA | <14 Ω | | A |
| 1N5933B | A3 | a1 | MO | Z Diode | | | 68 mA | 1.5 W | | 22 V | 17 mA | <17.5 Ω | | A |
| 1N5934B | A3 | a1 | MO | Z Diode | | | 62 mA | 1.5 W | | 24 V | 15.6 mA | <19 Ω | | A |
| 1N5935B | A3 | a1 | MO | Z Diode | | | 55 mA | 1.5 W | | 27 V | 13.9 mA | <23 Ω | | A |
| 1N5936B | A3 | a1 | MO | Z Diode | | | 50 mA | 1.5 W | | 30 V | 12.5 mA | <26 Ω | | A |
| 1N5937B | A3 | a1 | MO | Z Diode | | | 45 mA | 1.5 W | | 33 V | 11.4 mA | <33 Ω | | A |
| 1N5938B | A3 | a1 | MO | Z Diode | | | 41 mA | 1.5 W | | 36 V | 10.4 mA | <38 Ω | | A |
| 1N5939B | A3 | a1 | MO | Z Diode | | | 38 mA | 1.5 W | | 39 V | 9.6 mA | <45 Ω | | A |
| 1N5940B | A3 | a1 | MO | Z Diode | | | 34 mA | 1.5 W | | 43 V | 8.7 mA | <53 Ω | | A |
| 1N5941B | A3 | a1 | MO | Z Diode | | | 31 mA | 1.5 W | | 47 V | 8 mA | <67 Ω | | A |
| 1N5942B | A3 | a1 | MO | Z Diode | | | 29 mA | 1.5 W | | 51 V | 7.3 mA | <70 Ω | | A |
| 1N5943B | A3 | a1 | MO | Z Diode | | | 26 mA | 1.5 W | | 56 V | 6.7 mA | <860 Ω | | A |
| 1N5944B | A3 | a1 | MO | Z Diode | | | 24 mA | 1.5 W | | 62 V | 6 mA | <100 Ω | | A |
| 1N5945B | A3 | a1 | MO | Z Diode | | | 22 mA | 1.5 W | | 68 V | 5.5 mA | <120 Ω | | A |
| 1N5946B | A3 | a1 | MO | Z Diode | | | 20 mA | 1.5 W | | 75 V | 5 mA | <140 Ω | | A |
| 1N5947B | A3 | a1 | MO | Z Diode | | | 18 mA | 1.5 W | | 82 V | 4.6 mA | <160 Ω | | A |
| 1N5948B | A3 | a1 | MO | Z Diode | | | 16 mA | 1.5 W | | 91 V | 4.1 mA | <200 Ω | | A |
| 1N5949B | A3 | a1 | MO | Z Diode | | | 15 mA | 1.5 W | | 100 V | 3.7 mA | <250 Ω | | A |
| 1N5950B | A3 | a1 | MO | Z Diode | | | 13 mA | 1.5 W | | 110 V | 3.4 mA | <300 Ω | | A |
| 1N5951B | A3 | a1 | MO | Z Diode | | | 12 mA | 1.5 W | | 120 V | 3.1 mA | <380 Ω | | A |
| 1N5952B | A3 | a1 | MO | Z Diode | | | 11 mA | 1.5 W | | 130 V | 2.9 mA | <450 Ω | | A |
| 1N5953B | A3 | a1 | MO | Z Diode | | | 10 mA | 1.5 W | | 150 V | 2.5 mA | <600 Ω | | A |
| 1N5954B | A3 | a1 | MO | Z Diode | | | 9 mA | 1.5 W | | 160 V | 2.3 mA | <700 Ω | | A |
| 1N5955B | A3 | a1 | MO | Z Diode | | | 8 mA | 1.5 W | | 180 V | 2.1 mA | <900 Ω | | A |
| 1N5956B | A3 | a1 | MO | Z Diode | | | 7 mA | 1.5 W | | 200 V | 1.9 mA | <1200 Ω | | A |
| 1N5985B | A1 | a1 | MO | Z Diode | | | 208 mA | 0.5 W | | 2.4 V | 5 mA | <100 Ω | -3.5 mV/°C | |

| Type | Case | Pin-code | | | Vcla Vbro | Its | Izm | Pv | Pvts | Vz | Iz Is | rz | TK | |
|------|------|----------|--|--|-----------|-----|-----|----|------|----|-------|----|----|--|
| | | | | | **Maximum Ratings** | | | | | **Electrical Characteristics** | | | | |
| 1N5986B | A1 | a1 | MO | Z Diode | | | 185 mA | 0.5 W | | 2.7 V | 5 mA | <100Ω | -3.5 mV/°C | |
| 1N5987B | A1 | a1 | MO | Z Diode | | | 167 mA | 0.5 W | | 3.0 V | 5 mA | <95Ω | -3.5 mV/°C | |
| 1N5988B | A1 | a1 | MO | Z Diode | | | 152 mA | 0.5 W | | 3.3 V | 5 mA | <95Ω | -3.5 mV/°C | P |
| 1N5989B | A1 | a1 | MO | Z Diode | | | 139 mA | 0.5 W | | 3.6 V | 5 mA | <90Ω | -3.5 mV/°C | |
| 1N5990B | A1 | a1 | MO | Z Diode | | | 128 mA | 0.5 W | | 3.9 V | 5 mA | <90Ω | -3.5 mV/°C | |
| 1N5991B | A1 | a1 | MO | Z Diode | | | 116 mA | 0.5 W | | 4.3 V | 5 mA | <90Ω | -3.5 mV/°C | |
| 1N5992B | A1 | a1 | MO | Z Diode | | | 106 mA | 0.5 W | | 4.7 V | 5 mA | <80Ω | -3.5 mV/°C | |
| 1N5993B | A1 | a1 | MO | Z Diode | | | 98 mA | 0.5 W | | 5.1 V | 5 mA | <60Ω | -2.7 mV/°C | P |
| 1N5994B | A1 | a1 | MO | Z Diode | | | 89 mA | 0.5 W | | 5.6 V | 5 mA | <40Ω | 2.5 mV/°C | P |
| 1N5995B | A1 | a1 | MO | Z Diode | | | 81 mA | 0.5 W | | 6.2 V | 5 mA | <10Ω | 3.7 mV/°C | |
| 1N5996B | A1 | a1 | MO | Z Diode | | | 74 mA | 0.5 W | | 6.8 V | 5 mA | <15Ω | 4.5 mV/°C | |
| 1N5997B | A1 | a1 | MO | Z Diode | | | 67 mA | 0.5 W | | 7.5 V | 5 mA | <15Ω | 5.3 mV/°C | |
| 1N5998B | A1 | a1 | MO | Z Diode | | | 61 mA | 0.5 W | | 8.2 V | 5 mA | <15Ω | 6.2 mV/°C | P |
| 1N5999B | A1 | a1 | MO | Z Diode | | | 55 mA | 0.5 W | | 9.1 V | 5 mA | <15Ω | 8 mV/°C | |
| 1N6000B | A1 | a1 | MO | Z Diode | | | 50 mA | 0.5 W | | 10 V | 5 mA | <20Ω | 8 mV/°C | |
| 1N6001B | A1 | a1 | MO | Z Diode | | | 45 mA | 0.5 W | | 11 V | 5 mA | <20Ω | 9 mV/°C | |
| 1N6002B | A1 | a1 | MO | Z Diode | | | 42 mA | 0.5 W | | 12 V | 5 mA | <25Ω | 10 mV/°C | |
| 1N6003B | A1 | a1 | MO | Z Diode | | | 38 mA | 0.5 W | | 13 V | 5 mA | <30Ω | 11 mV/°C | |
| 1N6004B | A1 | a1 | MO | Z Diode | | | 33 mA | 0.5 W | | 15 V | 5 mA | <30Ω | 13 mV/°C | |
| 1N6005B | A1 | a1 | MO | Z Diode | | | 31 mA | 0.5 W | | 16 V | 5 mA | <40Ω | 14 mV/°C | |
| 1N6006B | A1 | a1 | MO | Z Diode | | | 28 mA | 0.5 W | | 18 V | 5 mA | <45Ω | 16 mV/°C | |
| 1N6007B | A1 | a1 | MO | Z Diode | | | 25 mA | 0.5 W | | 20 V | 5 mA | <55Ω | 18 mV/°C | P |
| 1N6008B | A1 | a1 | MO | Z Diode | | | 23 mA | 0.5 W | | 22 V | 5 mA | <55Ω | 20 mV/°C | |
| 1N6009B | A1 | a1 | MO | Z Diode | | | 21 mA | 0.5 W | | 24 V | 5 mA | <70Ω | 22 mV/°C | |
| 1N6010B | A1 | a1 | MO | Z Diode | | | 19 mA | 0.5 W | | 27 V | 2 mA | <80Ω | 23.5 mV/°C | |
| 1N6011B | A1 | a1 | MO | Z Diode | | | 17 mA | 0.5 W | | 30 V | 2 mA | <80Ω | 26 mV/°C | |
| 1N6012B | A1 | a1 | MO | Z Diode | | | 15 mA | 0.5 W | | 33 V | 2 mA | <80Ω | 29 mV/°C | |
| 1N6013B | A1 | a1 | MO | Z Diode | | | 14 mA | 0.5 W | | 36 V | 2 mA | <90Ω | 31 mV/°C | |
| 1N6014B | A1 | a1 | MO | Z Diode | | | 13 mA | 0.5 W | | 39 V | 2 mA | <130Ω | 34 mV/°C | |
| 1N6015B | A1 | a1 | MO | Z Diode | | | 12 mA | 0.5 W | | 43 V | 2 mA | <150Ω | 37 mV/°C | |
| 1N6016B | A1 | a1 | MO | Z Diode | | | 11 mA | 0.5 W | | 47 V | 2 mA | <170Ω | 40 mV/°C | |
| 1N6017B | A1 | a1 | MO | Z Diode | | | 9.8 mA | 0.5 W | | 51 V | 2 mA | <180Ω | 44 mV/°C | |
| 1N6018B | A1 | a1 | MO | Z Diode | | | 8.9 mA | 0.5 W | | 56 V | 2 mA | <200Ω | 47 mV/°C | |
| 1N6019B | A1 | a1 | MO | Z Diode | | | 8 mA | 0.5 W | | 62 V | 2 mA | <215Ω | 51 mV/°C | |
| 1N6020B | A1 | a1 | MO | Z Diode | | | 7.4 mA | 0.5 W | | 68 V | 2 mA | <240Ω | 56 mV/°C | |
| 1N6021B | A1 | a1 | MO | Z Diode | | | 6.7 mA | 0.5 W | | 75 V | 2 mA | <255Ω | 60 mV/°C | |
| 1N6022B | A1 | a1 | MO | Z Diode | | | 6.1 mA | 0.5 W | | 82 V | 2 mA | <280Ω | 95 mV/°C | |
| 1N6023B | A1 | a1 | MO | Z Diode | | | 5.5 mA | 0.5 W | | 91 V | 2 mA | <300Ω | 107 mV/°C | |
| 1N6024B | A1 | a1 | MO | Z Diode | | | 5 mA | 0.5 W | | 100 V | 2 mA | <500Ω | 119 mV/°C | |
| 1N6025B | A1 | a1 | MO | Z Diode | | | 4.5 mA | 0.5 W | | 110 V | 2 mA | <650Ω | 131 mV/°C | |

| Type | Case | Pin-code | | | Vcla Vbro | Its | Izm | Pv | Pvts | Vz | Iz Is | rz | TK | |
|---|---|---|---|---|---|---|---|---|---|---|---|---|---|---|
| | | | | | | **Maximum Ratings** | | | | **Electrical Characteristics** | | | | |
| 1SMB5943BT3 | G1 | a1 | MO | Z Diode | | | 26 mA | 1.5 W | | 56 V | 6.7 mA | <860Ω | | |
| 1SMB5913BT3 | G1 | a1 | MO | Z Diode | | | 454 mA | 1.5 W | | 3.3 V | 113.6 mA | <10Ω | | |
| 1SMB5914BT3 | G1 | a1 | MO | Z Diode | | | 416 mA | 1.5 W | | 3.6 V | 104.2 mA | <9Ω | | |
| 1SMB5915BT3 | G1 | a1 | MO | Z Diode | | | 284 mA | 1.5 W | | 3.9 V | 96.1 mA | <7.5Ω | | |
| 1SMB5916BT3 | G1 | a1 | MO | Z Diode | | | 248 mA | 1.5 W | | 4.3 V | 87.2 mA | <6Ω | | |
| 1SMB5917BT3 | G1 | a1 | MO | Z Diode | | | 319 mA | 1.5 W | | 4.7 V | 79.8 mA | <5Ω | | |
| 1SMB5918BT3 | G1 | a1 | MO | Z Diode | | | 294 mA | 1.5 W | | 5.1 V | 73.5 mA | <4Ω | | |
| 1SMB5919BT3 | G1 | a1 | MO | Z Diode | | | 267 mA | 1.5 W | | 5.6 V | 66.9 mA | <2Ω | | |
| 1SMB5920BT3 | G1 | a1 | MO | Z Diode | | | 241 mA | 1.5 W | | 6.2 V | 60.5 mA | <2Ω | | |
| 1SMB5921BT3 | G1 | a1 | MO | Z Diode | | | 220 mA | 1.5 W | | 6.8 V | 55.1 mA | <2.5Ω | | |
| 1SMB5922BT3 | G1 | a1 | MO | Z Diode | | | 200 mA | 1.5 W | | 7.5 V | 50 mA | <3Ω | | |
| 1SMB5923BT3 | G1 | a1 | MO | Z Diode | | | 182 mA | 1.5 W | | 8.2 V | 45.7 mA | <3.5Ω | | |
| 1SMB5924BT3 | G1 | a1 | MO | Z Diode | | | 164 mA | 1.5 W | | 9.1 V | 41.2 mA | <4Ω | | |
| 1SMB5925BT3 | G1 | a1 | MO | Z Diode | | | 150 mA | 1.5 W | | 10 V | 37.5 mA | <4.5Ω | | |
| 1SMB5926BT3 | G1 | a1 | MO | Z Diode | | | 136 mA | 1.5 W | | 11 V | 34.1 mA | <5.5Ω | | |
| 1SMB5927BT3 | G1 | a1 | MO | Z Diode | | | 125 mA | 1.5 W | | 12 V | 31.2 mA | <6.5Ω | | |
| 1SMB5928BT3 | G1 | a1 | MO | Z Diode | | | 115 mA | 1.5 W | | 13 V | 28.8 mA | <7Ω | | |
| 1SMB5929BT3 | G1 | a1 | MO | Z Diode | | | 100 mA | 1.5 W | | 15 V | 25 mA | <9Ω | | |
| 1SMB5930BT3 | G1 | a1 | MO | Z Diode | | | 93 mA | 1.5 W | | 16 V | 23.4 mA | <10Ω | | |
| 1SMB5931BT3 | G1 | a1 | MO | Z Diode | | | 83 mA | 1.5 W | | 18 V | 20.8 mA | <12Ω | | |
| 1SMB5932BT3 | G1 | a1 | MO | Z Diode | | | 75 mA | 1.5 W | | 20 V | 18.7 mA | <14Ω | | |
| 1SMB5933BT3 | G1 | a1 | MO | Z Diode | | | 68 mA | 1.5 W | | 22 V | 17.5 mA | <17.5Ω | | |
| 1SMB5934BT3 | G1 | a1 | MO | Z Diode | | | 62 mA | 1.5 W | | 24 V | 15.6 mA | <19Ω | | |
| 1SMB5935BT3 | G1 | a1 | MO | Z Diode | | | 55 mA | 1.5 W | | 27 V | 13.9 mA | <23Ω | | |
| 1SMB5936BT3 | G1 | a1 | MO | Z Diode | | | 50 mA | 1.5 W | | 30 V | 12.5 mA | <26Ω | | |
| 1SMB5937BT3 | G1 | a1 | MO | Z Diode | | | 45 mA | 1.5 W | | 33 V | 11.4 mA | <33Ω | | |
| 1SMB5938BT3 | G1 | a1 | MO | Z Diode | | | 41 mA | 1.5 W | | 36 V | 10.4 mA | <38Ω | | |
| 1SMB5939BT3 | G1 | a1 | MO | Z Diode | | | 38 mA | 1.5 W | | 39 V | 9.6 mA | <45Ω | | |
| 1SMB5940BT3 | G1 | a1 | MO | Z Diode | | | 34 mA | 1.5 W | | 43 V | 8.7 mA | <63Ω | | |
| 1SMB5941BT3 | G1 | a1 | MO | Z Diode | | | 31 mA | 1.5 W | | 47 V | 8 mA | <67Ω | | |
| 1SMB5942BT3 | G1 | a1 | MO | Z Diode | | | 29 mA | 1.5 W | | 51 V | 7.3 mA | <70Ω | | |
| 1SMB5944BT3 | G1 | a1 | MO | Z Diode | | | 24 mA | 1.5 W | | 62 V | 6 mA | <100Ω | | |
| 1SMB5945BT3 | G1 | a1 | MO | Z Diode | | | 22 mA | 1.5 W | | 68 V | 5.5 mA | <120Ω | | |
| 1SMB5946BT3 | G1 | a1 | MO | Z Diode | | | 20 mA | 1.5 W | | 75 V | 5 mA | <140Ω | | |
| 1SMB5947BT3 | G1 | a1 | MO | Z Diode | | | 18 mA | 1.5 W | | 82 V | 4.6 mA | <160Ω | | |
| 1SMB5948BT3 | G1 | a1 | MO | Z Diode | | | 16 mA | 1.5 W | | 91 V | 4.1 mA | <200Ω | | |
| 1SMB5949BT3 | G1 | a1 | MO | Z Diode | | | 15 mA | 1.5 W | | 100 V | 3.7 mA | <250Ω | | |
| 1SMB5950BT3 | G1 | a1 | MO | Z Diode | | | 13 mA | 1.5 W | | 110 V | 3.4 mA | <300Ω | | |
| 1SMB5951BT3 | G1 | a1 | MO | Z Diode | | | 12 mA | 1.5 W | | 120 V | 3.1 mA | <380Ω | | |
| 1SMB5952BT3 | G1 | a1 | MO | Z Diode | | | 11 mA | 1.5 W | | 130 V | 2.9 mA | <450Ω | | |

| Type | Case | Pin-code | | | Maximum Ratings | | | | | Electrical Characteristics | | | | |
|---|---|---|---|---|---|---|---|---|---|---|---|---|---|---|
| | | | | | Vcla / Vbro | Its | Izm | Pv | Pvts | Vz | Iz / Is | rz | TK | |
| 1SMB5953BT3 | G1 | a1 | MO | Z Diode | | | 10 mA | 1.5 W | | 150 V | 2.5 mA | <6000 Ω | | |
| 1SMB5954BT3 | G1 | a1 | MO | Z Diode | | | 9 mA | 1.5 W | | 170 V | 2.3 mA | <7000 Ω | | |
| 1SMB5955BT3 | G1 | a1 | MO | Z Diode | | | 8 mA | 1.5 W | | 180 V | 2.1 mA | <9000 Ω | | |
| 1SMB5956BT3 | G1 | a1 | MO | Z Diode | | | 7 mA | 1.5 W | | 200 V | 1.9 mA | <1200 Ω | | |
| 1SMB5.0A | G1 | a1 | MO | TVS | 9.2 V | 65.2 mA | 65.2 mA | | 500 W | | | | | |
| 1SMB6.0A | G1 | a1 | MO | TVS | 10.3 V | 58.3 mA | 58.3 mA | | 500 W | | | | | |
| 1SMB6.5A | G1 | a1 | MO | TVS | 11.2 V | 53.6 mA | 53.6 mA | | 500 W | | | | | |
| 1SMB7.0A | G1 | a1 | MO | TVS | 12 V | 50 mA | 50 mA | | 500 W | | | | | |
| 1SMB7.5A | G1 | a1 | MO | TVS | 12.9 V | 56.5 mA | 56.5 mA | | 500 W | | | | | |
| 1SMB8.0A | G1 | a1 | MO | TVS | 13.6 V | 44.1 mA | 44.1 mA | | 500 W | | | | | |
| 1SMB8.5A | G1 | a1 | MO | TVS | 14.4 V | 41.7 mA | 41.7 mA | | 500 W | | | | | |
| 1SMB9.1A | G1 | a1 | MO | TVS | 15.4 V | 39 mA | 39 mA | | 500 W | | | | | |
| 1SMB10A | G1 | a1 | MO | TVS | 17 V | 35.3 mA | 35.3 mA | | 500 W | | | | | |
| 1SMB11A | G1 | a1 | MO | TVS | 18.2 V | 33 mA | 33 mA | | 500 W | | | | | |
| 1SMB12A | G1 | a1 | MO | TVS | 19.9 V | 30.2 mA | 30.2 mA | | 500 W | | | | | |
| 1SMB13A | G1 | a1 | MO | TVS | 21.5 V | 27.9 mA | 27.9 mA | | 500 W | | | | | |
| 1SMB14A | G1 | a1 | MO | TVS | 23.2 V | 25.8 mA | 25.8 mA | | 500 W | | | | | |
| 1SMB15A | G1 | a1 | MO | TVS | 24.4 V | 24 mA | 24 mA | | 500 W | | | | | |
| 1SMB16A | G1 | a1 | MO | TVS | 26 V | 23.1 mA | 23.1 mA | | 500 W | | | | | |
| 1SMB17A | G1 | a1 | MO | TVS | 27.6 V | 21.7 mA | 21.7 mA | | 500 W | | | | | |
| 1SMB18A | G1 | a1 | MO | TVS | 29.2 V | 20.5 mA | 20.5 mA | | 500 W | | | | | |
| 1SMB20A | G1 | a1 | MO | TVS | 32.4 V | 18.5 mA | 18.5 mA | | 500 W | | | | | |
| 1SMB22A | G1 | a1 | MO | TVS | 35.5 V | 16.9 mA | 16.9 mA | | 500 W | | | | | |
| 1SMB24A | G1 | a1 | MO | TVS | 38.9 V | 15.4 mA | 15.4 mA | | 500 W | | | | | |
| 1SMB26A | G1 | a1 | MO | TVS | 42.1 V | 14.2 mA | 14.2 mA | | 500 W | | | | | |
| 1SMB28A | G1 | a1 | MO | TVS | 45.4 V | 13.2 mA | 13.2 mA | | 500 W | | | | | |
| 1SMB30A | G1 | a1 | MO | TVS | 48.4 V | 12.4 mA | 12.4 mA | | 500 W | | | | | |
| 1SMB33A | G1 | a1 | MO | TVS | 53.3 V | 11.3 mA | 11.3 mA | | 500 W | | | | | |
| 1SMB36A | G1 | a1 | MO | TVS | 58.1 V | 10.3 mA | 10.3 mA | | 500 W | | | | | |
| 1SMB40A | G1 | a1 | MO | TVS | 64.5 V | 9.3 mA | 9.3 mA | | 500 W | | | | | |
| 1SMB43A | G1 | a1 | MO | TVS | 69.4 V | 8.6 mA | 8.6 mA | | 500 W | | | | | |
| 1SMB45A | G1 | a1 | MO | TVS | 72.7 V | 8.3 mA | 8.3 mA | | 500 W | | | | | |
| 1SMB48A | G1 | a1 | MO | TVS | 77.4 V | 7.7 mA | 7.7 mA | | 500 W | | | | | |
| 1SMB51A | G1 | a1 | MO | TVS | 82.4 V | 7.3 mA | 7.3 mA | | 500 W | | | | | |
| 1SMB54A | G1 | a1 | MO | TVS | 87.1 V | 6.9 mA | 6.9 mA | | 500 W | | | | | |
| 1SMB58A | G1 | a1 | MO | TVS | 93.6 V | 6.4 mA | 6.4 mA | | 500 W | | | | | |
| 1SMB60A | G1 | a1 | MO | TVS | 96.8 V | 6.2 mA | 6.2 mA | | 500 W | | | | | |
| 1SMB64A | G1 | a1 | MO | TVS | 103 V | 5.8 mA | 5.8 mA | | 500 W | | | | | |
| 1SMB70A | G1 | a1 | MO | TVS | 113 V | 5.3 mA | 5.3 mA | | 500 W | | | | | |
| 1SMB75A | G1 | a1 | MO | TVS | 121 V | 4.9 mA | 4.9 mA | | 500 W | | | | | |

| Type | Case | Pin-code | | | Maximum Ratings Vcla *Vbro* | Its | Izm | Pv | Pvts | Electrical Characteristics Vz | Iz *Is* | rz | TK | |
|------|------|----------|--|--|------|-----|-----|----|------|------|------|----|----|--|
| 1SMB78A | G1 | a1 | MO | TVS | 126 V | 4.7 mA | 4.7 mA | | 500 W | | | | | |
| 1SMB85A | G1 | a1 | MO | TVS | 137 V | 4.4 mA | 4.4 mA | | 500 W | | | | | |
| 1SMB90A | G1 | a1 | MO | TVS | 146 V | 4.1 mA | 4.1 mA | | 500 W | | | | | |
| 1SMB100A | G1 | a1 | MO | TVS | 162 V | 3.7 mA | 3.7 mA | | 500 W | | | | | |
| 1SMB110A | G1 | a1 | MO | TVS | 177 V | 3.4 mA | 3.4 mA | | 500 W | | | | | |
| 1SMB120A | G1 | a1 | MO | TVS | 193 V | 3.1 mA | 3.1 mA | | 500 W | | | | | |
| 1SMB130A | G1 | a1 | MO | TVS | 209 V | 2.9 mA | 2.9 mA | | 500 W | | | | | |
| 1SMB150A | G1 | a1 | MO | TVS | 243 V | 2.5 mA | 2.5 mA | | 500 W | | | | | |
| 1SMB160A | G1 | a1 | MO | TVS | 259 V | 2.3 mA | 2.3 mA | | 500 W | | | | | |
| 1SMB170A | G1 | a1 | MO | TVS | 275 V | 2.2 mA | 2.2 mA | | 500 W | | | | | |
| 1SMC5.0A | G2 | a1 | MO | TVS | 9.2 V | 163 mA | 163 mA | | 1.5 kW | | | | | |
| 1SMC6.0A | G2 | a1 | MO | TVS | 10.3 V | 145.6 mA | 145.6 mA | | 1.5 kW | | | | | |
| 1SMC6.5A | G2 | a1 | MO | TVS | 11.2 V | 133.9 mA | 133.9 mA | | 1.5 kW | | | | | |
| 1SMC7.0A | G2 | a1 | MO | TVS | 12 V | 125 mA | 125 mA | | 1.5 kW | | | | | |
| 1SMC7.5A | G2 | a1 | MO | TVS | 12.9 V | 116.3 mA | 116.3 mA | | 1.5 kW | | | | | |
| 1SMC8.0A | G2 | a1 | MO | TVS | 13.6 V | 110.3 mA | 110.3 mA | | 1.5 kW | | | | | |
| 1SMC8.5A | G2 | a1 | MO | TVS | 14.4 V | 104.2 mA | 104.2 mA | | 1.5 kW | | | | | |
| 1SMC9.1A | G2 | a1 | MO | TVS | 15.4 V | 97.4 mA | 97.4 mA | | 1.5 kW | | | | | |
| 1SMC10A | G2 | a1 | MO | TVS | 17 V | 88.2 mA | 88.2 mA | | 1.5 kW | | | | | |
| 1SMC11A | G2 | a1 | MO | TVS | 18.2 V | 82.4 mA | 82.4 mA | | 1.5 kW | | | | | |
| 1SMC12A | G2 | a1 | MO | TVS | 19.9 V | 75.3 mA | 75.3 mA | | 1.5 kW | | | | | |
| 1SMC13A | G2 | a1 | MO | TVS | 21.5 V | 69.7 mA | 69.7 mA | | 1.5 kW | | | | | |
| 1SMC14A | G2 | a1 | MO | TVS | 23.2 V | 64.7 mA | 64.7 mA | | 1.5 kW | | | | | |
| 1SMC15A | G2 | a1 | MO | TVS | 24.4 V | 61.5 mA | 61.5 mA | | 1.5 kW | | | | | |
| 1SMC16A | G2 | a1 | MO | TVS | 26 V | 57.7 mA | 57.7 mA | | 1.5 kW | | | | | |
| 1SMC17A | G2 | a1 | MO | TVS | 27.6 V | 53.3 mA | 53.3 mA | | 1.5 kW | | | | | |
| 1SMC18A | G2 | a1 | MO | TVS | 29.2 V | 51.4 mA | 51.4 mA | | 1.5 kW | | | | | |
| 1SMC20A | G2 | a1 | MO | TVS | 32.4 V | 46.3 mA | 46.3 mA | | 1.5 kW | | | | | |
| 1SMC22A | G2 | a1 | MO | TVS | 35.5 V | 52.2 mA | 52.2 mA | | 1.5 kW | | | | | |
| 1SMC24A | G2 | a1 | MO | TVS | 38.9 V | 38.6 mA | 38.6 mA | | 1.5 kW | | | | | |
| 1SMC26A | G2 | a1 | MO | TVS | 42.1 V | 35.6 mA | 35.6 mA | | 1.5 kW | | | | | |
| 1SMC28A | G2 | a1 | MO | TVS | 45.4 V | 33 mA | 33 mA | | 1.5 kW | | | | | |
| 1SMC30A | G2 | a1 | MO | TVS | 48.4 V | 31 mA | 31 mA | | 1.5 kW | | | | | |
| 1SMC33A | G2 | a1 | MO | TVS | 53.3 V | 28.1 mA | 28.1 mA | | 1.5 kW | | | | | |
| 1SMC36A | G2 | a1 | MO | TVS | 58.1 V | 25.8 mA | 25.8 mA | | 1.5 kW | | | | | |
| 1SMC40A | G2 | a1 | MO | TVS | 64.5 V | 23.2 mA | 23.2 mA | | 1.5 kW | | | | | |
| 1SMC43A | G2 | a1 | MO | TVS | 69.4 V | 21.6 mA | 21.6 mA | | 1.5 kW | | | | | |
| 1SMC45A | G2 | a1 | MO | TVS | 72.7 V | 20.6 mA | 20.6 mA | | 1.5 kW | | | | | |
| 1SMC48A | G2 | a1 | MO | TVS | 77.4 V | 19.4 mA | 19.4 mA | | 1.5 kW | | | | | |
| 1SMC51A | G2 | a1 | MO | TVS | 82.4 V | 18.2 mA | 18.2 mA | | 1.5 kW | | | | | |

| Type | Case | Pin-code | | | Vcla Vbro | Its | Izm | Pv | Pvts | Vz | Iz Is | rz | TK | |
|------|------|----------|---|---|-----------|-----|-----|-----|------|-----|-------|-----|-----|---|
| 1SMC54A | G2 | a1 | MO | TVS | 87.1 V | 17.2 mA | 17.2 mA | | 1.5 kW | | | | | |
| 1SMC58A | G2 | a1 | MO | TVS | 93.6 V | 16 mA | 16 mA | | 1.5 kW | | | | | |
| 1SMC60A | G2 | a1 | MO | TVS | 96.8 V | 15.5 mA | 15.5 mA | | 1.5 kW | | | | | |
| 1SMC64A | G2 | a1 | MO | TVS | 103 V | 14.6 mA | 14.6 mA | | 1.5 kW | | | | | |
| 1SMC70A | G2 | a1 | MO | TVS | 113 V | 13.3 mA | 13.3 mA | | 1.5 kW | | | | | |
| 1SMC75A | G2 | a1 | MO | TVS | 121 V | 12.4 mA | 12.4 mA | | 1.5 kW | | | | | |
| 1SMC78A | G2 | a1 | MO | TVS | 126 V | 11.4 mA | 11.4 mA | | 1.5 kW | | | | | |
| 1Z33 | B1 | a1 | TO | Z Diode, TVS | | | | 1 W | 200 W | 33 V | 10 mA | <30 Ω | 41 mV/°C | Vz ±10% |
| 1Z36 | B1 | a1 | TO | Z Diode, TVS | | | | 1 W | 200 W | 36 V | 9 mA | <30 Ω | 45 mV/°C | Vz ±10% |
| 1Z43 | B1 | a1 | TO | Z Diode, TVS | | | | 1 W | 200 W | 43 V | 7 mA | <40 Ω | 53 mV/°C | Vz ±10% |
| 1Z47 | B1 | a1 | TO | Z Diode, TVS | | | | 1 W | 200 W | 47 V | 6 mA | <65 Ω | 60 mV/°C | Vz ±10% |
| 1Z51 | B1 | a1 | TO | Z Diode, TVS | | | | 1 W | 200 W | 51 V | 6 mA | <65 Ω | 68 mV/°C | Vz ±10% |
| 1Z68 | B1 | a1 | TO | Z Diode, TVS | | | | 1 W | 200 W | 68 V | 4 mA | <120 Ω | 90 mV/°C | Vz ±10% |
| 1Z75 | B1 | a1 | TO | Z Diode, TVS | | | | 1 W | 200 W | 75 V | 4 mA | <150 Ω | 104 mV/°C | Vz ±10% |
| 1Z82 | B1 | a1 | TO | Z Diode, TVS | | | | 1 W | 200 W | 82 V | 3 mA | <170 Ω | 113 mV/°C | Vz ±10% |
| 1Z100 | B1 | a1 | TO | Z Diode, TVS | | | | 1 W | 200 W | 100 V | 3 mA | <300 Ω | 138 mV/°C | Vz ±10% |
| 1Z110 | B1 | a1 | TO | Z Diode, TVS | | | | 1 W | 200 W | 110 V | 3 mA | <300 Ω | 152 mV/°C | Vz ±10% |
| 1Z150 | B1 | a1 | TO | Z Diode, TVS | | | | 1 W | 200 W | 150 V | 2 mA | <450 Ω | 212 mV/°C | Vz ±10% |
| 1Z180 | B1 | a1 | TO | Z Diode, TVS | | | | 1 W | 200 W | 180 V | 1.5 mA | <500 Ω | 155 mV/°C | Vz ±10% |
| 1Z330 | B1 | a1 | TO | Z Diode, TVS | | | | 1 W | 200 W | 330 V | 1 mA | <5k Ω | 472 mV/°C | Vz ±10% |
| 1Z390 | B1 | a1 | TO | Z Diode, TVS | | | | 1 W | 200 W | 390 V | 0.5 mA | <10k Ω | 555 mV/°C | Vz ±10% |
| 1Z6.2 | B1 | a1 | TO | Z Diode | | | | 1 W | 200 W | 6.2 V | 10 mA | <60 Ω | 2 mV/°C | Vz ±10% |
| 1Z6.8 | B1 | a1 | TO | Z Diode | | | | 1 W | 200 W | 6.8 V | 10 mA | <60 Ω | 4 mV/°C | Vz ±10% |
| 1Z7.5 | B1 | a1 | TO | Z Diode | | | | 1 W | 200 W | 7.5 V | 10 mA | <30 Ω | 5 mV/°C | Vz ±10% |
| 1Z8.2 | B1 | a1 | TO | Z Diode | | | | 1 W | 200 W | 8.2 V | 10 mA | <30 Ω | 6 mV/°C | Vz ±10% |
| 1Z9.1 | B1 | a1 | TO | Z Diode | | | | 1 W | 200 W | 9.1 V | 10 mA | <30 Ω | 8 mV/°C | Vz ±10% |
| 1Z10 | B1 | a1 | TO | Z Diode | | | | 1 W | 200 W | 10 V | 10 mA | <30 Ω | 9 mV/°C | Vz ±10% |
| 1Z11 | B1 | a1 | TO | Z Diode | | | | 1 W | 200 W | 11 V | 10 mA | <30 Ω | 11 mV/°C | Vz ±10% |
| 1Z12 | B1 | a1 | TO | Z Diode | | | | 1 W | 200 W | 12 V | 10 mA | <30 Ω | 13 mV/°C | Vz ±10% |
| 1Z13 | B1 | a1 | TO | Z Diode | | | | 1 W | 200 W | 13 V | 10 mA | <30 Ω | 14 mV/°C | Vz ±10% |
| 1Z15 | B1 | a1 | TO | Z Diode | | | | 1 W | 200 W | 15 V | 10 mA | <30 Ω | 17 mV/°C | Vz ±10% |
| 1Z16 | B1 | a1 | TO | Z Diode | | | | 1 W | 200 W | 16 V | 10 mA | <30 Ω | 19 mV/°C | Vz ±10% |
| 1Z18 | B1 | a1 | TO | Z Diode | | | | 1 W | 200 W | 18 V | 10 mA | <30 Ω | 23 mV/°C | Vz ±10% |
| 1Z20 | B1 | a1 | TO | Z Diode | | | | 1 W | 200 W | 20 V | 10 mA | <30 Ω | 26 mV/°C | Vz ±10% |
| 1Z22 | B1 | a1 | TO | Z Diode | | | | 1 W | 200 W | 22 V | 10 mA | <30 Ω | 28 mV/°C | Vz ±10% |
| 1Z24 | B1 | a1 | TO | Z Diode | | | | 1 W | 200 W | 24 V | 10 mA | <30 Ω | 32 mV/°C | Vz ±10% |
| 1Z27 | B1 | a1 | TO | Z Diode | | | | 1 W | 200 W | 27 V | 10 mA | <30 Ω | 36 mV/°C | Vz ±10% |
| 1Z30 | B1 | a1 | TO | Z Diode | | | | 1 W | 200 W | 30 V | 10 mA | <30 Ω | 40 mV/°C | Vz ±10% |
| 2Z12 | B16 | a1 | TO | TVS | 16.7 V | 36 mA | 36 mA | 2 W | 600 W | 12 V | 10 mA | | | Vz ±10% |
| 2Z13 | B16 | a1 | TO | TVS | 18.2 V | 33 mA | 33 mA | 2 W | 600 W | 13 V | 10 mA | | | Vz ±10% |

129

| Type | Case | Pin-code | | | Maximum Ratings | | | | | Electrical Characteristics | | | | |
|---|---|---|---|---|---|---|---|---|---|---|---|---|---|---|
| | | | | | Vcla Vbro | Its | Izm | Pv | Pvts | Vz | Iz Is | rz | TK | |
| 2Z15 | B16 | a1 | TO | TVS | 21.2 V | 28 mA | 28 mA | 2 W | 600 W | 15 V | 10 mA | | | Vz ±10% |
| 2Z16 | B16 | a1 | TO | TVS | 22.5 V | 27 mA | 27 mA | 2 W | 600 W | 16 V | 10 mA | | | Vz ±10% |
| 2Z18 | B16 | a1 | TO | TVS | 25.2 V | 24 mA | 24 mA | 2 W | 600 W | 18 V | 10 mA | | | Vz ±10% |
| 2Z20 | B16 | a1 | TO | TVS | 27.7 V | 22 mA | 22 mA | 2 W | 600 W | 20 V | 10 mA | | | Vz ±10% |
| 2Z22 | B16 | a1 | TO | TVS | 30.6 V | 20 mA | 20 mA | 2 W | 600 W | 22 V | 10 mA | | | Vz ±10% |
| 2Z24 | B16 | a1 | TO | TVS | 33.2 V | 18 mA | 18 mA | 2 W | 600 W | 24 V | 10 mA | | | Vz ±10% |
| 2Z27 | B16 | a1 | TO | TVS | 37.5 V | 16 mA | 16 mA | 2 W | 600 W | 27 V | 10 mA | | | Vz ±10% |
| 2Z30 | B16 | a1 | TO | TVS | 41.4 V | 14.5 mA | 14.5 mA | 2 W | 600 W | 30 V | 10 mA | | | Vz ±10% |
| 2Z33 | B16 | a1 | TO | TVS | 45.7 V | 13.1 mA | 13.1 mA | 2 W | 600 W | 33 V | 10 mA | | | Vz ±10% |
| 2Z36 | B16 | a1 | TO | TVS | 49.9 V | 12 mA | 12 mA | 2 W | 600 W | 36 V | 9 mA | | | Vz ±10% |
| 2Z47 | B16 | a1 | TO | TVS | 67.8 V | 8.8 mA | 8.8 mA | 2 W | 600 W | 47 V | 6 mA | | | Vz ±10% |
| 2Z51 | B16 | a1 | TO | TVS | 73.5 V | 8.2 mA | 8.2 mA | 2 W | 600 W | 51 V | 6 mA | | | Vz ±10% |
| 2Z16A | B16 | a1 | TO | TVS | 22.5 V | 27 mA | 27 mA | 2 W | 600 W | | | | | Vz ±10% |
| 2Z18A | B16 | a1 | TO | TVS | 25.2 V | 24 mA | 24 mA | 2 W | 600 W | | | | | Vz ±10% |
| 2Z27A | B16 | a1 | TO | TVS | 37.5 V | 16 mA | 16 mA | 2 W | 600 W | | | | | Vz ±10% |
| 3EZ3.9D5 | A3 | a1 | MO | Z Diode | | | 630 mA | 1 W | | 3.9 V | 194 mA | <4.5Ω | | |
| 3EZ4.3D5 | A3 | a1 | MO | Z Diode | | | 590 mA | 1 W | | 4.3 V | 174 mA | <4.5Ω | | |
| 3EZ4.7D5 | A3 | a1 | MO | Z Diode | | | 550 mA | 1 W | | 4.7 V | 160 mA | <4Ω | | |
| 3EZ5.1D5 | A3 | a1 | MO | Z Diode | | | 520 mA | 1 W | | 5.1 V | 147 mA | <3.5Ω | | |
| 3EZ5.6D5 | A3 | a1 | MO | Z Diode | | | 480 mA | 1 W | | 5.6 V | 134 mA | <2.5Ω | | |
| 3EZ6.2D5 | A3 | a1 | MO | Z Diode | | | 435 mA | 1 W | | 6.2 V | 121 mA | <1.5Ω | | |
| 3EZ6.8D5 | A3 | a1 | MO | Z Diode | | | 393 mA | 1 W | | 6.8 V | 110 mA | <2Ω | | |
| 3EZ7.5D5 | A3 | a1 | MO | Z Diode | | | 360 mA | 1 W | | 7.5 V | 100 mA | <2Ω | | |
| 3EZ8.2D5 | A3 | a1 | MO | Z Diode | | | 330 mA | 1 W | | 8.2 V | 91 mA | <2.3Ω | | |
| 3EZ9.1D5 | A3 | a1 | MO | Z Diode | | | 297 mA | 1 W | | 9.1 V | 82 mA | <2.5Ω | | |
| 3EZ10D5 | A3 | a1 | MO | Z Diode | | | 270 mA | 1 W | | 10 V | 75 mA | <3.5Ω | | |
| 3EZ11D5 | A3 | a1 | MO | Z Diode | | | 245 mA | 1 W | | 11 V | 68 mA | <4Ω | | |
| 3EZ12D5 | A3 | a1 | MO | Z Diode | | | 225 mA | 1 W | | 12 V | 63 mA | <4.5Ω | | |
| 3EZ13D5 | A3 | a1 | MO | Z Diode | | | 208 mA | 1 W | | 13 V | 58 mA | <4.5Ω | | |
| 3EZ14D5 | A3 | a1 | MO | Z Diode | | | 193 mA | 1 W | | 14 V | 53 mA | <5Ω | | |
| 3EZ15D5 | A3 | a1 | MO | Z Diode | | | 180 mA | 1 W | | 15 V | 50 mA | <5.5Ω | | |
| 3EZ16D5 | A3 | a1 | MO | Z Diode | | | 169 mA | 1 W | | 16 V | 47 mA | <5.5Ω | | |
| 3EZ17D5 | A3 | a1 | MO | Z Diode | | | 159 mA | 1 W | | 17 V | 44 mA | <6Ω | | |
| 3EZ18D5 | A3 | a1 | MO | Z Diode | | | 150 mA | 1 W | | 18 V | 42 mA | <6Ω | | |
| 3EZ19D5 | A3 | a1 | MO | Z Diode | | | 142 mA | 1 W | | 19 V | 40 mA | <7Ω | | |
| 3EZ20D5 | A3 | a1 | MO | Z Diode | | | 135 mA | 1 W | | 20 V | 37 mA | <7Ω | | |
| 3EZ22D5 | A3 | a1 | MO | Z Diode | | | 123 mA | 1 W | | 22 V | 34 mA | <8Ω | | |
| 3EZ24D5 | A3 | a1 | MO | Z Diode | | | 112 mA | 1 W | | 24 V | 31 mA | <9Ω | | |
| 3EZ27D5 | A3 | a1 | MO | Z Diode | | | 100 mA | 1 W | | 27 V | 28 mA | <10Ω | | |
| 3EZ28D5 | A3 | a1 | MO | Z Diode | | | 960 mA | 1 W | | 28 V | 27 mA | <12Ω | | |

| Type | Case | Pin-code | | | Maximum Ratings | | | | | Electrical Characteristics | | | | |
|---|---|---|---|---|---|---|---|---|---|---|---|---|---|---|
| | | | | | Vcla Vbro | Its | Izm | Pv | Pvts | Vz | Iz / Is | rz | TK | |
| 3EZ30D5 | A3 | a1 | MO | Z Diode | | | 908 mA | 1 W | | 30 V | 25 mA | <16Ω | | |
| 3EZ33D5 | A3 | a1 | MO | Z Diode | | | 824 mA | 1 W | | 33 V | 23 mA | <20Ω | | |
| 3EZ36D5 | A3 | a1 | MO | Z Diode | | | 752 mA | 1 W | | 36 V | 21 mA | <22Ω | | |
| 3EZ39D5 | A3 | a1 | MO | Z Diode | | | 692 mA | 1 W | | 39 V | 19 mA | <28Ω | | |
| 3EZ43D5 | A3 | a1 | MO | Z Diode | | | 630 mA | 1 W | | 43 V | 17 mA | <33Ω | | |
| 3EZ47D5 | A3 | a1 | MO | Z Diode | | | 570 mA | 1 W | | 47 V | 16 mA | <38Ω | | |
| 3EZ51D5 | A3 | a1 | MO | Z Diode | | | 53 mA | 1 W | | 51 V | 15 mA | <45Ω | | |
| 3EZ56D5 | A3 | a1 | MO | Z Diode | | | 48 mA | 1 W | | 56 V | 13 mA | <50Ω | | |
| 3EZ62D5 | A3 | a1 | MO | Z Diode | | | 44 mA | 1 W | | 62 V | 12 mA | <55Ω | | |
| 3EZ68D5 | A3 | a1 | MO | Z Diode | | | 40 mA | 1 W | | 68 V | 11 mA | <70Ω | | |
| 3EZ75D5 | A3 | a1 | MO | Z Diode | | | 36 mA | 1 W | | 75 V | 10 mA | <85Ω | | |
| 3EZ82D5 | A3 | a1 | MO | Z Diode | | | 33 mA | 1 W | | 82 V | 9.1 mA | <95Ω | | |
| 3EZ91D5 | A3 | a1 | MO | Z Diode | | | 30 mA | 1 W | | 91 V | 8.2 mA | <115Ω | | |
| 3EZ100D5 | A3 | a1 | MO | Z Diode | | | 27 mA | 1 W | | 100 V | 7.5 mA | <160Ω | | |
| 3EZ110D5 | A3 | a1 | MO | Z Diode | | | 25 mA | 1 W | | 110 V | 6.8 mA | <225Ω | | |
| 3EZ120D5 | A3 | a1 | MO | Z Diode | | | 22 mA | 1 W | | 120 V | 6.3 mA | <300Ω | | |
| 3EZ130D5 | A3 | a1 | MO | Z Diode | | | 21 mA | 1 W | | 130 V | 5.8 mA | <375Ω | | |
| 3EZ140D5 | A3 | a1 | MO | Z Diode | | | 19 mA | 1 W | | 140 V | 5.3 mA | <475Ω | | |
| 3EZ150D5 | A3 | a1 | MO | Z Diode | | | 18 mA | 1 W | | 150 V | 5 mA | <550Ω | | |
| 3EZ160D5 | A3 | a1 | MO | Z Diode | | | 17 mA | 1 W | | 160 V | 4.7 mA | <625Ω | | |
| 3EZ170D5 | A3 | a1 | MO | Z Diode | | | 16 mA | 1 W | | 170 V | 4.4 mA | <650Ω | | |
| 3EZ180D5 | A3 | a1 | MO | Z Diode | | | 15 mA | 1 W | | 180 V | 4.2 mA | <700Ω | | |
| 3EZ190D5 | A3 | a1 | MO | Z Diode | | | 14 mA | 1 W | | 190 V | 4 mA | <800Ω | | |
| 3EZ200D5 | A3 | a1 | MO | Z Diode | | | 13 mA | 1 W | | 200 V | 3.7 mA | <875Ω | | |
| 3EZ220D5 | A3 | a1 | MO | Z Diode | | | 12 mA | 1 W | | 220 V | 3.4 mA | <1600Ω | | |
| 3EZ240D5 | A3 | a1 | MO | Z Diode | | | 11 mA | 1 W | | 240 V | 3.1 mA | <1700Ω | | |
| 3EZ270D5 | A3 | a1 | MO | Z Diode | | | 10 mA | 1 W | | 270 V | 2.8 mA | <1800Ω | | |
| 3EZ300D5 | A3 | a1 | MO | Z Diode | | | 9 mA | 1 W | | 300 V | 2.5 mA | <1900Ω | | |
| 3EZ330D5 | A3 | a1 | MO | Z Diode | | | 8 mA | 1 W | | 330 V | 2.3 mA | <2200Ω | | |
| 3EZ360D5 | A3 | a1 | MO | Z Diode | | | 8 mA | 1 W | | 360 V | 2.1 mA | <2700Ω | | |
| 3EZ400D5 | A3 | a1 | MO | Z Diode | | | 7 mA | 1 W | | 400 V | 1.9 mA | <3500Ω | | |
| 3Z12 | B10 | a1 | TO | Z Diode | | | | 3 W | 1.5 kW | 12 V | 10 mA | <30Ω | 13 mV/°C | Vz ±10% |
| 3Z13 | B10 | a1 | TO | Z Diode | | | | 3 W | 1.5 kW | 13 V | 10 mA | <30Ω | 14 mV/°C | Vz ±10% |
| 3Z15 | B10 | a1 | TO | Z Diode | | | | 3 W | 1.5 kW | 15 V | 10 mA | <30Ω | 17 mV/°C | Vz ±10% |
| 3Z16 | B10 | a1 | TO | Z Diode | | | | 3 W | 1.5 kW | 16 V | 10 mA | <30Ω | 19 mV/°C | Vz ±10% |
| 3Z18 | B10 | a1 | TO | Z Diode | | | | 3 W | 1.5 kW | 18 V | 10 mA | <30Ω | 23 mV/°C | Vz ±10% |
| 3Z20 | B10 | a1 | TO | Z Diode | | | | 3 W | 1.5 kW | 20 V | 10 mA | <30Ω | 26 mV/°C | Vz ±10% |
| 3Z22 | B10 | a1 | TO | Z Diode | | | | 3 W | 1.5 kW | 22 V | 10 mA | <30Ω | 28 mV/°C | Vz ±10% |
| 3Z24 | B10 | a1 | TO | Z Diode | | | | 3 W | 1.5 kW | 24 V | 10 mA | <30Ω | 32 mV/°C | Vz ±10% |
| 3Z27 | B10 | a1 | TO | Z Diode | | | | 3 W | 1.5 kW | 27 V | 10 mA | <30Ω | 36 mV/°C | Vz ±10% |

**3Z30 – 1.5KE36**

| Type | Case | Pin-code | | | Maximum Ratings | | | | | Electrical Characteristics | | | | |
|---|---|---|---|---|---|---|---|---|---|---|---|---|---|---|
| | | | | | Vcla / Vbro | Its | Izm | Pv | Pvts | Vz | Iz / Is | rz | TK | |
| 3Z30 | B10 | a1 | TO | Z Diode | | | | 3 W | 1.5 kW | 30 V | 10 mA | <30 Ω | 40 mV/°C | Vz ±10% |
| 3Z33 | B10 | a1 | TO | Z Diode | | | | 3 W | 1.5 kW | 33 V | 10 mA | <30 Ω | 41 mV/°C | Vz ±10% |
| 3Z36 | B10 | a1 | TO | Z Diode | | | | 3 W | 1.5 kW | 36 V | 9 mA | <30 Ω | 45 mV/°C | Vz ±10% |
| 3Z43 | B10 | a1 | TO | Z Diode | | | | 3 W | 1.5 kW | 43 V | 7 mA | <30 Ω | 53 mV/°C | Vz ±10% |
| 3Z47 | B10 | a1 | TO | Z Diode | | | | 3 W | 1.5 kW | 47 V | 6 mA | <65 Ω | 60 mV/°C | Vz ±10% |
| 3Z51 | B10 | a1 | TO | Z Diode | | | | 3 W | 1.5 kW | 51 V | 6 mA | <65 Ω | 68 mV/°C | Vz ±10% |
| 3Z68 | B10 | a1 | TO | Z Diode | | | | 3 W | 1.5 kW | 68 V | 4 mA | <120 Ω | 90 mV/°C | Vz ±10% |
| 3Z75 | B10 | a1 | TO | Z Diode | | | | 3 W | 1.5 kW | 75 V | 4 mA | <150 Ω | 104 mV/°C | Vz ±10% |
| 3Z82 | B10 | a1 | TO | Z Diode | | | | 3 W | 1.5 kW | 82 V | 3 mA | <170 Ω | 113 mV/°C | Vz ±10% |
| 3Z100 | B10 | a1 | TO | Z Diode | | | | 3 W | 1.5 kW | 100 V | 3 mA | <300 Ω | 138 mV/°C | Vz ±10% |
| 3Z110 | B10 | a1 | TO | Z Diode | | | | 3 W | 1.5 kW | 110 V | 3 mA | <300 Ω | 152 mV/°C | Vz ±10% |
| 3Z150 | B10 | a1 | TO | Z Diode | | | | 3 W | 1.5 kW | 150 V | 2 mA | <450 Ω | 212 mV/°C | Vz ±10% |
| 3Z180 | B10 | a1 | TO | Z Diode | | | | 3 W | 1.5 kW | 180 V | 1.5 mA | <500 Ω | 155 mV/°C | Vz ±10% |
| 3Z200 | B10 | a1 | TO | Z Diode | | | | 3 W | 1.5 kW | 200 V | 1.5 mA | <500 Ω | 169 mV/°C | Vz ±10% |
| 3Z220 | B10 | a1 | TO | Z Diode | | | | 3 W | 1.5 kW | 220 V | 0.5 mA | <5 kΩ | 309 mV/°C | Vz ±10% |
| 3Z240 | B10 | a1 | TO | Z Diode | | | | 3 W | 1.5 kW | 240 V | 0.5 mA | <5 kΩ | 243 mV/°C | Vz ±10% |
| 3Z270 | B10 | a1 | TO | Z Diode | | | | 3 W | 1.5 kW | 270 V | 0.5 mA | <5 kΩ | 385 mV/°C | Vz ±10% |
| 3Z300 | B10 | a1 | TO | Z Diode | | | | 3 W | 1.5 kW | 300 V | 0.5 mA | <5 kΩ | 428 mV/°C | Vz ±10% |
| 3Z330 | B10 | a1 | TO | Z Diode | | | | 3 W | 1.5 kW | 330 V | 0.5 mA | <5 kΩ | 470 mV/°C | Vz ±10% |
| 3Z390 | B10 | a1 | TO | Z Diode | | | | 3 W | 1.5 kW | 390 V | 0.5 mA | <10 kΩ | 555 mV/°C | Vz ±10% |
| 5Z27 | B15 | a1 | TO | TVS, Z Diode | | 62 A | 62 A | 5 W | | 27 V | 10 mA | <50 Ω | | |
| 5Z30 | B15 | a1 | TO | TVS, Z Diode | | 62 A | 62 A | 5 W | | 30 V | 10 mA | <50 Ω | | |
| 1.5KE6.8 | B2 | a1 | MO | TVS | 10.8 V | 139 mA | 139 mA | 5 W | 1.5 kW | | | | | |
| 1.5KE7.5 | B2 | a1 | MO | TVS | 11.7 V | 128 mA | 128 mA | 5 W | 1.5 kW | | | | | |
| 1.5KE8.2 | B2 | a1 | MO | TVS | 12.5 V | 120 mA | 120 mA | 5 W | 1.5 kW | | | | | |
| 1.5KE9.1 | B2 | a1 | MO | TVS | 13.8 V | 109 mA | 109 mA | 5 W | 1.5 kW | | | | | |
| 1.5KE10 | B2 | a1 | MO | TVS | 15 V | 100 mA | 100 mA | 5 W | 1.5 kW | | | | | |
| 1.5KE11 | B2 | a1 | MO | TVS | 16.2 V | 93 mA | 93 mA | 5 W | 1.5 kW | | | | | |
| 1.5KE12 | B2 | a1 | MO | TVS | 17.3 V | 87 mA | 87 mA | 5 W | 1.5 kW | | | | | |
| 1.5KE13 | B2 | a1 | MO | TVS | 19 V | 79 mA | 79 mA | 5 W | 1.5 kW | | | | | |
| 1.5KE15 | B2 | a1 | MO | TVS | 22 V | 68 mA | 68 mA | 5 W | 1.5 kW | | | | | |
| 1.5KE16 | B2 | a1 | MO | TVS | 23.5 V | 64 mA | 64 mA | 5 W | 1.5 kW | | | | | |
| 1.5KE18 | B2 | a1 | MO | TVS | 26.5 V | 56.5 mA | 56.5 mA | 5 W | 1.5 kW | | | | | |
| 1.5KE20 | B2 | a1 | MO | TVS | 29.1 V | 51.5 mA | 51.5 mA | 5 W | 1.5 kW | | | | | |
| 1.5KE22 | B2 | a1 | MO | TVS | 31.9 V | 47 mA | 47 mA | 5 W | 1.5 kW | | | | | |
| 1.5KE24 | B2 | a1 | MO | TVS | 34.7 V | 43 mA | 43 mA | 5 W | 1.5 kW | | | | | |
| 1.5KE27 | B2 | a1 | MO | TVS | 39.1 V | 38.5 mA | 38.5 mA | 5 W | 1.5 kW | | | | | |
| 1.5KE30 | B2 | a1 | MO | TVS | 43.5 V | 34.5 mA | 34.5 mA | 5 W | 1.5 kW | | | | | |
| 1.5KE33 | B2 | a1 | MO | TVS | 47.7 V | 31.5 mA | 31.5 mA | 5 W | 1.5 kW | | | | | |
| 1.5KE36 | B2 | a1 | MO | TVS | 52 V | 29 mA | 29 mA | 5 W | 1.5 kW | | | | | |

| Type | Case | Pin-code | | | Vcla Vbro | Its | Izm | Pv | Pvts | Vz | Iz Is | rz | TK | |
|------|------|----------|---|---|-----------|-----|-----|----|----|----|----|----|----|---|
| 1.5KE39 | B2 | a1 | MO | TVS | 56.4 V | 26.5 mA | 26.5 mA | 5 W | 1.5 kW | | | | | |
| 1.5KE43 | B2 | a1 | MO | TVS | 61.9 V | 24 mA | 24 mA | 5 W | 1.5 kW | | | | | |
| 1.5KE47 | B2 | a1 | MO | TVS | 67.8 V | 22.2 mA | 22.2 mA | 5 W | 1.5 kW | | | | | |
| 1.5KE51 | B2 | a1 | MO | TVS | 73.5 V | 20.4 mA | 20.4 mA | 5 W | 1.5 kW | | | | | |
| 1.5KE56 | B2 | a1 | MO | TVS | 80.5 V | 18.6 mA | 18.6 mA | 5 W | 1.5 kW | | | | | |
| 1.5KE62 | B2 | a1 | MO | TVS | 89 V | 16.9 mA | 16.9 mA | 5 W | 1.5 kW | | | | | |
| 1.5KE68 | B2 | a1 | MO | TVS | 98 V | 15.3 mA | 15.3 mA | 5 W | 1.5 kW | | | | | |
| 1.5KE75 | B2 | a1 | MO | TVS | 108 V | 13.9 mA | 13.9 mA | 5 W | 1.5 kW | | | | | |
| 1.5KE82 | B2 | a1 | MO | TVS | 118 V | 12.7 mA | 12.7 mA | 5 W | 1.5 kW | | | | | |
| 1.5KE91 | B2 | a1 | MO | TVS | 131 V | 11.4 mA | 11.4 mA | 5 W | 1.5 kW | | | | | |
| 1.5KE100 | B2 | a1 | MO | TVS | 144 V | 10.4 mA | 10.4 mA | 5 W | 1.5 kW | | | | | |
| 1.5KE110 | B2 | a1 | MO | TVS | 158 V | 9.5 mA | 9.5 mA | 5 W | 1.5 kW | | | | | |
| 1.5KE120 | B2 | a1 | MO | TVS | 173 V | 8.7 mA | 8.7 mA | 5 W | 1.5 kW | | | | | |
| 1.5KE130 | B2 | a1 | MO | TVS | 187 V | 8 mA | 8 mA | 5 W | 1.5 kW | | | | | |
| 1.5KE150 | B2 | a1 | MO | TVS | 215 V | 7 mA | 7 mA | 5 W | 1.5 kW | | | | | |
| 1.5KE160 | B2 | a1 | MO | TVS | 230 V | 6.5 mA | 6.5 mA | 5 W | 1.5 kW | | | | | |
| 1.5KE170 | B2 | a1 | MO | TVS | 244 V | 6.2 mA | 6.2 mA | 5 W | 1.5 kW | | | | | |
| 1.5KE180 | B2 | a1 | MO | TVS | 258 V | 5.8 mA | 5.8 mA | 5 W | 1.5 kW | | | | | |
| 1.5KE200 | B2 | a1 | MO | TVS | 287 V | 5.2 mA | 5.2 mA | 5 W | 1.5 kW | | | | | |
| 1.5KE220 | B2 | a1 | MO | TVS | 344 V | 4.3 mA | 4.3 mA | 5 W | 1.5 kW | | | | | |
| 1.5KE250 | B2 | a1 | MO | TVS | 360 V | 5 mA | 5 mA | 5 W | 1.5 kW | | | | | |
| 1.5KE6.8A | B2 | a1 | MO | TVS | 10.5 V | 143 mA | 143 mA | 5 W | 1.5 kW | | | | P | |
| 1.5KE7.5A | B2 | a1 | MO | TVS | 11.3 V | 132 mA | 132 mA | 5 W | 1.5 kW | | | | | |
| 1.5KE8.2A | B2 | a1 | MO | TVS | 12.1 V | 124 mA | 124 mA | 5 W | 1.5 kW | | | | | |
| 1.5KE9.1A | B2 | a1 | MO | TVS | 13.4 V | 112 mA | 112 mA | 5 W | 1.5 kW | | | | | |
| 1.5KE10A | B2 | a1 | MO | TVS | 14.5 V | 103 mA | 103 mA | 5 W | 1.5 kW | | | | | |
| 1.5KE11A | B2 | a1 | MO | TVS | 15.6 V | 96 mA | 96 mA | 5 W | 1.5 kW | | | | | |
| 1.5KE12A | B2 | a1 | MO | TVS | 16.7 V | 90 mA | 90 mA | 5 W | 1.5 kW | | | | | |
| 1.5KE13A | B2 | a1 | MO | TVS | 18.2 V | 82 mA | 82 mA | 5 W | 1.5 kW | | | | P | |
| 1.5KE15A | B2 | a1 | MO | TVS | 21.2 V | 71 mA | 71 mA | 5 W | 1.5 kW | | | | P | |
| 1.5KE16A | B2 | a1 | MO | TVS | 22.5 V | 67 mA | 67 mA | 5 W | 1.5 kW | | | | | |
| 1.5KE18A | B2 | a1 | MO | TVS | 25.2 V | 59.5 mA | 59.5 mA | 5 W | 1.5 kW | | | | | |
| 1.5KE20A | B2 | a1 | MO | TVS | 27.7 V | 54 mA | 54 mA | 5 W | 1.5 kW | | | | | |
| 1.5KE22A | B2 | a1 | MO | TVS | 30.6 V | 49 mA | 49 mA | 5 W | 1.5 kW | | | | | |
| 1.5KE24A | B2 | a1 | MO | TVS | 33.2 V | 45 mA | 45 mA | 5 W | 1.5 kW | | | | | |
| 1.5KE27A | B2 | a1 | MO | TVS | 37.5 V | 40 mA | 40 mA | 5 W | 1.5 kW | | | | P | |
| 1.5KE30A | B2 | a1 | MO | TVS | 41.4 V | 36 mA | 36 mA | 5 W | 1.5 kW | | | | | |
| 1.5KE33A | B2 | a1 | MO | TVS | 45.7 V | 33 mA | 33 mA | 5 W | 1.5 kW | | | | P | |
| 1.5KE36A | B2 | a1 | MO | TVS | 49.9 V | 30 mA | 30 mA | 5 W | 1.5 kW | | | | P | |
| 1.5KE39A | B2 | a1 | MO | TVS | 53.9 V | 28 mA | 28 mA | 5 W | 1.5 kW | | | | | |

| Type | Case | Pin-code | | | Maximum Ratings | | | | | Electrical Characteristics | | | | |
|---|---|---|---|---|---|---|---|---|---|---|---|---|---|---|
| | | | | | $V_{cla}$ $V_{bro}$ | Its | Izm | Pv | Pvts | Vz | Iz Is | rz | TK | |
| 1.5KE43A | B2 | a1 | MO | TVS | 59.3 V | 25.3 mA | 25.3 mA | 5 W | 1.5 kW | | | | | |
| 1.5KE47A | B2 | a1 | MO | TVS | 64.8 V | 23.2 mA | 23.2 mA | 5 W | 1.5 kW | | | | | |
| 1.5KE51A | B2 | a1 | MO | TVS | 70.1 V | 21.4 mA | 21.4 mA | 5 W | 1.5 kW | | | | | |
| 1.5KE56A | B2 | a1 | MO | TVS | 77 V | 19.5 mA | 19.5 mA | 5 W | 1.5 kW | | | | | |
| 1.5KE62A | B2 | a1 | MO | TVS | 85 V | 17.7 mA | 17.7 mA | 5 W | 1.5 kW | | | | P | |
| 1.5KE68A | B2 | a1 | MO | TVS | 92 V | 16.3 mA | 16.3 mA | 5 W | 1.5 kW | | | | | |
| 1.5KE75A | B2 | a1 | MO | TVS | 103 V | 14.6 mA | 14.6 mA | 5 W | 1.5 kW | | | | | |
| 1.5KE82A | B2 | a1 | MO | TVS | 113 V | 13.3 mA | 13.3 mA | 5 W | 1.5 kW | | | | | |
| 1.5KE91A | B2 | a1 | MO | TVS | 125 V | 12 mA | 12 mA | 5 W | 1.5 kW | | | | | |
| 1.5KE100A | B2 | a1 | MO | TVS | 137 V | 11 mA | 11 mA | 5 W | 1.5 kW | | | | | |
| 1.5KE110A | B2 | a1 | MO | TVS | 152 V | 9.9 mA | 9.9 mA | 5 W | 1.5 kW | | | | | |
| 1.5KE120A | B2 | a1 | MO | TVS | 165 V | 9.1 mA | 9.1 mA | 5 W | 1.5 kW | | | | | |
| 1.5KE130A | B2 | a1 | MO | TVS | 179 V | 8.4 mA | 8.4 mA | 5 W | 1.5 kW | | | | | |
| 1.5KE150A | B2 | a1 | MO | TVS | 207 V | 7.2 mA | 7.2 mA | 5 W | 1.5 kW | | | | | |
| 1.5KE160A | B2 | a1 | MO | TVS | 219 V | 6.8 mA | 6.8 mA | 5 W | 1.5 kW | | | | | |
| 1.5KE170A | B2 | a1 | MO | TVS | 234 V | 6.4 mA | 6.4 mA | 5 W | 1.5 kW | | | | | |
| 1.5KE180A | B2 | a1 | MO | TVS | 246 V | 6.1 mA | 6.1 mA | 5 W | 1.5 kW | | | | | |
| 1.5KE200A | B2 | a1 | MO | TVS | 274 V | 5.5 mA | 5.5 mA | 5 W | 1.5 kW | | | | | |
| 1.5KE220A | B2 | a1 | MO | TVS | 328 V | 4.6 mA | 4.6 mA | 5 W | 1.5 kW | | | | | |
| 1.5KE250A | B2 | a1 | MO | TVS | 344 V | 5 mA | 5 mA | 5 W | 1.5 kW | | | | | |
| 1.5KE6.8C | B2 | a2 | MO | Bidir. TVS | 10.8 V | 139 mA | 139 mA | 5 W | 1.5 kW | | | | | |
| 1.5KE7.5C | B2 | a2 | MO | Bidir. TVS | 11.7 V | 128 mA | 128 mA | 5 W | 1.5 kW | | | | | |
| 1.5KE8.2C | B2 | a2 | MO | Bidir. TVS | 12.5 V | 120 mA | 120 mA | 5 W | 1.5 kW | | | | | |
| 1.5KE9.1C | B2 | a2 | MO | Bidir. TVS | 13.8 V | 109 mA | 109 mA | 5 W | 1.5 kW | | | | | |
| 1.5KE10C | B2 | a2 | MO | Bidir. TVS | 15 V | 100 mA | 100 mA | 5 W | 1.5 kW | | | | | |
| 1.5KE11C | B2 | a2 | MO | Bidir. TVS | 16.2 V | 93 mA | 93 mA | 5 W | 1.5 kW | | | | | |
| 1.5KE12C | B2 | a2 | MO | Bidir. TVS | 17.3 V | 87 mA | 87 mA | 5 W | 1.5 kW | | | | | |
| 1.5KE13C | B2 | a2 | MO | Bidir. TVS | 19 V | 79 mA | 79 mA | 5 W | 1.5 kW | | | | | |
| 1.5KE15C | B2 | a2 | MO | Bidir. TVS | 22 V | 68 mA | 68 mA | 5 W | 1.5 kW | | | | | |
| 1.5KE16C | B2 | a2 | MO | Bidir. TVS | 23.5 V | 64 mA | 64 mA | 5 W | 1.5 kW | | | | | |
| 1.5KE18C | B2 | a2 | MO | Bidir. TVS | 26.5 V | 56.5 mA | 56.5 mA | 5 W | 1.5 kW | | | | | |
| 1.5KE20C | B2 | a2 | MO | Bidir. TVS | 29.1 V | 51.5 mA | 51.5 mA | 5 W | 1.5 kW | | | | | |
| 1.5KE22C | B2 | a2 | MO | Bidir. TVS | 31.9 V | 47 mA | 47 mA | 5 W | 1.5 kW | | | | | |
| 1.5KE24C | B2 | a2 | MO | Bidir. TVS | 34.7 V | 43 mA | 43 mA | 5 W | 1.5 kW | | | | | |
| 1.5KE27C | B2 | a2 | MO | Bidir. TVS | 39.1 V | 38.5 mA | 38.5 mA | 5 W | 1.5 kW | | | | | |
| 1.5KE30C | B2 | a2 | MO | Bidir. TVS | 43.5 V | 34.5 mA | 34.5 mA | 5 W | 1.5 kW | | | | | |
| 1.5KE33C | B2 | a2 | MO | Bidir. TVS | 47.7 V | 31.5 mA | 31.5 mA | 5 W | 1.5 kW | | | | | |
| 1.5KE36C | B2 | a2 | MO | Bidir. TVS | 52 V | 29 mA | 29 mA | 5 W | 1.5 kW | | | | | |
| 1.5KE39C | B2 | a2 | MO | Bidir. TVS | 56.4 V | 26.5 mA | 26.5 mA | 5 W | 1.5 kW | | | | | |
| 1.5KE43C | B2 | a2 | MO | Bidir. TVS | 61.9 V | 24 mA | 24 mA | 5 W | 1.5 kW | | | | | |

| Type | Case | Pin-code | | | Maximum Ratings | | | | | Electrical Characteristics | | | | |
|---|---|---|---|---|---|---|---|---|---|---|---|---|---|---|
| | | | | | Vcla Vbro | Its | Izm | Pv | Pvts | Vz | Iz / Is | rz | TK | |
| 1.5KE47C | B2 | a2 | MO | Bidir. TVS | 67.8 V | 22.2 mA | 22.2 mA | 5 W | 1.5 kW | | | | | |
| 1.5KE51C | B2 | a2 | MO | Bidir. TVS | 73.5 V | 20.4 mA | 20.4 mA | 5 W | 1.5 kW | | | | | |
| 1.5KE56C | B2 | a2 | MO | Bidir. TVS | 80.5 V | 18.6 mA | 18.6 mA | 5 W | 1.5 kW | | | | | |
| 1.5KE62C | B2 | a2 | MO | Bidir. TVS | 89 V | 16.9 mA | 16.9 mA | 5 W | 1.5 kW | | | | | |
| 1.5KE68C | B2 | a2 | MO | Bidir. TVS | 98 V | 15.3 mA | 15.3 mA | 5 W | 1.5 kW | | | | | |
| 1.5KE75C | B2 | a2 | MO | Bidir. TVS | 108 V | 13.9 mA | 13.9 mA | 5 W | 1.5 kW | | | | | |
| 1.5KE82C | B2 | a2 | MO | Bidir. TVS | 118 V | 12.7 mA | 12.7 mA | 5 W | 1.5 kW | | | | | |
| 1.5KE91C | B2 | a2 | MO | Bidir. TVS | 131 V | 11.4 mA | 11.4 mA | 5 W | 1.5 kW | | | | | |
| 1.5KE100C | B2 | a2 | MO | Bidir. TVS | 144 V | 10.4 mA | 10.4 mA | 5 W | 1.5 kW | | | | | |
| 1.5KE110C | B2 | a2 | MO | Bidir. TVS | 158 V | 9.5 mA | 9.5 mA | 5 W | 1.5 kW | | | | | |
| 1.5KE120C | B2 | a2 | MO | Bidir. TVS | 173 V | 8.7 mA | 8.7 mA | 5 W | 1.5 kW | | | | | |
| 1.5KE130C | B2 | a2 | MO | Bidir. TVS | 187 V | 8 mA | 8 mA | 5 W | 1.5 kW | | | | | |
| 1.5KE150C | B2 | a2 | MO | Bidir. TVS | 215 V | 7 mA | 7 mA | 5 W | 1.5 kW | | | | | |
| 1.5KE160C | B2 | a2 | MO | Bidir. TVS | 230 V | 6.5 mA | 6.5 mA | 5 W | 1.5 kW | | | | | |
| 1.5KE170C | B2 | a2 | MO | Bidir. TVS | 244 V | 6.2 mA | 6.2 mA | 5 W | 1.5 kW | | | | | |
| 1.5KE180C | B2 | a2 | MO | Bidir. TVS | 258 V | 5.8 mA | 5.8 mA | 5 W | 1.5 kW | | | | | |
| 1.5KE200C | B2 | a2 | MO | Bidir. TVS | 287 V | 5.2 mA | 5.2 mA | 5 W | 1.5 kW | | | | | |
| 1.5KE220C | B2 | a2 | MO | Bidir. TVS | 344 V | 4.3 mA | 4.3 mA | 5 W | 1.5 kW | | | | | |
| 1.5KE250C | B2 | a2 | MO | Bidir. TVS | 360 V | 5 mA | 5 mA | 5 W | 1.5 kW | | | | | |
| 1.5KE6.8CA | B2 | a2 | MO | Bidir. TVS | 10.5 V | 143 mA | 143 mA | 5 W | 1.5 kW | | | | | P |
| 1.5KE7.5CA | B2 | a2 | MO | Bidir. TVS | 11.3 V | 132 mA | 132 mA | 5 W | 1.5 kW | | | | | |
| 1.5KE8.2CA | B2 | a2 | MO | Bidir. TVS | 12.1 V | 124 mA | 124 mA | 5 W | 1.5 kW | | | | | |
| 1.5KE9.1CA | B2 | a2 | MO | Bidir. TVS | 13.4 V | 112 mA | 112 mA | 5 W | 1.5 kW | | | | | |
| 1.5KE10CA | B2 | a2 | MO | Bidir. TVS | 14.5 V | 103 mA | 103 mA | 5 W | 1.5 kW | | | | | |
| 1.5KE11CA | B2 | a2 | MO | Bidir. TVS | 15.6 V | 96 mA | 96 mA | 5 W | 1.5 kW | | | | | |
| 1.5KE12CA | B2 | a2 | MO | Bidir. TVS | 16.7 V | 90 mA | 90 mA | 5 W | 1.5 kW | | | | | |
| 1.5KE13CA | B2 | a2 | MO | Bidir. TVS | 18.2 V | 82 mA | 82 mA | 5 W | 1.5 kW | | | | | P |
| 1.5KE15CA | B2 | a2 | MO | Bidir. TVS | 21.2 V | 71 mA | 71 mA | 5 W | 1.5 kW | | | | | P |
| 1.5KE16CA | B2 | a2 | MO | Bidir. TVS | 22.5 V | 67 mA | 67 mA | 5 W | 1.5 kW | | | | | |
| 1.5KE18CA | B2 | a2 | MO | Bidir. TVS | 25.2 V | 59.5 mA | 59.5 mA | 5 W | 1.5 kW | | | | | |
| 1.5KE20CA | B2 | a2 | MO | Bidir. TVS | 27.7 V | 54 mA | 54 mA | 5 W | 1.5 kW | | | | | |
| 1.5KE22CA | B2 | a2 | MO | Bidir. TVS | 30.6 V | 49 mA | 49 mA | 5 W | 1.5 kW | | | | | |
| 1.5KE24CA | B2 | a2 | MO | Bidir. TVS | 33.2 V | 45 mA | 45 mA | 5 W | 1.5 kW | | | | | |
| 1.5KE27CA | B2 | a2 | MO | Bidir. TVS | 37.5 V | 40 mA | 40 mA | 5 W | 1.5 kW | | | | | P |
| 1.5KE30CA | B2 | a2 | MO | Bidir. TVS | 41.4 V | 36 mA | 36 mA | 5 W | 1.5 kW | | | | | |
| 1.5KE33CA | B2 | a2 | MO | Bidir. TVS | 45.7 V | 33 mA | 33 mA | 5 W | 1.5 kW | | | | | P |
| 1.5KE36CA | B2 | a2 | MO | Bidir. TVS | 49.9 V | 30 mA | 30 mA | 5 W | 1.5 kW | | | | | P |
| 1.5KE39CA | B2 | a2 | MO | Bidir. TVS | 53.9 V | 28 mA | 28 mA | 5 W | 1.5 kW | | | | | |
| 1.5KE43CA | B2 | a2 | MO | Bidir. TVS | 59.3 V | 25.3 mA | 25.3 mA | 5 W | 1.5 kW | | | | | |
| 1.5KE47CA | B2 | a2 | MO | Bidir. TVS | 64.8 V | 23.2 mA | 23.2 mA | 5 W | 1.5 kW | | | | | |

| Type | Case | Pin-code | | | Maximum Ratings | | | | | Electrical Characteristics | | | | |
|---|---|---|---|---|---|---|---|---|---|---|---|---|---|---|
| | | | | | Vcla Vbro | Its | Izm | Pv | Pvts | Vz | Iz Is | rz | TK | |
| 1.5KE51CA | B2 | a2 | MO | Bidir. TVS | 70.1 V | 21.4 mA | 21.4 mA | 5 W | 1.5 kW | | | | | |
| 1.5KE56CA | B2 | a2 | MO | Bidir. TVS | 77 V | 19.5 mA | 19.5 mA | 5 W | 1.5 kW | | | | | |
| 1.5KE62CA | B2 | a2 | MO | Bidir. TVS | 85 V | 17.7 mA | 17.7 mA | 5 W | 1.5 kW | | | | | P |
| 1.5KE68CA | B2 | a2 | MO | Bidir. TVS | 92 V | 16.3 mA | 16.3 mA | 5 W | 1.5 kW | | | | | |
| 1.5KE75CA | B2 | a2 | MO | Bidir. TVS | 103 V | 14.6 mA | 14.6 mA | 5 W | 1.5 kW | | | | | |
| 1.5KE82CA | B2 | a2 | MO | Bidir. TVS | 113 V | 13.3 mA | 13.3 mA | 5 W | 1.5 kW | | | | | |
| 1.5KE91CA | B2 | a2 | MO | Bidir. TVS | 125 V | 12 mA | 12 mA | 5 W | 1.5 kW | | | | | |
| 1.5KE100CA | B2 | a2 | MO | Bidir. TVS | 137 V | 11 mA | 11 mA | 5 W | 1.5 kW | | | | | |
| 1.5KE110CA | B2 | a2 | MO | Bidir. TVS | 152 V | 9.9 mA | 9.9 mA | 5 W | 1.5 kW | | | | | |
| 1.5KE120CA | B2 | a2 | MO | Bidir. TVS | 165 V | 9.1 mA | 9.1 mA | 5 W | 1.5 kW | | | | | |
| 1.5KE130CA | B2 | a2 | MO | Bidir. TVS | 179 V | 8.4 mA | 8.4 mA | 5 W | 1.5 kW | | | | | |
| 1.5KE150CA | B2 | a2 | MO | Bidir. TVS | 207 V | 7.2 mA | 7.2 mA | 5 W | 1.5 kW | | | | | |
| 1.5KE160CA | B2 | a2 | MO | Bidir. TVS | 219 V | 6.8 mA | 6.8 mA | 5 W | 1.5 kW | | | | | |
| 1.5KE170CA | B2 | a2 | MO | Bidir. TVS | 234 V | 6.4 mA | 6.4 mA | 5 W | 1.5 kW | | | | | |
| 1.5KE180CA | B2 | a2 | MO | Bidir. TVS | 246 V | 6.1 mA | 6.1 mA | 5 W | 1.5 kW | | | | | |
| 1.5KE200CA | B2 | a2 | MO | Bidir. TVS | 274 V | 5.5 mA | 5.5 mA | 5 W | 1.5 kW | | | | | |
| 1.5KE220CA | B2 | a2 | MO | Bidir. TVS | 328 V | 4.6 mA | 4.6 mA | 5 W | 1.5 kW | | | | | |
| 1.5KE250CA | B2 | a2 | MO | Bidir. TVS | 344 V | 5 mA | 5 mA | 5 W | 1.5 kW | | | | | |
| 1.5SMC6.8A | G2 | a1 | MO | TVS | 10.5 V | 143 mA | 143 mA | | 1.5 kW | | | | | P |
| 1.5SMC7.5A | G2 | a1 | MO | TVS | 11.3 V | 132 mA | 132 mA | | 1.5 kW | | | | | |
| 1.5SMC8.2A | G2 | a1 | MO | TVS | 12.1 V | 124 mA | 124 mA | | 1.5 kW | | | | | |
| 1.5SMC9.1A | G2 | a1 | MO | TVS | 13.4 V | 112 mA | 112 mA | | 1.5 kW | | | | | |
| 1.5SMC10A | G2 | a1 | MO | TVS | 14.5 V | 103 mA | 103 mA | | 1.5 kW | | | | | |
| 1.5SMC11A | G2 | a1 | MO | TVS | 15.6 V | 96 mA | 96 mA | | 1.5 kW | | | | | |
| 1.5SMC12A | G2 | a1 | MO | TVS | 16.7 V | 90 mA | 90 mA | | 1.5 kW | | | | | |
| 1.5SMC13A | G2 | a1 | MO | TVS | 18.2 V | 82 mA | 82 mA | | 1.5 kW | | | | | P |
| 1.5SMC15A | G2 | a1 | MO | TVS | 21.2 V | 71 mA | 71 mA | | 1.5 kW | | | | | P |
| 1.5SMC16A | G2 | a1 | MO | TVS | 22.5 V | 67 mA | 67 mA | | 1.5 kW | | | | | |
| 1.5SMC18A | G2 | a1 | MO | TVS | 25.2 V | 59.5 mA | 59.5 mA | | 1.5 kW | | | | | |
| 1.5SMC20A | G2 | a1 | MO | TVS | 27.7 V | 54 mA | 54 mA | | 1.5 kW | | | | | |
| 1.5SMC22A | G2 | a1 | MO | TVS | 30.6 V | 49 mA | 49 mA | | 1.5 kW | | | | | |
| 1.5SMC24A | G2 | a1 | MO | TVS | 33.2 V | 45 mA | 45 mA | | 1.5 kW | | | | | |
| 1.5SMC27A | G2 | a1 | MO | TVS | 37.5 V | 40 mA | 40 mA | | 1.5 kW | | | | | P |
| 1.5SMC30A | G2 | a1 | MO | TVS | 41.4 V | 36 mA | 36 mA | | 1.5 kW | | | | | |
| 1.5SMC33A | G2 | a1 | MO | TVS | 45.7 V | 33 mA | 33 mA | | 1.5 kW | | | | | P |
| 1.5SMC36A | G2 | a1 | MO | TVS | 49.9 V | 30 mA | 30 mA | | 1.5 kW | | | | | P |
| 1.5SMC39A | G2 | a1 | MO | TVS | 53.9 V | 28 mA | 28 mA | | 1.5 kW | | | | | |
| 1.5SMC43A | G2 | a1 | MO | TVS | 59.3 V | 25.3 mA | 25.3 mA | | 1.5 kW | | | | | |
| 1.5SMC47A | G2 | a1 | MO | TVS | 64.8 V | 23.2 mA | 23.2 mA | | 1.5 kW | | | | | |
| 1.5SMC51A | G2 | a1 | MO | TVS | 70.1 V | 21.4 mA | 21.4 mA | | 1.5 kW | | | | | |

| Type | Case | Pin-code | | | Maximum Ratings | | | | | Electrical Characteristics | | | | |
|---|---|---|---|---|---|---|---|---|---|---|---|---|---|---|
| | | | | | Vcla / Vbro | Its | Izm | Pv | Pvts | Vz / Is | Iz / Is | rz | TK | |
| 1.5SMC56A | G2 | a1 | MO | TVS | 77 V | 19.5 mA | 19.5 mA | | 1.5 kW | | | | | |
| 1.5SMC62A | G2 | a1 | MO | TVS | 85 V | 17.7 mA | 17.7 mA | | 1.5 kW | | | | | P |
| 1.5SMC68A | G2 | a1 | MO | TVS | 92 V | 16.3 mA | 16.3 mA | | 1.5 kW | | | | | |
| 1.5SMC75A | G2 | a1 | MO | TVS | 103 V | 14.6 mA | 14.6 mA | | 1.5 kW | | | | | |
| 1.5SMC82A | G2 | a1 | MO | TVS | 113 V | 13.3 mA | 13.3 mA | | 1.5 kW | | | | | |
| 1.5SMC91A | G2 | a1 | MO | TVS | 125 V | 13 mA | 13 mA | | 1.5 kW | | | | | |
| BA314 | A1 | a1 | PH | Stabistor | | | | | | <0.78 | 10 | 3.5 Ω | -2300 ·10$^6$/°C | |
| BA315 | A1 | a1 | PH | Stabistor | | | | | | <0.75 | 10 | 6 Ω | -2800 ·10$^6$/°C | |
| BAS17 | F1 | c10 | PH | Stabistor | | | | | | 0.915 | 100 | | -1800 ·10$^6$/°C | |
| BR210-100 | I5 | a3 | PH | Breakover | 112 V | 150 A | 150 A | (40) W | 400 W | | 200 mA | | 1000 ·10$^6$/°C | |
| BR210-120 | I5 | a3 | PH | Breakover | 135 V | 150 A | 150 A | (40) W | 400 W | | 200 mA | | 1000 ·10$^6$/°C | |
| BR210-140 | I5 | a3 | PH | Breakover | 157 V | 150 A | 150 A | (40) W | 400 W | | 200 mA | | 1000 ·10$^6$/°C | |
| BR210-160 | I5 | a3 | PH | Breakover | 180 V | 150 A | 150 A | (40) W | 400 W | | 200 mA | | 1000 ·10$^6$/°C | |
| BR210-240 | I5 | a3 | PH | Breakover | 269 V | 150 A | 150 A | (40) W | 400 W | | 200 mA | | 1000 ·10$^6$/°C | |
| BR210-260 | I5 | a3 | PH | Breakover | 292 V | 150 A | 150 A | (40) W | 400 W | | 200 mA | | 1000 ·10$^6$/°C | |
| BR210-280 | I5 | a3 | PH | Breakover | 314 V | 150 A | 150 A | (40) W | 400 W | | 200 mA | | 1000 ·10$^6$/°C | |
| BR211-100 | A6 | a3 | PH | Breakover | 112 V | 40 A | 40 A | 1.2 W | 50 W | | 200 mA | | 1000 ·10$^6$/°C | |
| BR211-120 | A6 | a3 | PH | Breakover | 135 V | 40 A | 40 A | 1.2 W | 50 W | | 200 mA | | 1000 ·10$^6$/°C | |
| BR211-140 | A6 | a3 | PH | Breakover | 157 V | 40 A | 40 A | 1.2 W | 50 W | | 200 mA | | 1000 ·10$^6$/°C | |
| BR211-160 | A6 | a3 | PH | Breakover | 180 V | 40 A | 40 A | 1.2 W | 50 W | | 200 mA | | 1000 ·10$^6$/°C | |
| BR211-180 | A6 | a3 | PH | Breakover | 202 V | 40 A | 40 A | 1.2 W | 50 W | | 200 mA | | 1000 ·10$^6$/°C | |
| BR211-200 | A6 | a3 | PH | Breakover | 224 V | 40 A | 40 A | 1.2 W | 50 W | | 200 mA | | 1000 ·10$^6$/°C | |
| BR211-220 | A6 | a3 | PH | Breakover | 247 V | 40 A | 40 A | 1.2 W | 50 W | | 200 mA | | 1000 ·10$^6$/°C | |
| BR211-240 | A6 | a3 | PH | Breakover | 269 V | 40 A | 40 A | 1.2 W | 50 W | | 200 mA | | 1000 ·10$^6$/°C | |
| BR211-260 | A6 | a3 | PH | Breakover | 292 V | 40 A | 40 A | 1.2 W | 50 W | | 200 mA | | 1000 ·10$^6$/°C | |
| BR211-280 | A6 | a3 | PH | Breakover | 314 V | 40 A | 40 A | 1.2 W | 50 W | | 200 mA | | 1000 ·10$^6$/°C | |
| BR213-100 | I4 | c19 | PH | Bidir. BRO | 112 V | 150 A | 150 A | (40) W | 400 W | | 200 mA | | 1000 ·10$^6$/°C | |
| BR213-120 | I4 | c19 | PH | Bidir. BRO | 135 V | 150 A | 150 A | (40) W | 400 W | | 200 mA | | 1000 ·10$^6$/°C | |
| BR213-140 | I4 | c19 | PH | Bidir. BRO | 157 V | 150 A | 150 A | (40) W | 400 W | | 200 mA | | 1000 ·10$^6$/°C | |
| BR213-160 | I4 | c19 | PH | Bidir. BRO | 180 V | 150 A | 150 A | (40) W | 400 W | | 200 mA | | 1000 ·10$^6$/°C | |
| BR213-240 | I4 | c19 | PH | Bidir. BRO | 269 V | 150 A | 150 A | (40) W | 400 W | | 200 mA | | 1000 ·10$^6$/°C | |
| BR213-260 | I4 | c19 | PH | Bidir. BRO | 292 V | 150 A | 150 A | (40) W | 400 W | | 200 mA | | 1000 ·10$^6$/°C | |
| BR213-280 | I4 | c19 | PH | Bidir. BRO | 314 V | 150 A | 150 A | (40) W | 400 W | | 200 mA | | 1000 ·10$^6$/°C | |
| BR216 | I4 | c18 | PH | Bidir. BRO | 78 V | 150 A | 150 A | (35) W | 110 W | | 200 mA | | 1000 ·10$^6$/°C | |
| BR220-100 | I4 | c16 | PH | Bidir. BRO | 62 V | 150 A | 150 A | (40) W | 400 W | | 200 mA | | 1000 ·10$^6$/°C | |
| BR220-120 | I4 | c16 | PH | Bidir. BRO | 135 V | 150 A | 150 A | (40) W | 400 W | | 200 mA | | 1000 ·10$^6$/°C | |
| BR220-140 | I4 | c16 | PH | Bidir. BRO | 157 V | 150 A | 150 A | (40) W | 400 W | | 200 mA | | 1000 ·10$^6$/°C | |
| BR220-160 | I4 | c16 | PH | Bidir. BRO | 180 V | 150 A | 150 A | (40) W | 400 W | | 200 mA | | 1000 ·10$^6$/°C | |
| BR220-240 | I4 | c16 | PH | Bidir. BRO | 269 V | 150 A | 150 A | (40) W | 400 W | | 200 mA | | 1000 ·10$^6$/°C | |
| BR220-260 | I4 | c16 | PH | Bidir. BRO | 292 V | 150 A | 150 A | (40) W | 400 W | | 200 mA | | 1000 ·10$^6$/°C | |

| Type | Case | Pin-code | | | Maximum Ratings | | | | | Electrical Characteristics | | | | |
|---|---|---|---|---|---|---|---|---|---|---|---|---|---|---|
| | | | | | $V_{cla}$ $V_{bro}$ | Its | Izm | Pv | Pvts | Vz | Iz Is | rz | TK | |
| BR220-280 | I4 | c16 | PH | Bidir. BRO | 314 V | 150 A | 150 A | (40) W | 400 W | | 200 mA | | $1000 \cdot 10^6$/°C | |
| BZD23C3V6 | A8 | a1 | PH | Z Diode, TVS | | 45 mA | 45 mA | 2 W | | 3.6 V | 100 mA | 4 Ω | $-1400 \cdot 10^6$/°C | ZD only |
| BZD23C3V9 | A8 | a1 | PH | Z Diode, TVS | | 43 mA | 43 mA | 2 W | | 3.9 V | 100 mA | 4 Ω | $-1400 \cdot 10^6$/°C | ZD only |
| BZD23C4V3 | A8 | a1 | PH | Z Diode, TVS | | 40 mA | 40 mA | 2 W | | 4.3 V | 100 mA | 4 Ω | $-1200 \cdot 10^6$/°C | ZD only |
| BZD23C4V7 | A8 | a1 | PH | Z Diode, TVS | | 38 mA | 38 mA | 2 W | | 4.7 V | 100 mA | 3 Ω | $-1000 \cdot 10^6$/°C | ZD only |
| BZD23C5V1 | A8 | a1 | PH | Z Diode, TVS | | 35 mA | 35 mA | 2 W | | 5.1 V | 100 mA | 3 Ω | $-800 \cdot 10^6$/°C | ZD only |
| BZD23C5V6 | A8 | a1 | PH | Z Diode, TVS | | 32 mA | 32 mA | 2 W | | 5.6 V | 100 mA | 2 Ω | $400 \cdot 10^6$/°C | ZD only |
| BZD23C6V2 | A8 | a1 | PH | Z Diode, TVS | | 28 mA | 28 mA | 2 W | | 6.2 V | 100 mA | 2 Ω | $600 \cdot 10^6$/°C | ZD only |
| BZD23C6V8 | A8 | a1 | PH | Z Diode, TVS | | 25 mA | 25 mA | 2 W | | 6.8 V | 100 mA | 1 Ω | $700 \cdot 10^6$/°C | ZD only |
| BZD23C7V5 | A8 | a1 | PH | Z Diode, TVS | 11.3 V | 23.3 mA | 23.3 mA | 2.5 W | 300 W | 7.5 V | 100 mA | 1 Ω | $700 \cdot 10^6$/°C | |
| BZD23C8V2 | A8 | a1 | PH | Z Diode, TVS | 12.3 V | 12.2 mA | 12.2 mA | 2.5 W | 300 W | 8.2 V | 100 mA | 1 Ω | $800 \cdot 10^6$/°C | |
| BZD23C9V1 | A8 | a1 | PH | Z Diode, TVS | 13.3 V | 11.3 mA | 11.3 mA | 2.5 W | 300 W | 9.1 V | 50 mA | 2 Ω | $800 \cdot 10^6$/°C | |
| BZD23C10 | A8 | a1 | PH | Z Diode, TVS | 14.8 V | 10.1 mA | 10.1 mA | 2.5 W | 300 W | 10 V | 50 mA | 2 Ω | $900 \cdot 10^6$/°C | |
| BZD23C11 | A8 | a1 | PH | Z Diode, TVS | 15.7 V | 9.6 mA | 9.6 mA | 2.5 W | 300 W | 11 V | 50 mA | 4 Ω | $1000 \cdot 10^6$/°C | |
| BZD23C12 | A8 | a1 | PH | Z Diode, TVS | 17 V | 8.8 mA | 8.8 mA | 2.5 W | 300 W | 12 V | 50 mA | 4 Ω | $1000 \cdot 10^6$/°C | |
| BZD23C13 | A8 | a1 | PH | Z Diode, TVS | 18.9 V | 7.9 mA | 7.9 mA | 2.5 W | 300 W | 13 V | 50 mA | 5 Ω | $1000 \cdot 10^6$/°C | |
| BZD23C15 | A8 | a1 | PH | Z Diode, TVS | 20.9 V | 7.2 mA | 7.2 mA | 2.5 W | 300 W | 15 V | 50 mA | 5 Ω | $1000 \cdot 10^6$/°C | |
| BZD23C16 | A8 | a1 | PH | Z Diode, TVS | 22.9 V | 6.6 mA | 6.6 mA | 2.5 W | 300 W | 16 V | 25 mA | 6 Ω | $1100 \cdot 10^6$/°C | |
| BZD23C18 | A8 | a1 | PH | Z Diode, TVS | 25.6 V | 5.9 mA | 5.9 mA | 2.5 W | 300 W | 18 V | 25 mA | 6 Ω | $1100 \cdot 10^6$/°C | |
| BZD23C20 | A8 | a1 | PH | Z Diode, TVS | 28.4 V | 5.3 mA | 5.3 mA | 2.5 W | 300 W | 20 V | 25 mA | 6 Ω | $1100 \cdot 10^6$/°C | |
| BZD23C22 | A8 | a1 | PH | Z Diode, TVS | 31 V | 4.8 mA | 4.8 mA | 2.5 W | 300 W | 22 V | 25 mA | 6 Ω | $1100 \cdot 10^6$/°C | |
| BZD23C24 | A8 | a1 | PH | Z Diode, TVS | 33.8 V | 4.4 mA | 4.4 mA | 2.5 W | 300 W | 24 V | 25 mA | 7 Ω | $1100 \cdot 10^6$/°C | |
| BZD23C27 | A8 | a1 | PH | Z Diode, TVS | 38.1 V | 3.9 mA | 3.9 mA | 2.5 W | 300 W | 27 V | 25 mA | 7 Ω | $1100 \cdot 10^6$/°C | |
| BZD23C30 | A8 | a1 | PH | Z Diode, TVS | 42.2 V | 3.6 mA | 3.6 mA | 2.5 W | 300 W | 30 V | 25 mA | 8 Ω | $1100 \cdot 10^6$/°C | |
| BZD23C33 | A8 | a1 | PH | Z Diode, TVS | 46.2 V | 3.2 mA | 3.2 mA | 2.5 W | 300 W | 33 V | 25 mA | 8 Ω | $1100 \cdot 10^6$/°C | |
| BZD23C36 | A8 | a1 | PH | Z Diode, TVS | 50.1 V | 3 mA | 3 mA | 2.5 W | 300 W | 36 V | 10 mA | 21 Ω | $1100 \cdot 10^6$/°C | |
| BZD23C39 | A8 | a1 | PH | Z Diode, TVS | 54.1 V | 2.8 mA | 2.8 mA | 2.5 W | 300 W | 39 V | 10 mA | 21 Ω | $1100 \cdot 10^6$/°C | |
| BZD23C43 | A8 | a1 | PH | Z Diode, TVS | 60.7 V | 2.5 mA | 2.5 mA | 2.5 W | 300 W | 43 V | 10 mA | 24 Ω | $1200 \cdot 10^6$/°C | |
| BZD23C47 | A8 | a1 | PH | Z Diode, TVS | 65.5 V | 2.3 mA | 2.3 mA | 2.5 W | 300 W | 47 V | 10 mA | 24 Ω | $1200 \cdot 10^6$/°C | |
| BZD23C51 | A8 | a1 | PH | Z Diode, TVS | 70.8 V | 2.1 mA | 2.1 mA | 2.5 W | 300 W | 51 V | 10 mA | 25 Ω | $1200 \cdot 10^6$/°C | |
| BZD23C56 | A8 | a1 | PH | Z Diode, TVS | 78.6 V | 1.9 mA | 1.9 mA | 2.5 W | 300 W | 56 V | 10 mA | 25 Ω | $1200 \cdot 10^6$/°C | |
| BZD23C62 | A8 | a1 | PH | Z Diode, TVS | 86.5 V | 1.7 mA | 1.7 mA | 2.5 W | 300 W | 62 V | 10 mA | 25 Ω | $1300 \cdot 10^6$/°C | |
| BZD23C68 | A8 | a1 | PH | Z Diode, TVS | 94.4 V | 1.6 mA | 1.6 mA | 2.5 W | 300 W | 68 V | 10 mA | 25 Ω | $1300 \cdot 10^6$/°C | |
| BZD23C75 | A8 | a1 | PH | Z Diode, TVS | 103.5 V | 1.5 mA | 1.5 mA | 2.5 W | 300 W | 75 V | 10 mA | 30 Ω | $1300 \cdot 10^6$/°C | |
| BZD23C82 | A8 | a1 | PH | Z Diode, TVS | 114 V | 1.3 mA | 1.3 mA | 2.5 W | 300 W | 82 V | 10 mA | 30 Ω | $1300 \cdot 10^6$/°C | |
| BZD23C91 | A8 | a1 | PH | Z Diode, TVS | 126 V | 1.2 mA | 1.2 mA | 2.5 W | 300 W | 91 V | 5 mA | 60 Ω | $1300 \cdot 10^6$/°C | |
| BZD23C100 | A8 | a1 | PH | Z Diode, TVS | 139 V | 1.1 mA | 1.1 mA | 2.5 W | 300 W | 100 V | 5 mA | 60 Ω | $1300 \cdot 10^6$/°C | |
| BZD23C110 | A8 | a1 | PH | Z Diode, TVS | 152 V | 1 mA | 1 mA | 2.5 W | 300 W | 110 V | 5 mA | 80 Ω | $1300 \cdot 10^6$/°C | |
| BZD23C120 | A8 | a1 | PH | Z Diode, TVS | 167 V | 0.9 mA | 0.9 mA | 2.5 W | 300 W | 120 V | 5 mA | 80 Ω | $1300 \cdot 10^6$/°C | |
| BZD23C130 | A8 | a1 | PH | Z Diode, TVS | 185 V | 0.81 mA | 0.81 mA | 2.5 W | 300 W | 130 V | 5 mA | 110 Ω | $1300 \cdot 10^6$/°C | |

| Type | Case | Pin-code | | | Maximum Ratings | | | | | Electrical Characteristics | | | | |
|---|---|---|---|---|---|---|---|---|---|---|---|---|---|---|
| | | | | | Vcla Vbro | Its | Izm | Pv | Pvts | Vz | Iz Is | rz | TK | |
| BZD23C150 | A8 | a1 | PH | Z Diode, TVS | 204 V | 0.73 mA | 0.73 mA | 2.5 W | 300 W | 150 V | 5 mA | 130 Ω | 1300 ·10⁶/°C | |
| BZD23C160 | A8 | a1 | PH | Z Diode, TVS | 224 V | 0.67 mA | 0.67 mA | 2.5 W | 300 W | 160 V | 5 mA | 150 Ω | 1300 ·10⁶/°C | |
| BZD23C180 | A8 | a1 | PH | Z Diode, TVS | 249 V | 0.6 mA | 0.6 mA | 2.5 W | 300 W | 180 V | 5 mA | 180 Ω | 1300 ·10⁶/°C | |
| BZD23C200 | A8 | a1 | PH | Z Diode, TVS | 276 V | 0.54 mA | 0.54 mA | 2.5 W | 300 W | 200 V | 5 mA | 200 Ω | 1300 ·10⁶/°C | |
| BZD23C220 | A8 | a1 | PH | Z Diode, TVS | 305 V | 0.5 mA | 0.5 mA | 2.5 W | 300 W | 220 V | 2 mA | 350 Ω | 1300 ·10⁶/°C | |
| BZD23C240 | A8 | a1 | PH | Z Diode, TVS | 336 V | 0.45 mA | 0.45 mA | 2.5 W | 300 W | 240 V | 2 mA | 400 Ω | 1300 ·10⁶/°C | |
| BZD23C270 | A8 | a1 | PH | Z Diode, TVS | 380 V | 0.4 mA | 0.4 mA | 2.5 W | 300 W | 270 V | 2 mA | 450 Ω | 1300 ·10⁶/°C | |
| BZD23C300 | A8 | a1 | PH | Z Diode, TVS | 419 V | 0.36 mA | 0.36 mA | 2.5 W | 300 W | | | | | TVS only |
| BZD23C330 | A8 | a1 | PH | Z Diode, TVS | 459 V | 0.33 mA | 0.33 mA | 2.5 W | 300 W | | | | | TVS only |
| BZD23C360 | A8 | a1 | PH | Z Diode, TVS | 498 V | 0.3 mA | 0.3 mA | 2.5 W | 300 W | | | | | TVS only |
| BZD23C390 | A8 | a1 | PH | Z Diode, TVS | 537 V | 0.28 mA | 0.28 mA | 2.5 W | 300 W | | | | | TVS only |
| BZD23C430 | A8 | a1 | PH | Z Diode, TVS | 603 V | 0.25 mA | 0.25 mA | 2.5 W | 300 W | | | | | TVS only |
| BZD23C470 | A8 | a1 | PH | Z Diode, TVS | 655 V | 0.23 mA | 0.23 mA | 2.5 W | 300 W | | | | | TVS only |
| BZD23C510 | A8 | a1 | PH | Z Diode, TVS | 707 V | 0.21 mA | 0.21 mA | 2.5 W | 300 W | | | | | TVS only |
| BZD27C3V6 | D5 | a1 | PH | Z Diode, TVS | | 45 mA | 45 mA | 1.7 W | | 3.6 V | 100 mA | 4 Ω | -1400 ·10⁶/°C | ZD only |
| BZD27C3V9 | D5 | a1 | PH | Z Diode, TVS | | 43 mA | 43 mA | 1.7 W | | 3.9 V | 100 mA | 4 Ω | -1400 ·10⁶/°C | ZD only |
| BZD27C4V3 | D5 | a1 | PH | Z Diode, TVS | | 40 mA | 40 mA | 1.7 W | | 4.3 V | 100 mA | 4 Ω | -1200 ·10⁶/°C | ZD only |
| BZD27C4V7 | D5 | a1 | PH | Z Diode, TVS | | 38 mA | 38 mA | 1.7 W | | 4.7 V | 100 mA | 3 Ω | -1000 ·10⁶/°C | ZD only |
| BZD27C5V1 | D5 | a1 | PH | Z Diode, TVS | | 35 mA | 35 mA | 1.7 W | | 5.1 V | 100 mA | 3 Ω | -800 ·10⁶/°C | ZD only |
| BZD27C5V6 | D5 | a1 | PH | Z Diode, TVS | | 32 mA | 32 mA | 1.7 W | | 5.6 V | 100 mA | 2 Ω | 400 ·10⁶/°C | ZD only |
| BZD27C6V2 | D5 | a1 | PH | Z Diode, TVS | | 28 mA | 28 mA | 1.7 W | | 6.2 V | 100 mA | 2 Ω | 600 ·10⁶/°C | ZD only |
| BZD27C6V8 | D5 | a1 | PH | Z Diode, TVS | | 25 mA | 25 mA | 1.7 W | | 6.8 V | 100 mA | 1 Ω | 700 ·10⁶/°C | ZD only |
| BZD27C7V5 | D5 | a1 | PH | Z Diode, TVS | 11.3 V | 23.3 mA | 23.3 mA | 2.3 W | 300 W | 7.5 V | 100 mA | 1 Ω | 700 ·10⁶/°C | |
| BZD27C8V2 | D5 | a1 | PH | Z Diode, TVS | 12.3 V | 12.2 mA | 12.2 mA | 2.3 W | 300 W | 8.2 V | 100 mA | 1 Ω | 800 ·10⁶/°C | |
| BZD27C9V1 | D5 | a1 | PH | Z Diode, TVS | 13.3 V | 11.3 mA | 11.3 mA | 2.3 W | 300 W | 9.1 V | 50 mA | 2 Ω | 800 ·10⁶/°C | |
| BZD27C10 | D5 | a1 | PH | Z Diode, TVS | 14.8 V | 10.1 mA | 10.1 mA | 2.3 W | 300 W | 10 V | 50 mA | 2 Ω | 900 ·10⁶/°C | |
| BZD27C11 | D5 | a1 | PH | Z Diode, TVS | 15.7 V | 9.6 mA | 9.6 mA | 2.3 W | 300 W | 11 V | 50 mA | 4 Ω | 1000 ·10⁶/°C | |
| BZD27C12 | D5 | a1 | PH | Z Diode, TVS | 17 V | 8.8 mA | 8.8 mA | 2.3 W | 300 W | 12 V | 50 mA | 4 Ω | 1000 ·10⁶/°C | |
| BZD27C13 | D5 | a1 | PH | Z Diode, TVS | 18.9 V | 7.9 mA | 7.9 mA | 2.3 W | 300 W | 13 V | 50 mA | 5 Ω | 1000 ·10⁶/°C | |
| BZD27C15 | D5 | a1 | PH | Z Diode, TVS | 20.9 V | 7.2 mA | 7.2 mA | 2.3 W | 300 W | 15 V | 50 mA | 5 Ω | 1000 ·10⁶/°C | |
| BZD27C16 | D5 | a1 | PH | Z Diode, TVS | 22.9 V | 6.6 mA | 6.6 mA | 2.3 W | 300 W | 16 V | 25 mA | 6 Ω | 1100 ·10⁶/°C | |
| BZD27C18 | D5 | a1 | PH | Z Diode, TVS | 25.6 V | 5.9 mA | 5.9 mA | 2.3 W | 300 W | 18 V | 25 mA | 6 Ω | 1100 ·10⁶/°C | |
| BZD27C20 | D5 | a1 | PH | Z Diode, TVS | 28.4 V | 5.3 mA | 5.3 mA | 2.3 W | 300 W | 20 V | 25 mA | 6 Ω | 1100 ·10⁶/°C | |
| BZD27C22 | D5 | a1 | PH | Z Diode, TVS | 31 V | 4.8 mA | 4.8 mA | 2.3 W | 300 W | 22 V | 25 mA | 6 Ω | 1100 ·10⁶/°C | |
| BZD27C24 | D5 | a1 | PH | Z Diode, TVS | 33.8 V | 4.4 mA | 4.4 mA | 2.3 W | 300 W | 24 V | 25 mA | 7 Ω | 1100 ·10⁶/°C | |
| BZD27C27 | D5 | a1 | PH | Z Diode, TVS | 38.1 V | 3.9 mA | 3.9 mA | 2.3 W | 300 W | 27 V | 25 mA | 7 Ω | 1100 ·10⁶/°C | |
| BZD27C30 | D5 | a1 | PH | Z Diode, TVS | 42.2 V | 3.6 mA | 3.6 mA | 2.3 W | 300 W | 30 V | 25 mA | 8 Ω | 1100 ·10⁶/°C | |
| BZD27C33 | D5 | a1 | PH | Z Diode, TVS | 46.2 V | 3.2 mA | 3.2 mA | 2.3 W | 300 W | 33 V | 25 mA | 8 Ω | 1100 ·10⁶/°C | |
| BZD27C36 | D5 | a1 | PH | Z Diode, TVS | 50.1 V | 3 mA | 3 mA | 2.3 W | 300 W | 36 V | 10 mA | 21 Ω | 1100 ·10⁶/°C | |
| BZD27C39 | D5 | a1 | PH | Z Diode, TVS | 54.1 V | 2.8 mA | 2.8 mA | 2.3 W | 300 W | 39 V | 10 mA | 21 Ω | 1100 ·10⁶/°C | |

| Type | Case | Pin-code | | | Vcla/Vbro | Its | Izm | Pv | Pvts | Vz | Iz/Is | rz | TK | |
|---|---|---|---|---|---|---|---|---|---|---|---|---|---|---|
| | | | | **Maximum Ratings** | | | | | | **Electrical Characteristics** | | | | |
| BZD27C43 | D5 | a1 | PH | Z Diode, TVS | 60.7 V | 2.5 mA | 2.5 mA | 2.3 W | 300 W | 43 V | 10 mA | 24 Ω | $1200 \cdot 10^6/°C$ | |
| BZD27C47 | D5 | a1 | PH | Z Diode, TVS | 65.5 V | 2.3 mA | 2.3 mA | 2.3 W | 300 W | 47 V | 10 mA | 24 Ω | $1200 \cdot 10^6/°C$ | |
| BZD27C51 | D5 | a1 | PH | Z Diode, TVS | 70.8 V | 2.1 mA | 2.1 mA | 2.3 W | 300 W | 51 V | 10 mA | 25 Ω | $1200 \cdot 10^6/°C$ | |
| BZD27C56 | D5 | a1 | PH | Z Diode, TVS | 78.6 V | 1.9 mA | 1.9 mA | 2.3 W | 300 W | 56 V | 10 mA | 25 Ω | $1200 \cdot 10^6/°C$ | |
| BZD27C62 | D5 | a1 | PH | Z Diode, TVS | 86.5 V | 1.7 mA | 1.7 mA | 2.3 W | 300 W | 62 V | 10 mA | 25 Ω | $1300 \cdot 10^6/°C$ | |
| BZD27C68 | D5 | a1 | PH | Z Diode, TVS | 94.4 V | 1.6 mA | 1.6 mA | 2.3 W | 300 W | 68 V | 10 mA | 25 Ω | $1300 \cdot 10^6/°C$ | |
| BZD27C75 | D5 | a1 | PH | Z Diode, TVS | 103.5 V | 1.5 mA | 1.5 mA | 2.3 W | 300 W | 75 V | 10 mA | 30 Ω | $1300 \cdot 10^6/°C$ | |
| BZD27C82 | D5 | a1 | PH | Z Diode, TVS | 114 V | 1.3 mA | 1.3 mA | 2.3 W | 300 W | 82 V | 10 mA | 30 Ω | $1300 \cdot 10^6/°C$ | |
| BZD27C91 | D5 | a1 | PH | Z Diode, TVS | 126 V | 1.2 mA | 1.2 mA | 2.3 W | 300 W | 91 V | 5 mA | 60 Ω | $1300 \cdot 10^6/°C$ | |
| BZD27C100 | D5 | a1 | PH | Z Diode, TVS | 139 V | 1.1 mA | 1.1 mA | 2.3 W | 300 W | 100 V | 5 mA | 60 Ω | $1300 \cdot 10^6/°C$ | |
| BZD27C110 | D5 | a1 | PH | Z Diode, TVS | 152 V | 1 mA | 1 mA | 2.3 W | 300 W | 110 V | 5 mA | 80 Ω | $1300 \cdot 10^6/°C$ | |
| BZD27C120 | D5 | a1 | PH | Z Diode, TVS | 167 V | 0.9 mA | 0.9 mA | 2.3 W | 300 W | 120 V | 5 mA | 80 Ω | $1300 \cdot 10^6/°C$ | |
| BZD27C130 | D5 | a1 | PH | Z Diode, TVS | 185 V | 0.81 mA | 0.81 mA | 2.3 W | 300 W | 130 V | 5 mA | 110 Ω | $1300 \cdot 10^6/°C$ | |
| BZD27C150 | D5 | a1 | PH | Z Diode, TVS | 204 V | 0.73 mA | 0.73 mA | 2.3 W | 300 W | 150 V | 5 mA | 130 Ω | $1300 \cdot 10^6/°C$ | |
| BZD27C160 | D5 | a1 | PH | Z Diode, TVS | 224 V | 0.67 mA | 0.67 mA | 2.3 W | 300 W | 160 V | 5 mA | 150 Ω | $1300 \cdot 10^6/°C$ | |
| BZD27C180 | D5 | a1 | PH | Z Diode, TVS | 249 V | 0.6 mA | 0.6 mA | 2.3 W | 300 W | 180 V | 5 mA | 180 Ω | $1300 \cdot 10^6/°C$ | |
| BZD27C200 | D5 | a1 | PH | Z Diode, TVS | 276 V | 0.54 mA | 0.54 mA | 2.3 W | 300 W | 200 V | 5 mA | 200 Ω | $1300 \cdot 10^6/°C$ | |
| BZD27C220 | D5 | a1 | PH | Z Diode, TVS | 305 V | 0.5 mA | 0.5 mA | 2.3 W | 300 W | 220 V | 2 mA | 350 Ω | $1300 \cdot 10^6/°C$ | |
| BZD27C240 | D5 | a1 | PH | Z Diode, TVS | 336 V | 0.45 mA | 0.45 mA | 2.3 W | 300 W | 240 V | 2 mA | 400 Ω | $1300 \cdot 10^6/°C$ | |
| BZD27C270 | D5 | a1 | PH | Z Diode, TVS | 380 V | 0.4 mA | 0.4 mA | 2.3 W | 300 W | 270 V | 2 mA | 450 Ω | $1300 \cdot 10^6/°C$ | |
| BZD27C300 | D5 | a1 | PH | Z Diode, TVS | 419 V | 0.36 mA | 0.36 mA | 2.3 W | 300 W | | | | TVS only | |
| BZD27C330 | D5 | a1 | PH | Z Diode, TVS | 459 V | 0.33 mA | 0.33 mA | 2.3 W | 300 W | | | | TVS only | |
| BZD27C360 | D5 | a1 | PH | Z Diode, TVS | 498 V | 0.3 mA | 0.3 mA | 2.3 W | 300 W | | | | TVS only | |
| BZD27C390 | D5 | a1 | PH | Z Diode, TVS | 537 V | 0.28 mA | 0.28 mA | 2.3 W | 300 W | | | | TVS only | |
| BZD27C430 | D5 | a1 | PH | Z Diode, TVS | 603 V | 0.25 mA | 0.25 mA | 2.3 W | 300 W | | | | TVS only | |
| BZD27C470 | D5 | a1 | PH | Z Diode, TVS | 655 V | 0.23 mA | 0.23 mA | 2.3 W | 300 W | | | | TVS only | |
| BZD27C510 | D5 | a1 | PH | Z Diode, TVS | 707 V | 0.21 mA | 0.21 mA | 2.3 W | 300 W | | | | TVS only | |
| BZM85C2V7 | D1 | a1 | SG | Z Diode | | | 370 mA | 1.3 W | | 2.7 V | 80 mA | <20 Ω | $-800 \cdot 10^6/°C$ | |
| BZM85C3V0 | D1 | a1 | SG | Z Diode | | | 340 mA | 1.3 W | | 3.0 V | 80 mA | <20 Ω | $-800 \cdot 10^6/°C$ | |
| BZM85C3V3 | D1 | a1 | SG | Z Diode | | | 320 mA | 1.3 W | | 3.3 V | 80 mA | <20 Ω | $-800 \cdot 10^6/°C$ | P |
| BZM85C3V6 | D1 | a1 | SG | Z Diode | | | 290 mA | 1.3 W | | 3.6 V | 60 mA | <20 Ω | $-800 \cdot 10^6/°C$ | P |
| BZM85C3V9 | D1 | a1 | SG | Z Diode | | | 280 mA | 1.3 W | | 3.9 V | 60 mA | <15 Ω | $-700 \cdot 10^6/°C$ | P |
| BZM85C4V3 | D1 | a1 | SG | Z Diode | | | 250 mA | 1.3 W | | 4.3 V | 50 mA | <13 Ω | $-500 \cdot 10^6/°C$ | P |
| BZM85C4V7 | D1 | a1 | SG | Z Diode | | | 215 mA | 1.3 W | | 4.7 V | 45 mA | <13 Ω | $400 \cdot 10^6/°C$ | P |
| BZM85C5V1 | D1 | a1 | SG | Z Diode | | | 200 mA | 1.3 W | | 5.1 V | 45 mA | <10 Ω | $400 \cdot 10^6/°C$ | P |
| BZM85C5V6 | D1 | a1 | SG | Z Diode | | | 190 mA | 1.3 W | | 5.6 V | 45 mA | <7 Ω | $450 \cdot 10^6/°C$ | P |
| BZM85C6V2 | D1 | a1 | SG | Z Diode | | | 170 mA | 1.3 W | | 6.2 V | 35 mA | <4 Ω | $550 \cdot 10^6/°C$ | P |
| BZM85C6V8 | D1 | a1 | SG | Z Diode | | | 155 mA | 1.3 W | | 6.8 V | 35 mA | <3.5 Ω | $600 \cdot 10^6/°C$ | P |
| BZM85C7V5 | D1 | a1 | SG | Z Diode | | | 140 mA | 1.3 W | | 7.5 V | 35 mA | <3 Ω | $650 \cdot 10^6/°C$ | P |
| BZM85C8V2 | D1 | a1 | SG | Z Diode | | | 130 mA | 1.3 W | | 8.2 V | 25 mA | <5 Ω | $700 \cdot 10^6/°C$ | P |

| Type | Case | Pin-code | | | Maximum Ratings | | | | | Electrical Characteristics | | | | |
|---|---|---|---|---|---|---|---|---|---|---|---|---|---|---|
| | | | | | Vcla Vbro | Its | Izm | Pv | Pvts | Vz | Iz Is | rz | TK | |
| BZM85C9V1 | D1 | a1 | SG | Z Diode | | | 120 mA | 1.3 W | | 9.1 V | 25 mA | <5 Ω | 750·10⁶/°C | P |
| BZM85C10 | D1 | a1 | SG | Z Diode | | | 105 mA | 1.3 W | | 10 V | 25 mA | <7 Ω | 800·10⁶/°C | P |
| BZM85C11 | D1 | a1 | SG | Z Diode | | | 97 mA | 1.3 W | | 11 V | 20 mA | <8 Ω | 800·10⁶/°C | |
| BZM85C12 | D1 | a1 | SG | Z Diode | | | 88 mA | 1.3 W | | 12 V | 20 mA | <9 Ω | 850·10⁶/°C | P |
| BZM85C13 | D1 | a1 | SG | Z Diode | | | 79 mA | 1.3 W | | 13 V | 20 mA | <10 Ω | 850·10⁶/°C | |
| BZM85C15 | D1 | a1 | SG | Z Diode | | | 71 mA | 1.3 W | | 15 V | 15 mA | <15 Ω | 900·10⁶/°C | P |
| BZM85C16 | D1 | a1 | SG | Z Diode | | | 66 mA | 1.3 W | | 16 V | 15 mA | <15 Ω | 900·10⁶/°C | |
| BZM85C18 | D1 | a1 | SG | Z Diode | | | 62 mA | 1.3 W | | 18 V | 15 mA | <20 Ω | 900·10⁶/°C | |
| BZM85C20 | D1 | a1 | SG | Z Diode | | | 56 mA | 1.3 W | | 20 V | 10 mA | <24 Ω | 900·10⁶/°C | |
| BZM85C22 | D1 | a1 | SG | Z Diode | | | 52 mA | 1.3 W | | 22 V | 10 mA | <25 Ω | 950·10⁶/°C | |
| BZM85C24 | D1 | a1 | SG | Z Diode | | | 47 mA | 1.3 W | | 24 V | 10 mA | <25 Ω | 950·10⁶/°C | |
| BZM85C27 | D1 | a1 | SG | Z Diode | | | 41 mA | 1.3 W | | 27 V | 8 mA | <30 Ω | 950·10⁶/°C | |
| BZM85C30 | D1 | a1 | SG | Z Diode | | | 36 mA | 1.3 W | | 30 V | 8 mA | <30 Ω | 950·10⁶/°C | |
| BZM85C33 | D1 | a1 | SG | Z Diode | | | 33 mA | 1.3 W | | 33 V | 8 mA | <35 Ω | 950·10⁶/°C | |
| BZM85C36 | D1 | a1 | SG | Z Diode | | | 30 mA | 1.3 W | | 36 V | 8 mA | <40 Ω | 950·10⁶/°C | |
| BZM85C39 | D1 | a1 | SG | Z Diode | | | 28 mA | 1.3 W | | 39 V | 6 mA | <50 Ω | 950·10⁶/°C | |
| BZM85C43 | D1 | a1 | SG | Z Diode | | | 26 mA | 1.3 W | | 43 V | 6 mA | <50 Ω | 950·10⁶/°C | |
| BZM85C47 | D1 | a1 | SG | Z Diode | | | 23 mA | 1.3 W | | 47 V | 4 mA | <90 Ω | 950·10⁶/°C | |
| BZM85C51 | D1 | a1 | SG | Z Diode | | | 21 mA | 1.3 W | | 51 V | 4 mA | <115 Ω | 950·10⁶/°C | |
| BZM85C56 | D1 | a1 | SG | Z Diode | | | 19 mA | 1.3 W | | 56 V | 4 mA | <120 Ω | 950·10⁶/°C | |
| BZM85C62 | D1 | a1 | SG | Z Diode | | | 16 mA | 1.3 W | | 62 V | 4 mA | <125 Ω | 950·10⁶/°C | |
| BZM85C68 | D1 | a1 | SG | Z Diode | | | 15 mA | 1.3 W | | 68 V | 4 mA | <130 Ω | 950·10⁶/°C | |
| BZM85C75 | D1 | a1 | SG | Z Diode | | | 14 mA | 1.3 W | | 75 V | 4 mA | <135 Ω | 950·10⁶/°C | |
| BZM85C82 | D1 | a1 | SG | Z Diode | | | 12 mA | 1.3 W | | 82 V | 2.7 mA | <200 Ω | 1200·10⁶/°C | |
| BZM85C91 | D1 | a1 | SG | Z Diode | | | 10 mA | 1.3 W | | 91 V | 2.7 mA | <250 Ω | 1200·10⁶/°C | |
| BZM85C100 | D1 | a1 | SG | Z Diode | | | 9 mA | 1.3 W | | 100 V | 2.7 mA | <350 Ω | 1200·10⁶/°C | |
| BZT03C7V5 | A4 | a1 | PH | Z Diode, TVS | 11.3 V | 26.5 mA | 26.5 mA | 3.25 W | 600 W | 7.5 V | 100 mA | <1 Ω | 700·10⁶/°C | |
| BZT03C8V2 | A4 | a1 | PH | Z Diode, TVS | 12.3 V | 24.4 mA | 24.4 mA | 3.25 W | 600 W | 8.2 V | 100 mA | <1 Ω | 800·10⁶/°C | |
| BZT03C9V1 | A4 | a1 | PH | Z Diode, TVS | 13.3 V | 22.7 mA | 22.7 mA | 3.25 W | 600 W | 9.1 V | 50 mA | <2 Ω | 800·10⁶/°C | |
| BZT03C10 | A4 | a1 | PH | Z Diode, TVS | 14.8 V | 20.3 mA | 20.3 mA | 3.25 W | 600 W | 10 V | 50 mA | <2 Ω | 900·10⁶/°C | |
| BZT03C11 | A4 | a1 | PH | Z Diode, TVS | 15.7 V | 19.1 mA | 19.1 mA | 3.25 W | 600 W | 11 V | 50 mA | <4 Ω | 1000·10⁶/°C | |
| BZT03C12 | A4 | a1 | PH | Z Diode, TVS | 17 V | 17.7 mA | 17.7 mA | 3.25 W | 600 W | 12 V | 50 mA | <4 Ω | 1000·10⁶/°C | |
| BZT03C13 | A4 | a1 | PH | Z Diode, TVS | 18.9 V | 15.9 mA | 15.9 mA | 3.25 W | 600 W | 13 V | 50 mA | <5 Ω | 1000·10⁶/°C | |
| BZT03C15 | A4 | a1 | PH | Z Diode, TVS | 20.9 V | 14.4 mA | 14.4 mA | 3.25 W | 600 W | 15 V | 50 mA | <5 Ω | 1000·10⁶/°C | |
| BZT03C16 | A4 | a1 | PH | Z Diode, TVS | 22.9 V | 13.1 mA | 13.1 mA | 3.25 W | 600 W | 16 V | 25 mA | <6 Ω | 1100·10⁶/°C | |
| BZT03C18 | A4 | a1 | PH | Z Diode, TVS | 25.6 V | 11.7 mA | 11.7 mA | 3.25 W | 600 W | 18 V | 25 mA | <6 Ω | 1100·10⁶/°C | |
| BZT03C20 | A4 | a1 | PH | Z Diode, TVS | 28.4 V | 10.6 mA | 10.6 mA | 3.25 W | 600 W | 20 V | 25 mA | <6 Ω | 1100·10⁶/°C | |
| BZT03C22 | A4 | a1 | PH | Z Diode, TVS | 31 V | 9.7 mA | 9.7 mA | 3.25 W | 600 W | 22 V | 25 mA | <6 Ω | 1100·10⁶/°C | |
| BZT03C24 | A4 | a1 | PH | Z Diode, TVS | 33.8 V | 8.9 mA | 8.9 mA | 3.25 W | 600 W | 24 V | 25 mA | <7 Ω | 1100·10⁶/°C | |
| BZT03C27 | A4 | a1 | PH | Z Diode, TVS | 38.1 V | 7.9 mA | 7.9 mA | 3.25 W | 600 W | 27 V | 25 mA | <7 Ω | 1100·10⁶/°C | |

| Type | Case | Pin-code | | | Vcla Vbro | Its | Izm | Pv | Pvts | Vz | Iz Is | rz | TK | |
|---|---|---|---|---|---|---|---|---|---|---|---|---|---|---|
| BZT03C30 | A4 | a1 | PH | Z Diode, TVS | 42.2 V | 7.1 mA | 7.1 mA | 3.25 W | 600 W | 30 V | 25 mA | <8 Ω | $1100 \cdot 10^6/°C$ | |
| BZT03C33 | A4 | a1 | PH | Z Diode, TVS | 46.2 V | 6.5 mA | 6.5 mA | 3.25 W | 600 W | 33 V | 25 mA | <8 Ω | $1100 \cdot 10^6/°C$ | |
| BZT03C36 | A4 | a1 | PH | Z Diode, TVS | 50.1 V | 6 mA | 6 mA | 3.25 W | 600 W | 36 V | 10 mA | <21 Ω | $1100 \cdot 10^6/°C$ | |
| BZT03C39 | A4 | a1 | PH | Z Diode, TVS | 54.1 V | 5.5 mA | 5.5 mA | 3.25 W | 600 W | 39 V | 10 mA | <21 Ω | $1100 \cdot 10^6/°C$ | |
| BZT03C43 | A4 | a1 | PH | Z Diode, TVS | 60.7 V | 4.9 mA | 4.9 mA | 3.25 W | 600 W | 43 V | 10 mA | <24 Ω | $1200 \cdot 10^6/°C$ | |
| BZT03C47 | A4 | a1 | PH | Z Diode, TVS | 65.5 V | 4.6 mA | 4.6 mA | 3.25 W | 600 W | 47 V | 10 mA | <24 Ω | $1200 \cdot 10^6/°C$ | |
| BZT03C51 | A4 | a1 | PH | Z Diode, TVS | 70.8 V | 4.2 mA | 4.2 mA | 3.25 W | 600 W | 51 V | 10 mA | <25 Ω | $1200 \cdot 10^6/°C$ | |
| BZT03C56 | A4 | a1 | PH | Z Diode, TVS | 78.6 V | 3.8 mA | 3.8 mA | 3.25 W | 600 W | 56 V | 10 mA | <25 Ω | $1200 \cdot 10^6/°C$ | |
| BZT03C62 | A4 | a1 | PH | Z Diode, TVS | 86.5 V | 3.5 mA | 3.5 mA | 3.25 W | 600 W | 62 V | 10 mA | <25 Ω | $1300 \cdot 10^6/°C$ | |
| BZT03C68 | A4 | a1 | PH | Z Diode, TVS | 94.4 V | 3.2 mA | 3.2 mA | 3.25 W | 600 W | 68 V | 10 mA | <25 Ω | $1300 \cdot 10^6/°C$ | |
| BZT03C75 | A4 | a1 | PH | Z Diode, TVS | 103.5 V | 2.9 mA | 2.9 mA | 3.25 W | 600 W | 75 V | 10 mA | <30 Ω | $1300 \cdot 10^6/°C$ | |
| BZT03C82 | A4 | a1 | PH | Z Diode, TVS | 114 V | 2.6 mA | 2.6 mA | 3.25 W | 600 W | 82 V | 10 mA | <30 Ω | $1300 \cdot 10^6/°C$ | |
| BZT03C91 | A4 | a1 | PH | Z Diode, TVS | 126 V | 2.4 mA | 2.4 mA | 3.25 W | 600 W | 91 V | 5 mA | <60 Ω | $1300 \cdot 10^6/°C$ | |
| BZT03C100 | A4 | a1 | PH | Z Diode, TVS | 139 V | 2.2 mA | 2.2 mA | 3.25 W | 600 W | 100 V | 5 mA | <60 Ω | $1300 \cdot 10^6/°C$ | |
| BZT03C110 | A4 | a1 | PH | Z Diode, TVS | 152 V | 2 mA | 2 mA | 3.25 W | 600 W | 110 V | 5 mA | <80 Ω | $1300 \cdot 10^6/°C$ | |
| BZT03C120 | A4 | a1 | PH | Z Diode, TVS | 167 V | 1.8 mA | 1.8 mA | 3.25 W | 600 W | 120 V | 5 mA | <80 Ω | $1300 \cdot 10^6/°C$ | |
| BZT03C130 | A4 | a1 | PH | Z Diode, TVS | 185 V | 1.6 mA | 1.6 mA | 3.25 W | 600 W | 130 V | 5 mA | <110 Ω | $1300 \cdot 10^6/°C$ | |
| BZT03C150 | A4 | a1 | PH | Z Diode, TVS | 204 V | 1.5 mA | 1.5 mA | 3.25 W | 600 W | 150 V | 5 mA | <130 Ω | $1300 \cdot 10^6/°C$ | |
| BZT03C160 | A4 | a1 | PH | Z Diode, TVS | 224 V | 1.3 mA | 1.3 mA | 3.25 W | 600 W | 160 V | 5 mA | <150 Ω | $1300 \cdot 10^6/°C$ | |
| BZT03C180 | A4 | a1 | PH | Z Diode, TVS | 249 V | 1.2 mA | 1.2 mA | 3.25 W | 600 W | 180 V | 5 mA | <180 Ω | $1300 \cdot 10^6/°C$ | |
| BZT03C200 | A4 | a1 | PH | Z Diode, TVS | 276 V | .1.1 mA | 1.1 mA | 3.25 W | 600 W | 200 V | 5 mA | <200 Ω | $1300 \cdot 10^6/°C$ | |
| BZT03C220 | A4 | a1 | PH | Z Diode, TVS | 305 V | 1 mA | 1 mA | 3.25 W | 600 W | 220 V | 2 mA | <350 Ω | $1300 \cdot 10^6/°C$ | |
| BZT03C240 | A4 | a1 | PH | Z Diode, TVS | 336 V | 0.9 mA | 0.9 mA | 3.25 W | 600 W | 240 V | 2 mA | <400 Ω | $1300 \cdot 10^6/°C$ | |
| BZT03C270 | A4 | a1 | PH | Z Diode, TVS | 380 V | 0.8 mA | 0.8 mA | 3.25 W | 600 W | 270 V | 2 mA | <450 Ω | $1300 \cdot 10^6/°C$ | |
| BZT03C300 | A4 | a1 | PH | Z Diode, TVS | 419 V | 0.72 mA | 0.72 mA | 3.25 W | 600 W | | | | | TVS only |
| BZT03C330 | A4 | a1 | PH | Z Diode, TVS | 459 V | 0.65 mA | 0.65 mA | 3.25 W | 600 W | | | | | TVS only |
| BZT03C360 | A4 | a1 | PH | Z Diode, TVS | 498 V | 0.6 mA | 0.6 mA | 3.25 W | 600 W | | | | | TVS only |
| BZT03C390 | A4 | a1 | PH | Z Diode, TVS | 537 V | 0.56 mA | 0.56 mA | 3.25 W | 600 W | | | | | TVS only |
| BZT03C430 | A4 | a1 | PH | Z Diode, TVS | 603 V | 0.5 mA | 0.5 mA | 3.25 W | 600 W | | | | | TVS only |
| BZT03C470 | A4 | a1 | PH | Z Diode, TVS | 655 V | 0.45 mA | 0.45 mA | 3.25 W | 600 W | | | | | TVS only |
| BZT03C510 | A4 | a1 | PH | Z Diode, TVS | 707 V | 0.42 mA | 0.42 mA | 3.25 W | 600 W | | | | | |
| BZT03D7V5 | A4 | a1 | TE | TVS, Z Diode | 11.6 V | 26.5 mA | 26.5 mA | 3.25 W | 600 W | 7.5 V | 100 mA | 1 Ω | $700 \cdot 10^6/°C$ | |
| BZT03D8V2 | A4 | a1 | TE | TVS, Z Diode | 12.6 V | 24.4 mA | 24.4 mA | 3.25 W | 600 W | 8.2 V | 100 mA | 1 Ω | $800 \cdot 10^6/°C$ | |
| BZT03D9V1 | A4 | a1 | TE | TVS, Z Diode | 13.7 V | 22.7 mA | 22.7 mA | 3.25 W | 600 W | 9.1 V | 50 mA | 2 Ω | $800 \cdot 10^6/°C$ | |
| BZT03D10 | A4 | a1 | TE | TVS, Z Diode | 15.2 V | 20.3 mA | 20.3 mA | 3.25 W | 600 W | 10 V | 50 mA | 2 Ω | $900 \cdot 10^6/°C$ | |
| BZT03D11 | A4 | a1 | TE | TVS, Z Diode | 16.2 V | 19.1 mA | 19.1 mA | 3.25 W | 600 W | 11 V | 50 mA | 4 Ω | $1000 \cdot 10^6/°C$ | |
| BZT03D12 | A4 | a1 | TE | TVS, Z Diode | 17.5 V | 17.7 mA | 17.7 mA | 3.25 W | 600 W | 12 V | 50 mA | 4 Ω | $1000 \cdot 10^6/°C$ | |
| BZT03D13 | A4 | a1 | TE | TVS, Z Diode | 19.1 V | 15.9 mA | 15.9 mA | 3.25 W | 600 W | 13 V | 50 mA | 5 Ω | $1000 \cdot 10^6/°C$ | |
| BZT03D15 | A4 | a1 | TE | TVS, Z Diode | 21.8 V | 14.4 mA | 14.4 mA | 3.25 W | 600 W | 15 V | 50 mA | 5 Ω | $1000 \cdot 10^6/°C$ | |
| BZT03D16 | A4 | a1 | TE | TVS, Z Diode | 23.4 V | 13.1 mA | 13.1 mA | 3.25 W | 600 W | 16 V | 25 mA | 6 Ω | $1100 \cdot 10^6/°C$ | |

142

| Type | Case | Pin-code | | | Maximum Ratings | | | | | Electrical Characteristics | | | | |
|---|---|---|---|---|---|---|---|---|---|---|---|---|---|---|
| | | | | | $V_{cla}$ / $V_{bro}$ | $I_{ts}$ | $I_{zm}$ | $P_v$ | $P_{vts}$ | $V_z$ | $I_z$ / $I_s$ | $r_z$ | TK | |
| BZT03D18 | A4 | a1 | TE | TVS, Z Diode | 26.3 V | 11.7 mA | 11.7 mA | 3.25 W | 600 W | 18 V | 25 mA | 6 Ω | 1100 ·10⁶/°C | |
| BZT03D20 | A4 | a1 | TE | TVS, Z Diode | 29.2 V | 10.6 mA | 10.6 mA | 3.25 W | 600 W | 20 V | 25 mA | 6 Ω | 1100 ·10⁶/°C | |
| BZT03D22 | A4 | a1 | TE | TVS, Z Diode | 31.9 V | 9.7 mA | 9.7 mA | 3.25 W | 600 W | 22 V | 25 mA | 6 Ω | 1100 ·10⁶/°C | |
| BZT03D24 | A4 | a1 | TE | TVS, Z Diode | 34.6 V | 8.9 mA | 8.9 mA | 3.25 W | 600 W | 24 V | 25 mA | 7 Ω | 1100 ·10⁶/°C | |
| BZT03D27 | A4 | a1 | TE | TVS, Z Diode | 39 V | 7.9 mA | 7.9 mA | 3.25 W | 600 W | 27 V | 25 mA | 7 Ω | 1100 ·10⁶/°C | |
| BZT03D30 | A4 | a1 | TE | TVS, Z Diode | 43.5 V | 7.1 mA | 7.1 mA | 3.25 W | 600 W | 30 V | 25 mA | 8 Ω | 1100 ·10⁶/°C | |
| BZT03D33 | A4 | a1 | TE | TVS, Z Diode | 47.5 V | 6.5 mA | 6.5 mA | 3.25 W | 600 W | 33 V | 25 mA | 8 Ω | 1100 ·10⁶/°C | |
| BZT03D36 | A4 | a1 | TE | TVS, Z Diode | 51.5 V | 6 mA | 6 mA | 3.25 W | 600 W | 36 V | 10 mA | 21 Ω | 1100 ·10⁶/°C | |
| BZT03D39 | A4 | a1 | TE | TVS, Z Diode | 56 V | 5.5 mA | 5.5 mA | 3.25 W | 600 W | 39 V | 10 mA | 21 Ω | 1100 ·10⁶/°C | |
| BZT03D43 | A4 | a1 | TE | TVS, Z Diode | 62 V | 4.9 mA | 4.9 mA | 3.25 W | 600 W | 43 V | 10 mA | 24 Ω | 1200 ·10⁶/°C | |
| BZT03D47 | A4 | a1 | TE | TVS, Z Diode | 67.5 V | 4.6 mA | 4.6 mA | 3.25 W | 600 W | 47 V | 10 mA | 24 Ω | 1200 ·10⁶/°C | |
| BZT03D51 | A4 | a1 | TE | TVS, Z Diode | 73 V | 4.2 mA | 4.2 mA | 3.25 W | 600 W | 51 V | 10 mA | 25 Ω | 1200 ·10⁶/°C | |
| BZT03D56 | A4 | a1 | TE | TVS, Z Diode | 81 V | 3.8 mA | 3.8 mA | 3.25 W | 600 W | 56 V | 10 mA | 25 Ω | 1200 ·10⁶/°C | |
| BZT03D62 | A4 | a1 | TE | TVS, Z Diode | 89 V | 3.5 mA | 3.5 mA | 3.25 W | 600 W | 62 V | 10 mA | 25 Ω | 1300 ·10⁶/°C | |
| BZT03D68 | A4 | a1 | TE | TVS, Z Diode | 97 V | 3.2 mA | 3.2 mA | 3.25 W | 600 W | 68 V | 10 mA | 25 Ω | 1300 ·10⁶/°C | |
| BZT03D75 | A4 | a1 | TE | TVS, Z Diode | 107 V | 2.9 mA | 2.9 mA | 3.25 W | 600 W | 75 V | 10 mA | 30 Ω | 1300 ·10⁶/°C | |
| BZT03D82 | A4 | a1 | TE | TVS, Z Diode | 117 V | 2.6 mA | 2.6 mA | 3.25 W | 600 W | 82 V | 10 mA | 30 Ω | 1300 ·10⁶/°C | |
| BZT03D91 | A4 | a1 | TE | TVS, Z Diode | 130 V | 2.4 mA | 2.4 mA | 3.25 W | 600 W | 91 V | 5 mA | 60 Ω | 1300 ·10⁶/°C | |
| BZT03D100 | A4 | a1 | TE | TVS, Z Diode | 143 V | 2.2 mA | 2.2 mA | 3.25 W | 600 W | 100 V | 5 mA | 60 Ω | 1300 ·10⁶/°C | |
| BZT03D110 | A4 | a1 | TE | TVS, Z Diode | 157 V | 2 mA | 2 mA | 3.25 W | 600 W | 110 V | 5 mA | 80 Ω | 1300 ·10⁶/°C | |
| BZT03D120 | A4 | a1 | TE | TVS, Z Diode | 172 V | 1.8 mA | 1.8 mA | 3.25 W | 600 W | 120 V | 5 mA | 80 Ω | 1300 ·10⁶/°C | |
| BZT03D130 | A4 | a1 | TE | TVS, Z Diode | 187 V | 1.6 mA | 1.6 mA | 3.25 W | 600 W | 130 V | 5 mA | 110 Ω | 1300 ·10⁶/°C | |
| BZT03D150 | A4 | a1 | TE | TVS, Z Diode | 213 V | 1.5 mA | 1.5 mA | 3.25 W | 600 W | 150 V | 5 mA | 130 Ω | 1300 ·10⁶/°C | |
| BZT03D160 | A4 | a1 | TE | TVS, Z Diode | 229 V | 1.3 mA | 1.3 mA | 3.25 W | 600 W | 160 V | 5 mA | 150 Ω | 1300 ·10⁶/°C | |
| BZT03D180 | A4 | a1 | TE | TVS, Z Diode | 256 V | 1.2 mA | 1.2 mA | 3.25 W | 600 W | 180 V | 5 mA | 180 Ω | 1300 ·10⁶/°C | |
| BZT03D200 | A4 | a1 | TE | TVS, Z Diode | 284 V | 1.1 mA | 1.1 mA | 3.25 W | 600 W | 200 V | 5 mA | 200 Ω | 1300 ·10⁶/°C | |
| BZT03D220 | A4 | a1 | TE | TVS, Z Diode | 314 V | 1 mA | 1 mA | 3.25 W | 600 W | 220 V | 2 mA | 350 Ω | 1300 ·10⁶/°C | |
| BZT03D240 | A4 | a1 | TE | TVS, Z Diode | 364 V | 0.9 mA | 0.9 mA | 3.25 W | 600 W | 240 V | 2 mA | 400 Ω | 1300 ·10⁶/°C | |
| BZT03D270 | A4 | a1 | TE | TVS, Z Diode | 388 V | 0.8 mA | 0.8 mA | 3.25 W | 600 W | 270 V | 2 mA | 450 Ω | 1300 ·10⁶/°C | |
| BZT52C2V7 | G4 | a1 | IT | Z Diode | | 134 mA | | 0.4 W | | 2.7 V | 5 mA | 75 Ω | -900 ·10⁶/°C | |
| BZT52C3V0 | G4 | a1 | IT | Z Diode | | 118 mA | | 0.4 W | | 3.0 V | 5 mA | 80 Ω | -900 ·10⁶/°C | |
| BZT52C3V3 | G4 | a1 | IT | Z Diode | | 109 mA | | 0.4 W | | 3.3 V | 5 mA | 80 Ω | -800 ·10⁶/°C | |
| BZT52C3V6 | G4 | a1 | IT | Z Diode | | 100 mA | | 0.4 W | | 3.6 V | 5 mA | 80 Ω | -800 ·10⁶/°C | |
| BZT52C3V9 | G4 | a1 | IT | Z Diode | | 92 mA | | 0.4 W | | 3.9 V | 5 mA | 80 Ω | -700 ·10⁶/°C | |
| BZT52C4V3 | G4 | a1 | IT | Z Diode | | 84 mA | | 0.4 W | | 4.3 V | 5 mA | 80 Ω | -600 ·10⁶/°C | |
| BZT52C4V7 | G4 | a1 | IT | Z Diode | | 76 mA | | 0.4 W | | 4.7 V | 5 mA | 70 Ω | -500 ·10⁶/°C | |
| BZT52C5V1 | G4 | a1 | IT | Z Diode | | 67 mA | | 0.4 W | | 5.1 V | 5 mA | 30 Ω | 400 ·10⁶/°C | |
| BZT52C5V6 | G4 | a1 | IT | Z Diode | | 59 mA | | 0.4 W | | 5.6 V | 5 mA | 10 Ω | 600 ·10⁶/°C | |
| BZT52C6V2 | G4 | a1 | IT | Z Diode | | 54 mA | | 0.4 W | | 6.2 V | 5 mA | 4.8 Ω | 700 ·10⁶/°C | |
| BZT52C6V8 | G4 | a1 | IT | Z Diode | | 49 mA | | 0.4 W | | 6.8 V | 5 mA | 4.5 Ω | 700 ·10⁶/°C | |

| Type | Case | Pin-code | | | Vcla Vbro | Its | Izm | Pv | Pvts | Vz | Iz Is | rz | TK | |
|------|------|----------|---|---|------|-----|-----|-----|------|-----|----|-----|------|---|
| | | | | | | | **Maximum Ratings** | | | | **Electrical Characteristics** | | | |
| BZT52C7V5 | G4 | a1 | IT | Z Diode | | | 44 mA | 0.4 W | | 7.5 V | 5 mA | 4 Ω | $700 \cdot 10^6/°C$ | |
| BZT52C8V2 | G4 | a1 | IT | Z Diode | | | 40 mA | 0.4 W | | 8.2 V | 5 mA | 4.5 Ω | $700 \cdot 10^6/°C$ | |
| BZT52C9V1 | G4 | a1 | IT | Z Diode | | | 36 mA | 0.4 W | | 9.1 V | 5 mA | 4.8 Ω | $800 \cdot 10^6/°C$ | |
| BZT52C10 | G4 | a1 | IT | Z Diode | | | 33 mA | 0.4 W | | 10 V | 5 mA | 5.2 Ω | $800 \cdot 10^6/°C$ | |
| BZT52C11 | G4 | a1 | IT | Z Diode | | | 30 mA | 0.4 W | | 11 V | 5 mA | 6 Ω | $900 \cdot 10^6/°C$ | |
| BZT52C12 | G4 | a1 | IT | Z Diode | | | 28 mA | 0.4 W | | 12 V | 5 mA | 7 Ω | $900 \cdot 10^6/°C$ | |
| BZT52C13 | G4 | a1 | IT | Z Diode | | | 25 mA | 0.4 W | | 13 V | 5 mA | 9 Ω | $900 \cdot 10^6/°C$ | |
| BZT52C15 | G4 | a1 | IT | Z Diode | | | 23 mA | 0.4 W | | 15 V | 5 mA | 11 Ω | $900 \cdot 10^6/°C$ | |
| BZT52C16 | G4 | a1 | IT | Z Diode | | | 20 mA | 0.4 W | | 16 V | 5 mA | 13 Ω | $950 \cdot 10^6/°C$ | |
| BZT52C18 | G4 | a1 | IT | Z Diode | | | 18 mA | 0.4 W | | 18 V | 5 mA | 18 Ω | $950 \cdot 10^6/°C$ | |
| BZT52C20 | G4 | a1 | IT | Z Diode | | | 17 mA | 0.4 W | | 20 V | 5 mA | 20 Ω | $1000 \cdot 10^6/°C$ | |
| BZT52C22 | G4 | a1 | IT | Z Diode | | | 16 mA | 0.4 W | | 22 V | 5 mA | 25 Ω | $1000 \cdot 10^6/°C$ | |
| BZT52C24 | G4 | a1 | IT | Z Diode | | | 13 mA | 0.4 W | | 24 V | 5 mA | 28 Ω | $1000 \cdot 10^6/°C$ | |
| BZT52C27 | G4 | a1 | IT | Z Diode | | | 12 mA | 0.4 W | | 27 V | 5 mA | 30 Ω | $1000 \cdot 10^6/°C$ | |
| BZT52C30 | G4 | a1 | IT | Z Diode | | | 10 mA | 0.4 W | | 30 V | 5 mA | 35 Ω | $1000 \cdot 10^6/°C$ | |
| BZT52C33 | G4 | a1 | IT | Z Diode | | | 9 mA | 0.4 W | | 33 V | 5 mA | 40 Ω | $1000 \cdot 10^6/°C$ | |
| BZT52C36 | G4 | a1 | IT | Z Diode | | | 9 mA | 0.4 W | | 36 V | 5 mA | 40 Ω | $1000 \cdot 10^6/°C$ | |
| BZT52C39 | G4 | a1 | IT | Z Diode | | | 8 mA | 0.4 W | | 39 V | 5 mA | 50 Ω | $1200 \cdot 10^6/°C$ | |
| BZT52C43 | G4 | a1 | IT | Z Diode | | | 7 mA | 0.4 W | | 43 V | 5 mA | 60 Ω | $1200 \cdot 10^6/°C$ | |
| BZT52C47 | G4 | a1 | IT | Z Diode | | | 6 mA | 0.4 W | | 47 V | 5 mA | 70 Ω | $1200 \cdot 10^6/°C$ | |
| BZT52C51 | G4 | a1 | IT | Z Diode | | | 6 mA | 0.4 W | | 51 V | 5 mA | 70 Ω | $1200 \cdot 10^6/°C$ | |
| BZT55C2V4 | -- | a1 | TE | Z Diode | | | 135 mA | | | 2.4 V | 5 mA | <85 Ω | $-800 \cdot 10^6/°C$ | |
| BZT55C2V7 | -- | a1 | TE | Z Diode | | | 125 mA | | | 2.7 V | 5 mA | <85 Ω | $-800 \cdot 10^6/°C$ | |
| BZT55C3V0 | -- | a1 | TE | Z Diode | | | 115 mA | | | 3.0 V | 5 mA | <85 Ω | $-800 \cdot 10^6/°C$ | |
| BZT55C3V3 | -- | a1 | TE | Z Diode | | | 110 mA | | | 3.3 V | 5 mA | <85 Ω | $-800 \cdot 10^6/°C$ | |
| BZT55C3V6 | -- | a1 | TE | Z Diode | | | 105 mA | | | 3.6 V | 5 mA | <85 Ω | $-800 \cdot 10^6/°C$ | |
| BZT55C3V9 | -- | a1 | TE | Z Diode | | | 95 mA | | | 3.9 V | 5 mA | <85 Ω | $-700 \cdot 10^6/°C$ | |
| BZT55C4V3 | -- | a1 | TE | Z Diode | | | 90 mA | | | 4.3 V | 5 mA | <75 Ω | $-400 \cdot 10^6/°C$ | |
| BZT55C4V7 | -- | a1 | TE | Z Diode | | | 85 mA | | | 4.7 V | 5 mA | <60 Ω | $-300 \cdot 10^6/°C$ | |
| BZT55C5V1 | -- | a1 | TE | Z Diode | | | 80 mA | | | 5.1 V | 5 mA | <35 Ω | $500 \cdot 10^6/°C$ | |
| BZT55C5V6 | -- | a1 | TE | Z Diode | | | 70 mA | | | 5.6 V | 5 mA | <25 Ω | $600 \cdot 10^6/°C$ | |
| BZT55C6V2 | -- | a1 | TE | Z Diode | | | 64 mA | | | 6.2 V | 5 mA | <10 Ω | $700 \cdot 10^6/°C$ | |
| BZT55C6V8 | -- | a1 | TE | Z Diode | | | 58 mA | | | 6.8 V | 5 mA | <8 Ω | $800 \cdot 10^6/°C$ | |
| BZT55C7V5 | -- | a1 | TE | Z Diode | | | 53 mA | | | 7.5 V | 5 mA | <7 Ω | $900 \cdot 10^6/°C$ | |
| BZT55C8V2 | -- | a1 | TE | Z Diode | | | 47 mA | | | 8.2 V | 5 mA | <7 Ω | $900 \cdot 10^6/°C$ | |
| BZT55C9V1 | -- | a1 | TE | Z Diode | | | 43 mA | | | 9.1 V | 5 mA | <10 Ω | $1000 \cdot 10^6/°C$ | |
| BZT55C10 | -- | a1 | TE | Z Diode | | | 40 mA | | | 10 V | 5 mA | <15 Ω | $1100 \cdot 10^6/°C$ | |
| BZT55C11 | -- | a1 | TE | Z Diode | | | 36 mA | | | 11 V | 5 mA | <20 Ω | $1100 \cdot 10^6/°C$ | |
| BZT55C12 | -- | a1 | TE | Z Diode | | | 32 mA | | | 12 V | 5 mA | <20 Ω | $1100 \cdot 10^6/°C$ | |
| BZT55C13 | -- | a1 | TE | Z Diode | | | 29 mA | | | 13 V | 5 mA | <26 Ω | $1100 \cdot 10^6/°C$ | |

| Type | Case | Pin-code | | | Vcla Vbro | Its | Izm | Pv | Pvts | Vz | Iz Is | rz | TK | |
|------|------|----------|---|---|-----------|-----|-----|----|----|----|----|----|----|---|
| BZT55C15 | -- | a1 | TE | Z Diode | | | 27 mA | | | 15 V | 5 mA | <30Ω | $1100 \cdot 10^6$/°C | |
| BZT55C16 | -- | a1 | TE | Z Diode | | | 24 mA | | | 16 V | 5 mA | <40Ω | $1100 \cdot 10^6$/°C | |
| BZT55C18 | -- | a1 | TE | Z Diode | | | 21 mA | | | 18 V | 5 mA | <50Ω | $1100 \cdot 10^6$/°C | |
| BZT55C20 | -- | a1 | TE | Z Diode | | | 20 mA | | | 20 V | 5 mA | <55Ω | $1100 \cdot 10^6$/°C | |
| BZT55C22 | -- | a1 | TE | Z Diode | | | 18 mA | | | 22 V | 5 mA | <55Ω | $1100 \cdot 10^6$/°C | |
| BZT55C24 | -- | a1 | TE | Z Diode | | | 16 mA | | | 24 V | 5 mA | <80Ω | $1200 \cdot 10^6$/°C | |
| BZT55C27 | -- | a1 | TE | Z Diode | | | 14 mA | | | 27 V | 5 mA | <80Ω | $1200 \cdot 10^6$/°C | |
| BZT55C30 | -- | a1 | TE | Z Diode | | | 13 mA | | | 30 V | 5 mA | <80Ω | $1200 \cdot 10^6$/°C | |
| BZT55C33 | -- | a1 | TE | Z Diode | | | 12 mA | | | 33 V | 5 mA | <80Ω | $1200 \cdot 10^6$/°C | |
| BZT55C36 | -- | a1 | TE | Z Diode | | | 11 mA | | | 36 V | 5 mA | <80Ω | $1200 \cdot 10^6$/°C | |
| BZT55C39 | -- | a1 | TE | Z Diode | | | 10 mA | | | 39 V | 5 mA | <90Ω | $1200 \cdot 10^6$/°C | |
| BZT55C43 | -- | a1 | TE | Z Diode | | | 9 mA | | | 43 V | 2.5 mA | <90Ω | $1200 \cdot 10^6$/°C | |
| BZT55C47 | -- | a1 | TE | Z Diode | | | 9 mA | | | 47 V | 2.5 mA | <110Ω | $1200 \cdot 10^6$/°C | |
| BZT55C51 | -- | a1 | TE | Z Diode | | | 8 mA | | | 51 V | 2.5 mA | <125Ω | $1200 \cdot 10^6$/°C | |
| BZT55C56 | -- | a1 | TE | Z Diode | | | 7 mA | | | 56 V | 2.5 mA | <135Ω | $1200 \cdot 10^6$/°C | |
| BZT55C62 | -- | a1 | TE | Z Diode | | | 6 mA | | | 62 V | 2.5 mA | <150Ω | $1200 \cdot 10^6$/°C | |
| BZT55C68 | -- | a1 | TE | Z Diode | | | 6 mA | | | 68 V | 2.5 mA | <200Ω | $1200 \cdot 10^6$/°C | |
| BZT55C75 | -- | a1 | TE | Z Diode | | | 5 mA | | | 75 V | 2.5 mA | <250Ω | $1200 \cdot 10^6$/°C | |
| BZV10 | A2 | a1 | PH | Ref. Z Diode | | | 50 mA | 0.4 W | | 6.2 V | 2 mA | 20 Ω | $100 \cdot 10^6$/°C | |
| BZV11 | A2 | a1 | PH | Ref. Z Diode | | | 50 mA | 0.4 W | | 6.2 V | 2 mA | 20 Ω | $50 \cdot 10^6$/°C | |
| BZV12 | A2 | a1 | PH | Ref. Z Diode | | | 50 mA | 0.4 W | | 6.2 V | 2 mA | 20 Ω | $20 \cdot 10^6$/°C | |
| BZV13 | A2 | a1 | PH | Ref. Z Diode | | | 50 mA | 0.4 W | | 6.2 V | 2 mA | 20 Ω | $10 \cdot 10^6$/°C | |
| BZV14 | A2 | a1 | PH | Ref. Z Diode | | | 50 mA | 0.4 W | | 6.2 V | 2 mA | 20 Ω | $5 \cdot 10^6$/°C | |
| BZV37 | A2 | a2 | PH,SG | Z Diode | | | 50 mA | 0.4 W | 40 W | 6.5 V | 5 mA | <20Ω | $1000 \cdot 10^6$/°C | |
| BZV47C3V3 | B4 | a1 | SG | Z Diode | | | 570 mA | 2 W | 55 W | 3.3 V | 100 mA | <10Ω | $-600 \cdot 10^6$/°C | |
| BZV47C3V6 | B4 | a1 | SG | Z Diode | | | 525 mA | 2 W | 55 W | 3.6 V | 100 mA | <10Ω | $-550 \cdot 10^6$/°C | |
| BZV47C3V9 | B4 | a1 | SG | Z Diode | | | 485 mA | 2 W | 55 W | 3.9 V | 100 mA | <7Ω | $-500 \cdot 10^6$/°C | |
| BZV47C4V3 | B4 | a1 | SG | Z Diode | | | 435 mA | 2 W | 55 W | 4.3 V | 100 mA | <7Ω | $-400 \cdot 10^6$/°C | |
| BZV47C4V7 | B4 | a1 | SG | Z Diode | | | 400 mA | 2 W | 55 W | 4.7 V | 100 mA | <7Ω | $-200 \cdot 10^6$/°C | |
| BZV47C5V1 | B4 | a1 | SG | Z Diode | | | 370 mA | 2 W | 55 W | 5.1 V | 100 mA | <5Ω | $100 \cdot 10^6$/°C | |
| BZV47C5V6 | B4 | a1 | SG | Z Diode | | | 330 mA | 2 W | 55 W | 5.6 V | 100 mA | <2Ω | $250 \cdot 10^6$/°C P | |
| BZV47C6V2 | B4 | a1 | SG | Z Diode | | | 300 mA | 2 W | 55 W | 6.2 V | 100 mA | <2Ω | $320 \cdot 10^6$/°C P | |
| BZV47C6V8 | B4 | a1 | SG | Z Diode | | | 275 mA | 2 W | 55 W | 6.8 V | 100 mA | <2Ω | $400 \cdot 10^6$/°C P | |
| BZV47C7V5 | B4 | a1 | SG | Z Diode | | | 250 mA | 2 W | 55 W | 7.5 V | 100 mA | <2Ω | $450 \cdot 10^6$/°C | |
| BZV47C8V2 | B4 | a1 | SG | Z Diode | | | 230 mA | 2 W | 55 W | 8.2 V | 100 mA | <2Ω | $480 \cdot 10^6$/°C | |
| BZV47C9V1 | B4 | a1 | SG | Z Diode | | | 205 mA | 2 W | 55 W | 9.1 V | 50 mA | <4Ω | $510 \cdot 10^6$/°C | |
| BZV47C10 | B4 | a1 | SG | Z Diode | | | 185 mA | 2 W | 55 W | 10 V | 50 mA | <4Ω | $550 \cdot 10^6$/°C | |
| BZV47C11 | B4 | a1 | SG | Z Diode | | | 170 mA | 2 W | 55 W | 11 V | 50 mA | <7Ω | $600 \cdot 10^6$/°C | |
| BZV47C12 | B4 | a1 | SG | Z Diode | | | 155 mA | 2 W | 55 W | 12 V | 50 mA | <7Ω | $650 \cdot 10^6$/°C P | |
| BZV47C13 | B4 | a1 | SG | Z Diode | | | 140 mA | 2 W | 55 W | 13 V | 50 mA | <10Ω | $650 \cdot 10^6$/°C | |

| Type | Case | Pin-code | | | Maximum Ratings | | | | | Electrical Characteristics | | | | |
|------|------|----------|---|---|---|---|---|---|---|---|---|---|---|---|
| | | | | | Vcla Vbro | Its | Izm | Pv | Pvts | Vz | Iz / Is | rz | TK | |
| BZV47C15 | B4 | a1 | SG | Z Diode | | | 130 mA | 2 W | 55 W | 15 V | 50 mA | <10 Ω | 700·10⁶/°C | P |
| BZV47C16 | B4 | a1 | SG | Z Diode | | | 115 mA | 2 W | 55 W | 16 V | 25 mA | <15 Ω | 700·10⁶/°C | |
| BZV47C18 | B4 | a1 | SG | Z Diode | | | 105 mA | 2 W | 55 W | 18 V | 25 mA | <15 Ω | 750·10⁶/°C | P |
| BZV47C20 | B4 | a1 | SG | Z Diode | | | 94 mA | 2 W | 55 W | 20 V | 25 mA | <15 Ω | 750·10⁶/°C | |
| BZV47C22 | B4 | a1 | SG | Z Diode | | | 86 mA | 2 W | 55 W | 22 V | 25 mA | <15 Ω | 800·10⁶/°C | |
| BZV47C24 | B4 | a1 | SG | Z Diode | | | 78 mA | 2 W | 55 W | 24 V | 25 mA | <15 Ω | 800·10⁶/°C | P |
| BZV47C27 | B4 | a1 | SG | Z Diode | | | 69 mA | 2 W | 55 W | 27 V | 25 mA | <15 Ω | 850·10⁶/°C | |
| BZV47C30 | B4 | a1 | SG | Z Diode | | | 62 mA | 2 W | 55 W | 30 V | 25 mA | <15 Ω | 850·10⁶/°C | P |
| BZV47C33 | B4 | a1 | SG | Z Diode | | | 57 mA | 2 W | 55 W | 33 V | 25 mA | <15 Ω | 850·10⁶/°C | |
| BZV47C36 | B4 | a1 | SG | Z Diode | | | 52 mA | 2 W | 55 W | 36 V | 10 mA | <40 Ω | 850·10⁶/°C | P |
| BZV47C39 | B4 | a1 | SG | Z Diode | | | 48 mA | 2 W | 55 W | 39 V | 10 mA | <40 Ω | 900·10⁶/°C | |
| BZV47C43 | B4 | a1 | SG | Z Diode | | | 43 mA | 2 W | 55 W | 43 V | 10 mA | <45 Ω | 900·10⁶/°C | |
| BZV47C47 | B4 | a1 | SG | Z Diode | | | 40 mA | 2 W | 55 W | 47 V | 10 mA | <45 Ω | 900·10⁶/°C | P |
| BZV47C51 | B4 | a1 | SG | Z Diode | | | 37 mA | 2 W | 55 W | 51 V | 10 mA | <60 Ω | 900·10⁶/°C | |
| BZV47C56 | B4 | a1 | SG | Z Diode | | | 33 mA | 2 W | 55 W | 56 V | 10 mA | <60 Ω | 900·10⁶/°C | |
| BZV47C62 | B4 | a1 | SG | Z Diode | | | 30 mA | 2 W | 55 W | 62 V | 10 mA | <80 Ω | 900·10⁶/°C | P |
| BZV47C68 | B4 | a1 | SG | Z Diode | | | 27 mA | 2 W | 55 W | 68 V | 10 mA | <80 Ω | 900·10⁶/°C | P |
| BZV47C75 | B4 | a1 | SG | Z Diode | | | 25 mA | 2 W | 55 W | 75 V | 10 mA | <100 Ω | 900·10⁶/°C | |
| BZV47C82 | B4 | a1 | SG | Z Diode | | | 23 mA | 2 W | 55 W | 82 V | 5 mA | <100 Ω | 900·10⁶/°C | |
| BZV47C91 | B4 | a1 | SG | Z Diode | | | 20 mA | 2 W | 55 W | 91 V | 5 mA | <200 Ω | 900·10⁶/°C | |
| BZV47C100 | B4 | a1 | SG | Z Diode | | | 18 mA | 2 W | 55 W | 100 V | 5 mA | <200 Ω | 900·10⁶/°C | P |
| BZV47C110 | B4 | a1 | SG | Z Diode | | | 17 mA | 2 W | 55 W | 110 V | 5 mA | <250 Ω | 900·10⁶/°C | |
| BZV47C120 | B4 | a1 | SG | Z Diode | | | 15 mA | 2 W | 55 W | 120 V | 5 mA | <250 Ω | 950·10⁶/°C | |
| BZV47C130 | B4 | a1 | SG | Z Diode | | | 14 mA | 2 W | 55 W | 130 V | 5 mA | <300 Ω | 950·10⁶/°C | P |
| BZV47C150 | B4 | a1 | SG | Z Diode | | | 13 mA | 2 W | 55 W | 150 V | 5 mA | <300 Ω | 950·10⁶/°C | P |
| BZV47C160 | B4 | a1 | SG | Z Diode | | | 12 mA | 2 W | 55 W | 160 V | 5 mA | <350 Ω | 950·10⁶/°C | |
| BZV47C180 | B4 | a1 | SG | Z Diode | | | 11 mA | 2 W | 55 W | 180 V | 5 mA | <350 Ω | 950·10⁶/°C | |
| BZV47C200 | B4 | a1 | SG | Z Diode | | | 9 mA | 2 W | 55 W | 200 V | 5 mA | <350 Ω | 950·10⁶/°C | P |
| BZV49C2V4 | F6 | c14 | PH | Z Diode | | | | 1 W | 40 W | 2.4 V | 5 mA | 70 Ω | | |
| BZV49C2V7 | F6 | c14 | PH | Z Diode | | | | 1 W | 40 W | 2.7 V | 5 mA | 75 Ω | | |
| BZV49C3V0 | F6 | c14 | PH | Z Diode | | | | 1 W | 40 W | 3.0 V | 5 mA | 80 Ω | | |
| BZV49C3V3 | F6 | c14 | PH | Z Diode | | | | 1 W | 40 W | 3.3 V | 5 mA | 85 Ω | | |
| BZV49C3V6 | F6 | c14 | PH | Z Diode | | | | 1 W | 40 W | 3.6 V | 5 mA | 85 Ω | | |
| BZV49C3V9 | F6 | c14 | PH | Z Diode | | | | 1 W | 40 W | 3.9 V | 5 mA | 85 Ω | | |
| BZV49C4V3 | F6 | c14 | PH | Z Diode | | | | 1 W | 40 W | 4.3 V | 5 mA | 80 Ω | | |
| BZV49C4V7 | F6 | c14 | PH | Z Diode | | | | 1 W | 40 W | 4.7 V | 5 mA | 50 Ω | | |
| BZV49C5V1 | F6 | c14 | PH | Z Diode | | | | 1 W | 40 W | 5.1 V | 5 mA | 40 Ω | | |
| BZV49C5V6 | F6 | c14 | PH | Z Diode | | | | 1 W | 40 W | 5.6 V | 5 mA | 15 Ω | | |
| BZV49C6V2 | F6 | c14 | PH | Z Diode | | | | 1 W | 40 W | 6.2 V | 5 mA | 6 Ω | | |
| BZV49C6V8 | F6 | c14 | PH | Z Diode | | | | 1 W | 40 W | 6.8 V | 5 mA | 6 Ω | | |

| Type | Case | Pin-code | 🏭 | ⚙️ | Vcla Vbro | \|\|ts | Izm | Pv | Pvts | Vz | Iz Is | rz | TK | |
|------|------|----------|----|----|-----------|--------|-----|----|------|----|-------|----|----|---|
| | | | | | **Maximum Ratings** | | | | | **Electrical Characteristics** | | | | |
| BZV49C7V5 | F6 | c14 | PH | Z Diode | | | | 1 W | 40 W | 7.5 V | 5 mA | 6 Ω | | |
| BZV49C8V2 | F6 | c14 | PH | Z Diode | | | | 1 W | 40 W | 8.2 V | 5 mA | 6 Ω | | |
| BZV49C9V1 | F6 | c14 | PH | Z Diode | | | | 1 W | 40 W | 9.1 V | 5 mA | 6 Ω | | |
| BZV49C10 | F6 | c14 | PH | Z Diode | | | | 1 W | 40 W | 10 V | 5 mA | 8 Ω | | |
| BZV49C11 | F6 | c14 | PH | Z Diode | | | | 1 W | 40 W | 11 V | 5 mA | 10 Ω | | |
| BZV49C12 | F6 | c14 | PH | Z Diode | | | | 1 W | 40 W | 12 V | 5 mA | 10 Ω | | |
| BZV49C13 | F6 | c14 | PH | Z Diode | | | | 1 W | 40 W | 13 V | 5 mA | 10 Ω | | |
| BZV49C15 | F6 | c14 | PH | Z Diode | | | | 1 W | 40 W | 15 V | 5 mA | 10 Ω | | |
| BZV49C16 | F6 | c14 | PH | Z Diode | | | | 1 W | 40 W | 16 V | 5 mA | 10 Ω | | |
| BZV49C18 | F6 | c14 | PH | Z Diode | | | | 1 W | 40 W | 18 V | 5 mA | 10 Ω | | |
| BZV49C20 | F6 | c14 | PH | Z Diode | | | | 1 W | 40 W | 20 V | 5 mA | 15 Ω | | |
| BZV49C22 | F6 | c14 | PH | Z Diode | | | | 1 W | 40 W | 22 V | 5 mA | 20 Ω | | |
| BZV49C24 | F6 | c14 | PH | Z Diode | | | | 1 W | 40 W | 24 V | 5 mA | 25 Ω | | |
| BZV49C27 | F6 | c14 | PH | Z Diode | | | | 1 W | 40 W | 27 V | 2 mA | 25 Ω | | |
| BZV49C30 | F6 | c14 | PH | Z Diode | | | | 1 W | 40 W | 30 V | 2 mA | 30 Ω | | |
| BZV49C33 | F6 | c14 | PH | Z Diode | | | | 1 W | 40 W | 33 V | 2 mA | 35 Ω | | |
| BZV49C36 | F6 | c14 | PH | Z Diode | | | | 1 W | 40 W | 36 V | 2 mA | 35 Ω | | |
| BZV49C39 | F6 | c14 | PH | Z Diode | | | | 1 W | 40 W | 39 V | 2 mA | 40 Ω | | |
| BZV49C43 | F6 | c14 | PH | Z Diode | | | | 1 W | 40 W | 43 V | 2 mA | 45 Ω | | |
| BZV49C47 | F6 | c14 | PH | Z Diode | | | | 1 W | 40 W | 47 V | 2 mA | 50 Ω | | |
| BZV49C51 | F6 | c14 | PH | Z Diode | | | | 1 W | 40 W | 51 V | 2 mA | 60 Ω | | |
| BZV49C56 | F6 | c14 | PH | Z Diode | | | | 1 W | 40 W | 56 V | 2 mA | 70 Ω | | |
| BZV49C62 | F6 | c14 | PH | Z Diode | | | | 1 W | 40 W | 62 V | 2 mA | 80 Ω | | |
| BZV49C68 | F6 | c14 | PH | Z Diode | | | | 1 W | 40 W | 68 V | 2 mA | 90 Ω | | |
| BZV49C75 | F6 | c14 | PH | Z Diode | | | | 1 W | 40 W | 75 V | 2 mA | 95 Ω | | |
| BZV55B33 | D2 | a1 | PH | Z Diode | | | | 0.5 W | 30 W | 33 V | 2 mA | 35 Ω | | |
| BZV55B36 | D2 | a1 | PH | Z Diode | | | | 0.5 W | 30 W | 36 V | 2 mA | 35 Ω | | |
| BZV55B39 | D2 | a1 | PH | Z Diode | | | | 0.5 W | 30 W | 39 V | 2 mA | 40 Ω | | |
| BZV55B43 | D2 | a1 | PH | Z Diode | | | | 0.5 W | 30 W | 43 V | 2 mA | 45 Ω | | |
| BZV55B47 | D2 | a1 | PH | Z Diode | | | | 0.5 W | 30 W | 47 V | 2 mA | 50 Ω | | |
| BZV55B51 | D2 | a1 | PH | Z Diode | | | | 0.5 W | 30 W | 51 V | 2 mA | 60 Ω | | |
| BZV55C2V4 | D2 | a1 | SG,PH,MO | Z Diode | | 155 mA | | 0.5 W | | 2.4 V | 5 mA | <85 Ω | $-800 \cdot 10^6/°C$ | |
| BZV55C2V7 | D2 | a1 | SG,PH,MO | Z Diode | | 135 mA | | 0.5 W | | 2.7 V | 5 mA | <85 Ω | $-800 \cdot 10^6/°C$ | |
| BZV55C3V0 | D2 | a1 | SG,PH,MO | Z Diode | | 125 mA | | 0.5 W | | 3.0 V | 5 mA | <85 Ω | $-800 \cdot 10^6/°C$ | |
| BZV55C3V3 | D2 | a1 | SG,PH,MO | Z Diode | | 115 mA | | 0.5 W | | 3.3 V | 5 mA | <85 Ω | $-800 \cdot 10^6/°C$ | P (SG) |
| BZV55C3V6 | D2 | a1 | SG,PH,MO | Z Diode | | 105 mA | | 0.5 W | | 3.6 V | 5 mA | <85 Ω | $-800 \cdot 10^6/°C$ | P (SG) |
| BZV55C3V9 | D2 | a1 | SG,PH,MO | Z Diode | | 95 mA | | 0.5 W | | 3.9 V | 5 mA | <85 Ω | $-700 \cdot 10^6/°C$ | P (SG) |
| BZV55C4V3 | D2 | a1 | SG,PH,MO | Z Diode | | 90 mA | | 0.5 W | | 4.3 V | 5 mA | <75 Ω | $-400 \cdot 10^6/°C$ | P (SG) |
| BZV55C4V7 | D2 | a1 | SG,PH,MO | Z Diode | | 85 mA | | 0.5 W | | 4.7 V | 5 mA | <60 Ω | $-300 \cdot 10^6/°C$ | P (SG) |
| BZV55C5V1 | D2 | a1 | SG,PH,MO | Z Diode | | 80 mA | | 0.5 W | | 5.1 V | 5 mA | <35 Ω | $500 \cdot 10^6/°C$ | P (SG) |

| Type | Case | Pin-code | | | Maximum Ratings | | | | | Electrical Characteristics | | | | |
|---|---|---|---|---|---|---|---|---|---|---|---|---|---|---|
| | | | | | $V_{cla}$ $V_{bro}$ | Its | Izm | Pv | Pvts | Vz | Iz / Is | rz | TK | |
| BZV55C5V6 | D2 | a1 | SG,PH,MO | Z Diode | | 70 mA | 0.5 W | | | 5.6 V | 5 mA | <25 Ω | $600 \cdot 10^6/°C$ | P (SG) |
| BZV55C6V2 | D2 | a1 | SG,PH,MO | Z Diode | | 64 mA | 0.5 W | | | 6.2 V | 5 mA | <10 Ω | $700 \cdot 10^6/°C$ | P (SG) |
| BZV55C6V8 | D2 | a1 | SG,PH,MO | Z Diode | | 58 mA | 0.5 W | | | 6.8 V | 5 mA | <8 Ω | $800 \cdot 10^6/°C$ | P (SG) |
| BZV55C7V5 | D2 | a1 | SG,PH,MO | Z Diode | | 53 mA | 0.5 W | | | 7.5 V | 5 mA | <7 Ω | $900 \cdot 10^6/°C$ | P (SG) |
| BZV55C8V2 | D2 | a1 | SG,PH,MO | Z Diode | | 47 mA | 0.5 W | | | 8.2 V | 5 mA | <7 Ω | $900 \cdot 10^6/°C$ | P (SG) |
| BZV55C9V1 | D2 | a1 | SG,PH,MO | Z Diode | | 43 mA | 0.5 W | | | 9.1 V | 5 mA | <10 Ω | $1000 \cdot 10^6/°C$ | P (SG) |
| BZV55C10 | D2 | a1 | SG,PH,MO | Z Diode | | 40 mA | 0.5 W | | | 10 V | 5 mA | <15 Ω | $1100 \cdot 10^6/°C$ | P (SG) |
| BZV55C11 | D2 | a1 | SG,PH,MO | Z Diode | | 36 mA | 0.5 W | | | 11 V | 5 mA | <20 Ω | $1100 \cdot 10^6/°C$ | |
| BZV55C12 | D2 | a1 | SG,PH,MO | Z Diode | | 32 mA | 0.5 W | | | 12 V | 5 mA | <20 Ω | $1100 \cdot 10^6/°C$ | P (SG) |
| BZV55C13 | D2 | a1 | SG,PH,MO | Z Diode | | 29 mA | 0.5 W | | | 13 V | 5 mA | <26 Ω | $1100 \cdot 10^6/°C$ | |
| BZV55C15 | D2 | a1 | SG,PH,MO | Z Diode | | 27 mA | 0.5 W | | | 15 V | 5 mA | <30 Ω | $1100 \cdot 10^6/°C$ | P (SG) |
| BZV55C16 | D2 | a1 | SG,PH,MO | Z Diode | | 24 mA | 0.5 W | | | 16 V | 5 mA | <40 Ω | $1100 \cdot 10^6/°C$ | |
| BZV55C18 | D2 | a1 | SG,PH,MO | Z Diode | | 21 mA | 0.5 W | | | 18 V | 5 mA | <50 Ω | $1100 \cdot 10^6/°C$ | |
| BZV55C20 | D2 | a1 | SG,PH,MO | Z Diode | | 20 mA | 0.5 W | | | 20 V | 5 mA | <55 Ω | $1100 \cdot 10^6/°C$ | |
| BZV55C22 | D2 | a1 | SG,PH,MO | Z Diode | | 18 mA | 0.5 W | | | 22 V | 5 mA | <55 Ω | $1100 \cdot 10^6/°C$ | |
| BZV55C24 | D2 | a1 | SG,PH,MO | Z Diode | | 16 mA | 0.5 W | | | 24 V | 5 mA | <80 Ω | $1200 \cdot 10^6/°C$ | |
| BZV55C27 | D2 | a1 | SG,PH,MO | Z Diode | | 14 mA | 0.5 W | | | 27 V | 5 mA | <80 Ω | $1200 \cdot 10^6/°C$ | |
| BZV55C30 | D2 | a1 | SG,PH,MO | Z Diode | | 13 mA | 0.5 W | | | 30 V | 5 mA | <80 Ω | $1200 \cdot 10^6/°C$ | |
| BZV55C33 | D2 | a1 | SG,PH,MO | Z Diode | | 12 mA | 0.5 W | | | 33 V | 5 mA | <80 Ω | $1200 \cdot 10^6/°C$ | |
| BZV55C36 | D2 | a1 | SG,PH,MO | Z Diode | | 11 mA | 0.5 W | | | 36 V | 5 mA | <80 Ω | $1200 \cdot 10^6/°C$ | |
| BZV55C39 | D2 | a1 | SG,PH,MO | Z Diode | | 10 mA | 0.5 W | | | 39 V | 5 mA | <90 Ω | $1200 \cdot 10^6/°C$ | |
| BZV55C43 | D2 | a1 | SG,PH,MO | Z Diode | | 9 mA | 0.5 W | | | 43 V | 2.5 mA | <90 Ω | $1200 \cdot 10^6/°C$ | |
| BZV55C47 | D2 | a1 | SG,PH,MO | Z Diode | | 9 mA | 0.5 W | | | 47 V | 2.5 mA | <110 Ω | $1200 \cdot 10^6/°C$ | |
| BZV55C51 | D2 | a1 | SG,PH,MO | Z Diode | | 8 mA | 0.5 W | | | 51 V | 2.5 mA | <125 Ω | $1200 \cdot 10^6/°C$ | |
| BZV55C56 | D2 | a1 | SG,PH,MO | Z Diode | | 7 mA | 0.5 W | | | 56 V | 2.5 mA | <135 Ω | $1200 \cdot 10^6/°C$ | |
| BZV55C62 | D2 | a1 | SG,PH | Z Diode | | 6 mA | 0.5 W | | | 62 V | 2.5 mA | <150 Ω | $1200 \cdot 10^6/°C$ | |
| BZV55C68 | D2 | a1 | SG,PH | Z Diode | | 6 mA | 0.5 W | | | 68 V | 2.5 mA | <200 Ω | $1200 \cdot 10^6/°C$ | |
| BZV55C75 | D2 | a1 | SG,PH | Z Diode | | 5 mA | 0.5 W | | | 75 V | 2.5 mA | <250 Ω | $1200 \cdot 10^6/°C$ | |
| BZV55C82 | D2 | a1 | SG | Z Diode | | 5 mA | 0.5 W | | | 82 V | 2.5 mA | <300 Ω | $1200 \cdot 10^6/°C$ | |
| BZV55C91 | D2 | a1 | SG | Z Diode | | 4 mA | 0.5 W | | | 91 V | 2.5 mA | <450 Ω | $1200 \cdot 10^6/°C$ | |
| BZV55C100 | D2 | a1 | SG,PH | Z Diode | | 4 mA | 0.5 W | | | 100 V | 1 mA | <450 Ω | $1200 \cdot 10^6/°C$ | |
| BZV58C3V3 | B3 | a1 | SG | Z Diode | | 1430 mA | 5 W | 110 W | | 3.3 V | 380 mA | <3 Ω | $-600 \cdot 10^6/°C$ | |
| BZV58C3V6 | B3 | a1 | SG | Z Diode | | 1310 mA | 5 W | 110 W | | 3.6 V | 350 mA | <2.5 Ω | $-550 \cdot 10^6/°C$ | |
| BZV58C3V9 | B3 | a1 | SG | Z Diode | | 1220 mA | 5 W | 110 W | | 3.9 V | 320 mA | <2 Ω | $-500 \cdot 10^6/°C$ | |
| BZV58C4V3 | B3 | a1 | SG | Z Diode | | 1090 mA | 5 W | 110 W | | 4.3 V | 290 mA | <2 Ω | $-400 \cdot 10^6/°C$ | |
| BZV58C4V7 | B3 | a1 | SG | Z Diode | | 1000 mA | 5 W | 110 W | | 4.7 V | 260 mA | <2 Ω | $-200 \cdot 10^6/°C$ | |
| BZV58C5V1 | B3 | a1 | SG | Z Diode | | 925 mA | 5 W | 110 W | | 5.1 V | 240 mA | <1.5 Ω | $250 \cdot 10^6/°C$ | |
| BZV58C5V6 | B3 | a1 | SG | Z Diode | | 830 mA | 5 W | 110 W | | 5.6 V | 220 mA | <1 Ω | $320 \cdot 10^6/°C$ | |
| BZV58C6V2 | B3 | a1 | SG | Z Diode | | 750 mA | 5 W | 110 W | | 6.2 V | 200 mA | <1 Ω | $400 \cdot 10^6/°C$ | |
| BZV58C6V8 | B3 | a1 | SG | Z Diode | | 690 mA | 5 W | 110 W | | 6.8 V | 175 mA | <1 Ω | $450 \cdot 10^6/°C$ | |

| Type | Case | Pin-code | | | Maximum Ratings | | | | | Electrical Characteristics | | | | |
|---|---|---|---|---|---|---|---|---|---|---|---|---|---|---|
| | | | | | Vcla Vbro | Its | Izm | Pv | Pvts | Vz | Iz Is | rz | TK | |
| BZV58C7V5 | B3 | a1 | SG | Z Diode | | | 630 mA | 5 W | 110 W | 7.5 V | 175 mA | <1.5 Ω | 480·10⁶/°C | |
| BZV58C8V2 | B3 | a1 | SG | Z Diode | | | 570 mA | 5 W | 110 W | 8.2 V | 150 mA | <1.5 Ω | 510·10⁶/°C | |
| BZV58C9V1 | B3 | a1 | SG | Z Diode | | | 520 mA | 5 W | 110 W | 9.1 V | 150 mA | <2 Ω | 550·10⁶/°C | |
| BZV58C10 | B3 | a1 | SG | Z Diode | | | 470 mA | 5 W | 110 W | 10 V | 125 mA | <2 Ω | 600·10⁶/°C | |
| BZV58C11 | B3 | a1 | SG | Z Diode | | | 430 mA | 5 W | 110 W | 11 V | 125 mA | <2.5 Ω | 650·10⁶/°C | |
| BZV58C12 | B3 | a1 | SG | Z Diode | | | 390 mA | 5 W | 110 W | 12 V | 100 mA | <2.5 Ω | 650·10⁶/°C | |
| BZV58C13 | B3 | a1 | SG | Z Diode | | | 350 mA | 5 W | 110 W | 13 V | 100 mA | <2.5 Ω | 700·10⁶/°C | |
| BZV58C15 | B3 | a1 | SG | Z Diode | | | 320 mA | 5 W | 110 W | 15 V | 75 mA | <2.5 Ω | 700·10⁶/°C | |
| BZV58C16 | B3 | a1 | SG | Z Diode | | | 290 mA | 5 W | 110 W | 16 V | 75 mA | <2.5 Ω | 750·10⁶/°C | |
| BZV58C18 | B3 | a1 | SG | Z Diode | | | 260 mA | 5 W | 110 W | 18 V | 65 mA | <2.5 Ω | 750·10⁶/°C | |
| BZV58C20 | B3 | a1 | SG | Z Diode | | | 235 mA | 5 W | 110 W | 20 V | 65 mA | <3 Ω | 800·10⁶/°C | |
| BZV58C22 | B3 | a1 | SG | Z Diode | | | 215 mA | 5 W | 110 W | 22 V | 50 mA | <3.5 Ω | 800·10⁶/°C | |
| BZV58C24 | B3 | a1 | SG | Z Diode | | | 195 mA | 5 W | 110 W | 24 V | 50 mA | <3.5 Ω | 850·10⁶/°C | |
| BZV58C27 | B3 | a1 | SG | Z Diode | | | 170 mA | 5 W | 110 W | 27 V | 50 mA | <5 Ω | 850·10⁶/°C | |
| BZV58C30 | B3 | a1 | SG | Z Diode | | | 155 mA | 5 W | 110 W | 30 V | 40 mA | <8 Ω | 850·10⁶/°C | |
| BZV58C33 | B3 | a1 | SG | Z Diode | | | 140 mA | 5 W | 110 W | 33 V | 40 mA | <10 Ω | 850·10⁶/°C | |
| BZV58C36 | B3 | a1 | SG | Z Diode | | | 130 mA | 5 W | 110 W | 36 V | 30 mA | <11 Ω | 900·10⁶/°C | |
| BZV58C39 | B3 | a1 | SG | Z Diode | | | 120 mA | 5 W | 110 W | 39 V | 30 mA | <14 Ω | 900·10⁶/°C | |
| BZV58C43 | B3 | a1 | SG | Z Diode | | | 110 mA | 5 W | 110 W | 43 V | 30 mA | <20 Ω | 900·10⁶/°C | |
| BZV58C47 | B3 | a1 | SG | Z Diode | | | 100 mA | 5 W | 110 W | 47 V | 25 mA | <25 Ω | 900·10⁶/°C | |
| BZV58C51 | B3 | a1 | SG | Z Diode | | | 92 mA | 5 W | 110 W | 51 V | 25 mA | <27 Ω | 900·10⁶/°C | |
| BZV58C56 | B3 | a1 | SG | Z Diode | | | 83 mA | 5 W | 110 W | 56 V | 20 mA | <35 Ω | 900·10⁶/°C | |
| BZV58C62 | B3 | a1 | SG | Z Diode | | | 75 mA | 5 W | 110 W | 62 V | 20 mA | <42 Ω | 900·10⁶/°C | |
| BZV58C68 | B3 | a1 | SG | Z Diode | | | 69 mA | 5 W | 110 W | 68 V | 20 mA | <44 Ω | 900·10⁶/°C | |
| BZV58C75 | B3 | a1 | SG | Z Diode | | | 63 mA | 5 W | 110 W | 75 V | 20 mA | <45 Ω | 900·10⁶/°C | |
| BZV58C82 | B3 | a1 | SG | Z Diode | | | 57 mA | 5 W | 110 W | 82 V | 15 mA | <65 Ω | 900·10⁶/°C | |
| BZV58C91 | B3 | a1 | SG | Z Diode | | | 52 mA | 5 W | 110 W | 91 V | 15 mA | <75 Ω | 900·10⁶/°C | |
| BZV58C100 | B3 | a1 | SG | Z Diode | | | 47 mA | 5 W | 110 W | 100 V | 12 mA | <90 Ω | 900·10⁶/°C | |
| BZV58C110 | B3 | a1 | SG | Z Diode | | | 43 mA | 5 W | 110 W | 110 V | 12 mA | <125 Ω | 950·10⁶/°C | |
| BZV58C120 | B3 | a1 | SG | Z Diode | | | 39 mA | 5 W | 110 W | 120 V | 10 mA | <170 Ω | 950·10⁶/°C | |
| BZV58C130 | B3 | a1 | SG | Z Diode | | | 35 mA | 5 W | 110 W | 130 V | 10 mA | <190 Ω | 950·10⁶/°C | |
| BZV58C150 | B3 | a1 | SG | Z Diode | | | 32 mA | 5 W | 110 W | 150 V | 8 mA | <330 Ω | 950·10⁶/°C | |
| BZV58C160 | B3 | a1 | SG | Z Diode | | | 29 mA | 5 W | 110 W | 160 V | 8 mA | <350 Ω | 950·10⁶/°C | |
| BZV58C180 | B3 | a1 | SG | Z Diode | | | 26 mA | 5 W | 110 W | 180 V | 5 mA | <430 Ω | 950·10⁶/°C | |
| BZV58C200 | B3 | a1 | SG | Z Diode | | | 23 mA | 5 W | 110 W | 200 V | 5 mA | <480 Ω | 1000·10⁶/°C | |
| BZV58C8V2 | B8 | a1 | RD | Z Diode | | | | 5 W | | 8.2 V | 150 mA | | | |
| BZV58C9V1 | B8 | a1 | RD | Z Diode | | | | 5 W | | 9.1 V | 150 mA | | | |
| BZV58C10 | B8 | a1 | RD | Z Diode | | | | 5 W | | 10 V | 125 mA | | | |
| BZV58C11 | B8 | a1 | RD | Z Diode | | | | 5 W | | 11 V | 125 mA | | | |
| BZV58C12 | B8 | a1 | RD | Z Diode | | | | 5 W | | 12 V | 100 mA | | | |

| Type | Case | Pin-code | | | Maximum Ratings | | | | | Electrical Characteristics | | | | |
|---|---|---|---|---|---|---|---|---|---|---|---|---|---|---|
| | | | | | Vcla / Vbro | Its | Izm | Pv | Pvts | Vz | Iz / Is | rz | TK | |
| BZV58C13 | B8 | a1 | RD | Z Diode | | | | 5 W | | 13 V | 100 mA | | | |
| BZV58C15 | B8 | a1 | RD | Z Diode | | | | 5 W | | 15 V | 75 mA | | | |
| BZV58C16 | B8 | a1 | RD | Z Diode | | | | 5 W | | 16 V | 75 mA | | | |
| BZV58C18 | B8 | a1 | RD | Z Diode | | | | 5 W | | 18 V | 65 mA | | | |
| BZV58C20 | B8 | a1 | RD | Z Diode | | | | 5 W | | 20 V | 65 mA | | | |
| BZV58C22 | B8 | a1 | RD | Z Diode | | | | 5 W | | 22 V | 50 mA | | | |
| BZV58C24 | B8 | a1 | RD | Z Diode | | | | 5 W | | 24 V | 50 mA | | | |
| BZV58C27 | B8 | a1 | RD | Z Diode | | | | 5 W | | 27 V | 50 mA | | | |
| BZV58C30 | B8 | a1 | RD | Z Diode | | | | 5 W | | 30 V | 40 mA | | | |
| BZV58C33 | B8 | a1 | RD | Z Diode | | | | 5 W | | 33 V | 40 mA | | | |
| BZV58C36 | B8 | a1 | RD | Z Diode | | | | 5 W | | 36 V | 30 mA | | | |
| BZV58C39 | B8 | a1 | RD | Z Diode | | | | 5 W | | 39 V | 30 mA | | | |
| BZV58C43 | B8 | a1 | RD | Z Diode | | | | 5 W | | 43 V | 30 mA | | | |
| BZV58C47 | B8 | a1 | RD | Z Diode | | | | 5 W | | 47 V | 25 mA | | | |
| BZV58C51 | B8 | a1 | RD | Z Diode | | | | 5 W | | 51 V | 25 mA | | | |
| BZV58C56 | B8 | a1 | RD | Z Diode | | | | 5 W | | 56 V | 20 mA | | | |
| BZV58C62 | B8 | a1 | RD | Z Diode | | | | 5 W | | 62 V | 20 mA | | | |
| BZV58C68 | B8 | a1 | RD | Z Diode | | | | 5 W | | 68 V | 20 mA | | | |
| BZV58C75 | B8 | a1 | RD | Z Diode | | | | 5 W | | 75 V | 20 mA | | | |
| BZV58C82 | B8 | a1 | RD | Z Diode | | | | 5 W | | 82 V | 15 mA | | | |
| BZV58C91 | B8 | a1 | RD | Z Diode | | | | 5 W | | 91 V | 15 mA | | | |
| BZV58C100 | B8 | a1 | RD | Z Diode | | | | 5 W | | 100 V | 12 mA | | | |
| BZV58C110 | B8 | a1 | RD | Z Diode | | | | 5 W | | 110 V | 12 mA | | | |
| BZV58C120 | B8 | a1 | RD | Z Diode | | | | 5 W | | 120 V | 10 mA | | | |
| BZV58C130 | B8 | a1 | RD | Z Diode | | | | 5 W | | 130 V | 10 mA | | | |
| BZV58C150 | B8 | a1 | RD | Z Diode | | | | 5 W | | 150 V | 8 mA | | | |
| BZV58C160 | B8 | a1 | RD | Z Diode | | | | 5 W | | 160 V | 8 mA | | | |
| BZV58C180 | B8 | a1 | RD | Z Diode | | | | 5 W | | 180 V | 5 mA | | | |
| BZV58C200 | B8 | a1 | RD | Z Diode | | | | 5 W | | 200 V | 5 mA | | | |
| BZV80 | D2 | a1 | PH | Ref. Z Diode | 50 mA | | | 0.4 W | | 6.2 V | 7.5 mA | <15 Ω | 100 ·10⁶/°C | |
| BZV81 | D2 | a1 | PH | Ref. Z Diode | 50 mA | | | 0.4 W | | 6.2 V | 7.5 mA | <15 Ω | 50 ·10⁶/°C | |
| BZV85C3V6 | A3 | a1 | PH | Z Diode | | 2 A | | 1.3 W | 60 W | 3.6 V | 60 mA | 15 Ω | -3.5 mV/°C | |
| BZV85C3V9 | A3 | a1 | PH | Z Diode | | 1.9 A | | 1.3 W | 60 W | 3.9 V | 60 mA | 15 Ω | -3.5 mV/°C | |
| BZV85C4V3 | A3 | a1 | PH | Z Diode | | 1.8 A | | 1.3 W | 60 W | 4.3 V | 50 mA | 13 Ω | -2.7 mV/°C | |
| BZV85C4V7 | A3 | a1 | PH | Z Diode | | 1.8 A | | 1.3 W | 60 W | 4.7 V | 45 mA | 13 Ω | -2 mV/°C | |
| BZV85C5V1 | A3 | a1 | PH | Z Diode | | 1.7 A | | 1.3 W | 60 W | 5.1 V | 45 mA | 10 Ω | 2.2 mV/°C | |
| BZV85C5V6 | A3 | a1 | PH | Z Diode | | 1.7 A | | 1.3 W | 60 W | 5.6 V | 45 mA | 7 Ω | 2.7 mV/°C | |
| BZV85C6V2 | A3 | a1 | PH | Z Diode | | 1.6 A | | 1.3 W | 60 W | 6.2 V | 35 mA | 4 Ω | 3.6 mV/°C | |
| BZV85C6V8 | A3 | a1 | PH | Z Diode | | 1.5 A | | 1.3 W | 60 W | 6.8 V | 35 mA | 3.5 Ω | 4.3 mV/°C | |
| BZV85C7V5 | A3 | a1 | PH | Z Diode | | 1.5 A | | 1.3 W | 60 W | 7.5 V | 35 mA | 3 Ω | 5.5 mV/°C | |

| Type | Case | Pin-code | | | Maximum Ratings | | | | | Electrical Characteristics | | | | |
|---|---|---|---|---|---|---|---|---|---|---|---|---|---|---|
| | | | | | Vcla Vbro | Its | Izm | Pv | Pvts | Vz / Is | Iz | rz | TK | |
| BZV85C8V2 | A3 | a1 | PH | Z Diode | | | 1.4 A | 1.3 W | 60 W | 8.2 V | 25 mA | 5 Ω | 6.1 mV/°C | |
| BZV85C9V1 | A3 | a1 | PH | Z Diode | | | 1.3 A | 1.3 W | 60 W | 9.1 V | 25 mA | 5 Ω | 7.2 mV/°C | |
| BZV85C10 | A3 | a1 | PH | Z Diode | | | 1.2 A | 1.3 W | 60 W | 10 V | 25 mA | 8 Ω | 8.5 mV/°C | |
| BZV85C11 | A3 | a1 | PH | Z Diode | | | 1.1 A | 1.3 W | 60 W | 11 V | 20 mA | 10 Ω | 9.3 mV/°C | |
| BZV85C12 | A3 | a1 | PH | Z Diode | | | 1 A | 1.3 W | 60 W | 12 V | 20 mA | 10 Ω | 10.8 mV/°C | |
| BZV85C13 | A3 | a1 | PH | Z Diode | | | 900 mA | 1.3 W | 60 W | 13 V | 20 mA | 10 Ω | 12 mV/°C | |
| BZV85C15 | A3 | a1 | PH | Z Diode | | | 760 mA | 1.3 W | 60 W | 15 V | 15 mA | 15 Ω | 13.6 mV/°C | |
| BZV85C16 | A3 | a1 | PH | Z Diode | | | 700 mA | 1.3 W | 60 W | 16 V | 15 mA | 15 Ω | 15.4 mV/°C | |
| BZV85C18 | A3 | a1 | PH | Z Diode | | | 600 mA | 1.3 W | 60 W | 18 V | 15 mA | 20 Ω | 17.1 mV/°C | |
| BZV85C20 | A3 | a1 | PH | Z Diode | | | 540 mA | 1.3 W | 60 W | 20 V | 10 mA | 24 Ω | 19.1 mV/°C | |
| BZV85C22 | A3 | a1 | PH | Z Diode | | | 500 mA | 1.3 W | 60 W | 22 V | 10 mA | 25 Ω | 22.1 mV/°C | |
| BZV85C24 | A3 | a1 | PH | Z Diode | | | 450 mA | 1.3 W | 60 W | 24 V | 10 mA | 30 Ω | 24.3 mV/°C | |
| BZV85C27 | A3 | a1 | PH | Z Diode | | | 400 mA | 1.3 W | 60 W | 27 V | 8 mA | 40 Ω | 27.5 mV/°C | |
| BZV85C30 | A3 | a1 | PH | Z Diode | | | 380 mA | 1.3 W | 60 W | 30 V | 8 mA | 45 Ω | 32 mV/°C | |
| BZV85C33 | A3 | a1 | PH | Z Diode | | | 350 mA | 1.3 W | 60 W | 33 V | 8 mA | 45 Ω | 35 mV/°C | |
| BZV85C36 | A3 | a1 | PH | Z Diode | | | 320 mA | 1.3 W | 60 W | 36 V | 8 mA | 50 Ω | 39.9 mV/°C | |
| BZV85C39 | A3 | a1 | PH | Z Diode | | | 296 mA | 1.3 W | 60 W | 39 V | 6 mA | 60 Ω | 43 mV/°C | |
| BZV85C43 | A3 | a1 | PH | Z Diode | | | 270 mA | 1.3 W | 60 W | 43 V | 6 mA | 75 Ω | 48.3 mV/°C | |
| BZV85C47 | A3 | a1 | PH | Z Diode | | | 246 mA | 1.3 W | 60 W | 47 V | 4 mA | 100 Ω | 52.5 mV/°C | |
| BZV85C51 | A3 | a1 | PH | Z Diode | | | 226 mA | 1.3 W | 60 W | 51 V | 4 mA | 125 Ω | 56.5 mV/°C | |
| BZV85C56 | A3 | a1 | PH | Z Diode | | | 208 mA | 1.3 W | 60 W | 56 V | 4 mA | 150 Ω | 63 mV/°C | |
| BZV85C62 | A3 | a1 | PH | Z Diode | | | 286 mA | 1.3 W | 60 W | 62 V | 4 mA | 175 Ω | 72.5 mV/°C | |
| BZV85C68 | A3 | a1 | PH | Z Diode | | | 171 mA | 1.3 W | 60 W | 68 V | 4 mA | 200 Ω | 81 mV/°C | |
| BZV85C75 | A3 | a1 | PH | Z Diode | | | 161 mA | 1.3 W | 60 W | 75 V | 4 mA | 225 Ω | 88 mV/°C | |
| BZV86-1V4 | A1 | a1 | PH | Stabistor | | | | 0.33 W | | <1.4 | 5 | | -3.8 mV/°C | |
| BZV86-2V0 | A1 | a1 | PH | Stabistor | | | | 0.33 W | | <2.0 | 5 | | -6 mV/°C | |
| BZV86-2V6 | A1 | a1 | PH | Stabistor | | | | 0.33 W | | <2.6 | 5 | | -8.5 mV/°C | |
| BZV86-3V2 | A1 | a1 | PH | Stabistor | | | | 0.33 W | | <3.25 | 5 | | -12 mV/°C | |
| BZV87-1V4 | D2 | a1 | PH | Stabistor | | | | 0.33 W | | <1.4 | 5 | | -3.8 mV/°C | |
| BZV87-2V0 | D2 | a1 | PH | Stabistor | | | | 0.33 W | | <2.0 | 5 | | -6 mV/°C | |
| BZV87-2V6 | D2 | a1 | PH | Stabistor | | | | 0.33 W | | <2.6 | 5 | | -8.5 mV/°C | |
| BZV87-3V2 | D2 | a1 | PH | Stabistor | | | | 0.33 W | | <3.25 | 5 | | -12 mV/°C | |
| BZV90C2V4 | F8 | d9 | PH | Z Diode | | | | 1.3 W | 40 W | 2.4 V | 5 mA | 70 Ω | -3.5 mV/°C | |
| BZV90C2V7 | F8 | d9 | PH | Z Diode | | | | 1.3 W | 40 W | 2.7 V | 5 mA | 75 Ω | -3.5 mV/°C | |
| BZV90C3V0 | F8 | d9 | PH | Z Diode | | | | 1.3 W | 40 W | 3.0 V | 5 mA | 80 Ω | -3.5 mV/°C | |
| BZV90C3V3 | F8 | d9 | PH | Z Diode | | | | 1.3 W | 40 W | 3.3 V | 5 mA | 85 Ω | -3.5 mV/°C | |
| BZV90C3V6 | F8 | d9 | PH | Z Diode | | | | 1.3 W | 40 W | 3.6 V | 5 mA | 85 Ω | -3.5 mV/°C | |
| BZV90C3V9 | F8 | d9 | PH | Z Diode | | | | 1.3 W | 40 W | 3.9 V | 5 mA | 85 Ω | -3.5 mV/°C | |
| BZV90C4V3 | F8 | d9 | PH | Z Diode | | | | 1.3 W | 40 W | 4.3 V | 5 mA | 80 Ω | -3.5 mV/°C | |
| BZV90C4V7 | F8 | d9 | PH | Z Diode | | | | 1.3 W | 40 W | 4.7 V | 5 mA | 50 Ω | -3.5 mV/°C | |

| Type | Case | Pin-code | | | Vcla Vbro | Its | Izm | Pv | Pvts | Vz | Iz Is | rz | TK | |
|---|---|---|---|---|---|---|---|---|---|---|---|---|---|---|
| | | | PH | | | | | **Maximum Ratings** | | | | **Electrical Characteristics** | | |
| BZV90C5V1 | F8 | d9 | PH | Z Diode | | | | 1.3 W | 40 W | 5.1 V | 5 mA | 40 Ω | -2.7 mV/°C | |
| BZV90C5V6 | F8 | d9 | PH | Z Diode | | | | 1.3 W | 40 W | 5.6 V | 5 mA | 15 Ω | 2.5 mV/°C | |
| BZV90C6V2 | F8 | d9 | PH | Z Diode | | | | 1.3 W | 40 W | 6.2 V | 5 mA | 6 Ω | 3.7 mV/°C | |
| BZV90C6V8 | F8 | d9 | PH | Z Diode | | | | 1.3 W | 40 W | 6.8 V | 5 mA | 6 Ω | 4.5 mV/°C | |
| BZV90C7V5 | F8 | d9 | PH | Z Diode | | | | 1.3 W | 40 W | 7.5 V | 5 mA | 6 Ω | 5.3 mV/°C | |
| BZV90C8V2 | F8 | d9 | PH | Z Diode | | | | 1.3 W | 40 W | 8.2 V | 5 mA | 6 Ω | 6.2 mV/°C | |
| BZV90C9V1 | F8 | d9 | PH | Z Diode | | | | 1.3 W | 40 W | 9.1 V | 5 mA | 6 Ω | 7 mV/°C | |
| BZV90C10 | F8 | d9 | PH | Z Diode | | | | 1.3 W | 40 W | 10 V | 5 mA | 6 Ω | 8 mV/°C | |
| BZV90C11 | F8 | d9 | PH | Z Diode | | | | 1.3 W | 40 W | 11 V | 5 mA | 10 Ω | 9 mV/°C | |
| BZV90C12 | F8 | d9 | PH | Z Diode | | | | 1.3 W | 40 W | 12 V | 5 mA | 10 Ω | 10 mV/°C | |
| BZV90C13 | F8 | d9 | PH | Z Diode | | | | 1.3 W | 40 W | 13 V | 5 mA | 10 Ω | 11 mV/°C | |
| BZV90C15 | F8 | d9 | PH | Z Diode | | | | 1.3 W | 40 W | 15 V | 5 mA | 10 Ω | 13 mV/°C | |
| BZV90C16 | F8 | d9 | PH | Z Diode | | | | 1.3 W | 40 W | 16 V | 5 mA | 10 Ω | 14 mV/°C | |
| BZV90C18 | F8 | d9 | PH | Z Diode | | | | 1.3 W | 40 W | 18 V | 5 mA | 10 Ω | 16 mV/°C | |
| BZV90C20 | F8 | d9 | PH | Z Diode | | | | 1.3 W | 40 W | 20 V | 5 mA | 15 Ω | 18 mV/°C | |
| BZV90C22 | F8 | d9 | PH | Z Diode | | | | 1.3 W | 40 W | 22 V | 5 mA | 20 Ω | 20 mV/°C | |
| BZV90C24 | F8 | d9 | PH | Z Diode | | | | 1.3 W | 40 W | 24 V | 5 mA | 25 Ω | 22 mV/°C | |
| BZV90C27 | F8 | d9 | PH | Z Diode | | | | 1.3 W | 40 W | 27 V | 2 mA | 25 Ω | 25.3 mV/°C | |
| BZV90C30 | F8 | d9 | PH | Z Diode | | | | 1.3 W | 40 W | 30 V | 2 mA | 30 Ω | 29.4 mV/°C | |
| BZV90C33 | F8 | d9 | PH | Z Diode | | | | 1.3 W | 40 W | 33 V | 2 mA | 35 Ω | 33.4 mV/°C | |
| BZV90C36 | F8 | d9 | PH | Z Diode | | | | 1.3 W | 40 W | 36 V | 2 mA | 35 Ω | 37.4 mV/°C | |
| BZV90C39 | F8 | d9 | PH | Z Diode | | | | 1.3 W | 40 W | 39 V | 2 mA | 40 Ω | 41.2 mV/°C | |
| BZV90C43 | F8 | d9 | PH | Z Diode | | | | 1.3 W | 40 W | 43 V | 2 mA | 45 Ω | 46.6 mV/°C | |
| BZV90C47 | F8 | d9 | PH | Z Diode | | | | 1.3 W | 40 W | 47 V | 2 mA | 50 Ω | 51.8 mV/°C | |
| BZV90C51 | F8 | d9 | PH | Z Diode | | | | 1.3 W | 40 W | 51 V | 2 mA | 60 Ω | 57.2 mV/°C | |
| BZV90C56 | F8 | d9 | PH | Z Diode | | | | 1.3 W | 40 W | 56 V | 2 mA | 70 Ω | 63.8 mV/°C | |
| BZV90C62 | F8 | d9 | PH | Z Diode | | | | 1.3 W | 40 W | 62 V | 2 mA | 80 Ω | 71.6 mV/°C | |
| BZV90C68 | F8 | d9 | PH | Z Diode | | | | 1.3 W | 40 W | 68 V | 2 mA | 90 Ω | 79.8 mV/°C | |
| BZV90C75 | F8 | d9 | PH | Z Diode | | | | 1.3 W | 40 W | 75 V | 2 mA | 95 Ω | 88.6 mV/°C | |
| BZW03C7V5 | A5 | a1 | PH | Z Diode, TVS | 11.3 V | 44.2 mA | 44.2 mA | 6 W | 1 kW | 7.5 V | 175 mA | 0.7 Ω | 700·10⁶/°C | |
| BZW03C8V2 | A5 | a1 | PH | Z Diode, TVS | 12.3 V | 40.6 mA | 40.6 mA | 6 W | 1 kW | 8.2 V | 150 mA | 0.8 Ω | 800·10⁶/°C | |
| BZW03C9V1 | A5 | a1 | PH | Z Diode, TVS | 13.3 V | 37.6 mA | 37.6 mA | 6 W | 1 kW | 9.1 V | 150 mA | 0.9 Ω | 800·10⁶/°C | |
| BZW03C10 | A5 | a1 | PH | Z Diode, TVS | 14.8 V | 34 mA | 34 mA | 6 W | 1 kW | 10 V | 125 mA | 1 Ω | 900·10⁶/°C | |
| BZW03C11 | A5 | a1 | PH | Z Diode, TVS | 15.7 V | 31.8 mA | 31.8 mA | 6 W | 1 kW | 11 V | 125 mA | 1.1 Ω | 1000·10⁶/°C | |
| BZW03C12 | A5 | a1 | PH | Z Diode, TVS | 17 V | 29.4 mA | 29.4 mA | 6 W | 1 kW | 12 V | 100 mA | 1.1 Ω | 1000·10⁶/°C | |
| BZW03C13 | A5 | a1 | PH | Z Diode, TVS | 18.9 V | 26.4 mA | 26.4 mA | 6 W | 1 kW | 13 V | 100 mA | 1.2 Ω | 1000·10⁶/°C | |
| BZW03C15 | A5 | a1 | PH | Z Diode, TVS | 20.9 V | 23.9 mA | 23.9 mA | 6 W | 1 kW | 15 V | 75 mA | 1.2 Ω | 1000·10⁶/°C | |
| BZW03C16 | A5 | a1 | PH | Z Diode, TVS | 22.9 V | 21.8 mA | 21.8 mA | 6 W | 1 kW | 16 V | 75 mA | 1.3 Ω | 1100·10⁶/°C | |
| BZW03C18 | A5 | a1 | PH | Z Diode, TVS | 25.6 V | 19.5 mA | 19.5 mA | 6 W | 1 kW | 18 V | 65 mA | 1.3 Ω | 1100·10⁶/°C | |
| BZW03C20 | A5 | a1 | PH | Z Diode, TVS | 28.4 V | 17.6 mA | 17.6 mA | 6 W | 1 kW | 20 V | 65 mA | 1.5 Ω | 1100·10⁶/°C | |

| Type | Case | Pin-code | | | Vcla Vbro | Its | Izm | Pv | Pvts | Vz | Iz Is | rz | TK | |
|------|------|----------|--|--|-----------|-----|-----|----|------|----|-------|----|----|--|
| BZW03C22 | A5 | a1 | PH | Z Diode, TVS | 31 V | 16.1 mA | 16.1 mA | 6 W | 1 kW | 22 V | 50 mA | 1.6 Ω | $1100 \cdot 10^6/°C$ | |
| BZW03C24 | A5 | a1 | PH | Z Diode, TVS | 33.8 V | 14.8 mA | 14.8 mA | 6 W | 1 kW | 24 V | 50 mA | 1.8 Ω | $1100 \cdot 10^6/°C$ | |
| BZW03C27 | A5 | a1 | PH | Z Diode, TVS | 38.1 V | 13.1 mA | 13.1 mA | 6 W | 1 kW | 27 V | 50 mA | 2.5 Ω | $1100 \cdot 10^6/°C$ | |
| BZW03C30 | A5 | a1 | PH | Z Diode, TVS | 42.2 V | 11.8 mA | 11.8 mA | 6 W | 1 kW | 30 V | 40 mA | 4 Ω | $1100 \cdot 10^6/°C$ | |
| BZW03C33 | A5 | a1 | PH | Z Diode, TVS | 46.2 V | 10.8 mA | 10.8 mA | 6 W | 1 kW | 33 V | 40 mA | 5 Ω | $1100 \cdot 10^6/°C$ | |
| BZW03C36 | A5 | a1 | PH | Z Diode, TVS | 50.1 V | 10 mA | 10 mA | 6 W | 1 kW | 36 V | 30 mA | 6 Ω | $1100 \cdot 10^6/°C$ | |
| BZW03C39 | A5 | a1 | PH | Z Diode, TVS | 54.1 V | 9.2 mA | 9.2 mA | 6 W | 1 kW | 39 V | 30 mA | 7 Ω | $1100 \cdot 10^6/°C$ | |
| BZW03C43 | A5 | a1 | PH | Z Diode, TVS | 60.7 V | 8.2 mA | 8.2 mA | 6 W | 1 kW | 43 V | 30 mA | 10 Ω | $1200 \cdot 10^6/°C$ | |
| BZW03C47 | A5 | a1 | PH | Z Diode, TVS | 65.5 V | 7.6 mA | 7.6 mA | 6 W | 1 kW | 47 V | 25 mA | 12 Ω | $1200 \cdot 10^6/°C$ | |
| BZW03C51 | A5 | a1 | PH | Z Diode, TVS | 70.8 V | 7 mA | 7 mA | 6 W | 1 kW | 51 V | 25 mA | 14 Ω | $1200 \cdot 10^6/°C$ | |
| BZW03C56 | A5 | a1 | PH | Z Diode, TVS | 78.6 V | 6.3 mA | 6.3 mA | 6 W | 1 kW | 56 V | 20 mA | 18 Ω | $1200 \cdot 10^6/°C$ | |
| BZW03C62 | A5 | a1 | PH | Z Diode, TVS | 86.5 V | 5.8 mA | 5.8 mA | 6 W | 1 kW | 62 V | 20 mA | 20 Ω | $1300 \cdot 10^6/°C$ | |
| BZW03C68 | A5 | a1 | PH | Z Diode, TVS | 94.4 V | 5.3 mA | 5.3 mA | 6 W | 1 kW | 68 V | 20 mA | 22 Ω | $1300 \cdot 10^6/°C$ | |
| BZW03C75 | A5 | a1 | PH | Z Diode, TVS | 103.5 V | 4.8 mA | 4.8 mA | 6 W | 1 kW | 75 V | 20 mA | 25 Ω | $1300 \cdot 10^6/°C$ | |
| BZW03C82 | A5 | a1 | PH | Z Diode, TVS | 114 V | 4.3 mA | 4.3 mA | 6 W | 1 kW | 82 V | 15 mA | 30 Ω | $1300 \cdot 10^6/°C$ | |
| BZW03C91 | A5 | a1 | PH | Z Diode, TVS | 126 V | 3.9 mA | 3.9 mA | 6 W | 1 kW | 91 V | 15 mA | 40 Ω | $1300 \cdot 10^6/°C$ | |
| BZW03C100 | A5 | a1 | PH | Z Diode, TVS | 139 V | 3.6 mA | 3.6 mA | 6 W | 1 kW | 100 V | 12 mA | 45 Ω | $1300 \cdot 10^6/°C$ | |
| BZW03C110 | A5 | a1 | PH | Z Diode, TVS | 152 V | 3.3 mA | 3.3 mA | 6 W | 1 kW | 110 V | 12 mA | 65 Ω | $1300 \cdot 10^6/°C$ | |
| BZW03C120 | A5 | a1 | PH | Z Diode, TVS | 167 V | 3 mA | 3 mA | 6 W | 1 kW | 120 V | 10 mA | 90 Ω | $1300 \cdot 10^6/°C$ | |
| BZW03C130 | A5 | a1 | PH | Z Diode, TVS | 185 V | 2.7 mA | 2.7 mA | 6 W | 1 kW | 130 V | 10 mA | 100 Ω | $1300 \cdot 10^6/°C$ | |
| BZW03C150 | A5 | a1 | PH | Z Diode, TVS | 204 V | 2.4 mA | 2.4 mA | 6 W | 1 kW | 150 V | 8 mA | 150 Ω | $1300 \cdot 10^6/°C$ | |
| BZW03C160 | A5 | a1 | PH | Z Diode, TVS | 224 V | 2.2 mA | 2.2 mA | 6 W | 1 kW | 160 V | 8 mA | 180 Ω | $1300 \cdot 10^6/°C$ | |
| BZW03C180 | A5 | a1 | PH | Z Diode, TVS | 249 V | 2 mA | 2 mA | 6 W | 1 kW | 180 V | 5 mA | 210 Ω | $1300 \cdot 10^6/°C$ | |
| BZW03C200 | A5 | a1 | PH | Z Diode, TVS | 276 V | 1.8 mA | 1.8 mA | 6 W | 1 kW | 200 V | 5 mA | 250 Ω | $1300 \cdot 10^6/°C$ | |
| BZW03C220 | A5 | a1 | PH | Z Diode, TVS | 305 V | 1.6 mA | 1.6 mA | 6 W | 1 kW | 220 V | 5 mA | 350 Ω | $1300 \cdot 10^6/°C$ | |
| BZW03C240 | A5 | a1 | PH | Z Diode, TVS | 336 V | 1.5 mA | 1.5 mA | 6 W | 1 kW | 240 V | 5 mA | 450 Ω | $1300 \cdot 10^6/°C$ | |
| BZW03C270 | A5 | a1 | PH | Z Diode, TVS | 380 V | 1.3 mA | 1.3 mA | 6 W | 1 kW | 270 V | 5 mA | 600 Ω | $1300 \cdot 10^6/°C$ | |
| BZW03C300 | A5 | a1 | PH | TVS | 419 V | 1.2 mA | 1.2 mA | 6 W | 1 kW | | | | | TVS only |
| BZW03C330 | A5 | a1 | PH | TVS | 459 V | 1.1 mA | 1.1 mA | 6 W | 1 kW | | | | | TVS only |
| BZW03C360 | A5 | a1 | PH | TVS | 498 V | 1 mA | 1 mA | 6 W | 1 kW | | | | | TVS only |
| BZW03C390 | A5 | a1 | PH | TVS | 537 V | 0.93 mA | 0.93 mA | 6 W | 1 kW | | | | | TVS only |
| BZW03C430 | A5 | a1 | PH | TVS | 603 V | 0.83 mA | 0.83 mA | 6 W | 1 kW | | | | | TVS only |
| BZW03C470 | A5 | a1 | PH | TVS | 655 V | 0.76 mA | 0.76 mA | 6 W | 1 kW | | | | | TVS only |
| BZW03C510 | A5 | a1 | PH | TVS | 707 V | 0.71 mA | 0.71 mA | 6 W | 1 kW | | | | | TVS only |
| BZW03C4V7 | A5 | a1 | PH | Z Diode, TVS | | 38 mA | 38 mA | 6 W | 1 kW | 4.7 V | | | | ZD only |
| BZW03C5V1 | A5 | a1 | PH | Z Diode, TVS | | 35 mA | 35 mA | 6 W | 1 kW | 5.1 V | | | | ZD only |
| BZW03C3V6 | A5 | a1 | PH | Z Diode | | | 45 mA | 6 W | 1 kW | 3.6 V | | | | ZD only |
| BZW03C3V9 | A5 | a1 | PH | Z Diode | | | 43 mA | 6 W | 1 kW | 3.9 V | | | | ZD only |
| BZW03C4V3 | A5 | a1 | PH | Z Diode | | | 40 mA | 6 W | 1 kW | 4.3 V | | | | ZD only |
| BZW03C5V6 | A5 | a1 | PH | Z Diode | | | 32 mA | 6 W | 1 kW | 5.6 V | | | | ZD only |

| Type | Case | Pin-code | | | Vcla Vbro | Its | Izm | Pv | Pvts | Vz | Iz Is | rz | TK | |
|---|---|---|---|---|---|---|---|---|---|---|---|---|---|---|
| | | | | | **Maximum Ratings** | | | | | **Electrical Characteristics** | | | | |
| BZW03C6V2 | A5 | a1 | PH | Z Diode | | | 28 mA | 6 W | 1 kW | 6.2 V | | | | ZD only |
| BZW03C6V8 | A5 | a1 | PH | Z Diode | | | 25 mA | 6 W | 1 kW | 6.8 V | | | | ZD only |
| BZW03D7V5 | A5 | a1 | TE | TVS, Z Diode | 11.7 V | 44.2 mA | 44.2 mA | 6 W | 1000 W | 7.5 V | 175 mA | 0.7 Ω | $700 \cdot 10^6/°C$ | |
| BZW03D8V2 | A5 | a1 | TE | TVS, Z Diode | 12.6 V | 40.6 mA | 40.6 mA | 6 W | 1000 W | 8.2 V | 150 mA | 0.8 Ω | $800 \cdot 10^6/°C$ | |
| BZW03D9V1 | A5 | a1 | TE | TVS, Z Diode | 13.6 V | 37.6 mA | 37.6 mA | 6 W | 1000 W | 9.1 V | 150 mA | 0.9 Ω | $800 \cdot 10^6/°C$ | |
| BZW03D10 | A5 | a1 | TE | TVS, Z Diode | 15.2 V | 34 mA | 34 mA | 6 W | 1000 W | 10 V | 125 mA | 1 Ω | $900 \cdot 10^6/°C$ | |
| BZW03D11 | A5 | a1 | TE | TVS, Z Diode | 16.2 V | 31.8 mA | 31.8 mA | 6 W | 1000 W | 11 V | 125 mA | 1.1 Ω | $1000 \cdot 10^6/°C$ | |
| BZW03D12 | A5 | a1 | TE | TVS, Z Diode | 17.5 V | 29.4 mA | 29.4 mA | 6 W | 1000 W | 12 V | 100 mA | 1.1 Ω | $1000 \cdot 10^6/°C$ | |
| BZW03D13 | A5 | a1 | TE | TVS, Z Diode | 19.1 V | 26.4 mA | 26.4 mA | 6 W | 1000 W | 13 V | 100 mA | 1.2 Ω | $1000 \cdot 10^6/°C$ | |
| BZW03D15 | A5 | a1 | TE | TVS, Z Diode | 21.8 V | 23.9 mA | 23.9 mA | 6 W | 1000 W | 15 V | 75 mA | 1.2 Ω | $1000 \cdot 10^6/°C$ | |
| BZW03D16 | A5 | a1 | TE | TVS, Z Diode | 23.4 V | 21.8 mA | 21.8 mA | 6 W | 1000 W | 16 V | 75 mA | 1.3 Ω | $1100 \cdot 10^6/°C$ | |
| BZW03D18 | A5 | a1 | TE | TVS, Z Diode | 26.3 V | 19.5 mA | 19.5 mA | 6 W | 1000 W | 18 V | 65 mA | 1.3 Ω | $1100 \cdot 10^6/°C$ | |
| BZW03D20 | A5 | a1 | TE | TVS, Z Diode | 29.2 V | 17.6 mA | 17.6 mA | 6 W | 1000 W | 20 V | 65 mA | 1.5 Ω | $1100 \cdot 10^6/°C$ | |
| BZW03D22 | A5 | a1 | TE | TVS, Z Diode | 32 V | 16.1 mA | 16.1 mA | 6 W | 1000 W | 22 V | 50 mA | 1.6 Ω | $1100 \cdot 10^6/°C$ | |
| BZW03D24 | A5 | a1 | TE | TVS, Z Diode | 34.6 V | 14.8 mA | 14.8 mA | 6 W | 1000 W | 24 V | 50 mA | 1.8 Ω | $1100 \cdot 10^6/°C$ | |
| BZW03D27 | A5 | a1 | TE | TVS, Z Diode | 39 V | 13.1 mA | 13.1 mA | 6 W | 1000 W | 27 V | 50 mA | 2.5 Ω | $1100 \cdot 10^6/°C$ | |
| BZW03D30 | A5 | a1 | TE | TVS, Z Diode | 43.2 V | 11.8 mA | 11.8 mA | 6 W | 1000 W | 30 V | 40 mA | 4 Ω | $1100 \cdot 10^6/°C$ | |
| BZW03D33 | A5 | a1 | TE | TVS, Z Diode | 47 V | 10.8 mA | 10.8 mA | 6 W | 1000 W | 33 V | 40 mA | 5 Ω | $1100 \cdot 10^6/°C$ | |
| BZW03D36 | A5 | a1 | TE | TVS, Z Diode | 51.7 V | 10 mA | 10 mA | 6 W | 1000 W | 36 V | 30 mA | 6 Ω | $1100 \cdot 10^6/°C$ | |
| BZW03D39 | A5 | a1 | TE | TVS, Z Diode | 56 V | 9.2 mA | 9.2 mA | 6 W | 1000 W | 39 V | 30 mA | 7 Ω | $1100 \cdot 10^6/°C$ | |
| BZW03D43 | A5 | a1 | TE | TVS, Z Diode | 62 V | 8.2 mA | 8.2 mA | 6 W | 1000 W | 43 V | 30 mA | 10 Ω | $1200 \cdot 10^6/°C$ | |
| BZW03D47 | A5 | a1 | TE | TVS, Z Diode | 66.7 V | 7.6 mA | 7.6 mA | 6 W | 1000 W | 47 V | 25 mA | 12 Ω | $1200 \cdot 10^6/°C$ | |
| BZW03D51 | A5 | a1 | TE | TVS, Z Diode | 73 V | 7 mA | 7 mA | 6 W | 1000 W | 51 V | 25 mA | 14 Ω | $1200 \cdot 10^6/°C$ | |
| BZW03D56 | A5 | a1 | TE | TVS, Z Diode | 80.2 V | 6.3 mA | 6.3 mA | 6 W | 1000 W | 56 V | 20 mA | 18 Ω | $1200 \cdot 10^6/°C$ | |
| BZW03D62 | A5 | a1 | TE | TVS, Z Diode | 88.7 V | 5.8 mA | 5.8 mA | 6 W | 1000 W | 62 V | 20 mA | 20 Ω | $1300 \cdot 10^6/°C$ | |
| BZW03D68 | A5 | a1 | TE | TVS, Z Diode | 97.2 V | 5.3 mA | 5.3 mA | 6 W | 1000 W | 68 V | 20 mA | 22 Ω | $1300 \cdot 10^6/°C$ | |
| BZW03D75 | A5 | a1 | TE | TVS, Z Diode | 107 V | 4.8 mA | 4.8 mA | 6 W | 1000 W | 75 V | 20 mA | 25 Ω | $1300 \cdot 10^6/°C$ | |
| BZW03D82 | A5 | a1 | TE | TVS, Z Diode | 117 V | 4.3 mA | 4.3 mA | 6 W | 1000 W | 82 V | 15 mA | 30 Ω | $1300 \cdot 10^6/°C$ | |
| BZW03D91 | A5 | a1 | TE | TVS, Z Diode | 130 V | 3.9 mA | 3.9 mA | 6 W | 1000 W | 91 V | 15 mA | 40 Ω | $1300 \cdot 10^6/°C$ | |
| BZW03D100 | A5 | a1 | TE | TVS, Z Diode | 143 V | 3.6 mA | 3.6 mA | 6 W | 1000 W | 100 V | 12 mA | 45 Ω | $1300 \cdot 10^6/°C$ | |
| BZW03D110 | A5 | a1 | TE | TVS, Z Diode | 157 V | 3.3 mA | 3.3 mA | 6 W | 1000 W | 110 V | 12 mA | 65 Ω | $1300 \cdot 10^6/°C$ | |
| BZW03D120 | A5 | a1 | TE | TVS, Z Diode | 172 V | 3 mA | 3 mA | 6 W | 1000 W | 120 V | 10 mA | 90 Ω | $1300 \cdot 10^6/°C$ | |
| BZW03D130 | A5 | a1 | TE | TVS, Z Diode | 187 V | 2.7 mA | 2.7 mA | 6 W | 1000 W | 130 V | 10 mA | 100 Ω | $1300 \cdot 10^6/°C$ | |
| BZW03D150 | A5 | a1 | TE | TVS, Z Diode | 213 V | 2.4 mA | 2.4 mA | 6 W | 1000 W | 150 V | 8 mA | 150 Ω | $1300 \cdot 10^6/°C$ | |
| BZW03D160 | A5 | a1 | TE | TVS, Z Diode | 229 V | 2.2 mA | 2.2 mA | 6 W | 1000 W | 160 V | 8 mA | 180 Ω | $1300 \cdot 10^6/°C$ | |
| BZW03D180 | A5 | a1 | TE | TVS, Z Diode | 256 V | 2 mA | 2 mA | 6 W | 1000 W | 180 V | 5 mA | 210 Ω | $1300 \cdot 10^6/°C$ | |
| BZW03D200 | A5 | a1 | TE | TVS, Z Diode | 284 V | 2.8 mA | 2.8 mA | 6 W | 1000 W | 200 V | 5 mA | 250 Ω | $1300 \cdot 10^6/°C$ | |
| BZW03D220 | A5 | a1 | TE | TVS, Z Diode | 314 V | 1.6 mA | 1.6 mA | 6 W | 1000 W | 220 V | 5 mA | 350 Ω | $1300 \cdot 10^6/°C$ | |
| BZW03D240 | A5 | a1 | TE | TVS, Z Diode | 364 V | 1.5 mA | 1.5 mA | 6 W | 1000 W | 240 V | 5 mA | 450 Ω | $1300 \cdot 10^6/°C$ | |
| BZW03D270 | A5 | a1 | TE | TVS, Z Diode | 388 V | 1.3 mA | 1.3 mA | 6 W | 1000 W | 270 V | 5 mA | 600 Ω | $1300 \cdot 10^6/°C$ | |

| Type | Case | Pin-code | 🏭 | ⚙ | Maximum Ratings | | | | Electrical Characteristics | | | | |
|------|------|----------|-----|-----|-----------------|-----|-----|-----|----------------------------|-----|-----|-----|-----|
| | | | | | Vcla Vbro | Its | Izm | Pv | Pvts | Vz | Iz Is | rz | TK | 📄 |
| BZW14 | A5 | a1 | PH | TVS, Z Diode | 28 V | 50 mA | 50 mA | | | | | | | |
| BZX55C0V8 | A1 | a1 | SG,IT,PH | Z Diode | | | 155 mA | 0.5 W | | 0.8 V | 5 mA | <8 Ω | $-800 \cdot 10^6$/°C | P (SG) |
| BZX55C2V4 | A1 | a1 | SG,TE,PH,MO | Z Diode | | | 135 mA | 0.5 W | | 2.4 V | 5 mA | <85 Ω | $-800 \cdot 10^6$/°C | P (SG) |
| BZX55C2V7 | A1 | a1 | SG,TE,PH,MO | Z Diode | | | 125 mA | 0.5 W | | 2.7 V | 5 mA | <85 Ω | $-800 \cdot 10^6$/°C | P (SG) |
| BZX55C3V0 | A1 | a1 | SG,TE,IT,PH,MO | Z Diode | | | 115 mA | 0.5 W | | 3.0 V | 5 mA | <85 Ω | $-800 \cdot 10^6$/°C | P (SG) |
| BZX55C3V3 | A1 | a1 | SG,TE,IT,PH,MO | Z Diode | | | 110 mA | 0.5 W | | 3.3 V | 5 mA | <85 Ω | $-800 \cdot 10^6$/°C | P (SG) |
| BZX55C3V6 | A1 | a1 | SG,TE,IT,PH,MO | Z Diode | | | 105 mA | 0.5 W | | 3.6 V | 5 mA | <85 Ω | $-800 \cdot 10^6$/°C | P (SG) |
| BZX55C3V9 | A1 | a1 | SG,TE,IT,PH,MO | Z Diode | | | 95 mA | 0.5 W | | 3.9 V | 5 mA | <85 Ω | $-700 \cdot 10^6$/°C | P (SG) |
| BZX55C4V3 | A1 | a1 | SG,TE,IT,PH,MO | Z Diode | | | 90 mA | 0.5 W | | 4.3 V | 5 mA | <75 Ω | $-400 \cdot 10^6$/°C | P (SG) |
| BZX55C4V7 | A1 | a1 | SG,TE,IT,PH,MO | Z Diode | | | 85 mA | 0.5 W | | 4.7 V | 5 mA | <60 Ω | $-300 \cdot 10^6$/°C | P (SG) |
| BZX55C5V1 | A1 | a1 | SG,TE,IT,PH,MO | Z Diode | | | 80 mA | 0.5 W | | 5.1 V | 5 mA | <35 Ω | $500 \cdot 10^6$/°C | P (SG) |
| BZX55C5V6 | A1 | a1 | SG,TE,IT,PH,MO | Z Diode | | | 70 mA | 0.5 W | | 5.6 V | 5 mA | <25 Ω | $600 \cdot 10^6$/°C | P (SG) |
| BZX55C6V2 | A1 | a1 | SG,TE,IT,PH,MO | Z Diode | | | 64 mA | 0.5 W | | 6.2 V | 5 mA | <10 Ω | $700 \cdot 10^6$/°C | P (SG) |
| BZX55C6V8 | A1 | a1 | SG,TE,IT,PH,MO | Z Diode | | | 58 mA | 0.5 W | | 6.8 V | 5 mA | <8 Ω | $800 \cdot 10^6$/°C | P (SG) |
| BZX55C7V5 | A1 | a1 | SG,TE,IT,PH,MO | Z Diode | | | 53 mA | 0.5 W | | 7.5 V | 5 mA | <7 Ω | $900 \cdot 10^6$/°C | P (SG) |
| BZX55C8V2 | A1 | a1 | SG,TE,IT,PH,MO | Z Diode | | | 47 mA | 0.5 W | | 8.2 V | 5 mA | <7 Ω | $900 \cdot 10^6$/°C | P (SG) |
| BZX55C9V1 | A1 | a1 | SG,TE,IT,PH,MO | Z Diode | | | 43 mA | 0.5 W | | 9.1 V | 5 mA | <10 Ω | $1000 \cdot 10^6$/°C | P (SG) |
| BZX55C10 | A1 | a1 | SG,TE,IT,PH,MO | Z Diode | | | 40 mA | 0.5 W | | 10 V | 5 mA | <15 Ω | $1100 \cdot 10^6$/°C | P (SG) |
| BZX55C11 | A1 | a1 | SG,TE,IT,PH,MO | Z Diode | | | 36 mA | 0.5 W | | 11 V | 5 mA | <20 Ω | $1100 \cdot 10^6$/°C | P (SG) |
| BZX55C12 | A1 | a1 | SG,TE,IT,PH,MO | Z Diode | | | 32 mA | 0.5 W | | 12 V | 5 mA | <20 Ω | $1100 \cdot 10^6$/°C | P (SG) |
| BZX55C13 | A1 | a1 | SG,TE,IT,PH,MO | Z Diode | | | 29 mA | 0.5 W | | 13 V | 5 mA | <26 Ω | $1100 \cdot 10^6$/°C | P (SG) |
| BZX55C15 | A1 | a1 | SG,TE,IT,PH,MO | Z Diode | | | 27 mA | 0.5 W | | 15 V | 5 mA | <30 Ω | $1100 \cdot 10^6$/°C | P (SG) |
| BZX55C16 | A1 | a1 | SG,TE,IT,PH,MO | Z Diode | | | 24 mA | 0.5 W | | 16 V | 5 mA | <40 Ω | $1100 \cdot 10^6$/°C | P (SG) |
| BZX55C18 | A1 | a1 | SG,TE,IT,PH,MO | Z Diode | | | 21 mA | 0.5 W | | 18 V | 5 mA | <50 Ω | $1100 \cdot 10^6$/°C | P (SG) |
| BZX55C20 | A1 | a1 | SG,TE,IT,PH,MO | Z Diode | | | 20 mA | 0.5 W | | 20 V | 5 mA | <55 Ω | $1100 \cdot 10^6$/°C | P (SG) |
| BZX55C22 | A1 | a1 | SG,TE,IT,PH,MO | Z Diode | | | 18 mA | 0.5 W | | 22 V | 5 mA | <55 Ω | $1100 \cdot 10^6$/°C | P (SG) |
| BZX55C24 | A1 | a1 | SG,TE,IT,PH,MO | Z Diode | | | 16 mA | 0.5 W | | 24 V | 5 mA | <80 Ω | $1200 \cdot 10^6$/°C | P (SG) |
| BZX55C27 | A1 | a1 | SG,TE,IT,PH,MO | Z Diode | | | 14 mA | 0.5 W | | 27 V | 5 mA | <80 Ω | $1200 \cdot 10^6$/°C | P (SG) |
| BZX55C30 | A1 | a1 | SG,TE,IT,PH,MO | Z Diode | | | 13 mA | 0.5 W | | 30 V | 5 mA | <80 Ω | $1200 \cdot 10^6$/°C | P (SG) |
| BZX55C33 | A1 | a1 | SG,TE,IT,PH,MO | Z Diode | | | 12 mA | 0.5 W | | 33 V | 5 mA | <80 Ω | $1200 \cdot 10^6$/°C | P (SG) |
| BZX55C36 | A1 | a1 | SG,TE,IT,PH,MO | Z Diode | | | 11 mA | 0.5 W | | 36 V | 5 mA | <80 Ω | $1200 \cdot 10^6$/°C | P (SG) |
| BZX55C39 | A1 | a1 | SG,TE,IT,PH,MO | Z Diode | | | 10 mA | 0.5 W | | 39 V | 5 mA | <90 Ω | $1200 \cdot 10^6$/°C | P (SG) |
| BZX55C43 | A1 | a1 | SG,TE,IT,PH,MO | Z Diode | | | 9 mA | 0.5 W | | 43 V | 2.5 mA | <90 Ω | $1200 \cdot 10^6$/°C | P (SG) |
| BZX55C47 | A1 | a1 | SG,TE,IT,PH,MO | Z Diode | | | 9 mA | 0.5 W | | 47 V | 2.5 mA | <110 Ω | $1200 \cdot 10^6$/°C | P (SG) |
| BZX55C51 | A1 | a1 | SG,TE,IT,PH,MO | Z Diode | | | 8 mA | 0.5 W | | 51 V | 2.5 mA | <125 Ω | $1200 \cdot 10^6$/°C | P (SG) |
| BZX55C56 | A1 | a1 | SG,TE,PH,MO | Z Diode | | | 7 mA | 0.5 W | | 56 V | 2.5 mA | <135 Ω | $1200 \cdot 10^6$/°C | P (SG) |
| BZX55C62 | A1 | a1 | SG,TE,PH,MO | Z Diode | | | 6 mA | 0.5 W | | 62 V | 2.5 mA | <150 Ω | $1200 \cdot 10^6$/°C | P (SG) |
| BZX55C68 | A1 | a1 | SG,TE,PH,MO | Z Diode | | | 6 mA | 0.5 W | | 68 V | 2.5 mA | <200 Ω | $1200 \cdot 10^6$/°C | P (SG) |
| BZX55C75 | A1 | a1 | SG,TE,PH,MO | Z Diode | | | 5 mA | 0.5 W | | 75 V | 2.5 mA | <250 Ω | $1200 \cdot 10^6$/°C | P (SG) |
| BZX55C82 | A1 | a1 | SG,MO | Z Diode | | | 5 mA | 0.5 W | | 82 V | 2.5 mA | <300 Ω | $1200 \cdot 10^6$/°C | P (SG) |

| Type | Case | Pin-code | | | $V_{cla}$ / $V_{bro}$ | Its | Izm | Pv | Pvts | Vz | Iz / Is | rz | TK | |
|------|------|----------|---|---|---|-----|-----|----|------|----|---------|----|----|---|
| BZX55C91 | A1 | a1 | SG,MO | Z Diode | | | 4 mA | 0.5 W | | 91 V | 1 mA | <450 Ω | $1200 \cdot 10^6$/°C | P (SG) |
| BZX55C100 | A1 | a1 | SG | Z Diode | | | 4 mA | 0.5 W | | 100 V | 1 mA | <450 Ω | $1200 \cdot 10^6$/°C | P (SG) |
| BZX55C110 | A1 | a1 | SG | Z Diode | | | 4 mA | 0.5 W | | 110 V | 1 mA | <600 Ω | $1200 \cdot 10^6$/°C | P (SG) |
| BZX55C120 | A1 | a1 | SG | Z Diode | | | 3 mA | 0.5 W | | 120 V | 1 mA | <800 Ω | $1200 \cdot 10^6$/°C | P (SG) |
| BZX55C130 | A1 | a1 | SG | Z Diode | | | 3 mA | 0.5 W | | 130 V | 1 mA | <1000 Ω | $1200 \cdot 10^6$/°C | P (SG) |
| BZX55C150 | A1 | a1 | SG | Z Diode | | | 3 mA | 0.5 W | | 150 V | 1 mA | <1200 Ω | $1200 \cdot 10^6$/°C | P (SG) |
| BZX55C160 | A1 | a1 | SG | Z Diode | | | 3 mA | 0.5 W | | 160 V | 1 mA | <1500 Ω | $1200 \cdot 10^6$/°C | P (SG) |
| BZX55C180 | A1 | a1 | SG | Z Diode | | | 2 mA | 0.5 W | | 180 V | 1 mA | <1800 Ω | $1200 \cdot 10^6$/°C | P (SG) |
| BZX55C200 | A1 | a1 | SG | Z Diode | | | 2 mA | 0.5 W | | 200 V | 1 mA | <2000 Ω | $1200 \cdot 10^6$/°C | P (SG) |
| BZX55C0V8S | A2 | a1 | IT | Z Diode | | | 93 mA | 0.5 W | | 0.8 V | 5 mA | <8 Ω | $-800 \cdot 10^6$/°C | |
| BZX55C2V7S | A2 | a1 | IT | Z Diode | | | 75 mA | 0.5 W | | 2.7 V | 5 mA | <85 Ω | $-800 \cdot 10^6$/°C | |
| BZX55C3V0S | A2 | a1 | IT | Z Diode | | | 69 mA | 0.5 W | | 3.0 V | 5 mA | <85 Ω | $-800 \cdot 10^6$/°C | |
| BZX55C3V3S | A2 | a1 | IT | Z Diode | | | 66 mA | 0.5 W | | 3.3 V | 5 mA | <85 Ω | $-800 \cdot 10^6$/°C | |
| BZX55C3V6S | A2 | a1 | IT | Z Diode | | | 63 mA | 0.5 W | | 3.6 V | 5 mA | <85 Ω | $-800 \cdot 10^6$/°C | |
| BZX55C3V9S | A2 | a1 | IT | Z Diode | | | 57 mA | 0.5 W | | 3.9 V | 5 mA | <85 Ω | $-700 \cdot 10^6$/°C | |
| BZX55C4V3S | A2 | a1 | IT | Z Diode | | | 54 mA | 0.5 W | | 4.3 V | 5 mA | <75 Ω | $-400 \cdot 10^6$/°C | |
| BZX55C4V7S | A2 | a1 | IT | Z Diode | | | 51 mA | 0.5 W | | 4.7 V | 5 mA | <60 Ω | $-300 \cdot 10^6$/°C | |
| BZX55C5V1S | A2 | a1 | IT | Z Diode | | | 48 mA | 0.5 W | | 5.1 V | 5 mA | <35 Ω | $500 \cdot 10^6$/°C | |
| BZX55C5V6S | A2 | a1 | IT | Z Diode | | | 42 mA | 0.5 W | | 5.6 V | 5 mA | <25 Ω | $600 \cdot 10^6$/°C | |
| BZX55C6V2S | A2 | a1 | IT | Z Diode | | | 39 mA | 0.5 W | | 6.2 V | 5 mA | <10 Ω | $700 \cdot 10^6$/°C | |
| BZX55C6V8S | A2 | a1 | IT | Z Diode | | | 35 mA | 0.5 W | | 6.8 V | 5 mA | <8 Ω | $800 \cdot 10^6$/°C | |
| BZX55C7V5S | A2 | a1 | IT | Z Diode | | | 32 mA | 0.5 W | | 7.5 V | 5 mA | <7 Ω | $900 \cdot 10^6$/°C | |
| BZX55C8V2S | A2 | a1 | IT | Z Diode | | | 28 mA | 0.5 W | | 8.2 V | 5 mA | <7 Ω | $900 \cdot 10^6$/°C | |
| BZX55C9V1S | A2 | a1 | IT | Z Diode | | | 26 mA | 0.5 W | | 9.1 V | 5 mA | <10 Ω | $1000 \cdot 10^6$/°C | |
| BZX55C10S | A2 | a1 | IT | Z Diode | | | 24 mA | 0.5 W | | 10 V | 5 mA | <15 Ω | $1100 \cdot 10^6$/°C | |
| BZX55C11S | A2 | a1 | IT | Z Diode | | | 22 mA | 0.5 W | | 11 V | 5 mA | <20 Ω | $1100 \cdot 10^6$/°C | |
| BZX55C12S | A2 | a1 | IT | Z Diode | | | 19 mA | 0.5 W | | 12 V | 5 mA | <20 Ω | $1100 \cdot 10^6$/°C | |
| BZX55C13S | A2 | a1 | IT | Z Diode | | | 17 mA | 0.5 W | | 13 V | 5 mA | <26 Ω | $1100 \cdot 10^6$/°C | |
| BZX55C15S | A2 | a1 | IT | Z Diode | | | 16 mA | 0.5 W | | 15 V | 5 mA | <30 Ω | $1100 \cdot 10^6$/°C | |
| BZX55C16S | A2 | a1 | IT | Z Diode | | | 14 mA | 0.5 W | | 16 V | 5 mA | <40 Ω | $1100 \cdot 10^6$/°C | |
| BZX55C18S | A2 | a1 | IT | Z Diode | | | 13 mA | 0.5 W | | 18 V | 5 mA | <50 Ω | $1100 \cdot 10^6$/°C | |
| BZX55C20S | A2 | a1 | IT | Z Diode | | | 12 mA | 0.5 W | | 20 V | 5 mA | <55 Ω | $1100 \cdot 10^6$/°C | |
| BZX55C22S | A2 | a1 | IT | Z Diode | | | 11 mA | 0.5 W | | 22 V | 5 mA | <55 Ω | $1100 \cdot 10^6$/°C | |
| BZX55C24S | A2 | a1 | IT | Z Diode | | | 10 mA | 0.5 W | | 24 V | 5 mA | <80 Ω | $1200 \cdot 10^6$/°C | |
| BZX55C27S | A2 | a1 | IT | Z Diode | | | 8 mA | 0.5 W | | 27 V | 5 mA | <80 Ω | $1200 \cdot 10^6$/°C | |
| BZX55C30S | A2 | a1 | IT | Z Diode | | | 8 mA | 0.5 W | | 30 V | 5 mA | <80 Ω | $1200 \cdot 10^6$/°C | |
| BZX55C33S | A2 | a1 | IT | Z Diode | | | 7 mA | 0.5 W | | 33 V | 5 mA | <80 Ω | $1200 \cdot 10^6$/°C | |
| BZX55C36S | A2 | a1 | IT | Z Diode | | | 7 mA | 0.5 W | | 36 V | 5 mA | <80 Ω | $1200 \cdot 10^6$/°C | |
| BZX55C39S | A2 | a1 | IT | Z Diode | | | 6 mA | 0.5 W | | 39 V | 5 mA | <90 Ω | $1200 \cdot 10^6$/°C | |
| BZX55C43S | A2 | a1 | IT | Z Diode | | | 5 mA | 0.5 W | | 43 V | 2.5 mA | <90 Ω | $1200 \cdot 10^6$/°C | |

**Maximum Ratings** · **Electrical Characteristics**

| Type | Case | Pin-code | | | Maximum Ratings | | | | | Electrical Characteristics | | | | |
|------|------|----------|---|---|---|---|---|---|---|---|---|---|---|---|
| | | | | | $V_{cla}$ / $V_{bro}$ | Its | Izm | Pv | Pvts | Vz | Iz / Is | rz | TK | |
| BZX55C47S | A2 | a1 | IT | Z Diode | | | 5 mA | 0.5 W | | 47 V | 2.5 mA | <110 Ω | 1200·10$^6$/°C | |
| BZX55C51S | A2 | a1 | IT | Z Diode | | | 5 mA | 0.5 W | | 51 V | 2.5 mA | <125 Ω | 1200·10$^6$/°C | |
| BZX70C7V5 | B11 | a1 | PH | Z Diode, TVS | 10 V | 20 A | 20 A | 2.5 W | 700 W | 7.5 V | 50 mA | 0.45 Ω | | |
| BZX70C8V2 | B11 | a1 | PH | Z Diode, TVS | 11.2 V | 20 A | 20 A | 2.5 W | 700 W | 8.2 V | 50 mA | 0.45 Ω | | |
| BZX70C9V1 | B11 | a1 | PH | Z Diode, TVS | 12.5 V | 20 A | 20 A | 2.5 W | 700 W | 9.1 V | 50 mA | 0.55 Ω | | |
| BZX70C10 | B11 | a1 | PH | Z Diode, TVS | 14 V | 20 A | 20 A | 2.5 W | 700 W | 10 V | 50 mA | 0.75 Ω | | |
| BZX70C11 | B11 | a1 | PH | Z Diode, TVS | 15.5 V | 20 A | 20 A | 2.5 W | 700 W | 11 V | 50 mA | 0.8 Ω | | |
| BZX70C12 | B11 | a1 | PH | Z Diode, TVS | 17.5 V | 20 A | 20 A | 2.5 W | 700 W | 12 V | 50 mA | 0.85 Ω | | |
| BZX70C13 | B11 | a1 | PH | Z Diode, TVS | 19 V | 20 A | 20 A | 2.5 W | 700 W | 13 V | 50 mA | 0.9 Ω | | |
| BZX70C15 | B11 | a1 | PH | Z Diode, TVS | 21 V | 20 A | 20 A | 2.5 W | 700 W | 15 V | 50 mA | 1.0 Ω | | |
| BZX70C16 | B11 | a1 | PH | Z Diode, TVS | 23 V | 20 A | 20 A | 2.5 W | 700 W | 16 V | 20 mA | 2.4 Ω | | |
| BZX70C18 | B11 | a1 | PH | Z Diode, TVS | 26 V | 20 A | 20 A | 2.5 W | 700 W | 18 V | 20 mA | 2.5 Ω | | |
| BZX70C20 | B11 | a1 | PH | Z Diode, TVS | 26 V | 10 A | 10 A | 2.5 W | 700 W | 20 V | 20 mA | 2.8 Ω | | |
| BZX70C22 | B11 | a1 | PH | Z Diode, TVS | 29 V | 10 A | 10 A | 2.5 W | 700 W | 22 V | 20 mA | 3.0 Ω | | |
| BZX70C24 | B11 | a1 | PH | Z Diode, TVS | 33 V | 10 A | 10 A | 2.5 W | 700 W | 24 V | 20 mA | 3.4 Ω | | |
| BZX70C27 | B11 | a1 | PH | Z Diode, TVS | 38 V | 10 A | 10 A | 2.5 W | 700 W | 27 V | 20 mA | 3.8 Ω | | |
| BZX70C30 | B11 | a1 | PH | Z Diode, TVS | 43 V | 10 A | 10 A | 2.5 W | 700 W | 30 V | 20 mA | 4.5 Ω | | |
| BZX70C33 | B11 | a1 | PH | Z Diode, TVS | 48 V | 10 A | 10 A | 2.5 W | 700 W | 33 V | 20 mA | 5.0 Ω | | |
| BZX70C36 | B11 | a1 | PH | Z Diode, TVS | 52 V | 10 A | 10 A | 2.5 W | 700 W | 36 V | 20 mA | 5.5 Ω | | |
| BZX70C39 | B11 | a1 | PH | Z Diode, TVS | 54 V | 10 A | 10 A | 2.5 W | 700 W | 39 V | 10 mA | 7 Ω | | |
| BZX70C43 | B11 | a1 | PH | Z Diode, TVS | 58 V | 5 A | 5 A | 2.5 W | 700 W | 43 V | 10 mA | 13 Ω | | |
| BZX70C47 | B11 | a1 | PH | Z Diode, TVS | 65 V | 5 A | 5 A | 2.5 W | 700 W | 47 V | 10 mA | 14 Ω | | |
| BZX70C51 | B11 | a1 | PH | Z Diode, TVS | 72 V | 5 A | 5 A | 2.5 W | 700 W | 51 V | 10 mA | 15 Ω | | |
| BZX70C56 | B11 | a1 | PH | Z Diode, TVS | 82 V | 5 A | 5 A | 2.5 W | 700 W | 56 V | 10 mA | 17 Ω | | |
| BZX70C62 | B11 | a1 | PH | Z Diode, TVS | 93 V | 5 A | 5 A | 2.5 W | 700 W | 62 V | 10 mA | 18 Ω | | |
| BZX70C68 | B11 | a1 | PH | Z Diode, TVS | 104 V | 5 A | 5 A | 2.5 W | 700 W | 68 V | 10 mA | 18 Ω | | |
| BZX70C75 | B11 | a1 | PH | Z Diode, TVS | 116 V | 5 A | 5 A | 2.5 W | 700 W | 75 V | 10 mA | 20 Ω | | |
| BZX79C2V4 | A1 | a1 | SG,PH,MO | Z Diode | | | 155 mA | 2 W | | 2.4 V | 5 mA | <100 Ω | -3.5 mV/°C | |
| BZX79C2V7 | A1 | a1 | SG,PH,MO | Z Diode | | | 135 mA | 2 W | | 2.7 V | 5 mA | <100 Ω | -3.5 mV/°C | |
| BZX79C3V0 | A1 | a1 | SG,PH,MO | Z Diode | | | 125 mA | 2 W | | 3.0 V | 5 mA | <95 Ω | -3.5 mV/°C | |
| BZX79C3V3 | A1 | a1 | SG,PH,MO,NS | Z Diode | | | 115 mA | 2 W | | 3.3 V | 5 mA | <95 Ω | -3.5 mV/°C | P (SG) |
| BZX79C3V6 | A1 | a1 | SG,PH,MO,NS | Z Diode | | | 105 mA | 2 W | | 3.6 V | 5 mA | <90 Ω | -3.5 mV/°C | P (SG) |
| BZX79C3V9 | A1 | a1 | SG,PH,MO,NS | Z Diode | | | 95 mA | 2 W | | 3.9 V | 5 mA | <90 Ω | -3.5 mV/°C | P (SG) |
| BZX79C4V3 | A1 | a1 | SG,PH,MO,NS | Z Diode | | | 90 mA | 2 W | | 4.3 V | 5 mA | <90 Ω | -3.5 mV/°C | P (SG) |
| BZX79C4V7 | A1 | a1 | SG,PH,MO,NS | Z Diode | | | 85 mA | 2 W | | 4.7 V | 5 mA | <80 Ω | -3.5 mV/°C | P (SG) |
| BZX79C5V1 | A1 | a1 | SG,PH,MO,NS | Z Diode | | | 80 mA | 2 W | | 5.1 V | 5 mA | <60 Ω | -2.7 mV/°C | P (SG) |
| BZX79C5V6 | A1 | a1 | SG,PH,MO,NS | Z Diode | | | 70 mA | 2 W | | 5.6 V | 5 mA | <40 Ω | 2.5 mV/°C | P (SG) |
| BZX79C6V2 | A1 | a1 | SG,PH,MO,NS | Z Diode | | | 64 mA | 2 W | | 6.2 V | 5 mA | <10 Ω | 3.7 mV/°C | P (SG) |
| BZX79C6V8 | A1 | a1 | SG,PH,MO,NS | Z Diode | | | 58 mA | 2 W | | 6.8 V | 5 mA | <15 Ω | 4.5 mV/°C | P (SG) |
| BZX79C7V5 | A1 | a1 | SG,PH,MO,NS | Z Diode | | | 53 mA | 2 W | | 7.5 V | 5 mA | <15 Ω | 5.3 mV/°C | P (SG) |

| Type | Case | Pin-code | | | Maximum Ratings | | | | | Electrical Characteristics | | | | |
|---|---|---|---|---|---|---|---|---|---|---|---|---|---|---|
| | | | | | Vcla Vbro | Its | Izm | Pv | Pvts | Vz | Iz Is | rz | TK | |
| BZX79C8V2 | A1 | a1 | SG,PH,MO,NS | Z Diode | | 47 mA | 2 W | | | 8.2 V | 5 mA | <15Ω | 6.2 mV/°C | |
| BZX79C9V1 | A1 | a1 | SG,PH,MO,NS | Z Diode | | 43 mA | 2 W | | | 9.1 V | 5 mA | <15Ω | 7 mV/°C | P (SG) |
| BZX79C10 | A1 | a1 | SG,PH,MO,NS | Z Diode | | 40 mA | 2 W | | | 10 V | 5 mA | <20Ω | 8 mV/°C | P (SG) |
| BZX79C11 | A1 | a1 | SG,PH,MO,NS | Z Diode | | 36 mA | 2 W | | | 11 V | 5 mA | <20Ω | 9 mV/°C | |
| BZX79C12 | A1 | a1 | SG,PH,MO,NS | Z Diode | | 32 mA | 2 W | | | 12 V | 5 mA | <25Ω | 10 mV/°C | P (SG) |
| BZX79C13 | A1 | a1 | SG,PH,MO,NS | Z Diode | | 29 mA | 2 W | | | 13 V | 5 mA | <30Ω | 11 mV/°C | |
| BZX79C15 | A1 | a1 | SG,PH,MO,NS | Z Diode | | 27 mA | 2 W | | | 15 V | 5 mA | <30Ω | 13 mV/°C | P (SG) |
| BZX79C16 | A1 | a1 | SG,PH,MO,NS | Z Diode | | 24 mA | 2 W | | | 16 V | 5 mA | <40Ω | 14 mV/°C | |
| BZX79C18 | A1 | a1 | SG,PH,MO,NS | Z Diode | | 21 mA | 2 W | | | 18 V | 5 mA | <45Ω | 16 mV/°C | P (SG) |
| BZX79C20 | A1 | a1 | SG,PH,MO,NS | Z Diode | | 20 mA | 2 W | | | 20 V | 5 mA | <55Ω | 18 mV/°C | P (SG) |
| BZX79C22 | A1 | a1 | SG,PH,MO,NS | Z Diode | | 18 mA | 2 W | | | 22 V | 5 mA | <55Ω | 20 mV/°C | P (SG) |
| BZX79C24 | A1 | a1 | SG,PH,MO,NS | Z Diode | | 16 mA | 2 W | | | 24 V | 5 mA | <70Ω | 22 mV/°C | P (SG) |
| BZX79C27 | A1 | a1 | SG,PH,MO,NS | Z Diode | | 14 mA | 2 W | | | 27 V | 2 mA | <80Ω | 25.3 mV/°C | P (SG) |
| BZX79C30 | A1 | a1 | SG,PH,MO,NS | Z Diode | | 13 mA | 2 W | | | 30 V | 2 mA | <80Ω | 29.4 mV/°C | |
| BZX79C33 | A1 | a1 | SG,PH,MO,NS | Z Diode | | 12 mA | 2 W | | | 33 V | 2 mA | <80Ω | 33.4 mV/°C | P (SG) |
| BZX79C36 | A1 | a1 | SG,PH,MO | Z Diode | | 11 mA | 2 W | | | 36 V | 2 mA | <90Ω | 37.4 mV/°C | |
| BZX79C39 | A1 | a1 | SG,PH,MO | Z Diode | | 10 mA | 2 W | | | 39 V | 2 mA | <130Ω | 41.2 mV/°C | |
| BZX79C43 | A1 | a1 | SG,PH,MO | Z Diode | | 9 mA | 2 W | | | 43 V | 2 mA | <150Ω | 46.6 mV/°C | |
| BZX79C47 | A1 | a1 | SG,PH,MO | Z Diode | | 9 mA | 2 W | | | 47 V | 2 mA | <170Ω | 51.8 mV/°C | |
| BZX79C51 | A1 | a1 | SG,PH,MO | Z Diode | | 8 mA | 2 W | | | 51 V | 2 mA | <180Ω | 57.2 mV/°C | |
| BZX79C56 | A1 | a1 | SG,PH,MO | Z Diode | | 7 mA | 2 W | | | 56 V | 2 mA | <200Ω | 63.8 mV/°C | |
| BZX79C62 | A1 | a1 | SG,PH,MO | Z Diode | | 6 mA | 2 W | | | 62 V | 2 mA | <215Ω | 71.6 mV/°C | |
| BZX79C68 | A1 | a1 | SG,PH,MO | Z Diode | | 6 mA | 2 W | | | 68 V | 2 mA | <240Ω | 79.8 mV/°C | |
| BZX79C75 | A1 | a1 | SG,PH,MO | Z Diode | | 5 mA | 2 W | | | 75 V | 2 mA | <255Ω | 88.6 mV/°C | |
| BZX79C82 | A1 | a1 | SG,MO | Z Diode | | 5 mA | 2 W | | | 82 V | 2 mA | <280Ω | 97.6 mV/°C | |
| BZX79C91 | A1 | a1 | SG,MO | Z Diode | | 4 mA | 2 W | | | 91 V | 2 mA | <300Ω | 109 mV/°C | |
| BZX79C100 | A1 | a1 | SG,MO | Z Diode | | 4 mA | 2 W | | | 100 V | 2 mA | <500Ω | 121 mV/°C | |
| BZX79C110 | A1 | a1 | MO | Z Diode | | 4 mA | 2 W | | | 110 V | 2 mA | <500Ω | 131 mV/°C | |
| BZX79C120 | A1 | a1 | MO | Z Diode | | 4 mA | 2 W | | | 120 V | 2 mA | <500Ω | 144 mV/°C | |
| BZX79C130 | A1 | a1 | MO | Z Diode | | 4 mA | 2 W | | | 130 V | 2 mA | <500Ω | 158 mV/°C | |
| BZX79C150 | A1 | a1 | MO | Z Diode | | 4 mA | 2 W | | | 150 V | 2 mA | <500Ω | 185 mV/°C | |
| BZX79C160 | A1 | a1 | MO | Z Diode | | 4 mA | 2 W | | | 160 V | 2 mA | <500Ω | 200 mV/°C | |
| BZX79C180 | A1 | a1 | MO | Z Diode | | 4 mA | 2 W | | | 180 V | 2 mA | <500Ω | 228 mV/°C | |
| BZX79C200 | A1 | a1 | MO | Z Diode | | 4 mA | 2 W | | | 200 V | 2 mA | <500Ω | 255 mV/°C | |
| BZX83C2V4 | A1 | a1 | TE | Z Diode | | | | 0.5 W | | 2.4 V | 5 mA | <90Ω | -900·10$^6$/°C | |
| BZX83C2V7 | A1 | a1 | TE,MO | Z Diode | | | | 0.5 W | | 2.7 V | 5 mA | <90Ω | -900·10$^6$/°C | |
| BZX83C3V0 | A1 | a1 | TE,MO | Z Diode | | | | 0.5 W | | 3.0 V | 5 mA | <90Ω | -800·10$^6$/°C | |
| BZX83C3V3 | A1 | a1 | TE,MO | Z Diode | | | | 0.5 W | | 3.3 V | 5 mA | <90Ω | -800·10$^6$/°C | |
| BZX83C3V6 | A1 | a1 | TE,MO | Z Diode | | | | 0.5 W | | 3.6 V | 5 mA | <90Ω | -800·10$^6$/°C | |
| BZX83C3V9 | A1 | a1 | TE,MO | Z Diode | | | | 0.5 W | | 3.9 V | 5 mA | <90Ω | -800·10$^6$/°C | |

| Type | Case | Pin-code | | | $V_{cla}$ $V_{bro}$ | $I_{ts}$ | $I_{zm}$ | $P_v$ | $P_{vts}$ | $V_z$ | $I_z$ $I_s$ | $r_z$ | TK | |
|---|---|---|---|---|---|---|---|---|---|---|---|---|---|---|
| | | | | | **Maximum Ratings** | | | | | **Electrical Characteristics** | | | | |
| BZX83C4V3 | A1 | a1 | TE,MO | Z Diode | | | | 0.5 W | | 4.3 V | 5 mA | <80 Ω | $-600 \cdot 10^6/°C$ | |
| BZX83C4V7 | A1 | a1 | TE,MO | Z Diode | | | | 0.5 W | | 4.7 V | 5 mA | <80 Ω | $-500 \cdot 10^6/°C$ | |
| BZX83C5V1 | A1 | a1 | TE,MO | Z Diode | | | | 0.5 W | | 5.1 V | 5 mA | <60 Ω | $500 \cdot 10^6/°C$ | |
| BZX83C5V6 | A1 | a1 | TE,MO | Z Diode | | | | 0.5 W | | 5.6 V | 5 mA | <40 Ω | $500 \cdot 10^6/°C$ | |
| BZX83C6V2 | A1 | a1 | TE,MO | Z Diode | | | | 0.5 W | | 6.2 V | 5 mA | <10 Ω | $600 \cdot 10^6/°C$ | |
| BZX83C6V8 | A1 | a1 | TE,MO | Z Diode | | | | 0.5 W | | 6.8 V | 5 mA | <8 Ω | $700 \cdot 10^6/°C$ | |
| BZX83C7V5 | A1 | a1 | TE,MO | Z Diode | | | | 0.5 W | | 7.5 V | 5 mA | <7 Ω | $700 \cdot 10^6/°C$ | |
| BZX83C8V2 | A1 | a1 | TE,MO | Z Diode | | | | 0.5 W | | 8.2 V | 5 mA | <7 Ω | $800 \cdot 10^6/°C$ | |
| BZX83C9V1 | A1 | a1 | TE,MO | Z Diode | | | | 0.5 W | | 9.1 V | 5 mA | <10 Ω | $900 \cdot 10^6/°C$ | |
| BZX83C10 | A1 | a1 | TE,MO | Z Diode | | | | 0.5 W | | 10 V | 5 mA | <15 Ω | $1000 \cdot 10^6/°C$ | |
| BZX83C11 | A1 | a1 | TE,MO | Z Diode | | | | 0.5 W | | 11 V | 5 mA | <20 Ω | $1100 \cdot 10^6/°C$ | |
| BZX83C12 | A1 | a1 | TE,MO | Z Diode | | | | 0.5 W | | 12 V | 5 mA | <20 Ω | $1100 \cdot 10^6/°C$ | |
| BZX83C13 | A1 | a1 | TE,MO | Z Diode | | | | 0.5 W | | 13 V | 5 mA | <25 Ω | $1100 \cdot 10^6/°C$ | |
| BZX83C15 | A1 | a1 | TE,MO | Z Diode | | | | 0.5 W | | 15 V | 5 mA | <30 Ω | $1100 \cdot 10^6/°C$ | |
| BZX83C16 | A1 | a1 | TE,MO | Z Diode | | | | 0.5 W | | 16 V | 5 mA | <40 Ω | $1100 \cdot 10^6/°C$ | |
| BZX83C18 | A1 | a1 | TE,MO | Z Diode | | | | 0.5 W | | 18 V | 5 mA | <55 Ω | $1100 \cdot 10^6/°C$ | |
| BZX83C20 | A1 | a1 | TE,MO | Z Diode | | | | 0.5 W | | 20 V | 5 mA | <55 Ω | $1100 \cdot 10^6/°C$ | |
| BZX83C22 | A1 | a1 | TE,MO | Z Diode | | | | 0.5 W | | 22 V | 5 mA | <58 Ω | $1200 \cdot 10^6/°C$ | |
| BZX83C24 | A1 | a1 | TE,MO | Z Diode | | | | 0.5 W | | 24 V | 5 mA | <80 Ω | $1200 \cdot 10^6/°C$ | |
| BZX83C27 | A1 | a1 | TE,MO | Z Diode | | | | 0.5 W | | 27 V | 5 mA | <80 Ω | $1200 \cdot 10^6/°C$ | |
| BZX83C30 | A1 | a1 | TE,MO | Z Diode | | | | 0.5 W | | 30 V | 5 mA | <90 Ω | $1200 \cdot 10^6/°C$ | |
| BZX83C33 | A1 | a1 | TE,MO | Z Diode | | | | 0.5 W | | 33 V | 5 mA | <90 Ω | $1200 \cdot 10^6/°C$ | |
| BZX83C36 | A1 | a1 | TE | Z Diode | | | | 0.5 W | | 36 V | 5 mA | <90 Ω | $1200 \cdot 10^6/°C$ | |
| BZX83C39 | A1 | a1 | TE | Z Diode | | | | 0.5 W | | 39 V | 2.5 mA | <110 Ω | $1200 \cdot 10^6/°C$ | |
| BZX84C2V4 | F1 | c3 | SG,RD,PH | Z Diode | | | 60 mA | 0.35 W | | 2.4 V | 5 mA | <85 Ω | $-600 \cdot 10^6/°C$ | |
| BZX84C2V7 | F1 | c3 | SG,RD,IT,PH | Z Diode | | | 54 mA | 0.35 W | | 2.7 V | 5 mA | <85 Ω | $-600 \cdot 10^6/°C$ | |
| BZX84C3V0 | F1 | c3 | SG,RD,IT,PH | Z Diode | | | 50 mA | 0.35 W | | 3.0 V | 5 mA | <85 Ω | $-600 \cdot 10^6/°C$ | |
| BZX84C3V3 | F1 | c3 | SG,RD,IT,PH | Z Diode | | | 47 mA | 0.35 W | | 3.3 V | 5 mA | <85 Ω | $-600 \cdot 10^6/°C$ | P (SG) |
| BZX84C3V6 | F1 | c3 | SG,RD,IT,PH | Z Diode | | | 45 mA | 0.35 W | | 3.6 V | 5 mA | <85 Ω | $-600 \cdot 10^6/°C$ | P (SG) |
| BZX84C3V9 | F1 | c3 | SG,RD,IT,PH | Z Diode | | | 43 mA | 0.35 W | | 3.9 V | 5 mA | <85 Ω | $-600 \cdot 10^6/°C$ | P (SG) |
| BZX84C4V3 | F1 | c3 | SG,RD,IT,PH | Z Diode | | | 40 mA | 0.35 W | | 4.3 V | 5 mA | <80 Ω | $-500 \cdot 10^6/°C$ | P (SG) |
| BZX84C4V7 | F1 | c3 | SG,RD,IT,PH,NS | Z Diode | | | 38 mA | 0.35 W | | 4.7 V | 5 mA | <80 Ω | $-300 \cdot 10^6/°C$ | P (SG) |
| BZX84C5V1 | F1 | c3 | SG,RD,IT,PH,NS | Z Diode | | | 35 mA | 0.35 W | | 5.1 V | 5 mA | <60 Ω | $200 \cdot 10^6/°C$ | P (SG) |
| BZX84C5V6 | F1 | c3 | SG,RD,IT,PH,NS | Z Diode | | | 32 mA | 0.35 W | | 5.6 V | 5 mA | <40 Ω | $300 \cdot 10^6/°C$ | P (SG) |
| BZX84C6V2 | F1 | c3 | SG,RD,IT,PH,NS | Z Diode | | | 28 mA | 0.35 W | | 6.2 V | 5 mA | <10 Ω | $400 \cdot 10^6/°C$ | P (SG) |
| BZX84C6V8 | F1 | c3 | SG,RD,IT,PH,NS | Z Diode | | | 25 mA | 0.35 W | | 6.8 V | 5 mA | <15 Ω | $500 \cdot 10^6/°C$ | P (SG) |
| BZX84C7V5 | F1 | c3 | SG,RD,IT,PH,NS | Z Diode | | | 23 mA | 0.35 W | | 7.5 V | 5 mA | <15 Ω | $500 \cdot 10^6/°C$ | P (SG) |
| BZX84C8V2 | F1 | c3 | SG,RD,IT,PH,NS | Z Diode | | | 21 mA | 0.35 W | | 8.2 V | 5 mA | <15 Ω | $600 \cdot 10^6/°C$ | P (SG) |
| BZX84C9V1 | F1 | c3 | SG,RD,IT,PH,NS | Z Diode | | | 18 mA | 0.35 W | | 9.1 V | 5 mA | <15 Ω | $600 \cdot 10^6/°C$ | P (SG) |
| BZX84C10 | F1 | c3 | SG,RD,IT,PH,NS | Z Diode | | | 16 mA | 0.35 W | | 10 V | 5 mA | <20 Ω | $700 \cdot 10^6/°C$ | |

| Type | Case | Pin code | | | Vcla Vbro | Its | Izm | Pv | Pvts | Vz | Iz Is | rz | TK | |
|------|------|----------|---|---|-----------|-----|-----|----|------|----|-------|----|----|---|
| | | | | | **Maximum Ratings** | | | | | **Electrical Characteristics** | | | | |
| BZX84C11 | F1 | c3 | SG,RD,IT,PH,NS | Z Diode | | | 15 mA | 0.35 W | | 11 V | 5 mA | <20 Ω | 700·10⁶/°C | P (SG) |
| BZX84C12 | F1 | c3 | SG,RD,IT,PH,NS | Z Diode | | | 13 mA | 0.35 W | | 12 V | 5 mA | <25 Ω | 700·10⁶/°C | P (SG) |
| BZX84C13 | F1 | c3 | SG,RD,IT,PH,NS | Z Diode | | | 12 mA | 0.35 W | | 13 V | 5 mA | <30 Ω | 800·10⁶/°C | |
| BZX84C15 | F1 | c3 | SG,RD,IT,PH,NS | Z Diode | | | 11 mA | 0.35 W | | 15 V | 5 mA | <30 Ω | 800·10⁶/°C | P (SG) |
| BZX84C16 | F1 | c3 | SG,RD,IT,PH,NS | Z Diode | | | 10 mA | 0.35 W | | 16 V | 5 mA | <40 Ω | 800·10⁶/°C | |
| BZX84C18 | F1 | c3 | SG,RD,IT,PH,NS | Z Diode | | | 9 mA | 0.35 W | | 18 V | 5 mA | <45 Ω | 800·10⁶/°C | |
| BZX84C20 | F1 | c3 | SG,RD,IT,PH,NS | Z Diode | | | 8 mA | 0.35 W | | 20 V | 5 mA | <55 Ω | 800·10⁶/°C | |
| BZX84C22 | F1 | c3 | SG,RD,IT,PH,NS | Z Diode | | | 8 mA | 0.35 W | | 22 V | 5 mA | <55 Ω | 900·10⁶/°C | |
| BZX84C24 | F1 | c3 | SG,RD,IT,PH,NS | Z Diode | | | 7 mA | 0.35 W | | 24 V | 5 mA | <70 Ω | 900·10⁶/°C | |
| BZX84C27 | F1 | c3 | SG,RD,IT,PH,NS | Z Diode | | | 6 mA | 0.35 W | | 27 V | 2 mA | <80 Ω | 900·10⁶/°C | |
| BZX84C30 | F1 | c3 | SG,RD,IT,PH,NS | Z Diode | | | 6 mA | 0.35 W | | 30 V | 2 mA | <80 Ω | 900·10⁶/°C | |
| BZX84C33 | F1 | c3 | SG,RD,IT,PH,NS | Z Diode | | | 5 mA | 0.35 W | | 33 V | 2 mA | <80 Ω | 900·10⁶/°C | |
| BZX84C36 | F1 | c3 | SG,RD,IT,PH | Z Diode | | | 5 mA | 0.35 W | | 36 V | 2 mA | <90 Ω | 900·10⁶/°C | |
| BZX84C39 | F1 | c3 | SG,RD,IT,PH | Z Diode | | | 4 mA | 0.35 W | | 39 V | 2 mA | <130 Ω | 900·10⁶/°C | |
| BZX84C43 | F1 | c3 | SG,RD,IT,PH | Z Diode | | | 4 mA | 0.35 W | | 43 V | 2 mA | <150 Ω | 900·10⁶/°C | |
| BZX84C47 | F1 | c3 | SG,RD,IT,PH | Z Diode | | | 4 mA | 0.35 W | | 47 V | 2 mA | <170 Ω | 900·10⁶/°C | |
| BZX84C51 | F1 | c3 | SG,RD,IT,PH | Z Diode | | | 3 mA | 0.35 W | | 51 V | 2 mA | <180 Ω | 900·10⁶/°C | |
| BZX84C56 | F1 | c3 | SG,RD,PH | Z Diode | | | 3 mA | 0.35 W | | 56 V | 2 mA | <200 Ω | 900·10⁶/°C | |
| BZX84C62 | F1 | c3 | SG,RD,PH | Z Diode | | | 3 mA | 0.35 W | | 62 V | 2 mA | <215 Ω | 900·10⁶/°C | |
| BZX84C68 | F1 | c3 | SG,RD,PH | Z Diode | | | 3 mA | 0.35 W | | 68 V | 2 mA | <240 Ω | 900·10⁶/°C | |
| BZX84C75 | F1 | c3 | SG,RD,PH | Z Diode | | | 2 mA | 0.35 W | | 75 V | 2 mA | <255 Ω | 900·10⁶/°C | |
| BZX84C2V4L | F1 | c3 | MO | Z Diode | | | 60 mA | 0.3 W | | 2.4 V | 5 mA | <100 Ω | -3.5 mV/°C | |
| BZX84C2V7L | F1 | c3 | MO | Z Diode | | | 54 mA | 0.3 W | | 2.7 V | 5 mA | <100 Ω | -3.5 mV/°C | |
| BZX84C3V0L | F1 | c3 | MO | Z Diode | | | 50 mA | 0.3 W | | 3.0 V | 5 mA | <95 Ω | -3.5 mV/°C | |
| BZX84C3V3L | F1 | c3 | MO | Z Diode | | | 47 mA | 0.3 W | | 3.3 V | 5 mA | <95 Ω | -3.5 mV/°C | |
| BZX84C3V6L | F1 | c3 | MO | Z Diode | | | 45 mA | 0.3 W | | 3.6 V | 5 mA | <90 Ω | -3.5 mV/°C | |
| BZX84C3V9L | F1 | c3 | MO | Z Diode | | | 43 mA | 0.3 W | | 3.9 V | 5 mA | <90 Ω | -3.5 mV/°C | |
| BZX84C4V3L | F1 | c3 | MO | Z Diode | | | 40 mA | 0.3 W | | 4.3 V | 5 mA | <90 Ω | -3.5 mV/°C | |
| BZX84C4V7L | F1 | c3 | MO | Z Diode | | | 38 mA | 0.3 W | | 4.7 V | 5 mA | <80 Ω | -3.5 mV/°C | P |
| BZX84C5V1L | F1 | c3 | MO | Z Diode | | | 35 mA | 0.3 W | | 5.1 V | 5 mA | <60 Ω | -2.7 mV/°C | P |
| BZX84C5V6L | F1 | c3 | MO | Z Diode | | | 32 mA | 0.3 W | | 5.6 V | 5 mA | <40 Ω | 2.5 mV/°C | P |
| BZX84C6V2L | F1 | c3 | MO | Z Diode | | | 28 mA | 0.3 W | | 6.2 V | 5 mA | <10 Ω | 3.7 mV/°C | P |
| BZX84C6V8L | F1 | c3 | MO | Z Diode | | | 25 mA | 0.3 W | | 6.8 V | 5 mA | <15 Ω | 4.5 mV/°C | P |
| BZX84C7V5L | F1 | c3 | MO | Z Diode | | | 23 mA | 0.3 W | | 7.5 V | 5 mA | <15 Ω | 5.3 mV/°C | |
| BZX84C8V2L | F1 | c3 | MO | Z Diode | | | 21 mA | 0.3 W | | 8.2 V | 5 mA | <15 Ω | 6.2 mV/°C | P |
| BZX84C9V1L | F1 | c3 | MO | Z Diode | | | 18 mA | 0.3 W | | 9.1 V | 5 mA | <15 Ω | 7 mV/°C | P |
| BZX84C10L | F1 | c3 | MO | Z Diode | | | 16 mA | 0.3 W | | 10 V | 5 mA | <20 Ω | 8 mV/°C | P |
| BZX84C11L | F1 | c3 | MO | Z Diode | | | 15 mA | 0.3 W | | 11 V | 5 mA | <20 Ω | 9 mV/°C | |
| BZX84C12L | F1 | c3 | MO | Z Diode | | | 13 mA | 0.3 W | | 12 V | 5 mA | <25 Ω | 10 mV/°C | P |
| BZX84C13L | F1 | c3 | MO | Z Diode | | | 12 mA | 0.3 W | | 13 V | 5 mA | <30 Ω | 11 mV/°C | |

| Type | Case | Pin-code | | | Vcla Vbro | Its | Izm | Pv | Pvts | Vz | Iz Is | rz | TK | |
|------|------|----------|---|---|-----------|-----|-----|----|----|----|-------|----|-----|---|
| | | | | | **Maximum Ratings** | | | | | **Electrical Characteristics** | | | | |
| BZX84C15L | F1 | c3 | MO | Z Diode | | 11 mA | | 0.3 W | | 15 V | 5 mA | <30 Ω | 13 mV/°C | P |
| BZX84C16L | F1 | c3 | MO | Z Diode | | 10 mA | | 0.3 W | | 16 V | 5 mA | <40 Ω | 14 mV/°C | |
| BZX84C18L | F1 | c3 | MO | Z Diode | | 9 mA | | 0.3 W | | 18 V | 5 mA | <45 Ω | 16 mV/°C | |
| BZX84C20L | F1 | c3 | MO | Z Diode | | 8 mA | | 0.3 W | | 20 V | 5 mA | <55 Ω | 18 mV/°C | |
| BZX84C22L | F1 | c3 | MO | Z Diode | | 8 mA | | 0.3 W | | 22 V | 5 mA | <55 Ω | 20 mV/°C | |
| BZX84C24L | F1 | c3 | MO | Z Diode | | 7 mA | | 0.3 W | | 24 V | 5 mA | <70 Ω | 22 mV/°C | |
| BZX84C27L | F1 | c3 | MO | Z Diode | | 6 mA | | 0.3 W | | 27 V | 2 mA | <80 Ω | 25.3 mV/°C | |
| BZX84C30L | F1 | c3 | MO | Z Diode | | 6 mA | | 0.3 W | | 30 V | 2 mA | <80 Ω | 29.4 mV/°C | P |
| BZX84C33L | F1 | c3 | MO | Z Diode | | 5 mA | | 0.3 W | | 33 V | 2 mA | <80 Ω | 33.4 mV/°C | |
| BZX84C36L | F1 | c3 | MO | Z Diode | | 5 mA | | 0.3 W | | 36 V | 2 mA | <90 Ω | 37.4 mV/°C | |
| BZX84C39L | F1 | c3 | MO | Z Diode | | 4 mA | | 0.3 W | | 39 V | 2 mA | <130 Ω | 41.2 mV/°C | |
| BZX84C43L | F1 | c3 | MO | Z Diode | | 4 mA | | 0.3 W | | 43 V | 2 mA | <150 Ω | 46.6 mV/°C | |
| BZX84C47L | F1 | c3 | MO | Z Diode | | 4 mA | | 0.3 W | | 47 V | 2 mA | <170 Ω | 51.8 mV/°C | |
| BZX84C51L | F1 | c3 | MO | Z Diode | | 3 mA | | 0.3 W | | 51 V | 2 mA | <180 Ω | 57.2 mV/°C | |
| BZX84C56L | F1 | c3 | MO | Z Diode | | 3 mA | | 0.3 W | | 56 V | 2 mA | <200 Ω | 63.8 mV/°C | |
| BZX84C62L | F1 | c3 | MO | Z Diode | | 3 mA | | 0.3 W | | 62 V | 2 mA | <215 Ω | 71.6 mV/°C | |
| BZX84C68L | F1 | c3 | MO | Z Diode | | 3 mA | | 0.3 W | | 68 V | 2 mA | <240 Ω | 79.8 mV/°C | |
| BZX84C75L | F1 | c3 | MO | Z Diode | | 2 mA | | 0.3 W | | 75 V | 2 mA | <255 Ω | 88.6 mV/°C | |
| BZX85C2V7 | A3 | a1 | SG,TE | Z Diode | | 370 mA | | 1.3 W | | 2.7 V | 80 mA | <20 Ω | -800·10⁻⁶/°C | |
| BZX85C3V0 | A3 | a1 | SG,TE | Z Diode | | 340 mA | | 1.3 W | | 3.0 V | 80 mA | <20 Ω | -800·10⁻⁶/°C | |
| BZX85C3V3 | A3 | a1 | SG,TE,MO,NS | Z Diode | | 320 mA | | 1.3 W | | 3.3 V | 80 mA | <20 Ω | -800·10⁻⁶/°C | ..B |
| BZX85C3V6 | A3 | a1 | SG,TE,IT,MO,NS | Z Diode | | 290 mA | | 1.3 W | | 3.6 V | 70 mA | <20 Ω | -800·10⁻⁶/°C | ..B |
| BZX85C3V9 | A3 | a1 | SG,TE,IT,MO,NS | Z Diode | | 280 mA | | 1.3 W | | 3.9 V | 60 mA | <15 Ω | -700·10⁻⁶/°C | |
| BZX85C4V3 | A3 | a1 | SG,TE,IT,MO,NS | Z Diode | | 250 mA | | 1.3 W | | 4.3 V | 50 mA | <13 Ω | -500·10⁻⁶/°C | |
| BZX85C4V7 | A3 | a1 | SG,TE,IT,MO,NS | Z Diode | | 215 mA | | 1.3 W | | 4.7 V | 45 mA | <13 Ω | 400·10⁻⁶/°C | |
| BZX85C5V1 | A3 | a1 | SG,TE,IT,MO,NS | Z Diode | | 200 mA | | 1.3 W | | 5.1 V | 45 mA | <10 Ω | 400·10⁻⁶/°C | |
| BZX85C5V6 | A3 | a1 | SG,TE,IT,MO,NS | Z Diode | | 190 mA | | 1.3 W | | 5.6 V | 45 mA | <7 Ω | 450·10⁻⁶/°C | |
| BZX85C6V2 | A3 | a1 | SG,TE,IT,MO,NS | Z Diode | | 170 mA | | 1.3 W | | 6.2 V | 35 mA | <4 Ω | 550·10⁻⁶/°C | |
| BZX85C6V8 | A3 | a1 | SG,TE,IT,MO,NS | Z Diode | | 155 mA | | 1.3 W | | 6.8 V | 35 mA | <3.5 Ω | 600·10⁻⁶/°C | |
| BZX85C7V5 | A3 | a1 | SG,TE,IT,MO,NS | Z Diode | | 140 mA | | 1.3 W | | 7.5 V | 35 mA | <3 Ω | 650·10⁻⁶/°C | |
| BZX85C8V2 | A3 | a1 | SG,TE,IT,MO,NS | Z Diode | | 130 mA | | 1.3 W | | 8.2 V | 25 mA | <5 Ω | 700·10⁻⁶/°C | |
| BZX85C9V1 | A3 | a1 | SG,TE,IT,MO,NS | Z Diode | | 120 mA | | 1.3 W | | 9.1 V | 25 mA | <5 Ω | 750·10⁻⁶/°C | |
| BZX85C10 | A3 | a1 | SG,TE,IT,MO,NS | Z Diode | | 105 mA | | 1.3 W | | 10 V | 25 mA | <7 Ω | 800·10⁻⁶/°C | |
| BZX85C11 | A3 | a1 | SG,TE,IT,MO,NS | Z Diode | | 97 mA | | 1.3 W | | 11 V | 20 mA | <8 Ω | 800·10⁻⁶/°C | |
| BZX85C12 | A3 | a1 | SG,TE,IT,MO,NS | Z Diode | | 88 mA | | 1.3 W | | 12 V | 20 mA | <9 Ω | 850·10⁻⁶/°C | |
| BZX85C13 | A3 | a1 | SG,TE,IT,MO,NS | Z Diode | | 79 mA | | 1.3 W | | 13 V | 20 mA | <10 Ω | 850·10⁻⁶/°C | |
| BZX85C15 | A3 | a1 | SG,TE,IT,MO,NS | Z Diode | | 71 mA | | 1.3 W | | 15 V | 15 mA | <15 Ω | 900·10⁻⁶/°C | |
| BZX85C16 | A3 | a1 | SG,TE,IT,MO,NS | Z Diode | | 66 mA | | 1.3 W | | 16 V | 15 mA | <15 Ω | 900·10⁻⁶/°C | |
| BZX85C18 | A3 | a1 | SG,TE,IT,MO,NS | Z Diode | | 62 mA | | 1.3 W | | 18 V | 15 mA | <20 Ω | 900·10⁻⁶/°C | |
| BZX85C20 | A3 | a1 | SG,TE,IT,MO,NS | Z Diode | | 56 mA | | 1.3 W | | 20 V | 10 mA | <24 Ω | 900·10⁻⁶/°C | |

| Type | Case | Pin-code | | | Vcla Vbro | Its | Izm | Pv | Pvts | Vz | Iz Is | rz | TK | |
|---|---|---|---|---|---|---|---|---|---|---|---|---|---|---|
| | | | | | **Maximum Ratings** | | | | | **Electrical Characteristics** | | | | |
| BZX85C22 | A3 | a1 | SG,TE,IT,MO,NS | Z Diode | | | 52 mA | 1.3 W | | 22 V | 10 mA | <25 Ω | 950·10⁶/°C | |
| BZX85C24 | A3 | a1 | SG,TE,IT,MO,NS | Z Diode | | | 47 mA | 1.3 W | | 24 V | 10 mA | <25 Ω | 950·10⁶/°C | |
| BZX85C27 | A3 | a1 | SG,TE,IT,MO,NS | Z Diode | | | 41 mA | 1.3 W | | 27 V | 8 mA | <30 Ω | 950·10⁶/°C | |
| BZX85C30 | A3 | a1 | SG,TE,IT,MO,NS | Z Diode | | | 36 mA | 1.3 W | | 30 V | 8 mA | <30 Ω | 950·10⁶/°C | |
| BZX85C33 | A3 | a1 | SG,TE,IT,MO,NS | Z Diode | | | 33 mA | 1.3 W | | 33 V | 8 mA | <35 Ω | 950·10⁶/°C | |
| BZX85C36 | A3 | a1 | SG,TE,IT,MO | Z Diode | | | 30 mA | 1.3 W | | 36 V | 8 mA | <40 Ω | 950·10⁶/°C | |
| BZX85C39 | A3 | a1 | SG,TE,IT,MO | Z Diode | | | 28 mA | 1.3 W | | 39 V | 6 mA | <50 Ω | 950·10⁶/°C | |
| BZX85C43 | A3 | a1 | SG,TE,IT,MO | Z Diode | | | 26 mA | 1.3 W | | 43 V | 6 mA | <50 Ω | 950·10⁶/°C | |
| BZX85C47 | A3 | a1 | SG,TE,IT,MO | Z Diode | | | 23 mA | 1.3 W | | 47 V | 4 mA | <90 Ω | 950·10⁶/°C | |
| BZX85C51 | A3 | a1 | SG,TE,IT,MO | Z Diode | | | 21 mA | 1.3 W | | 51 V | 4 mA | <115 Ω | 950·10⁶/°C | |
| BZX85C56 | A3 | a1 | SG,TE,IT,MO | Z Diode | | | 19 mA | 1.3 W | | 56 V | 4 mA | <120 Ω | 950·10⁶/°C | |
| BZX85C62 | A3 | a1 | SG,TE,IT,MO | Z Diode | | | 16 mA | 1.3 W | | 62 V | 4 mA | <125 Ω | 950·10⁶/°C | |
| BZX85C68 | A3 | a1 | SG,TE,MO | Z Diode | | | 15 mA | 1.3 W | | 68 V | 4 mA | <130 Ω | 950·10⁶/°C | |
| BZX85C75 | A3 | a1 | SG,TE,MO | Z Diode | | | 14 mA | 1.3 W | | 75 V | 4 mA | <135 Ω | 950·10⁶/°C | |
| BZX85C82 | A3 | a1 | SG,MO | Z Diode | | | 12 mA | 1.3 W | | 82 V | 2.7 mA | <200 Ω | 1200·10⁶/°C | |
| BZX85C91 | A3 | a1 | SG,MO | Z Diode | | | 10 mA | 1.3 W | | 91 V | 2.7 mA | <250 Ω | 1200·10⁶/°C | |
| BZX85C100 | A3 | a1 | SG,MO | Z Diode | | | 9 mA | 1.3 W | | 100 V | 2.7 mA | <350 Ω | 1200·10⁶/°C | |
| BZX85C110 | A3 | a1 | SG | Z Diode | | | 9 mA | 1.3 W | | 110 V | 2.7 mA | <450 Ω | 1200·10⁶/°C | |
| BZX85C120 | A3 | a1 | SG | Z Diode | | | 8 mA | 1.3 W | | 120 V | 2 mA | <550 Ω | 1200·10⁶/°C | |
| BZX85C130 | A3 | a1 | SG | Z Diode | | | 7 mA | 1.3 W | | 130 V | 2 mA | <700 Ω | 1200·10⁶/°C | |
| BZX85C150 | A3 | a1 | SG | Z Diode | | | 6 mA | 1.3 W | | 150 V | 2 mA | <1000 Ω | 1200·10⁶/°C | |
| BZX85C160 | A3 | a1 | SG | Z Diode | | | 6 mA | 1.3 W | | 160 V | 1.5 mA | <1100 Ω | 1200·10⁶/°C | |
| BZX85C180 | A3 | a1 | SG | Z Diode | | | 5 mA | 1.3 W | | 180 V | 1.5 mA | <1200 Ω | 1200·10⁶/°C | |
| BZX85C200 | A3 | a1 | SG | Z Diode | | | 5 mA | 1.3 W | | 200 V | 1.5 mA | <1500 Ω | 1200·10⁶/°C | |
| BZY91C7V5 | E4 | a1 | PH | Z Diode, TVS | | | | (100) W | 9.5 kW | 7.5 V | 5A mA | 0.2 Ω | 900·10⁶/°C | |
| BZY91C8V2 | E4 | a1 | PH | Z Diode, TVS | 9.5 V | 150 mA | 150 mA | (100) W | 9.5 kW | 8.2 V | 5A mA | 0.3 Ω | 900·10⁶/°C | |
| BZY91C9V1 | E4 | a1 | PH | Z Diode, TVS | 10 V | 150 mA | 150 mA | (100) W | 9.5 kW | 9.1 V | 2A mA | 0.4 Ω | 700·10⁶/°C | |
| BZY91C10 | E4 | a1 | PH | Z Diode, TVS | 11 V | 150 mA | 150 mA | (100) W | 9.5 kW | 10 V | 2A mA | 0.4 Ω | 700·10⁶/°C | |
| BZY91C11 | E4 | a1 | PH | Z Diode, TVS | 12 V | 150 mA | 150 mA | (100) W | 9.5 kW | 11 V | 2A mA | 0.4 Ω | 700·10⁶/°C | |
| BZY91C12 | E4 | a1 | PH | Z Diode, TVS | 13 V | 150 mA | 150 mA | (100) W | 9.5 kW | 12 V | 2A mA | 0.5 Ω | 700·10⁶/°C | |
| BZY91C13 | E4 | a1 | PH | Z Diode, TVS | 14.5 V | 150 mA | 150 mA | (100) W | 9.5 kW | 13 V | 2A mA | 0.5 Ω | 700·10⁶/°C | |
| BZY91C15 | E4 | a1 | PH | Z Diode, TVS | 16 V | 150 mA | 150 mA | (100) W | 9.5 kW | 15 V | 2A mA | 0.6 Ω | 750·10⁶/°C | |
| BZY91C16 | E4 | a1 | PH | Z Diode, TVS | 17.5 V | 150 mA | 150 mA | (100) W | 9.5 kW | 16 V | 2A mA | 0.6 Ω | 750·10⁶/°C | |
| BZY91C18 | E4 | a1 | PH | Z Diode, TVS | 19 V | 150 mA | 150 mA | (100) W | 9.5 kW | 18 V | 2A mA | 0.7 Ω | 750·10⁶/°C | |
| BZY91C20 | E4 | a1 | PH | Z Diode, TVS | 22 V | 100 mA | 100 mA | (100) W | 9.5 kW | 20 V | 1A mA | 0.8 Ω | 750·10⁶/°C | |
| BZY91C22 | E4 | a1 | PH | Z Diode, TVS | 24 V | 100 mA | 100 mA | (100) W | 9.5 kW | 22 V | 1A mA | 0.8 Ω | 750·10⁶/°C | |
| BZY91C24 | E4 | a1 | PH | Z Diode, TVS | 26 V | 100 mA | 100 mA | (100) W | 9.5 kW | 24 V | 1A mA | 0.9 Ω | 800·10⁶/°C | |
| BZY91C27 | E4 | a1 | PH | Z Diode, TVS | 28 V | 100 mA | 100 mA | (100) W | 9.5 kW | 27 V | 1A mA | 1 Ω | 820·10⁶/°C | |
| BZY91C30 | E4 | a1 | PH | Z Diode, TVS | 31 V | 100 mA | 100 mA | (100) W | 9.5 kW | 30 V | 1A mA | 1.1 Ω | 850·10⁶/°C | |
| BZY91C33 | E4 | a1 | PH | Z Diode, TVS | 34 V | 100 mA | 100 mA | (100) W | 9.5 kW | 33 V | 1A mA | 1.2 Ω | 880·10⁶/°C | |

| Type | Case | Pin-code | | | Maximum Ratings | | | | | Electrical Characteristics | | | | |
|---|---|---|---|---|---|---|---|---|---|---|---|---|---|---|
| | | | | | Vcla Vbro | Its | Izm | Pv | Pvts | Vz | Iz / Is | rz | TK | |
| BZY91C36 | E4 | a1 | PH | Z Diode, TVS | 38 V | 100 mA | 100 mA | (100) W | 9.5 kW | 36 V | 1A mA | 1.3 Ω | 900 ·10⁶/°C | |
| BZY91C39 | E4 | a1 | PH | Z Diode, TVS | 40 V | 50 mA | 50 mA | (100) W | 9.5 kW | 39 V | 500 mA | 1.4 Ω | 900 ·10⁶/°C | |
| BZY91C43 | E4 | a1 | PH | Z Diode, TVS | 44 V | 50 mA | 50 mA | (100) W | 9.5 kW | 43 V | 500 mA | 1.5 Ω | 920 ·10⁶/°C | |
| BZY91C47 | E4 | a1 | PH | Z Diode, TVS | 49 V | 50 mA | 50 mA | (100) W | 9.5 kW | 47 V | 500 mA | 1.7 Ω | 930 ·10⁶/°C | |
| BZY91C51 | E4 | a1 | PH | Z Diode, TVS | 54 V | 50 mA | 50 mA | (100) W | 9.5 kW | 51 V | 500 mA | 1.8 Ω | 930 ·10⁶/°C | |
| BZY91C56 | E4 | a1 | PH | Z Diode, TVS | 60 V | 50 mA | 50 mA | (100) W | 9.5 kW | 56 V | 500 mA | 2 Ω | 940 ·10⁶/°C | |
| BZY91C62 | E4 | a1 | PH | Z Diode, TVS | 66 V | 50 mA | 50 mA | (100) W | 9.5 kW | 62 V | 500 mA | 2.2 Ω | 940 ·10⁶/°C | |
| BZY91C68 | E4 | a1 | PH | Z Diode, TVS | 72 V | 50 mA | 50 mA | (100) W | 9.5 kW | 68 V | 500 mA | 2.4 Ω | 940 ·10⁶/°C | |
| BZY91C75 | E4 | a1 | PH | Z Diode, TVS | 79 V | 50 mA | 50 mA | (100) W | 9.5 kW | 75 V | 500 mA | 2.6 Ω | 950 ·10⁶/°C | |
| BZY91C7V5R | E4 | b1 | PH | Z Diode, TVS | | | | (100) W | 9.5 kW | 7.5 V | 5A mA | 0.2 Ω | 900 ·10⁶/°C | |
| BZY91C8V2R | E4 | b1 | PH | Z Diode, TVS | 9.5 V | 150 mA | 150 mA | (100) W | 9.5 kW | 8.2 V | 5A mA | 0.3 Ω | 900 ·10⁶/°C | |
| BZY91C9V1R | E4 | b1 | PH | Z Diode, TVS | 10 V | 150 mA | 150 mA | (100) W | 9.5 kW | 9.1 V | 2A mA | 0.4 Ω | 700 ·10⁶/°C | |
| BZY91C10R | E4 | b1 | PH | Z Diode, TVS | 11 V | 150 mA | 150 mA | (100) W | 9.5 kW | 10 V | 2A mA | 0.4 Ω | 700 ·10⁶/°C | |
| BZY91C11R | E4 | b1 | PH | Z Diode, TVS | 12 V | 150 mA | 150 mA | (100) W | 9.5 kW | 11 V | 2A mA | 0.4 Ω | 700 ·10⁶/°C | |
| BZY91C12R | E4 | b1 | PH | Z Diode, TVS | 13 V | 150 mA | 150 mA | (100) W | 9.5 kW | 12 V | 2A mA | 0.5 Ω | 700 ·10⁶/°C | |
| BZY91C13R | E4 | b1 | PH | Z Diode, TVS | 14.5 V | 150 mA | 150 mA | (100) W | 9.5 kW | 13 V | 2A mA | 0.5 Ω | 700 ·10⁶/°C | |
| BZY91C15R | E4 | b1 | PH | Z Diode, TVS | 16 V | 150 mA | 150 mA | (100) W | 9.5 kW | 15 V | 2A mA | 0.6 Ω | 750 ·10⁶/°C | |
| BZY91C16R | E4 | b1 | PH | Z Diode, TVS | 17.5 V | 150 mA | 150 mA | (100) W | 9.5 kW | 16 V | 2A mA | 0.6 Ω | 750 ·10⁶/°C | |
| BZY91C18R | E4 | b1 | PH | Z Diode, TVS | 19 V | 150 mA | 150 mA | (100) W | 9.5 kW | 18 V | 2A mA | 0.7 Ω | 750 ·10⁶/°C | |
| BZY91C20R | E4 | b1 | PH | Z Diode, TVS | 22 V | 100 mA | 100 mA | (100) W | 9.5 kW | 20 V | 1A mA | 0.8 Ω | 750 ·10⁶/°C | |
| BZY91C22R | E4 | b1 | PH | Z Diode, TVS | 24 V | 100 mA | 100 mA | (100) W | 9.5 kW | 22 V | 1A mA | 0.8 Ω | 750 ·10⁶/°C | |
| BZY91C24R | E4 | b1 | PH | Z Diode, TVS | 26 V | 100 mA | 100 mA | (100) W | 9.5 kW | 24 V | 1A mA | 0.9 Ω | 800 ·10⁶/°C | |
| BZY91C27R | E4 | b1 | PH | Z Diode, TVS | 28 V | 100 mA | 100 mA | (100) W | 9.5 kW | 27 V | 1A mA | 1 Ω | 820 ·10⁶/°C | |
| BZY91C30R | E4 | b1 | PH | Z Diode, TVS | 31 V | 100 mA | 100 mA | (100) W | 9.5 kW | 30 V | 1A mA | 1.1 Ω | 850 ·10⁶/°C | |
| BZY91C33R | E4 | b1 | PH | Z Diode, TVS | 34 V | 100 mA | 100 mA | (100) W | 9.5 kW | 33 V | 1A mA | 1.2 Ω | 880 ·10⁶/°C | |
| BZY91C36R | E4 | b1 | PH | Z Diode, TVS | 38 V | 100 mA | 100 mA | (100) W | 9.5 kW | 36 V | 1A mA | 1.3 Ω | 900 ·10⁶/°C | |
| BZY91C39R | E4 | b1 | PH | Z Diode, TVS | 40 V | 50 mA | 50 mA | (100) W | 9.5 kW | 39 V | 500 mA | 1.4 Ω | 900 ·10⁶/°C | |
| BZY91C43R | E4 | b1 | PH | Z Diode, TVS | 44 V | 50 mA | 50 mA | (100) W | 9.5 kW | 43 V | 500 mA | 1.5 Ω | 920 ·10⁶/°C | |
| BZY91C47R | E4 | b1 | PH | Z Diode, TVS | 49 V | 50 mA | 50 mA | (100) W | 9.5 kW | 47 V | 500 mA | 1.7 Ω | 930 ·10⁶/°C | |
| BZY91C51R | E4 | b1 | PH | Z Diode, TVS | 54 V | 50 mA | 50 mA | (100) W | 9.5 kW | 51 V | 500 mA | 1.8 Ω | 930 ·10⁶/°C | |
| BZY91C56R | E4 | b1 | PH | Z Diode, TVS | 60 V | 50 mA | 50 mA | (100) W | 9.5 kW | 56 V | 500 mA | 2 Ω | 940 ·10⁶/°C | |
| BZY91C62R | E4 | b1 | PH | Z Diode, TVS | 66 V | 50 mA | 50 mA | (100) W | 9.5 kW | 62 V | 500 mA | 2.2 Ω | 940 ·10⁶/°C | |
| BZY91C68R | E4 | b1 | PH | Z Diode, TVS | 72 V | 50 mA | 50 mA | (100) W | 9.5 kW | 68 V | 500 mA | 2.4 Ω | 940 ·10⁶/°C | |
| BZY91C75R | E4 | b1 | PH | Z Diode, TVS | 79 V | 50 mA | 50 mA | (100) W | 9.5 kW | 75 V | 500 mA | 2.6 Ω | 950 ·10⁶/°C | |
| BZY93C7V5 | E2 | a1 | PH | Z Diode, TVS | 8 V | 20 mA | 20 mA | (20) W | 700 W | 7.5 V | 2A mA | 0.04 Ω | 3 mV/°C | |
| BZY93C8V2 | E2 | a1 | PH | Z Diode, TVS | 9 V | 20 mA | 20 mA | (20) W | 700 W | 8.2 V | 2A mA | 0.05 Ω | 4 mV/°C | |
| BZY93C9V1 | E2 | a1 | PH | Z Diode, TVS | 10 V | 20 mA | 20 mA | (20) W | 700 W | 9.1 V | 1A mA | 0.07 Ω | 5 mV/°C | |
| BZY93C10 | E2 | a1 | PH | Z Diode, TVS | 11 V | 20 mA | 20 mA | (20) W | 700 W | 10 V | 1A mA | 0.07 Ω | 7 mV/°C | |
| BZY93C11 | E2 | a1 | PH | Z Diode, TVS | 12.3 V | 20 mA | 20 mA | (20) W | 700 W | 11 V | 1A mA | 0.08 Ω | 7.5 mV/°C | |
| BZY93C12 | E2 | a1 | PH | Z Diode, TVS | 14 V | 20 mA | 20 mA | (20) W | 700 W | 12 V | 1A mA | 0.08 Ω | 8 mV/°C | |

| Type | Case | Pin-code | | | Maximum Ratings | | | | | Electrical Characteristics | | | | |
|---|---|---|---|---|---|---|---|---|---|---|---|---|---|---|
| | | | | | Vcla Vbro | Its | Izm | Pv | Pvts | Vz | Iz Is | rz | TK | |
| BZY93C13 | E2 | a1 | PH | Z Diode, TVS | 15.3 V | 20 mA | 20 mA | (20) W | 700 W | 13 V | 1A mA | 0.08 Ω | 8.5 mV/°C | |
| BZY93C15 | E2 | a1 | PH | Z Diode, TVS | 17 V | 20 mA | 20 mA | (20) W | 700 W | 15 V | 1A mA | 0.1 Ω | 10 mV/°C | |
| BZY93C16 | E2 | a1 | PH | Z Diode, TVS | 19.3 V | 20 mA | 20 mA | (20) W | 700 W | 16 V | 2A mA | 0.18 Ω | 11 mV/°C | |
| BZY93C18 | E2 | a1 | PH | Z Diode, TVS | 21 V | 20 mA | 20 mA | (20) W | 700 W | 18 V | 500 mA | 0.2 Ω | 13 mV/°C | |
| BZY93C20 | E2 | a1 | PH | Z Diode, TVS | 23 V | 10 mA | 10 mA | (20) W | 700 W | 20 V | 500 mA | 0.2 Ω | 14 mV/°C | |
| BZY93C22 | E2 | a1 | PH | Z Diode, TVS | 26 V | 10 mA | 10 mA | (20) W | 700 W | 22 V | 500 mA | 0.21 Ω | 16 mV/°C | |
| BZY93C24 | E2 | a1 | PH | Z Diode, TVS | 29 V | 10 mA | 10 mA | (20) W | 700 W | 24 V | 500 mA | 0.22 Ω | 18 mV/°C | |
| BZY93C27 | E2 | a1 | PH | Z Diode, TVS | 33 V | 10 mA | 10 mA | (20) W | 700 W | 27 V | 500 mA | 0 25 Ω | 21 mV/°C | |
| BZY93C30 | E2 | a1 | PH | Z Diode, TVS | 38 V | 10 mA | 10 mA | (20) W | 700 W | 30 V | 500 mA | 0.3 Ω | 25 mV/°C | |
| BZY93C33 | E2 | a1 | PH | Z Diode, TVS | 42 V | 10 mA | 10 mA | (20) W | 700 W | 33 V | 500 mA | 0.32 Ω | 30 mV/°C | |
| BZY93C36 | E2 | a1 | PH | Z Diode, TVS | 47 V | 10 mA | 10 mA | (20) W | 700 W | 36 V | 200 mA | 0.75 Ω | 32 mV/°C | |
| BZY93C39 | E2 | a1 | PH | Z Diode, TVS | 40 V | 5 mA | 5 mA | (20) W | 700 W | 39 V | 200 mA | 0.85 Ω | 35 mV/°C | |
| BZY93C43 | E2 | a1 | PH | Z Diode, TVS | 45 V | 5 mA | 5 mA | (20) W | 700 W | 43 V | 200 mA | 0.9 Ω | 40 mV/°C | |
| BZY93C47 | E2 | a1 | PH | Z Diode, TVS | 51 V | 5 mA | 5 mA | (20) W | 700 W | 47 V | 200 mA | 1 Ω | 45 mV/°C | |
| BZY93C51 | E2 | a1 | PH | Z Diode, TVS | 57 V | 5 mA | 5 mA | (20) W | 700 W | 51 V | 200 mA | 1.2 Ω | 50 mV/°C | |
| BZY93C56 | E2 | a1 | PH | Z Diode, TVS | 64 V | 5 mA | 5 mA | (20) W | 700 W | 56 V | 200 mA | 1.3 Ω | 55 mV/°C | |
| BZY93C62 | E2 | a1 | PH | Z Diode, TVS | 73 V | 5 mA | 5 mA | (20) W | 700 W | 62 V | 200 mA | 1.5 Ω | 60 mV/°C | |
| BZY93C68 | E2 | a1 | PH | Z Diode, TVS | 81 V | 5 mA | 5 mA | (20) W | 700 W | 68 V | 200 mA | 1.8 Ω | 65 mV/°C | |
| BZY93C75 | E2 | a1 | PH | Z Diode, TVS | 90 V | 5 mA | 5 mA | (20) W | 700 W | 75 V | 200 mA | 2 Ω | 70 mV/°C | |
| BZY93C7V5R | E2 | b1 | PH | Z Diode, TVS | 8 V | 20 mA | 20 mA | (20) W | 700 W | 7.5 V | 2A mA | 0.04 Ω | 3 mV/°C | |
| BZY93C8V2R | E2 | b1 | PH | Z Diode, TVS | 9 V | 20 mA | 20 mA | (20) W | 700 W | 8.2 V | 2A mA | 0.05 Ω | 4 mV/°C | |
| BZY93C9V1R | E2 | b1 | PH | Z Diode, TVS | 10 V | 20 mA | 20 mA | (20) W | 700 W | 9.1 V | 1A mA | 0.07 Ω | 5 mV/°C | |
| BZY93C10R | E2 | b1 | PH | Z Diode, TVS | 11 V | 20 mA | 20 mA | (20) W | 700 W | 10 V | 1A mA | 0.07 Ω | 7 mV/°C | |
| BZY93C11R | E2 | b1 | PH | Z Diode, TVS | 12.3 V | 20 mA | 20 mA | (20) W | 700 W | 11 V | 1A mA | 0.08 Ω | 7.5 mV/°C | |
| BZY93C12R | E2 | b1 | PH | Z Diode, TVS | 14 V | 20 mA | 20 mA | (20) W | 700 W | 12 V | 1A mA | 0.08 Ω | 8 mV/°C | |
| BZY93C13R | E2 | b1 | PH | Z Diode, TVS | 15.3 V | 20 mA | 20 mA | (20) W | 700 W | 13 V | 1A mA | 0.08 Ω | 8.5 mV/°C | |
| BZY93C15R | E2 | b1 | PH | Z Diode, TVS | 17 V | 20 mA | 20 mA | (20) W | 700 W | 15 V | 1A mA | 0.1 Ω | 10 mV/°C | |
| BZY93C16R | E2 | b1 | PH | Z Diode, TVS | 19.3 V | 20 mA | 20 mA | (20) W | 700 W | 16 V | 2A mA | 0.18 Ω | 11 mV/°C | |
| BZY93C18R | E2 | b1 | PH | Z Diode, TVS | 21 V | 20 mA | 20 mA | (20) W | 700 W | 18 V | 500 mA | 0.2 Ω | 13 mV/°C | |
| BZY93C20R | E2 | b1 | PH | Z Diode, TVS | 23 V | 10 mA | 10 mA | (20) W | 700 W | 20 V | 500 mA | 0.2 Ω | 14 mV/°C | |
| BZY93C22R | E2 | b1 | PH | Z Diode, TVS | 26 V | 10 mA | 10 mA | (20) W | 700 W | 22 V | 500 mA | 0.21 Ω | 16 mV/°C | |
| BZY93C24R | E2 | b1 | PH | Z Diode, TVS | 29 V | 10 mA | 10 mA | (20) W | 700 W | 24 V | 500 mA | 0.22 Ω | 18 mV/°C | |
| BZY93C27R | E2 | b1 | PH | Z Diode, TVS | 33 V | 10 mA | 10 mA | (20) W | 700 W | 27 V | 500 mA | 0 25 Ω | 21 mV/°C | |
| BZY93C30R | E2 | b1 | PH | Z Diode, TVS | 38 V | 10 mA | 10 mA | (20) W | 700 W | 30 V | 500 mA | 0.3 Ω | 25 mV/°C | |
| BZY93C33R | E2 | b1 | PH | Z Diode, TVS | 42 V | 10 mA | 10 mA | (20) W | 700 W | 33 V | 500 mA | 0.32 Ω | 30 mV/°C | |
| BZY93C36R | E2 | b1 | PH | Z Diode, TVS | 47 V | 10 mA | 10 mA | (20) W | 700 W | 36 V | 200 mA | 0.75 Ω | 32 mV/°C | |
| BZY93C39R | E2 | b1 | PH | Z Diode, TVS | 40 V | 5 mA | 5 mA | (20) W | 700 W | 39 V | 200 mA | 0.85 Ω | 35 mV/°C | |
| BZY93C43R | E2 | b1 | PH | Z Diode, TVS | 45 V | 5 mA | 5 mA | (20) W | 700 W | 43 V | 200 mA | 0.9 Ω | 40 mV/°C | |
| BZY93C47R | E2 | b1 | PH | Z Diode, TVS | 51 V | 5 mA | 5 mA | (20) W | 700 W | 47 V | 200 mA | 1 Ω | 45 mV/°C | |
| BZY93C51R | E2 | b1 | PH | Z Diode, TVS | 57 V | 5 mA | 5 mA | (20) W | 700 W | 51 V | 200 mA | 1.2 Ω | 50 mV/°C | |

| Type | Case | Pin-code | | | Maximum Ratings $V_{cla}/V_{bro}$ | Its | Izm | Pv | Pvts | Electrical Characteristics Vz | Iz / Is | rz | TK | |
|---|---|---|---|---|---|---|---|---|---|---|---|---|---|---|
| BZY93C56R | E2 | b1 | PH | Z Diode, TVS | 64 V | 5 mA | 5 mA | (20) W | 700 W | 56 V | 200 mA | 1.3 Ω | 55 mV/°C | |
| BZY93C62R | E2 | b1 | PH | Z Diode, TVS | 73 V | 5 mA | 5 mA | (20) W | 700 W | 62 V | 200 mA | 1.5 Ω | 60 mV/°C | |
| BZY93C68R | E2 | b1 | PH | Z Diode, TVS | 81 V | 5 mA | 5 mA | (20) W | 700 W | 68 V | 200 mA | 1.8 Ω | 65 mV/°C | |
| BZY93C75R | E2 | b1 | PH | Z Diode, TVS | 90 V | 5 mA | 5 mA | (20) W | 700 W | 75 V | 200 mA | 2 Ω | 70 mV/°C | |
| BZY97C3V3 | B4 | a1 | SG | Z Diode | | | 429 mA | 1.5 W | 20 W | 3.3 V | 100 mA | <10 Ω | $-1000 \cdot 10^6$/°C | |
| BZY97C3V6 | B4 | a1 | SG | Z Diode | | | 395 mA | 1.5 W | 20 W | 3.6 V | 100 mA | <10 Ω | $-800 \cdot 10^6$/°C | |
| BZY97C3V9 | B4 | a1 | SG | Z Diode | | | 366 mA | 1.5 W | 20 W | 3.9 V | 100 mA | <7 Ω | $-700 \cdot 10^6$/°C | |
| BZY97C4V3 | B4 | a1 | SG | Z Diode | | | 327 mA | 1.5 W | 20 W | 4.3 V | 100 mA | <7 Ω | $-700 \cdot 10^6$/°C | |
| BZY97C4V7 | B4 | a1 | SG | Z Diode | | | 300 mA | 1.5 W | 20 W | 4.7 V | 100 mA | <7 Ω | $-700 \cdot 10^6$/°C | |
| BZY97C5V1 | B4 | a1 | SG | Z Diode | | | 278 mA | 1.5 W | 20 W | 5.1 V | 100 mA | <6 Ω | $-600 \cdot 10^6$/°C P | |
| BZY97C5V6 | B4 | a1 | SG | Z Diode | | | 250 mA | 1.5 W | 20 W | 5.6 V | 100 mA | <2 Ω | $500 \cdot 10^6$/°C P | |
| BZY97C6V2 | B4 | a1 | SG | Z Diode | | | 227 mA | 1.5 W | 20 W | 6.2 V | 100 mA | <2 Ω | $600 \cdot 10^6$/°C P | |
| BZY97C6V8 | B4 | a1 | SG | Z Diode | | | 208 mA | 1.5 W | 20 W | 6.8 V | 100 mA | <2 Ω | $700 \cdot 10^6$/°C P | |
| BZY97C7V5 | B4 | a1 | SG | Z Diode | | | 190 mA | 1.5 W | 20 W | 7.5 V | 100 mA | <2 Ω | $700 \cdot 10^6$/°C | |
| BZY97C8V2 | B4 | a1 | SG | Z Diode | | | 172 mA | 1.5 W | 20 W | 8.2 V | 100 mA | <2 Ω | $800 \cdot 10^6$/°C | |
| BZY97C9V1 | B4 | a1 | SG | Z Diode | | | 156 mA | 1.5 W | 20 W | 9.1 V | 50 mA | <4 Ω | $800 \cdot 10^6$/°C | |
| BZY97C10 | B4 | a1 | SG | Z Diode | | | 142 mA | 1.5 W | 20 W | 10 V | 50 mA | <4 Ω | $900 \cdot 10^6$/°C | |
| BZY97C11 | B4 | a1 | SG | Z Diode | | | 129 mA | 1.5 W | 20 W | 11 V | 50 mA | <7 Ω | $1000 \cdot 10^6$/°C | |
| BZY97C12 | B4 | a1 | SG | Z Diode | | | 118 mA | 1.5 W | 20 W | 12 V | 50 mA | <7 Ω | $1000 \cdot 10^6$/°C | |
| BZY97C13 | B4 | a1 | SG | Z Diode | | | 106 mA | 1.5 W | 20 W | 13 V | 50 mA | <10 Ω | $1000 \cdot 10^6$/°C P | |
| BZY97C15 | B4 | a1 | SG | Z Diode | | | 96 mA | 1.5 W | 20 W | 15 V | 50 mA | <10 Ω | $1000 \cdot 10^6$/°C P | |
| BZY97C16 | B4 | a1 | SG | Z Diode | | | 88 mA | 1.5 W | 20 W | 16 V | 25 mA | <15 Ω | $1100 \cdot 10^6$/°C | |
| BZY97C18 | B4 | a1 | SG | Z Diode | | | 79 mA | 1.5 W | 20 W | 18 V | 25 mA | <15 Ω | $1100 \cdot 10^6$/°C P | |
| BZY97C20 | B4 | a1 | SG | Z Diode | | | 71 mA | 1.5 W | 20 W | 20 V | 25 mA | <15 Ω | $1100 \cdot 10^6$/°C P | |
| BZY97C22 | B4 | a1 | SG | Z Diode | | | 64 mA | 1.5 W | 20 W | 22 V | 25 mA | <15 Ω | $1100 \cdot 10^6$/°C P | |
| BZY97C24 | B4 | a1 | SG | Z Diode | | | 59 mA | 1.5 W | 20 W | 24 V | 25 mA | <15 Ω | $1100 \cdot 10^6$/°C P | |
| BZY97C27 | B4 | a1 | SG | Z Diode | | | 52 mA | 1.5 W | 20 W | 27 V | 25 mA | <15 Ω | $1100 \cdot 10^6$/°C P | |
| BZY97C30 | B4 | a1 | SG | Z Diode | | | 47 mA | 1.5 W | 20 W | 30 V | 25 mA | <15 Ω | $1100 \cdot 10^6$/°C P | |
| BZY97C33 | B4 | a1 | SG | Z Diode | | | 42 mA | 1.5 W | 20 W | 33 V | 25 mA | <15 Ω | $1100 \cdot 10^6$/°C P | |
| BZY97C36 | B4 | a1 | SG | Z Diode | | | 40 mA | 1.5 W | 20 W | 36 V | 10 mA | <40 Ω | $1100 \cdot 10^6$/°C P | |
| BZY97C39 | B4 | a1 | SG | Z Diode | | | 37 mA | 1.5 W | 20 W | 39 V | 10 mA | <40 Ω | $1100 \cdot 10^6$/°C | |
| BZY97C43 | B4 | a1 | SG | Z Diode | | | 33 mA | 1.5 W | 20 W | 43 V | 10 mA | <45 Ω | $1200 \cdot 10^6$/°C | |
| BZY97C47 | B4 | a1 | SG | Z Diode | | | 30 mA | 1.5 W | 20 W | 47 V | 10 mA | <45 Ω | $1200 \cdot 10^6$/°C P | |
| BZY97C51 | B4 | a1 | SG | Z Diode | | | 28 mA | 1.5 W | 20 W | 51 V | 10 mA | <60 Ω | $1200 \cdot 10^6$/°C | |
| BZY97C56 | B4 | a1 | SG | Z Diode | | | 25 mA | 1.5 W | 20 W | 56 V | 10 mA | <60 Ω | $1200 \cdot 10^6$/°C | |
| BZY97C62 | B4 | a1 | SG | Z Diode | | | 23 mA | 1.5 W | 20 W | 62 V | 10 mA | <80 Ω | $1200 \cdot 10^6$/°C P | |
| BZY97C68 | B4 | a1 | SG | Z Diode | | | 21 mA | 1.5 W | 20 W | 68 V | 10 mA | <80 Ω | $1200 \cdot 10^6$/°C P | |
| BZY97C75 | B4 | a1 | SG | Z Diode | | | 19 mA | 1.5 W | 20 W | 75 V | 10 mA | <100 Ω | $1200 \cdot 10^6$/°C | |
| BZY97C82 | B4 | a1 | SG | Z Diode | | | 17 mA | 1.5 W | 20 W | 82 V | 10 mA | <100 Ω | $1200 \cdot 10^6$/°C | |
| BZY97C91 | B4 | a1 | SG | Z Diode | | | 16 mA | 1.5 W | 20 W | 91 V | 5 mA | <200 Ω | $1300 \cdot 10^6$/°C | |

| Type | Case | Pin-code | | | Vcla Vbro | Its | Izm | Pv | Pvts | Vz | Iz / Is | rz | TK | |
|------|------|----------|---|---|------|-----|-----|-----|------|-----|---------|-----|-----|---|
| | | | | | | | **Maximum Ratings** | | | | **Electrical Characteristics** | | | |
| BZY97C100 | B4 | a1 | SG | Z Diode | | 14 mA | | 1.5 W | 20 W | 100 V | 5 mA | <200Ω | 1300·10⁶/°C | |
| BZY97C110 | B4 | a1 | SG | Z Diode | | 13 mA | | 1.5 W | 20 W | 110 V | 5 mA | <250Ω | 1300·10⁶/°C | |
| BZY97C120 | B4 | a1 | SG | Z Diode | | 12 mA | | 1.5 W | 20 W | 120 V | 5 mA | <250Ω | 1300·10⁶/°C | |
| BZY97C130 | B4 | a1 | SG | Z Diode | | 11 mA | | 1.5 W | 20 W | 130 V | 5 mA | <300Ω | 1300·10⁶/°C | P |
| BZY97C150 | B4 | a1 | SG | Z Diode | | 10 mA | | 1.5 W | 20 W | 150 V | 5 mA | <300Ω | 1300·10⁶/°C | P |
| BZY97C160 | B4 | a1 | SG | Z Diode | | 9 mA | | 1.5 W | 20 W | 160 V | 5 mA | <350Ω | 1300·10⁶/°C | |
| BZY97C180 | B4 | a1 | SG | Z Diode | | 8 mA | | 1.5 W | 20 W | 180 V | 5 mA | <350Ω | 1300·10⁶/°C | |
| BZY97C200 | B4 | a1 | SG | Z Diode | | 7 mA | | 1.5 W | 20 W | 200 V | 5 mA | <350Ω | 1300·10⁶/°C | P |
| BZY97C7V5 | B1 | a1 | RD | Z Diode | | | | 1.5 W | | 7.5 V | 100 mA | | | |
| BZY97C8V2 | B1 | a1 | RD | Z Diode | | | | 1.5 W | | 8.2 V | 100 mA | | | |
| BZY97C9V1 | B1 | a1 | RD | Z Diode | | | | 1.5 W | | 9.1 V | 50 mA | | | |
| BZY97C10 | B1 | a1 | RD | Z Diode | | | | 1.5 W | | 10 V | 50 mA | | | |
| BZY97C11 | B1 | a1 | RD | Z Diode | | | | 1.5 W | | 11 V | 50 mA | | | |
| BZY97C12 | B1 | a1 | RD | Z Diode | | | | 1.5 W | | 12 V | 50 mA | | | |
| BZY97C13 | B1 | a1 | RD | Z Diode | | | | 1.5 W | | 13 V | 50 mA | | | |
| BZY97C15 | B1 | a1 | RD | Z Diode | | | | 1.5 W | | 15 V | 50 mA | | | |
| BZY97C16 | B1 | a1 | RD | Z Diode | | | | 1.5 W | | 16 V | 25 mA | | | |
| BZY97C18 | B1 | a1 | RD | Z Diode | | | | 1.5 W | | 18 V | 25 mA | | | |
| BZY97C20 | B1 | a1 | RD | Z Diode | | | | 1.5 W | | 20 V | 25 mA | | | |
| BZY97C22 | B1 | a1 | RD | Z Diode | | | | 1.5 W | | 22 V | 25 mA | | | |
| BZY97C24 | B1 | a1 | RD | Z Diode | | | | 1.5 W | | 24 V | 25 mA | | | |
| BZY97C27 | B1 | a1 | RD | Z Diode | | | | 1.5 W | | 27 V | 25 mA | | | |
| BZY97C30 | B1 | a1 | RD | Z Diode | | | | 1.5 W | | 30 V | 25 mA | | | |
| BZY97C33 | B1 | a1 | RD | Z Diode | | | | 1.5 W | | 33 V | 25 mA | | | |
| BZY97C36 | B1 | a1 | RD | Z Diode | | | | 1.5 W | | 36 V | 10 mA | | | |
| BZY97C39 | B1 | a1 | RD | Z Diode | | | | 1.5 W | | 39 V | 10 mA | | | |
| BZY97C43 | B1 | a1 | RD | Z Diode | | | | 1.5 W | | 43 V | 10 mA | | | |
| BZY97C47 | B1 | a1 | RD | Z Diode | | | | 1.5 W | | 47 V | 10 mA | | | |
| BZY97C51 | B1 | a1 | RD | Z Diode | | | | 1.5 W | | 51 V | 10 mA | | | |
| BZY97C56 | B1 | a1 | RD | Z Diode | | | | 1.5 W | | 56 V | 10 mA | | | |
| BZY97C62 | B1 | a1 | RD | Z Diode | | | | 1.5 W | | 62 V | 10 mA | | | |
| BZY97C68 | B1 | a1 | RD | Z Diode | | | | 1.5 W | | 68 V | 10 mA | | | |
| BZY97C75 | B1 | a1 | RD | Z Diode | | | | 1.5 W | | 75 V | 10 mA | | | |
| BZY97C82 | B1 | a1 | RD | Z Diode | | | | 1.5 W | | 82 V | 10 mA | | | |
| BZY97C91 | B1 | a1 | RD | Z Diode | | | | 1.5 W | | 91 V | 5 mA | | | |
| BZY97C100 | B1 | a1 | RD | Z Diode | | | | 1.5 W | | 100 V | 5 mA | | | |
| BZY97C110 | B1 | a1 | RD | Z Diode | | | | 1.5 W | | 110 V | 5 mA | | | |
| BZY97C120 | B1 | a1 | RD | Z Diode | | | | 1.5 W | | 120 V | 5 mA | | | |
| BZY97C130 | B1 | a1 | RD | Z Diode | | | | 1.5 W | | 130 V | 5 mA | | | |
| BZY97C150 | B1 | a1 | RD | Z Diode | | | | 1.5 W | | 150 V | 5 mA | | | |

| Type | Case | Pin-code | | | Maximum Ratings Vcla Vbro | Its | Izm | Pv | Pvts | Electrical Characteristics Vz | Iz / Is | rz | TK | |
|---|---|---|---|---|---|---|---|---|---|---|---|---|---|---|
| BZY97C160 | B1 | a1 | RD | Z Diode | | | | 1.5 W | | 160 V | 5 mA | | | |
| BZY97C180 | B1 | a1 | RD | Z Diode | | | | 1.5 W | | 180 V | 5 mA | | | |
| BZY97C200 | B1 | a1 | RD | Z Diode | | | | 1.5 W | | 200 V | 5 mA | | | |
| DZ23C2V7 | F1 | c7 | IT | Bidir. ZD | | | | 0.35 W | | 2.7 V | 5 mA | $<100\,\Omega$ | $-650 \cdot 10^6/°C$ | |
| DZ23C3 | F1 | c7 | IT | Bidir. ZD | | | | 0.35 W | | 3.0 V | 5 mA | $<100\,\Omega$ | $-600 \cdot 10^6/°C$ | |
| DZ23C3V3 | F1 | c7 | IT | Bidir. ZD | | | | 0.35 W | | 3.3 V | 5 mA | $<95\,\Omega$ | $-550 \cdot 10^6/°C$ | |
| DZ23C3V6 | F1 | c7 | IT | Bidir. ZD | | | | 0.35 W | | 3.6 V | 5 mA | $<95\,\Omega$ | $-550 \cdot 10^6/°C$ | |
| DZ23C3V9 | F1 | c7 | IT | Bidir. ZD | | | | 0.35 W | | 3.9 V | 5 mA | $<90\,\Omega$ | $-500 \cdot 10^6/°C$ | |
| DZ23C4V3 | F1 | c7 | IT | Bidir. ZD | | | | 0.35 W | | 4.3 V | 5 mA | $<90\,\Omega$ | $-350 \cdot 10^6/°C$ | |
| DZ23C4V7 | F1 | c7 | IT | Bidir. ZD | | | | 0.35 W | | 4.7 V | 5 mA | $<80\,\Omega$ | $-150 \cdot 10^6/°C$ | |
| DZ23C5V1 | F1 | c7 | IT | Bidir. ZD | | | | 0.35 W | | 5.1 V | 5 mA | $<60\,\Omega$ | $50 \cdot 10^6/°C$ | |
| DZ23C5V6 | F1 | c7 | IT | Bidir. ZD | | | | 0.35 W | | 5.6 V | 5 mA | $<40\,\Omega$ | $200 \cdot 10^6/°C$ | |
| DZ23C6V2 | F1 | c7 | IT | Bidir. ZD | | | | 0.35 W | | 6.2 V | 5 mA | $<10\,\Omega$ | $300 \cdot 10^6/°C$ | |
| DZ23C6V8 | F1 | c7 | IT | Bidir. ZD | | | | 0.35 W | | 6.8 V | 5 mA | $<15\,\Omega$ | $450 \cdot 10^6/°C$ | |
| DZ23C7V5 | F1 | c7 | IT | Bidir. ZD | | | | 0.35 W | | 7.5 V | 5 mA | $<15\,\Omega$ | $500 \cdot 10^6/°C$ | |
| DZ23C8V2 | F1 | c7 | IT | Bidir. ZD | | | | 0.35 W | | 8.2 V | 5 mA | $<15\,\Omega$ | $550 \cdot 10^6/°C$ | |
| DZ23C9V1 | F1 | c7 | IT | Bidir. ZD | | | | 0.35 W | | 9.1 V | 5 mA | $<15\,\Omega$ | $650 \cdot 10^6/°C$ | |
| DZ23C10 | F1 | c7 | IT | Bidir. ZD | | | | 0.35 W | | 10 V | 5 mA | $<20\,\Omega$ | $650 \cdot 10^6/°C$ | |
| DZ23C11 | F1 | c7 | IT | Bidir. ZD | | | | 0.35 W | | 11 V | 5 mA | $<20\,\Omega$ | $700 \cdot 10^6/°C$ | |
| DZ23C12 | F1 | c7 | IT | Bidir. ZD | | | | 0.35 W | | 12 V | 5 mA | $<25\,\Omega$ | $750 \cdot 10^6/°C$ | |
| DZ23C13 | F1 | c7 | IT | Bidir. ZD | | | | 0.35 W | | 13 V | 5 mA | $<30\,\Omega$ | $800 \cdot 10^6/°C$ | |
| DZ23C15 | F1 | c7 | IT | Bidir. ZD | | | | 0.35 W | | 15 V | 5 mA | $<30\,\Omega$ | $800 \cdot 10^6/°C$ | |
| DZ23C16 | F1 | c7 | IT | Bidir. ZD | | | | 0.35 W | | 16 V | 5 mA | $<40\,\Omega$ | $900 \cdot 10^6/°C$ | |
| DZ23C18 | F1 | c7 | IT | Bidir. ZD | | | | 0.35 W | | 18 V | 5 mA | $<45\,\Omega$ | $900 \cdot 10^6/°C$ | |
| DZ23C20 | F1 | c7 | IT | Bidir. ZD | | | | 0.35 W | | 20 V | 5 mA | $<55\,\Omega$ | $900 \cdot 10^6/°C$ | |
| DZ23C22 | F1 | c7 | IT | Bidir. ZD | | | | 0.35 W | | 22 V | 5 mA | $<55\,\Omega$ | $900 \cdot 10^6/°C$ | |
| DZ23C24 | F1 | c7 | IT | Bidir. ZD | | | | 0.35 W | | 24 V | 5 mA | $<70\,\Omega$ | $900 \cdot 10^6/°C$ | |
| DZ23C27 | F1 | c7 | IT | Bidir. ZD | | | | 0.35 W | | 27 V | 2 mA | $<80\,\Omega$ | $900 \cdot 10^6/°C$ | |
| DZ23C30 | F1 | c7 | IT | Bidir. ZD | | | | 0.35 W | | 30 V | 2 mA | $<80\,\Omega$ | $900 \cdot 10^6/°C$ | |
| DZ23C33 | F1 | c7 | IT | Bidir. ZD | | | | 0.35 W | | 33 V | 2 mA | $<80\,\Omega$ | $900 \cdot 10^6/°C$ | |
| DZ23C36 | F1 | c7 | IT | Bidir. ZD | | | | 0.35 W | | 36 V | 2 mA | $<90\,\Omega$ | $900 \cdot 10^6/°C$ | |
| DZ23C39 | F1 | c7 | IT | Bidir. ZD | | | | 0.35 W | | 39 V | 2 mA | $<130\,\Omega$ | $1100 \cdot 10^6/°C$ | |
| DZ23C43 | F1 | c7 | IT | Bidir. ZD | | | | 0.35 W | | 43 V | 2 mA | $<150\,\Omega$ | $1100 \cdot 10^6/°C$ | |
| DZ23C47 | F1 | c7 | IT | Bidir. ZD | | | | 0.35 W | | 47 V | 2 mA | $<170\,\Omega$ | $1100 \cdot 10^6/°C$ | |
| DZ23C51 | F1 | c7 | IT | Bidir. ZD | | | | 0.35 W | | 51 V | 2 mA | $<180\,\Omega$ | $1100 \cdot 10^6/°C$ | |
| DZ89C3V9 | F7 | c7 | IT | Bidir. ZD | | 290 mA | | 2 W | | 3.9 V | 100 mA | $3.8\,\Omega$ | $-700 \cdot 10^6/°C$ | |
| DZ89C4V3 | F7 | c7 | IT | Bidir. ZD | | 260 mA | | 2 W | | 4.3 V | 100 mA | $3.8\,\Omega$ | $-700 \cdot 10^6/°C$ | |
| DZ89C4V7 | F7 | c7 | IT | Bidir. ZD | | 235 mA | | 2 W | | 4.7 V | 100 mA | $3.8\,\Omega$ | $-700 \cdot 10^6/°C$ | |
| DZ89C5V1 | F7 | c7 | IT | Bidir. ZD | | 215 mA | | 2 W | | 5.1 V | 100 mA | $2\,\Omega$ | $-600 \cdot 10^6/°C$ | |
| DZ89C5V6 | F7 | c7 | IT | Bidir. ZD | | 193 mA | | 2 W | | 5.6 V | 100 mA | $1\,\Omega$ | $500 \cdot 10^6/°C$ | |

| Type | Case | Pin-code | | | Maximum Ratings | | | | | Electrical Characteristics | | | | |
|---|---|---|---|---|---|---|---|---|---|---|---|---|---|---|
| | | | | | Vcla / Vbro | Its | Izm | Pv | Pvts | Vz | Iz / Is | rz | TK | |
| DZ89C6V2 | F7 | c7 | IT | Bidir. ZD | | | 183 mA | 2 W | | 6.2 V | 100 mA | 1 Ω | $600 \cdot 10^6/°C$ | |
| DZ89C6V8 | F7 | c7 | IT | Bidir. ZD | | | 157 mA | 2 W | | 6.8 V | 100 mA | 1 Ω | $700 \cdot 10^6/°C$ | |
| DZ89C7V5 | F7 | c7 | IT | Bidir. ZD | | | 143 mA | 2 W | | 7.5 V | 100 mA | 1 Ω | $700 \cdot 10^6/°C$ | |
| DZ89C8V2 | F7 | c7 | IT | Bidir. ZD | | | 127 mA | 2 W | | 8.2 V | 100 mA | 1 Ω | $800 \cdot 10^6/°C$ | |
| DZ89C9V1 | F7 | c7 | IT | Bidir. ZD | | | 117 mA | 2 W | | 9.1 V | 50 mA | 2 Ω | $800 \cdot 10^6/°C$ | |
| DZ89C10 | F7 | c7 | IT | Bidir. ZD | | | 105 mA | 2 W | | 10 V | 50 mA | 2 Ω | $900 \cdot 10^6/°C$ | |
| DZ89C11 | F7 | c7 | IT | Bidir. ZD | | | 94 mA | 2 W | | 11 V | 50 mA | 4 Ω | $1000 \cdot 10^6/°C$ | |
| DZ89C12 | F7 | c7 | IT | Bidir. ZD | | | 85 mA | 2 W | | 12 V | 50 mA | 4 Ω | $1000 \cdot 10^6/°C$ | |
| DZ89C13 | F7 | c7 | IT | Bidir. ZD | | | 78 mA | 2 W | | 13 V | 50 mA | 5 Ω | $1000 \cdot 10^6/°C$ | |
| DZ89C15 | F7 | c7 | IT | Bidir. ZD | | | 70 mA | 2 W | | 15 V | 50 mA | 5 Ω | $1000 \cdot 10^6/°C$ | |
| DZ89C16 | F7 | c7 | IT | Bidir. ZD | | | 63 mA | 2 W | | 16 V | 25 mA | 6 Ω | $1100 \cdot 10^6/°C$ | |
| DZ89C18 | F7 | c7 | IT | Bidir. ZD | | | 57 mA | 2 W | | 18 V | 25 mA | 6 Ω | $1100 \cdot 10^6/°C$ | |
| DZ89C20 | F7 | c7 | IT | Bidir. ZD | | | 52 mA | 2 W | | 20 V | 25 mA | 6 Ω | $1100 \cdot 10^6/°C$ | |
| DZ89C22 | F7 | c7 | IT | Bidir. ZD | | | 48 mA | 2 W | | 22 V | 25 mA | 6 Ω | $1100 \cdot 10^6/°C$ | |
| DZ89C24 | F7 | c7 | IT | Bidir. ZD | | | 42 mA | 2 W | | 24 V | 25 mA | 7 Ω | $1100 \cdot 10^6/°C$ | |
| DZ89C27 | F7 | c7 | IT | Bidir. ZD | | | 38 mA | 2 W | | 27 V | 25 mA | 7 Ω | $1100 \cdot 10^6/°C$ | |
| DZ89C30 | F7 | c7 | IT | Bidir. ZD | | | 35 mA | 2 W | | 30 V | 25 mA | 8 Ω | $1100 \cdot 10^6/°C$ | |
| DZ89C33 | F7 | c7 | IT | Bidir. ZD | | | 31 mA | 2 W | | 33 V | 10 mA | 8 Ω | $1100 \cdot 10^6/°C$ | |
| DZ89C36 | F7 | c7 | IT | Bidir. ZD | | | 29 mA | 2 W | | 36 V | 10 mA | 21 Ω | $1100 \cdot 10^6/°C$ | |
| DZ89C39 | F7 | c7 | IT | Bidir. ZD | | | 26 mA | 2 W | | 39 V | 10 mA | 21 Ω | $1100 \cdot 10^6/°C$ | |
| DZ89C43 | F7 | c7 | IT | Bidir. ZD | | | 24 mA | 2 W | | 43 V | 10 mA | 24 Ω | $1200 \cdot 10^6/°C$ | |
| DZ89C47 | F7 | c7 | IT | Bidir. ZD | | | 22 mA | 2 W | | 47 V | 10 mA | 24 Ω | $1200 \cdot 10^6/°C$ | |
| DZ89C51 | F7 | c7 | IT | Bidir. ZD | | | 20 mA | 2 W | | 51 V | 10 mA | 25 Ω | $1200 \cdot 10^6/°C$ | |
| DZ89C56 | F7 | c7 | IT | Bidir. ZD | | | 18 mA | 2 W | | 56 V | 10 mA | 25 Ω | $1200 \cdot 10^6/°C$ | |
| DZ89C62 | F7 | c7 | IT | Bidir. ZD | | | 16 mA | 2 W | | 62 V | 10 mA | 25 Ω | $1300 \cdot 10^6/°C$ | |
| DZ89C68 | F7 | c7 | IT | Bidir. ZD | | | 14 mA | 2 W | | 68 V | 10 mA | 25 Ω | $1300 \cdot 10^6/°C$ | |
| DZ89C75 | F7 | c7 | IT | Bidir. ZD | | | 13 mA | 2 W | | 75 V | 10 mA | 30 Ω | $1300 \cdot 10^6/°C$ | |
| DZ89C82 | F7 | c7 | IT | Bidir. ZD | | | 12 mA | 2 W | | 82 V | 10 mA | 30 Ω | $1300 \cdot 10^6/°C$ | |
| DZ89C91 | F7 | c7 | IT | Bidir. ZD | | | 11 mA | 2 W | | 91 V | 5 mA | 60 Ω | $1300 \cdot 10^6/°C$ | |
| DZ89C100 | F7 | c7 | IT | Bidir. ZD | | | 10 mA | 2 W | | 100 V | 5 mA | 60 Ω | $1300 \cdot 10^6/°C$ | |
| DZ89C110 | F7 | c7 | IT | Bidir. ZD | | | 9 mA | 2 W | | 110 V | 5 mA | 80 Ω | $1300 \cdot 10^6/°C$ | |
| DZ89C120 | F7 | c7 | IT | Bidir. ZD | | | 8 mA | 2 W | | 120 V | 5 mA | 80 Ω | $1300 \cdot 10^6/°C$ | |
| DZ89C130 | F7 | c7 | IT | Bidir. ZD | | | 7 mA | 2 W | | 130 V | 5 mA | 110 Ω | $1300 \cdot 10^6/°C$ | |
| DZ89C150 | F7 | c7 | IT | Bidir. ZD | | | 6.5 mA | 2 W | | 150 V | 5 mA | 110 Ω | $1300 \cdot 10^6/°C$ | |
| DZ89C160 | F7 | c7 | IT | Bidir. ZD | | | 5 mA | 2 W | | 160 V | 5 mA | 150 Ω | $1300 \cdot 10^6/°C$ | |
| DZ89C180 | F7 | c7 | IT | Bidir. ZD | | | 5.5 mA | 2 W | | 180 V | 5 mA | 150 Ω | $1300 \cdot 10^6/°C$ | |
| DZ89C200 | F7 | c7 | IT | Bidir. ZD | | | 5.5 mA | 2 W | | 200 V | 5 mA | 150 Ω | $1300 \cdot 10^6/°C$ | |
| DZT2.4A | G6 | a1 | RO | Z Diode | | | | 0.2 W | | 2.4 V | 5 mA | <100 Ω | | Vz ±2.5% |
| DZT2.7A | G6 | a1 | RO | Z Diode | | | | 0.2 W | | 2.7 V | 5 mA | <110 Ω | | Vz ±2.5% |
| DZT3.0A | G6 | a1 | RO | Z Diode | | | | 0.2 W | | 3 V | 5 mA | <120 Ω | | Vz ±2.5% |

| Type | Case | Pin-code | | | Maximum Ratings | | | | | Electrical Characteristics | | | | |
|------|------|----------|---|---|---|---|---|---|---|---|---|---|---|---|
| | | | | | Vcla/Vbro | Its | Izm | Pv | Pvts | Vz | Iz/Is | rz | TK | |
| DZT3.3A | G6 | a1 | RO | Z Diode | | | | 0.2 W | | 3.3 V | 5 mA | <120Ω | | Vz ±2.5% |
| DZT3.6A | G6 | a1 | RO | Z Diode | | | | 0.2 W | | 3.6 V | 5 mA | <100Ω | | Vz ±2.5% |
| DZT3.9A | G6 | a1 | RO | Z Diode | | | | 0.2 W | | 3.9 V | 5 mA | <100Ω | | Vz ±2.5% |
| DZT4.3A | G6 | a1 | RO | Z Diode | | | | 0.2 W | | 4.2 V | 5 mA | <100Ω | | Vz ±2.5% |
| DZT4.7A | G6 | a1 | RO | Z Diode | | | | 0.2 W | | 4.5 V | 5 mA | <100Ω | | Vz ±2.5% |
| DZT5.1A | G6 | a1 | RO | Z Diode | | | | 0.2 W | | 4.9 V | 5 mA | <80Ω | | Vz ±2.5% |
| DZT5.6A | G6 | a1 | RO | Z Diode | | | | 0.2 W | | 5.5 V | 5 mA | <60Ω | | Vz ±2.5% |
| DZT6.2A | G6 | a1 | RO | Z Diode | | | | 0.2 W | | 6 V | 5 mA | <60Ω | | Vz ±2.5% |
| DZT6.8A | G6 | a1 | RO | Z Diode | | | | 0.2 W | | 6.6 V | 5 mA | <40Ω | | Vz ±2.5% |
| DZT7.5A | G6 | a1 | RO | Z Diode | | | | 0.2 W | | 7.2 V | 5 mA | <30Ω | | Vz ±2.5% |
| DZT8.2A | G6 | a1 | RO | Z Diode | | | | 0.2 W | | 7.9 V | 5 mA | <30Ω | | Vz ±2.5% |
| DZT9.1A | G6 | a1 | RO | Z Diode | | | | 0.2 W | | 8.8 V | 5 mA | <30Ω | | Vz ±2.5% |
| DZT10A | G6 | a1 | RO | Z Diode | | | | 0.2 W | | 9.7 V | 5 mA | <30Ω | | Vz ±2.5% |
| DZT11A | G6 | a1 | RO | Z Diode | | | | 0.2 W | | 10.7 V | 5 mA | <30Ω | | Vz ±2.5% |
| DZT12A | G6 | a1 | RO | Z Diode | | | | 0.2 W | | 11.7 V | 5 mA | <30Ω | | Vz ±2.5% |
| DZT13A | G6 | a1 | RO | Z Diode | | | | 0.2 W | | 12.7 V | 5 mA | <37Ω | | Vz ±2.5% |
| DZT15A | G6 | a1 | RO | Z Diode | | | | 0.2 W | | 14.2 V | 5 mA | <42Ω | | Vz ±2.5% |
| DZT16A | G6 | a1 | RO | Z Diode | | | | 0.2 W | | 15.7 V | 5 mA | <50Ω | | Vz ±2.5% |
| DZT18A | G6 | a1 | RO | Z Diode | | | | 0.2 W | | 17.3 V | 5 mA | <65Ω | | Vz ±2.5% |
| DZT20A | G6 | a1 | RO | Z Diode | | | | 0.2 W | | 19.3 V | 5 mA | <85Ω | | Vz ±2.5% |
| DZT22A | G6 | a1 | RO | Z Diode | | | | 0.2 W | | 21.3 V | 5 mA | <100Ω | | Vz ±2.5% |
| DZT24A | G6 | a1 | RO | Z Diode | | | | 0.2 W | | 23.4 V | 5 mA | <120Ω | | Vz ±2.5% |
| DZT27A | G6 | a1 | RO | Z Diode | | | | 0.2 W | | 26.3 V | 5 mA | <150Ω | | Vz ±2.5% |
| DZT30A | G6 | a1 | RO | Z Diode | | | | 0.2 W | | 29 V | 5 mA | <200Ω | | Vz ±2.5% |
| DZT33A | G6 | a1 | RO | Z Diode | | | | 0.2 W | | 32 V | 5 mA | <250Ω | | Vz ±2.5% |
| DZT36A | G6 | a1 | RO | Z Diode | | | | 0.2 W | | 35 V | 5 mA | <300Ω | | Vz ±2.5% |
| DZT2.4B | G6 | a1 | RO | Z Diode | | | | 0.2 W | | 2.5 V | 5 mA | <100Ω | | Vz ±2.5% |
| DZT2.7B | G6 | a1 | RO | Z Diode | | | | 0.2 W | | 2.8 V | 5 mA | <110Ω | | Vz ±2.5% |
| DZT3.0B | G6 | a1 | RO | Z Diode | | | | 0.2 W | | 3.1 V | 5 mA | <120Ω | | Vz ±2.5% |
| DZT3.3B | G6 | a1 | RO | Z Diode | | | | 0.2 W | | 3.4 V | 5 mA | <120Ω | | Vz ±2.5% |
| DZT3.6B | G6 | a1 | RO | Z Diode | | | | 0.2 W | | 3.7 V | 5 mA | <100Ω | | Vz ±2.5% |
| DZT3.9B | G6 | a1 | RO | Z Diode | | | | 0.2 W | | 4 V | 5 mA | <100Ω | | Vz ±2.5% |
| DZT4.3B | G6 | a1 | RO | Z Diode | | | | 0.2 W | | 4.3 V | 5 mA | <100Ω | | Vz ±2.5% |
| DZT4.7B | G6 | a1 | RO | Z Diode | | | | 0.2 W | | 4.6 V | 5 mA | <100Ω | | Vz ±2.5% |
| DZT5.1B | G6 | a1 | RO | Z Diode | | | | 0.2 W | | 5.1 V | 5 mA | <80Ω | | Vz ±2.5% |
| DZT5.6B | G6 | a1 | RO | Z Diode | | | | 0.2 W | | 5.6 V | 5 mA | <60Ω | | Vz ±2.5% |
| DZT6.2B | G6 | a1 | RO | Z Diode | | | | 0.2 W | | 6.2 V | 5 mA | <60Ω | | Vz ±2.5% |
| DZT6.8B | G6 | a1 | RO | Z Diode | | | | 0.2 W | | 6.8 V | 5 mA | <40Ω | | Vz ±2.5% |
| DZT7.5B | G6 | a1 | RO | Z Diode | | | | 0.2 W | | 7.4 V | 5 mA | <30Ω | | Vz ±2.5% |
| DZT8.2B | G6 | a1 | RO | Z Diode | | | | 0.2 W | | 7.2 V | 5 mA | <30Ω | | Vz ±2.5% |

| Type | Case | Pin-code | | | Maximum Ratings Vcla/Vbro | Its | Izm | Pv | Pvts | Electrical Characteristics Vz | Iz/Is | rz | TK | |
|---|---|---|---|---|---|---|---|---|---|---|---|---|---|---|
| DZT9.1B | G6 | a1 | RO | Z Diode | | | | 0.2 W | | 9.1 V | 5 mA | <30Ω | | Vz ±2.5% |
| DZT10B | G6 | a1 | RO | Z Diode | | | | 0.2 W | | 10 V | 5 mA | <30Ω | | Vz ±2.5% |
| DZT11B | G6 | a1 | RO | Z Diode | | | | 0.2 W | | 11 V | 5 mA | <30Ω | | Vz ±2.5% |
| DZT12B | G6 | a1 | RO | Z Diode | | | | 0.2 W | | 12 V | 5 mA | <30Ω | | Vz ±2.5% |
| DZT13B | G6 | a1 | RO | Z Diode | | | | 0.2 W | | 13.2 V | 5 mA | <37Ω | | Vz ±2.5% |
| DZT15B | G6 | a1 | RO | Z Diode | | | | 0.2 W | | 14.7 V | 5 mA | <42Ω | | Vz ±2.5% |
| DZT16B | G6 | a1 | RO | Z Diode | | | | 0.2 W | | 16.2 V | 5 mA | <50Ω | | Vz ±2.5% |
| DZT18B | G6 | a1 | RO | Z Diode | | | | 0.2 W | | 17.9 V | 5 mA | <65Ω | | Vz ±2.5% |
| DZT20B | G6 | a1 | RO | Z Diode | | | | 0.2 W | | 20 V | 5 mA | <85Ω | | Vz ±2.5% |
| DZT22B | G6 | a1 | RO | Z Diode | | | | 0.2 W | | 22 V | 5 mA | <100Ω | | Vz ±2.5% |
| DZT24B | G6 | a1 | RO | Z Diode | | | | 0.2 W | | 24.1 V | 5 mA | <120Ω | | Vz ±2.5% |
| DZT27B | G6 | a1 | RO | Z Diode | | | | 0.2 W | | 26.9 V | 5 mA | <150Ω | | Vz ±2.5% |
| DZT30B | G6 | a1 | RO | Z Diode | | | | 0.2 W | | 29.9 V | 5 mA | <200Ω | | Vz ±2.5% |
| DZT33B | G6 | a1 | RO | Z Diode | | | | 0.2 W | | 33.1 V | 5 mA | <250Ω | | Vz ±2.5% |
| DZT36B | G6 | a1 | RO | Z Diode | | | | 0.2 W | | 35.9 V | 5 mA | <300Ω | | Vz ±2.5% |
| DZT4.3C | G6 | a1 | RO | Z Diode | | | | 0.2 W | | 4.4 V | 5 mA | <100Ω | | Vz ±2.5% |
| DZT4.7C | G6 | a1 | RO | Z Diode | | | | 0.2 W | | 4.8 V | 5 mA | <100Ω | | Vz ±2.5% |
| DZT5.1C | G6 | a1 | RO | Z Diode | | | | 0.2 W | | 5.2 V | 5 mA | <80Ω | | Vz ±2.5% |
| DZT5.6C | G6 | a1 | RO | Z Diode | | | | 0.2 W | | 5.8 V | 5 mA | <60Ω | | Vz ±2.5% |
| DZT6.2C | G6 | a1 | RO | Z Diode | | | | 0.2 W | | 6.4 V | 5 mA | <60Ω | | Vz ±2.5% |
| DZT6.8C | G6 | a1 | RO | Z Diode | | | | 0.2 W | | 7 V | 5 mA | <40Ω | | Vz ±2.5% |
| DZT7.5C | G6 | a1 | RO | Z Diode | | | | 0.2 W | | 7.7 V | 5 mA | <30Ω | | Vz ±2.5% |
| DZT8.2C | G6 | a1 | RO | Z Diode | | | | 0.2 W | | 8.5 V | 5 mA | <30Ω | | Vz ±2.5% |
| DZT9.1C | G6 | a1 | RO | Z Diode | | | | 0.2 W | | 9.6 V | 5 mA | <30Ω | | Vz ±2.5% |
| DZT10C | G6 | a1 | RO | Z Diode | | | | 0.2 W | | 10.3 V | 5 mA | <30Ω | | Vz ±2.5% |
| DZT11C | G6 | a1 | RO | Z Diode | | | | 0.2 W | | 11.3 V | 5 mA | <30Ω | | Vz ±2.5% |
| DZT12C | G6 | a1 | RO | Z Diode | | | | 0.2 W | | 12.3 V | 5 mA | <30Ω | | Vz ±2.5% |
| DZT13C | G6 | a1 | RO | Z Diode | | | | 0.2 W | | 13.7 V | 5 mA | <37Ω | | Vz ±2.5% |
| DZT15C | G6 | a1 | RO | Z Diode | | | | 0.2 W | | 15.2 V | 5 mA | <42Ω | | Vz ±2.5% |
| DZT16C | G6 | a1 | RO | Z Diode | | | | 0.2 W | | 16.6 V | 5 mA | <50Ω | | Vz ±2.5% |
| DZT18C | G6 | a1 | RO | Z Diode | | | | 0.2 W | | 18.6 V | 5 mA | <65Ω | | Vz ±2.5% |
| DZT20C | G6 | a1 | RO | Z Diode | | | | 0.2 W | | 20.6 V | 5 mA | <85Ω | | Vz ±2.5% |
| DZT22C | G6 | a1 | RO | Z Diode | | | | 0.2 W | | 22.7 V | 5 mA | <100Ω | | Vz ±2.5% |
| DZT24C | G6 | a1 | RO | Z Diode | | | | 0.2 W | | 24.5 V | 5 mA | <120Ω | | Vz ±2.5% |
| DZT27C | G6 | a1 | RO | Z Diode | | | | 0.2 W | | 27.8 V | 5 mA | <150Ω | | Vz ±2.5% |
| DZT30C | G6 | a1 | RO | Z Diode | | | | 0.2 W | | 31 V | 5 mA | <200Ω | | Vz ±2.5% |
| DZT33C | G6 | a1 | RO | Z Diode | | | | 0.2 W | | 34 V | 5 mA | <250Ω | | Vz ±2.5% |
| DZT36C | G6 | a1 | RO | Z Diode | | | | 0.2 W | | 37 V | 5 mA | <300Ω | | Vz ±2.5% |
| F1C518 | G1 | a1 | RD | TVS | 25 V | 20 mA | 20 mA | | 0.5 kW | | | | | |
| F1C527 | G1 | a1 | RD | TVS | 38 V | 13 mA | 13 mA | | 0.5 kW | | | | | |

| Type | Case | Pin-code | | | Maximum Ratings Vcla Vbro | Its | Izm | Pv | Pvts | Electrical Characteristics Vz | Iz Is | rz | TK | |
|---|---|---|---|---|---|---|---|---|---|---|---|---|---|---|
| F1C2260 | G1 | a1 | RD | TVS | 360 V | 1 mA | 1 mA | | 0.2 kW | | | | | |
| LL1.5 | D2 | a1 | IT | Z Diode | | | 120 mA | 0.3 W | | 1.45 V | 5 mA | 13 Ω | -2600 ·10^6/°C | |
| LL2 | D2 | a1 | IT | Z Diode | | | 120 mA | 0.3 W | | 2.15 V | 5 mA | 18 Ω | -2600 ·10^6/°C | |
| LL2.4 | D2 | a1 | IT | Z Diode | | | 120 mA | 0.3 W | | 2.38 V | 5 mA | 14 Ω | -3400 ·10^6/°C | |
| LL2.7 | D2 | a1 | IT | Z Diode | | | 105 mA | 0.3 W | | 2.7 V | 5 mA | 15 Ω | -3400 ·10^6/°C | |
| LL3 | D2 | a1 | IT | Z Diode | | | 95 mA | 0.3 W | | 3.0 V | 5 mA | 15 Ω | -3400 ·10^6/°C | |
| LL3.3 | D2 | a1 | IT | Z Diode | | | 90 mA | 0.3 W | | 3.3 V | 5 mA | 16 Ω | -3400 ·10^6/°C | |
| LL3.6 | D2 | a1 | IT | Z Diode | | | 80 mA | 0.3 W | | 3.6 V | 5 mA | 16 Ω | -3400 ·10^6/°C | |
| LL3.9 | D2 | a1 | IT | Z Diode | | | 75 mA | 0.3 W | | 3.9 V | 5 mA | 17 Ω | -3400 ·10^6/°C | |
| LL4.3 | D2 | a1 | IT | Z Diode | | | 65 mA | 0.3 W | | 4.3 V | 5 mA | 17 Ω | -3400 ·10^6/°C | |
| LL4.7 | D2 | a1 | IT | Z Diode | | | 60 mA | 0.3 W | | 4.7 V | 5 mA | 18 Ω | -3400 ·10^6/°C | |
| LL5.1 | D2 | a1 | IT | Z Diode | | | 55 mA | 0.3 W | | 5.1 V | 5 mA | 18 Ω | -3400 ·10^6/°C | |
| MLL4678 | D2 | a1 | MO | Z Diode | | | 120 mA | 0.5 W | | 1.8 V | 50 µA | | | |
| MLL4679 | D2 | a1 | MO | Z Diode | | | 110 mA | 0.5 W | | 2.0 V | 50 µA | | | |
| MLL4680 | D2 | a1 | MO | Z Diode | | | 100 mA | 0.5 W | | 2.2 V | 50 µA | | | |
| MLL4681 | D2 | a1 | MO | Z Diode | | | 95 mA | 0.5 W | | 2.4 V | 50 µA | | | |
| MLL4682 | D2 | a1 | MO | Z Diode | | | 90 mA | 0.5 W | | 2.7 V | 50 µA | | | |
| MLL4683 | D2 | a1 | MO | Z Diode | | | 85 mA | 0.5 W | | 3.0 V | 50 µA | | | |
| MLL4684 | D2 | a1 | MO | Z Diode | | | 80 mA | 0.5 W | | 3.3 V | 50 µA | | | P |
| MLL4685 | D2 | a1 | MO | Z Diode | | | 75 mA | 0.5 W | | 3.6 V | 50 µA | | | |
| MLL4686 | D2 | a1 | MO | Z Diode | | | 70 mA | 0.5 W | | 3.9 V | 50 µA | | | |
| MLL4687 | D2 | a1 | MO | Z Diode | | | 65 mA | 0.5 W | | 4.3 V | 50 µA | | | P |
| MLL4688 | D2 | a1 | MO | Z Diode | | | 60 mA | 0.5 W | | 4.7 V | 50 µA | | | P |
| MLL4689 | D2 | a1 | MO | Z Diode | | | 55 mA | 0.5 W | | 5.1 V | 50 µA | | | P |
| MLL4690 | D2 | a1 | MO | Z Diode | | | 50 mA | 0.5 W | | 5.6 V | 50 µA | | | P |
| MLL4691 | D2 | a1 | MO | Z Diode | | | 45 mA | 0.5 W | | 6.2 V | 50 µA | | | P |
| MLL4692 | D2 | a1 | MO | Z Diode | | | 35 mA | 0.5 W | | 6.8 V | 50 µA | | | P |
| MLL4693 | D2 | a1 | MO | Z Diode | | | 31.8 mA | 0.5 W | | 7.0 V | 50 µA | | | P |
| MLL4694 | D2 | a1 | MO | Z Diode | | | 29 mA | 0.5 W | | 8.2 V | 50 µA | | | P |
| MLL4695 | D2 | a1 | MO | Z Diode | | | 27.4 mA | 0.5 W | | 8.7 V | 50 µA | | | |
| MLL4696 | D2 | a1 | MO | Z Diode | | | 26.2 mA | 0.5 W | | 9.1 V | 50 µA | | | P |
| MLL4697 | D2 | a1 | MO | Z Diode | | | 24.8 mA | 0.5 W | | 10 V | 50 µA | | | P |
| MLL4698 | D2 | a1 | MO | Z Diode | | | 21.6 mA | 0.5 W | | 11 V | 50 µA | | | |
| MLL4699 | D2 | a1 | MO | Z Diode | | | 20.4 mA | 0.5 W | | 12 V | 50 µA | | | P |
| MLL4700 | D2 | a1 | MO | Z Diode | | | 19 mA | 0.5 W | | 13 V | 50 µA | | | |
| MLL4701 | D2 | a1 | MO | Z Diode | | | 17.5 mA | 0.5 W | | 14 V | 50 µA | | | |
| MLL4702 | D2 | a1 | MO | Z Diode | | | 16.3 mA | 0.5 W | | 15 V | 50 µA | | | P |
| MLL4703 | D2 | a1 | MO | Z Diode | | | 15.4 mA | 0.5 W | | 16 V | 50 µA | | | |
| MLL4704 | D2 | a1 | MO | Z Diode | | | 14.5 mA | 0.5 W | | 17 V | 50 µA | | | |
| MLL4705 | D2 | a1 | MO | Z Diode | | | 13.2 mA | 0.5 W | | 18 V | 50 µA | | | |

| Type | Case | Pin-code | | | Maximum Ratings | | | | | Electrical Characteristics | | | | |
|---|---|---|---|---|---|---|---|---|---|---|---|---|---|---|
| | | | | | $V_{cla}$ $V_{bro}$ | Its | Izm | Pv | Pvts | Vz | Iz Is | rz | TK | |
| MLL4706 | D2 | a1 | MO | Z Diode | | | 12.5 mA | 0.5 W | | 19 V | 50 µA | | | |
| MLL4707 | D2 | a1 | MO | Z Diode | | | 11.9 mA | 0.5 W | | 20 V | 50 µA | | | |
| MLL4708 | D2 | a1 | MO | Z Diode | | | 10.8 mA | 0.5 W | | 22 V | 50 µA | | | |
| MLL4709 | D2 | a1 | MO | Z Diode | | | 9.9 mA | 0.5 W | | 24 V | 50 µA | | | |
| MLL4710 | D2 | a1 | MO | Z Diode | | | 9.5 mA | 0.5 W | | 25 V | 50 µA | | | |
| MLL4711 | D2 | a1 | MO | Z Diode | | | 8.8 mA | 0.5 W | | 27 V | 50 µA | | | P |
| MLL4712 | D2 | a1 | MO | Z Diode | | | 8.5 mA | 0.5 W | | 28 V | 50 µA | | | P |
| MLL4713 | D2 | a1 | MO | Z Diode | | | 7.9 mA | 0.5 W | | 30 V | 50 µA | | | |
| MLL4714 | D2 | a1 | MO | Z Diode | | | 7.2 mA | 0.5 W | | 33 V | 50 µA | | | |
| MLL4715 | D2 | a1 | MO | Z Diode | | | 6.6 mA | 0.5 W | | 36 V | 50 µA | | | |
| MLL4716 | D2 | a1 | MO | Z Diode | | | 6.1 mA | 0.5 W | | 39 V | 50 µA | | | |
| MLL4717 | D2 | a1 | MO | Z Diode | | | 5.5 mA | 0.5 W | | 43 V | 50 µA | | | |
| MLL5221B | D4 | a1 | MO | Z Diode | | | | 0.5 W | | 2.4 V | 20 mA | <30 Ω | $-850 \cdot 10^6/°C$ | |
| MLL5222B | D4 | a1 | MO | Z Diode | | | | 0.5 W | | 2.5 V | 20 mA | <30 Ω | $-850 \cdot 10^6/°C$ | |
| MLL5223B | D4 | a1 | MO | Z Diode | | | | 0.5 W | | 2.7 V | 20 mA | <30 Ω | $-800 \cdot 10^6/°C$ | |
| MLL5224B | D4 | a1 | MO | Z Diode | | | | 0.5 W | | 2.8 V | 20 mA | <30 Ω | $-800 \cdot 10^6/°C$ | |
| MLL5225B | D4 | a1 | MO | Z Diode | | | | 0.5 W | | 3.0 V | 20 mA | <29 Ω | $-750 \cdot 10^6/°C$ | |
| MLL5226B | D4 | a1 | MO | Z Diode | | | | 0.5 W | | 3.3 V | 20 mA | <28 Ω | $-700 \cdot 10^6/°C$ | |
| MLL5227B | D4 | a1 | MO | Z Diode | | | | 0.5 W | | 3.6 V | 20 mA | <24 Ω | $-650 \cdot 10^6/°C$ | |
| MLL5228B | D4 | a1 | MO | Z Diode | | | | 0.5 W | | 3.9 V | 20 mA | <23 Ω | $-600 \cdot 10^6/°C$ | |
| MLL5229B | D4 | a1 | MO | Z Diode | | | | 0.5 W | | 4.3 V | 20 mA | <22 Ω | $550 \cdot 10^6/°C$ | |
| MLL5230B | D4 | a1 | MO | Z Diode | | | | 0.5 W | | 4.7 V | 20 mA | <19 Ω | $300 \cdot 10^6/°C$ | |
| MLL5231B | D4 | a1 | MO | Z Diode | | | | 0.5 W | | 5.1 V | 20 mA | <17 Ω | $300 \cdot 10^6/°C$ P | |
| MLL5232B | D4 | a1 | MO | Z Diode | | | | 0.5 W | | 5,6 V | 20 mA | <11 Ω | $380 \cdot 10^6/°C$ | |
| MLL5233B | D4 | a1 | MO | Z Diode | | | | 0.5 W | | 6.0 V | 20 mA | <7 Ω | $380 \cdot 10^6/°C$ P | |
| MLL5234B | D4 | a1 | MO | Z Diode | | | | 0.5 W | | 6.2 V | 20 mA | <7 Ω | $450 \cdot 10^6/°C$ | |
| MLL5235B | D4 | a1 | MO | Z Diode | | | | 0.5 W | | 6.8 V | 20 mA | <5 Ω | $500 \cdot 10^6/°C$ | |
| MLL5236B | D4 | a1 | MO | Z Diode | | | | 0.5 W | | 7.0 V | 20 mA | <6 Ω | $580 \cdot 10^6/°C$ | |
| MLL5237B | D4 | a1 | MO | Z Diode | | | | 0.5 W | | 8.2 V | 20 mA | <8 Ω | $620 \cdot 10^6/°C$ | |
| MLL5238B | D4 | a1 | MO | Z Diode | | | | 0.5 W | | 8.7 V | 20 mA | <8 Ω | $650 \cdot 10^6/°C$ | |
| MLL5239B | D4 | a1 | MO | Z Diode | | | | 0.5 W | | 9.1 V | 20 mA | <10 Ω | $680 \cdot 10^6/°C$ | |
| MLL5240B | D4 | a1 | MO | Z Diode | | | | 0.5 W | | 10 V | 20 mA | <17 Ω | $750 \cdot 10^6/°C$ | |
| MLL5241B | D4 | a1 | MO | Z Diode | | | | 0.5 W | | 11 V | 20 mA | <22 Ω | $760 \cdot 10^6/°C$ | |
| MLL5242B | D4 | a1 | MO | Z Diode | | | | 0.5 W | | 12 V | 20 mA | <30 Ω | $770 \cdot 10^6/°C$ | |
| MLL5243B | D4 | a1 | MO | Z Diode | | | | 0.5 W | | 13 V | 9.5 mA | <13 Ω | $790 \cdot 10^6/°C$ | |
| MLL5244B | D4 | a1 | MO | Z Diode | | | | 0.5 W | | 14 V | 9.0 mA | <15 Ω | $820 \cdot 10^6/°C$ P | |
| MLL5245B | D4 | a1 | MO | Z Diode | | | | 0.5 W | | 15 V | 8.5 mA | <16 Ω | $820 \cdot 10^6/°C$ | |
| MLL5246B | D4 | a1 | MO | Z Diode | | | | 0.5 W | | 16 V | 7.8 mA | <17 Ω | $830 \cdot 10^6/°C$ | |
| MLL5247B | D4 | a1 | MO | Z Diode | | | | 0.5 W | | 17 V | 7.4 mA | <19 Ω | $840 \cdot 10^6/°C$ | |
| MLL5248B | D4 | a1 | MO | Z Diode | | | | 0.5 W | | 18 V | 7.0 mA | <21 Ω | $850 \cdot 10^6/°C$ | |

| Type | Case | Pin-code | | | **Maximum Ratings** Vcla/Vbro | Its | Izm | Pv | Pvts | **Electrical Characteristics** Vz | Iz / Is | rz | TK | |
|---|---|---|---|---|---|---|---|---|---|---|---|---|---|---|
| MLL5249B | D4 | a1 | MO | Z Diode | | | | 0.5 W | | 19 V | 6.6 mA | <23Ω | $860 \cdot 10^6$/°C | |
| MLL5250B | D4 | a1 | MO | Z Diode | | | | 0.5 W | | 20 V | 6.2 mA | <25Ω | $860 \cdot 10^6$/°C | |
| MLL5251B | D4 | a1 | MO | Z Diode | | | | 0.5 W | | 22 V | 5.6 mA | <29Ω | $870 \cdot 10^6$/°C | |
| MLL5252B | D4 | a1 | MO | Z Diode | | | | 0.5 W | | 24 V | 5.2 mA | <33Ω | $880 \cdot 10^6$/°C P | |
| MLL5253B | D4 | a1 | MO | Z Diode | | | | 0.5 W | | 25 V | 5.0 mA | <35Ω | $890 \cdot 10^6$/°C | |
| MLL5254B | D4 | a1 | MO | Z Diode | | | | 0.5 W | | 27 V | 4.6 mA | <41Ω | $900 \cdot 10^6$/°C | |
| MLL5255B | D4 | a1 | MO | Z Diode | | | | 0.5 W | | 28 V | 4.5 mA | <44Ω | $910 \cdot 10^6$/°C | |
| MLL5256B | D4 | a1 | MO | Z Diode | | | | 0.5 W | | 30 V | 4.2 mA | <49Ω | $910 \cdot 10^6$/°C | |
| MLL5257B | D4 | a1 | MO | Z Diode | | | | 0.5 W | | 33 V | 3.8 mA | <58Ω | $920 \cdot 10^6$/°C | |
| MLL5258B | D4 | a1 | MO | Z Diode | | | | 0.5 W | | 36 V | 3.4 mA | <70Ω | $930 \cdot 10^6$/°C | |
| MLL5259B | D4 | a1 | MO | Z Diode | | | | 0.5 W | | 39 V | 3.2 mA | <80Ω | $940 \cdot 10^6$/°C | |
| MLL5260B | D4 | a1 | MO | Z Diode | | | | 0.5 W | | 43 V | 3.0 mA | <93Ω | $950 \cdot 10^6$/°C | |
| MLL5261B | D4 | a1 | MO | Z Diode | | | | 0.5 W | | 47 V | 2.7 mA | <105Ω | $950 \cdot 10^6$/°C | |
| MLL5262B | D4 | a1 | MO | Z Diode | | | | 0.5 W | | 51 V | 2.5 mA | <125Ω | $960 \cdot 10^6$/°C | |
| MLL5263B | D4 | a1 | MO | Z Diode | | | | 0.5 W | | 56 V | 2.3 mA | <150Ω | $960 \cdot 10^6$/°C | |
| MLL5264B | D4 | a1 | MO | Z Diode | | | | 0.5 W | | 60 V | 2.1 mA | <170Ω | $920 \cdot 10^6$/°C | |
| MLL5265B | D4 | a1 | MO | Z Diode | | | | 0.5 W | | 62 V | 2.0 mA | <185Ω | $930 \cdot 10^6$/°C | |
| MLL5266B | D4 | a1 | MO | Z Diode | | | | 0.5 W | | 68 V | 1.8 mA | <230Ω | $940 \cdot 10^6$/°C | |
| MLL5267B | D4 | a1 | MO | Z Diode | | | | 0.5 W | | 75 V | 1.7 mA | <270Ω | $950 \cdot 10^6$/°C | |
| MLL5268B | D4 | a1 | MO | Z Diode | | | | 0.5 W | | 82 V | 1.7 mA | <270Ω | $950 \cdot 10^6$/°C | |
| MLL5269B | D4 | a1 | MO | Z Diode | | | | 0.5 W | | 87 V | 1.7 mA | <270Ω | $960 \cdot 10^6$/°C | |
| MLL5270B | D4 | a1 | MO | Z Diode | | | | 0.5 W | | 91 V | 1.7 mA | <270Ω | $960 \cdot 10^6$/°C | |
| MMBZ5226B | F1 | c3 | NS | Z Diode | | | | 0.5 W | | 3.3 V | 20 mA | <28Ω | $-700 \cdot 10^6$/°C | |
| MMBZ5227B | F1 | c3 | NS | Z Diode | | | | 0.5 W | | 3.6 V | 20 mA | <24Ω | $-650 \cdot 10^6$/°C | |
| MMBZ5228B | F1 | c3 | NS | Z Diode | | | | 0.5 W | | 3.9 V | 20 mA | <23Ω | $-600 \cdot 10^6$/°C | |
| MMBZ5229B | F1 | c3 | NS | Z Diode | | | | 0.5 W | | 4.3 V | 20 mA | <22Ω | $550 \cdot 10^6$/°C | |
| MMBZ5230B | F1 | c3 | NS | Z Diode | | | | 0.5 W | | 4.7 V | 20 mA | <19Ω | $300 \cdot 10^6$/°C | |
| MMBZ5231B | F1 | c3 | NS | Z Diode | | | | 0.5 W | | 5.1 V | 20 mA | <17Ω | $300 \cdot 10^6$/°C | |
| MMBZ5232B | F1 | c3 | NS | Z Diode | | | | 0.5 W | | 5,6 V | 20 mA | <11Ω | $380 \cdot 10^6$/°C | |
| MMBZ5233B | F1 | c3 | NS | Z Diode | | | | 0.5 W | | 6.0 V | 20 mA | <7Ω | $380 \cdot 10^6$/°C | |
| MMBZ5234B | F1 | c3 | NS | Z Diode | | | | 0.5 W | | 6.2 V | 20 mA | <7Ω | $450 \cdot 10^6$/°C | |
| MMBZ5235B | F1 | c3 | NS | Z Diode | | | | 0.5 W | | 6.8 V | 20 mA | <5Ω | $500 \cdot 10^6$/°C | |
| MMBZ5236B | F1 | c3 | NS | Z Diode | | | | 0.5 W | | 7.0 V | 20 mA | <6Ω | $580 \cdot 10^6$/°C | |
| MMBZ5237B | F1 | c3 | NS | Z Diode | | | | 0.5 W | | 8.2 V | 20 mA | <8Ω | $620 \cdot 10^6$/°C | |
| MMBZ5238B | F1 | c3 | NS | Z Diode | | | | 0.5 W | | 8.7 V | 20 mA | <8Ω | $650 \cdot 10^6$/°C | |
| MMBZ5239B | F1 | c3 | NS | Z Diode | | | | 0.5 W | | 9.1 V | 20 mA | <10Ω | $680 \cdot 10^6$/°C | |
| MMBZ5240B | F1 | c3 | NS | Z Diode | | | | 0.5 W | | 10 V | 20 mA | <17Ω | $750 \cdot 10^6$/°C | |
| MMBZ5241B | F1 | c3 | NS | Z Diode | | | | 0.5 W | | 11 V | 20 mA | <22Ω | $760 \cdot 10^6$/°C | |
| MMBZ5242B | F1 | c3 | NS | Z Diode | | | | 0.5 W | | 12 V | 20 mA | <30Ω | $770 \cdot 10^6$/°C | |
| MMBZ5243B | F1 | c3 | NS | Z Diode | | | | 0.5 W | | 13 V | 9.5 mA | <13Ω | $790 \cdot 10^6$/°C | |

173

| Type | Case | Pin-code | | | Vcla Vbro | Its | Izm | Pv | Pvts | Vz | Iz Is | rz | TK | |
|---|---|---|---|---|---|---|---|---|---|---|---|---|---|---|
| | | | | | | | | **Maximum Ratings** | | | **Electrical Characteristics** | | | |
| MMBZ5244B | F1 | c3 | NS | Z Diode | | | | 0.5 W | | 14 V | 9.0 mA | <15Ω | $820 \cdot 10^6$/°C | |
| MMBZ5245B | F1 | c3 | NS | Z Diode | | | | 0.5 W | | 15 V | 8.5 mA | <16Ω | $820 \cdot 10^6$/°C | |
| MMBZ5246B | F1 | c3 | NS | Z Diode | | | | 0.5 W | | 16 V | 7.8 mA | <17Ω | $830 \cdot 10^6$/°C | |
| MMBZ5247B | F1 | c3 | NS | Z Diode | | | | 0.5 W | | 17 V | 7.4 mA | <19Ω | $840 \cdot 10^6$/°C | |
| MMBZ5248B | F1 | c3 | NS | Z Diode | | | | 0.5 W | | 18 V | 7.0 mA | <21Ω | $850 \cdot 10^6$/°C | |
| MMBZ5249B | F1 | c3 | NS | Z Diode | | | | 0.5 W | | 19 V | 6.6 mA | <23Ω | $860 \cdot 10^6$/°C | |
| MMBZ5250B | F1 | c3 | NS | Z Diode | | | | 0.5 W | | 20 V | 6.2 mA | <25Ω | $860 \cdot 10^6$/°C | |
| MMBZ5251B | F1 | c3 | NS | Z Diode | | | | 0.5 W | | 22 V | 5.6 mA | <29Ω | $870 \cdot 10^6$/°C | |
| MMBZ5252B | F1 | c3 | NS | Z Diode | | | | 0.5 W | | 24 V | 5.2 mA | <33Ω | $880 \cdot 10^6$/°C | |
| MMBZ5253B | F1 | c3 | NS | Z Diode | | | | 0.5 W | | 25 V | 5.0 mA | <35Ω | $890 \cdot 10^6$/°C | |
| MMBZ5254B | F1 | c3 | NS | Z Diode | | | | 0.5 W | | 27 V | 4.6 mA | <41Ω | $900 \cdot 10^6$/°C | |
| MMBZ5255B | F1 | c3 | NS | Z Diode | | | | 0.5 W | | 28 V | 4.5 mA | <44Ω | $910 \cdot 10^6$/°C | |
| MMBZ5256B | F1 | c3 | NS | Z Diode | | | | 0.5 W | | 30 V | 4.2 mA | <49Ω | $910 \cdot 10^6$/°C | |
| MMBZ5257B | F1 | c3 | NS | Z Diode | | | | 0.5 W | | 33 V | 3.8 mA | <58Ω | $920 \cdot 10^6$/°C | |
| MMBZ221BL | F1 | c3 | MO | Z Diode | | | | 0.3 W | | 2.4 V | 20 mA | <30Ω | $-850 \cdot 10^6$/°C | |
| MMBZ222BL | F1 | c3 | MO | Z Diode | | | | 0.3 W | | 2.5 V | 20 mA | <30Ω | $-850 \cdot 10^6$/°C | |
| MMBZ223BL | F1 | c3 | MO | Z Diode | | | | 0.3 W | | 2.7 V | 20 mA | <30Ω | $-800 \cdot 10^6$/°C | |
| MMBZ224BL | F1 | c3 | MO | Z Diode | | | | 0.3 W | | 2.8 V | 20 mA | <30Ω | $-800 \cdot 10^6$/°C | |
| MMBZ225BL | F1 | c3 | MO | Z Diode | | | | 0.3 W | | 3.0 V | 20 mA | <29Ω | $-750 \cdot 10^6$/°C | |
| MMBZ226BL | F1 | c3 | MO | Z Diode | | | | 0.3 W | | 3.3 V | 20 mA | <28Ω | $-700 \cdot 10^6$/°C | P |
| MMBZ227BL | F1 | c3 | MO | Z Diode | | | | 0.3 W | | 3.6 V | 20 mA | <24Ω | $-650 \cdot 10^6$/°C | |
| MMBZ228BL | F1 | c3 | MO | Z Diode | | | | 0.3 W | | 3.9 V | 20 mA | <23Ω | $-600 \cdot 10^6$/°C | |
| MMBZ229BL | F1 | c3 | MO | Z Diode | | | | 0.3 W | | 4.3 V | 20 mA | <22Ω | $550 \cdot 10^6$/°C | P |
| MMBZ230BL | F1 | c3 | MO | Z Diode | | | | 0.3 W | | 4.7 V | 20 mA | <19Ω | $300 \cdot 10^6$/°C | P |
| MMBZ231BL | F1 | c3 | MO | Z Diode | | | | 0.3 W | | 5.1 V | 20 mA | <17Ω | $300 \cdot 10^6$/°C | P |
| MMBZ232BL | F1 | c3 | MO | Z Diode | | | | 0.3 W | | 5,6 V | 20 mA | <11Ω | $380 \cdot 10^6$/°C | P |
| MMBZ233BL | F1 | c3 | MO | Z Diode | | | | 0.3 W | | 6.0 V | 20 mA | <7Ω | $380 \cdot 10^6$/°C | |
| MMBZ234BL | F1 | c3 | MO | Z Diode | | | | 0.3 W | | 6.2 V | 20 mA | <7Ω | $450 \cdot 10^6$/°C | P |
| MMBZ235BL | F1 | c3 | MO | Z Diode | | | | 0.3 W | | 6.8 V | 20 mA | <5Ω | $500 \cdot 10^6$/°C | P |
| MMBZ236BL | F1 | c3 | MO | Z Diode | | | | 0.3 W | | 7.0 V | 20 mA | <6Ω | $580 \cdot 10^6$/°C | P |
| MMBZ237BL | F1 | c3 | MO | Z Diode | | | | 0.3 W | | 8.2 V | 20 mA | <8Ω | $620 \cdot 10^6$/°C | P |
| MMBZ238BL | F1 | c3 | MO | Z Diode | | | | 0.3 W | | 8.7 V | 20 mA | <8Ω | $650 \cdot 10^6$/°C | |
| MMBZ239BL | F1 | c3 | MO | Z Diode | | | | 0.3 W | | 9.1 V | 20 mA | <10Ω | $680 \cdot 10^6$/°C | P |
| MMBZ240BL | F1 | c3 | MO | Z Diode | | | | 0.3 W | | 10 V | 20 mA | <17Ω | $750 \cdot 10^6$/°C | P |
| MMBZ241BL | F1 | c3 | MO | Z Diode | | | | 0.3 W | | 11 V | 20 mA | <22Ω | $760 \cdot 10^6$/°C | |
| MMBZ242BL | F1 | c3 | MO | Z Diode | | | | 0.3 W | | 12 V | 20 mA | <30Ω | $770 \cdot 10^6$/°C | P |
| MMBZ243BL | F1 | c3 | MO | Z Diode | | | | 0.3 W | | 13 V | 9.5 mA | <13Ω | $790 \cdot 10^6$/°C | |
| MMBZ244BL | F1 | c3 | MO | Z Diode | | | | 0.3 W | | 14 V | 9.0 mA | <15Ω | $820 \cdot 10^6$/°C | |
| MMBZ245BL | F1 | c3 | MO | Z Diode | | | | 0.3 W | | 15 V | 8.5 mA | <16Ω | $820 \cdot 10^6$/°C | P |
| MMBZ246BL | F1 | c3 | MO | Z Diode | | | | 0.3 W | | 16 V | 7.8 mA | <17Ω | $830 \cdot 10^6$/°C | |

| Type | Case | Pin-code | | | Maximum Ratings | | | | | Electrical Characteristics | | | | |
|------|------|----------|---|---|-----------------|---|---|---|---|----------------------------|---|---|---|---|
| | | | | | $V_{cla}$ $V_{bro}$ | Its | Izm | Pv | Pvts | Vz | Iz / Is | rz | TK | |
| MMBZ247BL | F1 | c3 | MO | Z Diode | | | | 0.3 W | | 17 V | 7.4 mA | <19 Ω | $840 \cdot 10^6$/°C | |
| MMBZ248BL | F1 | c3 | MO | Z Diode | | | | 0.3 W | | 18 V | 7.0 mA | <21 Ω | $850 \cdot 10^6$/°C | |
| MMBZ249BL | F1 | c3 | MO | Z Diode | | | | 0.3 W | | 19 V | 6.6 mA | <23 Ω | $860 \cdot 10^6$/°C | |
| MMBZ250BL | F1 | c3 | MO | Z Diode | | | | 0.3 W | | 20 V | 6.2 mA | <25 Ω | $860 \cdot 10^6$/°C | |
| MMBZ251BL | F1 | c3 | MO | Z Diode | | | | 0.3 W | | 22 V | 5.6 mA | <29 Ω | $870 \cdot 10^6$/°C | |
| MMBZ252BL | F1 | c3 | MO | Z Diode | | | | 0.3 W | | 24 V | 5.2 mA | <33 Ω | $880 \cdot 10^6$/°C | |
| MMBZ253BL | F1 | c3 | MO | Z Diode | | | | 0.3 W | | 25 V | 5.0 mA | <35 Ω | $890 \cdot 10^6$/°C | |
| MMBZ254BL | F1 | c3 | MO | Z Diode | | | | 0.3 W | | 27 V | 4.6 mA | <41 Ω | $900 \cdot 10^6$/°C | P |
| MMBZ255BL | F1 | c3 | MO | Z Diode | | | | 0.3 W | | 28 V | 4.5 mA | <44 Ω | $910 \cdot 10^6$/°C | P |
| MMBZ256BL | F1 | c3 | MO | Z Diode | | | | 0.3 W | | 30 V | 4.2 mA | <49 Ω | $910 \cdot 10^6$/°C | |
| MMBZ257BL | F1 | c3 | MO | Z Diode | | | | 0.3 W | | 33 V | 3.8 mA | <58 Ω | $920 \cdot 10^6$/°C | |
| MMBZ258BL | F1 | c3 | MO | Z Diode | | | | 0.3 W | | 36 V | 3.4 mA | <70 Ω | $930 \cdot 10^6$/°C | |
| MMBZ259BL | F1 | c3 | MO | Z Diode | | | | 0.3 W | | 39 V | 3.2 mA | <80 Ω | $940 \cdot 10^6$/°C | |
| MMBZ260BL | F1 | c3 | MO | Z Diode | | | | 0.3 W | | 43 V | 3.0 mA | <93 Ω | $950 \cdot 10^6$/°C | |
| MMBZ261BL | F1 | c3 | MO | Z Diode | | | | 0.3 W | | 47 V | 2.7 mA | <105 Ω | $950 \cdot 10^6$/°C | |
| MMBZ262BL | F1 | c3 | MO | Z Diode | | | | 0.3 W | | 51 V | 2.5 mA | <125 Ω | $960 \cdot 10^6$/°C | |
| MMBZ263BL | F1 | c3 | MO | Z Diode | | | | 0.3 W | | 56 V | 2.3 mA | <150 Ω | $960 \cdot 10^6$/°C | |
| MMBZ264BL | F1 | c3 | MO | Z Diode | | | | 0.3 W | | 60 V | 2.1 mA | <170 Ω | $920 \cdot 10^6$/°C | |
| MMBZ265BL | F1 | c3 | MO | Z Diode | | | | 0.3 W | | 62 V | 2.0 mA | <185 Ω | $930 \cdot 10^6$/°C | |
| MMBZ266BL | F1 | c3 | MO | Z Diode | | | | 0.3 W | | 68 V | 1.8 mA | <230 Ω | $940 \cdot 10^6$/°C | |
| MMBZ267BL | F1 | c3 | MO | Z Diode | | | | 0.3 W | | 75 V | 1.7 mA | <270 Ω | $950 \cdot 10^6$/°C | |
| MMBZ268BL | F1 | c3 | MO | Z Diode | | | | 0.3 W | | 82 V | 1.7 mA | <270 Ω | $950 \cdot 10^6$/°C | |
| MMBZ269BL | F1 | c3 | MO | Z Diode | | | | 0.3 W | | 87 V | 1.7 mA | <270 Ω | $960 \cdot 10^6$/°C | |
| MMBZ270BL | F1 | c3 | MO | Z Diode | | | | 0.3 W | | 91 V | 1.7 mA | <270 Ω | $960 \cdot 10^6$/°C | |
| MR2535L | B14 | a1 | MO | TVS | 62 A | 62 A | | | | | | | | |
| MZ4614 | A1 | a1 | MO | Z Diode | | 120 mA | | 0.5 W | | 1.8 V | 250 µA | 1200 Ω | | Vz ±5% |
| MZ4615 | A1 | a1 | MO | Z Diode | | 110 mA | | 0.5 W | | 2.0 V | 250 µA | 1250 Ω | | Vz ±5% |
| MZ4616 | A1 | a1 | MO | Z Diode | | 100 mA | | 0.5 W | | 2.2 V | 250 µA | 1300 Ω | | Vz ±5% |
| MZ4617 | A1 | a1 | MO | Z Diode | | 95 mA | | 0.5 W | | 2.4 V | 250 µA | 1400 Ω | | Vz ±5% |
| MZ4618 | A1 | a1 | MO | Z Diode | | 90 mA | | 0.5 W | | 2.7 V | 250 µA | 1500 Ω | | Vz ±5% |
| MZ4619 | A1 | a1 | MO | Z Diode | | 85 mA | | 0.5 W | | 3.0 V | 250 µA | 1600 Ω | | Vz ±5% |
| MZ4620 | A1 | a1 | MO | Z Diode | | 80 mA | | 0.5 W | | 3.3 V | 250 µA | 1650 Ω | | Vz ±5% |
| MZ4621 | A1 | a1 | MO | Z Diode | | 75 mA | | 0.5 W | | 3.6 V | 250 µA | 1700 Ω | | Vz ±5% |
| MZ4622 | A1 | a1 | MO | Z Diode | | 70 mA | | 0.5 W | | 3.9 V | 250 µA | 1650 Ω | | Vz ±5% |
| MZ4623 | A1 | a1 | MO | Z Diode | | 65 mA | | 0.5 W | | 4.3 V | 250 µA | 1600 Ω | | Vz ±5% |
| MZ4624 | A1 | a1 | MO | Z Diode | | 60 mA | | 0.5 W | | 4.7 V | 250 µA | 1550 Ω | | Vz ±5% |
| MZ4625 | A1 | a1 | MO | Z Diode | | 55 mA | | 0.5 W | | 5.1 V | 250 µA | 1500 Ω | | Vz ±5% |
| MZ4626 | A1 | a1 | MO | Z Diode | | 50 mA | | 0.5 W | | 5.6 V | 250 µA | 1400 Ω | | Vz ±5% |
| MZ4627 | A1 | a1 | MO | Z Diode | | 45 mA | | 0.5 W | | 6.2 V | 250 µA | 1300 Ω | | Vz ±5% |
| MZ4099 | A1 | a1 | MO | Z Diode | | 35 mA | | 0.5 W | | 6.8 V | 250 µA | 200 Ω | | Vz ±5% |

**MZ4100 – MZD36**

| | | | | | Maximum Ratings | | | | | Electrical Characteristics | | | | |
|---|---|---|---|---|---|---|---|---|---|---|---|---|---|---|
| Type | Case | Pin-code | | | Vcla / Vbro | Its | Izm | Pv | Pvts | Vz | Iz / Is | rz | TK | |
| MZ4100 | A1 | a1 | MO | Z Diode | | | 31.8 mA | 0.5 W | | 7.5 V | 250 µA | 200 Ω | | Vz ±5% |
| MZ4101 | A1 | a1 | MO | Z Diode | | | 29 mA | 0.5 W | | 8.2 V | 250 µA | 200 Ω | | Vz ±5% |
| MZ4102 | A1 | a1 | MO | Z Diode | | | 27.4 mA | 0.5 W | | 8.7 V | 250 µA | 200 Ω | | Vz ±5% |
| MZ4103 | A1 | a1 | MO | Z Diode | | | 26.2 mA | 0.5 W | | 9.1 V | 250 µA | 200 Ω | | Vz ±5% |
| MZ4104 | A1 | a1 | MO | Z Diode | | | 24.8 mA | 0.5 W | | 10 V | 250 µA | 200 Ω | | Vz ±5% |
| MZ5520B | A1 | a1 | MO | Z Diode | | | 98 mA | 0.5 W | | 3.9 V | 20 mA | <22 Ω | | Vz ±5% |
| MZ5521B | A1 | a1 | MO | Z Diode | | | 88 mA | 0.5 W | | 4.3 V | 20 mA | <18 Ω | | Vz ±5% |
| MZ5522B | A1 | a1 | MO | Z Diode | | | 81 mA | 0.5 W | | 4.7 V | 10 mA | <22 Ω | | Vz ±5% |
| MZ5523B | A1 | a1 | MO | Z Diode | | | 75 mA | 0.5 W | | 5.1 V | 5 mA | <26 Ω | | Vz ±5% |
| MZ5524B | A1 | a1 | MO | Z Diode | | | 68 mA | 0.5 W | | 5.6 V | 3 mA | <30 Ω | | Vz ±5% |
| MZ5525B | A1 | a1 | MO | Z Diode | | | 61 mA | 0.5 W | | 6.2 V | 1 mA | <30 Ω | | Vz ±5% |
| MZ5526B | A1 | a1 | MO | Z Diode | | | 56 mA | 0.5 W | | 6.8 V | 1 mA | <30 Ω | | Vz ±5% |
| MZ5527B | A1 | a1 | MO | Z Diode | | | 51 mA | 0.5 W | | 7.5 V | 1 mA | <35 Ω | | Vz ±5% |
| MZ5528B | A1 | a1 | MO | Z Diode | | | 46 mA | 0.5 W | | 8.2 V | 1 mA | <40 Ω | | Vz ±5% |
| MZ5529B | A1 | a1 | MO | Z Diode | | | 42 mA | 0.5 W | | 9.1 V | 1 mA | <45 Ω | | Vz ±5% |
| MZ5530B | A1 | a1 | MO | Z Diode | | | 38 mA | 0.5 W | | 10 V | 1 mA | <60 Ω | | Vz ±5% |
| MZD3.9 | A3 | a1 | MO | Z Diode | | | 1380 mA | 1.3 W | | 3.9 V | 100 mA | <7 Ω | -600 ·10⁶/°C | Vz ±5-8.5% |
| MZD4.3 | A3 | a1 | MO | Z Diode | | | 1260 mA | 1.3 W | | 4.3 V | 100 mA | <7 Ω | -550 ·10⁶/°C | Vz ±5-8.5% |
| MZD4.7 | A3 | a1 | MO | Z Diode | | | 1190 mA | 1.3 W | | 4.7 V | 100 mA | <7 Ω | -300 ·10⁶/°C | Vz ±5-8.5% |
| MZD5.1 | A3 | a1 | MO | Z Diode | | | 1070 mA | 1.3 W | | 5.1 V | 100 mA | <5 Ω | -300 ·10⁶/°C | Vz ±5-8.5% |
| MZD5.6 | A3 | a1 | MO | Z Diode | | | 970 mA | 1.3 W | | 5.6 V | 100 mA | <2 Ω | 380 ·10⁶/°C | Vz ±5-8.5% |
| MZD6.2 | A3 | a1 | MO | Z Diode | | | 890 mA | 1.3 W | | 6.2 V | 100 mA | <2 Ω | 450 ·10⁶/°C | Vz ±5-8.5% |
| MZD6.8 | A3 | a1 | MO | Z Diode | | | 810 mA | 1.3 W | | 6.8 V | 100 mA | <2 Ω | 500 ·10⁶/°C | Vz ±5-8.5% |
| MZD7.5 | A3 | a1 | MO | Z Diode | | | 730 mA | 1.3 W | | 7.5 V | 100 mA | <2 Ω | 580 ·10⁶/°C | Vz ±5-8.5% |
| MZD8.2 | A3 | a1 | MO | Z Diode | | | 660 mA | 1.3 W | | 8.2 V | 100 mA | <2 Ω | 620 ·10⁶/°C | Vz ±5-8.5% |
| MZD9.1 | A3 | a1 | MO | Z Diode | | | 605 mA | 1.3 W | | 9.1 V | 50 mA | <4 Ω | 680 ·10⁶/°C | Vz ±5-8.5% |
| MZD10 | A3 | a1 | MO | Z Diode | | | 550 mA | 1.3 W | | 10 V | 50 mA | <7 Ω | 750 ·10⁶/°C | Vz ±5-8.5% |
| MZD11 | A3 | a1 | MO | Z Diode | | | 500 mA | 1.3 W | | 11 V | 50 mA | <7 Ω | 760 ·10⁶/°C | Vz ±5-8.5% |
| MZD12 | A3 | a1 | MO | Z Diode | | | 454 mA | 1.3 W | | 12 V | 50 mA | <10 Ω | 770 ·10⁶/°C | Vz ±5-8.5% |
| MZD13 | A3 | a1 | MO | Z Diode | | | 414 mA | 1.3 W | | 13 V | 50 mA | <10 Ω | 790 ·10⁶/°C | Vz ±5-8.5% |
| MZD15 | A3 | a1 | MO | Z Diode | | | 380 mA | 1.3 W | | 15 V | 50 mA | <15 Ω | 820 ·10⁶/°C | Vz ±5-8.5% |
| MZD16 | A3 | a1 | MO | Z Diode | | | 344 mA | 1.3 W | | 16 V | 25 mA | <15 Ω | 830 ·10⁶/°C | Vz ±5-8.5% |
| MZD18 | A3 | a1 | MO | Z Diode | | | 304 mA | 1.3 W | | 18 V | 25 mA | <15 Ω | 850 ·10⁶/°C | Vz ±5-8.5% |
| MZD20 | A3 | a1 | MO | Z Diode | | | 285 mA | 1.3 W | | 20 V | 25 mA | <15 Ω | 860 ·10⁶/°C | Vz ±5-8.5% |
| MZD22 | A3 | a1 | MO | Z Diode | | | 250 mA | 1.3 W | | 22 V | 25 mA | <15 Ω | 870 ·10⁶/°C | Vz ±5-8.5% |
| MZD24 | A3 | a1 | MO | Z Diode | | | 225 mA | 1.3 W | | 24 V | 25 mA | <15 Ω | 880 ·10⁶/°C | Vz ±5-8.5% |
| MZD27 | A3 | a1 | MO | Z Diode | | | 205 mA | 1.3 W | | 27 V | 25 mA | <15 Ω | 900 ·10⁶/°C | Vz ±5-8.5% |
| MZD30 | A3 | a1 | MO | Z Diode | | | 190 mA | 1.3 W | | 30 V | 25 mA | <15 Ω | 910 ·10⁶/°C | Vz ±5-8.5% |
| MZD33 | A3 | a1 | MO | Z Diode | | | 170 mA | 1.3 W | | 33 V | 25 mA | <15 Ω | 920 ·10⁶/°C | Vz ±5-8.5% |
| MZD36 | A3 | a1 | MO | Z Diode | | | 150 mA | 1.3 W | | 36 V | 10 mA | <40 Ω | 930 ·10⁶/°C | Vz ±5-8.5% |

| Type | Case | Pin code | | | Maximum Ratings | | | | | Electrical Characteristics | | | | |
|------|------|----------|---|---|---|---|---|---|---|---|---|---|---|---|
| | | | | | Vcla Vbro | Its | Izm | Pv | Pvts | Vz | Iz Is | rz | TK | |
| MZD39 | A3 | a1 | MO | Z Diode | | | 135 mA | 1.3 W | | 39 V | 10 mA | <40 Ω | $940 \cdot 10^6/°C$ | Vz ±5-8.5% |
| MZD43 | A3 | a1 | MO | Z Diode | | | 125 mA | 1.3 W | | 43 V | 10 mA | <45 Ω | $950 \cdot 10^6/°C$ | Vz ±5-8.5% |
| MZD47 | A3 | a1 | MO | Z Diode | | | 115 mA | 1.3 W | | 47 V | 10 mA | <45 Ω | $950 \cdot 10^6/°C$ | Vz ±5-8.5% |
| MZD51 | A3 | a1 | MO | Z Diode | | | 110 mA | 1.3 W | | 51 V | 10 mA | <60 Ω | $960 \cdot 10^6/°C$ | Vz ±5-8.5% |
| MZD56 | A3 | a1 | MO | Z Diode | | | 95 mA | 1.3 W | | 56 V | 10 mA | <600 Ω | $960 \cdot 10^6/°C$ | Vz ±5-8.5% |
| MZD62 | A3 | a1 | MO | Z Diode | | | 90 mA | 1.3 W | | 62 V | 10 mA | <800 Ω | $970 \cdot 10^6/°C$ | Vz ±5-8.5% |
| MZD68 | A3 | a1 | MO | Z Diode | | | 80 mA | 1.3 W | | 68 V | 10 mA | <800 Ω | $970 \cdot 10^6/°C$ | Vz ±5-8.5% |
| MZD75 | A3 | a1 | MO | Z Diode | | | 70 mA | 1.3 W | | 75 V | 10 mA | <100 Ω | $980 \cdot 10^6/°C$ | Vz ±5-8.5% |
| MZD82 | A3 | a1 | MO | Z Diode | | | 65 mA | 1.3 W | | 82 V | 10 mA | <100 Ω | $980 \cdot 10^6/°C$ | Vz ±5-8.5% |
| MZD91 | A3 | a1 | MO | Z Diode | | | 60 mA | 1.3 W | | 91 V | 5 mA | <200 Ω | $990 \cdot 10^6/°C$ | Vz ±5-8.5% |
| MZD100 | A3 | a1 | MO | Z Diode | | | 55 mA | 1.3 W | | 100 V | 5 mA | <200 Ω | $1100 \cdot 10^6/°C$ | Vz ±5-8.5% |
| MZD110 | A3 | a1 | MO | Z Diode | | | 50 mA | 1.3 W | | 110 V | 5 mA | <250 Ω | $1100 \cdot 10^6/°C$ | Vz ±5-8.5% |
| MZD120 | A3 | a1 | MO | Z Diode | | | 45 mA | 1.3 W | | 120 V | 5 mA | <250 Ω | $1100 \cdot 10^6/°C$ | Vz ±5-8.5% |
| MZD130 | A3 | a1 | MO | Z Diode | | | | 1.3 W | | 130 V | 5 mA | <300 Ω | $1100 \cdot 10^6/°C$ | Vz ±5-8.5% |
| MZD150 | A3 | a1 | MO | Z Diode | | | | 1.3 W | | 150 V | 5 mA | <300 Ω | $1100 \cdot 10^6/°C$ | Vz ±5-8.5% |
| MZD160 | A3 | a1 | MO | Z Diode | | | | 1.3 W | | 160 V | 5 mA | <350 Ω | $1100 \cdot 10^6/°C$ | Vz ±5-8.5% |
| MZD180 | A3 | a1 | MO | Z Diode | | | | 1.3 W | | 180 V | 5 mA | <350 Ω | $1100 \cdot 10^6/°C$ | Vz ±5-8.5% |
| MZD200 | A3 | a1 | MO | Z Diode | | | | 1.3 W | | 200 V | 5 mA | <350 Ω | $1100 \cdot 10^6/°C$ | Vz ±5-8.5% |
| MZP4728A | A3 | a1 | MO | Z Diode | | 1380 mA | | 1 W | | 3.3 V | 76 mA | <10 Ω | $-600 \cdot 10^6/°C$ | B |
| MZP4729A | A3 | a1 | MO | Z Diode | | 1550 mA | | 1 W | | 3.6 V | 69 mA | <10 Ω | $-600 \cdot 10^6/°C$ | B |
| MZP4730A | A3 | a1 | MO | Z Diode | | 1190 mA | | 1 W | | 3.9 V | 64 mA | <9 Ω | $-500 \cdot 10^6/°C$ | B |
| MZP4731A | A3 | a1 | MO | Z Diode | | 1070 mA | | 1 W | | 4.3 V | 58 mA | <9 Ω | $-300 \cdot 10^6/°C$ | B |
| MZP4732A | A3 | a1 | MO | Z Diode | | 970 mA | | 1 W | | 4.7 V | 53 mA | <8 Ω | $-100 \cdot 10^6/°C$ | B |
| MZP4733A | A3 | a1 | MO | Z Diode | | 890 mA | | 1 W | | 5.1 V | 49 mA | <7 Ω | $100 \cdot 10^6/°C$ | B |
| MZP4734A | A3 | a1 | MO | Z Diode | | 810 mA | | 1 W | | 5.6 V | 45 mA | <5 Ω | $300 \cdot 10^6/°C$ | B |
| MZP4735B | A3 | a1 | MO | Z Diode | | 730 mA | | 1 W | | 6.2 V | 41 mA | <2 Ω | $400 \cdot 10^6/°C$ | B |
| MZP4736A | A3 | a1 | MO | Z Diode | | 660 mA | | 1 W | | 6.8 V | 37 mA | <3.5 Ω | $500 \cdot 10^6/°C$ | B |
| MZP4737A | A3 | a1 | MO | Z Diode | | 605 mA | | 1 W | | 7.5 V | 34 mA | <4 Ω | $500 \cdot 10^6/°C$ | B |
| MZP4738A | A3 | a1 | MO | Z Diode | | 550 mA | | 1 W | | 8.2 V | 31 mA | <4.5 Ω | $600 \cdot 10^6/°C$ | B |
| MZP4739A | A3 | a1 | MO | Z Diode | | 500 mA | | 1 W | | 9.1 V | 28 mA | <5 Ω | $600 \cdot 10^6/°C$ | B |
| MZP4740A | A3 | a1 | MO | Z Diode | | 454 mA | | 1 W | | 10 V | 25 mA | <7 Ω | $700 \cdot 10^6/°C$ | B |
| MZP4741A | A3 | a1 | MO | Z Diode | | 414 mA | | 1 W | | 11 V | 23 mA | <8 Ω | $700 \cdot 10^6/°C$ | B |
| MZP4742A | A3 | a1 | MO | Z Diode | | 380 mA | | 1 W | | 12 V | 21 mA | <9 Ω | $700 \cdot 10^6/°C$ | B |
| MZP4743A | A3 | a1 | MO | Z Diode | | 344 mA | | 1 W | | 13 V | 19 mA | <10 Ω | $700 \cdot 10^6/°C$ | B |
| MZP4744A | A3 | a1 | MO | Z Diode | | 304 mA | | 1 W | | 15 V | 17 mA | <14 Ω | $800 \cdot 10^6/°C$ | B |
| MZP4745A | A3 | a1 | MO | Z Diode | | 285 mA | | 1 W | | 16 V | 15.5 mA | <16 Ω | $800 \cdot 10^6/°C$ | B |
| MZP4746A | A3 | a1 | MO | Z Diode | | 250 mA | | 1 W | | 18 V | 14 mA | <20 Ω | $800 \cdot 10^6/°C$ | B |
| MZP4747A | A3 | a1 | MO | Z Diode | | 225 mA | | 1 W | | 20 V | 12.5 mA | <22 Ω | $800 \cdot 10^6/°C$ | B |
| MZP4748A | A3 | a1 | MO | Z Diode | | 205 mA | | 1 W | | 22 V | 11.5 mA | <23 Ω | $800 \cdot 10^6/°C$ | B |
| MZP4749A | A3 | a1 | MO | Z Diode | | 190 mA | | 1 W | | 24 V | 10.5 mA | <25 Ω | $800 \cdot 10^6/°C$ | B |

| Type | Case | Pin-code | | | Vcla Vbro | Its | Izm | Pv | Pvts | Vz | Iz Is | rz | TK | |
|------|------|----------|---|---|-----------|-----|-----|-----|------|-----|-------|-----|-----|---|
| | | | | | | **Maximum Ratings** | | | | **Electrical Characteristics** | | | | |
| MZP4750A | A3 | a1 | MO | Z Diode | | | 170 mA | 1 W | | 27 V | 9.5 mA | <35Ω | 900·10⁶/°C | B |
| MZP4751A | A3 | a1 | MO | Z Diode | | | 150 mA | 1 W | | 30 V | 8.5 mA | <40Ω | 900·10⁶/°C | B |
| MZP4752A | A3 | a1 | MO | Z Diode | | | 135 mA | 1 W | | 33 V | 7.5 mA | <45Ω | 900·10⁶/°C | B |
| MZP4753A | A3 | a1 | MO | Z Diode | | | 125 mA | 1 W | | 36 V | 7 mA | <50Ω | 900·10⁶/°C | B |
| MZP4754A | A3 | a1 | MO | Z Diode | | | 115 mA | 1 W | | 39 V | 6.5 mA | <60Ω | 900·10⁶/°C | B |
| MZP4755A | A3 | a1 | MO | Z Diode | | | 110 mA | 1 W | | 43 V | 6 mA | <70Ω | 900·10⁶/°C | B |
| MZP4756A | A3 | a1 | MO | Z Diode | | | 95 mA | 1 W | | 47 V | 5.5 mA | <80Ω | 900·10⁶/°C | B |
| MZP4757A | A3 | a1 | MO | Z Diode | | | 90 mA | 1 W | | 51 V | 5 mA | <95Ω | 900·10⁶/°C | B |
| MZP4758A | A3 | a1 | MO | Z Diode | | | 80 mA | 1 W | | 56 V | 4.5 mA | <110Ω | 900·10⁶/°C | B |
| MZP4759A | A3 | a1 | MO | Z Diode | | | 70 mA | 1 W | | 62 V | 4 mA | <125Ω | 900·10⁶/°C | B |
| MZP4760A | A3 | a1 | MO | Z Diode | | | 65 mA | 1 W | | 68 V | 3.7 mA | <150Ω | 900·10⁶/°C | B |
| MZP4761A | A3 | a1 | MO | Z Diode | | | 60 mA | 1 W | | 75 V | 3.3 mA | <175Ω | 900·10⁶/°C | B |
| MZP4762A | A3 | a1 | MO | Z Diode | | | 55 mA | 1 W | | 82 V | 3 mA | <200Ω | 900·10⁶/°C | B |
| MZP4763A | A3 | a1 | MO | Z Diode | | | 50 mA | 1 W | | 91 V | 2.8 mA | <250Ω | 900·10⁶/°C | B |
| MZP4764A | A3 | a1 | MO | Z Diode | | | 45 mA | 1 W | | 100 V | 2.5 mA | <350Ω | 900·10⁶/°C | B |
| MZP4187B | A3 | a1 | MO | Z Diode | | | | 1 W | | 110 V | 2.3 mA | <450Ω | 1000·10⁶/°C | B |
| MZP4188B | A3 | a1 | MO | Z Diode | | | | 1 W | | 120 V | 2 mA | <550Ω | 1000·10⁶/°C | B |
| MZP4189B | A3 | a1 | MO | Z Diode | | | | 1 W | | 130 V | 1.9 mA | <700Ω | 1000·10⁶/°C | B |
| MZP4190B | A3 | a1 | MO | Z Diode | | | | 1 W | | 150 V | 1.7 mA | <1000Ω | 1000·10⁶/°C | B |
| MZP4191B | A3 | a1 | MO | Z Diode | | | | 1 W | | 170 V | 1.6 mA | <1100Ω | 1000·10⁶/°C | B |
| MZP4192B | A3 | a1 | MO | Z Diode | | | | 1 W | | 180 V | 1.4 mA | <1200Ω | 1000·10⁶/°C | B |
| MZP4193B | A3 | a1 | MO | Z Diode | | | | 1 W | | 200 V | 1.2 mA | <1500Ω | 1000·10⁶/°C | B |
| MZPY3V9 | A3 | a1 | MO | Z Diode | | | 1190 mA | 1 W | | 3.9 V | 100 mA | <7Ω | 200·10⁶/°C | CD |
| MZPY4V3 | A3 | a1 | MO | Z Diode | | | 1070 mA | 1 W | | 4.3 V | 100 mA | <7Ω | 300·10⁶/°C | CD |
| MZPY4V7 | A3 | a1 | MO | Z Diode | | | 9700 mA | 1 W | | 4.7 V | 100 mA | <7Ω | 400·10⁶/°C | CD |
| MZPY5V1 | A3 | a1 | MO | Z Diode | | | 890 mA | 1 W | | 5.1 V | 100 mA | <5Ω | 500·10⁶/°C | CD |
| MZPY5V6 | A3 | a1 | MO | Z Diode | | | 810 mA | 1 W | | 5.6 V | 100 mA | <2Ω | 500·10⁶/°C | CD |
| MZPY6V2 | A3 | a1 | MO | Z Diode | | | 730 mA | 1 W | | 6.2 V | 100 mA | <2Ω | 600·10⁶/°C | CD |
| MZPY6V8 | A3 | a1 | MO | Z Diode | | | 660 mA | 1 W | | 6.8 V | 100 mA | <2Ω | 700·10⁶/°C | CD |
| MZPY7V5 | A3 | a1 | MO | Z Diode | | | 605 mA | 1 W | | 7.5 V | 100 mA | <2Ω | 700·10⁶/°C | CD |
| MZPY8V2 | A3 | a1 | MO | Z Diode | | | 550 mA | 1 W | | 8.2 V | 100 mA | <2Ω | 800·10⁶/°C | CD |
| MZPY9V1 | A3 | a1 | MO | Z Diode | | | 500 mA | 1 W | | 9.1 V | 50 mA | <4Ω | 800·10⁶/°C | CD |
| MZPY10 | A3 | a1 | MO | Z Diode | | | 454 mA | 1 W | | 10 V | 50 mA | <4Ω | 900·10⁶/°C | CD |
| MZPY11 | A3 | a1 | MO | Z Diode | | | 414 mA | 1 W | | 11 V | 50 mA | <7Ω | 1000·10⁶/°C | CD |
| MZPY12 | A3 | a1 | MO | Z Diode | | | 380 mA | 1 W | | 12 V | 50 mA | <7Ω | 1000·10⁶/°C | CD |
| MZPY13 | A3 | a1 | MO | Z Diode | | | 244 mA | 1 W | | 13 V | 50 mA | <9Ω | 1000·10⁶/°C | CD |
| MZPY15 | A3 | a1 | MO | Z Diode | | | 304 mA | 1 W | | 15 V | 50 mA | <9Ω | 1000·10⁶/°C | CD |
| MZPY16 | A3 | a1 | MO | Z Diode | | | 285 mA | 1 W | | 16 V | 25 mA | <10Ω | 1100·10⁶/°C | CD |
| MZPY18 | A3 | a1 | MO | Z Diode | | | 250 mA | 1 W | | 18 V | 25 mA | <11Ω | 1100·10⁶/°C | CD |
| MZPY20 | A3 | a1 | MO | Z Diode | | | 225 mA | 1 W | | 20 V | 25 mA | <12Ω | 1100·10⁶/°C | CD |

| Type | Case | Pin-code | | | Maximum Ratings | | | | | Electrical Characteristics | | | | |
|---|---|---|---|---|---|---|---|---|---|---|---|---|---|---|
| | | | | | Vcla/Vbro | Its | Izm | Pv | Pvts | Vz | Iz/Is | rz | TK | |
| MZPY22 | A3 | a1 | MO | Z Diode | | | 205 mA | 1 W | | 22 V | 25 mA | <13Ω | $1100 \cdot 10^6/°C$ | CD |
| MZPY24 | A3 | a1 | MO | Z Diode | | | 190 mA | 1 W | | 24 V | 25 mA | <14Ω | $1200 \cdot 10^6/°C$ | CD |
| MZPY27 | A3 | a1 | MO | Z Diode | | | 170 mA | 1 W | | 27 V | 25 mA | <15Ω | $1200 \cdot 10^6/°C$ | CD |
| MZPY30 | A3 | a1 | MO | Z Diode | | | 150 mA | 1 W | | 30 V | 25 mA | <20Ω | $1200 \cdot 10^6/°C$ | CD |
| MZPY33 | A3 | a1 | MO | Z Diode | | | 135 mA | 1 W | | 33 V | 10 mA | <20Ω | $1200 \cdot 10^6/°C$ | CD |
| MZPY36 | A3 | a1 | MO | Z Diode | | | 125 mA | 1 W | | 36 V | 10 mA | <60Ω | $1200 \cdot 10^6/°C$ | CD |
| MZPY39 | A3 | a1 | MO | Z Diode | | | 115 mA | 1 W | | 39 V | 10 mA | <60Ω | $1200 \cdot 10^6/°C$ | CD |
| MZPY43 | A3 | a1 | MO | Z Diode | | | 110 mA | 1 W | | 43 V | 10 mA | <80Ω | $1300 \cdot 10^6/°C$ | CD |
| MZPY47 | A3 | a1 | MO | Z Diode | | | 95 mA | 1 W | | 47 V | 10 mA | <80Ω | $1300 \cdot 10^6/°C$ | CD |
| MZPY51 | A3 | a1 | MO | Z Diode | | | 90 mA | 1 W | | 51 V | 10 mA | <100Ω | $1300 \cdot 10^6/°C$ | CD |
| MZPY56 | A3 | a1 | MO | Z Diode | | | 80 mA | 1 W | | 56 V | 10 mA | <100Ω | $1300 \cdot 10^6/°C$ | CD |
| MZPY62 | A3 | a1 | MO | Z Diode | | | 70 mA | 1 W | | 62 V | 10 mA | <130Ω | $1300 \cdot 10^6/°C$ | CD |
| MZPY68 | A3 | a1 | MO | Z Diode | | | 65 mA | 1 W | | 68 V | 10 mA | <130Ω | $1300 \cdot 10^6/°C$ | CD |
| MZPY75 | A3 | a1 | MO | Z Diode | | | 60 mA | 1 W | | 75 V | 10 mA | <160Ω | $1300 \cdot 10^6/°C$ | CD |
| MZPY82 | A3 | a1 | MO | Z Diode | | | 55 mA | 1 W | | 82 V | 10 mA | <160Ω | $1300 \cdot 10^6/°C$ | CD |
| MZPY91 | A3 | a1 | MO | Z Diode | | | 50 mA | 1 W | | 91 V | 5 mA | <250Ω | $1300 \cdot 10^6/°C$ | CD |
| MZPY100 | A3 | a1 | MO | Z Diode | | | 45 mA | 1 W | | 100 V | 5 mA | <250Ω | $1300 \cdot 10^6/°C$ | CD |
| P6KE6.8 | B7 | a1 | MO | TVS | 10.8 V | 56 mA | 56 mA | 5 W | 600 W | | | | | |
| P6KE7.5 | B7 | a1 | MO | TVS | 11.7 V | 51 mA | 51 mA | 5 W | 600 W | | | | | |
| P6KE8.2 | B7 | a1 | MO | TVS | 12.5 V | 48 mA | 48 mA | 5 W | 600 W | | | | | |
| P6KE9.1 | B7 | a1 | MO | TVS | 13.8 V | 44 mA | 44 mA | 5 W | 600 W | | | | | |
| P6KE10 | B7 | a1 | MO | TVS | 15 V | 40 mA | 40 mA | 5 W | 600 W | | | | | |
| P6KE11 | B7 | a1 | MO | TVS | 16.2 V | 37 mA | 37 mA | 5 W | 600 W | | | | | |
| P6KE12 | B7 | a1 | MO | TVS | 17.3 V | 35 mA | 35 mA | 5 W | 600 W | | | | | |
| P6KE13 | B7 | a1 | MO | TVS | 19 V | 32 mA | 32 mA | 5 W | 600 W | | | | | |
| P6KE15 | B7 | a1 | MO | TVS | 22 V | 27 mA | 27 mA | 5 W | 600 W | | | | | |
| P6KE16 | B7 | a1 | MO | TVS | 23.5 V | 26 mA | 26 mA | 5 W | 600 W | | | | | |
| P6KE18 | B7 | a1 | MO | TVS | 26.5 V | 23 mA | 23 mA | 5 W | 600 W | | | | | |
| P6KE20 | B7 | a1 | MO | TVS | 29.1 V | 21 mA | 21 mA | 5 W | 600 W | | | | | |
| P6KE22 | B7 | a1 | MO | TVS | 31.9 V | 19 mA | 19 mA | 5 W | 600 W | | | | | |
| P6KE24 | B7 | a1 | MO | TVS | 34.7 V | 17 mA | 17 mA | 5 W | 600 W | | | | | |
| P6KE27 | B7 | a1 | MO | TVS | 39.1 V | 15 mA | 15 mA | 5 W | 600 W | | | | | |
| P6KE30 | B7 | a1 | MO | TVS | 43.5 V | 14 mA | 14 mA | 5 W | 600 W | | | | | |
| P6KE33 | B7 | a1 | MO | TVS | 47.7 V | 12.6 mA | 12.6 mA | 5 W | 600 W | | | | | |
| P6KE36 | B7 | a1 | MO | TVS | 52 V | 11.6 mA | 11.6 mA | 5 W | 600 W | | | | | |
| P6KE39 | B7 | a1 | MO | TVS | 56.4 V | 10.6 mA | 10.6 mA | 5 W | 600 W | | | | | |
| P6KE43 | B7 | a1 | MO | TVS | 61.9 V | 9.6 mA | 9.6 mA | 5 W | 600 W | | | | | |
| P6KE47 | B7 | a1 | MO | TVS | 67.8 V | 8.9 mA | 8.9 mA | 5 W | 600 W | | | | | |
| P6KE51 | B7 | a1 | MO | TVS | 73.5 V | 8.2 mA | 8.2 mA | 5 W | 600 W | | | | | |
| P6KE56 | B7 | a1 | MO | TVS | 80.5 V | 7.4 mA | 7.4 mA | 5 W | 600 W | | | | | |

| Type | Case | Pin code | | | Maximum Ratings | | | | | Electrical Characteristics | | | | |
|------|------|------|------|------|------|------|------|------|------|------|------|------|------|------|
| | | | MO | TVS | Vcla Vbro | Its | Izm | Pv | Pvts | Vz | Iz Is | rz | TK | |
| P6KE62 | B7 | a1 | MO | TVS | 89 V | 6.8 mA | 6.8 mA | 5 W | 600 W | | | | | |
| P6KE68 | B7 | a1 | MO | TVS | 98 V | 6.1 mA | 6.1 mA | 5 W | 600 W | | | | | |
| P6KE75 | B7 | a1 | MO | TVS | 108 V | 5.5 mA | 5.5 mA | 5 W | 600 W | | | | | |
| P6KE82 | B7 | a1 | MO | TVS | 118 V | 5.1 mA | 5.1 mA | 5 W | 600 W | | | | | |
| P6KE91 | B7 | a1 | MO | TVS | 131 V | 4.5 mA | 4.5 mA | 5 W | 600 W | | | | | |
| P6KE100 | B7 | a1 | MO | TVS | 144 V | 4.2 mA | 4.2 mA | 5 W | 600 W | | | | | |
| P6KE110 | B7 | a1 | MO | TVS | 158 V | 3.8 mA | 3.8 mA | 5 W | 600 W | | | | | |
| P6KE120 | B7 | a1 | MO | TVS | 173 V | 3.5 mA | 3.5 mA | 5 W | 600 W | | | | | |
| P6KE130 | B7 | a1 | MO | TVS | 187 V | 3.2 mA | 3.2 mA | 5 W | 600 W | | | | | |
| P6KE150 | B7 | a1 | MO | TVS | 215 V | 2.8 mA | 2.8 mA | 5 W | 600 W | | | | | |
| P6KE160 | B7 | a1 | MO | TVS | 230 V | 2.6 mA | 2.6 mA | 5 W | 600 W | | | | | |
| P6KE170 | B7 | a1 | MO | TVS | 244 V | 2.5 mA | 2.5 mA | 5 W | 600 W | | | | | |
| P6KE180 | B7 | a1 | MO | TVS | 258 V | 2.3 mA | 2.3 mA | 5 W | 600 W | | | | | |
| P6KE200 | B7 | a1 | MO | TVS | 287 V | 2.1 mA | 2.1 mA | 5 W | 600 W | | | | | |
| P6KE6.8A | B7 | a1 | MO | TVS | 10.5 V | 57 mA | 57 mA | 5 W | 600 W | | | | | P |
| P6KE7.5A | B7 | a1 | MO | TVS | 11.3 V | 53 mA | 53 mA | 5 W | 600 W | | | | | |
| P6KE8.2A | B7 | a1 | MO | TVS | 12.1 V | 50 mA | 50 mA | 5 W | 600 W | | | | | |
| P6KE9.1A | B7 | a1 | MO | TVS | 13.4 V | 45 mA | 45 mA | 5 W | 600 W | | | | | |
| P6KE10A | B7 | a1 | MO | TVS | 14.5 V | 41 mA | 41 mA | 5 W | 600 W | | | | | |
| P6KE11A | B7 | a1 | MO | TVS | 15.6 V | 38 mA | 38 mA | 5 W | 600 W | | | | | |
| P6KE12A | B7 | a1 | MO | TVS | 16.7 V | 36 mA | 36 mA | 5 W | 600 W | | | | | |
| P6KE13A | B7 | a1 | MO | TVS | 18.2 V | 33 mA | 33 mA | 5 W | 600 W | | | | | P |
| P6KE15A | B7 | a1 | MO | TVS | 21.2 V | 28 mA | 28 mA | 5 W | 600 W | | | | | P |
| P6KE16A | B7 | a1 | MO | TVS | 22.5 V | 27 mA | 27 mA | 5 W | 600 W | | | | | |
| P6KE18A | B7 | a1 | MO | TVS | 25.2 V | 24 mA | 24 mA | 5 W | 600 W | | | | | |
| P6KE20A | B7 | a1 | MO | TVS | 27.7 V | 22 mA | 22 mA | 5 W | 600 W | | | | | |
| P6KE22A | B7 | a1 | MO | TVS | 30.6 V | 10 mA | 10 mA | 5 W | 600 W | | | | | |
| P6KE24A | B7 | a1 | MO | TVS | 33.2 V | 18 mA | 18 mA | 5 W | 600 W | | | | | |
| P6KE27A | B7 | a1 | MO | TVS | 37.5 V | 16 mA | 16 mA | 5 W | 600 W | | | | | P |
| P6KE30A | B7 | a1 | MO | TVS | 41.4 V | 14.4 mA | 14.4 mA | 5 W | 600 W | | | | | |
| P6KE33A | B7 | a1 | MO | TVS | 45.7 V | 13.2 mA | 13.2 mA | 5 W | 600 W | | | | | P |
| P6KE36A | B7 | a1 | MO | TVS | 49.9 V | 12 mA | 12 mA | 5 W | 600 W | | | | | P |
| P6KE39A | B7 | a1 | MO | TVS | 53.9 V | 11.2 mA | 11.2 mA | 5 W | 600 W | | | | | |
| P6KE43A | B7 | a1 | MO | TVS | 59.3 V | 10.1 mA | 10.1 mA | 5 W | 600 W | | | | | |
| P6KE47A | B7 | a1 | MO | TVS | 64.8 V | 9.3 mA | 9.3 mA | 5 W | 600 W | | | | | |
| P6KE51A | B7 | a1 | MO | TVS | 70.1 V | 8.6 mA | 8.6 mA | 5 W | 600 W | | | | | |
| P6KE56A | B7 | a1 | MO | TVS | 77 V | 7.8 mA | 7.8 mA | 5 W | 600 W | | | | | |
| P6KE62A | B7 | a1 | MO | TVS | 85 V | 7.1 mA | 7.1 mA | 5 W | 600 W | | | | | P |
| P6KE68A | B7 | a1 | MO | TVS | 92 V | 6.5 mA | 6.5 mA | 5 W | 600 W | | | | | |
| P6KE75A | B7 | a1 | MO | TVS | 103 V | 5.8 mA | 5.8 mA | 5 W | 600 W | | | | | |

| Type | Case | Pin-code | | | Maximum Ratings | | | | | Electrical Characteristics | | | | |
|---|---|---|---|---|---|---|---|---|---|---|---|---|---|---|
| | | | | | Vcla / Vbro | Its | Izm | Pv | Pvts | Vz | Iz / Is | rz | TK | |
| P6KE82A | B7 | a1 | MO | TVS | 113 V | 5.3 mA | 5.3 mA | 5 W | 600 W | | | | | |
| P6KE91A | B7 | a1 | MO | TVS | 125 V | 4.8 mA | 4.8 mA | 5 W | 600 W | | | | | |
| P6KE100A | B7 | a1 | MO | TVS | 137 V | 4.4 mA | 4.4 mA | 5 W | 600 W | | | | | |
| P6KE110A | B7 | a1 | MO | TVS | 152 V | 4 mA | 4 mA | 5 W | 600 W | | | | | |
| P6KE120A | B7 | a1 | MO | TVS | 165 V | 3.6 mA | 3.6 mA | 5 W | 600 W | | | | | |
| P6KE130A | B7 | a1 | MO | TVS | 179 V | 3.3 mA | 3.3 mA | 5 W | 600 W | | | | | |
| P6KE150A | B7 | a1 | MO | TVS | 207 V | 2.9 mA | 2.9 mA | 5 W | 600 W | | | | | |
| P6KE160A | B7 | a1 | MO | TVS | 219 V | 2.7 mA | 2.7 mA | 5 W | 600 W | | | | | |
| P6KE170A | B7 | a1 | MO | TVS | 234 V | 2.6 mA | 2.6 mA | 5 W | 600 W | | | | | |
| P6KE180A | B7 | a1 | MO | TVS | 246 V | 2.4 mA | 2.4 mA | 5 W | 600 W | | | | | |
| P6KE200A | B7 | a1 | MO | TVS | 274 V | 2.2 mA | 2.2 mA | 5 W | 600 W | | | | | |
| P6KE6.8C | B7 | a2 | MO | Bidir. TVS | 10.8 V | 56 mA | 56 mA | 5 W | 600 W | | | | | |
| P6KE7.5C | B7 | a2 | MO | Bidir. TVS | 11.7 V | 51 mA | 51 mA | 5 W | 600 W | | | | | |
| P6KE8.2C | B7 | a2 | MO | Bidir. TVS | 12.5 V | 48 mA | 48 mA | 5 W | 600 W | | | | | |
| P6KE9.1C | B7 | a2 | MO | Bidir. TVS | 13.8 V | 44 mA | 44 mA | 5 W | 600 W | | | | | |
| P6KE10C | B7 | a2 | MO | Bidir. TVS | 15 V | 40 mA | 40 mA | 5 W | 600 W | | | | | |
| P6KE11C | B7 | a2 | MO | Bidir. TVS | 16.2 V | 37 mA | 37 mA | 5 W | 600 W | | | | | |
| P6KE12C | B7 | a2 | MO | Bidir. TVS | 17.3 V | 35 mA | 35 mA | 5 W | 600 W | | | | | |
| P6KE13C | B7 | a2 | MO | Bidir. TVS | 19 V | 32 mA | 32 mA | 5 W | 600 W | | | | | |
| P6KE15C | B7 | a2 | MO | Bidir. TVS | 22 V | 27 mA | 27 mA | 5 W | 600 W | | | | | |
| P6KE16C | B7 | a2 | MO | Bidir. TVS | 23.5 V | 26 mA | 26 mA | 5 W | 600 W | | | | | |
| P6KE18C | B7 | a2 | MO | Bidir. TVS | 26.5 V | 23 mA | 23 mA | 5 W | 600 W | | | | | |
| P6KE20C | B7 | a2 | MO | Bidir. TVS | 29.1 V | 21 mA | 21 mA | 5 W | 600 W | | | | | |
| P6KE22C | B7 | a2 | MO | Bidir. TVS | 31.9 V | 19 mA | 19 mA | 5 W | 600 W | | | | | |
| P6KE24C | B7 | a2 | MO | Bidir. TVS | 34.7 V | 17 mA | 17 mA | 5 W | 600 W | | | | | |
| P6KE27C | B7 | a2 | MO | Bidir. TVS | 39.1 V | 15 mA | 15 mA | 5 W | 600 W | | | | | |
| P6KE30C | B7 | a2 | MO | Bidir. TVS | 43.5 V | 14 mA | 14 mA | 5 W | 600 W | | | | | |
| P6KE33C | B7 | a2 | MO | Bidir. TVS | 47.7 V | 12.6 mA | 12.6 mA | 5 W | 600 W | | | | | |
| P6KE36C | B7 | a2 | MO | Bidir. TVS | 52 V | 11.6 mA | 11.6 mA | 5 W | 600 W | | | | | |
| P6KE39C | B7 | a2 | MO | Bidir. TVS | 56.4 V | 10.6 mA | 10.6 mA | 5 W | 600 W | | | | | |
| P6KE43C | B7 | a2 | MO | Bidir. TVS | 61.9 V | 9.6 mA | 9.6 mA | 5 W | 600 W | | | | | |
| P6KE47C | B7 | a2 | MO | Bidir. TVS | 67.8 V | 8.9 mA | 8.9 mA | 5 W | 600 W | | | | | |
| P6KE51C | B7 | a2 | MO | Bidir. TVS | 73.5 V | 8.2 mA | 8.2 mA | 5 W | 600 W | | | | | |
| P6KE56C | B7 | a2 | MO | Bidir. TVS | 80.5 V | 7.4 mA | 7.4 mA | 5 W | 600 W | | | | | |
| P6KE62C | B7 | a2 | MO | Bidir. TVS | 89 V | 6.8 mA | 6.8 mA | 5 W | 600 W | | | | | |
| P6KE68C | B7 | a2 | MO | Bidir. TVS | 98 V | 6.1 mA | 6.1 mA | 5 W | 600 W | | | | | |
| P6KE75C | B7 | a2 | MO | Bidir. TVS | 108 V | 5.5 mA | 5.5 mA | 5 W | 600 W | | | | | |
| P6KE82C | B7 | a2 | MO | Bidir. TVS | 118 V | 5.1 mA | 5.1 mA | 5 W | 600 W | | | | | |
| P6KE91C | B7 | a2 | MO | Bidir. TVS | 131 V | 4.5 mA | 4.5 mA | 5 W | 600 W | | | | | |
| P6KE100C | B7 | a2 | MO | Bidir. TVS | 144 V | 4.2 mA | 4.2 mA | 5 W | 600 W | | | | | |

| Type | Case | Pin-code | | | Maximum Ratings | | | | | Electrical Characteristics | | | | |
|------|------|----------|---|---|---|---|---|---|---|---|---|---|---|---|
| | | | | | $V_{cla}$ / $V_{bro}$ | Its | Izm | Pv | Pvts | Vz | Iz / Is | rz | TK | |
| P6KE110C | B7 | a2 | MO | Bidir. TVS | 158 V | 3.8 mA | 3.8 mA | 5 W | 600 W | | | | | |
| P6KE120C | B7 | a2 | MO | Bidir. TVS | 173 V | 3.5 mA | 3.5 mA | 5 W | 600 W | | | | | |
| P6KE130C | B7 | a2 | MO | Bidir. TVS | 187 V | 3.2 mA | 3.2 mA | 5 W | 600 W | | | | | |
| P6KE150C | B7 | a2 | MO | Bidir. TVS | 215 V | 2.8 mA | 2.8 mA | 5 W | 600 W | | | | | |
| P6KE160C | B7 | a2 | MO | Bidir. TVS | 230 V | 2.6 mA | 2.6 mA | 5 W | 600 W | | | | | |
| P6KE170C | B7 | a2 | MO | Bidir. TVS | 244 V | 2.5 mA | 2.5 mA | 5 W | 600 W | | | | | |
| P6KE180C | B7 | a2 | MO | Bidir. TVS | 258 V | 2.3 mA | 2.3 mA | 5 W | 600 W | | | | | |
| P6KE200C | B7 | a2 | MO | Bidir. TVS | 287 V | 2.1 mA | 2.1 mA | 5 W | 600 W | | | | | |
| P6KE6.8CA | B7 | a2 | MO | Bidir. TVS | 10.5 V | 57 mA | 57 mA | 5 W | 600 W | | | | | P |
| P6KE7.5CA | B7 | a2 | MO | Bidir. TVS | 11.3 V | 53 mA | 53 mA | 5 W | 600 W | | | | | |
| P6KE8.2CA | B7 | a2 | MO | Bidir. TVS | 12.1 V | 50 mA | 50 mA | 5 W | 600 W | | | | | |
| P6KE9.1CA | B7 | a2 | MO | Bidir. TVS | 13.4 V | 45 mA | 45 mA | 5 W | 600 W | | | | | |
| P6KE10CA | B7 | a2 | MO | Bidir. TVS | 14.5 V | 41 mA | 41 mA | 5 W | 600 W | | | | | |
| P6KE11CA | B7 | a2 | MO | Bidir. TVS | 15.6 V | 38 mA | 38 mA | 5 W | 600 W | | | | | |
| P6KE12CA | B7 | a2 | MO | Bidir. TVS | 16.7 V | 36 mA | 36 mA | 5 W | 600 W | | | | | |
| P6KE13CA | B7 | a2 | MO | Bidir. TVS | 18.2 V | 33 mA | 33 mA | 5 W | 600 W | | | | | P |
| P6KE15CA | B7 | a2 | MO | Bidir. TVS | 21.2 V | 28 mA | 28 mA | 5 W | 600 W | | | | | P |
| P6KE16CA | B7 | a2 | MO | Bidir. TVS | 22.5 V | 27 mA | 27 mA | 5 W | 600 W | | | | | |
| P6KE18CA | B7 | a2 | MO | Bidir. TVS | 25.2 V | 24 mA | 24 mA | 5 W | 600 W | | | | | |
| P6KE20CA | B7 | a2 | MO | Bidir. TVS | 27.7 V | 22 mA | 22 mA | 5 W | 600 W | | | | | |
| P6KE22CA | B7 | a2 | MO | Bidir. TVS | 30.6 V | 10 mA | 10 mA | 5 W | 600 W | | | | | |
| P6KE24CA | B7 | a2 | MO | Bidir. TVS | 33.2 V | 18 mA | 18 mA | 5 W | 600 W | | | | | |
| P6KE27CA | B7 | a2 | MO | Bidir. TVS | 37.5 V | 16 mA | 16 mA | 5 W | 600 W | | | | | P |
| P6KE30CA | B7 | a2 | MO | Bidir. TVS | 41.4 V | 14.4 mA | 14.4 mA | 5 W | 600 W | | | | | |
| P6KE33CA | B7 | a2 | MO | Bidir. TVS | 45.7 V | 13.2 mA | 13.2 mA | 5 W | 600 W | | | | | P |
| P6KE36CA | B7 | a2 | MO | Bidir. TVS | 49.9 V | 12 mA | 12 mA | 5 W | 600 W | | | | | P |
| P6KE39CA | B7 | a2 | MO | Bidir. TVS | 53.9 V | 11.2 mA | 11.2 mA | 5 W | 600 W | | | | | |
| P6KE43CA | B7 | a2 | MO | Bidir. TVS | 59.3 V | 10.1 mA | 10.1 mA | 5 W | 600 W | | | | | |
| P6KE47CA | B7 | a2 | MO | Bidir. TVS | 64.8 V | 9.3 mA | 9.3 mA | 5 W | 600 W | | | | | |
| P6KE51CA | B7 | a2 | MO | Bidir. TVS | 70.1 V | 8.6 mA | 8.6 mA | 5 W | 600 W | | | | | |
| P6KE56CA | B7 | a2 | MO | Bidir. TVS | 77 V | 7.8 mA | 7.8 mA | 5 W | 600 W | | | | | |
| P6KE62CA | B7 | a2 | MO | Bidir. TVS | 85 V | 7.1 mA | 7.1 mA | 5 W | 600 W | | | | | P |
| P6KE68CA | B7 | a2 | MO | Bidir. TVS | 92 V | 6.5 mA | 6.5 mA | 5 W | 600 W | | | | | |
| P6KE75CA | B7 | a2 | MO | Bidir. TVS | 103 V | 5.8 mA | 5.8 mA | 5 W | 600 W | | | | | |
| P6KE82CA | B7 | a2 | MO | Bidir. TVS | 113 V | 5.3 mA | 5.3 mA | 5 W | 600 W | | | | | |
| P6KE91CA | B7 | a2 | MO | Bidir. TVS | 125 V | 4.8 mA | 4.8 mA | 5 W | 600 W | | | | | |
| P6KE100CA | B7 | a2 | MO | Bidir. TVS | 137 V | 4.4 mA | 4.4 mA | 5 W | 600 W | | | | | |
| P6KE110CA | B7 | a2 | MO | Bidir. TVS | 152 V | 4 mA | 4 mA | 5 W | 600 W | | | | | |
| P6KE120CA | B7 | a2 | MO | Bidir. TVS | 165 V | 3.6 mA | 3.6 mA | 5 W | 600 W | | | | | |
| P6KE130CA | B7 | a2 | MO | Bidir. TVS | 179 V | 3.3 mA | 3.3 mA | 5 W | 600 W | | | | | |

| Type | Case | Pin-code | | | Maximum Ratings | | | | | Electrical Characteristics | | | | |
|---|---|---|---|---|---|---|---|---|---|---|---|---|---|---|
| | | | | | Vcla Vbro | Its | Izm | Pv | Pvts | Vz Is | Iz | rz | TK | |
| P6KE150CA | B7 | a2 | MO | Bidir. TVS | 207 V | 2.9 mA | 2.9 mA | 5 W | 600 W | | | | | |
| P6KE160CA | B7 | a2 | MO | Bidir. TVS | 219 V | 2.7 mA | 2.7 mA | 5 W | 600 W | | | | | |
| P6KE170CA | B7 | a2 | MO | Bidir. TVS | 234 V | 2.6 mA | 2.6 mA | 5 W | 600 W | | | | | |
| P6KE180CA | B7 | a2 | MO | Bidir. TVS | 246 V | 2.4 mA | 2.4 mA | 5 W | 600 W | | | | | |
| P6KE200CA | B7 | a2 | MO | Bidir. TVS | 274 V | 2.2 mA | 2.2 mA | 5 W | 600 W | | | | | |
| P6SMB6.8A | G1 | a1 | MO | TVS | 10.5 V | 57 mA | 57 mA | | 500 W | | | | | P |
| P6SMB7.5A | G1 | a1 | MO | TVS | 11.3 V | 53 mA | 53 mA | | 500 W | | | | | |
| P6SMB8.2A | G1 | a1 | MO | TVS | 12.1 V | 50 mA | 50 mA | | 500 W | | | | | |
| P6SMB9.1A | G1 | a1 | MO | TVS | 13.4 V | 45 mA | 45 mA | | 500 W | | | | | |
| P6SMB10A | G1 | a1 | MO | TVS | 14.5 V | 41 mA | 41 mA | | 500 W | | | | | |
| P6SMB11A | G1 | a1 | MO | TVS | 15.6 V | 38 mA | 38 mA | | 500 W | | | | | |
| P6SMB12A | G1 | a1 | MO | TVS | 16.7 V | 36 mA | 36 mA | | 500 W | | | | | |
| P6SMB13A | G1 | a1 | MO | TVS | 18.2 V | 33 mA | 33 mA | | 500 W | | | | | |
| P6SMB15A | G1 | a1 | MO | TVS | 21.2 V | 28 mA | 28 mA | | 500 W | | | | | P |
| P6SMB16A | G1 | a1 | MO | TVS | 22.5 V | 27 mA | 27 mA | | 500 W | | | | | P |
| P6SMB18A | G1 | a1 | MO | TVS | 25.2 V | 24 mA | 24 mA | | 500 W | | | | | |
| P6SMB20A | G1 | a1 | MO | TVS | 27.7 V | 22 mA | 22 mA | | 500 W | | | | | |
| P6SMB22A | G1 | a1 | MO | TVS | 30.6 V | 20 mA | 20 mA | | 500 W | | | | | |
| P6SMB24A | G1 | a1 | MO | TVS | 33.2 V | 18 mA | 18 mA | | 500 W | | | | | |
| P6SMB27A | G1 | a1 | MO | TVS | 37.5 V | 16 mA | 16 mA | | 500 W | | | | | P |
| P6SMB30A | G1 | a1 | MO | TVS | 41.4 V | 14.4 mA | 14.4 mA | | 500 W | | | | | |
| P6SMB33A | G1 | a1 | MO | TVS | 45.7 V | 13.2 mA | 13.2 mA | | 500 W | | | | | P |
| P6SMB36A | G1 | a1 | MO | TVS | 49.9 V | 12 mA | 12 mA | | 500 W | | | | | P |
| P6SMB39A | G1 | a1 | MO | TVS | 53.9 V | 11.2 mA | 11.2 mA | | 500 W | | | | | |
| P6SMB43A | G1 | a1 | MO | TVS | 59.3 V | 10.1 mA | 10.1 mA | | 500 W | | | | | |
| P6SMB47A | G1 | a1 | MO | TVS | 64.8 V | 9.3 mA | 9.3 mA | | 500 W | | | | | |
| P6SMB51A | G1 | a1 | MO | TVS | 70.1 V | 8.6 mA | 8.6 mA | | 500 W | | | | | |
| P6SMB56A | G1 | a1 | MO | TVS | 77 V | 7.8 mA | 7.8 mA | | 500 W | | | | | |
| P6SMB62A | G1 | a1 | MO | TVS | 85 V | 7.1 mA | 7.1 mA | | 500 W | | | | | P |
| P6SMB68A | G1 | a1 | MO | TVS | 92 V | 6.5 mA | 6.5 mA | | 500 W | | | | | |
| P6SMB75A | G1 | a1 | MO | TVS | 103 V | 5.8 mA | 5.8 mA | | 500 W | | | | | |
| P6SMB82A | G1 | a1 | MO | TVS | 113 V | 5.3 mA | 5.3 mA | | 500 W | | | | | |
| P6SMB91A | G1 | a1 | MO | TVS | 125 V | 4.8 mA | 4.8 mA | | 500 W | | | | | |
| P6SMB100A | G1 | a1 | MO | TVS | 137 V | 4.4 mA | 4.4 mA | | 500 W | | | | | |
| P6SMB110A | G1 | a1 | MO | TVS | 152 V | 4 mA | 4 mA | | 500 W | | | | | |
| P6SMB120A | G1 | a1 | MO | TVS | 165 V | 3.6 mA | 3.6 mA | | 500 W | | | | | |
| P6SMB130A | G1 | a1 | MO | TVS | 179 V | 3.3 mA | 3.3 mA | | 500 W | | | | | |
| P6SMB150A | G1 | a1 | MO | TVS | 207 V | 2.9 mA | 2.9 mA | | 500 W | | | | | |
| P6SMB160A | G1 | a1 | MO | TVS | 219 V | 2.7 mA | 2.7 mA | | 500 W | | | | | |
| P6SMB170A | G1 | a1 | MO | TVS | 234 V | 2.6 mA | 2.6 mA | | 500 W | | | | | |

| Type | Case | Pin-code | | | Maximum Ratings | | | | | Electrical Characteristics | | | | |
|------|------|----------|---|---|---|---|---|---|---|---|---|---|---|---|
| | | | | | Vcla $V_{bro}$ | Its | Izm | Pv | Pvts | Vz | Iz $I_s$ | rz | TK | |
| P6SMB180A | G1 | a1 | MO | TVS | 246 V | 2.4 mA | 2.4 mA | | 500 W | | | | | |
| P6SMB200A | G1 | a1 | MO | TVS | 274 V | 2.2 mA | 2.2 mA | | 500 W | | | | | |
| PLE0.7 | B4 | a1 | SG | Stabistor | | | | | | 0.7 V | 5 µA | <10 Ω | -3000·10⁶/°C | |
| PLE1.5 | B4 | a1 | SG | Stabistor | | | | | | 1.45 V | 5 µA | <20 Ω | -3000·10⁶/°C | |
| PLVA450A | A1 | a1 | PH | Avalanche | | | | 0.4 W | 30 W | 5.0 V | 250 µA | <700 Ω | | Nd=1µV/√Hz |
| PLVA453A | A1 | a1 | PH | Avalanche | | | | 0.4 W | 30 W | 5.3 V | 250 µA | <250 Ω | | Nd=1µV/√Hz |
| PLVA456A | A1 | a1 | PH | Avalanche | | | | 0.4 W | 30 W | 5.6 V | 250 µA | <100 Ω | | Nd=1µV/√Hz |
| PLVA459A | A1 | a1 | PH | Avalanche | | | | 0.4 W | 30 W | 5.9 V | 250 µA | <100 Ω | | Nd=1µV/√Hz |
| PLVA462A | A1 | a1 | PH | Avalanche | | | | 0.4 W | 30 W | 6.2 V | 250 µA | <100 Ω | | Nd=1µV/√Hz |
| PLVA465A | A1 | a1 | PH | Avalanche | | | | 0.4 W | 30 W | 6.5 V | 250 µA | <100 Ω | | Nd=1µV/√Hz |
| PLVA468A | A1 | a1 | PH | Avalanche | | | | 0.4 W | 30 W | 6.8 V | 250 µA | <100 Ω | | Nd=1µV/√Hz |
| PLVA650A | F1 | c3 | PH | Avalanche | | | | 0.25 W | 30 W | 5.0 V | 250 µA | <700 Ω | | Nd=1µV/√Hz |
| PLVA653A | F1 | c3 | PH | Avalanche | | | | 0.25 W | 30 W | 5.3 V | 250 µA | <250 Ω | | Nd=1µV/√Hz |
| PLVA656A | F1 | c3 | PH | Avalanche | | | | 0.25 W | 30 W | 5.6 V | 250 µA | <100 Ω | | Nd=1µV/√Hz |
| PLVA659A | F1 | c3 | PH | Avalanche | | | | 0.25 W | 30 W | 5.9 V | 250 µA | <100 Ω | | Nd=1µV/√Hz |
| PLVA662A | F1 | c3 | PH | Avalanche | | | | 0.25 W | 30 W | 6.2 V | 250 µA | <100 Ω | | Nd=1µV/√Hz |
| PLVA665A | F1 | c3 | PH | Avalanche | | | | 0.25 W | 30 W | 6.5 V | 250 µA | <100 Ω | | Nd=1µV/√Hz |
| PLVA668A | F1 | c3 | PH | Avalanche | | | | 0.25 W | 30 W | 6.8 V | 250 µA | <100 Ω | | Nd=1µV/√Hz |
| PMBZ5226B | F1 | c3 | PH | Z Diode | | | | 0.3 W | | 3.3 V | 20 mA | 28 Ω | -640·10⁶/°C | |
| PMBZ5227B | F1 | c3 | PH | Z Diode | | | | 0.3 W | | 3.6 V | 20 mA | 26 Ω | -650·10⁶/°C | |
| PMBZ5228B | F1 | c3 | PH | Z Diode | | | | 0.3 W | | 3.9 V | 20 mA | 25 Ω | -630·10⁶/°C | |
| PMBZ5229B | F1 | c3 | PH | Z Diode | | | | 0.3 W | | 4.3 V | 20 mA | 22 Ω | -580·10⁶/°C | |
| PMBZ5230B | F1 | c3 | PH | Z Diode | | | | 0.3 W | | 4.7 V | 20 mA | 19 Ω | -470·10⁶/°C | |
| PMBZ5231B | F1 | c3 | PH | Z Diode | | | | 0.3 W | | 5.1 V | 20 mA | 17 Ω | -130·10⁶/°C | |
| PMBZ5232B | F1 | c3 | PH | Z Diode | | | | 0.3 W | | 5,6 V | 20 mA | 11 Ω | 230·10⁶/°C | |
| PMBZ5233B | F1 | c3 | PH | Z Diode | | | | 0.3 W | | 6.0 V | 20 mA | 7 Ω | 230·10⁶/°C | |
| PMBZ5234B | F1 | c3 | PH | Z Diode | | | | 0.3 W | | 6.2 V | 20 mA | 7 Ω | 390·10⁶/°C | |
| PMBZ5235B | F1 | c3 | PH | Z Diode | | | | 0.3 W | | 6.8 V | 20 mA | 5 Ω | 400·10⁶/°C | |
| PMBZ5236B | F1 | c3 | PH | Z Diode | | | | 0.3 W | | 7.0 V | 20 mA | 6 Ω | 470·10⁶/°C | |
| PMBZ5237B | F1 | c3 | PH | Z Diode | | | | 0.3 W | | 8.2 V | 20 mA | 8 Ω | 520·10⁶/°C | |
| PMBZ5238B | F1 | c3 | PH | Z Diode | | | | 0.3 W | | 8.7 V | 20 mA | 8 Ω | 530·10⁶/°C | |
| PMBZ5239B | F1 | c3 | PH | Z Diode | | | | 0.3 W | | 9.1 V | 20 mA | 10 Ω | 560·10⁶/°C | |
| PMBZ5240B | F1 | c3 | PH | Z Diode | | | | 0.3 W | | 10 V | 20 mA | 17 Ω | 560·10⁶/°C | |
| PMBZ5241B | F1 | c3 | PH | Z Diode | | | | 0.3 W | | 11 V | 20 mA | 22 Ω | 580·10⁶/°C | |
| PMBZ5242B | F1 | c3 | PH | Z Diode | | | | 0.3 W | | 12 V | 20 mA | 30 Ω | 620·10⁶/°C | |
| PMBZ5243B | F1 | c3 | PH | Z Diode | | | | 0.3 W | | 13 V | 9.5 mA | 13 Ω | 650·10⁶/°C | |
| PMBZ5244B | F1 | c3 | PH | Z Diode | | | | 0.3 W | | 14 V | 9.0 mA | 15 Ω | 670·10⁶/°C | |
| PMBZ5245B | F1 | c3 | PH | Z Diode | | | | 0.3 W | | 15 V | 8.5 mA | 16 Ω | 730·10⁶/°C | |
| PMBZ5246B | F1 | c3 | PH | Z Diode | | | | 0.3 W | | 16 V | 7.8 mA | 17 Ω | 730·10⁶/°C | |
| PMBZ5247B | F1 | c3 | PH | Z Diode | | | | 0.3 W | | 17 V | 7.4 mA | 19 Ω | 730·10⁶/°C | |

| Type | Case | Pin-code | | | | Vcla Vbro | Its | Izm | Pv | Pvts | Vz | Iz / Is | rz | TK | |
|------|------|------|---|---|---|------|-----|-----|-----|------|-----|-----|-----|-----|---|
| PMBZ5248B | F1 | c3 | PH | Z Diode | | | | | 0.3 W | | 18 V | 7.0 mA | 21 Ω | 788·10^6/°C | |
| PMBZ5249B | F1 | c3 | PH | Z Diode | | | | | 0.3 W | | 19 V | 6.6 mA | 23 Ω | 780·10^6/°C | |
| PMBZ5250B | F1 | c3 | PH | Z Diode | | | | | 0.3 W | | 20 V | 6.2 mA | 25 Ω | 800·10^6/°C | |
| PMBZ5251B | F1 | c3 | PH | Z Diode | | | | | 0.3 W | | 22 V | 5.6 mA | 29 Ω | 800·10^6/°C | |
| PMBZ5252B | F1 | c3 | PH | Z Diode | | | | | 0.3 W | | 24 V | 5.2 mA | 33 Ω | 810·10^6/°C | |
| PMBZ5253B | F1 | c3 | PH | Z Diode | | | | | 0.3 W | | 25 V | 5.0 mA | 35 Ω | 820·10^6/°C | |
| PMBZ5254B | F1 | c3 | PH | Z Diode | | | | | 0.3 W | | 27 V | 4.6 mA | 41 Ω | 850·10^6/°C | |
| PMBZ5255B | F1 | c3 | PH | Z Diode | | | | | 0.3 W | | 28 V | 4.5 mA | 44 Ω | 850·10^6/°C | |
| PMBZ5256B | F1 | c3 | PH | Z Diode | | | | | 0.3 W | | 30 V | 4.2 mA | 49 Ω | 850·10^6/°C | |
| PMBZ5257B | F1 | c3 | PH | Z Diode | | | | | 0.3 W | | 33 V | 3.8 mA | 58 Ω | 850·10^6/°C | |
| PMLL5225B | D4 | a1 | PH | Z Diode | | | | | 0.5 W | 10 W | 3.0 V | 20 mA | <29 Ω | -750·10^6/°C | |
| PMLL5226B | D4 | a1 | PH | Z Diode | | | | | 0.5 W | 10 W | 3.3 V | 20 mA | <28 Ω | -700·10^6/°C | |
| PMLL5227B | D4 | a1 | PH | Z Diode | | | | | 0.5 W | 10 W | 3.6 V | 20 mA | <24 Ω | -650·10^6/°C | |
| PMLL5228B | D4 | a1 | PH | Z Diode | | | | | 0.5 W | 10 W | 3.9 V | 20 mA | <23 Ω | -600·10^6/°C | |
| PMLL5229B | D4 | a1 | PH | Z Diode | | | | | 0.5 W | 10 W | 4.3 V | 20 mA | <22 Ω | 550·10^6/°C | |
| PMLL5230B | D4 | a1 | PH | Z Diode | | | | | 0.5 W | 10 W | 4.7 V | 20 mA | <19 Ω | 300·10^6/°C | |
| PMLL5231B | D4 | a1 | PH | Z Diode | | | | | 0.5 W | 10 W | 5.1 V | 20 mA | <17 Ω | 300·10^6/°C | |
| PMLL5232B | D4 | a1 | PH | Z Diode | | | | | 0.5 W | 10 W | 5,6 V | 20 mA | <11 Ω | 380·10^6/°C | |
| PMLL5233B | D4 | a1 | PH | Z Diode | | | | | 0.5 W | 10 W | 6.0 V | 20 mA | <7 Ω | 380·10^6/°C | |
| PMLL5234B | D4 | a1 | PH | Z Diode | | | | | 0.5 W | 10 W | 6.2 V | 20 mA | <7 Ω | 450·10^6/°C | |
| PMLL5235B | D4 | a1 | PH | Z Diode | | | | | 0.5 W | 10 W | 6.8 V | 20 mA | <5 Ω | 500·10^6/°C | |
| PMLL5236B | D4 | a1 | PH | Z Diode | | | | | 0.5 W | 10 W | 7.0 V | 20 mA | <6 Ω | 580·10^6/°C | |
| PMLL5237B | D4 | a1 | PH | Z Diode | | | | | 0.5 W | 10 W | 8.2 V | 20 mA | <8 Ω | 620·10^6/°C | |
| PMLL5238B | D4 | a1 | PH | Z Diode | | | | | 0.5 W | 10 W | 8.7 V | 20 mA | <8 Ω | 650·10^6/°C | |
| PMLL5239B | D4 | a1 | PH | Z Diode | | | | | 0.5 W | 10 W | 9.1 V | 20 mA | <10 Ω | 680·10^6/°C | |
| PMLL5240B | D4 | a1 | PH | Z Diode | | | | | 0.5 W | 10 W | 10 V | 20 mA | <17 Ω | 750·10^6/°C | |
| PMLL5241B | D4 | a1 | PH | Z Diode | | | | | 0.5 W | 10 W | 11 V | 20 mA | <22 Ω | 760·10^6/°C | |
| PMLL5242B | D4 | a1 | PH | Z Diode | | | | | 0.5 W | 10 W | 12 V | 20 mA | <30 Ω | 770·10^6/°C | |
| PMLL5243B | D4 | a1 | PH | Z Diode | | | | | 0.5 W | 10 W | 13 V | 9.5 mA | <13 Ω | 790·10^6/°C | |
| PMLL5244B | D4 | a1 | PH | Z Diode | | | | | 0.5 W | 10 W | 14 V | 9.0 mA | <15 Ω | 820·10^6/°C | |
| PMLL5245B | D4 | a1 | PH | Z Diode | | | | | 0.5 W | 10 W | 15 V | 8.5 mA | <16 Ω | 820·10^6/°C | |
| PMLL5246B | D4 | a1 | PH | Z Diode | | | | | 0.5 W | 10 W | 16 V | 7.8 mA | <17 Ω | 830·10^6/°C | |
| PMLL5247B | D4 | a1 | PH | Z Diode | | | | | 0.5 W | 10 W | 17 V | 7.4 mA | <19 Ω | 840·10^6/°C | |
| PMLL5248B | D4 | a1 | PH | Z Diode | | | | | 0.5 W | 10 W | 18 V | 7.0 mA | <21 Ω | 850·10^6/°C | |
| PMLL5249B | D4 | a1 | PH | Z Diode | | | | | 0.5 W | 10 W | 19 V | 6.6 mA | <23 Ω | 860·10^6/°C | |
| PMLL5250B | D4 | a1 | PH | Z Diode | | | | | 0.5 W | 10 W | 20 V | 6.2 mA | <25 Ω | 860·10^6/°C | |
| PMLL5251B | D4 | a1 | PH | Z Diode | | | | | 0.5 W | 10 W | 22 V | 5.6 mA | <29 Ω | 870·10^6/°C | |
| PMLL5252B | D4 | a1 | PH | Z Diode | | | | | 0.5 W | 10 W | 24 V | 5.2 mA | <33 Ω | 880·10^6/°C | |
| PMLL5253B | D4 | a1 | PH | Z Diode | | | | | 0.5 W | 10 W | 25 V | 5.0 mA | <35 Ω | 890·10^6/°C | |
| PMLL5254B | D4 | a1 | PH | Z Diode | | | | | 0.5 W | 10 W | 27 V | 4.6 mA | <41 Ω | 900·10^6/°C | |

**PMBZ5248B – PMLL5254B**

Maximum Ratings — Electrical Characteristics

| Type | Case | Pin-code | | | Maximum Ratings | | | | | Electrical Characteristics | | | | |
|------|------|----------|---|---|---|---|---|---|---|---|---|---|---|---|
| | | | | | Vcla Vbro | Its | Izm | Pv | Pvts | Vz | Iz / Is | rz | TK | |
| PMLL5255B | D4 | a1 | PH | Z Diode | | | | 0.5 W | 10 W | 28 V | 4.5 mA | <44 Ω | $910 \cdot 10^{6}/°C$ | |
| PMLL5256B | D4 | a1 | PH | Z Diode | | | | 0.5 W | 10 W | 30 V | 4.2 mA | <49 Ω | $910 \cdot 10^{6}/°C$ | |
| PMLL5257B | D4 | a1 | PH | Z Diode | | | | 0.5 W | 10 W | 33 V | 3.8 mA | <58 Ω | $920 \cdot 10^{6}/°C$ | |
| PMLL5258B | D4 | a1 | PH | Z Diode | | | | 0.5 W | 10 W | 36 V | 3.4 mA | <70 Ω | $930 \cdot 10^{6}/°C$ | |
| PMLL5259B | D4 | a1 | PH | Z Diode | | | | 0.5 W | 10 W | 39 V | 3.2 mA | <80 Ω | $940 \cdot 10^{6}/°C$ | |
| PMLL5260B | D4 | a1 | PH | Z Diode | | | | 0.5 W | 10 W | 43 V | 3.0 mA | <93 Ω | $950 \cdot 10^{6}/°C$ | |
| PMLL5261B | D4 | a1 | PH | Z Diode | | | | 0.5 W | 10 W | 47 V | 2.7 mA | <105 Ω | $950 \cdot 10^{6}/°C$ | |
| PMLL5262B | D4 | a1 | PH | Z Diode | | | | 0.5 W | 10 W | 51 V | 2.5 mA | <125 Ω | $960 \cdot 10^{6}/°C$ | |
| PMLL5263B | D4 | a1 | PH | Z Diode | | | | 0.5 W | 10 W | 56 V | 2.3 mA | <150 Ω | $960 \cdot 10^{6}/°C$ | |
| PMLL5264B | D4 | a1 | PH | Z Diode | | | | 0.5 W | 10 W | 60 V | 2.1 mA | <170 Ω | $970 \cdot 10^{6}/°C$ | |
| PMLL5265B | D4 | a1 | PH | Z Diode | | | | 0.5 W | 10 W | 62 V | 2.0 mA | <185 Ω | $970 \cdot 10^{6}/°C$ | |
| PMLL5266B | D4 | a1 | PH | Z Diode | | | | 0.5 W | 10 W | 68 V | 1.8 mA | <230 Ω | $970 \cdot 10^{6}/°C$ | |
| PMLL5267B | D4 | a1 | PH | Z Diode | | | | 0.5 W | 10 W | 75 V | 1.7 mA | <270 Ω | $980 \cdot 10^{6}/°C$ | |
| PZ127 | B16 | a1 | RD | TVS | | | | | 0.3 kW | | | | | |
| PZ227 | B16 | a1 | RD | TVS | | | | | 0.6 kW | | | | | |
| PZ427 | B17 | a1 | RD | TVS | | | | | 0.9 kW | | | | | |
| PZ627 | B18 | a1 | RD | TVS | | | | | 2.8 kW | | | | | |
| PZ628 | B18 | a1 | RD | TVS | | | | | 2.8 kW | | | | | |
| PZT2.4A | G5 | a1 | RO | Z Diode | | | | 1 W | | 2.4 V | 40 mA | <15 Ω | | Vz ±5% |
| PZT2.7A | G5 | a1 | RO | Z Diode | | | | 1 W | | 2.7 V | 40 mA | <15 Ω | | Vz ±5% |
| PZT3.0A | G5 | a1 | RO | Z Diode | | | | 1 W | | 3 V | 40 mA | <15 Ω | | Vz ±5% |
| PZT3.3A | G5 | a1 | RO | Z Diode | | | | 1 W | | 3.3 V | 40 mA | <15 Ω | | Vz ±5% |
| PZT3.6A | G5 | a1 | RO | Z Diode | | | | 1 W | | 3.6 V | 40 mA | <15 Ω | | Vz ±5% |
| PZT3.9A | G5 | a1 | RO | Z Diode | | | | 1 W | | 3.9 V | 40 mA | <15 Ω | | Vz ±5% |
| PZT4.3A | G5 | a1 | RO | Z Diode | | | | 1 W | | 4.3 V | 40 mA | <15 Ω | | Vz ±5% |
| PZT4.7A | G5 | a1 | RO | Z Diode | | | | 1 W | | 4.7 V | 40 mA | <10 Ω | | Vz ±5% |
| PZT5.1A | G5 | a1 | RO | Z Diode | | | | 1 W | | 5.1 V | 40 mA | <8 Ω | | Vz ±5% |
| PZT5.6A | G5 | a1 | RO | Z Diode | | | | 1 W | | 5.6 V | 40 mA | <8 Ω | | Vz ±5% |
| PZT6.2A | G5 | a1 | RO | Z Diode | | | | 1 W | | 6.2 V | 40 mA | <6 Ω | | Vz ±5% |
| PZT6.8A | G5 | a1 | RO | Z Diode | | | | 1 W | | 6.8 V | 40 mA | <6 Ω | | Vz ±5% |
| PZT7.5A | G5 | a1 | RO | Z Diode | | | | 1 W | | 7.5 V | 40 mA | <4 Ω | | Vz ±5% |
| PZT8.2A | G5 | a1 | RO | Z Diode | | | | 1 W | | 8.2 V | 40 mA | <4 Ω | | Vz ±5% |
| PZT9.1A | G5 | a1 | RO | Z Diode | | | | 1 W | | 9.1 V | 40 mA | <6 Ω | | Vz ±5% |
| PZT10A | G5 | a1 | RO | Z Diode | | | | 1 W | | 10 V | 40 mA | <6 Ω | | Vz ±5% |
| PZT11A | G5 | a1 | RO | Z Diode | | | | 1 W | | 11 V | 20 mA | <8 Ω | | Vz ±5% |
| PZT12A | G5 | a1 | RO | Z Diode | | | | 1 W | | 12.1 V | 20 mA | <8 Ω | | Vz ±5% |
| PZT13A | G5 | a1 | RO | Z Diode | | | | 1 W | | 13.2 V | 20 mA | <10 Ω | | Vz ±5% |
| PZT15A | G5 | a1 | RO | Z Diode | | | | 1 W | | 15.2 V | 20 mA | <10 Ω | | Vz ±5% |
| PZT16A | G5 | a1 | RO | Z Diode | | | | 1 W | | 16.1 V | 20 mA | <12 Ω | | Vz ±5% |
| PZT18A | G5 | a1 | RO | Z Diode | | | | 1 W | | 18 V | 20 mA | <12 Ω | | Vz ±5% |

| Type | Case | Pin-code | | | Vcla Vbro | Its | Izm | Pv | Pvts | Vz | Iz Is | rz | TK | |
|---|---|---|---|---|---|---|---|---|---|---|---|---|---|---|
| PZT20A | G5 | a1 | RO | Z Diode | | | | 1 W | | 20 V | 20 mA | <14 Ω | | Vz ±5% |
| PZT22A | G5 | a1 | RO | Z Diode | | | | 1 W | | 22 V | 10 mA | <14 Ω | | Vz ±5% |
| PZT24A | G5 | a1 | RO | Z Diode | | | | 1 W | | 24.1 V | 10 mA | <16 Ω | | Vz ±5% |
| PZT27A | G5 | a1 | RO | Z Diode | | | | 1 W | | 27.1 V | 10 mA | <16 Ω | | Vz ±5% |
| PZT30A | G5 | a1 | RO | Z Diode | | | | 1 W | | 30 V | 10 mA | <18 Ω | | Vz ±5% |
| PZT33A | G5 | a1 | RO | Z Diode | | | | 1 W | | 33 V | 10 mA | <18 Ω | | Vz ±5% |
| PZT36A | G5 | a1 | RO | Z Diode | | | | 1 W | | 36 V | 10 mA | <20 Ω | | Vz ±5% |
| PZT39A | G5 | a1 | RO | Z Diode | | | | 1 W | | 39 V | 10 mA | <50 Ω | | Vz ±5% |
| PZT43A | G5 | a1 | RO | Z Diode | | | | 1 W | | 43 V | 10 mA | <50 Ω | | Vz ±5% |
| PZT2.4B | G5 | a1 | RO | Z Diode | | | | 1 W | | 2.6 V | 40 mA | <15 Ω | | Vz ±5% |
| PZT2.7B | G5 | a1 | RO | Z Diode | | | | 1 W | | 2.9 V | 40 mA | <15 Ω | | Vz ±5% |
| PZT3.0B | G5 | a1 | RO | Z Diode | | | | 1 W | | 3.2 V | 40 mA | <15 Ω | | Vz ±5% |
| PZT3.3B | G5 | a1 | RO | Z Diode | | | | 1 W | | 3.5 V | 40 mA | <15 Ω | | Vz ±5% |
| PZT3.6B | G5 | a1 | RO | Z Diode | | | | 1 W | | 3.8 V | 40 mA | <15 Ω | | Vz ±5% |
| PZT3.9B | G5 | a1 | RO | Z Diode | | | | 1 W | | 4.1 V | 40 mA | <15 Ω | | Vz ±5% |
| PZT4.3B | G5 | a1 | RO | Z Diode | | | | 1 W | | 4.6 V | 40 mA | <15 Ω | | Vz ±5% |
| PZT4.7B | G5 | a1 | RO | Z Diode | | | | 1 W | | 5 V | 40 mA | <10 Ω | | Vz ±5% |
| PZT5.1B | G5 | a1 | RO | Z Diode | | | | 1 W | | 5.4 V | 40 mA | <8 Ω | | Vz ±5% |
| PZT5.6B | G5 | a1 | RO | Z Diode | | | | 1 W | | 6 V | 40 mA | <8 Ω | | Vz ±5% |
| PZT6.2B | G5 | a1 | RO | Z Diode | | | | 1 W | | 6.6 V | 40 mA | <6 Ω | | Vz ±5% |
| PZT6.8B | G5 | a1 | RO | Z Diode | | | | 1 W | | 7.3 V | 40 mA | <6 Ω | | Vz ±5% |
| PZT7.5B | G6 | a1 | RO | Z Diode | | | | 1 W | | 8 V | 40 mA | <4 Ω | | Vz ±5% |
| PZT8.2B | G5 | a1 | RO | Z Diode | | | | 1 W | | 8.8 V | 40 mA | <4 Ω | | Vz ±5% |
| PZT9.1B | G5 | a1 | RO | Z Diode | | | | 1 W | | 9.7 V | 40 mA | <6 Ω | | Vz ±5% |
| PZT10B | G5 | a1 | RO | Z Diode | | | | 1 W | | 10.6 V | 40 mA | <6 Ω | | Vz ±5% |
| PZT11B | G5 | a1 | RO | Z Diode | | | | 1 W | | 11.7 V | 20 mA | <8 Ω | | Vz ±5% |
| PZT12B | G5 | a1 | RO | Z Diode | | | | 1 W | | 12.7 V | 20 mA | <8 Ω | | Vz ±5% |
| PZT13B | G5 | a1 | RO | Z Diode | | | | 1 W | | 14.1 V | 20 mA | <10 Ω | | Vz ±5% |
| PZT15B | G5 | a1 | RO | Z Diode | | | | 1 W | | 15.6 V | 20 mA | <10 Ω | | Vz ±5% |
| PZT16B | G5 | a1 | RO | Z Diode | | | | 1 W | | 17.3 V | 20 mA | <12 Ω | | Vz ±5% |
| PZT18B | G5 | a1 | RO | Z Diode | | | | 1 W | | 19.2 V | 20 mA | <12 Ω | | Vz ±5% |
| PZT20B | G5 | a1 | RO | Z Diode | | | | 1 W | | 21.2 V | 20 mA | <14 Ω | | Vz ±5% |
| PZT22B | G5 | a1 | RO | Z Diode | | | | 1 W | | 23.3 V | 10 mA | <14 Ω | | Vz ±5% |
| PZT24B | G5 | a1 | RO | Z Diode | | | | 1 W | | 25.8 V | 10 mA | <16 Ω | | Vz ±5% |
| PZT27B | G5 | a1 | RO | Z Diode | | | | 1 W | | 28.9 V | 10 mA | <16 Ω | | Vz ±5% |
| PZT30B | G5 | a1 | RO | Z Diode | | | | 1 W | | 32 V | 10 mA | <18 Ω | | Vz ±5% |
| PZT33B | G5 | a1 | RO | Z Diode | | | | 1 W | | 35 V | 10 mA | <18 Ω | | Vz ±5% |
| PZT36B | G5 | a1 | RO | Z Diode | | | | 1 W | | 38 V | 10 mA | <20 Ω | | Vz ±5% |
| RLZ2.4A | D2 | a1 | RO | Z Diode | | | | 0.4 W | | 2.4 V | 20 mA | <100 Ω | | Vz ±2.5% |
| RLZ2.7A* | D2 | a1 | RO | Z Diode | | | | 0.4 W | | 2.6 V | 20 mA | <100 Ω | | Vz ±2.5% |

| Type | Case | Pin-code | ⚙ | ⚙ | Maximum Ratings | | | | | Electrical Characteristics | | | | |
|------|------|----------|---|---|-----------------|---|---|---|---|----------------------------|---|---|---|---|
| | | | | | Vcla Vbro | Its | Izm | Pv | Pvts | Vz | Iz Is | rz | TK | |
| RLZ3.0A | D2 | a1 | RO | Z Diode | | | | 0.4 W | | 2.9 V | 20 mA | <80Ω | | Vz ±2.5% |
| RLZ3.3A | D2 | a1 | RO | Z Diode | | | | 0.4 W | | 3.2 V | 20 mA | <70Ω | | Vz ±2.5% |
| RLZ3.6A | D2 | a1 | RO | Z Diode | | | | 0.4 W | | 3.6 V | 20 mA | <60Ω | | Vz ±2.5% |
| RLZ3.9A | D2 | a1 | RO | Z Diode | | | | 0.4 W | | 3.9 V | 20 mA | <50Ω | | Vz ±2.5% |
| RLZ4.3A | D2 | a1 | RO | Z Diode | | | | 0.4 W | | 4.2 V | 20 mA | <40Ω | | Vz ±2.5% |
| RLZ4.7A | D2 | a1 | RO | Z Diode | | | | 0.4 W | | 4.6 V | 20 mA | <25Ω | | Vz ±2.5% |
| RLZ5.1A | D2 | a1 | RO | Z Diode | | | | 0.4 W | | 5 V | 20 mA | <20Ω | | Vz ±2.5% |
| RLZ5.6A | D2 | a1 | RO | Z Diode | | | | 0.4 W | | 5.5 V | 20 mA | <13Ω | | Vz ±2.5% |
| RLZ6.2A | D2 | a1 | RO | Z Diode | | | | 0.4 W | | 6 V | 20 mA | <10Ω | | Vz ±2.5% |
| RLZ6.8A | D2 | a1 | RO | Z Diode | | | | 0.4 W | | 6.5 V | 20 mA | <8Ω | | Vz ±2.5% |
| RLZ7.5A | D2 | a1 | RO | Z Diode | | | | 0.4 W | | 7.1 V | 20 mA | <8Ω | | Vz ±2.5% |
| RLZ8.2A | D2 | a1 | RO | Z Diode | | | | 0.4 W | | 7.7 V | 20 mA | <8Ω | | Vz ±2.5% |
| RLZ9.1A | D2 | a1 | RO | Z Diode | | | | 0.4 W | | 8.5 V | 20 mA | <8Ω | | Vz ±2.5% |
| RLZ10A | D2 | a1 | RO | Z Diode | | | | 0.4 W | | 9.4 V | 20 mA | <8Ω | | Vz ±2.5% |
| RLZ11A | D2 | a1 | RO | Z Diode | | | | 0.4 W | | 10.3 V | 20 mA | <10Ω | | Vz ±2.5% |
| RLZ12A | D2 | a1 | RO | Z Diode | | | | 0.4 W | | 11.4 V | 20 mA | <12Ω | | Vz ±2.5% |
| RLZ13A | D2 | a1 | RO | Z Diode | | | | 0.4 W | | 12.4 V | 20 mA | <14Ω | | Vz ±2.5% |
| RLZ15A | D2 | a1 | RO | Z Diode | | | | 0.4 W | | 13.7 V | 20 mA | <16Ω | | Vz ±2.5% |
| RLZ16A | D2 | a1 | RO | Z Diode | | | | 0.4 W | | 15.2 V | 20 mA | <18Ω | | Vz ±2.5% |
| RLZ18A | D2 | a1 | RO | Z Diode | | | | 0.4 W | | 16.6 V | 20 mA | <23Ω | | Vz ±2.5% |
| RLZ20A | D2 | a1 | RO | Z Diode | | | | 0.4 W | | 18.5 V | 20 mA | <28Ω | | Vz ±2.5% |
| RLZ22A | D2 | a1 | RO | Z Diode | | | | 0.4 W | | 20.6 V | 20 mA | <30Ω | | Vz ±2.5% |
| RLZ24A | D2 | a1 | RO | Z Diode | | | | 0.4 W | | 23.2 V | 20 mA | <35Ω | | Vz ±2.5% |
| RLZ27A | D2 | a1 | RO | Z Diode | | | | 0.4 W | | 24.9 V | 20 mA | <45Ω | | Vz ±2.5% |
| RLZ30A | D2 | a1 | RO | Z Diode | | | | 0.4 W | | 27.7 V | 20 mA | <55Ω | | Vz ±2.5% |
| RLZ33A | D2 | a1 | RO | Z Diode | | | | 0.4 W | | 29.9 V | 20 mA | <65Ω | | Vz ±2.5% |
| RLZ36A | D2 | a1 | RO | Z Diode | | | | 0.4 W | | 32.9 V | 20 mA | <75Ω | | Vz ±2.5% |
| RLZ39A | D2 | a1 | RO | Z Diode | | | | 0.4 W | | 35.3 V | 20 mA | <85Ω | | Vz ±2.5% |
| RLZ39E | D2 | a1 | RO | Z Diode | | | | 0.4 W | | 38.6 V | 5 mA | <85Ω | | Vz ±2.5% |
| RLZ39F | D2 | a1 | RO | Z Diode | | | | 0.4 W | | 39.1 V | 5 mA | <85Ω | | Vz ±2.5% |
| RLZ39G | D2 | a1 | RO | Z Diode | | | | 0.4 W | | 39.7 V | 5 mA | <85Ω | | Vz ±2.5% |
| RLZ43 | D2 | a1 | RO | Z Diode | | | | 0.4 W | | 42.5 V | 5 mA | <90Ω | | Vz ±2.5% |
| RLZ47 | D2 | a1 | RO | Z Diode | | | | 0.4 W | | 46.5 V | 5 mA | <90Ω | | Vz ±2.5% |
| RLZ51 | D2 | a1 | RO | Z Diode | | | | 0.4 W | | 51 V | 5 mA | <110Ω | | Vz ±2.5% |
| RLZ56 | D2 | a1 | RO | Z Diode | | | | 0.4 W | | 56.5 V | 5 mA | <110Ω | | Vz ±2.5% |
| RLZ2.4B | D2 | a1 | RO | Z Diode | | | | 0.4 W | | 2.5 V | 20 mA | <100Ω | | Vz ±2.5% |
| RLZ2.7B | D2 | a1 | RO | Z Diode | | | | 0.4 W | | 2.8 V | 20 mA | <100Ω | | Vz ±2.5% |
| RLZ3.0B | D2 | a1 | RO | Z Diode | | | | 0.4 W | | 3.1 V | 20 mA | <80Ω | | Vz ±2.5% |
| RLZ3.3B | D2 | a1 | RO | Z Diode | | | | 0.4 W | | 3.4 V | 20 mA | <70Ω | | Vz ±2.5% |
| RLZ3.6B | D2 | a1 | RO | Z Diode | | | | 0.4 W | | 3.7 V | 20 mA | <60Ω | | Vz ±2.5% |

| Type | Case | Pin-code | | | Maximum Ratings | | | | | Electrical Characteristics | | | | |
| --- | --- | --- | --- | --- | Vcla Vbro | Its | Izm | Pv | Pvts | Vz | Iz Is | rz | TK | Vz ±2.5% |
| RLZ3.9B | D2 | a1 | RO | Z Diode | | | | 0.4 W | | 4 V | 20 mA | <50 Ω | | Vz ±2.5% |
| RLZ4.3B | D2 | a1 | RO | Z Diode | | | | 0.4 W | | 4.3 V | 20 mA | <40 Ω | | Vz ±2.5% |
| RLZ4.7B | D2 | a1 | RO | Z Diode | | | | 0.4 W | | 5 V | 20 mA | <25 Ω | | Vz ±2.5% |
| RLZ5.1B | D2 | a1 | RO | Z Diode | | | | 0.4 W | | 5.1 V | 20 mA | <20 Ω | | Vz ±2.5% |
| RLZ5.6B | D2 | a1 | RO | Z Diode | | | | 0.4 W | | 5.6 V | 20 mA | <13 Ω | | Vz ±2.5% |
| RLZ6.2B | D2 | a1 | RO | Z Diode | | | | 0.4 W | | 6.1 V | 20 mA | <10 Ω | | Vz ±2.5% |
| RLZ6.8B | D2 | a1 | RO | Z Diode | | | | 0.4 W | | 6.7 V | 20 mA | <8 Ω | | Vz ±2.5% |
| RLZ7.5B | D2 | a1 | RO | Z Diode | | | | 0.4 W | | 7.3 V | 20 mA | <8 Ω | | Vz ±2.5% |
| RLZ8.2B | D2 | a1 | RO | Z Diode | | | | 0.4 W | | 8 V | 20 mA | <8 Ω | | Vz ±2.5% |
| RLZ9.1B | D2 | a1 | RO | Z Diode | | | | 0.4 W | | 8.8 V | 20 mA | <8 Ω | | Vz ±2.5% |
| RLZ10B | D2 | a1 | RO | Z Diode | | | | 0.4 W | | 9.6 V | 20 mA | <8 Ω | | Vz ±2.5% |
| RLZ11B | D2 | a1 | RO | Z Diode | | | | 0.4 W | | 10.7 V | 20 mA | <10 Ω | | Vz ±2.5% |
| RLZ12B | D2 | a1 | RO | Z Diode | | | | 0.4 W | | 11.7 V | 20 mA | <12 Ω | | Vz ±2.5% |
| RLZ13B | D2 | a1 | RO | Z Diode | | | | 0.4 W | | 12.8 V | 20 mA | <14 Ω | | Vz ±2.5% |
| RLZ15B | D2 | a1 | RO | Z Diode | | | | 0.4 W | | 14.3 V | 20 mA | <16 Ω | | Vz ±2.5% |
| RLZ16B | D2 | a1 | RO | Z Diode | | | | 0.4 W | | 15.9 V | 20 mA | <18 Ω | | Vz ±2.5% |
| RLZ18B | D2 | a1 | RO | Z Diode | | | | 0.4 W | | 17.3 V | 20 mA | <23 Ω | | Vz ±2.5% |
| RLZ20B | D2 | a1 | RO | Z Diode | | | | 0.4 W | | 19.1 V | 20 mA | <28 Ω | | Vz ±2.5% |
| RLZ22B | D2 | a1 | RO | Z Diode | | | | 0.4 W | | 21.2 V | 20 mA | <30 Ω | | Vz ±2.5% |
| RLZ24B | D2 | a1 | RO | Z Diode | | | | 0.4 W | | 23.1 V | 20 mA | <35 Ω | | Vz ±2.5% |
| RLZ27B | D2 | a1 | RO | Z Diode | | | | 0.4 W | | 25.6 V | 20 mA | <45 Ω | | Vz ±2.5% |
| RLZ30B | D2 | a1 | RO | Z Diode | | | | 0.4 W | | 29.1 V | 20 mA | <55 Ω | | Vz ±2.5% |
| RLZ33B | D2 | a1 | RO | Z Diode | | | | 0.4 W | | 31.1 V | 20 mA | <65 Ω | | Vz ±2.5% |
| RLZ36B | D2 | a1 | RO | Z Diode | | | | 0.4 W | | 33.5 V | 20 mA | <75 Ω | | Vz ±2.5% |
| RLZ39B | D2 | a1 | RO | Z Diode | | | | 0.4 W | | 36.6 V | 20 mA | <85 Ω | | Vz ±2.5% |
| RLZ4.3C | D2 | a1 | RO | Z Diode | | | | 0.4 W | | 4.4 V | 20 mA | <40 Ω | | Vz ±2.5% |
| RLZ4.7C | D2 | a1 | RO | Z Diode | | | | 0.4 W | | 4.8 V | 20 mA | <25 Ω | | Vz ±2.5% |
| RLZ5.1C | D2 | a1 | RO | Z Diode | | | | 0.4 W | | 5.2 V | 20 mA | <20 Ω | | Vz ±2.5% |
| RLZ5.6C | D2 | a1 | RO | Z Diode | | | | 0.4 W | | 5.8 V | 20 mA | <13 Ω | | Vz ±2.5% |
| RLZ6.2C | D2 | a1 | RO | Z Diode | | | | 0.4 W | | 6.3 V | 20 mA | <10 Ω | | Vz ±2.5% |
| RLZ6.8C | D2 | a1 | RO | Z Diode | | | | 0.4 W | | 6.9 V | 20 mA | <8 Ω | | Vz ±2.5% |
| RLZ7.5C | D2 | a1 | RO | Z Diode | | | | 0.4 W | | 7.5 V | 20 mA | <8 Ω | | Vz ±2.5% |
| RLZ8.2C | D2 | a1 | RO | Z Diode | | | | 0.4 W | | 8.2 V | 20 mA | <8 Ω | | Vz ±2.5% |
| RLZ9.1C | D2 | a1 | RO | Z Diode | | | | 0.4 W | | 9.1 V | 20 mA | <8 Ω | | Vz ±2.5% |
| RLZ10C | D2 | a1 | RO | Z Diode | | | | 0.4 W | | 10 V | 20 mA | <8 Ω | | Vz ±2.5% |
| RLZ11C | D2 | a1 | RO | Z Diode | | | | 0.4 W | | 11 V | 20 mA | <10 Ω | | Vz ±2.5% |
| RLZ12C | D2 | a1 | RO | Z Diode | | | | 0.4 W | | 12.1 V | 20 mA | <12 Ω | | Vz ±2.5% |
| RLZ13C | D2 | a1 | RO | Z Diode | | | | 0.4 W | | 13.3 V | 20 mA | <14 Ω | | Vz ±2.5% |
| RLZ15C | D2 | a1 | RO | Z Diode | | | | 0.4 W | | 14.7 V | 20 mA | <16 Ω | | Vz ±2.5% |
| RLZ16C | D2 | a1 | RO | Z Diode | | | | 0.4 W | | 16.1 V | 20 mA | <18 Ω | | Vz ±2.5% |

| Type | Case | Pin-code | | | Maximum Ratings | | | | | Electrical Characteristics | | | | |
|------|------|----------|---|---|-----------------|----|----|----|-----|----------------------------|----|----|----|----|
| | | | | | Vcla / Vbro | Its | Izm | Pv | Pvts | Vz | Iz / Is | rz | TK | |
| RLZ18C | D2 | a1 | RO | Z Diode | | | | 0.4 W | | 17.9 V | 20 mA | <23 Ω | | Vz ±2.5% |
| RLZ20C | D2 | a1 | RO | Z Diode | | | | 0.4 W | | 20.1 V | 20 mA | <28 Ω | | Vz ±2.5% |
| RLZ22C | D2 | a1 | RO | Z Diode | | | | 0.4 W | | 21.6 V | 20 mA | <30 Ω | | Vz ±2.5% |
| RLZ24C | D2 | a1 | RO | Z Diode | | | | 0.4 W | | 23.7 V | 20 mA | <35 Ω | | Vz ±2.5% |
| RLZ27C | D2 | a1 | RO | Z Diode | | | | 0.4 W | | 26.3 V | 20 mA | <45 Ω | | Vz ±2.5% |
| RLZ30C | D2 | a1 | RO | Z Diode | | | | 0.4 W | | 29.1 V | 20 mA | <55 Ω | | Vz ±2.5% |
| RLZ33C | D2 | a1 | RO | Z Diode | | | | 0.4 W | | 31.7 V | 20 mA | <65 Ω | | Vz ±2.5% |
| RLZ36C | D2 | a1 | RO | Z Diode | | | | 0.4 W | | 34.2 V | 20 mA | <75 Ω | | Vz ±2.5% |
| RLZ39C | D2 | a1 | RO | Z Diode | | | | 0.4 W | | 36.9 V | 20 mA | <85 Ω | | Vz ±2.5% |
| RLZ10D | D2 | a1 | RO | Z Diode | | | | 0.4 W | | 10.2 V | 20 mA | <8 Ω | | Vz ±2.5% |
| RLZ20D | D2 | a1 | RO | Z Diode | | | | 0.4 W | | 20.2 V | 20 mA | <28 Ω | | Vz ±2.5% |
| RLZ22D | D2 | a1 | RO | Z Diode | | | | 0.4 W | | 22.1 V | 20 mA | <30 Ω | | Vz ±2.5% |
| RLZ24D | D2 | a1 | RO | Z Diode | | | | 0.4 W | | 24.2 V | 20 mA | <35 Ω | | Vz ±2.5% |
| RLZ27D | D2 | a1 | RO | Z Diode | | | | 0.4 W | | 27 V | 20 mA | <45 Ω | | Vz ±2.5% |
| RLZ30D | D2 | a1 | RO | Z Diode | | | | 0.4 W | | 29.8 V | 20 mA | <55 Ω | | Vz ±2.5% |
| RLZ33D | D2 | a1 | RO | Z Diode | | | | 0.4 W | | 31.8 V | 20 mA | <65 Ω | | Vz ±2.5% |
| RLZ36D | D2 | a1 | RO | Z Diode | | | | 0.4 W | | 34.9 V | 20 mA | <75 Ω | | Vz ±2.5% |
| RLZ39D | D2 | a1 | RO | Z Diode | | | | 0.4 W | | 37.6 V | 20 mA | <85 Ω | | Vz ±2.5% |
| RLZJ3.6A | D2 | a1 | RO | Z Diode | | | | 0.4 W | | 3.5 V | 5 mA | <130 Ω | | Vz ±2.5% |
| RLZJ3.9A | D2 | a1 | RO | Z Diode | | | | 0.4 W | | 3.8 V | 5 mA | <130 Ω | | Vz ±2.5% |
| RLZJ4.3A | D2 | a1 | RO | Z Diode | | | | 0.4 W | | 4.1 V | 5 mA | <130 Ω | | Vz ±2.5% |
| RLZJ4.7A | D2 | a1 | RO | Z Diode | | | | 0.4 W | | 4.5 V | 5 mA | <130 Ω | | Vz ±2.5% |
| RLZJ5.1A | D2 | a1 | RO | Z Diode | | | | 0.4 W | | 4.9 V | 5 mA | <130 Ω | | Vz ±2.5% |
| RLZJ5.6A | D2 | a1 | RO | Z Diode | | | | 0.4 W | | 5.5 V | 5 mA | <80 Ω | | Vz ±2.5% |
| RLZJ6.2A | D2 | a1 | RO | Z Diode | | | | 0.4 W | | 6 V | 5 mA | <50 Ω | | Vz ±2.5% |
| RLZJ6.8A | D2 | a1 | RO | Z Diode | | | | 0.4 W | | 6.6 V | 5 mA | <30 Ω | | Vz ±2.5% |
| RLZJ7.5A | D2 | a1 | RO | Z Diode | | | | 0.4 W | | 7.2 V | 5 mA | <30 Ω | | Vz ±2.5% |
| RLZJ8.2A | D2 | a1 | RO | Z Diode | | | | 0.4 W | | 7.9 V | 5 mA | <30 Ω | | Vz ±2.5% |
| RLZJ9.1A | D2 | a1 | RO | Z Diode | | | | 0.4 W | | 8.8 V | 5 mA | <30 Ω | | Vz ±2.5% |
| RLZJ10A | D2 | a1 | RO | Z Diode | | | | 0.4 W | | 9.7 V | 5 mA | <30 Ω | | Vz ±2.5% |
| RLZJ11A | D2 | a1 | RO | Z Diode | | | | 0.4 W | | 10.7 V | 5 mA | <30 Ω | | Vz ±2.5% |
| RLZJ12A | D2 | a1 | RO | Z Diode | | | | 0.4 W | | 11.7 V | 5 mA | <35 Ω | | Vz ±2.5% |
| RLZJ13A | D2 | a1 | RO | Z Diode | | | | 0.4 W | | 12.7 V | 5 mA | <35 Ω | | Vz ±2.5% |
| RLZJ15A | D2 | a1 | RO | Z Diode | | | | 0.4 W | | 14.2 V | 5 mA | <40 Ω | | Vz ±2.5% |
| RLZJ16A | D2 | a1 | RO | Z Diode | | | | 0.4 W | | 16.5 V | 5 mA | <40 Ω | | Vz ±2.5% |
| RLZJ18A | D2 | a1 | RO | Z Diode | | | | 0.4 W | | 17.6 V | 5 mA | <45 Ω | | Vz ±2.5% |
| RLZJ20A | D2 | a1 | RO | Z Diode | | | | 0.4 W | | 19.3 V | 5 mA | <50 Ω | | Vz ±2.5% |
| RLZJ22A | D2 | a1 | RO | Z Diode | | | | 0.4 W | | 21.3 V | 5 mA | <55 Ω | | Vz ±2.5% |
| RLZJ24A | D2 | a1 | RO | Z Diode | | | | 0.4 W | | 24.4 V | 5 mA | <60 Ω | | Vz ±2.5% |
| RLZJ3.6B | D2 | a1 | RO | Z Diode | | | | 0.4 W | | 3.7 V | 5 mA | <130 Ω | | Vz ±2.5% |

| Type | Case | Pin-code | | | Maximum Ratings | | | | | Electrical Characteristics | | | TK | |
|---|---|---|---|---|---|---|---|---|---|---|---|---|---|---|
| | | | | | $V_{cla}$ $V_{bro}$ | Its | Izm | Pv | Pvts | Vz | Iz Is | rz | | |
| RLZJ3.9B | D2 | a1 | RO | Z Diode | | | | 0.4 W | | 4 V | 5 mA | <130 Ω | | Vz ±2.5% |
| RLZJ4.3B | D2 | a1 | RO | Z Diode | | | | 0.4 W | | 4.2 V | 5 mA | <130 Ω | | Vz ±2.5% |
| RLZJ4.7B | D2 | a1 | RO | Z Diode | | | | 0.4 W | | 4.6 V | 5 mA | <130 Ω | | Vz ±2.5% |
| RLZJ5.1B | D2 | a1 | RO | Z Diode | | | | 0.4 W | | 5.1 V | 5 mA | <130 Ω | | Vz ±2.5% |
| RLZJ5.6B | D2 | a1 | RO | Z Diode | | | | 0.4 W | | 5.6 V | 5 mA | <80 Ω | | Vz ±2.5% |
| RLZJ6.2B | D2 | a1 | RO | Z Diode | | | | 0.4 W | | 6.2 V | 5 mA | <50 Ω | | Vz ±2.5% |
| RLZJ6.8B | D2 | a1 | RO | Z Diode | | | | 0.4 W | | 6.8 V | 5 mA | <30 Ω | | Vz ±2.5% |
| RLZJ7.5B | D2 | a1 | RO | Z Diode | | | | 0.4 W | | 7.4 V | 5 mA | <30 Ω | | Vz ±2.5% |
| RLZJ8.2B | D2 | a1 | RO | Z Diode | | | | 0.4 W | | 8.2 V | 5 mA | <30 Ω | | Vz ±2.5% |
| RLZJ9.1B | D2 | a1 | RO | Z Diode | | | | 0.4 W | | 9.1 V | 5 mA | <30 Ω | | Vz ±2.5% |
| RLZJ10B | D2 | a1 | RO | Z Diode | | | | 0.4 W | | 10 V | 5 mA | <30 Ω | | Vz ±2.5% |
| RLZJ11B | D2 | a1 | RO | Z Diode | | | | 0.4 W | | 11 V | 5 mA | <30 Ω | | Vz ±2.5% |
| RLZJ12B | D2 | a1 | RO | Z Diode | | | | 0.4 W | | 12 V | 5 mA | <35 Ω | | Vz ±2.5% |
| RLZJ13B | D2 | a1 | RO | Z Diode | | | | 0.4 W | | 12.2 V | 5 mA | <35 Ω | | Vz ±2.5% |
| RLZJ15B | D2 | a1 | RO | Z Diode | | | | 0.4 W | | 14.7 V | 5 mA | <40 Ω | | Vz ±2.5% |
| RLZJ16B | D2 | a1 | RO | Z Diode | | | | 0.4 W | | 15.1 V | 5 mA | <40 Ω | | Vz ±2.5% |
| RLZJ18B | D2 | a1 | RO | Z Diode | | | | 0.4 W | | 18 V | 5 mA | <45 Ω | | Vz ±2.5% |
| RLZJ20B | D2 | a1 | RO | Z Diode | | | | 0.4 W | | 19 V | 5 mA | <50 Ω | | Vz ±2.5% |
| RLZJ22B | D2 | a1 | RO | Z Diode | | | | 0.4 W | | 21 V | 5 mA | <55 Ω | | Vz ±2.5% |
| RLZJ24B | D2 | a1 | RO | Z Diode | | | | 0.4 W | | 24.2 V | 5 mA | <60 Ω | | Vz ±2.5% |
| RLZJ4.3C | D2 | a1 | RO | Z Diode | | | | 0.4 W | | 4.4 V | 5 mA | <130 Ω | | Vz ±2.5% |
| RLZJ4.7C | D2 | a1 | RO | Z Diode | | | | 0.4 W | | 4.8 V | 5 mA | <130 Ω | | Vz ±2.5% |
| RLZJ5.1C | D2 | a1 | RO | Z Diode | | | | 0.4 W | | 5.3 V | 5 mA | <130 Ω | | Vz ±2.5% |
| RLZJ5.6C | D2 | a1 | RO | Z Diode | | | | 0.4 W | | 5.8 V | 5 mA | <80 Ω | | Vz ±2.5% |
| RLZJ6.2C | D2 | a1 | RO | Z Diode | | | | 0.4 W | | 6.4 V | 5 mA | <50 Ω | | Vz ±2.5% |
| RLZJ6.8C | D2 | a1 | RO | Z Diode | | | | 0.4 W | | 7 V | 5 mA | <30 Ω | | Vz ±2.5% |
| RLZJ7.5C | D2 | a1 | RO | Z Diode | | | | 0.4 W | | 7.7 V | 5 mA | <30 Ω | | Vz ±2.5% |
| RLZJ8.2C | D2 | a1 | RO | Z Diode | | | | 0.4 W | | 8.5 V | 5 mA | <30 Ω | | Vz ±2.5% |
| RLZJ9.1C | D2 | a1 | RO | Z Diode | | | | 0.4 W | | 9.4 V | 5 mA | <30 Ω | | Vz ±2.5% |
| RLZJ10C | D2 | a1 | RO | Z Diode | | | | 0.4 W | | 10.3 V | 5 mA | <30 Ω | | Vz ±2.5% |
| RLZJ11C | D2 | a1 | RO | Z Diode | | | | 0.4 W | | 11.3 V | 5 mA | <30 Ω | | Vz ±2.5% |
| RLZJ12C | D2 | a1 | RO | Z Diode | | | | 0.4 W | | 12.3 V | 5 mA | <35 Ω | | Vz ±2.5% |
| RLZJ13C | D2 | a1 | RO | Z Diode | | | | 0.4 W | | 13.7 V | 5 mA | <35 Ω | | Vz ±2.5% |
| RLZJ15C | D2 | a1 | RO | Z Diode | | | | 0.4 W | | 15.2 V | 5 mA | <40 Ω | | Vz ±2.5% |
| RLZJ16C | D2 | a1 | RO | Z Diode | | | | 0.4 W | | 16.7 V | 5 mA | <40 Ω | | Vz ±2.5% |
| RLZJ18C | D2 | a1 | RO | Z Diode | | | | 0.4 W | | 18.6 V | 5 mA | <45 Ω | | Vz ±2.5% |
| RLZJ20C | D2 | a1 | RO | Z Diode | | | | 0.4 W | | 20.7 V | 5 mA | <50 Ω | | Vz ±2.5% |
| RLZJ22C | D2 | a1 | RO | Z Diode | | | | 0.4 W | | 22.7 V | 5 mA | <55 Ω | | Vz ±2.5% |
| RLZJ24C | D2 | a1 | RO | Z Diode | | | | 0.4 W | | 25 V | 5 mA | <60 Ω | | Vz ±2.5% |
| SA5.0 | B1 | a1 | MO | TVS | 9.6 V | 52 mA | 52 mA | | 500 W | | | | | |

| Type | Case | Pin-code | | | Maximum Ratings | | | | | Electrical Characteristics | | | | |
|------|------|----------|---|---|---|---|---|---|---|---|---|---|---|---|
| | | | | | Vcla Vbro | Its | Izm | Pv | Pvts | Vz Is | Iz | rz | TK | |
| SA6.0 | B1 | a1 | MO | TVS | 11.4 V | 43.9 mA | 43.9 mA | | 500 W | | | | | |
| SA6.5 | B1 | a1 | MO | TVS | 12.3 V | 40.7 mA | 40.7 mA | | 500 W | | | | | |
| SA7.0 | B1 | a1 | MO | TVS | 13.3 V | 37.8 mA | 37.8 mA | | 500 W | | | | | |
| SA7.5 | B1 | a1 | MO | TVS | 14.3 V | 35 mA | 35 mA | | 500 W | | | | | |
| SA8.0 | B1 | a1 | MO | TVS | 15 V | 33.3 mA | 33.3 mA | | 500 W | | | | | |
| SA8.5 | B1 | a1 | MO | TVS | 15.9 V | 31.4 mA | 31.4 mA | | 500 W | | | | | |
| SA9.1 | B1 | a1 | MO | TVS | 16.9 V | 29.5 mA | 29.5 mA | | 500 W | | | | | |
| SA10 | B1 | a1 | MO | TVS | 18.8 V | 26.6 mA | 26.6 mA | | 500 W | | | | | |
| SA11 | B1 | a1 | MO | TVS | 20.1 V | 24.9 mA | 24.9 mA | | 500 W | | | | | |
| SA12 | B1 | a1 | MO | TVS | 22 V | 22.7 mA | 22.7 mA | | 500 W | | | | | |
| SA13 | B1 | a1 | MO | TVS | 23.8 V | 21 mA | 21 mA | | 500 W | | | | | |
| SA14 | B1 | a1 | MO | TVS | 25.8 V | 19.4 mA | 19.4 mA | | 500 W | | | | | |
| SA15 | B1 | a1 | MO | TVS | 26.9 V | 18.8 mA | 18.8 mA | | 500 W | | | | | |
| SA16 | B1 | a1 | MO | TVS | 28.8 V | 17.6 mA | 17.6 mA | | 500 W | | | | | |
| SA17 | B1 | a1 | MO | TVS | 30.5 V | 16.4 mA | 16.4 mA | | 500 W | | | | | |
| SA18 | B1 | a1 | MO | TVS | 32.2 V | 15.5 mA | 15.5 mA | | 500 W | | | | | |
| SA20 | B1 | a1 | MO | TVS | 35.8 V | 13.9 mA | 13.9 mA | | 500 W | | | | | |
| SA22 | B1 | a1 | MO | TVS | 39.4 V | 12.7 mA | 12.7 mA | | 500 W | | | | | |
| SA24 | B1 | a1 | MO | TVS | 43 V | 11.6 mA | 11.6 mA | | 500 W | | | | | |
| SA26 | B1 | a1 | MO | TVS | 46.6 V | 10.7 mA | 10.7 mA | | 500 W | | | | | |
| SA28 | B1 | a1 | MO | TVS | 50 V | 9.9 mA | 9.9 mA | | 500 W | | | | | |
| SA30 | B1 | a1 | MO | TVS | 53.5 V | 9.3 mA | 9.3 mA | | 500 W | | | | | |
| SA33 | B1 | a1 | MO | TVS | 59 V | 8.5 mA | 8.5 mA | | 500 W | | | | | |
| SA36 | B1 | a1 | MO | TVS | 64.3 V | 7.8 mA | 7.8 mA | | 500 W | | | | | |
| SA40 | B1 | a1 | MO | TVS | 71.4 V | 7 mA | 7 mA | | 500 W | | | | | |
| SA43 | B1 | a1 | MO | TVS | 76.7 V | 6.5 mA | 6.5 mA | | 500 W | | | | | |
| SA45 | B1 | a1 | MO | TVS | 80.3 V | 6.2 mA | 6.2 mA | | 500 W | | | | | |
| SA48 | B1 | a1 | MO | TVS | 85.5 V | 5.8 mA | 5.8 mA | | 500 W | | | | | |
| SA51 | B1 | a1 | MO | TVS | 91.1 V | 5.5 mA | 5.5 mA | | 500 W | | | | | |
| SA54 | B1 | a1 | MO | TVS | 96.3 V | 5.2 mA | 5.2 mA | | 500 W | | | | | |
| SA58 | B1 | a1 | MO | TVS | 103 V | 4.9 mA | 4.9 mA | | 500 W | | | | | |
| SA60 | B1 | a1 | MO | TVS | 107 V | 4.7 mA | 4.7 mA | | 500 W | | | | | |
| SA64 | B1 | a1 | MO | TVS | 114 V | 4.4 mA | 4.4 mA | | 500 W | | | | | |
| SA70 | B1 | a1 | MO | TVS | 125 V | 4 mA | 4 mA | | 500 W | | | | | |
| SA75 | B1 | a1 | MO | TVS | 134 V | 3.6 mA | 3.6 mA | | 500 W | | | | | |
| SA78 | B1 | a1 | MO | TVS | 139 V | 3.4 mA | 3.4 mA | | 500 W | | | | | |
| SA85 | B1 | a1 | MO | TVS | 151 V | 3.1 mA | 3.1 mA | | 500 W | | | | | |
| SA90 | B1 | a1 | MO | TVS | 160 V | 2.8 mA | 2.8 mA | | 500 W | | | | | |
| SA100 | B1 | a1 | MO | TVS | 179 V | 2.5 mA | 2.5 mA | | 500 W | | | | | |
| SA110 | B1 | a1 | MO | TVS | 196 V | 2.4 mA | 2.4 mA | | 500 W | | | | | |

| Type | Case | Pin-code | | | Maximum Ratings Vcla/Vbro | Its | Izm | Pv | Pvts | Vz/Is | Iz | rz | TK | |
|------|------|----------|---|---|------|------|------|------|------|------|------|------|------|---|
| SA120 | B1 | a1 | MO | TVS | 214 V | 2.3 mA | 2.3 mA | | 500 W | | | | | |
| SA130 | B1 | a1 | MO | TVS | 231 V | 2.2 mA | 2.2 mA | | 500 W | | | | | |
| SA150 | B1 | a1 | MO | TVS | 268 V | 1.9 mA | 1.9 mA | | 500 W | | | | | |
| SA160 | B1 | a1 | MO | TVS | 287 V | 1.7 mA | 1.7 mA | | 500 W | | | | | |
| SA170 | B1 | a1 | MO | TVS | 304 V | 1.6 mA | 1.6 mA | | 500 W | | | | | |
| SA5.0A | B1 | a1 | MO | TVS | 9.2 V | 54.3 mA | 54.3 mA | | 500 W | | | | | P |
| SA6.0A | B1 | a1 | MO | TVS | 10.3 V | 48.5 mA | 48.5 mA | | 500 W | | | | | P |
| SA6.5A | B1 | a1 | MO | TVS | 11.2 V | 44.7 mA | 44.7 mA | | 500 W | | | | | |
| SA7.0A | B1 | a1 | MO | TVS | 12 V | 41.7 mA | 41.7 mA | | 500 W | | | | | |
| SA7.5A | B1 | a1 | MO | TVS | 12.9 V | 38.8 mA | 38.8 mA | | 500 W | | | | | |
| SA8.0A | B1 | a1 | MO | TVS | 13.6 V | 36.7 mA | 36.7 mA | | 500 W | | | | | |
| SA8.5A | B1 | a1 | MO | TVS | 14.4 V | 34.7 mA | 34.7 mA | | 500 W | | | | | |
| SA9.1A | B1 | a1 | MO | TVS | 15.4 V | 32.5 mA | 32.5 mA | | 500 W | | | | | |
| SA10A | B1 | a1 | MO | TVS | 17 V | 29.4 mA | 29.4 mA | | 500 W | | | | | |
| SA11A | B1 | a1 | MO | TVS | 18.2 V | 27.4 mA | 27.4 mA | | 500 W | | | | | |
| SA12A | B1 | a1 | MO | TVS | 19.9 V | 25.1 mA | 25.1 mA | | 500 W | | | | | P |
| SA13A | B1 | a1 | MO | TVS | 21.5 V | 23.2 mA | 23.2 mA | | 500 W | | | | | P |
| SA14A | B1 | a1 | MO | TVS | 23.2 V | 21.5 mA | 21.5 mA | | 500 W | | | | | P |
| SA15A | B1 | a1 | MO | TVS | 24.4 V | 20.6 mA | 20.6 mA | | 500 W | | | | | P |
| SA16A | B1 | a1 | MO | TVS | 26 V | 19.2 mA | 19.2 mA | | 500 W | | | | | |
| SA17A | B1 | a1 | MO | TVS | 27.6 V | 18.1 mA | 18.1 mA | | 500 W | | | | | |
| SA18A | B1 | a1 | MO | TVS | 29.2 V | 17.2 mA | 17.2 mA | | 500 W | | | | | |
| SA20A | B1 | a1 | MO | TVS | 32.4 V | 15.4 mA | 15.4 mA | | 500 W | | | | | |
| SA22A | B1 | a1 | MO | TVS | 35.5 V | 14.1 mA | 14.1 mA | | 500 W | | | | | |
| SA24A | B1 | a1 | MO | TVS | 38.9 V | 12.8 mA | 12.8 mA | | 500 W | | | | | |
| SA26A | B1 | a1 | MO | TVS | 42.1 V | 11.9 mA | 11.9 mA | | 500 W | | | | | |
| SA28A | B1 | a1 | MO | TVS | 45.4 V | 11 mA | 11 mA | | 500 W | | | | | |
| SA30A | B1 | a1 | MO | TVS | 48.4 V | 10.3 mA | 10.3 mA | | 500 W | | | | | |
| SA33A | B1 | a1 | MO | TVS | 53.3 V | 9.4 mA | 9.4 mA | | 500 W | | | | | |
| SA36A | B1 | a1 | MO | TVS | 58.1 V | 8.6 mA | 8.6 mA | | 500 W | | | | | |
| SA40A | B1 | a1 | MO | TVS | 64.5 V | 7.8 mA | 7.8 mA | | 500 W | | | | | |
| SA43A | B1 | a1 | MO | TVS | 69.4 V | 7.2 mA | 7.2 mA | | 500 W | | | | | |
| SA45A | B1 | a1 | MO | TVS | 72.7 V | 6.9 mA | 6.9 mA | | 500 W | | | | | |
| SA48A | B1 | a1 | MO | TVS | 77.4 V | 6.5 mA | 6.5 mA | | 500 W | | | | | |
| SA51A | B1 | a1 | MO | TVS | 82.4 V | 6.1 mA | 6.1 mA | | 500 W | | | | | |
| SA54A | B1 | a1 | MO | TVS | 87.1 V | 5.7 mA | 5.7 mA | | 500 W | | | | | |
| SA58A | B1 | a1 | MO | TVS | 93.6 V | 5.3 mA | 5.3 mA | | 500 W | | | | | |
| SA60A | B1 | a1 | MO | TVS | 96.8 V | 5.2 mA | 5.2 mA | | 500 W | | | | | |
| SA64A | B1 | a1 | MO | TVS | 103 V | 4.9 mA | 4.9 mA | | 500 W | | | | | |
| SA70A | B1 | a1 | MO | TVS | 113 V | 4.4 mA | 4.4 mA | | 500 W | | | | | |

| Type | Case | Pin-code | | | Maximum Ratings | | | | | Electrical Characteristics | | | | |
|---|---|---|---|---|---|---|---|---|---|---|---|---|---|---|
| | | | | | $V_{cla}$ / $V_{bro}$ | Its | Izm | Pv | Pvts | Vz | Iz / Is | rz | TK | |
| SA75A | B1 | a1 | MO | TVS | 121 V | 4.1 mA | 4.1 mA | | 500 W | | | | | |
| SA78A | B1 | a1 | MO | TVS | 126 V | 4 mA | 4 mA | | 500 W | | | | | |
| SA85A | B1 | a1 | MO | TVS | 137 V | 3.6 mA | 3.6 mA | | 500 W | | | | | |
| SA90A | B1 | a1 | MO | TVS | 146 V | 3.4 mA | 3.4 mA | | 500 W | | | | | |
| SA100A | B1 | a1 | MO | TVS | 162 V | 3.1 mA | 3.1 mA | | 500 W | | | | | |
| SA110A | B1 | a1 | MO | TVS | 177 V | 2.8 mA | 2.8 mA | | 500 W | | | | | |
| SA120A | B1 | a1 | MO | TVS | 193 V | 2.5 mA | 2.5 mA | | 500 W | | | | | |
| SA130A | B1 | a1 | MO | TVS | 209 V | 2.4 mA | 2.4 mA | | 500 W | | | | | |
| SA150A | B1 | a1 | MO | TVS | 243 V | 2.1 mA | 2.1 mA | | 500 W | | | | | |
| SA160A | B1 | a1 | MO | TVS | 259 V | 1.9 mA | 1.9 mA | | 500 W | | | | | |
| SA170A | B1 | a1 | MO | TVS | 275 V | 1.8 mA | 1.8 mA | | 500 W | | | | | |
| SA5.0C | B1 | a2 | MO | Bidir. TVS | 9.6 V | 52 mA | 52 mA | | 500 W | | | | | |
| SA6.0C | B1 | a2 | MO | Bidir. TVS | 11.4 V | 43.9 mA | 43.9 mA | | 500 W | | | | | |
| SA6.5C | B1 | a2 | MO | Bidir. TVS | 12.3 V | 40.7 mA | 40.7 mA | | 500 W | | | | | |
| SA7.0C | B1 | a2 | MO | Bidir. TVS | 13.3 V | 37.8 mA | 37.8 mA | | 500 W | | | | | |
| SA7.5C | B1 | a2 | MO | Bidir. TVS | 14.3 V | 35 mA | 35 mA | | 500 W | | | | | |
| SA8.0C | B1 | a2 | MO | Bidir. TVS | 15 V | 33.3 mA | 33.3 mA | | 500 W | | | | | |
| SA8.5C | B1 | a2 | MO | Bidir. TVS | 15.9 V | 31.4 mA | 31.4 mA | | 500 W | | | | | |
| SA9.1C | B1 | a2 | MO | Bidir. TVS | 16.9 V | 29.5 mA | 29.5 mA | | 500 W | | | | | |
| SA10C | B1 | a2 | MO | Bidir. TVS | 18.8 V | 26.6 mA | 26.6 mA | | 500 W | | | | | |
| SA11C | B1 | a2 | MO | Bidir. TVS | 20.1 V | 24.9 mA | 24.9 mA | | 500 W | | | | | |
| SA12C | B1 | a2 | MO | Bidir. TVS | 22 V | 22.7 mA | 22.7 mA | | 500 W | | | | | |
| SA13C | B1 | a2 | MO | Bidir. TVS | 23.8 V | 21 mA | 21 mA | | 500 W | | | | | |
| SA14C | B1 | a2 | MO | Bidir. TVS | 25.8 V | 19.4 mA | 19.4 mA | | 500 W | | | | | |
| SA15C | B1 | a2 | MO | Bidir. TVS | 26.9 V | 18.8 mA | 18.8 mA | | 500 W | | | | | |
| SA16C | B1 | a2 | MO | Bidir. TVS | 28.8 V | 17.6 mA | 17.6 mA | | 500 W | | | | | |
| SA17C | B1 | a2 | MO | Bidir. TVS | 30.5 V | 16.4 mA | 16.4 mA | | 500 W | | | | | |
| SA18C | B1 | a2 | MO | Bidir. TVS | 32.2 V | 15.5 mA | 15.5 mA | | 500 W | | | | | |
| SA20C | B1 | a2 | MO | Bidir. TVS | 35.8 V | 13.9 mA | 13.9 mA | | 500 W | | | | | |
| SA22C | B1 | a2 | MO | Bidir. TVS | 39.4 V | 12.7 mA | 12.7 mA | | 500 W | | | | | |
| SA24C | B1 | a2 | MO | Bidir. TVS | 43 V | 11.6 mA | 11.6 mA | | 500 W | | | | | |
| SA26C | B1 | a2 | MO | Bidir. TVS | 46.6 V | 10.7 mA | 10.7 mA | | 500 W | | | | | |
| SA28C | B1 | a2 | MO | Bidir. TVS | 50 V | 9.9 mA | 9.9 mA | | 500 W | | | | | |
| SA30C | B1 | a2 | MO | Bidir. TVS | 53.5 V | 9.3 mA | 9.3 mA | | 500 W | | | | | |
| SA33C | B1 | a2 | MO | Bidir. TVS | 59 V | 8.5 mA | 8.5 mA | | 500 W | | | | | |
| SA36C | B1 | a2 | MO | Bidir. TVS | 64.3 V | 7.8 mA | 7.8 mA | | 500 W | | | | | |
| SA40C | B1 | a2 | MO | Bidir. TVS | 71.4 V | 7 mA | 7 mA | | 500 W | | | | | |
| SA43C | B1 | a2 | MO | Bidir. TVS | 76.7 V | 6.5 mA | 6.5 mA | | 500 W | | | | | |
| SA45C | B1 | a2 | MO | Bidir. TVS | 80.3 V | 6.2 mA | 6.2 mA | | 500 W | | | | | |
| SA48C | B1 | a2 | MO | Bidir. TVS | 85.5 V | 5.8 mA | 5.8 mA | | 500 W | | | | | |

| Type | Case | Pin-code | | | Maximum Ratings | | | | Electrical Characteristics | | | | |
|------|------|----------|------|------|------|------|------|------|------|------|------|------|------|
| | | | | | Vcla *Vbro* | Its | Izm | Pv | Pvts | Vz | Iz *Is* | rz | TK | |
| SA51C | B1 | a2 | MO | Bidir. TVS | 91.1 V | 5.5 mA | 5.5 mA | | 500 W | | | | | |
| SA54C | B1 | a2 | MO | Bidir. TVS | 96.3 V | 5.2 mA | 5.2 mA | | 500 W | | | | | |
| SA58C | B1 | a2 | MO | Bidir. TVS | 103 V | 4.9 mA | 4.9 mA | | 500 W | | | | | |
| SA60C | B1 | a2 | MO | Bidir. TVS | 107 V | 4.7 mA | 4.7 mA | | 500 W | | | | | |
| SA64C | B1 | a2 | MO | Bidir. TVS | 114 V | 4.4 mA | 4.4 mA | | 500 W | | | | | |
| SA70C | B1 | a2 | MO | Bidir. TVS | 125 V | 4 mA | 4 mA | | 500 W | | | | | |
| SA75C | B1 | a2 | MO | Bidir. TVS | 134 V | 3.6 mA | 3.6 mA | | 500 W | | | | | |
| SA78C | B1 | a2 | MO | Bidir. TVS | 139 V | 3.4 mA | 3.4 mA | | 500 W | | | | | |
| SA85C | B1 | a2 | MO | Bidir. TVS | 151 V | 3.1 mA | 3.1 mA | | 500 W | | | | | |
| SA90C | B1 | a2 | MO | Bidir. TVS | 160 V | 2.8 mA | 2.8 mA | | 500 W | | | | | |
| SA100C | B1 | a2 | MO | Bidir. TVS | 179 V | 2.5 mA | 2.5 mA | | 500 W | | | | | |
| SA110C | B1 | a2 | MO | Bidir. TVS | 196 V | 2.4 mA | 2.4 mA | | 500 W | | | | | |
| SA120C | B1 | a2 | MO | Bidir. TVS | 214 V | 2.3 mA | 2.3 mA | | 500 W | | | | | |
| SA130C | B1 | a2 | MO | Bidir. TVS | 231 V | 2.2 mA | 2.2 mA | | 500 W | | | | | |
| SA150C | B1 | a2 | MO | Bidir. TVS | 268 V | 1.9 mA | 1.9 mA | | 500 W | | | | | |
| SA160C | B1 | a2 | MO | Bidir. TVS | 287 V | 1.7 mA | 1.7 mA | | 500 W | | | | | |
| SA170C | B1 | a2 | MO | Bidir. TVS | 304 V | 1.6 mA | 1.6 mA | | 500 W | | | | | |
| SA5.0CA | B1 | a2 | MO | Bidir. TVS | 9.2 V | 54.3 mA | 54.3 mA | | 500 W | | | | | P |
| SA6.0CA | B1 | a2 | MO | Bidir. TVS | 10.3 V | 48.5 mA | 48.5 mA | | 500 W | | | | | P |
| SA6.5CA | B1 | a2 | MO | Bidir. TVS | 11.2 V | 44.7 mA | 44.7 mA | | 500 W | | | | | |
| SA7.0CA | B1 | a2 | MO | Bidir. TVS | 12 V | 41.7 mA | 41.7 mA | | 500 W | | | | | |
| SA7.5CA | B1 | a2 | MO | Bidir. TVS | 12.9 V | 38.8 mA | 38.8 mA | | 500 W | | | | | |
| SA8.0CA | B1 | a2 | MO | Bidir. TVS | 13.6 V | 36.7 mA | 36.7 mA | | 500 W | | | | | |
| SA8.5CA | B1 | a2 | MO | Bidir. TVS | 14.4 V | 34.7 mA | 34.7 mA | | 500 W | | | | | |
| SA9.1CA | B1 | a2 | MO | Bidir. TVS | 15.4 V | 32.5 mA | 32.5 mA | | 500 W | | | | | |
| SA10CA | B1 | a2 | MO | Bidir. TVS | 17 V | 29.4 mA | 29.4 mA | | 500 W | | | | | |
| SA11CA | B1 | a2 | MO | Bidir. TVS | 18.2 V | 27.4 mA | 27.4 mA | | 500 W | | | | | |
| SA12CA | B1 | a2 | MO | Bidir. TVS | 19.9 V | 25.1 mA | 25.1 mA | | 500 W | | | | | P |
| SA13CA | B1 | a2 | MO | Bidir. TVS | 21.5 V | 23.2 mA | 23.2 mA | | 500 W | | | | | P |
| SA14CA | B1 | a2 | MO | Bidir. TVS | 23.2 V | 21.5 mA | 21.5 mA | | 500 W | | | | | |
| SA15CA | B1 | a2 | MO | Bidir. TVS | 24.4 V | 20.6 mA | 20.6 mA | | 500 W | | | | | P |
| SA16CA | B1 | a2 | MO | Bidir. TVS | 26 V | 19.2 mA | 19.2 mA | | 500 W | | | | | |
| SA17CA | B1 | a2 | MO | Bidir. TVS | 27.6 V | 18.1 mA | 18.1 mA | | 500 W | | | | | |
| SA18CA | B1 | a2 | MO | Bidir. TVS | 29.2 V | 17.2 mA | 17.2 mA | | 500 W | | | | | |
| SA20CA | B1 | a2 | MO | Bidir. TVS | 32.4 V | 15.4 mA | 15.4 mA | | 500 W | | | | | |
| SA22CA | B1 | a2 | MO | Bidir. TVS | 35.5 V | 14.1 mA | 14.1 mA | | 500 W | | | | | |
| SA24CA | B1 | a2 | MO | Bidir. TVS | 38.9 V | 12.8 mA | 12.8 mA | | 500 W | | | | | |
| SA26CA | B1 | a2 | MO | Bidir. TVS | 42.1 V | 11.9 mA | 11.9 mA | | 500 W | | | | | |
| SA28CA | B1 | a2 | MO | Bidir. TVS | 45.4 V | 11 mA | 11 mA | | 500 W | | | | | |
| SA30CA | B1 | a2 | MO | Bidir. TVS | 48.4 V | 10.3 mA | 10.3 mA | | 500 W | | | | | |

| Type | Case | Pin-code | | | Vcla Vbro | Its | Izm | Pv | Pvts | Vz | Iz Is | rz | TK | |
|------|------|----------|---|---|-----------|-----|-----|----|------|----|-------|----|----|---|
| | | | | | **Maximum Ratings** | | | | | **Electrical Characteristics** | | | | |
| SA33CA | B1 | a2 | MO | Bidir. TVS | 53.3 V | 9.4 mA | 9.4 mA | | 500 W | | | | | |
| SA36CA | B1 | a2 | MO | Bidir. TVS | 58.1 V | 8.6 mA | 8.6 mA | | 500 W | | | | | |
| SA40CA | B1 | a2 | MO | Bidir. TVS | 64.5 V | 7.8 mA | 7.8 mA | | 500 W | | | | | |
| SA43CA | B1 | a2 | MO | Bidir. TVS | 69.4 V | 7.2 mA | 7.2 mA | | 500 W | | | | | |
| SA45CA | B1 | a2 | MO | Bidir. TVS | 72.7 V | 6.9 mA | 6.9 mA | | 500 W | | | | | |
| SA48CA | B1 | a2 | MO | Bidir. TVS | 77.4 V | 6.5 mA | 6.5 mA | | 500 W | | | | | |
| SA51CA | B1 | a2 | MO | Bidir. TVS | 82.4 V | 6.1 mA | 6.1 mA | | 500 W | | | | | |
| SA54CA | B1 | a2 | MO | Bidir. TVS | 87.1 V | 5.7 mA | 5.7 mA | | 500 W | | | | | |
| SA58CA | B1 | a2 | MO | Bidir. TVS | 93.6 V | 5.3 mA | 5.3 mA | | 500 W | | | | | |
| SA60CA | B1 | a2 | MO | Bidir. TVS | 96.8 V | 5.2 mA | 5.2 mA | | 500 W | | | | | |
| SA64CA | B1 | a2 | MO | Bidir. TVS | 103 V | 4.9 mA | 4.9 mA | | 500 W | | | | | |
| SA70CA | B1 | a2 | MO | Bidir. TVS | 113 V | 4.4 mA | 4.4 mA | | 500 W | | | | | |
| SA75CA | B1 | a2 | MO | Bidir. TVS | 121 V | 4.1 mA | 4.1 mA | | 500 W | | | | | |
| SA78CA | B1 | a2 | MO | Bidir. TVS | 126 V | 4 mA | 4 mA | | 500 W | | | | | |
| SA85CA | B1 | a2 | MO | Bidir. TVS | 137 V | 3.6 mA | 3.6 mA | | 500 W | | | | | |
| SA90CA | B1 | a2 | MO | Bidir. TVS | 146 V | 3.4 mA | 3.4 mA | | 500 W | | | | | |
| SA100CA | B1 | a2 | MO | Bidir. TVS | 162 V | 3.1 mA | 3.1 mA | | 500 W | | | | | |
| SA110CA | B1 | a2 | MO | Bidir. TVS | 177 V | 2.8 mA | 2.8 mA | | 500 W | | | | | |
| SA120CA | B1 | a2 | MO | Bidir. TVS | 193 V | 2.5 mA | 2.5 mA | | 500 W | | | | | |
| SA130CA | B1 | a2 | MO | Bidir. TVS | 209 V | 2.4 mA | 2.4 mA | | 500 W | | | | | |
| SA150CA | B1 | a2 | MO | Bidir. TVS | 243 V | 2.1 mA | 2.1 mA | | 500 W | | | | | |
| SA160CA | B1 | a2 | MO | Bidir. TVS | 259 V | 1.9 mA | 1.9 mA | | 500 W | | | | | |
| SA170CA | B1 | a2 | MO | Bidir. TVS | 275 V | 1.8 mA | 1.8 mA | | 500 W | | | | | |
| SFPZ68 | G1 | a1 | RD | TVS | | | | | 0.4 kW | | | | | |
| SM5Z3V3A | G1 | a1 | SG | Z Diode | | | | 5 W | 180 W | 3.3 V | 380 mA | $<3\,\Omega$ | $-600 \cdot 10^6/°C$ | |
| SM5Z3V6A | G1 | a1 | SG | Z Diode | | | | 5 W | 180 W | 3.6 V | 350 mA | $<2.5\,\Omega$ | $-550 \cdot 10^6/°C$ | |
| SM5Z3V9A | G1 | a1 | SG | Z Diode | | | | 5 W | 180 W | 3.9 V | 320 mA | $<2\,\Omega$ | $-500 \cdot 10^6/°C$ | |
| SM5Z4V3A | G1 | a1 | SG | Z Diode | | | | 5 W | 180 W | 4.3 V | 290 mA | $<2\,\Omega$ | $-400 \cdot 10^6/°C$ | |
| SM5Z4V7A | G1 | a1 | SG | Z Diode | | | | 5 W | 180 W | 4.7 V | 260 mA | $<2\,\Omega$ | $-200 \cdot 10^6/°C$ | |
| SM5Z5V1A | G1 | a1 | SG | Z Diode | | | | 5 W | 180 W | 5.1 V | 240 mA | $<1.5\,\Omega$ | $100 \cdot 10^6/°C$ P | |
| SM5Z5V6A | G1 | a1 | SG | Z Diode | | | | 5 W | 180 W | 5.6 V | 220 mA | $<1\,\Omega$ | $250 \cdot 10^6/°C$ P | |
| SM5Z6V2A | G1 | a1 | SG | Z Diode | | | | 5 W | 180 W | 6.2 V | 200 mA | $<1\,\Omega$ | $320 \cdot 10^6/°C$ P | |
| SM5Z6V8A | G1 | a1 | SG | Z Diode | | | | 5 W | 180 W | 6.8 V | 175 mA | $<1\,\Omega$ | $400 \cdot 10^6/°C$ | |
| SM5Z7V5A | G1 | a1 | SG | Z Diode | | | | 5 W | 180 W | 7.5 V | 175 mA | $<1.5\,\Omega$ | $450 \cdot 10^6/°C$ P | |
| SM5Z8V2A | G1 | a1 | SG | Z Diode | | | | 5 W | 180 W | 8.2 V | 150 mA | $<1.5\,\Omega$ | $480 \cdot 10^6/°C$ P | |
| SM5Z9V1A | G1 | a1 | SG | Z Diode | | | | 5 W | 180 W | 9.1 V | 150 mA | $<2\,\Omega$ | $510 \cdot 10^6/°C$ | |
| SM5Z10A | G1 | a1 | SG | Z Diode | | | | 5 W | 180 W | 10 V | 125 mA | $<2\,\Omega$ | $650 \cdot 10^6/°C$ P | |
| SM5Z12A | G1 | a1 | SG | Z Diode | | | | 5 W | 180 W | 12 V | 100 mA | $<2.5\,\Omega$ | $650 \cdot 10^6/°C$ P | |
| SM5Z13A | G1 | a1 | SG | Z Diode | | | | 5 W | 180 W | 13 V | 100 mA | $<2.5\,\Omega$ | $650 \cdot 10^6/°C$ P | |
| SM5Z14A | G1 | a1 | SG | Z Diode | | | | 5 W | 180 W | 14 V | 100 mA | $<2.5\,\Omega$ | $700 \cdot 10^6/°C$ | |

| Type | Case | Pin-code | | | Maximum Ratings Vcla Vbro | Its | Izm | Pv | Pvts | Electrical Characteristics Vz | Iz Is | rz | TK | |
|------|------|------|---|---|---|---|---|---|---|---|---|---|---|---|
| SM5Z15A | G1 | a1 SG | | Z Diode | | | | 5 W | 180 W | 15 V | 75 mA | <2.5 Ω | $700 \cdot 10^6/°C$ | P |
| SM5Z16A | G1 | a1 SG | | Z Diode | | | | 5 W | 180 W | 16 V | 75 mA | <2.5 Ω | $700 \cdot 10^6/°C$ | |
| SM5Z18A | G1 | a1 SG | | Z Diode | | | | 5 W | 180 W | 18 V | 65 mA | <2.5 Ω | $750 \cdot 10^6/°C$ | P |
| SM5Z20A | G1 | a1 SG | | Z Diode | | | | 5 W | 180 W | 20 V | 65 mA | <3 Ω | $750 \cdot 10^6/°C$ | P |
| SM5Z22A | G1 | a1 SG | | Z Diode | | | | 5 W | 180 W | 22 V | 50 mA | <3.5 Ω | $800 \cdot 10^6/°C$ | P |
| SM5Z24A | G1 | a1 SG | | Z Diode | | | | 5 W | 180 W | 24 V | 50 mA | <3.5 Ω | $800 \cdot 10^6/°C$ | P |
| SM5Z27A | G1 | a1 SG | | Z Diode | | | | 5 W | 180 W | 27 V | 50 mA | <5 Ω | $850 \cdot 10^6/°C$ | P |
| SM5Z30A | G1 | a1 SG | | Z Diode | | | | 5 W | 180 W | 30 V | 40 mA | <8 Ω | $850 \cdot 10^6/°C$ | P |
| SM5Z33A | G1 | a1 SG | | Z Diode | | | | 5 W | 180 W | 33 V | 40 mA | <10 Ω | $850 \cdot 10^6/°C$ | P |
| SM5Z36A | G1 | a1 SG | | Z Diode | | | | 5 W | 180 W | 36 V | 30 mA | <11 Ω | $900 \cdot 10^6/°C$ | P |
| SM5Z39A | G1 | a1 SG | | Z Diode | | | | 5 W | 180 W | 39 V | 30 mA | <14 Ω | $900 \cdot 10^6/°C$ | P |
| SM5Z47A | G1 | a1 SG | | Z Diode | | | | 5 W | 180 W | 47 V | 25 mA | <25 Ω | $900 \cdot 10^6/°C$ | P |
| SM5Z62A | G1 | a1 SG | | Z Diode | | | | 5 W | 180 W | 62 V | 20 mA | <42 Ω | $900 \cdot 10^6/°C$ | P |
| SM5Z82A | G1 | a1 SG | | Z Diode | | | | 5 W | 180 W | 82 V | 15 mA | <65 Ω | $900 \cdot 10^6/°C$ | P |
| SM5Z91A | G1 | a1 SG | | Z Diode | | | | 5 W | 180 W | 91 V | 15 mA | <75 Ω | $900 \cdot 10^6/°C$ | |
| SM5Z100A | G1 | a1 SG | | Z Diode | | | | 5 W | 180 W | 100 V | 12 mA | <90 Ω | $950 \cdot 10^6/°C$ | P |
| SM5Z110A | G1 | a1 SG | | Z Diode | | | | 5 W | 180 W | 110 V | 12 mA | <125 Ω | $950 \cdot 10^6/°C$ | P |
| SM5Z150A | G1 | a1 SG | | Z Diode | | | | 5 W | 180 W | 150 V | 8 mA | <330 Ω | $950 \cdot 10^6/°C$ | P |
| SM5Z180A | G1 | a1 SG | | Z Diode | | | | 5 W | 180 W | 180 V | 5 mA | <430 Ω | $950 \cdot 10^6/°C$ | P |
| SM5Z200A | G1 | a1 SG | | Z Diode | | | | 5 W | 180 W | 200 V | 5 mA | <480 Ω | $1000 \cdot 10^6/°C$ | P |
| STZ6.8T | F1 | c5 RO | | Bidir. ZD | | | | 0.2 W | | 6.8 V | 5 mA | <40 Ω | | at 3.5V |
| T-LVA347A | A1 | a1 SG | | Z Diode | | | | 0.5 W | | 4.7 V | 10 mA | <10 Ω | | $Nd=1μV/\sqrt{Hz}$ |
| T-LVA351A | A1 | a1 SG | | Z Diode | | | | 0.5 W | | 5.1 V | 5 mA | <10 Ω | | $Nd=1μV/\sqrt{Hz}$ |
| T-LVA356A | A1 | a1 SG | | Z Diode | | | | 0.5 W | | 5.6 V | 1 mA | <40 Ω | | $Nd=1μV/\sqrt{Hz}$ |
| T-LVA362A | A1 | a1 SG | | Z Diode | | | | 0.5 W | | 6.2 V | 1 mA | <45 Ω | | $Nd=1μV/\sqrt{Hz}$ |
| T-LVA368A | A1 | a1 SG | | Z Diode | | | | 0.5 W | | 6.8 V | 1 mA | <50 Ω | | $Nd=1μV/\sqrt{Hz}$ |
| T-LVA375A | A1 | a1 SG | | Z Diode | | | | 0.5 W | | 7.5 V | 1 mA | <50 Ω | | $Nd=1μV/\sqrt{Hz}$ |
| T-LVA382A | A1 | a1 SG | | Z Diode | | | | 0.5 W | | 8.2 V | 1 mA | <60 Ω | | $Nd=1μV/\sqrt{Hz}$ |
| T-LVA391A | A1 | a1 SG | | Z Diode | | | | 0.5 W | | 9.1 V | 1 mA | <60 Ω | | $Nd=2μV/\sqrt{Hz}$ |
| T-LVA3100A | A1 | a1 SG | | Z Diode | | | | 0.5 W | | 10.0 V | 1 mA | <60 Ω | | $Nd=2μV/\sqrt{Hz}$ |
| T-LVA450A | A1 | a1 SG | | Z Diode | | | | 0.25 W | | 5.0 V | 0.25 mA | <700 Ω | $150 \cdot 10^6/°C$ | $Nd=1μV/\sqrt{Hz}$ |
| T-LVA453A | A1 | a1 SG | | Z Diode | | | | 0.25 W | | 5.3 V | 0.25 mA | <250 Ω | $250 \cdot 10^6/°C$ | $Nd=1μV/\sqrt{Hz}$ |
| T-LVA456A | A1 | a1 SG | | Z Diode | | | | 0.25 W | | 5.6 V | 0.25 mA | <100 Ω | $350 \cdot 10^6/°C$ | $Nd=1μV/\sqrt{Hz}$ |
| T-LVA459A | A1 | a1 SG | | Z Diode | | | | 0.25 W | | 5.9 V | 0.25 mA | <100 Ω | $390 \cdot 10^6/°C$ | $Nd=1μV/\sqrt{Hz}$ |
| T-LVA462A | A1 | a1 SG | | Z Diode | | | | 0.25 W | | 6.2 V | 0.25 mA | <100 Ω | $430 \cdot 10^6/°C$ | $Nd=1μV/\sqrt{Hz}$ |
| T-LVA465A | A1 | a1 SG | | Z Diode | | | | 0.25 W | | 6.5 V | 0.25 mA | <100 Ω | $460 \cdot 10^6/°C$ | $Nd=1μV/\sqrt{Hz}$ |
| T-LVA468A | A1 | a1 SG | | Z Diode | | | | 0.25 W | | 6.8 V | 0.25 mA | <175 Ω | $500 \cdot 10^6/°C$ | $Nd=1μV/\sqrt{Hz}$ |
| T-LVA471A | A1 | a1 SG | | Z Diode | | | | 0.25 W | | 7.1 V | 0.25 mA | <175 Ω | $530 \cdot 10^6/°C$ | $Nd=1μV/\sqrt{Hz}$ |
| T-LVA474A | A1 | a1 SG | | Z Diode | | | | 0.25 W | | 7.4 V | 0.25 mA | <175 Ω | $540 \cdot 10^6/°C$ | $Nd=1μV/\sqrt{Hz}$ |
| T-LVA477A | A1 | a1 SG | | Z Diode | | | | 0.25 W | | 7.7 V | 0.25 mA | <175 Ω | $580 \cdot 10^6/°C$ | $Nd=1μV/\sqrt{Hz}$ |

| Type | Case | Pin-code | | | Maximum Ratings | | | | | Electrical Characteristics | | | | |
|---|---|---|---|---|---|---|---|---|---|---|---|---|---|---|
| | | | | | Vcla Vbro | Its | Izm | Pv | Pvts | Vz | Iz Is | rz | TK | |
| T-LVA480A | A1 | a1 | SG | Z Diode | | | | 0.25 W | | 8.0 V | 0.25 mA | <175Ω | 600·10^6/°C | Nd=1µV/√Hz |
| T-LVA483A | A1 | a1 | SG | Z Diode | | | | 0.25 W | | 8.3 V | 0.25 mA | <175Ω | 620·10^6/°C | Nd=1µV/√Hz |
| T-LVA486A | A1 | a1 | SG | Z Diode | | | | 0.25 W | | 8.6 V | 0.25 mA | <175Ω | 640·10^6/°C | Nd=1µV/√Hz |
| T-LVA489A | A1 | a1 | SG | Z Diode | | | | 0.25 W | | 8.9 V | 0.25 mA | <175Ω | 660·10^6/°C | Nd=1µV/√Hz |
| T-LVA492A | A1 | a1 | SG | Z Diode | | | | 0.25 W | | 9.2 V | 0.25 mA | <175Ω | 670·10^6/°C | Nd=1µV/√Hz |
| T-LVA495A | A1 | a1 | SG | Z Diode | | | | 0.25 W | | 9.5 V | 0.25 mA | <175Ω | 680·10^6/°C | Nd=1µV/√Hz |
| T-LVA498A | A1 | a1 | SG | Z Diode | | | | 0.25 W | | 9.8 V | 0.25 mA | <175Ω | 700·10^6/°C | Nd=1µV/√Hz |
| T-LVA47A | A1 | a1 | SG | Z Diode | | | | 0.5 W | | 4.7 V | 10 mA | <15Ω | | Nd=4µV/√Hz |
| T-LVA51A | A1 | a1 | SG | Z Diode | | | | 0.5 W | | 5.1 V | 5 mA | <15Ω | | Nd=4µV/√Hz |
| T-LVA56A | A1 | a1 | SG | Z Diode | | | | 0.5 W | | 5.6 V | 1 mA | <40Ω | | Nd=4µV/√Hz |
| T-LVA62A | A1 | a1 | SG | Z Diode | | | | 0.5 W | | 6.2 V | 1 mA | <50Ω | | Nd=4µV/√Hz |
| T-LVA68A | A1 | a1 | SG | Z Diode | | | | 0.5 W | | 6.8 V | 1 mA | <50Ω | | Nd=4µV/√Hz |
| T-LVA75A | A1 | a1 | SG | Z Diode | | | | 0.5 W | | 7.5 V | 1 mA | <100Ω | | Nd=4µV/√Hz |
| T-LVA82A | A1 | a1 | SG | Z Diode | | | | 0.5 W | | 8.2 V | 1 mA | <100Ω | | Nd=4µV/√Hz |
| T-LVA91A | A1 | a1 | SG | Z Diode | | | | 0.5 W | | 9.1 V | 1 mA | <100Ω | | Nd=4µV/√Hz |
| T-LVA100A | A1 | a1 | SG | Z Diode | | | | 0.5 W | | 10.0 V | 1 mA | <100Ω | | Nd=4µV/√Hz |
| TM4728A | D1 | a1 | SG | Z Diode | | | 276 mA | 1 W | | 3.3 V | 76 mA | <10Ω | -600·10^6/°C | P |
| TM4729A | D1 | a1 | SG | Z Diode | | | 252 mA | 1 W | | 3.6 V | 69 mA | <10Ω | -600·10^6/°C | |
| TM4730A | D1 | a1 | SG | Z Diode | | | 234 mA | 1 W | | 3.9 V | 64 mA | <9Ω | -500·10^6/°C | P |
| TM4731A | D1 | a1 | SG | Z Diode | | | 217 mA | 1 W | | 4.3 V | 58 mA | <9Ω | -300·10^6/°C | |
| TM4732A | D1 | a1 | SG | Z Diode | | | 193 mA | 1 W | | 4.7 V | 53 mA | <8Ω | -100·10^6/°C | P |
| TM4733A | D1 | a1 | SG | Z Diode | | | 178 mA | 1 W | | 5.1 V | 49 mA | <7Ω | 100·10^6/°C | |
| TM4734A | D1 | a1 | SG | Z Diode | | | 162 mA | 1 W | | 5.6 V | 45 mA | <5Ω | 3400·10^6/°C | P |
| TM4735A | D1 | a1 | SG | Z Diode | | | 146 mA | 1 W | | 6.2 V | 41 mA | <2Ω | 400·10^6/°C | P |
| TM4736A | D1 | a1 | SG | Z Diode | | | 133 mA | 1 W | | 6.8 V | 37 mA | <3.5Ω | 500·10^6/°C | P |
| TM4737A | D1 | a1 | SG | Z Diode | | | 121 mA | 1 W | | 7.5 V | 34 mA | <4Ω | 500·10^6/°C | P |
| TM4738A | D1 | a1 | SG | Z Diode | | | 110 mA | 1 W | | 8.2 V | 31 mA | <4.5Ω | 600·10^6/°C | P |
| TM4739A | D1 | a1 | SG | Z Diode | | | 100 mA | 1 W | | 9.1 V | 28 mA | <5Ω | 600·10^6/°C | P |
| TM4740A | D1 | a1 | SG | Z Diode | | | 91 mA | 1 W | | 10 V | 25 mA | 7Ω | 700·10^6/°C | P |
| TM4741A | D1 | a1 | SG | Z Diode | | | 83 mA | 1 W | | 11 V | 23 mA | <8Ω | 700·10^6/°C | |
| TM4742A | D1 | a1 | SG | Z Diode | | | 76 mA | 1 W | | 12 V | 21 mA | <9Ω | 700·10^6/°C | P |
| TM4743A | D1 | a1 | SG | Z Diode | | | 69 mA | 1 W | | 13 V | 19 mA | <10Ω | 700·10^6/°C | |
| TM4744A | D1 | a1 | SG | Z Diode | | | 61 mA | 1 W | | 15 V | 17 mA | <14Ω | 800·10^6/°C | P |
| TM4745A | D1 | a1 | SG | Z Diode | | | 57 mA | 1 W | | 16 V | 15.5 mA | <16Ω | 800·10^6/°C | |
| TM4746A | D1 | a1 | SG | Z Diode | | | 50 mA | 1 W | | 18 V | 14 mA | <20Ω | 800·10^6/°C | |
| TM4747A | D1 | a1 | SG | Z Diode | | | 45 mA | 1 W | | 20 V | 12.5 mA | <22Ω | 800·10^6/°C | |
| TM4748A | D1 | a1 | SG | Z Diode | | | 41 mA | 1 W | | 22 V | 11.5 mA | <23Ω | 800·10^6/°C | |
| TM4749A | D1 | a1 | SG | Z Diode | | | 38 mA | 1 W | | 24 V | 10.5 mA | <25Ω | 800·10^6/°C | |
| TM4750A | D1 | a1 | SG | Z Diode | | | 34 mA | 1 W | | 27 V | 9.5 mA | <35Ω | 900·10^6/°C | |
| TM4751A | D1 | a1 | SG | Z Diode | | | 30 mA | 1 W | | 30 V | 8.5 mA | <40Ω | 900·10^6/°C | |

| Type | Case | Pin-code | | | Vcla Vbro | Its | Izm | Pv | Pvts | Vz | Iz Is | rz | TK | |
|------|------|----------|---|---|-----------|-----|-----|-----|------|-----|-------|-----|----|---|
| | | | | | | | **Maximum Ratings** | | | | **Electrical Characteristics** | | | |
| TM4752A | D1 | a1 | SG | Z Diode | | | 27 mA | 1 W | | 33 V | 7.5 mA | <45 Ω | $900 \cdot 10^6/°C$ | |
| TM4753A | D1 | a1 | SG | Z Diode | | | 25 mA | 1 W | | 36 V | 7.0 mA | <50 Ω | $900 \cdot 10^6/°C$ | |
| TM4754A | D1 | a1 | SG | Z Diode | | | 23 mA | 1 W | | 39 V | 6.5 mA | <60 Ω | $900 \cdot 10^6/°C$ | |
| TM4755A | D1 | a1 | SG | Z Diode | | | 22 mA | 1 W | | 43 V | 6.0 mA | <70 Ω | $900 \cdot 10^6/°C$ | |
| TM4756A | D1 | a1 | SG | Z Diode | | | 19 mA | 1 W | | 47 V | 5.5 mA | <80 Ω | $900 \cdot 10^6/°C$ | |
| TM4757A | D1 | a1 | SG | Z Diode | | | 18 mA | 1 W | | 51 V | 5.0 mA | <95 Ω | $900 \cdot 10^6/°C$ | |
| TM4758A | D1 | a1 | SG | Z Diode | | | 16 mA | 1 W | | 56 V | 4.5 mA | <110 Ω | $900 \cdot 10^6/°C$ | |
| TM4759A | D1 | a1 | SG | Z Diode | | | 14 mA | 1 W | | 62 V | 4.0 mA | <125 Ω | $900 \cdot 10^6/°C$ | |
| TM4760A | D1 | a1 | SG | Z Diode | | | 13 mA | 1 W | | 68 V | 3.7 mA | <150 Ω | $900 \cdot 10^6/°C$ | |
| TM4761A | D1 | a1 | SG | Z Diode | | | 12 mA | 1 W | | 75 V | 3.3 mA | <175 Ω | $900 \cdot 10^6/°C$ | |
| TM4762A | D1 | a1 | SG | Z Diode | | | 11 mA | 1 W | | 82 V | 3.0 mA | <200 Ω | $900 \cdot 10^6/°C$ | |
| TM4763A | D1 | a1 | SG | Z Diode | 69.2 V | | 10 mA | 1 W | | 91 V | 2.8 mA | <250 Ω | $900 \cdot 10^6/°C$ | |
| TM4764A | D1 | a1 | SG | Z Diode | | | 9 mA | 1 W | | 100 V | 2.5 mA | <350 Ω | $900 \cdot 10^6/°C$ | |
| TMM821 | D2 | a1 | SG | Ref. Z Diode | | | | 0.4 W | | 6.2 V | 7.5 mA | <15 Ω | $100 \cdot 10^6/°C$ | |
| TMM823 | D2 | a1 | SG | Ref. Z Diode | | | | 0.4 W | | 6.2 V | 7.5 mA | <15 Ω | $50 \cdot 10^6/°C$ | |
| TMM825 | D2 | a1 | SG | Ref. Z Diode | | | | 0.4 W | | 6.2 V | 7.5 mA | <15 Ω | $20 \cdot 10^6/°C$ | |
| TMM827 | D2 | a1 | SG | Ref. Z Diode | | | | 0.4 W | | 6.2 V | 7.5 mA | <15 Ω | $10 \cdot 10^6/°C$ | |
| TMM829 | D2 | a1 | SG | Ref. Z Diode | | | | 0.4 W | | 6.2 V | 7.5 mA | <15 Ω | $5 \cdot 10^6/°C$ | |
| TMM821A | D2 | a1 | SG | Ref. Z Diode | | | | 0.4 W | | 6.2 V | 7.5 mA | <10 Ω | $100 \cdot 10^6/°C$ | |
| TMM823A | D2 | a1 | SG | Ref. Z Diode | | | | 0.4 W | | 6.2 V | 7.5 mA | <10 Ω | $50 \cdot 10^6/°C$ | |
| TMM825A | D2 | a1 | SG | Ref. Z Diode | | | | 0.4 W | | 6.2 V | 7.5 mA | <10 Ω | $20 \cdot 10^6/°C$ | |
| TMM827A | D2 | a1 | SG | Ref. Z Diode | | | | 0.4 W | | 6.2 V | 7.5 mA | <10 Ω | $10 \cdot 10^6/°C$ | |
| TMM829A | D2 | a1 | SG | Ref. Z Diode | | | | 0.4 W | | 6.2 V | 7.5 mA | <10 Ω | $5 \cdot 10^6/°C$ | |
| TMM4565 | D2 | a1 | SG | Ref. Z Diode | | | | 0.4 W | | 6.4 V | 0.5 mA | <200 Ω | $100 \cdot 10^6/°C$ | |
| TMM4566 | D2 | a1 | SG | Ref. Z Diode | | | | 0.4 W | | 6.4 V | 0.5 mA | <200 Ω | $50 \cdot 10^6/°C$ | |
| TMM4567 | D2 | a1 | SG | Ref. Z Diode | | | | 0.4 W | | 6.4 V | 0.5 mA | <200 Ω | $20 \cdot 10^6/°C$ | |
| TMM4568 | D2 | a1 | SG | Ref. Z Diode | | | | 0.4 W | | 6.4 V | 0.5 mA | <200 Ω | $10 \cdot 10^6/°C$ | |
| TMM4569 | D2 | a1 | SG | Ref. Z Diode | | | | 0.4 W | | 6.4 V | 0.5 mA | <200 Ω | $5 \cdot 10^6/°C$ | |
| TMM4565A | D2 | a1 | SG | Ref. Z Diode | | | | 0.4 W | | 6.4 V | 0.5 mA | <200 Ω | $100 \cdot 10^6/°C$ | |
| TMM4566A | D2 | a1 | SG | Ref. Z Diode | | | | 0.4 W | | 6.4 V | 0.5 mA | <200 Ω | $50 \cdot 10^6/°C$ | |
| TMM4567A | D2 | a1 | SG | Ref. Z Diode | | | | 0.4 W | | 6.4 V | 0.5 mA | <200 Ω | $20 \cdot 10^6/°C$ | |
| TMM4568A | D2 | a1 | SG | Ref. Z Diode | | | | 0.4 W | | 6.4 V | 0.5 mA | <200 Ω | $10 \cdot 10^6/°C$ | |
| TMM4569A | D2 | a1 | SG | Ref. Z Diode | | | | 0.4 W | | 6.4 V | 0.5 mA | <200 Ω | $5 \cdot 10^6/°C$ | |
| TMM4575 | D2 | a1 | SG | Ref. Z Diode | | | | 0.4 W | | 8.5 V | 1 mA | <100 Ω | $100 \cdot 10^6/°C$ | |
| TMM4576 | D2 | a1 | SG | Ref. Z Diode | | | | 0.4 W | | 8.5 V | 1 mA | <100 Ω | $50 \cdot 10^6/°C$ | |
| TMM4577 | D2 | a1 | SG | Ref. Z Diode | | | | 0.4 W | | 8.5 V | 1 mA | <100 Ω | $20 \cdot 10^6/°C$ | |
| TMM4578 | D2 | a1 | SG | Ref. Z Diode | | | | 0.4 W | | 8.5 V | 1 mA | <100 Ω | $10 \cdot 10^6/°C$ | |
| TMM4579 | D2 | a1 | SG | Ref. Z Diode | | | | 0.4 W | | 8.5 V | 1 mA | <100 Ω | $5 \cdot 10^6/°C$ | |
| TMM4575A | D2 | a1 | SG | Ref. Z Diode | | | | 0.4 W | | 8.5 V | 1 mA | <100 Ω | $100 \cdot 10^6/°C$ | |
| TMM4576A | D2 | a1 | SG | Ref. Z Diode | | | | 0.4 W | | 8.5 V | 1 mA | <100 Ω | $50 \cdot 10^6/°C$ | |

| Type | Case | Pin-code | | | $V_{cla}$ $V_{bro}$ / Its | Izm | Pv | Pvts | Vz | Iz / Is | rz | TK | |
|------|------|----------|---|---|------|------|------|------|------|------|------|------|---|
| | | | | | Maximum Ratings | | | | Electrical Characteristics | | | | |
| TMM4577A | D2 | a1 | SG | Ref. Z Diode | | | 0.4 W | | 8.5 V | 1 mA | <100Ω | $20 \cdot 10^6/°C$ | |
| TMM4578A | D2 | a1 | SG | Ref. Z Diode | | | 0.4 W | | 8.5 V | 1 mA | <100Ω | $10 \cdot 10^6/°C$ | |
| TMM4579A | D2 | a1 | SG | Ref. Z Diode | | | 0.4 W | | 8.5 V | 1 mA | <100Ω | $5 \cdot 10^6/°C$ | |
| TMM4614 | D2 | a1 | SG | Z Diode | | 120 mA | 0.25 W | | 1.8 V | 0.25 mA | <1200Ω | | |
| TMM4615 | D2 | a1 | SG | Z Diode | | 110 mA | 0.25 W | | 2.0 V | 0.25 mA | <1250Ω | | |
| TMM4616 | D2 | a1 | SG | Z Diode | | 100 mA | 0.25 W | | 2.2 V | 0.25 mA | <1300Ω | | |
| TMM4617 | D2 | a1 | SG | Z Diode | | 95 mA | 0.25 W | | 2.4 V | 0.25 mA | <1400Ω | | |
| TMM4618 | D2 | a1 | SG | Z Diode | | 90 mA | 0.25 W | | 2.7 V | 0.25 mA | <1500Ω | | |
| TMM4619 | D2 | a1 | SG | Z Diode | | 85 mA | 0.25 W | | 3.0 V | 0.25 mA | <1600Ω | | |
| TMM4620 | D2 | a1 | SG | Z Diode | | 80 mA | 0.25 W | | 3.3 V | 0.25 mA | <1650Ω | | |
| TMM4621 | D2 | a1 | SG | Z Diode | | 75 mA | 0.25 W | | 3.6 V | 0.25 mA | <1700Ω | | |
| TMM4622 | D2 | a1 | SG | Z Diode | | 70 mA | 0.25 W | | 3.9 V | 0.25 mA | <1650Ω | | |
| TMM4623 | D2 | a1 | SG | Z Diode | | 65 mA | 0.25 W | | 4.3 V | 0.25 mA | <1600Ω | | |
| TMM4624 | D2 | a1 | SG | Z Diode | | 60 mA | 0.25 W | | 4.7 V | 0.25 mA | <1550Ω | | |
| TMM4625 | D2 | a1 | SG | Z Diode | | 55 mA | 0.25 W | | 5.1 V | 0.25 mA | <1500Ω | | |
| TMM4626 | D2 | a1 | SG | Z Diode | | 50 mA | 0.25 W | | 5.6 V | 0.25 mA | <1400Ω | | |
| TMM4627 | D2 | a1 | SG | Z Diode | | 45 mA | 0.25 W | | 6.2 V | 0.25 mA | <1200Ω | | |
| TMM5221B | D2 | a1 | SG | Z Diode | | 291 mA | 0.5 W | | 2.4 V | 20 mA | <30Ω | $-850 \cdot 10^6/°C$ | |
| TMM5222B | D2 | a1 | SG | Z Diode | | 182 mA | 0.5 W | | 2.5 V | 20 mA | <30Ω | $-850 \cdot 10^6/°C$ | |
| TMM5223B | D2 | a1 | SG | Z Diode | | 168 mA | 0.5 W | | 2.7 V | 20 mA | <30Ω | $-800 \cdot 10^6/°C$ | |
| TMM5224B | D2 | a1 | SG | Z Diode | | 162 mA | 0.5 W | | 2.8 V | 20 mA | <30Ω | $-800 \cdot 10^6/°C$ | |
| TMM5225B | D2 | a1 | SG | Z Diode | | 151 mA | 0.5 W | | 3.0 V | 20 mA | <29Ω | $-760 \cdot 10^6/°C$ | |
| TMM5226B | D2 | a1 | SG | Z Diode | | 138 mA | 0.5 W | | 3.3 V | 20 mA | <28Ω | $-700 \cdot 10^6/°C$ P | |
| TMM5227B | D2 | a1 | SG | Z Diode | | 126 mA | 0.5 W | | 3.6 V | 20 mA | <24Ω | $-650 \cdot 10^6/°C$ P | |
| TMM5228B | D2 | a1 | SG | Z Diode | | 115 mA | 0.5 W | | 3.9 V | 20 mA | <23Ω | $-600 \cdot 10^6/°C$ P | |
| TMM5229B | D2 | a1 | SG | Z Diode | | 106 mA | 0.5 W | | 4.3 V | 20 mA | <22Ω | $550 \cdot 10^6/°C$ P | |
| TMM5230B | D2 | a1 | SG | Z Diode | | 97 mA | 0.5 W | | 4.7 V | 20 mA | <19Ω | $300 \cdot 10^6/°C$ P | |
| TMM5231B | D2 | a1 | SG | Z Diode | | 89 mA | 0.5 W | | 5.1 V | 20 mA | <17Ω | $300 \cdot 10^6/°C$ P | |
| TMM5232B | D2 | a1 | SG | Z Diode | | 81 mA | 0.5 W | | 5.6 V | 20 mA | <11Ω | $380 \cdot 10^6/°C$ P | |
| TMM5233B | D2 | a1 | SG | Z Diode | | 76 mA | 0.5 W | | 6.0 V | 20 mA | <7Ω | $380 \cdot 10^6/°C$ P | |
| TMM5234B | D2 | a1 | SG | Z Diode | | 73 mA | 0.5 W | | 6.2 V | 20 mA | <7Ω | $450 \cdot 10^6/°C$ P | |
| TMM5235B | D2 | a1 | SG | Z Diode | | 67 mA | 0.5 W | | 6.8 V | 20 mA | <5Ω | $500 \cdot 10^6/°C$ P | |
| TMM5236B | D2 | a1 | SG | Z Diode | | 61 mA | 0.5 W | | 7.5 V | 20 mA | <6Ω | $580 \cdot 10^6/°C$ P | |
| TMM5237B | D2 | a1 | SG | Z Diode | | 55 mA | 0.5 W | | 8.2 V | 20 mA | <8Ω | $620 \cdot 10^6/°C$ P | |
| TMM5238B | D2 | a1 | SG | Z Diode | | 52 mA | 0.5 W | | 8.7 V | 20 mA | <8Ω | $650 \cdot 10^6/°C$ | |
| TMM5239B | D2 | a1 | SG | Z Diode | | 50 mA | 0.5 W | | 9.1 V | 20 mA | <10Ω | $680 \cdot 10^6/°C$ P | |
| TMM5240B | D2 | a1 | SG | Z Diode | | 45 mA | 0.5 W | | 10 V | 20 mA | <17Ω | $750 \cdot 10^6/°C$ P | |
| TMM5241B | D2 | a1 | SG | Z Diode | | 41 mA | 0.5 W | | 11 V | 20 mA | <22Ω | $760 \cdot 10^6/°C$ | |
| TMM5242B | D2 | a1 | SG | Z Diode | | 38 mA | 0.5 W | | 12 V | 20 mA | <30Ω | $770 \cdot 10^6/°C$ P | |
| TMM5243B | D2 | a1 | SG | Z Diode | | 35 mA | 0.5 W | | 13 V | 9.5 mA | <13Ω | $790 \cdot 10^6/°C$ | |

| Type | Case | Pin-code | | | Maximum Ratings | | | | | Electrical Characteristics | | | | |
|---|---|---|---|---|---|---|---|---|---|---|---|---|---|---|
| | | | | | $V_{cla}$ $V_{bro}$ | Its | Izm | Pv | Pvts | Vz | Iz Is | rz | TK | |
| TMM5244B | D2 | a1 | SG | Z Diode | | | 32 mA | 0.5 W | | 14 V | 9.0 mA | <15 Ω | $820 \cdot 10^6/°C$ | P |
| TMM5245B | D2 | a1 | SG | Z Diode | | | 30 mA | 0.5 W | | 15 V | 8.5 mA | <16 Ω | $820 \cdot 10^6/°C$ | P |
| TMM5246B | D2 | a1 | SG | Z Diode | | | 28 mA | 0.5 W | | 16 V | 7.8 mA | <17 Ω | $830 \cdot 10^6/°C$ | |
| TMM5247B | D2 | a1 | SG | Z Diode | | | 27 mA | 0.5 W | | 17 V | 7.4 mA | <19 Ω | $840 \cdot 10^6/°C$ | |
| TMM5248B | D2 | a1 | SG | Z Diode | | | 25 mA | 0.5 W | | 18 V | 7.0 mA | <21 Ω | $850 \cdot 10^6/°C$ | |
| TMM5249B | D2 | a1 | SG | Z Diode | | | 24 mA | 0.5 W | | 19 V | 6.6 mA | <23 Ω | $860 \cdot 10^6/°C$ | |
| TMM5250B | D2 | a1 | SG | Z Diode | | | 23 mA | 0.5 W | | 20 V | 6.2 mA | <25 Ω | $860 \cdot 10^6/°C$ | |
| TMM5251B | D2 | a1 | SG | Z Diode | | | 21 mA | 0.5 W | | 22 V | 5.6 mA | <29 Ω | $870 \cdot 10^6/°C$ | |
| TMM5252B | D2 | a1 | SG | Z Diode | | | 19 mA | 0.5 W | | 24 V | 5.2 mA | <33 Ω | $880 \cdot 10^6/°C$ | |
| TMM5253B | D2 | a1 | SG | Z Diode | | | 18 mA | 0.5 W | | 25 V | 5.0 mA | <35 Ω | $890 \cdot 10^6/°C$ | |
| TMM5254B | D2 | a1 | SG | Z Diode | | | 17 mA | 0.5 W | | 27 V | 4.6 mA | <41 Ω | $900 \cdot 10^6/°C$ | |
| TMM5255B | D2 | a1 | SG | Z Diode | | | 16 mA | 0.5 W | | 28 V | 4.5 mA | <44 Ω | $910 \cdot 10^6/°C$ | |
| TMM5256B | D2 | a1 | SG | Z Diode | | | 15 mA | 0.5 W | | 30 V | 4.2 mA | <49 Ω | $910 \cdot 10^6/°C$ | |
| TMM5257B | D2 | a1 | SG | Z Diode | | | 14 mA | 0.5 W | | 33 V | 3.8 mA | <58 Ω | $920 \cdot 10^6/°C$ | |
| TMM5258B | D2 | a1 | SG | Z Diode | | | 13 mA | 0.5 W | | 36 V | 3.4 mA | <70 Ω | $930 \cdot 10^6/°C$ | |
| TMM5259B | D2 | a1 | SG | Z Diode | | | 12 mA | 0.5 W | | 39 V | 3.2 mA | <80 Ω | $940 \cdot 10^6/°C$ | |
| TMM5260B | D2 | a1 | SG | Z Diode | | | 11 mA | 0.5 W | | 43 V | 3.0 mA | <93 Ω | $950 \cdot 10^6/°C$ | |
| TMM5261B | D2 | a1 | SG | Z Diode | | | 10 mA | 0.5 W | | 47 V | 2.7 mA | <105 Ω | $950 \cdot 10^6/°C$ | |
| TMM5262B | D2 | a1 | SG | Z Diode | | | 9 mA | 0.5 W | | 51 V | 2.5 mA | <125 Ω | $960 \cdot 10^6/°C$ | |
| TMM5263B | D2 | a1 | SG | Z Diode | | | 8 mA | 0.5 W | | 56 V | 2.2 mA | <150 Ω | $960 \cdot 10^6/°C$ | |
| TMM5264B | D2 | a1 | SG | Z Diode | | | 8 mA | 0.5 W | | 60 V | 2.1 mA | <170 Ω | $970 \cdot 10^6/°C$ | |
| TMM5265B | D2 | a1 | SG | Z Diode | | | 7 mA | 0.5 W | | 62 V | 2.0 mA | <185 Ω | $970 \cdot 10^6/°C$ | |
| TMM5266B | D2 | a1 | SG | Z Diode | | | 7 mA | 0.5 W | | 68 V | 1.8 mA | <230 Ω | $970 \cdot 10^6/°C$ | |
| TMM5267B | D2 | a1 | SG | Z Diode | | | 6 mA | 0.5 W | | 75 V | 1.7 mA | <270 Ω | $980 \cdot 10^6/°C$ | |
| TMM5268B | D2 | a1 | SG | Z Diode | | | 6 mA | 0.5 W | | 82 V | 1.5 mA | <330 Ω | $980 \cdot 10^6/°C$ | |
| TMM5269B | D2 | a1 | SG | Z Diode | | | 5 mA | 0.5 W | | 87 V | 1.4 mA | <370 Ω | $990 \cdot 10^6/°C$ | |
| TMM5270B | D2 | a1 | SG | Z Diode | | | 5 mA | 0.5 W | | 910 V | 1.4 mA | <400 Ω | $990 \cdot 10^6/°C$ | |
| TMM5271B | D2 | a1 | SG | Z Diode | | | 5 mA | 0.5 W | | 100 V | 1.3 mA | <500 Ω | $1100 \cdot 10^6/°C$ | |
| TRLG3210 | M1 | a1 | TE | Ref. LED | | | | | | | | 20 Ω | $800 \cdot 10^6/°C$ | green |
| TRLR3160 | M1 | a1 | TE | Ref. LED | | | | | | | | 10 Ω | $1200 \cdot 10^6/°C$ | red |
| TZM55C2V4 | D2 | a1 | TE | Z Diode | | | | 0.5 W | | 2.4 V | 5 mA | <85 Ω | $-900 \cdot 10^6/°C$ | |
| TZM55C2V7 | D2 | a1 | TE | Z Diode | | | | 0.5 W | | 2.7 V | 5 mA | <85 Ω | $-900 \cdot 10^6/°C$ | |
| TZM55C3V0 | D2 | a1 | TE | Z Diode | | | | 0.5 W | | 3.0 V | 5 mA | <90 Ω | $-800 \cdot 10^6/°C$ | |
| TZM55C3V3 | D2 | a1 | TE | Z Diode | | | | 0.5 W | | 3.3 V | 5 mA | <90 Ω | $-800 \cdot 10^6/°C$ | |
| TZM55C3V6 | D2 | a1 | TE | Z Diode | | | | 0.5 W | | 3.6 V | 5 mA | <90 Ω | $-800 \cdot 10^6/°C$ | |
| TZM55C3V9 | D2 | a1 | TE | Z Diode | | | | 0.5 W | | 3.9 V | 5 mA | <90 Ω | $-800 \cdot 10^6/°C$ | |
| TZM55C4V3 | D2 | a1 | TE | Z Diode | | | | 0.5 W | | 4.3 V | 5 mA | <90 Ω | $-600 \cdot 10^6/°C$ | |
| TZM55C4V7 | D2 | a1 | TE | Z Diode | | | | 0.5 W | | 4.7 V | 5 mA | <80 Ω | $-500 \cdot 10^6/°C$ | |
| TZM55C5V1 | D2 | a1 | TE | Z Diode | | | | 0.5 W | | 5.1 V | 5 mA | <60 Ω | $200 \cdot 10^6/°C$ | |
| TZM55C5V6 | D2 | a1 | TE | Z Diode | | | | 0.5 W | | 5.6 V | 5 mA | <40 Ω | $500 \cdot 10^6/°C$ | |

| Type | Case | Pin-code | | | $V_{cla}$ $V_{bro}$ | Its | Izm | Pv | Pvts | Vz | Iz Is | rz | TK | |
|------|------|----------|---|---|------|-----|-----|-----|------|-----|-------|-----|-----|---|
| | | | | | **Maximum Ratings** | | | | | **Electrical Characteristics** | | | | |
| TZM55C6V2 | D2 | a1 | TE | Z Diode | | | | 0.5 W | | 6.2 V | 5 mA | $<10\,\Omega$ | $600 \cdot 10^6/°C$ | |
| TZM55C6V8 | D2 | a1 | TE | Z Diode | | | | 0.5 W | | 6.8 V | 5 mA | $<8\,\Omega$ | $700 \cdot 10^6/°C$ | |
| TZM55C7V5 | D2 | a1 | TE | Z Diode | | | | 0.5 W | | 7.5 V | 5 mA | $<7\,\Omega$ | $700 \cdot 10^6/°C$ | |
| TZM55C8V2 | D2 | a1 | TE | Z Diode | | | | 0.5 W | | 8.2 V | 5 mA | $<7\,\Omega$ | $800 \cdot 10^6/°C$ | |
| TZM55C9V1 | D2 | a1 | TE | Z Diode | | | | 0.5 W | | 9.1 V | 5 mA | $<10\,\Omega$ | $900 \cdot 10^6/°C$ | |
| TZM55C10 | D2 | a1 | TE | Z Diode | | | | 0.5 W | | 10 V | 5 mA | $<15\,\Omega$ | $1000 \cdot 10^6/°C$ | |
| TZM55C11 | D2 | a1 | TE | Z Diode | | | | 0.5 W | | 11 V | 5 mA | $<20\,\Omega$ | $1100 \cdot 10^6/°C$ | |
| TZM55C12 | D2 | a1 | TE | Z Diode | | | | 0.5 W | | 12 V | 5 mA | $<20\,\Omega$ | $1100 \cdot 10^6/°C$ | |
| TZM55C13 | D2 | a1 | TE | Z Diode | | | | 0.5 W | | 13 V | 5 mA | $<26\,\Omega$ | $1100 \cdot 10^6/°C$ | |
| TZM55C15 | D2 | a1 | TE | Z Diode | | | | 0.5 W | | 15 V | 5 mA | $<30\,\Omega$ | $1100 \cdot 10^6/°C$ | |
| TZM55C16 | D2 | a1 | TE | Z Diode | | | | 0.5 W | | 16 V | 5 mA | $<40\,\Omega$ | $1100 \cdot 10^6/°C$ | |
| TZM55C18 | D2 | a1 | TE | Z Diode | | | | 0.5 W | | 18 V | 5 mA | $<50\,\Omega$ | $1100 \cdot 10^6/°C$ | |
| TZM55C20 | D2 | a1 | TE | Z Diode | | | | 0.5 W | | 20 V | 5 mA | $<55\,\Omega$ | $1100 \cdot 10^6/°C$ | |
| TZM55C22 | D2 | a1 | TE | Z Diode | | | | 0.5 W | | 22 V | 5 mA | $<55\,\Omega$ | $1200 \cdot 10^6/°C$ | |
| TZM55C24 | D2 | a1 | TE | Z Diode | | | | 0.5 W | | 24 V | 5 mA | $<80\,\Omega$ | $1200 \cdot 10^6/°C$ | |
| TZM55C27 | D2 | a1 | TE | Z Diode | | | | 0.5 W | | 27 V | 5 mA | $<80\,\Omega$ | $1200 \cdot 10^6/°C$ | |
| TZM55C30 | D2 | a1 | TE | Z Diode | | | | 0.5 W | | 30 V | 5 mA | $<80\,\Omega$ | $1200 \cdot 10^6/°C$ | |
| TZM55C33 | D2 | a1 | TE | Z Diode | | | | 0.5 W | | 33 V | 5 mA | $<80\,\Omega$ | $1200 \cdot 10^6/°C$ | |
| TZM55C36 | D2 | a1 | TE | Z Diode | | | | 0.5 W | | 36 V | 5 mA | $<80\,\Omega$ | $1200 \cdot 10^6/°C$ | |
| TZM55C39 | D2 | a1 | TE | Z Diode | | | | 0.5 W | | 39 V | 2.5 mA | $<90\,\Omega$ | $1200 \cdot 10^6/°C$ | |
| TZM55C43 | D2 | a1 | TE | Z Diode | | | | 0.5 W | | 43 V | 2.5 mA | $<90\,\Omega$ | $1200 \cdot 10^6/°C$ | |
| TZM55C47 | D2 | a1 | TE | Z Diode | | | | 0.5 W | | 47 V | 2.5 mA | $<110\,\Omega$ | $1200 \cdot 10^6/°C$ | |
| TZM55C51 | D2 | a1 | TE | Z Diode | | | | 0.5 W | | 51 V | 2.5 mA | $<125\,\Omega$ | $1200 \cdot 10^6/°C$ | |
| TZM55C56 | D2 | a1 | TE | Z Diode | | | | 0.5 W | | 56 V | 2.5 mA | $<135\,\Omega$ | $1200 \cdot 10^6/°C$ | |
| TZM55C62 | D2 | a1 | TE | Z Diode | | | | 0.5 W | | 62 V | 2.5 mA | $<150\,\Omega$ | $1200 \cdot 10^6/°C$ | |
| TZM55C68 | D2 | a1 | TE | Z Diode | | | | 0.5 W | | 68 V | 2.5 mA | $<200\,\Omega$ | $1200 \cdot 10^6/°C$ | |
| TZM55C75 | D2 | a1 | TE | Z Diode | | | | 0.5 W | | 75 V | 2.5 mA | $<250\,\Omega$ | $1200 \cdot 10^6/°C$ | |
| TZM5221B | D2 | a1 | TE | Z Diode | | 191 mA | | 0.5 W | | 2.4 V | 20 mA | $<30\,\Omega$ | $-850 \cdot 10^6/°C$ | |
| TZM5222B | D2 | a1 | TE | Z Diode | | 182 mA | | 0.5 W | | 2.5 V | 20 mA | $<30\,\Omega$ | $-850 \cdot 10^6/°C$ | |
| TZM5223B | D2 | a1 | TE | Z Diode | | 168 mA | | 0.5 W | | 2.7 V | 20 mA | $<30\,\Omega$ | $-800 \cdot 10^6/°C$ | |
| TZM5224B | D2 | a1 | TE | Z Diode | | 162 mA | | 0.5 W | | 2.8 V | 20 mA | $<30\,\Omega$ | $-800 \cdot 10^6/°C$ | |
| TZM5225B | D2 | a1 | TE | Z Diode | | 151 mA | | 0.5 W | | 3.0 V | 20 mA | $<29\,\Omega$ | $-750 \cdot 10^6/°C$ | |
| TZM5226B | D2 | a1 | TE | Z Diode | | 138 mA | | 0.5 W | | 3.3 V | 20 mA | $<28\,\Omega$ | $-700 \cdot 10^6/°C$ | |
| TZM5227B | D2 | a1 | TE | Z Diode | | 126 mA | | 0.5 W | | 3.6 V | 20 mA | $<24\,\Omega$ | $-650 \cdot 10^6/°C$ | |
| TZM5228B | D2 | a1 | TE | Z Diode | | 115 mA | | 0.5 W | | 3.9 V | 20 mA | $<23\,\Omega$ | $-600 \cdot 10^6/°C$ | |
| TZM5229B | D2 | a1 | TE | Z Diode | | 106 mA | | 0.5 W | | 4.3 V | 20 mA | $<22\,\Omega$ | $550 \cdot 10^6/°C$ | |
| TZM5230B | D2 | a1 | TE | Z Diode | | 97 mA | | 0.5 W | | 4.7 V | 20 mA | $<19\,\Omega$ | $300 \cdot 10^6/°C$ | |
| TZM5231B | D2 | a1 | TE | Z Diode | | 89 mA | | 0.5 W | | 5.1 V | 20 mA | $<17\,\Omega$ | $300 \cdot 10^6/°C$ | |
| TZM5232B | D2 | a1 | TE | Z Diode | | 81 mA | | 0.5 W | | 5,6 V | 20 mA | $<11\,\Omega$ | $380 \cdot 10^6/°C$ | |
| TZM5233B | D2 | a1 | TE | Z Diode | | 76 mA | | 0.5 W | | 6.0 V | 20 mA | $<7\,\Omega$ | $380 \cdot 10^6/°C$ | |

| Type | Case | Pin-code | | | Maximum Ratings | | | | | Electrical Characteristics | | | | |
|------|------|----------|---|---|---|---|---|---|---|---|---|---|---|---|
| | | | | | Vcla Vbro | Its | Izm | Pv | Pvts | Vz | Iz Is | rz | TK | |
| TZM5234B | D2 | a1 | TE | Z Diode | | | 73 mA | 0.5 W | | 6.2 V | 20 mA | <7 Ω | 450·10⁶/°C | |
| TZM5235B | D2 | a1 | TE | Z Diode | | | 67 mA | 0.5 W | | 6.8 V | 20 mA | <5 Ω | 500·10⁶/°C | |
| TZM5236B | D2 | a1 | TE | Z Diode | | | 61 mA | 0.5 W | | 7.0 V | 20 mA | <6 Ω | 580·10⁶/°C | |
| TZM5237B | D2 | a1 | TE | Z Diode | | | 55 mA | 0.5 W | | 8.2 V | 20 mA | <8 Ω | 620·10⁶/°C | |
| TZM5238B | D2 | a1 | TE | Z Diode | | | 52 mA | 0.5 W | | 8.7 V | 20 mA | <8 Ω | 650·10⁶/°C | |
| TZM5239B | D2 | a1 | TE | Z Diode | | | 50 mA | 0.5 W | | 9.1 V | 20 mA | <10 Ω | 680·10⁶/°C | |
| TZM5240B | D2 | a1 | TE | Z Diode | | | 45 mA | 0.5 W | | 10 V | 20 mA | <17 Ω | 750·10⁶/°C | |
| TZM5241B | D2 | a1 | TE | Z Diode | | | 41 mA | 0.5 W | | 11 V | 20 mA | <22 Ω | 760·10⁶/°C | |
| TZM5242B | D2 | a1 | TE | Z Diode | | | 38 mA | 0.5 W | | 12 V | 20 mA | <30 Ω | 770·10⁶/°C | |
| TZM5243B | D2 | a1 | TE | Z Diode | | | 35 mA | 0.5 W | | 13 V | 9.5 mA | <13 Ω | 790·10⁶/°C | |
| TZM5244B | D2 | a1 | TE | Z Diode | | | 32 mA | 0.5 W | | 14 V | 9.0 mA | <15 Ω | 820·10⁶/°C | |
| TZM5245B | D2 | a1 | TE | Z Diode | | | 30 mA | 0.5 W | | 15 V | 8.5 mA | <16 Ω | 820·10⁶/°C | |
| TZM5246B | D2 | a1 | TE | Z Diode | | | 28 mA | 0.5 W | | 16 V | 7.8 mA | <17 Ω | 830·10⁶/°C | |
| TZM5247B | D2 | a1 | TE | Z Diode | | | 27 mA | 0.5 W | | 17 V | 7.4 mA | <19 Ω | 840·10⁶/°C | |
| TZM5248B | D2 | a1 | TE | Z Diode | | | 25 mA | 0.5 W | | 18 V | 7.0 mA | <21 Ω | 850·10⁶/°C | |
| TZM5249B | D2 | a1 | TE | Z Diode | | | 24 mA | 0.5 W | | 19 V | 6.6 mA | <23 Ω | 860·10⁶/°C | |
| TZM5250B | D2 | a1 | TE | Z Diode | | | 23 mA | 0.5 W | | 20 V | 6.2 mA | <25 Ω | 860·10⁶/°C | |
| TZM5251B | D2 | a1 | TE | Z Diode | | | 21 mA | 0.5 W | | 22 V | 5.6 mA | <29 Ω | 870·10⁶/°C | |
| TZM5252B | D2 | a1 | TE | Z Diode | | | 19 mA | 0.5 W | | 24 V | 5.2 mA | <33 Ω | 880·10⁶/°C | |
| TZM5253B | D2 | a1 | TE | Z Diode | | | 18 mA | 0.5 W | | 25 V | 5.0 mA | <35 Ω | 890·10⁶/°C | |
| TZM5254B | D2 | a1 | TE | Z Diode | | | 17 mA | 0.5 W | | 27 V | 4.6 mA | <41 Ω | 900·10⁶/°C | |
| TZM5255B | D2 | a1 | TE | Z Diode | | | 16 mA | 0.5 W | | 28 V | 4.5 mA | <44 Ω | 910·10⁶/°C | |
| TZM5256B | D2 | a1 | TE | Z Diode | | | 15 mA | 0.5 W | | 30 V | 4.2 mA | <49 Ω | 910·10⁶/°C | |
| TZM5257B | D2 | a1 | TE | Z Diode | | | 14 mA | 0.5 W | | 33 V | 3.8 mA | <58 Ω | 920·10⁶/°C | |
| TZM5258B | D2 | a1 | TE | Z Diode | | | 13 mA | 0.5 W | | 36 V | 3.4 mA | <70 Ω | 930·10⁶/°C | |
| TZM5259B | D2 | a1 | TE | Z Diode | | | 12 mA | 0.5 W | | 39 V | 3.2 mA | <80 Ω | 940·10⁶/°C | |
| TZM5260B | D2 | a1 | TE | Z Diode | | | 11 mA | 0.5 W | | 43 V | 3.0 mA | <93 Ω | 950·10⁶/°C | |
| TZM5261B | D2 | a1 | TE | Z Diode | | | 10 mA | 0.5 W | | 47 V | 2.7 mA | <105 Ω | 950·10⁶/°C | |
| TZM5262B | D2 | a1 | TE | Z Diode | | | 9 mA | 0.5 W | | 51 V | 2.5 mA | <125 Ω | 960·10⁶/°C | |
| TZM5263B | D2 | a1 | TE | Z Diode | | | 8 mA | 0.5 W | | 56 V | 2.3 mA | <150 Ω | 960·10⁶/°C | |
| TZM5264B | D2 | a1 | TE | Z Diode | | | 8 mA | 0.5 W | | 60 V | 2.1 mA | <170 Ω | 970·10⁶/°C | |
| TZM5265B | D2 | a1 | TE | Z Diode | | | 7 mA | 0.5 W | | 62 V | 2.0 mA | <185 Ω | 970·10⁶/°C | |
| TZM5266B | D2 | a1 | TE | Z Diode | | | 7 mA | 0.5 W | | 68 V | 1.8 mA | <230 Ω | 970·10⁶/°C | |
| TZM5267B | D2 | a1 | TE | Z Diode | | | 6 mA | 0.5 W | | 75 V | 1.7 mA | <270 Ω | | |
| U1ZB12 | G5 | a1 | TO | Z Diode | | | | 1 W | | 12 V | 10 mA | <30 Ω | 13 mV | Vz ±10% |
| U1ZB13 | G5 | a1 | TO | Z Diode | | | | 1 W | | 13 V | 10 mA | <30 Ω | 14 mV | Vz ±10% |
| U1ZB15 | G5 | a1 | TO | Z Diode | | | | 1 W | | 15 V | 10 mA | <30 Ω | 17 mV | Vz ±10% |
| U1ZB16 | G5 | a1 | TO | Z Diode | | | | 1 W | | 16 V | 10 mA | <30 Ω | 19 mV | Vz ±10% |
| U1ZB18 | G5 | a1 | TO | Z Diode | | | | 1 W | | 18 V | 10 mA | <30 Ω | 23 mV | Vz ±10% |
| U1ZB20 | G5 | a1 | TO | Z Diode | | | | 1 W | | 20 V | 10 mA | <30 Ω | 26 mV | Vz ±10% |

**U1ZB22 – ZM4729**

| Type | Case | Pin-code | | | Maximum Ratings | | | | | Electrical Characteristics | | | | |
|---|---|---|---|---|---|---|---|---|---|---|---|---|---|---|
| | | | | | Vcla Vbro | Its | Izm | Pv | Pvts | Vz | Iz Is | rz | TK | |
| U1ZB22 | G5 | a1 | TO | Z Diode | | | | 1 W | | 22 V | 10 mA | <30Ω | 28 mV | Vz ±10% |
| U1ZB24 | G5 | a1 | TO | Z Diode | | | | 1 W | | 24 V | 10 mA | <30Ω | 32 mV | Vz ±10% |
| U1ZB27 | G5 | a1 | TO | Z Diode | | | | 1 W | | 27 V | 10 mA | <30Ω | 36 mV | Vz ±10% |
| U1ZB30 | G5 | a1 | TO | Z Diode | | | | 1 W | | 30 V | 10 mA | <30Ω | 40 mV | Vz ±10% |
| U1ZB33 | G5 | a1 | TO | Z Diode | | | | 1 W | | 33 V | 10 mA | <30Ω | 41 mV | Vz ±10% |
| U1ZB36 | G5 | a1 | TO | Z Diode | | | | 1 W | | 36 V | 9 mA | <30Ω | 45 mV | Vz ±10% |
| U1ZB43 | G5 | a1 | TO | Z Diode | | | | 1 W | | 43 V | 7 mA | <30Ω | 53 mV | Vz ±10% |
| U1ZB47 | G5 | a1 | TO | Z Diode | | | | 1 W | | 47 V | 6 mA | <65Ω | 60 mV | Vz ±10% |
| U1ZB51 | G5 | a1 | TO | Z Diode | | | | 1 W | | 51 V | 6 mA | <65Ω | 68 mV | Vz ±10% |
| U1ZB68 | G5 | a1 | TO | Z Diode | | | | 1 W | | 68 V | 4 mA | <120Ω | 90 mV | Vz ±10% |
| U1ZB75 | G5 | a1 | TO | Z Diode | | | | 1 W | | 75 V | 4 mA | <150Ω | 104 mV | Vz ±10% |
| U1ZB82 | G5 | a1 | TO | Z Diode | | | | 1 W | | 82 V | 3 mA | <170Ω | 113 mV | Vz ±10% |
| U1ZB100 | G5 | a1 | TO | Z Diode | | | | 1 W | | 100 V | 3 mA | <300Ω | 138 mV | Vz ±10% |
| U1ZB110 | G5 | a1 | TO | Z Diode | | | | 1 W | | 110 V | 3 mA | <300Ω | 152 mV | Vz ±10% |
| U1ZB150 | G5 | a1 | TO | Z Diode | | | | 1 W | | 150 V | 2 mA | <450Ω | 212 mV | Vz ±10% |
| U1ZB180 | G5 | a1 | TO | Z Diode | | | | 1 W | | 180 V | 1.5 mA | <500Ω | 155 mV | Vz ±10% |
| U1ZB200 | G5 | a1 | TO | Z Diode | | | | 1 W | | 200 V | 0.5 mA | <500Ω | 169 mV | Vz ±10% |
| U1ZB200-Y | G5 | a1 | TO | Z Diode | | | | 1 W | | 200 V | 0.5 mA | <500Ω | 169 mV | Vz ±5% |
| U1ZB200-Z | G5 | a1 | TO | Z Diode | | | | 1 W | | 210 V | 0.5 mA | <500Ω | 169 mV | Vz ±5% |
| U1ZB220 | G5 | a1 | TO | Z Diode | | | | 1 W | | 220 V | 0.5 mA | <5kΩ | 309 mV | Vz ±10% |
| U1ZB220-Y | G5 | a1 | TO | Z Diode | | | | 1 W | | 220 V | 0.5 mA | <5kΩ | 309 mV | Vz ±5% |
| U1ZB220-Z | G5 | a1 | TO | Z Diode | | | | 1 W | | 230 V | 0.5 mA | <5kΩ | 309 mV | Vz ±5% |
| U1ZB240 | G5 | a1 | TO | Z Diode | | | | 1 W | | 240 V | 0.5 mA | <5kΩ | 243 mV | Vz ±10% |
| U1ZB240-Y | G5 | a1 | TO | Z Diode | | | | 1 W | | 240 V | 0.5 mA | <5kΩ | 243 mV | Vz ±5% |
| U1ZB240-Z | G5 | a1 | TO | Z Diode | | | | 1 W | | 250 V | 0.5 mA | <5kΩ | 243 mV | Vz ±5% |
| U1ZB270 | G5 | a1 | TO | Z Diode | | | | 1 W | | 270 V | 0.5 mA | <5kΩ | 385 mV | Vz ±10% |
| U1ZB270-X | G5 | a1 | TO | Z Diode | | | | 1 W | | 260 V | 0.5 mA | <5kΩ | 385 mV | Vz ±5% |
| U1ZB270-Y | G5 | a1 | TO | Z Diode | | | | 1 W | | 270 V | 0.5 mA | <5kΩ | 385 mV | Vz ±5% |
| U1ZB270-Z | G5 | a1 | TO | Z Diode | | | | 1 W | | 280 V | 0.5 mA | <5kΩ | 385 mV | Vz ±5% |
| U1ZB300 | G5 | a1 | TO | Z Diode | | | | 1 W | | 300 V | 0.5 mA | <5kΩ | 428 mV | Vz ±10% |
| U1ZB300-X | G5 | a1 | TO | Z Diode | | | | 1 W | | 290 V | 0.5 mA | <5kΩ | 428 mV | Vz ±5% |
| U1ZB300-Y | G5 | a1 | TO | Z Diode | | | | 1 W | | 300 V | 0.5 mA | <5kΩ | 428 mV | Vz ±5% |
| U1ZB300-Z | G5 | a1 | TO | Z Diode | | | | 1 W | | 311 V | 0.5 mA | <5kΩ | 428 mV | Vz ±5% |
| U1ZB330 | G5 | a1 | TO | Z Diode | | | | 1 W | | 330 V | 0.5 mA | <5kΩ | 470 mV | Vz ±10% |
| U1ZB330-X | G5 | a1 | TO | Z Diode | | | | 1 W | | 320 V | 0.5 mA | <5kΩ | 470 mV | Vz ±5% |
| U1ZB330-Y | G5 | a1 | TO | Z Diode | | | | 1 W | | 330 V | 0.5 mA | <5kΩ | 470 mV | Vz ±5% |
| U1ZB330-Z | G5 | a1 | TO | Z Diode | | | | 1 W | | 340 V | 0.5 mA | <5kΩ | 470 mV | Vz ±5% |
| U1ZB390 | G5 | a1 | TO | Z Diode | | | | 1 W | | 390 V | 0.5 mA | <10kΩ | 555 mV | Vz ±10% |
| UMZ8.2T | F2 | c5 | RO | Bidir. ZD | | | | 0.2 W | | 8.2 V | 5 mA | <30Ω | | |
| ZM4729 | D1 | a1 | IT | Z Diode | | 252 mA | | 1 W | | 3.6 V | 69 mA | <10Ω | -600·10⁶/°C | Vz ±10% |

| Type | Case | Pin-code | | | Maximum Ratings | | | | | Electrical Characteristics | | | | |
|------|------|----------|---|---|---|---|---|---|---|---|---|---|---|---|
| | | | | | Vcla Vbro | Its | Izm | Pv | Pvts | Vz | Iz / Is | rz | TK | |
| ZM4730 | D1 | a1 | IT | Z Diode | | | 234 mA | 1 W | | 3.9 V | 64 mA | <9 Ω | -500·10⁶/°C | Vz ±10% |
| ZM4731 | D1 | a1 | IT | Z Diode | | | 217 mA | 1 W | | 4.3 V | 58 mA | <9 Ω | -300·10⁶/°C | Vz ±10% |
| ZM4732 | D1 | a1 | IT | Z Diode | | | 193 mA | 1 W | | 4.7 V | 53 mA | <8 Ω | -100·10⁶/°C | Vz ±10% |
| ZM4733 | D1 | a1 | IT | Z Diode | | | 178 mA | 1 W | | 5.1 V | 49 mA | <7 Ω | 100·10⁶/°C | Vz ±10% |
| ZM4734 | D1 | a1 | IT | Z Diode | | | 162 mA | 1 W | | 5.6 V | 45 mA | <5 Ω | 300·10⁶/°C | Vz ±10% |
| ZM4735 | D1 | a1 | IT | Z Diode | | | 146 mA | 1 W | | 6.2 V | 41 mA | <2 Ω | 400·10⁶/°C | Vz ±10% |
| ZM4736 | D1 | a1 | IT | Z Diode | | | 133 mA | 1 W | | 6.8 V | 37 mA | <3.5 Ω | 500·10⁶/°C | Vz ±10% |
| ZM4737 | D1 | a1 | IT | Z Diode | | | 121 mA | 1 W | | 7.5 V | 34 mA | <4 Ω | 500·10⁶/°C | Vz ±10% |
| ZM4738 | D1 | a1 | IT | Z Diode | | | 110 mA | 1 W | | 8.2 V | 31 mA | <4.5 Ω | 600·10⁶/°C | Vz ±10% |
| ZM4739 | D1 | a1 | IT | Z Diode | | | 100 mA | 1 W | | 9.1 V | 28 mA | <5 Ω | 600·10⁶/°C | Vz ±10% |
| ZM4740 | D1 | a1 | IT | Z Diode | | | 91 mA | 1 W | | 10 V | 25 mA | <7 Ω | 700·10⁶/°C | Vz ±10% |
| ZM4741 | D1 | a1 | IT | Z Diode | | | 83 mA | 1 W | | 11 V | 23 mA | <8 Ω | 700·10⁶/°C | Vz ±10% |
| ZM4742 | D1 | a1 | IT | Z Diode | | | 76 mA | 1 W | | 12 V | 21 mA | <9 Ω | 700·10⁶/°C | Vz ±10% |
| ZM4743 | D1 | a1 | IT | Z Diode | | | 69 mA | 1 W | | 13 V | 19 mA | <10 Ω | 700·10⁶/°C | Vz ±10% |
| ZM4744 | D1 | a1 | IT | Z Diode | | | 61 mA | 1 W | | 15 V | 17 mA | <14 Ω | 800·10⁶/°C | Vz ±10% |
| ZM4745 | D1 | a1 | IT | Z Diode | | | 57 mA | 1 W | | 16 V | 15.5 mA | <16 Ω | 800·10⁶/°C | Vz ±10% |
| ZM4746 | D1 | a1 | IT | Z Diode | | | 50 mA | 1 W | | 18 V | 14 mA | <20 Ω | 800·10⁶/°C | Vz ±10% |
| ZM4747 | D1 | a1 | IT | Z Diode | | | 45 mA | 1 W | | 20 V | 12.5 mA | <22 Ω | 800·10⁶/°C | Vz ±10% |
| ZM4748 | D1 | a1 | IT | Z Diode | | | 41 mA | 1 W | | 22 V | 11.5 mA | <23 Ω | 800·10⁶/°C | Vz ±10% |
| ZM4749 | D1 | a1 | IT | Z Diode | | | 38 mA | 1 W | | 24 V | 10.5 mA | <25 Ω | 800·10⁶/°C | Vz ±10% |
| ZM4750 | D1 | a1 | IT | Z Diode | | | 34 mA | 1 W | | 27 V | 9.5 mA | <35 Ω | 900·10⁶/°C | Vz ±10% |
| ZM4751 | D1 | a1 | IT | Z Diode | | | 30 mA | 1 W | | 30 V | 8.5 mA | <40 Ω | 900·10⁶/°C | Vz ±10% |
| ZM4752 | D1 | a1 | IT | Z Diode | | | 27 mA | 1 W | | 33 V | 7.5 mA | <45 Ω | 900·10⁶/°C | Vz ±10% |
| ZM4753 | D1 | a1 | IT | Z Diode | | | 25 mA | 1 W | | 36 V | 7 mA | <50 Ω | 900·10⁶/°C | Vz ±10% |
| ZM4754 | D1 | a1 | IT | Z Diode | | | 23 mA | 1 W | | 39 V | 6.5 mA | <60 Ω | 900·10⁶/°C | Vz ±10% |
| ZM4755 | D1 | a1 | IT | Z Diode | | | 22 mA | 1 W | | 43 V | 6 mA | <70 Ω | 900·10⁶/°C | Vz ±10% |
| ZM4756 | D1 | a1 | IT | Z Diode | | | 19 mA | 1 W | | 47 V | 5.5 mA | <80 Ω | 900·10⁶/°C | Vz ±10% |
| ZM4757 | D1 | a1 | IT | Z Diode | | | 18 mA | 1 W | | 51 V | 5 mA | <95 Ω | 900·10⁶/°C | Vz ±10% |
| ZM4758 | D1 | a1 | IT | Z Diode | | | 16 mA | 1 W | | 56 V | 4.5 mA | <110 Ω | 900·10⁶/°C | Vz ±10% |
| ZM4759 | D1 | a1 | IT | Z Diode | | | 14 mA | 1 W | | 62 V | 4 mA | <125 Ω | 900·10⁶/°C | Vz ±10% |
| ZM4760 | D1 | a1 | IT | Z Diode | | | 13 mA | 1 W | | 68 V | 3.7 mA | <150 Ω | 900·10⁶/°C | Vz ±10% |
| ZM4761 | D1 | a1 | IT | Z Diode | | | 12 mA | 1 W | | 75 V | 3.3 mA | <175 Ω | 900·10⁶/°C | Vz ±10% |
| ZM4762 | D1 | a1 | IT | Z Diode | | | 11 mA | 1 W | | 82 V | 3 mA | <200 Ω | 900·10⁶/°C | Vz ±10% |
| ZM4763 | D1 | a1 | IT | Z Diode | | | 10 mA | 1 W | | 91 V | 2.8 mA | <250 Ω | 900·10⁶/°C | Vz ±10% |
| ZM4764 | D1 | a1 | IT | Z Diode | | | 9 mA | 1 W | | 100 V | 2.5 mA | <350 Ω | 900·10⁶/°C | Vz ±10% |
| ZMM1 | F1 | a1 | IT | Z Diode | | | 340 mA | 0.5 W | | 0.8 V | 5 mA | 6.5 Ω | -2600·10⁶/°C | |
| ZMM2.4 | F1 | a1 | RD | Z Diode | | | | 0.5 W | | 2.4 V | 5 mA | | | |
| ZMM2.7 | F1 | a1 | RD,IT | Z Diode | | | 160 mA | 0.5 W | | 2.7 V | 5 mA | 75 Ω | -900·10⁶/°C | |
| ZMM3.0 | F1 | a1 | RD,IT | Z Diode | | | 140 mA | 0.5 W | | 3.0 V | 5 mA | 80 Ω | -900·10⁶/°C | |
| ZMM3.3 | F1 | a1 | RD,IT | Z Diode | | | 130 mA | 0.5 W | | 3.3 V | 5 mA | 80 Ω | -800·10⁶/°C | |

| Type | Case | Pin-code | | | Vcla Vbro | Its | Izm | Pv | Pvts | Vz | Iz Is | rz | TK | |
|------|------|----------|--|--|-----------|-----|-----|-----|------|-----|-------|-----|-----|--|
| | | | | | **Maximum Ratings** | | | | | **Electrical Characteristics** | | | | |
| ZMM3.6 | F1 | a1 | RD,IT | Z Diode | | | 120 mA | 0.5 W | | 3.6 V | 5 mA | 80 Ω | $-800 \cdot 10^6/°C$ | |
| ZMM3.9 | F1 | a1 | RD,IT | Z Diode | | | 110 mA | 0.5 W | | 3.9 V | 5 mA | 80 Ω | $-700 \cdot 10^6/°C$ | |
| ZMM4.3 | F1 | a1 | RD,IT | Z Diode | | | 100 mA | 0.5 W | | 4.3 V | 5 mA | 80 Ω | $-600 \cdot 10^6/°C$ | |
| ZMM4.7 | F1 | a1 | RD,IT | Z Diode | | | 90 mA | 0.5 W | | 4.7 V | 5 mA | 70 Ω | $-500 \cdot 10^6/°C$ | |
| ZMM5.1 | F1 | a1 | RD,IT | Z Diode | | | 80 mA | 0.5 W | | 5.1 V | 5 mA | 30 Ω | $400 \cdot 10^6/°C$ | |
| ZMM5.6 | F1 | a1 | RD,IT | Z Diode | | | 780 mA | 0.5 W | | 5.6 V | 5 mA | 10 Ω | $600 \cdot 10^6/°C$ | |
| ZMM6.2 | F1 | a1 | RD,IT | Z Diode | | | 64 mA | 0.5 W | | 6.2 V | 5 mA | 4.8 Ω | $700 \cdot 10^6/°C$ | |
| ZMM6.8 | F1 | a1 | RD,IT | Z Diode | | | 58 mA | 0.5 W | | 6.8 V | 5 mA | 4.5 Ω | $700 \cdot 10^6/°C$ | |
| ZMM7.5 | F1 | a1 | RD,IT | Z Diode | | | 53 mA | 0.5 W | | 7.5 V | 5 mA | 4 Ω | $700 \cdot 10^6/°C$ | |
| ZMM8.2 | F1 | a1 | RD,IT | Z Diode | | | 47 mA | 0.5 W | | 8.2 V | 5 mA | 4.5 Ω | $700 \cdot 10^6/°C$ | |
| ZMM9.1 | F1 | a1 | RD,IT | Z Diode | | | 43 mA | 0.5 W | | 9.1 V | 5 mA | 4.8 Ω | $800 \cdot 10^6/°C$ | |
| ZMM10 | F1 | a1 | RD,IT | Z Diode | | | 40 mA | 0.5 W | | 10 V | 5 mA | 5.2 Ω | $800 \cdot 10^6/°C$ | |
| ZMM11 | F1 | a1 | RD,IT | Z Diode | | | 36 mA | 0.5 W | | 11 V | 5 mA | 6 Ω | $900 \cdot 10^6/°C$ | |
| ZMM12 | F1 | a1 | RD,IT | Z Diode | | | 32 mA | 0.5 W | | 12 V | 5 mA | 7 Ω | $900 \cdot 10^6/°C$ | |
| ZMM13 | F1 | a1 | RD,IT | Z Diode | | | 29 mA | 0.5 W | | 13 V | 5 mA | 9 Ω | $900 \cdot 10^6/°C$ | |
| ZMM15 | F1 | a1 | RD,IT | Z Diode | | | 27 mA | 0.5 W | | 15 V | 5 mA | 11 Ω | $900 \cdot 10^6/°C$ | |
| ZMM16 | F1 | a1 | RD,IT | Z Diode | | | 24 mA | 0.5 W | | 16 V | 5 mA | 13 Ω | $950 \cdot 10^6/°C$ | |
| ZMM18 | F1 | a1 | RD,IT | Z Diode | | | 21 mA | 0.5 W | | 18 V | 5 mA | 18 Ω | $950 \cdot 10^6/°C$ | |
| ZMM20 | F1 | a1 | RD,IT | Z Diode | | | 20 mA | 0.5 W | | 20 V | 5 mA | 20 Ω | $1000 \cdot 10^6/°C$ | |
| ZMM22 | F1 | a1 | RD,IT | Z Diode | | | 18 mA | 0.5 W | | 22 V | 5 mA | 25 Ω | $1000 \cdot 10^6/°C$ | |
| ZMM24 | F1 | a1 | RD,IT | Z Diode | | | 16 mA | 0.5 W | | 24 V | 5 mA | 28 Ω | $1000 \cdot 10^6/°C$ | |
| ZMM27 | F1 | a1 | RD,IT | Z Diode | | | 14 mA | 0.5 W | | 27 V | 5 mA | 30 Ω | $1000 \cdot 10^6/°C$ | |
| ZMM30 | F1 | a1 | RD,IT | Z Diode | | | 13 mA | 0.5 W | | 30 V | 5 mA | 35 Ω | $1000 \cdot 10^6/°C$ | |
| ZMM33 | F1 | a1 | RD,IT | Z Diode | | | 12 mA | 0.5 W | | 33 V | 5 mA | 40 Ω | $1000 \cdot 10^6/°C$ | |
| ZMM36 | F1 | a1 | RD,IT | Z Diode | | | 11 mA | 0.5 W | | 36 V | 5 mA | 40 Ω | $1000 \cdot 10^6/°C$ | |
| ZMM39 | F1 | a1 | RD,IT | Z Diode | | | 10 mA | 0.5 W | | 39 V | 5 mA | 50 Ω | $1200 \cdot 10^6/°C$ | |
| ZMM43 | F1 | a1 | RD,IT | Z Diode | | | 9.2 mA | 0.5 W | | 43 V | 5 mA | 60 Ω | $1200 \cdot 10^6/°C$ | |
| ZMM47 | F1 | a1 | RD,IT | Z Diode | | | 8.5 mA | 0.5 W | | 47 V | 5 mA | 70 Ω | $1200 \cdot 10^6/°C$ | |
| ZMM51 | F1 | a1 | RD,IT | Z Diode | | | 7.8 mA | 0.5 W | | 51 V | 5 mA | 70 Ω | $1200 \cdot 10^6/°C$ | |
| ZMM5225 | D2 | a1 | IT | Z Diode | | | 151 mA | 0.5 W | | 3.0 V | 20 mA | <29 Ω | $-750 \cdot 10^6/°C$ | Vz ±20% |
| ZMM5226 | D2 | a1 | IT | Z Diode | | | 138 mA | 0.5 W | | 3.3 V | 20 mA | <28 Ω | $-700 \cdot 10^6/°C$ | Vz ±20% |
| ZMM5227 | D2 | a1 | IT | Z Diode | | | 126 mA | 0.5 W | | 3.6 V | 20 mA | <24 Ω | $-650 \cdot 10^6/°C$ | Vz ±20% |
| ZMM5228 | D2 | a1 | IT | Z Diode | | | 115 mA | 0.5 W | | 3.9 V | 20 mA | <23 Ω | $-600 \cdot 10^6/°C$ | Vz ±20% |
| ZMM5229 | D2 | a1 | IT | Z Diode | | | 106 mA | 0.5 W | | 4.3 V | 20 mA | <22 Ω | $550 \cdot 10^6/°C$ | Vz ±20% |
| ZMM5230 | D2 | a1 | IT | Z Diode | | | 97 mA | 0.5 W | | 4.7 V | 20 mA | <19 Ω | $300 \cdot 10^6/°C$ | Vz ±20% |
| ZMM5231 | D2 | a1 | IT | Z Diode | | | 89 mA | 0.5 W | | 5.1 V | 20 mA | <17 Ω | $300 \cdot 10^6/°C$ | Vz ±20% |
| ZMM5232 | D2 | a1 | IT | Z Diode | | | 81 mA | 0.5 W | | 5.6 V | 20 mA | <11 Ω | $380 \cdot 10^6/°C$ | Vz ±20% |
| ZMM5233 | D2 | a1 | IT | Z Diode | | | 76 mA | 0.5 W | | 6.0 V | 20 mA | <7 Ω | $380 \cdot 10^6/°C$ | Vz ±20% |
| ZMM5234 | D2 | a1 | IT | Z Diode | | | 73 mA | 0.5 W | | 6.2 V | 20 mA | <7 Ω | $450 \cdot 10^6/°C$ | Vz ±20% |
| ZMM5235 | D2 | a1 | IT | Z Diode | | | 67 mA | 0.5 W | | 6.8 V | 20 mA | <5 Ω | $500 \cdot 10^6/°C$ | Vz ±20% |

| Type | Case | Pin code | | | Maximum Ratings Vcla/Vbro | Its | Izm | Pv | Pvts | Electrical Characteristics Vz | Iz / Is | rz | TK | |
|---|---|---|---|---|---|---|---|---|---|---|---|---|---|---|
| ZMM5236 | D2 | a1 | IT | Z Diode | | | 61 mA | 0.5 W | | 7.0 V | 20 mA | <6 Ω | 580·10⁶/°C | Vz ±20% |
| ZMM5237 | D2 | a1 | IT | Z Diode | | | 55 mA | 0.5 W | | 8.2 V | 20 mA | <8 Ω | 620·10⁶/°C | Vz ±20% |
| ZMM5238 | D2 | a1 | IT | Z Diode | | | 52 mA | 0.5 W | | 8.7 V | 20 mA | <8 Ω | 650·10⁶/°C | Vz ±20% |
| ZMM5239 | D2 | a1 | IT | Z Diode | | | 50 mA | 0.5 W | | 9.1 V | 20 mA | <10 Ω | 680·10⁶/°C | Vz ±20% |
| ZMM5240 | D2 | a1 | IT | Z Diode | | | 45 mA | 0.5 W | | 10 V | 20 mA | <17 Ω | 750·10⁶/°C | Vz ±20% |
| ZMM5241 | D2 | a1 | IT | Z Diode | | | 41 mA | 0.5 W | | 11 V | 20 mA | <22 Ω | 760·10⁶/°C | Vz ±20% |
| ZMM5242 | D2 | a1 | IT | Z Diode | | | 38 mA | 0.5 W | | 12 V | 20 mA | <30 Ω | 770·10⁶/°C | Vz ±20% |
| ZMM5243 | D2 | a1 | IT | Z Diode | | | 35 mA | 0.5 W | | 13 V | 9.5 mA | <13 Ω | 790·10⁶/°C | Vz ±20% |
| ZMM5244 | D2 | a1 | IT | Z Diode | | | 32 mA | 0.5 W | | 14 V | 9.0 mA | <15 Ω | 820·10⁶/°C | Vz ±20% |
| ZMM5245 | D2 | a1 | IT | Z Diode | | | 30 mA | 0.5 W | | 15 V | 8.5 mA | <16 Ω | 820·10⁶/°C | Vz ±20% |
| ZMM5246 | D2 | a1 | IT | Z Diode | | | 28 mA | 0.5 W | | 16 V | 7.8 mA | <17 Ω | 830·10⁶/°C | Vz ±20% |
| ZMM5247 | D2 | a1 | IT | Z Diode | | | 27 mA | 0.5 W | | 17 V | 7.4 mA | <19 Ω | 840·10⁶/°C | Vz ±20% |
| ZMM5248 | D2 | a1 | IT | Z Diode | | | 25 mA | 0.5 W | | 18 V | 7.0 mA | <21 Ω | 850·10⁶/°C | Vz ±20% |
| ZMM5249 | D2 | a1 | IT | Z Diode | | | 24 mA | 0.5 W | | 19 V | 6.6 mA | <23 Ω | 860·10⁶/°C | Vz ±20% |
| ZMM5250 | D2 | a1 | IT | Z Diode | | | 23 mA | 0.5 W | | 20 V | 6.2 mA | <25 Ω | 860·10⁶/°C | Vz ±20% |
| ZMM5251 | D2 | a1 | IT | Z Diode | | | 21 mA | 0.5 W | | 22 V | 5.6 mA | <29 Ω | 870·10⁶/°C | Vz ±20% |
| ZMM5252 | D2 | a1 | IT | Z Diode | | | 19 mA | 0.5 W | | 24 V | 5.2 mA | <33 Ω | 880·10⁶/°C | Vz ±20% |
| ZMM5253 | D2 | a1 | IT | Z Diode | | | 18 mA | 0.5 W | | 25 V | 5.0 mA | <35 Ω | 890·10⁶/°C | Vz ±20% |
| ZMM5254 | D2 | a1 | IT | Z Diode | | | 17 mA | 0.5 W | | 27 V | 4.6 mA | <41 Ω | 900·10⁶/°C | Vz ±20% |
| ZMM5255 | D2 | a1 | IT | Z Diode | | | 16 mA | 0.5 W | | 28 V | 4.5 mA | <44 Ω | 910·10⁶/°C | Vz ±20% |
| ZMM5256 | D2 | a1 | IT | Z Diode | | | 15 mA | 0.5 W | | 30 V | 4.2 mA | <49 Ω | 910·10⁶/°C | Vz ±20% |
| ZMM5257 | D2 | a1 | IT | Z Diode | | | 14 mA | 0.5 W | | 33 V | 3.8 mA | <58 Ω | 920·10⁶/°C | Vz ±20% |
| ZMM5258 | D2 | a1 | IT | Z Diode | | | 13 mA | 0.5 W | | 36 V | 3.4 mA | <70 Ω | 930·10⁶/°C | Vz ±20% |
| ZMM5259 | D2 | a1 | IT | Z Diode | | | 12 mA | 0.5 W | | 39 V | 3.2 mA | <80 Ω | 940·10⁶/°C | Vz ±20% |
| ZMM5260 | D2 | a1 | IT | Z Diode | | | 11 mA | 0.5 W | | 43 V | 3.0 mA | <93 Ω | 950·10⁶/°C | Vz ±20% |
| ZMM5261 | D2 | a1 | IT | Z Diode | | | 10 mA | 0.5 W | | 47 V | 2.7 mA | <105 Ω | 950·10⁶/°C | Vz ±20% |
| ZMM5262 | D2 | a1 | IT | Z Diode | | | 9 mA | 0.5 W | | 51 V | 2.5 mA | <125 Ω | 960·10⁶/°C | Vz ±20% |
| ZMU100 | D1 | a1 | IT | Z Diode | | | 7 mA | 1 W | | 100 V | 5 mA | 140 Ω | 1300·10⁶/°C | |
| ZMU120 | D1 | a1 | IT | Z Diode | | | 6 mA | 1 W | | 120 V | 5 mA | 170 Ω | 1300·10⁶/°C | |
| ZMU150 | D1 | a1 | IT | Z Diode | | | 5 mA | 1 W | | 150 V | 5 mA | 200 Ω | 1300·10⁶/°C | |
| ZMU180 | D1 | a1 | IT | Z Diode | | | 4 mA | 1 W | | 180 V | 5 mA | 220 Ω | 1300·10⁶/°C | |
| ZMY1 | D1 | a1 | IT | Z Diode | | | 406 mA | 1 W | | 0.8 V | 5 mA | 6.5 Ω | -2600·10⁶/°C | |
| ZMY3.9 | D1 | a1 | RD,IT | Z Diode | | | 203 mA | 1 W | | 3.9 V | 100 mA | 3 Ω | -700·10⁶/°C | |
| ZMY4.3 | D1 | a1 | RD,IT | Z Diode | | | 182 mA | 1 W | | 4.3 V | 100 mA | 3 Ω | -700·10⁶/°C | |
| ZMY4.7 | D1 | a1 | RD,IT | Z Diode | | | 165 mA | 1 W | | 4.7 V | 100 mA | 3 Ω | -700·10⁶/°C | |
| ZMY5.1 | D1 | a1 | RD,IT | Z Diode | | | 150 mA | 1 W | | 5.1 V | 100 mA | 2 Ω | -600·10⁶/°C | |
| ZMY5.6 | D1 | a1 | RD,IT | Z Diode | | | 135 mA | 1 W | | 5.6 V | 100 mA | 1 Ω | 500·10⁶/°C | |
| ZMY6.2 | D1 | a1 | RD,IT | Z Diode | | | 128 mA | 1 W | | 6.2 V | 100 mA | 1 Ω | 600·10⁶/°C | |
| ZMY6.8 | D1 | a1 | RD,IT | Z Diode | | | 110 mA | 1 W | | 6.8 V | 100 mA | 1 Ω | 700·10⁶/°C | |
| ZMY7.5 | D1 | a1 | RD,IT | Z Diode | | | 100 mA | 1 W | | 7.5 V | 100 mA | 1 Ω | 700·10⁶/°C | |

| Type | Case | Pin-code | | | Maximum Ratings | | | | | Electrical Characteristics | | | | |
|------|------|----------|---|---|---------------|-----|-----|------|------|------|------|------|------|---|
| | | | | | Vcla Vbro | Its | Izm | Pv | Pvts | Vz | Iz Is | rz | TK | |
| ZMY8.2 | D1 | a1 | RD,IT | Z Diode | | | 89 mA | 1 W | | 8.2 V | 100 mA | 1 Ω | 800·10⁶/°C | |
| ZMY9.1 | D1 | a1 | RD,IT | Z Diode | | | 82 mA | 1 W | | 9.1 V | 50 mA | 2 Ω | 800·10⁶/°C | |
| ZMY10 | D1 | a1 | RD,IT | Z Diode | | | 74 mA | 1 W | | 10 V | 50 mA | 2 Ω | 900·10⁶/°C | |
| ZMY11 | D1 | a1 | RD,IT | Z Diode | | | 66 mA | 1 W | | 11 V | 50 mA | 3 Ω | 1000·10⁶/°C | |
| ZMY12 | D1 | a1 | RD,IT | Z Diode | | | 60 mA | 1 W | | 12 V | 50 mA | 3 Ω | 1000·10⁶/°C | |
| ZMY13 | D1 | a1 | RD,IT | Z Diode | 10 V | | 55 mA | 1 W | | 13 V | 50 mA | 4 Ω | 1000·10⁶/°C | |
| ZMY15 | D1 | a1 | RD,IT | Z Diode | | | 49 mA | 1 W | | 15 V | 50 mA | 4 Ω | 1000·10⁶/°C | |
| ZMY16 | D1 | a1 | RD,IT | Z Diode | | | 44 mA | 1 W | | 16 V | 25 mA | 5 Ω | 1100·10⁶/°C | |
| ZMY18 | D1 | a1 | RD,IT | Z Diode | | | 40 mA | 1 W | | 18 V | 25 mA | 5 Ω | 1100·10⁶/°C | |
| ZMY20 | D1 | a1 | RD,IT | Z Diode | | | 36 mA | 1 W | | 20 V | 25 mA | 6 Ω | 1100·10⁶/°C | |
| ZMY22 | D1 | a1 | RD,IT | Z Diode | | | 34 mA | 1 W | | 22 V | 25 mA | 7 Ω | 1100·10⁶/°C | |
| ZMY24 | D1 | a1 | RD,IT | Z Diode | | | 29 mA | 1 W | | 24 V | 25 mA | 8 Ω | 1200·10⁶/°C | |
| ZMY27 | D1 | a1 | RD,IT | Z Diode | | | 27 mA | 1 W | | 27 V | 25 mA | 9 Ω | 1200·10⁶/°C | |
| ZMY30 | D1 | a1 | RD,IT | Z Diode | | | 25 mA | 1 W | | 30 V | 25 mA | 10 Ω | 1200·10⁶/°C | |
| ZMY33 | D1 | a1 | RD,IT | Z Diode | | | 22 mA | 1 W | | 33 V | 25 mA | 11 Ω | 1200·10⁶/°C | |
| ZMY36 | D1 | a1 | RD,IT | Z Diode | | | 20 mA | 1 W | | 36 V | 10 mA | 25 Ω | 1200·10⁶/°C | |
| ZMY39 | D1 | a1 | RD,IT | Z Diode | | | 18 mA | 1 W | | 39 V | 10 mA | 30 Ω | 1200·10⁶/°C | |
| ZMY43 | D1 | a1 | RD,IT | Z Diode | | | 17 mA | 1 W | | 43 V | 10 mA | 35 Ω | 1300·10⁶/°C | |
| ZMY47 | D1 | a1 | RD,IT | Z Diode | | | 15 mA | 1 W | | 47 V | 10 mA | 40 Ω | 1300·10⁶/°C | |
| ZMY51 | D1 | a1 | RD,IT | Z Diode | | | 14 mA | 1 W | | 51 V | 10 mA | 45 Ω | 1300·10⁶/°C | |
| ZMY56 | D1 | a1 | RD,IT | Z Diode | | | 13 mA | 1 W | | 56 V | 10 mA | 50 Ω | 1300·10⁶/°C | |
| ZMY62 | D1 | a1 | RD,IT | Z Diode | | | 11 mA | 1 W | | 62 V | 10 mA | 60 Ω | 1300·10⁶/°C | |
| ZMY68 | D1 | a1 | RD,IT | Z Diode | | | 10 mA | 1 W | | 68 V | 10 mA | 65 Ω | 1300·10⁶/°C | |
| ZMY75 | D1 | a1 | RD,IT | Z Diode | | | 9 mA | 1 W | | 75 V | 10 mA | 70 Ω | 1300·10⁶/°C | |
| ZMY82 | D1 | a1 | RD,IT | Z Diode | | | 8 mA | 1 W | | 82 V | 10 mA | 80 Ω | 1300·10⁶/°C | |
| ZMY91 | D1 | a1 | RD,IT | Z Diode | | | 7.5 mA | 1 W | | 91 V | 5 mA | 120 Ω | 1300·10⁶/°C | |
| ZMY100 | D1 | a1 | RD,IT | Z Diode | | | 7 mA | 1 W | | 100 V | 5 mA | 130 Ω | 1300·10⁶/°C | |
| ZPD1 | A1 | a1 | IT | Z Diode | | | 340 mA | 0.5 W | | 0.8 V | 5 mA | 6.5 Ω | -2600·10⁶/°C | |
| ZPD2.4 | A1 | a1 | RD | Z Diode | | | | 0.5 W | | 2.4 V | 5 mA | | | |
| ZPD2.7 | A1 | a1 | RD,IT,MO | Z Diode | | | 150 mA | 0.5 W | | 2.7 V | 5 mA | 75 Ω | -900·10⁶/°C | |
| ZPD3.0 | A1 | a1 | RD,IT,MO | Z Diode | | | 140 mA | 0.5 W | | 3.0 V | 5 mA | 80 Ω | -900·10⁶/°C | |
| ZPD3.3 | A1 | a1 | RD,IT,MO | Z Diode | | | 130 mA | 0.5 W | | 3.3 V | 5 mA | 80 Ω | -800·10⁶/°C | |
| ZPD3.6 | A1 | a1 | RD,IT,MO | Z Diode | | | 120 mA | 0.5 W | | 3.6 V | 5 mA | 80 Ω | -800·10⁶/°C | |
| ZPD3.9 | A1 | a1 | RD,IT,MO | Z Diode | | | 110 mA | 0.5 W | | 3.9 V | 5 mA | 80 Ω | -700·10⁶/°C | |
| ZPD4.3 | A1 | a1 | RD,IT,MO | Z Diode | | | 100 mA | 0.5 W | | 4.3 V | 5 mA | 80 Ω | -600·10⁶/°C | |
| ZPD4.7 | A1 | a1 | RD,IT,MO | Z Diode | | | 90 mA | 0.5 W | | 4.7 V | 5 mA | 70 Ω | -500·10⁶/°C | |
| ZPD5.1 | A1 | a1 | RD,IT,MO | Z Diode | | | 80 mA | 0.5 W | | 5.1 V | 5 mA | 30 Ω | 400·10⁶/°C | |
| ZPD5.6 | A1 | a1 | RD,IT,MO | Z Diode | | | 70 mA | 0.5 W | | 5.6 V | 5 mA | 10 Ω | 600·10⁶/°C | |
| ZPD6.2 | A1 | a1 | RD,IT,MO | Z Diode | | | 64 mA | 0.5 W | | 6.2 V | 5 mA | 4.8 Ω | 700·10⁶/°C | |
| ZPD6.8 | A1 | a1 | RD,IT,MO | Z Diode | | | 58 mA | 0.5 W | | 6.8 V | 5 mA | 4.5 Ω | 700·10⁶/°C | |

| Type | Case | Pin-code | | | Maximum Ratings | | | | | Electrical Characteristics | | | | |
|------|------|----------|---|---|---|---|---|---|---|---|---|---|---|---|
| | | | | | Vcla/Vbro | Its | Izm | Pv | Pvts | Vz | Iz/Is | rz | TK | |
| ZPD7.5 | A1 | a1 | RD,IT,MO | Z Diode | | | 53 mA | 0.5 W | | 7.5 V | 5 mA | 4 Ω | $700 \cdot 10^6$/°C | |
| ZPD8.2 | A1 | a1 | RD,IT,MO | Z Diode | | | 47 mA | 0.5 W | | 8.2 V | 5 mA | 4.5 Ω | $700 \cdot 10^6$/°C | |
| ZPD9.1 | A1 | a1 | RD,IT,MO | Z Diode | | | 43 mA | 0.5 W | | 9.1 V | 5 mA | 4.8 Ω | $800 \cdot 10^6$/°C | |
| ZPD10 | A1 | a1 | RD,IT,MO | Z Diode | | | 40 mA | 0.5 W | | 10 V | 5 mA | 5.2 Ω | $800 \cdot 10^6$/°C | |
| ZPD11 | A1 | a1 | RD,IT,MO | Z Diode | | | 36 mA | 0.5 W | | 11 V | 5 mA | 6 Ω | $900 \cdot 10^6$/°C | |
| ZPD12 | A1 | a1 | RD,IT,MO | Z Diode | | | 32 mA | 0.5 W | | 12 V | 5 mA | 7 Ω | $900 \cdot 10^6$/°C | |
| ZPD13 | A1 | a1 | RD,IT,MO | Z Diode | | | 29 mA | 0.5 W | | 13 V | 5 mA | 9 Ω | $900 \cdot 10^6$/°C | |
| ZPD15 | A1 | a1 | RD,IT,MO | Z Diode | | | 27 mA | 0.5 W | | 15 V | 5 mA | 11 Ω | $900 \cdot 10^6$/°C | |
| ZPD16 | A1 | a1 | RD,IT,MO | Z Diode | | | 24 mA | 0.5 W | | 16 V | 5 mA | 13 Ω | $950 \cdot 10^6$/°C | |
| ZPD18 | A1 | a1 | RD,IT,MO | Z Diode | | | 21 mA | 0.5 W | | 18 V | 5 mA | 18 Ω | $950 \cdot 10^6$/°C | |
| ZPD20 | A1 | a1 | RD,IT,MO | Z Diode | | | 20 mA | 0.5 W | | 20 V | 5 mA | 20 Ω | $1000 \cdot 10^6$/°C | |
| ZPD22 | A1 | a1 | RD,IT,MO | Z Diode | | | 18 mA | 0.5 W | | 22 V | 5 mA | 25 Ω | $1000 \cdot 10^6$/°C | |
| ZPD24 | A1 | a1 | RD,IT,MO | Z Diode | | | 16 mA | 0.5 W | | 24 V | 5 mA | 28 Ω | $1000 \cdot 10^6$/°C | |
| ZPD27 | A1 | a1 | RD,IT,MO | Z Diode | | | 14 mA | 0.5 W | | 27 V | 5 mA | 30 Ω | $1000 \cdot 10^6$/°C | |
| ZPD30 | A1 | a1 | RD,IT,MO | Z Diode | | | 13 mA | 0.5 W | | 30 V | 5 mA | 35 Ω | $1000 \cdot 10^6$/°C | |
| ZPD33 | A1 | a1 | RD,IT,MO | Z Diode | | | 12 mA | 0.5 W | | 33 V | 5 mA | 40 Ω | $1000 \cdot 10^6$/°C | |
| ZPD36 | A1 | a1 | RD,IT | Z Diode | | | 11 mA | 0.5 W | | 36 V | 5 mA | 40 Ω | $1000 \cdot 10^6$/°C | |
| ZPD39 | A1 | a1 | RD,IT | Z Diode | | | 10 mA | 0.5 W | | 39 V | 5 mA | 50 Ω | $1200 \cdot 10^6$/°C | |
| ZPD43 | A1 | a1 | RD,IT | Z Diode | | | 9.2 mA | 0.5 W | | 43 V | 5 mA | 60 Ω | $1200 \cdot 10^6$/°C | |
| ZPD47 | A1 | a1 | RD,IT | Z Diode | | | 8.5 mA | 0.5 W | | 47 V | 5 mA | 70 Ω | $1200 \cdot 10^6$/°C | |
| ZPD51 | A1 | a1 | RD,IT | Z Diode | | | 7.8 mA | 0.5 W | | 51 V | 5 mA | 70 Ω | $1200 \cdot 10^6$/°C | |
| ZPD1S | A2 | a1 | IT | Z Diode | | | 205 mA | 0.3 W | | 0.8 V | 5 mA | 6.5 Ω | $-2600 \cdot 10^6$/°C | |
| ZPD2.7S | A2 | a1 | IT | Z Diode | | | 90 mA | 0.5 W | | 2.7 V | 5 mA | 75 Ω | $-900 \cdot 10^6$/°C | |
| ZPD3.0S | A2 | a1 | IT | Z Diode | | | 84 mA | 0.5 W | | 3.0 V | 5 mA | 80 Ω | $-900 \cdot 10^6$/°C | |
| ZPD3.3S | A2 | a1 | IT | Z Diode | | | 78 mA | 0.5 W | | 3.3 V | 5 mA | 80 Ω | $-800 \cdot 10^6$/°C | |
| ZPD3.6S | A2 | a1 | IT | Z Diode | | | 72 mA | 0.5 W | | 3.6 V | 5 mA | 80 Ω | $-800 \cdot 10^6$/°C | |
| ZPD3.9S | A2 | a1 | IT | Z Diode | | | 66 mA | 0.5 W | | 3.9 V | 5 mA | 80 Ω | $-700 \cdot 10^6$/°C | |
| ZPD4.3S | A2 | a1 | IT | Z Diode | | | 60 mA | 0.5 W | | 4.3 V | 5 mA | 80 Ω | $-600 \cdot 10^6$/°C | |
| ZPD4.7S | A2 | a1 | IT | Z Diode | | | 54 mA | 0.5 W | | 4.7 V | 5 mA | 70 Ω | $-500 \cdot 10^6$/°C | |
| ZPD5.1S | A2 | a1 | IT | Z Diode | | | 48 mA | 0.5 W | | 5.1 V | 5 mA | 30 Ω | $400 \cdot 10^6$/°C | |
| ZPD5.6S | A2 | a1 | IT | Z Diode | | | 42 mA | 0.5 W | | 5.6 V | 5 mA | 10 Ω | $600 \cdot 10^6$/°C | |
| ZPD6.2S | A2 | a1 | IT | Z Diode | | | 39 mA | 0.5 W | | 6.2 V | 5 mA | 4.8 Ω | $700 \cdot 10^6$/°C | |
| ZPD6.8S | A2 | a1 | IT | Z Diode | | | 35 mA | 0.5 W | | 6.8 V | 5 mA | 4.5 Ω | $700 \cdot 10^6$/°C | |
| ZPD7.5S | A2 | a1 | IT | Z Diode | | | 32 mA | 0.5 W | | 7.5 V | 5 mA | 4 Ω | $700 \cdot 10^6$/°C | |
| ZPD8.2S | A2 | a1 | IT | Z Diode | | | 28 mA | 0.5 W | | 8.2 V | 5 mA | 4.5 Ω | $700 \cdot 10^6$/°C | |
| ZPD9.1S | A2 | a1 | IT | Z Diode | | | 26 mA | 0.5 W | | 9.1 V | 5 mA | 4.8 Ω | $800 \cdot 10^6$/°C | |
| ZPD10S | A2 | a1 | IT | Z Diode | | | 24 mA | 0.5 W | | 10 V | 5 mA | 5.2 Ω | $800 \cdot 10^6$/°C | |
| ZPD11S | A2 | a1 | IT | Z Diode | | | 22 mA | 0.5 W | | 11 V | 5 mA | 6 Ω | $900 \cdot 10^6$/°C | |
| ZPD12S | A2 | a1 | IT | Z Diode | | | 19 mA | 0.5 W | | 12 V | 5 mA | 7 Ω | $900 \cdot 10^6$/°C | |
| ZPD13S | A2 | a1 | IT | Z Diode | | | 17 mA | 0.5 W | | 13 V | 5 mA | 9 Ω | $900 \cdot 10^6$/°C | |

| Type | Case | Pin-code | | | Maximum Ratings | | | | | Electrical Characteristics | | | | |
|------|------|----------|---|---|----------------|-----|------|------|------|---------------------------|------|------|------|---|
| | | | | | $V_{cla}$ $V_{bro}$ | Its | Izm | Pv | Pvts | Vz | Iz $I_s$ | rz | TK | |
| ZPD15S | A2 | a1 | IT | Z Diode | | | 16 mA | 0.5 W | | 15 V | 5 mA | 11 Ω | $900 \cdot 10^6$/°C | |
| ZPD16S | A2 | a1 | IT | Z Diode | | | 14 mA | 0.5 W | | 16 V | 5 mA | 13 Ω | $950 \cdot 10^6$/°C | |
| ZPD18S | A2 | a1 | IT | Z Diode | | | 13 mA | 0.5 W | | 18 V | 5 mA | 18 Ω | $950 \cdot 10^6$/°C | |
| ZPD20S | A2 | a1 | IT | Z Diode | | | 12 mA | 0.5 W | | 20 V | 5 mA | 20 Ω | $1000 \cdot 10^6$/°C | |
| ZPD22S | A2 | a1 | IT | Z Diode | | | 11 mA | 0.5 W | | 22 V | 5 mA | 25 Ω | $1000 \cdot 10^6$/°C | |
| ZPD24S | A2 | a1 | IT | Z Diode | | | 10 mA | 0.5 W | | 24 V | 5 mA | 28 Ω | $1000 \cdot 10^6$/°C | |
| ZPD27S | A2 | a1 | IT | Z Diode | | | 8 mA | 0.5 W | | 27 V | 5 mA | 30 Ω | $1000 \cdot 10^6$/°C | |
| ZPD30S | A2 | a1 | IT | Z Diode | | | 8 mA | 0.5 W | | 30 V | 5 mA | 35 Ω | $1000 \cdot 10^6$/°C | |
| ZPD33S | A2 | a1 | IT | Z Diode | | | 7 mA | 0.5 W | | 33 V | 5 mA | 40 Ω | $1000 \cdot 10^6$/°C | |
| ZPD36S | A2 | a1 | IT | Z Diode | | | 7 mA | 0.5 W | | 36 V | 5 mA | 40 Ω | $1000 \cdot 10^6$/°C | |
| ZPD39S | A2 | a1 | IT | Z Diode | | | 6 mA | 0.5 W | | 39 V | 5 mA | 50 Ω | $1200 \cdot 10^6$/°C | |
| ZPD43S | A2 | a1 | IT | Z Diode | | | 6 mA | 0.5 W | | 43 V | 5 mA | 60 Ω | $1200 \cdot 10^6$/°C | |
| ZPD47S | A2 | a1 | IT | Z Diode | | | 5 mA | 0.5 W | | 47 V | 5 mA | 70 Ω | $1200 \cdot 10^6$/°C | |
| ZPD51S | A2 | a1 | IT | Z Diode | | | 5 mA | 0.5 W | | 51 V | 5 mA | 70 Ω | $1200 \cdot 10^6$/°C | |
| ZPU100 | A3 | a1 | IT | Z Diode | | | 10 mA | 1.3 W | | 100 V | 5 mA | 140 Ω | $1300 \cdot 10^6$/°C | |
| ZPU120 | A3 | a1 | IT | Z Diode | | | 8.5 mA | 1.3 W | | 120 V | 5 mA | 170 Ω | $1300 \cdot 10^6$/°C | |
| ZPU150 | A3 | a1 | IT | Z Diode | | | 7 mA | 1.3 W | | 150 V | 5 mA | 200 Ω | $1300 \cdot 10^6$/°C | |
| ZPU180 | A3 | a1 | IT | Z Diode | | | 5.5 mA | 1.3 W | | 180 V | 5 mA | 220 Ω | $1300 \cdot 10^6$/°C | |
| ZPY1 | A3 | a1 | IT | Z Diode | | | 580 mA | 1.3 W | | 0.8 V | 5 mA | 6.5 Ω | $-2600 \cdot 10^6$/°C | |
| ZPY3V9 | A3 | a1 | SG,RD,IT | Z Diode | | | 290 mA | 1.3 W | | 3.9 V | 100 mA | <7 Ω | $200 \cdot 10^6$/°C | |
| ZPY4V3 | A3 | a1 | SG,RD,IT | Z Diode | | | 260 mA | 1.3 W | | 4.3 V | 100 mA | <7 Ω | $300 \cdot 10^6$/°C | |
| ZPY4V7 | A3 | a1 | SG,RD,IT | Z Diode | | | 235 mA | 1.3 W | | 4.7 V | 100 mA | <7 Ω | $400 \cdot 10^6$/°C | |
| ZPY5V1 | A3 | a1 | SG,RD,IT | Z Diode | | | 215 mA | 1.3 W | | 5.1 V | 100 mA | <5 Ω | $500 \cdot 10^6$/°C | |
| ZPY5V6 | A3 | a1 | SG,RD,IT | Z Diode | | | 193 mA | 1.3 W | | 5.6 V | 100 mA | <2 Ω | $500 \cdot 10^6$/°C | |
| ZPY6V2 | A3 | a1 | SG,RD,IT | Z Diode | | | 183 mA | 1.3 W | | 6.2 V | 100 mA | <2 Ω | $600 \cdot 10^6$/°C | |
| ZPY6V8 | A3 | a1 | SG,RD,IT | Z Diode | | | 157 mA | 1.3 W | | 6.8 V | 100 mA | <2 Ω | $700 \cdot 10^6$/°C | |
| ZPY7V5 | A3 | a1 | SG,RD,IT | Z Diode | | | 143 mA | 1.3 W | | 7.5 V | 100 mA | <2 Ω | $700 \cdot 10^6$/°C | |
| ZPY8V2 | A3 | a1 | SG,RD,IT | Z Diode | | | 127 mA | 1.3 W | | 8.2 V | 100 mA | <2 Ω | $800 \cdot 10^6$/°C | |
| ZPY9V1 | A3 | a1 | SG,RD,IT | Z Diode | | | 117 mA | 1.3 W | | 9.1 V | 50 mA | <4 Ω | $800 \cdot 10^6$/°C | |
| ZPY10 | A3 | a1 | SG,RD,IT | Z Diode | | | 105 mA | 1.3 W | | 10 V | 50 mA | <4 Ω | $900 \cdot 10^6$/°C | |
| ZPY11 | A3 | a1 | SG,RD,IT | Z Diode | | | 94 mA | 1.3 W | | 11 V | 50 mA | <7 Ω | $1000 \cdot 10^6$/°C | |
| ZPY12 | A3 | a1 | SG,RD,IT | Z Diode | | | 85 mA | 1.3 W | | 12 V | 50 mA | <7 Ω | $1000 \cdot 10^6$/°C | |
| ZPY13 | A3 | a1 | SG,RD,IT | Z Diode | | | 78 mA | 1.3 W | | 13 V | 50 mA | <9 Ω | $1000 \cdot 10^6$/°C | |
| ZPY15 | A3 | a1 | SG,RD,IT | Z Diode | | | 70 mA | 1.3 W | | 15 V | 50 mA | <9 Ω | $1000 \cdot 10^6$/°C | |
| ZPY16 | A3 | a1 | SG,RD,IT | Z Diode | | | 63 mA | 1.3 W | | 16 V | 25 mA | <10 Ω | $1100 \cdot 10^6$/°C | |
| ZPY18 | A3 | a1 | SG,RD,IT | Z Diode | | | 57 mA | 1.3 W | | 18 V | 25 mA | <11 Ω | $1100 \cdot 10^6$/°C | |
| ZPY20 | A3 | a1 | SG,RD,IT | Z Diode | | | 52 mA | 1.3 W | | 20 V | 25 mA | <12 Ω | $1100 \cdot 10^6$/°C | |
| ZPY22 | A3 | a1 | SG,RD,IT | Z Diode | | | 48 mA | 1.3 W | | 22 V | 25 mA | <13 Ω | $1100 \cdot 10^6$/°C | |
| ZPY24 | A3 | a1 | SG,RD,IT | Z Diode | | | 42 mA | 1.3 W | | 24 V | 25 mA | <14 Ω | $1200 \cdot 10^6$/°C | |
| ZPY27 | A3 | a1 | SG,RD,IT | Z Diode | | | 38 mA | 1.3 W | | 27 V | 25 mA | <15 Ω | $1200 \cdot 10^6$/°C | |

| Type | Case | Pin-code | | | Maximum Ratings | | | | | Electrical Characteristics | | | | |
|---|---|---|---|---|---|---|---|---|---|---|---|---|---|---|
| | | | | | $V_{cla}/V_{bro}$ | Its | Izm | Pv | Pvts | Vz | Iz / Is | rz | TK | |
| ZPY30 | A3 | a1 | SG,RD,IT | Z Diode | | | 35 mA | 1.3 W | | 30 V | 25 mA | <20 Ω | $1200 \cdot 10^6/°C$ | |
| ZPY33 | A3 | a1 | SG,RD,IT | Z Diode | | | 31 mA | 1.3 W | | 33 V | 10 mA | <20 Ω | $1200 \cdot 10^6/°C$ | |
| ZPY36 | A3 | a1 | SG,RD,IT | Z Diode | | | 29 mA | 1.3 W | | 36 V | 10 mA | <60 Ω | $1200 \cdot 10^6/°C$ | |
| ZPY39 | A3 | a1 | SG,RD,IT | Z Diode | | | 26 mA | 1.3 W | | 39 V | 10 mA | <60 Ω | $1200 \cdot 10^6/°C$ | |
| ZPY43 | A3 | a1 | SG,RD,IT | Z Diode | | | 24 mA | 1.3 W | | 43 V | 10 mA | <80 Ω | $1300 \cdot 10^6/°C$ | |
| ZPY47 | A3 | a1 | SG,RD,IT | Z Diode | | | 22 mA | 1.3 W | | 47 V | 10 mA | <80 Ω | $1300 \cdot 10^6/°C$ | |
| ZPY51 | A3 | a1 | SG,RD,IT | Z Diode | | | 20 mA | 1.3 W | | 51 V | 10 mA | <100 Ω | $1300 \cdot 10^6/°C$ | |
| ZPY56 | A3 | a1 | SG,RD,IT | Z Diode | | | 18 mA | 1.3 W | | 56 V | 10 mA | <100 Ω | $1300 \cdot 10^6/°C$ | |
| ZPY62 | A3 | a1 | SG,RD,IT | Z Diode | | | 16 mA | 1.3 W | | 62 V | 10 mA | <130 Ω | $1300 \cdot 10^6/°C$ | |
| ZPY68 | A3 | a1 | SG,RD,IT | Z Diode | | | 14 mA | 1.3 W | | 68 V | 10 mA | <130 Ω | $1300 \cdot 10^6/°C$ | |
| ZPY75 | A3 | a1 | SG,RD,IT | Z Diode | | | 13 mA | 1.3 W | | 75 V | 10 mA | <160 Ω | $1300 \cdot 10^6/°C$ | |
| ZPY82 | A3 | a1 | SG,RD,IT | Z Diode | | | 12 mA | 1.3 W | | 82 V | 10 mA | <160 Ω | $1300 \cdot 10^6/°C$ | |
| ZPY91 | A3 | a1 | SG,RD,IT | Z Diode | | | 11 mA | 1.3 W | | 91 V | 5 mA | <250 Ω | $1300 \cdot 10^6/°C$ | |
| ZPY100 | A3 | a1 | SG,RD,IT | Z Diode | | | 10 mA | 1.3 W | | 100 V | 5 mA | <250 Ω | $1300 \cdot 10^6/°C$ | |
| ZTE1.5 | A1 | a1 | IT | Z Diode | | | 120 mA | 0.3 W | | 1.45 V | 5 mA | 13 Ω | $-2600 \cdot 10^6/°C$ | |
| ZTE2 | A1 | a1 | IT | Z Diode | | | 120 mA | 0.3 W | | 2.15 V | 5 mA | 18 Ω | $-2600 \cdot 10^6/°C$ | |
| ZTE2.4 | A1 | a1 | IT | Z Diode | | | 120 mA | 0.3 W | | 2.38 V | 5 mA | 14 Ω | $-3400 \cdot 10^6/°C$ | |
| ZTE2.7 | A1 | a1 | IT | Z Diode | | | 105 mA | 0.3 W | | 2.7 V | 5 mA | 15 Ω | $-3400 \cdot 10^6/°C$ | |
| ZTE3 | A1 | a1 | IT | Z Diode | | | 95 mA | 0.3 W | | 3.0 V | 5 mA | 15 Ω | $-3400 \cdot 10^6/°C$ | |
| ZTE3.3 | A1 | a1 | IT | Z Diode | | | 90 mA | 0.3 W | | 3.3 V | 5 mA | 16 Ω | $-3400 \cdot 10^6/°C$ | |
| ZTE3.6 | A1 | a1 | IT | Z Diode | | | 80 mA | 0.3 W | | 3.6 V | 5 mA | 16 Ω | $-3400 \cdot 10^6/°C$ | |
| ZTE3.9 | A1 | a1 | IT | Z Diode | | | 75 mA | 0.3 W | | 3.9 V | 5 mA | 17 Ω | $-3400 \cdot 10^6/°C$ | |
| ZTE4.3 | A1 | a1 | IT | Z Diode | | | 65 mA | 0.3 W | | 4.3 V | 5 mA | 17 Ω | $-3400 \cdot 10^6/°C$ | |
| ZTE4.7 | A1 | a1 | IT | Z Diode | | | 60 mA | 0.3 W | | 4.7 V | 5 mA | 18 Ω | $-3400 \cdot 10^6/°C$ | |
| ZTE5.1 | A1 | a1 | IT | Z Diode | | | 55 mA | 0.3 W | | 5.1 V | 5 mA | 18 Ω | $-3400 \cdot 10^6/°C$ | |
| ZTK6.8 | A1 | a1 | IT | Ref. Z Diode | | | 36 mA | | | 6.8 V | 5 mA | 10 Ω | $-20 \cdot 10^6/°C$ | |
| ZTK9 | A1 | a1 | IT | Ref. Z Diode | | | 27 mA | | | 9.0 V | 5 mA | 10 Ω | $-20 \cdot 10^6/°C$ | |
| ZTK11 | A1 | a1 | IT | Ref. Z Diode | | | 19 mA | | | 11.0 V | 5 mA | 10 Ω | $-20 \cdot 10^6/°C$ | |
| ZTK18 | A1 | a1 | IT | Ref. Z Diode | | | 13 mA | | | 18.0 V | 5 mA | 11 Ω | $-20 \cdot 10^6/°C$ | |
| ZTK22 | A1 | a1 | IT | Ref. Z Diode | | | 10 mA | | | 22.0 V | 5 mA | 11 Ω | $-20 \cdot 10^6/°C$ | |
| ZTK27 | A1 | a1 | IT | Ref. Z Diode | | | 8 mA | | | 27.0 V | 5 mA | 12 Ω | $-20 \cdot 10^6/°C$ | |
| ZTK33A | A1 | a1 | IT | Ref. Z Diode | | | 7 mA | | | 31.5 V | 5 mA | 12 Ω | $-20 \cdot 10^6/°C$ | |
| ZTK33B | A1 | a1 | IT | Ref. Z Diode | | | 7 mA | | | 33.0 V | 5 mA | 12 Ω | $-20 \cdot 10^6/°C$ | |
| ZTK33C | A1 | a1 | IT | Ref. Z Diode | | | 7 mA | | | 35.0 V | 5 mA | 12 Ω | $-20 \cdot 10^6/°C$ | |
| ZY1 | B1 | a1 | IT | Z Diode | | 1000 mA | | 2 W | | 0.8 V | 100 mA | 0.5 Ω | $-2600 \cdot 10^6/°C$ | |
| ZY3.3 | B1 | a1 | RD | Z Diode | | | | 2 W | | 3.3 V | 100 mA | 3.8 Ω | | |
| ZY3.6 | B1 | a1 | RD | Z Diode | | | | 2 W | | 3.6 V | 100 mA | 3.8 Ω | | |
| ZY3.9 | B1 | a1 | RD,IT | Z Diode | | | 410 mA | 2 W | | 3.9 V | 100 mA | 3.8 Ω | $-700 \cdot 10^6/°C$ | |
| ZY4.3 | B1 | a1 | RD,IT | Z Diode | | | 260 mA | 2 W | | 4.3 V | 100 mA | 3.8 Ω | $-700 \cdot 10^6/°C$ | |
| ZY4.7 | B1 | a1 | RD,IT | Z Diode | | | 330 mA | 2 W | | 4.7 V | 100 mA | 3.8 Ω | $-700 \cdot 10^6/°C$ | |

| Type | Case | Pin-code | | | Vcla Vbro | Its | Izm | Pv | Pvts | Vz | Iz Is | rz | TK | |
|------|------|----------|---|---|-----------|-----|-----|-----|------|-----|-------|-----|-----|---|
| ZY5.1 | B1 | a1 | RD,IT | Z Diode | | | 300 mA | 2 W | | 5.1 V | 100 mA | 2 Ω | $-600 \cdot 10^6/°C$ | |
| ZY5.6 | B1 | a1 | RD,IT | Z Diode | | | 275 mA | 2 W | | 5.6 V | 100 mA | 1 Ω | $500 \cdot 10^6/°C$ | |
| ZY6.2 | B1 | a1 | RD,IT | Z Diode | | | 245 mA | 2 W | | 6.2 V | 100 mA | 1 Ω | $600 \cdot 10^6/°C$ | |
| ZY6.8 | B1 | a1 | RD,IT | Z Diode | | | 220 mA | 2 W | | 6.8 V | 100 mA | 1 Ω | $700 \cdot 10^6/°C$ | |
| ZY7.5 | B1 | a1 | RD,IT | Z Diode | | | 200 mA | 2 W | | 7.5 V | 100 mA | 1 Ω | $700 \cdot 10^6/°C$ | |
| ZY8.2 | B1 | a1 | RD,IT | Z Diode | | | 180 mA | 2 W | | 8.2 V | 100 mA | 1 Ω | $800 \cdot 10^6/°C$ | |
| ZY9.1 | B1 | a1 | RD,IT | Z Diode | | | 165 mA | 2 W | | 9.1 V | 50 mA | 2 Ω | $800 \cdot 10^6/°C$ | |
| ZY10 | B1 | a1 | RD,IT | Z Diode | | | 145 mA | 2 W | | 10 V | 50 mA | 2 Ω | $900 \cdot 10^6/°C$ | |
| ZY11 | B1 | a1 | RD,IT | Z Diode | | | 135 mA | 2 W | | 11 V | 50 mA | 4 Ω | $1000 \cdot 10^6/°C$ | |
| ZY12 | B1 | a1 | RD,IT | Z Diode | | | 120 mA | 2 W | | 12 V | 50 mA | 4 Ω | $1000 \cdot 10^6/°C$ | |
| ZY13 | B1 | a1 | RD,IT | Z Diode | | | 110 mA | 2 W | | 13 V | 50 mA | 5 Ω | $1000 \cdot 10^6/°C$ | |
| ZY15 | B1 | a1 | RD,IT | Z Diode | | | 98 mA | 2 W | | 15 V | 50 mA | 5 Ω | $1000 \cdot 10^6/°C$ | |
| ZY16 | B1 | a1 | RD,IT | Z Diode | | | 90 mA | 2 W | | 16 V | 25 mA | 6 Ω | $1100 \cdot 10^6/°C$ | |
| ZY18 | B1 | a1 | RD,IT | Z Diode | | | 80 mA | 2 W | | 18 V | 25 mA | 6 Ω | $1100 \cdot 10^6/°C$ | |
| ZY20 | B1 | a1 | RD,IT | Z Diode | | | 72 mA | 2 W | | 20 V | 25 mA | 6 Ω | $1100 \cdot 10^6/°C$ | |
| ZY22 | B1 | a1 | RD,IT | Z Diode | | | 66 mA | 2 W | | 22 V | 25 mA | 6 Ω | $1100 \cdot 10^6/°C$ | |
| ZY24 | B1 | a1 | RD,IT | Z Diode | | | 60 mA | 2 W | | 24 V | 25 mA | 7 Ω | $1100 \cdot 10^6/°C$ | |
| ZY27 | B1 | a1 | RD,IT | Z Diode | | | 53 mA | 2 W | | 27 V | 25 mA | 7 Ω | $1100 \cdot 10^6/°C$ | |
| ZY30 | B1 | a1 | RD,IT | Z Diode | | | 48 mA | 2 W | | 30 V | 25 mA | 8 Ω | $1100 \cdot 10^6/°C$ | |
| ZY33 | B1 | a1 | RD,IT | Z Diode | | | 44 mA | 2 W | | 33 V | 25 mA | 8 Ω | $1100 \cdot 10^6/°C$ | |
| ZY36 | B1 | a1 | RD,IT | Z Diode | | | 40 mA | 2 W | | 36 V | 10 mA | 21 Ω | $1100 \cdot 10^6/°C$ | |
| ZY39 | B1 | a1 | RD,IT | Z Diode | | | 37 mA | 2 W | | 39 V | 10 mA | 21 Ω | $1100 \cdot 10^6/°C$ | |
| ZY43 | B1 | a1 | RD,IT | Z Diode | | | 33 mA | 2 W | | 43 V | 10 mA | 24 Ω | $1200 \cdot 10^6/°C$ | |
| ZY47 | B1 | a1 | RD,IT | Z Diode | | | 30 mA | 2 W | | 47 V | 10 mA | 24 Ω | $1200 \cdot 10^6/°C$ | |
| ZY51 | B1 | a1 | RD,IT | Z Diode | | | 27 mA | 2 W | | 51 V | 10 mA | 25 Ω | $1200 \cdot 10^6/°C$ | |
| ZY56 | B1 | a1 | RD,IT | Z Diode | | | 25 mA | 2 W | | 56 V | 10 mA | 25 Ω | $1200 \cdot 10^6/°C$ | |
| ZY62 | B1 | a1 | RD,IT | Z Diode | | | 21 mA | 2 W | | 62 V | 10 mA | 25 Ω | $1300 \cdot 10^6/°C$ | |
| ZY68 | B1 | a1 | RD,IT | Z Diode | | | 20 mA | 2 W | | 68 V | 10 mA | 25 Ω | $1300 \cdot 10^6/°C$ | |
| ZY75 | B1 | a1 | RD,IT | Z Diode | | | 18 mA | 2 W | | 75 V | 10 mA | 30 Ω | $1300 \cdot 10^6/°C$ | |
| ZY82 | B1 | a1 | RD,IT | Z Diode | | | 16 mA | 2 W | | 82 V | 10 mA | 30 Ω | $1300 \cdot 10^6/°C$ | |
| ZY91 | B1 | a1 | RD,IT | Z Diode | | | 15 mA | 2 W | | 91 V | 5 mA | 60 Ω | $1300 \cdot 10^6/°C$ | |
| ZY100 | B1 | a1 | RD,IT | Z Diode | | | 13 mA | 2 W | | 100 V | 5 mA | 60 Ω | $1300 \cdot 10^6/°C$ | |
| ZY110 | B1 | a1 | RD,IT | Z Diode | | | 12 mA | 2 W | | 110 V | 5 mA | 80 Ω | $1300 \cdot 10^6/°C$ | |
| ZY120 | B1 | a1 | RD,IT | Z Diode | | | 11 mA | 2 W | | 120 V | 5 mA | 80 Ω | $1300 \cdot 10^6/°C$ | |
| ZY130 | B1 | a1 | RD,IT | Z Diode | | | 10 mA | 2 W | | 130 V | 5 mA | 110 Ω | $1300 \cdot 10^6/°C$ | |
| ZY150 | B1 | a1 | RD,IT | Z Diode | | | 9 mA | 2 W | | 150 V | 5 mA | 110 Ω | $1300 \cdot 10^6/°C$ | |
| ZY160 | B1 | a1 | RD,IT | Z Diode | | | 8.6 mA | 2 W | | 160 V | 5 mA | 150 Ω | $1300 \cdot 10^6/°C$ | |
| ZY180 | B1 | a1 | RD,IT | Z Diode | | | 8 mA | 2 W | | 180 V | 5 mA | 150 Ω | $1300 \cdot 10^6/°C$ | |
| ZY200 | B1 | a1 | RD,IT | Z Diode | | | 7.5 mA | 2 W | | 200 V | 5 mA | 150 Ω | $1300 \cdot 10^6/°C$ | |
| ZZ16 | B7 | a2 | IT | Bidir. TVS | 30 V | 300 A | 300 A | | | 13.0 V | 5 mA | | $<100 \cdot 10^6/°C$ | |

| Type | Case | Pin-code | | | $V_{cla}$ $V_{bro}$ | Maximum Ratings | | | | Electrical Characteristics | | | | |
|------|------|----------|---|---|------|-----|-----|-----|------|------|------------|----|----|---|
| | | | | | | Its | Izm | Pv | Pvts | Vz | Iz Is | rz | TK | |
| ZZ22 | B7 | a2 | IT | Bidir. TVS | 38 V | 200 A | 200 A | | | 18.0 V | 5 mA | | $<100 \cdot 10^6 /°C$ | |
| ZZ36 | B7 | a2 | IT | Bidir. TVS | 60 V | 130 A | 130 A | | | 30.0 V | 5 mA | | $<110 \cdot 10^6 /°C$ | |
| ZZ62 | B7 | a2 | IT | Bidir. TVS | 105 V | 80 A | 80 A | | | 52.0 V | 5 mA | | $<120 \cdot 10^6 /°C$ | |
| ZZ75 | B7 | a2 | IT | Bidir. TVS | 122 V | 68 A | 68 A | | | 63.0 V | 5 mA | | $<120 \cdot 10^6 /°C$ | |
| ZZ91 | B7 | a2 | IT | Bidir. TVS | 146 V | 56 A | 56 A | | | 76.0 V | 5 mA | | $<120 \cdot 10^6 /°C$ | |
| ZZ110 | B7 | a2 | IT | Bidir. TVS | 178 V | 45 A | 45 A | | | 92.0 V | 5 mA | | $<120 \cdot 10^6 /°C$ | |
| ZZ160 | B7 | a2 | IT | Bidir. TVS | 255 V | 30 A | 30 A | | | 135.0 V | 5 mA | | $<120 \cdot 10^6 /°C$ | |
| ZZY16 | B7 | a2 | IT | Bidir. TVS | 35 V | 200 A | 200 A | | | 13.0 V | 5 mA | | $<100 \cdot 10^6 /°C$ | |
| ZZY22 | B7 | a2 | IT | Bidir. TVS | 45 V | 130 A | 130 A | | | 18.0 V | 5 mA | | $<100 \cdot 10^6 /°C$ | |
| ZZY36 | B7 | a2 | IT | Bidir. TVS | 75 V | 90 A | 90 A | | | 30.0 V | 5 mA | | $<110 \cdot 10^6 /°C$ | |
| ZZY62 | B7 | a2 | IT | Bidir. TVS | 125 V | 60 A | 60 A | | | 52.0 V | 5 mA | | $<120 \cdot 10^6 /°C$ | |
| ZZY75 | B7 | a2 | IT | Bidir. TVS | 145 V | 50 A | 50 A | | | 63.0 V | 5 mA | | $<120 \cdot 10^6 /°C$ | |
| ZZY91 | B7 | a2 | IT | Bidir. TVS | 175 V | 40 A | 40 A | | | 76.0 V | 5 mA | | $<120 \cdot 10^6 /°C$ | |
| ZZY110 | B7 | a2 | IT | Bidir. TVS | 210 V | 30 A | 30 A | | | 92.0 V | 5 mA | | $<120 \cdot 10^6 /°C$ | |
| ZZY160 | B7 | a2 | IT | Bidir. TVS | 305 V | 20 A | 20 A | | | 135.0 V | 5 mA | | $<120 \cdot 10^6 /°C$ | |

# Chapter 2
# Kapitel 2
# Chapitre 2
# Capitulo 2

# Type Designation Codes
# Typenschlüssel
# Caractérisation des types
# Clasificación de tipos

# Type Designation Codes

## Pro-Electron Type Codes

The Pro-Electron semiconductor type code consists of two letters plus a consecutive identifer. This type code is used for all devices registered with Pro-Electron.

### The first letter identifies the semiconductor base material:

| | |
|---|---|
| A | Band gap 0.6 - 1.0 eV (e.g. Ge) |
| B | Band gap 1.0 - 1.3 eV (e.g. Si) |
| C | Band gap 1.3 eV (e.g. GaAs) |
| D | Band gap 0.6 eV (e.g. InSb) |
| R | Compound semiconductors (e.g. CdS) |

### The second letter identifies the device main function:

| | |
|---|---|
| A | Diode: rectifier, mixer, general switching purpose |
| B | Diode: variable capacitance |
| C | Transistor: small signal, audio frequencies |
| D | Transistor: power, audio frequencies (Rtjc °C/W) |
| E | Diode: tunnel diode |
| F | Transistor: small signal, high frequencies |
| G | Diode: oscillator, microwave diode |
| H | Diode: magnetic field sender |
| K | Hall element: in magnetic open circuits |
| L | Transistor: power, high frequencies (Rthjc; 15 °C/W) |
| M | Hall element: in magnetic closed loop |
| N | Optocoupler |
| P | Radiation receiver |
| Q | Radiation transmitter |
| R | Thyristor: low power |
| S | Transistor: small signal general switching purpose |
| T | Thyristor: power |
| U | Transistor: power switching purpose (Rthjc; 15 °C/W) |
| X | Diode: multiplier |
| Y | Diode: power diode, rectifier, booster |
| Z | Diode: reference diode, limiter, voltage regulator |

The consecutive identifier consists of a three digit number for commercial devices or of a single letter and a two digit number for professional devices. The size of this number does not imply any technical specifications. An additional letter that follows the identifer number may be used to state the device tolerances (e.g. Zener diodes):

| | | |
|---|---|---|
| A | ± | 1 % |
| B | ± | 2 % |
| C | ± | 5 % |
| D | ± | 10 % |
| E | ± | 20% |

## Pro-Electron Color Codes

The device type code is marked using colored rings. The first two rings – which are double in width – mark the cathode:

| wide rings 1st and 2nd letter | | small rings 3rd letter/number | | | |
|---|---|---|---|---|---|
| brown | AA | white | Z | black | 0 |
| red | BA | grey | Y | brown | 1 |
| | | black | X | red | 2 |
| | | blue | W | orange | 3 |
| | | green | V | yellow | 4 |
| | | yellow | T | green | 5 |
| | | orange | S | blue | 6 |
| | | | | violet | 7 |
| | | | | grey | 8 |
| | | | | white | 9 |

# Type Designation Codes

## Type Codes According JEDEC

JEDEC type codes use an 1N identifier for diodes or a 2N identifier for transistors, plus a four digit number that may be followed by a single letter.

## JEDEC Color Codes

For JEDEC types, the cathode is marked with one double wide ring. There are four/five more rings which identify the device as follows:

| Color | 1st..4th ring | 5th ring |
|-------|---------------|----------|
| black | 0 | - |
| brown | 1 | A |
| red | 2 | B |
| orange | 3 | C |
| yellow | 4 | D |
| green | 5 | E |
| blue | 6 | F |
| violet | 7 | G |
| grey | 8 | H |
| white | 0 | J |

The preceding identifiers 1N or 2N are not color coded.

## Individual Codes for Special Type Series

**Intermetall**
1 Series
2 Voltage

| *example* | **ZPD** | **51** |
|-----------|---------|--------|
|  | 1 | 2 |

1 Type
2 Toleranz
   A     ± 5%
   blank  ± 10%
   other tolerances on request

| *example* | **1N4764A** |  |
|-----------|-------------|--|
|  | 1 | 2 |

**Rohm**
1 Series
2 Type number

| *example* | **RLS** | **4446** |
|-----------|---------|----------|
|  | 1 | 2 |

1 Series
2 Voltage

| *example* | **MTZ** | **4.7** |
|-----------|---------|---------|
|  | 1 | 2 |

**Philips**
1 Series
2 Case
3 Voltage
4 Polarity (R- reverse)

| *example* | **BZV32** | **C** | **10** | **R** |
|-----------|-----------|-------|--------|-------|
|  | 1 | 2 | 3 | 4 |

**Motorola**
1 Series
2 Current
3 Voltage
4 Suffix

| *example* | **MBDR** | **100** | **25** | **xx** |
|-----------|----------|---------|--------|--------|
|  | 1 | 2 | 3 | 4 |

1 Series
2 Tolerance
   A     ±5%
   B     ±10%
   blank  ±20%

| *example* | **MZT** | **2778** | **A** |
|-----------|---------|----------|-------|
|  | 1 | 2 | 3 |

1 Power
2 Prefix
3 Voltage
4 Diode type
5 Tolerance in %

| *example* | **3** | **M** | **75** | **DZ** | **5** |
|-----------|-------|-------|--------|--------|-------|
|  | 1 | 2 | 3 | 4 | 5 |

# Type Designation Codes

## Other tolerances for special series

| | | |
|---|---|---|
| BZX84C2V4L, | | ±5%-±8.5% |
| BZX83C2V7, ZPD2.7, MZD3.9 | | ±5%-±8.5% |
| MMBZ5221BL, MLL4678, MZ4615 | | ±5% |
| 1SMB5913BT3, MZ5520 | | ±5% |
| 1N4370A, 1N957B, 1N4728B | A | ±5% |
| | B | ±2% |
| | C | ±1% |
| | blank | ±10% |
| BZX85C3V3 | C | ±5%-±8.5% |
| | B | ±2% |
| 1N957, 1N5221B, 1N5985B | A | ±10% |
| | B | ±5% |
| | C | ±2% |
| | D | ±1% |
| BZX55C2V4, BZX79C2.7 | C | ±5%-±8.5% |
| | B | ±2% |
| | A | ±1% |
| MZPY3.9 | C | ±2% |
| | D | ±1% |
| | blank | ±5%-±8.5% |
| MZP4726A | A | ±5% |
| | blank | ±10% |

## Toshiba

1 SMD (U)
2 Power
3 Z or ZM  (Zener Diode or bidirectional Zener diode)
4 Packing
5 Voltage
6 Tolerance     A        ±5%
                X, Y, Z  ±10V
                blank    ±10%

| example | **U** | **1** | **Z** | **B** | **270** | **X** |
|---|---|---|---|---|---|---|
| | 1 | 2 | 3 | 4 | 5 | 6 |

1 SMD (U)
2 Forward current
3 Reverse voltage
4 Diode type
5 Packing
6 Suffix

| example | **U** | **1** | **D** | **L** | **44** | **A** |
|---|---|---|---|---|---|---|
| | 1 | 2 | 3 | 4 | 5 | 6 |

1 Series
2 Reverse voltage

| example | **S5866** | **N** |
|---|---|---|
| | 1 | 2 |

1 Application
    TVS - TV
    TVR - strobes
2 Series
3 Reverse voltage

| example | **TVR** | **6** | **1** |
|---|---|---|---|
| | 1 | 2 | 3 |

1 Output current
2 Reverse voltage
3 Diode type
4 Number of rectifier units
5 Circuit
6 Isolated case (Z)
7 Serial number
8 Suffix

| example | **10** | **D** | **L** | **2** | **C** | **Z** | **47** | **A** |
|---|---|---|---|---|---|---|---|---|
| | 1 | 2 | 3 | 4 | 5 | 6 | 7 | 8 |

# Typenschlüssel

## Typkennzeichnung Pro-Electron

Die Typbezeichnung für Halbleiter-Bauelemente besteht aus zwei Buchstaben und einer laufenden Kennung. Sie wird bei Bauelementen verwendet, die bei Pro-Electron angemeldet sind.

Der erste Buchstabe benennt das Ausgangsmaterial:

| | |
|---|---|
| A | Bandabstand 0.6 - 1.0 eV (z.B. Germanium) |
| B | Bandabstand 1.0 - 1.3 eV (z.B. Silizium) |
| C | Bandabstand 1.3 eV (z.B. Gallium-Arsenid) |
| D | Bandabstand 0.6 eV (z.B. Indium-Antimonid) |
| R | Verbindungshalbleiter (z.B. Cadmium-Sulfid) |

Der zweite Buchstabe beschreibt die Hauptfunktion des Bauelementes:

| | |
|---|---|
| A | Diode: Gleichrichtung, Mischen, Schaltzwecke |
| B | Diode: variable Kapazität |
| C | Transistor: Kleinleistung, NF-Bereich |
| D | Transistor: Leistung, NF-Bereich (Rtjc °C/W) |
| E | Diode: Tunneldiode |
| F | Transistor: Kleinleistung, HF-Bereich |
| G | Diode: Oszillator, Mikrowellendiode |
| H | Diode: auf magnetische Felder ansprechend |
| K | Hallgenerator: im magnetisch offenen Kreis |
| M | Hallgenerator: im magnetisch geschlossenen Kreis |
| L | Transistor: Leistung, HF-Bereich  (Rthjc;15 °C/W) |
| N | Optokoppler |
| P | Strahlungsempfänger |
| Q | Strahlungssender |
| R | Thyristor: für kleine Leistungen |
| S | Transistor: Kleinleistung, Schaltzwecke |
| T | Thyristor: für große Leistungen |
| U | Transistor: Leistungsschalttransistor (Rthjc;15 °C/W) |
| X | Diode: Vervielfacher |
| Y | Diode: Leistungsdiode, Gleichrichter, Booster |
| Z | Diode: Referenzdiode, Begrenzer, Spannungsregler |

Die laufende Kennung besteht aus einer dreistelligen Zahl für Bauelemente der Rundfunk-, Fernseh- und Magnettontechnik bzw. aus einem Buchstaben und einer zweistelligen Zahl für solche für professionelle Anwendungen. Sie beinhaltet keine technische Aussage. Ein weiterer Buchstabe, der an die Bezeichnung des Grundtyps angehängt werden kann, kennzeichnet Toleranzen (z.B. bei Z-Dioden).

Dabei bedeuten:

| | | |
|---|---|---|
| A | ± | 1 % |
| B | ± | 2 % |
| C | ± | 5 % |
| D | ± | 10 % |
| E | ± | 20 % |

## Farbbezeichnung nach Pro-Electron:

Die Typbezeichnung wird durch Farbringe gekennzeichnet. Die beiden ersten Farbringe besitzen doppelte Breite und markieren die Katode. Es bedeuten:

| breite Ringe 1. und 2. Buchstabe | | schmale Ringe 3. Buchstabe/Ziffer | | | |
|---|---|---|---|---|---|
| braun | AA | weiß | Z | schwarz | 0 |
| rot | BA | grau | Y | braun | |
| | | schwarz | X | rot | 2 |
| | | blau | W | orange | 3 |
| | | grün | V | gelb | 4 |
| | | gelb | T | grün | 5 |
| | | orange | S | blau | 6 |
| | | | | violett | 7 |
| | | | | grau | 8 |
| | | | | weiß | |

# Typenschlüssel

## Typkennzeichnung nach JEDEC

Die Typbezeichnung besteht aus der Kennung 1N für Dioden bzw. 2N für Transistoren, der eine vierstellige Zahl und gegebenenfalls ein Buchstabe folgen.

## Farbbezeichnung nach JEDEC

Beim Farbcode für JEDEC-Typen wird die Katode durch einen doppelt breiten Ring gekennzeichnet. Vier weitere schmale Ringe bezeichnen den Typ des Bauelementes mit folgender Bedeutung.

| Farbe | 1.-4. Ring | 5. Ring |
|-------|-----------|---------|
| schwarz | 0 | - |
| braun | 1 | A |
| rot | 2 | B |
| orange | 3 | C |
| gelb | 4 | D |
| grün | 5 | E |
| blau | 6 | F |
| violett | 7 | G |
| grau | 8 | H |
| weiß | 0 | J |

Die vorangestellte Kombination 1N bzw. 2N wird nicht kodiert.

## Spezielle Typenschlüssel einzelner Hersteller

### Intermetall

| | | Beispiel | ZPD | 51 |
|---|---|---|---|---|
| 1 | Serie | | 1 | 2 |
| 2 | Spannung | | | |

| | | Beispiel | 1N4764 | A |
|---|---|---|---|---|
| 1 | Typ | | 1 | 2 |
| 2 | Toleranz | | | |

| A | ±5% |
|---|---|
| blank | ±10% |

andere Toleranzen auf Anfrage

### Rohm

| | | Beispiel | RLS | 4446 |
|---|---|---|---|---|
| 1 | Serie | | 1 | 2 |
| 2 | Typnummer | | | |

| | | Beispiel | MTZ | 4.7 |
|---|---|---|---|---|
| 1 | Serie | | 1 | 2 |
| 2 | Spannung | | | |

### Philips

| | | Beispiel | BZV32 | C | 10 | R |
|---|---|---|---|---|---|---|
| 1 | Serie | | 1 | 2 | 3 | 4 |
| 2 | Gehäuse | | | | | |
| 3 | Spannung | | | | | |
| 4 | Polarität (R- reverse) | | | | | |

### Motorola

| | | Beispiel | MBDR | 100 | 25 | xx |
|---|---|---|---|---|---|---|
| 1 | Serie | | 1 | 2 | 3 | 4 |
| 2 | Strom | | | | | |
| 3 | Spannung | | | | | |
| 4 | Suffix | | | | | |

| | | Beispiel | MZT | 2778 | A |
|---|---|---|---|---|---|
| 1 | Serie | | 1 | 2 | 3 |
| 2 | Toleranz | | | | |

| A | ±5% |
|---|---|
| B | ±10% |
| blank | ±20% |

# Typenschlüssel

| | | Beispiel | **3** | **M** | **75** | **DZ** | **5** |
|---|---|---|---|---|---|---|---|
| 1 Leistung | | | 1 | 2 | 3 | 4 | 5 |
| 2 Präfix | | | | | | | |
| 3 Spannung | | | | | | | |
| 4 Diodenart | | | | | | | |
| 5 Toleranz in % | | | | | | | |

### Abweichende Toleranzangaben für einzelne Baureihen

| | | |
|---|---|---|
| BZX84C2V4L, | | ±5% - ±8.5% |
| BZX83C2V7, ZPD2.7, MZD3.9 | | ±5% - ±8.5% |
| MMBZ5221BL, MLL4678, MZ4615 | | ±5% |
| 1SMB5913BT3, MZ5520 | | ±5% |
| 1N4370A, 1N957B, 1N4728B | A | ±5% |
| | B | ±2% |
| | C | ±1% |
| | blank | ±10% |
| BZX85C3V3 | C | ±5%-±8.5% |
| | B | ±2% |
| 1N957, 1N5221B, 1N5985B | A | ±10% |
| | B | ±5% |
| | C | ±2% |
| | D | ±1% |
| BZX55C2V4, BZX79C2.7 | C | ±5%-±8.5% |
| | B | ±2% |
| | A | ±1% |
| MZPY3.9 | C | ±2% |
| | D | ±1% |
| | blank | ±5%-±8.5% |
| MZP4726A | A | ±5% |
| | blank | ±10% |

### Toshiba

| | | Beispiel | **U** | **1** | **Z** | **B** | **270** | **X** |
|---|---|---|---|---|---|---|---|---|
| 1 SMD (U) | | | 1 | 2 | 3 | 4 | 5 | 6 |
| 2 Leistung | | | | | | | | |

3 Z oder ZM (Z-Diode, bidirektional)
4 Verpackung
5 Spannung

| 6 Toleranz | A | ±5% |
|---|---|---|
| | X, Y, Z | ±10V |
| | blank | ±10% |

| | Beispiel | **U** | **1** | **D** | **L** | **44** | **A** |
|---|---|---|---|---|---|---|---|
| 1 SMD (U) | | 1 | 2 | 3 | 4 | 5 | 6 |
| 2 Flußstrom | | | | | | | |

3 Sperrspannung
4 Diodenart
5 Verpackung
6 Suffix

| | Beispiel | **S5866** | **N** |
|---|---|---|---|
| 1 Serie | | 1 | 2 |
| 2 Sperrspannung | | | |

| | Beispiel | **TVR** | **6** | **1** |
|---|---|---|---|---|
| 1 Applikation | | 1 | 2 | 3 |
|   TVS - TV | | | | |
|   TVR - Strobes | | | | |

2 Serie
3 Sperrspannung

| | Beispiel | **10** | **D** | **L** | **2** | **C** | **Z** | **47** | **A** |
|---|---|---|---|---|---|---|---|---|---|
| 1 Ausgangsstrom | | 1 | 2 | 3 | 4 | 5 | 6 | 7 | 8 |
| 2 Sperrspannung | | | | | | | | | |

3 Diodenart
4 Zahl der Gleichrichtereinheiten
5 Schaltung
6 isoliertes Gehäuse (Z)
7 Seriennummer
8 Suffix

## Codes de références de ProElectron

Le code de caractérisation d'un composant à semiconducteur comprend deux lettres suivies d'un identificateur. Il est utilisé pour les composants inscrits chez ProElectron.

La première lettre désigne le matériau de base:

| | |
|---|---|
| A | Bande interdite de 0,6 à 1,0 eV (Germanium (Ge)) |
| B | Bande interdite de 1,0 à 1,3 eV (Silicium (Si)) |
| C | Bande interdite 1,3 eV (Gallium Arsenic (GaAs)) |
| D | Bande interdite 0;6 eV (Indium Antimoine (InSb)) |
| R | Autres semiconducteurs III-V ou II-VI (Cadmium Soufre (CdS)) |

La deuxième lettre décrit la fonction principale du composant :

| | |
|---|---|
| A | Diode: redresseur, mélangeur, fonctionnement en interrupteur |
| B | Diode: capacité variable |
| C | Transistor: faible puissance, basses fréquences |
| D | Transistor: puissance, basses fréquences (Rtjc 15°C/W) |
| E | Diode: diode à effet tunnel |
| F | Transistor: faible puissance, hautes fréquences |
| G | Diode: oscillateur, diode à microondes |
| H | Diode: détecteur de champs magnétiques |
| K | Elément à effet Hall en boucle magnétique ouverte |
| L | Transistor: puissance, hautes fréquences (Rthjc 15°C/W) |
| N | Coupleur optique |
| P | Récepteur d'onde |
| M | Elément à effet Hall en boucle magnétique fermée |
| Q | Emetteur d'onde |
| R | Thyristor: faibles puissances |
| S | Transistor: faibles puissances, fonctionnement en interrupteur |
| T | Thyristor: fortes puissances |
| U | Transistor: interrupteur aux fortes puissances (Rthjc 15°C/W) |

| | |
|---|---|
| X | Diode: multiplicateur |
| Y | Diode: diode de puissance, redresseur, »booster« |
| Z | Diode: diode de référence, limitateur, régulateur de tension |

L'identificateur qui suit les deux lettres est un nombre à trois chiffres pour les composants commerciaux des techniques radiophonique, télévisuelle et sonore, et l'ensemble d'une lettre et d'un nombre à deux chiffres pour leurs équivalents dans les applications professionnelles. Il ne contient aucune information technique. Une autre lettre qui peut être ajoutée à la description du type de base désigne les tolérances, selon la correspondance suivante:

| | | |
|---|---|---|
| A | ± | 1 % |
| B | ± | 2 % |
| C | ± | 5 % |
| D | ± | 10 % |
| E | ± | 20 % |

## Code des couleurs ProElectron

Le type est indiqué par des anneaux de couleurs. Les deux premiers anneaux ont une largeur double et marquent la cathode. Les significations des couleurs sont les suivantes:

| Anneaux larges deux premières lettres | | Anneaux minces troisième lettre ou chiffre | | | |
|---|---|---|---|---|---|
| marron | AA | blanc | Z | noir | 0 |
| rouge | BA | gris | Y | marron | 1 |
| | | noir | X | rouge | 2 |
| | | bleu | W | orange | 3 |
| | | vert | V | jaune | 4 |
| | | jaune | T | vert | 5 |
| | | orange | S | bleu | 6 |
| | | | | violet | 7 |
| | | | | gris | 8 |
| | | | | blanc | 9 |

# Caractérisation des types

## Codes de références de JEDEC

Le code comprend la mention »1N« pour les diodes, »2N« pour les transistors, suivie d'un nombre à quatre chiffres et parfois d'une lettre.

## Codes de couleurs de JEDEC

Dans le système de codes de couleurs de JEDEC, la cathode est marquée par un anneau de largeur double. Quatre autres anneaux plus minces décrivent le type du composant avec les significations suivantes:

| Couleur | Anneaux 1 à 4 | Anneau 5 |
|---------|---------------|----------|
| noir    | 0 | - |
| marron  | 1 | A |
| rouge   | 2 | B |
| orange  | 3 | C |
| jaune   | 4 | D |
| vert    | 5 | E |
| bleu    | 6 | F |
| violet  | 7 | G |
| gris    | 8 | H |
| blanc   | 0 | J |

La mention »1N« (ou »2N«) précédant ce code n'est pas retranscrite avec des couleurs.

## Codes de références par fabricant

### Intermetall

| | Exemple | | |
|---|---|---|---|
| 1 Série | | ZPD | 51 |
| 2 Tension | | 1 | 2 |

| | Exemple | | |
|---|---|---|---|
| 1 Type | | 1N4764 | A |
| 2 Tolérance | | 1 | 2 |

| A | ±5% |
|---|---|
| rien | ±10% |
| Autres tolérances sur demande | |

### Rohm

| | Exemple | | |
|---|---|---|---|
| 1 Série | | RLS | 4446 |
| 2 Numéro du type | | 1 | 2 |

| | Exemple | | |
|---|---|---|---|
| 1 Série | | MTZ | 4.7 |
| 2 Tension | | 1 | 2 |

### Philips

| | Exemple | | | |
|---|---|---|---|---|
| 1 Série | | BZV32 | C | 10 | R |
| 2 Boîtier | | 1 | 2 | 3 | 4 |
| 3 Tension | | | | | |
| 4 Polarisation (R pour la polarisation inverse) | | | | | |

### Motorola

| | Exemple | | | |
|---|---|---|---|---|
| 1 Série | | MBDR | 100 | 25 | xx |
| 2 Courant | | 1 | 2 | 3 | 4 |
| 3 Tension | | | | | |
| 4 Suffixe | | | | | |

| | Exemple | | |
|---|---|---|---|
| 1 Série | | MZT 2778 | A |
| 2 Tolérance | | 1   2 | 3 |

| A | ±5% |
|---|---|
| B | ±10% |
| rien | ±20% |

| | Exemple | | | | |
|---|---|---|---|---|---|
| 1 Puissance | | 3 | M | 75 | DZ | 5 |
| 2 Préfixe | | 1 | 2 | 3 | 4 | 5 |
| 3 Tension | | | | | | |
| 4 Type de diode | | | | | | |
| 5 Tolérance en % | | | | | | |

**Indications différentes de la tolérance pour certaines séries de composants:**

| | |
|---|---|
| BZX84C2V4L, | ±5% - ±8.5% |
| BZX83C2V7, ZPD2.7, MZD3.9 | ±5% - ±8.5% |

# Caractérisation des types

| | | | |
|---|---|---|---|
| MMBZ5221BL, MLL4678, MZ4615 | | | ±5% |
| 1SMB5913BT3, MZ5520 | | | ±5% |
| 1N4370A, 1N957B, 1N4728B | | A | ±5% |
| | | B | ±2% |
| | | C | ±1% |
| | | rien | ±10% |
| BZX85C3V3 | | C | ±5%-±8.5% |
| | | B | ±2% |
| 1N957, 1N5221B, 1N5985B | | A | ±10% |
| | | B | ±5% |
| | | C | ±2% |
| | | D | ±1% |
| BZX55C2V4, BZX79C2.7 | | C | ±5%-±8.5% |
| | | B | ±2% |
| | | A | ±1% |
| MZPY3.9 | | C | ±2% |
| | | D | ±1% |
| | | rien | ±5%-±8.5% |
| MZP4726A | | A | ±5% |
| | | rien | ±10% |

**Toshiba**

1 SMD (U)
2 Puissance
3 Z ou ZM (Diode Zener, bidirectionnelle)
4 Emballage
5 Tension
6 Tolérance

| | A | ±5% |
|---|---|---|
| | X, Y, Z | ±10V |
| | rien | ±10% |

| *Exemple* | **U** | **1** | **Z** | **B** | **270** | **X** |
|---|---|---|---|---|---|---|
| | 1 | 2 | 3 | 4 | 5 | 6 |

1 SMD (U)
2 Courant passant
3 Polarisation inverse
4 Type de diode
5 Emballage
6 Suffixe

| *Exemple* | **U** | **1** | **D** | **L** | **44** | **A** |
|---|---|---|---|---|---|---|
| | 1 | 2 | 3 | 4 | 5 | 6 |

1 Série
2 Polarisation inverse

| *Exemple* | **S5866** | **N** |
|---|---|---|
| | 1 | 2 |

1 Utilisation
    TVS - TV
    TVR - Strobes
2 Série
3 Polarisation inverse

| *Exemple* | **TVR** | **6** | **1** |
|---|---|---|---|
| | 1 | 2 | 3 |

1 Courant de sortie
2 Polarisation inverse
3 Type de diode
4 Nombre d'unités de redressement
5 Circuit
6 Boîtier isolé (Z)
7 Numéro de série
8 Suffixe

| *Exemple:* | **10** | **D** | **L** | **2** | **C** | **Z** | **47** | **A** |
|---|---|---|---|---|---|---|---|---|
| | 1 | 2 | 3 | 4 | 5 | 6 | 7 | 8 |

# Clasificación de tipos

## Caracterización de tipo según Pro-Electron

La caracterizacion para dispositivos semiconductores consiste de dos letras y una indicación correlativa. Se usa en dispositivos dados de alta en Pro-Electron.

La primera letra designa al material de partida del dispositivo:

A   Energía de enlace 0.6–1.00 eV (p.e. germanio)
B   Energía de enlace 1.0–1.3 eV (p.e. silicio)
C   Energía de enlace; 1.3 eV (p.e. arseniuro de galio)
D   Energía de enlace 0.6 eV (p.e. indio antimoniuro)
R   Semiconductor de unión (pe. sulfuro cádmico)

La segunda letra designa la función principal del dispositivo:

A   Diodo Rectificador, Mezcla, Conmutación
B   Diodo de Capacidad variable
C   Transistor de pequeña potencia, Aplicación a bajas frecuencias
D   Transistor de potencia a bajas frecuencias
E   Diodo túnel
F   Transistor de pequeña potencia a altas frecuencias
G   Diodo oscilador,diodo microondas
H   Diodo aplicable a campos magnéticos
K   Generador Hall en circuito magnético abierto
L   Transistor de potencia a altas frecuencias, $R_{thjc}$ ; 15 °C/W
M   Generador Hall en circuito magnético cerrado
N   Acoplador óptico
P   Sensor de radiaciones
Q   Emisor de radiaciones
R   Tiristor de pequeña potencia
S   Transistor de pequeña potencia para conmutación
T   Tiristor de potencia
U   Transistor de potencia de conmutación
X   Diodo multiplicador
Y   Diodo de potencia, rectificador, booster
Z   Diodo de referencia, limitador, reglador de voltaje

La indicación correlativa se compone de un número de tres cifras para componentes de técnicas de radio, televisión y magnetofónicas o de una letra y un número de dos cifras para aplicaciones profesionales. No incluyen ninguna característica técnica. Una letra adicional, que se pospone a la del tipo de dispositivo, indica las tolerancia de elemento (p.e. en diodos Zener)

Significan:

| | | |
|---|---|---|
| A | ± | 1 % |
| B | ± | 2 % |
| C | ± | 5 % |
| D | ± | 10 % |
| E | ± | 20 % |

## Caracterización de color según Pro-Electrón

La caracterización de tipo se realiza mediante diferentes colores. Los dos primeros son de doble anchura y marcan los cátodos. Significan:

| anillos anchos 1ª y 2ª letra | | anillos estrechos 3ª letra / Cifra | | | |
|---|---|---|---|---|---|
| marrón | AA | blanco | Z | negro | 0 |
| rojo | BA | gris | Y | marrón | 1 |
| | | negro | X | rojo | 2 |
| | | azul | W | naranja | 3 |
| | | verde | V | amarillo | 4 |
| | | amarillo | T | verde | 5 |
| | | naranja | S | azul | |
| | | | | violeta | 7 |
| | | | | gris | 8 |
| | | | | blanco | 9 |

# Clasificación de tipos

## Caracterización de tipo según JEDEC

a caracterización de tipo consiste de identificación 1N para diodos y 2N para transistores, a la que sigue un número de cuatro cifras o una letra.

## Caracterización de color según JEDEC

El código de color para dispositivos JEDEC se caracteriza por marcar el cátodo con un anillo ancho doble. Cuatro anillos más indican el tipo de dispositivo, significando :

| Color | 1er a 4º anillo | 5º anillonegro |
|---|---|---|
|  | 0 | – |
| marrón | 1 | A |
| rojo | 2 | B |
| naranja | 3 | C |
| amarillo | 4 | D |
| verde | 5 | E |
| azul | 6 | F |
| violeta | 7 | G |
| gris | 8 | H |
| blanco | 0 | J |

La combinación previa 1N o 2N no se codifica.

## Caracterización especial propia de fabricantes

**Intermetall**
1 Serie
2 Voltaje

| | Ejemplo | ZPD | 51 |
|---|---|---|---|
| | | 1 | 2 |

---

1 Tipo
2 Tolerancia

| | Ejemplo | 1N4764 | A |
|---|---|---|---|
| | | 1 | 2 |

A      $\pm 5\,\%$
descubierto   $\pm 10\,\%$
otras tolerancias previa consulta

**Rohm**
1 Serie
2 Número de tipo

| | Ejemplo | RLS | 4446 |
|---|---|---|---|
| | | 1 | 2 |

1 Serie
2 Voltaje

| | Ejemplo | MTZ | 4.7 |
|---|---|---|---|
| | | 1 | 2 |

**Philips**
1 Serie
2 Encapsulado
3 Voltaje
4 Polaridad

| | Ejemplo | BZV32 | C | 10 | R |
|---|---|---|---|---|---|
| | | 1 | 2 | 3 | 4 |

**Motorola**
1 Serie
2 Corriente
3 Voltaje
4 Sufijo

| | Ejemplo | MBDR | 100 | 25 | xx |
|---|---|---|---|---|---|
| | | 1 | 2 | 3 | 4 |

1 Serie
2 Tolerancia

| | Ejemplo | MZT | 2278 | A |
|---|---|---|---|---|
| | | 1 | 2 | 3 |

A      $\pm 5\,\%$
B      $\pm 10\,\%$
descubierto   $\pm 20\,\%$

1 Potencia
2 Prefijo
3 Voltaje
4 Tipo de diodo
5 Tolerancia en %

| | Ejemplo | 3 | M | 75 | DZ | 5 |
|---|---|---|---|---|---|---|
| | | 1 | 2 | 3 | 4 | 5 |

# Clasificación de tipos

## Tolerancias fuera de norma para algunas series

| | | |
|---|---|---|
| BZX84C2V4L | | ±5 %-±8.5% |
| BZX83C2V7, ZPD2.7, MZD3.9 | | ±5 %-±8.5% |
| MMBZ5221BL, MLL4678, MZ4615 | | ±5% |
| 1SMB5913BT3, MZ5520 | | ±5% |
| 1N4370,1N957B,1N4728B | A | ± 5% |
| | B | ± 2% |
| | C | ± 1% |
| | descubierto | ±10% |
| BZX85C3V3 | C | ±5%-±8.5% |
| | B | ±2% |
| 1N957,1N5221B, 1N5985B | A | ±10% |
| | B | ±5% |
| | C | ±2% |
| | D | ±1% |
| BZ55C2V4, BNZX79C2.7 | C | ±5%-±8.5% |
| | B | ±2% |
| | A | ±1% |
| MZPY3.9 | C | ±2% |
| | D | ±1% |
| | descubierto | ±5%-±8.5% |
| MZP4726A | A | ±5% |
| | descubierto | ±10% |

## Toshiba

1 SMD(U)
2 Potencia
3 Z o ZM (Diodo Z, bidireccional)
4 Embalaje, Encapsulado
5 Voltaje
6 Tolerancia   A      ±5%
             X, Y, Z  ±10V
             descubierto  ±10%

| Ejemplo | U | 1 | Z | B | 270 | X |
|---|---|---|---|---|---|---|
| | 1 | 2 | 3 | 4 | 5 | 6 |

1 SMD(U)
2 Corriente de flujo
3 Tensión de corte
4 Tipo de diodo
5 Embalaje, Encapsulado
6 Sufijo

| Ejemplo | U | 1 | D | L | 44 | A |
|---|---|---|---|---|---|---|
| | 1 | 2 | 3 | 4 | 5 | 6 |

1 Serie
2 Tensión de corte

| Ejemplo | S5866 | N |
|---|---|---|
| | 1 | 2 |

1 Aplicación
   TVS - TV
   TVS - Strobes
2 Serie
3 Tensión de corte

| Ejemplo | TVR | 6 | 1 |
|---|---|---|---|
| | | 1 | 2 | 3 |

1 Corriente de salida
2 Tensión de corte
3 Tipo de diodo
4 Número de unidades rectificadoras
5 Circuito
6 Encapsulado aislado (Z)
7 Número de serie
8 Sufijo

| Ejemplo | 10 | DL | 2 | C | Z | 4 | 7 | A |
|---|---|---|---|---|---|---|---|---|
| | 1 | 2 | 3 | 4 | 5 | 6 | 7 | 8 |

# Pincodes
# Pinbelegungen
# Codes-Pin
# Código de pin

## Pincodes
## Pinbelegungen

## Codes-Pin
## Código de pin

An individual pin number is assigned to all pins in the case outline drawings (chapter 4). In the data tables an additional short reference for the device pinout is supplied. The following tables and circuit diagrams show in which way references in the data tables and pinout numbers correlate. If no pinout number is supplied in the data table the pin assignment is included in the case drawing.

Sur les schémas des boîtiers (chapitre 4), les connexions des composants sont désignées par des numéros. Dans les tables, une courte information à propos des branchements est également présente. Les tables et schémas internes suivants montrent les correspondances entre les informations des tables et les connexions du composant. Lorsqu'aucune désignation particulière pour les pattes n'est donnée, c'est que le schéma du boîtier contient déjà une complète description des branchements.

In den Gehäusezeichnungen (Kapitel 4) sind die Anschlüsse der Bauelemente durch Nummern gekennzeichnet. In den Datentabellen ist zusätzlich eine Kurzbezeichnung für die Pinbelegung angegeben. Die folgenden Tabellen und Innenschaltungen zeigen die Zuordnung zwischen den Angaben zur Pinbelegung in den Datentabellen und den Anschlüssen des Bauelementes. Wenn keine Pinbelegung angegeben ist, enthält die Gehäusezeichnung die vollständige Anschlußbelegung.

En los planos de los encapsulados (capítulo 4) se indican las conexiones externas de los dispositivos mediante números. En las tablas de valores se ha incluido una breve descripción de los pins del dispositivo. Las siguientes tablas y símbolos de circuito muestran la relación entre los datos de las tablas de valores y los planos de los encapsulados. Si no se indica ninguna descripción de pins en las tablas de valores, significa que ésta puede leerse directamente de los planos de los encapsulados.

# Pincodes
# Pinbelegungen

| CODE | PIN 1 | PIN 2 | PIN 3 | CODE |
|------|-------|-------|-------|------|
| a1 | K | A | | a1 |
| a2 | K1 | K2 | | a2 |
| a3 | T1 | T2 | | a3 |
| b1 | A | K | | b1 |
| b2 | A1 | A2 | | b2 |
| c1 | A | K | NC | c1 |
| c2 | K1 | K2 | A1/A2 | c2 |
| c3 | NC | A | K | c3 |
| c4 | K1 | A1/A2 | K2 | c4 |
| c5 | A1 | A2 | K1/K2 | c5 |
| c6 | K1 | A2 | A1/K2 | c6 |
| c7 | A1 | K1/K2 | A2 | c7 |
| c8 | K1 | A1/A2 | K2 | c8 |
| c9 | A | K | A | c9 |
| c10 | A1 | K1/A2 | K2 | c10 |
| c11 | K1 | A1/K2 | A2 | c11 |
| c12 | K | K | A | c12 |
| c13 | NC | K | A | c13 |
| c14 | A | A | K | c14 |
| c15 | K | NC | A | c15 |
| c16 | T1 | T2 | T3 | c16 |
| c17 | A | NC | K | c17 |
| c18 | T1 | T2 | T3 | c18 |
| c19 | T1 | T2 | T3 | c19 |
| c20 | A1/K2 | K1 | A2 | c20 |

# Codes-Pin
# Código de pin

| CODE | PIN 1 | PIN 2 | PIN 3 | PIN 4 | CODE |
|------|-------|-------|-------|-------|------|
| d1 | K2 | A1 | K1 | A2 | d1 |
| d2 | K2 | A2 | A1 | A2 | d2 |
| d3 | K1 | A1 | A2 | K2 | d3 |
| d4 | NC | K | A | K | d4 |
| d5 | A1 | K1/K2 | A2 | K1/K2 | d5 |
| d6 | A1 | K1 | A2 | K2 | d6 |
| d7 | A | K | NC | NC | d7 |
| d8 | K | A1 | A2 | A3 | d8 |
| d9 | A | K | A | K | d9 |
| d10 | K1 | K2 | A2 | A1 | d10 |
| d20 | - | + | ~ | ~ | d20 |
| d21 | ~ | + | ~ | - | d21 |
| d22 | + | ~ | ~ | - | d22 |
| d23 | ~ | ~ | + | - | d23 |
| d24 | ~ | - | ~ | + | d24 |
| d25 | ~ | ~ | - | + | d25 |
| d26 | + | ~ | - | ~ | d26 |

# Pincodes
# Pinbelegungen

Codes-Pin
Código de pin

| CODE | PIN 1 | PIN 2 | PIN 3 | PIN 4 | PIN 5 | PIN 6 | PIN 7 | PIN 8 | PIN 9 | PIN 10 | PIN 11 | PIN 12 | CODE |
|------|-----|-----|-----|-----|-----|-----|-----|-----|-----|------|------|------|------|
| e1 | K | K1 | A2 | A3 | A4 | | | | | | | | e1 |
| e2 | A | K1 | K2 | K3 | K4 | | | | | | | | e2 |
| e3 | K1 | K2 | A1 | NC | A2 | | | | | | | | e3 |
| e4 | + | ~ | ~ | ~ | ~ | | | | | | | | e4 |
| f1 | K1 | A1 | K2 | A2 | K3 | A3 | | | | | | | f1 |
| f2 | A1 | K1 | A2 | K2 | A3 | K3 | | | | | | | f2 |
| f3 | K1 | K2 | K3 | A1 | A2 | A3 | | | | | | | f3 |
| f4 | A1 | A2 | A3 | K1 | K2 | K3 | | | | | | | f4 |
| h1 | K1 | A1 | K2 | A2 | K3 | A3 | K4 | A4 | | | | | h1 |
| h2 | A1 | K1 | A2 | K2 | A3 | K3 | A4 | K4 | | | | | h2 |
| h3 | K1 | K2 | K3 | K4 | A1 | A2 | A3 | A4 | | | | | h3 |
| h4 | A1 | A2 | A3 | A4 | K1 | K2 | K3 | K4 | | | | | h4 |
| i1 | A | K1 | K2 | K3 | K4 | K5 | K6 | K7 | K8 | | | | i1 |
| i2 | K | A1 | A2 | A3 | A4 | A5 | A6 | A7 | A8 | | | | i2 |
| j1 | K1 | A1 | K2 | A2 | K3 | A3 | K4 | A4 | K5 | A5 | | | i1 |
| j2 | A1 | K1 | A2 | K2 | A3 | K3 | A4 | K4 | A5 | k5 | | | i2 |
| l1 | K1 | A1 | K2 | A2 | K3 | A3 | K4 | A4 | K5 | A5 | K6 | A6 | l1 |
| l2 | A1 | K1 | A2 | K2 | A3 | K3 | A4 | K4 | A5 | K5 | A6 | K6 | l2 |

234

# Circuit symbols
# Innenschaltungen
# Symboles de circuit
# Simbolos de cirquito

A ▷|— K

a1, b1, c1, c3, c9, c12, c13
c14, c15, c17, d4, d7, d9

A1 ▷|—|◁ A2

a2

T1 ⧲ T2

a3

K1 —|◁ ▷|— K2

b2

A1 ◁•▷ A2

c2, c4, c8

A1/2
K1 ◁•▷ K2

c5, c7, d5

K1/A2
A1 ▷•▷ K2

c6, c10, c11, c20

T1 ⧲•⧲ T3
T2

c16

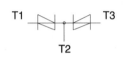

c18

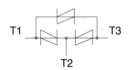

c19

d1, d2, d3, d6, d10, e3

d8

d9

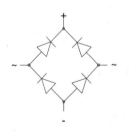

d20, d21, d22, d23, d24
d25, d26

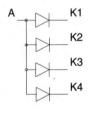

e1

e2

# Circuit symbols
## Innenschaltungen

# Symboles de circuit
## Simbolos de cirquito

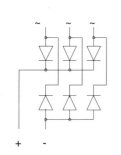

e4

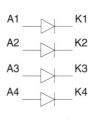

f1, f2, f3, f4

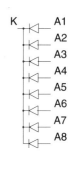

h1, h2, h3, h4

i1

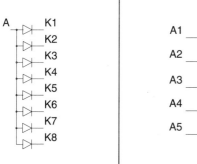

i2

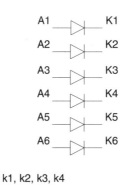

j1, j2

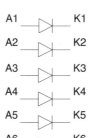

k1, k2, k3, k4

# Chapter 3
# Kapitel 3
# Chapitre 3
# Capitulo 3

# Type Identifiers
# Typkennungen
# Codes-tipe
# Código de Tipos

Due to minimum space available on the sub miniature device, type codes normally put onto these devices in abbrivated or ciphered format. In case the type identifier for an specific diode is known, the following table can provide the complete type code for the device. The overview is sorted alphabetically on type identifiers. Additionally information on manufacturer, standard case name and reference to the case outline drawing is provided. In case that there is more than one type identifier, the exact type code can be found either using additional manufacturers information or by comparing the case outline drawings.

Par manque de place sur les composants miniatures, la marque du type qui y est imprimée est généralement raccourcie ou codée. A la lecture de cette marque, les tables qui suivent permettent de retrouver la description complète du type correspondant au composant. Le sommaire est trié par ordre alphabétique des marques raccourcies ou codées. De plus, le fabricant, le nom usuel et le numéro du schéma du boîtier sont indiqués. Dans le cas où une même marque apparaît plusieurs fois dans la liste, le type exact du composant peut être déterminé grâce à au nom du fabricant et/ou à la forme du boîtier.

Bei Miniaturtypen wird aus Platzgründen eine verkürzte oder verschlüsselte Typbezeichnung (Typkennung) aufgestempelt. Ist diese Typkennung einer Diode bekannt, kann aus der nachstehenden Tabelle die vollständige Typbezeichnung entnommen werden. Die Übersicht ist alphabetisch nach der Typkennung sortiert, angegeben werden zusätzlich der Hersteller, die Gehäusebezeichnung und die Nummer der Gehäusezeichnung. Liegt eine Typkennung mehrfach vor, so kann der Typ durch Hinzuziehen der Herstellerangabe und/oder der Gehäuseform ermittelt werden.

En los tipos de dispositivo miniatura se sella por problemas de espacio una identificación abreviada o codificada ó codificada sobre el encapsulado. En caso de ser conocida la indentificatión del diodo, la siguiente table la decodifica y muestra la información completa del dispositivo. La tabla se ha ordenado alfabéticamente e incluye adicionalmente el nombre del fabricante, la denominación y el número del plano del encapsulado. En caso de aparecer una codificación varias veces en la lista, ésta puede diferenciarse por los datos del fabricante y/o del encapsulado.

| Code | 🏭 | 🔌 | | Type |
|---|---|---|---|---|
| A05 | SG | G1 | SOD6 | SMBYW02-50 |
| A1 | RD | F1 | SOT23 | BAW56 |
| A1 | NS | F1 | SOT23 | BAW56 |
| A10 | SG | G1 | SOD6 | SMBYW02-100 |
| A15 | SG | G1 | SOD6 | SMBYW02-150 |
| A1p | PH | F1 | SOT23 | BAW56 |
| A2 | PH | F1 | SOT23 | BAT18 |
| A20 | SG | G1 | SOD6 | SMBYW02-200 |
| A3 | SG | F1 | SOT23 | BAT17 |
| A3p | PH | F1 | SOT23 | BAT17 |
| A4 | RD | F1 | SOT23 | BAV70 |
| A4 | NS | F1 | SOT23 | BAV70 |
| A4p | PH | F1 | SOT23 | BAV70 |
| A6 | RD | F1 | SOT23 | BAS16 |
| A6 | NS | F1 | SOT23 | BAS16 |
| A6p | PH | F1 | SOT23 | BAS16 |
| A7 | RD | F1 | SOT23 | BAV99 |
| A7 | NS | F1 | SOT23 | BAV99 |
| A7p | PH | F1 | SOT23 | BAV99 |
| A8 | NS | F1 | SOT23 | BAS19 |
| A81 | NS | F1 | SOT23 | BAS20 |
| A82 | NS | F1 | SOT23 | BAS21 |
| A91 | PH | F1 | SOT23 | BAS17 |
| B | TO | O1 | | 1B4B1 |
| B | TO | F16 | MINIDIP4 | 1B4B42 |
| B | TO | A16 | DO41S | S5566B |
| B | TO | F13 | MINIFLAT | U1B4B42 |
| B3 | SG | G1 | SOD6 | SMBYT01-300 |
| B4 | SG | G1 | SOD6 | SMBYT01-400 |
| BA | TO | F1 | SOT23 | 1SS154 |
| BB | TO | F1 | SOT23 | 1SV128 |
| BB | TO | F12 | | 1SV237 |
| BC | TO | G5 | DO214AC | U1BC44 |
| BD | TO | F1 | SOT23 | 1SS271 |
| BE | TO | F1 | SOT23 | 1SV172 |
| BE | TO | F1 | SOT23 | 1SV252 |
| BF | TO | F1 | SOT23 | 1SS268 |
| BF | TO | F1 | SOT23 | 1SS312 |
| BF | TO | F1 | SOT23 | 1SS364 |
| BG | TO | F1 | SOT23 | 1SS269 |

| Code | 🏭 | 🔌 | | Type |
|---|---|---|---|---|
| BG | TO | F1 | SOT23 | 1SS313 |
| BH | TO | F1 | SOT23 | 1SS295 |
| blk/brn | NS | D2 | SOD80 | FDLL4148 |
| blk/orn | NS | D2 | SOD80 | FDLL4150 |
| blu | TO | A17 | DO41SS | S5688G |
| brn/blk | NS | D2 | SOD80 | FDLL4448 |
| brn/grn | NS | D2 | SOD80 | FDLL300 |
| brn/yel | NS | D2 | SOD80 | FDLL3595 |
| C2 | SG | G2 | SOD15 | SMBYT03-300 |
| C3 | SG | G2 | SOD15 | SMBYT03-300 |
| C4 | SG | G2 | SOD15 | SMBYT03-400 |
| D05 | SG | G2 | SOD15 | SMBYW04-50 |
| D10 | SG | G2 | SOD15 | SMBYW04-100 |
| D15 | SG | G2 | SOD15 | SMBYW04-150 |
| D20 | SG | G2 | SOD15 | SMBYW04-200 |
| D76 | SG | F1 | SOT23 | BAR18 |
| D85 | SG | F1 | SOT23 | BAT17DS |
| D94 | SG | F1 | SOT23 | BAR42 |
| D95 | SG | F1 | SOT23 | BAR43 |
| D96 | SG | F1 | SOT23 | BAS70-04 |
| D97 | SG | F1 | SOT23 | BAS70-05 |
| D98 | SG | F1 | SOT23 | BAS70-06 |
| DA5 | SG | F1 | SOT23 | BAR43S |
| DB1 | SG | F1 | SOT23 | BAR43A |
| DB2 | SG | F1 | SOT23 | BAR43C |
| DL | TO | G5 | DO214AC | U1DL44A |
| DL | TO | F6 | SOT89 | U1DL49 |
| DLA | TO | A16 | DO41S | 1DL41A |
| DLA | TO | A17 | DO41SS | 1DL42A |
| DLA | TO | B16 | DO15L | 1R5DL41A |
| DLA | TO | B10 | DO201AD | 3DL41A |
| FR1N | TO | A3 | DO41 | TFR1N |
| FR1T | TO | A3 | DO41 | TFR1T |
| FR2N | TO | A3 | DO41 | TFR2N |
| FR2T | TO | A3 | DO41 | TFR2T |
| FR3N | TO | A3 | DO41 | TFR3N |
| FR3T | TO | A3 | DO41 | TFR3T |
| FR4N | TO | A3 | DO41 | TFR4N |
| FR4T | TO | A3 | DO41 | TFR4T |
| G | TO | O1 | | 1G4B1 |

| Code | 🏭 | 🔌 | | Type |
|---|---|---|---|---|
| G | TO | F16 | MINIDIP4 | 1G4B42 |
| G | TO | A16 | DO41S | S5566G |
| G | TO | F13 | MINIFLAT | U1G4B42 |
| GC | TO | G5 | DO214AC | U1GC44 |
| GDE | MO | G2 | SOD15 | 1SMC5.0A |
| GDG | MO | G2 | SOD15 | 1SMC6.0A |
| GDK | MO | G2 | SOD15 | 1SMC6.5A |
| GDM | MO | G2 | SOD15 | 1SMC7.0A |
| GDP | MO | G2 | SOD15 | 1SMC7.5A |
| GDR | MO | G2 | SOD15 | 1SMC8.0A |
| GDT | MO | G2 | SOD15 | 1SMC8.5A |
| GDV | MO | G2 | SOD15 | 1SMC9.1A |
| GDX | MO | G2 | SOD15 | 1SMC10A |
| GDZ | MO | G2 | SOD15 | 1SMC11A |
| GEE | MO | G2 | SOD15 | 1SMC12A |
| GEG | MO | G2 | SOD15 | 1SMC13A |
| GEK | MO | G2 | SOD15 | 1SMC14A |
| GEM | MO | G2 | SOD15 | 1SMC15A |
| GEP | MO | G2 | SOD15 | 1SMC16A |
| GER | MO | G2 | SOD15 | 1SMC17A |
| GET | MO | G2 | SOD15 | 1SMC18A |
| GEV | MO | G2 | SOD15 | 1SMC20A |
| GEX | MO | G2 | SOD15 | 1SMC22A |
| GEZ | MO | G2 | SOD15 | 1SMC24A |
| GFE | MO | G2 | SOD15 | 1SMC26A |
| GFG | MO | G2 | SOD15 | 1SMC28A |
| GFK | MO | G2 | SOD15 | 1SMC30A |
| GFM | MO | G2 | SOD15 | 1SMC33A |
| GFP | MO | G2 | SOD15 | 1SMC36A |
| GFR | MO | G2 | SOD15 | 1SMC40A |
| GFT | MO | G2 | SOD15 | 1SMC43A |
| GFV | MO | G2 | SOD15 | 1SMC45A |
| GFX | MO | G2 | SOD15 | 1SMC48A |
| GFZ | MO | G2 | SOD15 | 1SMC51A |
| GGE | MO | G2 | SOD15 | 1SMC54A |
| GGG | MO | G2 | SOD15 | 1SMC58A |
| GGK | MO | G2 | SOD15 | 1SMC60A |
| GGM | MO | G2 | SOD15 | 1SMC64A |
| GGP | MO | G2 | SOD15 | 1SMC70A |
| GGR | MO | G2 | SOD15 | 1SMC75A |

| Code | | | Type |
|------|----|----|------|
| GGT | MO | G2 SOD15 | 1SMC78A |
| GH | TO | G5 DO214AC | U05GH44 |
| GH5 | TO | A16 DO41S | 1GH45 |
| GH5 | TO | B16 DO15L | 1R5GH45 |
| GH5 | TO | B10 DO201AD | 3GH45 |
| GH6 | TO | A16 DO41S | 1GH46 |
| gre | TO | A17 DO41SS | S5688N |
| GU | TO | A17 DO41SS | 1GU42 |
| GU | TO | F14 MINIDIP4 | O5GU4B48 |
| GU | TO | F6 SOT89 | U1GU44 |
| GU | TO | F15 H-FLAT | U05GU4B48 |
| GW | TO | G5 DO214AC | U1GWJ44 |
| GWJ | TO | A17 DO41SS | 1GWJ43 |
| J | TO | O1 | 1J4B1 |
| J | TO | F16 MINIDIP4 | 1J4B42 |
| J | TO | A16 DO41S | S5566J |
| J | TO | F13 MINIFLAT | U1J4B42 |
| JAp | PH | F1 SOT23 | BAV74 |
| JC | TO | G5 DO214AC | U1JC44 |
| JCp | PH | F1 SOT23 | BAL74 |
| JFp | PH | F1 SOT23 | BAL99 |
| JH | TO | G5 DO214AC | U05JH44 |
| JH5 | TO | A16 DO41S | 1JH45 |
| JH5 | TO | B16 DO15L | 1R5JH45 |
| JH5 | TO | B10 DO201AD | 3JH45 |
| JH6 | TO | A17 DO41SS | 1JH46 |
| JPp | PH | F1 SOT23 | BAS19 |
| JRp | PH | F1 SOT23 | BAS20 |
| JSp | PH | F1 SOT23 | BAS21 |
| JTp | PH | F3 SOT143 | BAS28 |
| JU | TO | A17 DO41SS | 1JU42 |
| JU | TO | G5 DO214AC | U1JU41 |
| K2 | RD | G1 SOD6 | D1FK20 |
| K2 | RD | F15 | S1ZAK20 |
| K20 | RD | G15 DO214AC | D2FK20 |
| K4 | RD | G1 SOD6 | D1FK40 |
| K4 | RD | F15 | S1ZAK40 |
| K40 | RD | G15 DO214AC | D2FK40 |
| KE | MO | G1 SOD6 | 1SMB5.0A |
| KG | MO | G1 SOD6 | 1SMB6.0A |
| KK | MO | G1 SOD6 | 1SMB6.5A |
| KM | MO | G1 SOD6 | 1SMB7.0A |
| KP | MO | G1 SOD6 | 1SMB7.5A |
| KR | MO | G1 SOD6 | 1SMB8.0A |
| KT | MO | G1 SOD6 | 1SMB8.5A |
| KV | MO | G1 SOD6 | 1SMB9.1A |
| KX | MO | G1 SOD6 | 1SMB10A |
| KZ | MO | G1 SOD6 | 1SMB11A |
| L2 | RD | G1 SOD6 | D1FL20 |
| L2 | RD | F15 | S1ZAL20 |
| L20 | PH | F1 SOT23 | BAS29 |
| L20 | NS | F1 SOT23 | BAS29 |
| L20 | PH | F1 SOT23 | BAS30 |
| L20 | RD | G15 DO214AC | D2FK60 |
| L21 | PH | F1 SOT23 | BAS31 |
| L21 | NS | F1 SOT23 | BAS31 |
| L22 | PH | F1 SOT23 | BAS35 |
| L22 | NS | F1 SOT23 | BAS35 |
| L30 | PH | F1 SOT23 | BAV23 |
| L31 | PH | F1 SOT23 | BAV23S |
| L41 | PH | F3 SOT143 | BAT74 |
| L42 | PH | F1 SOT23 | BAT54A |
| L43 | PH | F1 SOT23 | BAT54C |
| L44 | PH | F1 SOT23 | BAT54S |
| L4p | PH | F1 SOT23 | BAT54 |
| L51 | PH | F3 SOT143 | BAS56 |
| L52 | PH | F1 SOT23 | BAS678 |
| L5p | PH | F1 SOT23 | BAS55 |
| LE | MO | G1 SOD6 | 1SMB12A |
| LG | MO | G1 SOD6 | 1SMB13A |
| LK | MO | G1 SOD6 | 1SMB14A |
| LM | MO | G1 SOD6 | 1SMB15A |
| LP | MO | G1 SOD6 | 1SMB16A |
| LR | MO | G1 SOD6 | 1SMB17A |
| LT | MO | G1 SOD6 | 1SMB18A |
| LV | MO | G1 SOD6 | 1SMB20A |
| LX | MO | G1 SOD6 | 1SMB22A |
| LZ | MO | G1 SOD6 | 1SMB24A |
| ME | MO | G1 SOD6 | 1SMB26A |
| MG | MO | G1 SOD6 | 1SMB28A |
| MK | MO | G1 SOD6 | 1SMB30A |
| MM | MO | G1 SOD6 | 1SMB33A |
| MP | MO | G1 SOD6 | 1SMB36A |
| MR | MO | G1 SOD6 | 1SMB40A |
| MT | MO | G1 SOD6 | 1SMB43A |
| MV | MO | G1 SOD6 | 1SMB45A |
| MX | MO | G1 SOD6 | 1SMB48A |
| MZ | MO | G1 SOD6 | 1SMB51A |
| N | TO | A16 DO41S | S5566N |
| NE | MO | G1 SOD6 | 1SMB54A |
| NG | MO | G1 SOD6 | 1SMB58A |
| NH | TO | A16 DO41S | 1NH41 |
| NH | TO | A17 DO41SS | 1NH42 |
| NH | TO | G5 DO214AC | U05NH44 |
| NH5 | TO | B16 DO15L | 1R5NH45 |
| NH5 | TO | B10 DO201AD | 2NH45 |
| NH5 | TO | A16 DO41S | O5NH45 |
| NH6 | TO | A17 DO41SS | O5NH46 |
| NK | MO | G1 SOD6 | 1SMB60A |
| NM | MO | G1 SOD6 | 1SMB64A |
| NP | MO | G1 SOD6 | 1SMB70A |
| NR | MO | G1 SOD6 | 1SMB75A |
| NT | MO | G1 SOD6 | 1SMB78A |
| NU | TO | A17 DO41SS | O5NU42 |
| NU | TO | G5 DO214AC | U05NU44 |
| NV | MO | G1 SOD6 | 1SMB85A |
| NX | MO | G1 SOD6 | 1SMB90A |
| NZ | MO | G1 SOD6 | 1SMB100A |
| O5NU | TO | A16 DO41S | O5NU41 |
| OR8GU | TO | A3 DO41 | OR8GU41 |
| P | PH | G4 SOD123 | BA582 |
| P | PH | G4 SOD123 | BB515 |
| P | PH | G4 SOD123 | BB619 |
| P | PH | G4 SOD123 | BB620 |
| P1 | PH | G3 SOD323 | BB131 |
| P2 | PH | G3 SOD323 | BB132 |
| P3 | PH | G3 SOD323 | BB133 |
| P4 | PH | G3 SOD323 | BB134 |
| P5 | PH | G3 SOD323 | BB135 |
| p8A | PH | F1 SOT23 | PMBZ5226B |

| Code | | | | Type |
|---|---|---|---|---|
| p8B | PH | F1 | SOT23 | PMBZ5227B |
| p8C | PH | F1 | SOT23 | PMBZ5228B |
| p8D | PH | F1 | SOT23 | PMBZ5229B |
| p8E | PH | F1 | SOT23 | PMBZ5230B |
| p8F | PH | F1 | SOT23 | PMBZ5231B |
| p8G | PH | F1 | SOT23 | PMBZ5232B |
| p8H | PH | F1 | SOT23 | PMBZ5233B |
| p8J | PH | F1 | SOT23 | PMBZ5234B |
| p8K | PH | F1 | SOT23 | PMBZ5235B |
| p8L | PH | F1 | SOT23 | PMBZ5236B |
| p8M | PH | F1 | SOT23 | PMBZ5237B |
| p8N | PH | F1 | SOT23 | PMBZ5238B |
| p8P | PH | F1 | SOT23 | PMBZ5239B |
| p8Q | PH | F1 | SOT23 | PMBZ5240B |
| p8R | PH | F1 | SOT23 | PMBZ5241B |
| p8S | PH | F1 | SOT23 | PMBZ5242B |
| p8T | PH | F1 | SOT23 | PMBZ5243B |
| p8U | PH | F1 | SOT23 | PMBZ5244B |
| p8V | PH | F1 | SOT23 | PMBZ5245B |
| p8W | PH | F1 | SOT23 | PMBZ5246B |
| p8X | PH | F1 | SOT23 | PMBZ5247B |
| p8Y | PH | F1 | SOT23 | PMBZ5248B |
| p8Z | PH | F1 | SOT23 | PMBZ5249B |
| p9A | PH | F1 | SOT23 | PLVA650A |
| p9B | PH | F1 | SOT23 | PLVA653A |
| p9C | PH | F1 | SOT23 | PLVA656A |
| p9D | PH | F1 | SOT23 | PLVA659A |
| p9E | PH | F1 | SOT23 | PLVA662A |
| p9F | PH | F1 | SOT23 | PLVA665A |
| p9G | PH | F1 | SOT23 | PLVA668A |
| PE | MO | G1 | SOD6 | 1SMB110A |
| PG | MO | G1 | SOD6 | 1SMB120A |
| PK | MO | G1 | SOD6 | 1SMB130A |
| PM | MO | G1 | SOD6 | 1SMB150A |
| PP | MO | G1 | SOD6 | 1SMB160A |
| PR | MO | G1 | SOD6 | 1SMB170A |
| red/wht | NS | D2 | SOD80 | FDLL600 |
| S1 | TO | G9 | | 1SS239 |
| S12 | PH | F1 | SOT23 | BBY39 |
| S12 | SG | F8 | SOT223 | STPS120E |

| Code | | | | Type |
|---|---|---|---|---|
| S13 | PH | F1 | SOT23 | BBY42 |
| S13 | SG | F8 | SOT223 | STPS130E |
| S14 | PH | F1 | SOT23 | BB901 |
| S14 | SG | F8 | SOT223 | STPS140E |
| S16 | SG | F8 | SOT223 | STPS160E |
| S2 | TO | G9 | | 1SS242 |
| S2 | TO | G6 | | 1SS315 |
| S2 | PH | F1 | SOT23 | BBY40 |
| S32 | SG | G2 | SOD15 | STPS320S |
| S33 | SG | G2 | SOD15 | STPS330S |
| S34 | SG | G2 | SOD15 | STPS340S |
| S4 | PH | F1 | SOT23 | BBY62 |
| S4 | RD | G1 | SOD6 | D1FS4 |
| S4 | RD | F15 | | S1ZAS4 |
| S40 | RD | G15 | DO214AC | D2FS4 |
| SF1 | PH | F1 | SOT23 | BB804-1 |
| SF2 | PH | F1 | SOT23 | BB804-2 |
| SF3 | PH | F1 | SOT23 | BB804-3 |
| SG | TO | F6 | SOT89 | U1GWJ49 |
| SI | TO | F6 | SOT89 | U1GWJ2C49 |
| T | PH | G4 | SOD123 | BB811 |
| T1 | TO | G9 | | 1SV153 |
| T1 | TO | G6 | | 1SV214 |
| T1 | IT | F7 | SOT89A | DZ89C3V9 |
| T10 | IT | F7 | SOT89A | DZ89C9V1 |
| T11 | IT | F7 | SOT89A | DZ89C10 |
| T12 | IT | F7 | SOT89A | DZ89C11 |
| T13 | IT | F7 | SOT89A | DZ89C12 |
| T14 | IT | F7 | SOT89A | DZ89C13 |
| T15 | IT | F7 | SOT89A | DZ89C15 |
| T16 | IT | F7 | SOT89A | DZ89C16 |
| T17 | IT | F7 | SOT89A | DZ89C18 |
| T18 | IT | F7 | SOT89A | DZ89C20 |
| T19 | IT | F7 | SOT89A | DZ89C22 |
| T2 | TO | G9 | | 1SV161 |
| T2 | TO | G6 | | 1SV215 |
| T2 | TO | G6 | | 1SV216 |
| T2 | IT | F7 | SOT89A | DZ89C4V3 |
| T20 | IT | F7 | SOT89A | DZ89C24 |
| T21 | IT | F7 | SOT89A | DZ89C27 |

| Code | | | | Type |
|---|---|---|---|---|
| T22 | IT | F7 | SOT89A | DZ89C30 |
| T22 | SG | F8 | SOT223 | STPS220CE |
| T23 | IT | F7 | SOT89A | DZ89C33 |
| T23 | SG | F8 | SOT223 | STPS230CE |
| T24 | IT | F7 | SOT89A | DZ89C36 |
| T24 | SG | F8 | SOT223 | STPS240CE |
| T25 | IT | F7 | SOT89A | DZ89C39 |
| T26 | IT | F7 | SOT89A | DZ89C43 |
| T26 | SG | F8 | SOT223 | STPS260CE |
| T27 | IT | F7 | SOT89A | DZ89C47 |
| T28 | IT | F7 | SOT89A | DZ89C51 |
| T29 | IT | F7 | SOT89A | DZ89C56 |
| T3 | TO | G6 | | 1SV245 |
| T3 | IT | F7 | SOT89A | DZ89C4V7 |
| T30 | IT | F7 | SOT89A | DZ89C62 |
| T31 | IT | F7 | SOT89A | DZ89C68 |
| T32 | IT | F7 | SOT89A | DZ89C75 |
| T33 | IT | F7 | SOT89A | DZ89C82 |
| T34 | IT | F7 | SOT89A | DZ89C91 |
| T35 | IT | F7 | SOT89A | DZ89C100 |
| T36 | IT | F7 | SOT89A | DZ89C110 |
| T37 | IT | F7 | SOT89A | DZ89C120 |
| T38 | IT | F7 | SOT89A | DZ89C130 |
| T39 | IT | F7 | SOT89A | DZ89C150 |
| T4 | TO | G9 | | 1SV186 |
| T4 | TO | G9 | | 1SV204 |
| T4 | IT | F7 | SOT89A | DZ89C5V1 |
| T40 | IT | F7 | SOT89A | DZ89C160 |
| T41 | IT | F7 | SOT89A | DZ89C180 |
| T42 | IT | F7 | SOT89A | DZ89C200 |
| T5 | TO | G9 | | 1SV153A |
| T5 | IT | F7 | SOT89A | DZ89C5V6 |
| T6 | TO | G9 | | 1SV211 |
| T6 | TO | G6 | | 1SV217 |
| T6 | IT | F7 | SOT89A | DZ89C6V2 |
| T7 | TO | G9 | | 1SV204 |
| T7 | TO | G6 | | 1SV230 |
| T7 | IT | F7 | SOT89A | DZ89C6V8 |
| T8 | TO | G9 | | 1SV212 |
| T8 | TO | G6 | | 1SV229 |

| Code | | | | Type |
|------|------|------|--------|------|
| T8 | IT | F7 | SOT89A | DZ89C7V5 |
| T9 | TO | G9 | | 1SV227 |
| T9 | TO | G6 | | 1SV232 |
| T9 | IT | F7 | SOT89A | DZ89C8V2 |
| TA | TO | G9 | | 1SV226 |
| TA | TO | G6 | | 1SV231 |
| TB | TO | G6 | | 1SV238 |
| TC | TO | G6 | | 1SV239 |
| TH | TO | G5 | DO214AC | U05TH44 |
| TY | TO | G9 | | 1SS241 |
| TY | TO | G6 | | 1SS314 |
| U32 | SG | G1 | SOD6 | STPS320U |
| U33 | SG | G1 | SOD6 | STPS330U |
| U34 | SG | G1 | SOD6 | STPS340U |
| V1 | TO | F1 | SOT23 | 1SV160 |
| V1 | RD | G1 | SOD6 | D1F10 |
| V1 | RD | F15 | | S1ZA10 |
| V10 | RD | G15 | DO214AC | D2F10 |
| V10 | IT | F1 | TO236 | DZ23C6V2 |
| V11 | IT | F1 | TO236 | DZ23C6V8 |
| V12 | IT | F1 | TO236 | DZ23C7V5 |
| V13 | IT | F1 | TO236 | DZ23C8V2 |
| V14 | IT | F1 | TO236 | DZ23C9V1 |
| V15 | IT | F1 | TO236 | DZ23C10 |
| V16 | IT | F1 | TO236 | DZ23C11 |
| V17 | IT | F1 | TO236 | DZ23C12 |
| V18 | IT | F1 | TO236 | DZ23C13 |
| V19 | IT | F1 | TO236 | DZ23C15 |
| V2 | RD | G1 | SOD6 | D1F20 |
| V2 | RD | F15 | | S1ZA20 |
| V20 | RD | G2 | SOD15 | D2F20 |
| V20 | IT | F1 | TO236 | DZ23C16 |
| V21 | IT | F1 | TO236 | DZ23C18 |
| V22 | IT | F1 | TO236 | DZ23C20 |
| V23 | IT | F1 | TO236 | DZ23C22 |
| V24 | IT | F1 | TO236 | DZ23C24 |
| V25 | IT | F1 | TO236 | DZ23C27 |
| V26 | IT | F1 | TO236 | DZ23C30 |
| V27 | IT | F1 | TO236 | DZ23C33 |
| V28 | IT | F1 | TO236 | DZ23C36 |
| V29 | IT | F1 | TO236 | DZ23C39 |
| V3 | TO | F1 | SOT23 | 1SV225 |
| V30 | IT | F1 | TO236 | DZ23C43 |
| V31 | IT | F1 | TO236 | DZ23C47 |
| V32 | IT | F1 | TO236 | DZ23C51 |
| V4 | TO | F1 | SOT23 | 1SV228 |
| V4 | RD | G1 | SOD6 | D1F40 |
| V4 | RD | F15 | | S1ZA40 |
| V40 | RD | G2 | SOD15 | D2F40 |
| V5 | TO | F1 | SOT23 | 1SV242 |
| V5 | IT | F1 | TO236 | DZ23C2V7 |
| V5 | IT | F1 | TO236 | DZ23C3 |
| V5 | IT | F1 | TO236 | DZ23C3V3 |
| V5 | IT | F1 | TO236 | DZ23C3V6 |
| V5 | IT | F1 | TO236 | DZ23C3V9 |
| V6 | RD | G1 | SOD6 | D1F60 |
| V6 | IT | F1 | TO236 | DZ23C4V3 |
| V6 | RD | F15 | | S1ZA60 |
| V60 | RD | G2 | SOD15 | D2F60 |
| V7 | IT | F1 | TO236 | DZ23C4V7 |
| V8 | IT | F1 | TO236 | DZ23C5V1 |
| V9 | IT | F1 | TO236 | DZ23C5V6 |
| VR1B | TO | A3 | DO41 | TVR1B |
| VR1G | TO | A3 | DO41 | TVR1G |
| VR1J | TO | A3 | DO41 | TVR1J |
| VR2B | TO | A3 | DO41 | TVR2B |
| VR2G | TO | A3 | DO41 | TVR2G |
| VR2J | TO | A3 | DO41 | TVR2J |
| VR4J | TO | B16 | DO15L | TVR4J |
| VR4N | TO | B16 | DO15L | TVR4N |
| VR5B | TO | A17 | DO41SS | TVR5B |
| VR5G | TO | A17 | DO41SS | TVR5G |
| VR5J | TO | A17 | DO41SS | TVR5J |
| W3 | SG | F1 | SOT23 | BZX84C2V4 |
| W4 | SG | F1 | SOT23 | BZX84C2V7 |
| W5 | SG | F1 | SOT23 | BZX84C3V0 |
| W6 | SG | F1 | SOT23 | BZX84C3V3 |
| W7 | SG | F1 | SOT23 | BZX84C3V6 |
| W8 | SG | F1 | SOT23 | BZX84C3V9 |
| W9 | SG | F1 | SOT23 | BZX84C4V3 |
| W9 | MO | F1 | SOT23 | BZX84C4V3L |
| whi | TO | A17 | DO41SS | S5688B |
| Y1 | SG | F1 | SOT23 | BZX84C11 |
| Y1 | IT | F1 | SOT23 | BZX84C11 |
| Y1 | NS | F1 | SOT23 | BZX84C11 |
| Y1 | MO | F1 | SOT23 | BZX84C11L |
| Y10 | SG | F1 | SOT23 | BZX84C27 |
| Y10 | IT | F1 | SOT23 | BZX84C27 |
| Y10 | PH | F1 | SOT23 | BZX84C27 |
| Y10 | NS | F1 | SOT23 | BZX84C27 |
| Y10 | MO | F1 | SOT23 | BZX84C27L |
| Y11 | SG | F1 | SOT23 | BZX84C30 |
| Y11 | IT | F1 | SOT23 | BZX84C30 |
| Y11 | PH | F1 | SOT23 | BZX84C30 |
| Y11 | NS | F1 | SOT23 | BZX84C30 |
| Y11 | MO | F1 | SOT23 | BZX84C30L |
| Y12 | SG | F1 | SOT23 | BZX84C33 |
| Y12 | IT | F1 | SOT23 | BZX84C33 |
| Y12 | PH | F1 | SOT23 | BZX84C33 |
| Y12 | NS | F1 | SOT23 | BZX84C33 |
| Y12 | MO | F1 | SOT23 | BZX84C33L |
| Y13 | SG | F1 | SOT23 | BZX84C36 |
| Y13 | IT | F1 | SOT23 | BZX84C36 |
| Y13 | PH | F1 | SOT23 | BZX84C36 |
| Y13 | MO | F1 | SOT23 | BZX84C36L |
| Y14 | SG | F1 | SOT23 | BZX84C39 |
| Y14 | IT | F1 | SOT23 | BZX84C39 |
| Y14 | PH | F1 | SOT23 | BZX84C39 |
| Y14 | MO | F1 | SOT23 | BZX84C39L |
| Y15 | SG | F1 | SOT23 | BZX84C43 |
| Y15 | IT | F1 | SOT23 | BZX84C43 |
| Y15 | PH | F1 | SOT23 | BZX84C43 |
| Y15 | MO | F1 | SOT23 | BZX84C43L |
| Y16 | SG | F1 | SOT23 | BZX84C47 |
| Y16 | IT | F1 | SOT23 | BZX84C47 |
| Y16 | PH | F1 | SOT23 | BZX84C47L |
| Y16 | MO | F1 | SOT23 | BZX84C47L |
| Y17 | SG | F1 | SOT23 | BZX84C51 |
| Y17 | IT | F1 | SOT23 | BZX84C51 |
| Y17 | PH | F1 | SOT23 | BZX84C51 |

| Code | 🏭 | ⧧ | | Type |
|------|------|------|------|------|
| Y17 | MO | F1 | SOT23 | BZX84C51L |
| Y18 | SG | F1 | SOT23 | BZX84C56 |
| Y18 | PH | F1 | SOT23 | BZX84C56 |
| Y18 | MO | F1 | SOT23 | BZX84C56L |
| Y19 | SG | F1 | SOT23 | BZX84C62 |
| Y19 | PH | F1 | SOT23 | BZX84C62 |
| Y19 | MO | F1 | SOT23 | BZX84C62L |
| Y1p | PH | F1 | SOT23 | BZX84C11 |
| Y2 | SG | F1 | SOT23 | BZX84C12 |
| Y2 | IT | F1 | SOT23 | BZX84C12 |
| Y2 | NS | F1 | SOT23 | BZX84C12 |
| Y2 | MO | F1 | SOT23 | BZX84C12L |
| Y20 | SG | F1 | SOT23 | BZX84C68 |
| Y20 | PH | F1 | SOT23 | BZX84C68 |
| Y20 | MO | F1 | SOT23 | BZX84C68L |
| Y21 | SG | F1 | SOT23 | BZX84C75 |
| Y21 | PH | F1 | SOT23 | BZX84C75 |
| Y21 | MO | F1 | SOT23 | BZX84C75L |
| Y2p | PH | F1 | SOT23 | BZX84C12 |
| Y3 | SG | F1 | SOT23 | BZX84C13 |
| Y3 | IT | F1 | SOT23 | BZX84C13 |
| Y3 | NS | F1 | SOT23 | BZX84C13 |
| Y3 | MO | F1 | SOT23 | BZX84C13L |
| Y3p | PH | F1 | SOT23 | BZX84C13 |
| Y4 | SG | F1 | SOT23 | BZX84C15 |
| Y4 | IT | F1 | SOT23 | BZX84C15 |
| Y4 | NS | F1 | SOT23 | BZX84C15 |
| Y4 | MO | F1 | SOT23 | BZX84C15L |
| Y4p | PH | F1 | SOT23 | BZX84C15 |
| Y5 | SG | F1 | SOT23 | BZX84C16 |
| Y5 | IT | F1 | SOT23 | BZX84C16 |
| Y5 | NS | F1 | SOT23 | BZX84C16 |
| Y5 | MO | F1 | SOT23 | BZX84C16L |
| Y5p | PH | F1 | SOT23 | BZX84C16 |
| Y6 | SG | F1 | SOT23 | BZX84C18 |
| Y6 | IT | F1 | SOT23 | BZX84C18 |
| Y6 | NS | F1 | SOT23 | BZX84C18 |
| Y6 | MO | F1 | SOT23 | BZX84C18L |
| Y6p | PH | F1 | SOT23 | BZX84C18 |
| Y7 | SG | F1 | SOT23 | BZX84C20 |
| Y7 | IT | F1 | SOT23 | BZX84C20 |
| Y7 | NS | F1 | SOT23 | BZX84C20 |
| Y7 | MO | F1 | SOT23 | BZX84C20L |
| Y7p | PH | F1 | SOT23 | BZX84C20 |
| Y8 | SG | F1 | SOT23 | BZX84C22 |
| Y8 | IT | F1 | SOT23 | BZX84C22 |
| Y8 | NS | F1 | SOT23 | BZX84C22 |
| Y8 | MO | F1 | SOT23 | BZX84C22L |
| Y8p | PH | F1 | SOT23 | BZX84C22 |
| Y9 | SG | F1 | SOT23 | BZX84C24 |
| Y9 | IT | F1 | SOT23 | BZX84C24 |
| Y9 | NS | F1 | SOT23 | BZX84C24 |
| Y9 | MO | F1 | SOT23 | BZX84C24L |
| Y9p | PH | F1 | SOT23 | BZX84C24 |
| yel | TO | A17 | DO41SS | S5688J |
| Z1 | SG | F1 | SOT23 | BZX84C4V7 |
| Z1 | IT | F1 | SOT23 | BZX84C4V7 |
| Z1 | NS | F1 | SOT23 | BZX84C4V7 |
| Z1 | MO | F1 | SOT23 | BZX84C4V7L |
| Z11 | PH | F1 | SOT23 | BZX84C2V4 |
| Z11 | MO | F1 | SOT23 | BZX84C2V4L |
| Z12 | IT | F1 | SOT23 | BZX84C2V7 |
| Z12 | PH | F1 | SOT23 | BZX84C2V7 |
| Z12 | MO | F1 | SOT23 | BZX84C2V7L |
| Z13 | IT | F1 | SOT23 | BZX84C3V0 |
| Z13 | PH | F1 | SOT23 | BZX84C3V0 |
| Z13 | MO | F1 | SOT23 | BZX84C3V0L |
| Z14 | IT | F1 | SOT23 | BZX84C3V3 |
| Z14 | PH | F1 | SOT23 | BZX84C3V3 |
| Z14 | MO | F1 | SOT23 | BZX84C3V3L |
| Z15 | IT | F1 | SOT23 | BZX84C3V6 |
| Z15 | PH | F1 | SOT23 | BZX84C3V6 |
| Z15 | MO | F1 | SOT23 | BZX84C3V6L |
| Z16 | IT | F1 | SOT23 | BZX84C3V9 |
| Z16 | PH | F1 | SOT23 | BZX84C3V9 |
| Z16 | MO | F1 | SOT23 | BZX84C3V9L |
| Z17 | IT | F1 | SOT23 | BZX84C4V3 |
| Z17 | PH | F1 | SOT23 | BZX84C4V3 |
| Z1p | PH | F1 | SOT23 | BZX84C4V7 |
| Z2 | SG | F1 | SOT23 | BZX84C5V1 |
| Z2 | IT | F1 | SOT23 | BZX84C5V1 |
| Z2 | NS | F1 | SOT23 | BZX84C5V1 |
| Z2 | MO | F1 | SOT23 | BZX84C5V1L |
| Z2p | PH | F1 | SOT23 | BZX84C5V1 |
| Z3 | SG | F1 | SOT23 | BZX84C5V6 |
| Z3 | IT | F1 | SOT23 | BZX84C5V6 |
| Z3 | NS | F1 | SOT23 | BZX84C5V6 |
| Z3 | MO | F1 | SOT23 | BZX84C5V6L |
| Z3p | PH | F1 | SOT23 | BZX84C5V6 |
| Z4 | SG | F1 | SOT23 | BZX84C6V2 |
| Z4 | IT | F1 | SOT23 | BZX84C6V2 |
| Z4 | NS | F1 | SOT23 | BZX84C6V2 |
| Z4 | MO | F1 | SOT23 | BZX84C6V2L |
| Z4p | PH | F1 | SOT23 | BZX84C6V2 |
| Z5 | SG | F1 | SOT23 | BZX84C6V8 |
| Z5 | IT | F1 | SOT23 | BZX84C6V8 |
| Z5 | NS | F1 | SOT23 | BZX84C6V8 |
| Z5 | MO | F1 | SOT23 | BZX84C6V8L |
| Z5p | PH | F1 | SOT23 | BZX84C6V8 |
| Z6 | SG | F1 | SOT23 | BZX84C7V5 |
| Z6 | IT | F1 | SOT23 | BZX84C7V5 |
| Z6 | NS | F1 | SOT23 | BZX84C7V5 |
| Z6 | MO | F1 | SOT23 | BZX84C7V5L |
| Z6p | PH | F1 | SOT23 | BZX84C7V5 |
| Z7 | SG | F1 | SOT23 | BZX84C8V2 |
| Z7 | IT | F1 | SOT23 | BZX84C8V2 |
| Z7 | NS | F1 | SOT23 | BZX84C8V2 |
| Z7 | MO | F1 | SOT23 | BZX84C8V2L |
| Z7p | PH | F1 | SOT23 | BZX84C8V2 |
| Z8 | SG | F1 | SOT23 | BZX84C9V1 |
| Z8 | IT | F1 | SOT23 | BZX84C9V1 |
| Z8 | NS | F1 | SOT23 | BZX84C9V1 |
| Z8 | MO | F1 | SOT23 | BZX84C9V1L |
| Z8p | PH | F1 | SOT23 | BZX84C9V1 |
| Z9 | SG | F1 | SOT23 | BZX84C10 |
| Z9 | IT | F1 | SOT23 | BZX84C10 |
| Z9 | NS | F1 | SOT23 | BZX84C10 |
| Z9 | MO | F1 | SOT23 | BZX84C10L |
| Z9p | PH | F1 | SOT23 | BZX84C10 |
| ZDD | SG | G1 | SOD6 | SM5Z3V3A |

# Type Identifiers
# Typkennungen

# Codes-tipe
# Código de Tipos

| Code | | | | Type |
|------|---|----|------|------|
| ZDE | SG | G1 | SOD6 | SM5Z3V6A |
| ZDF | SG | G1 | SOD6 | SM5Z3V9A |
| ZDG | SG | G1 | SOD6 | SM5Z4V3A |
| ZDH | SG | G1 | SOD6 | SM5Z4V7A |
| ZDK | SG | G1 | SOD6 | SM5Z5V1A |
| ZDL | SG | G1 | SOD6 | SM5Z5V6A |
| ZDN | SG | G1 | SOD6 | SM5Z6V2A |
| ZDP | SG | G1 | SOD6 | SM5Z6V8A |
| ZDQ | SG | G1 | SOD6 | SM5Z7V5A |
| ZDR | SG | G1 | SOD6 | SM5Z8V2A |
| ZDT | SG | G1 | SOD6 | SM5Z9V1A |
| ZDU | SG | G1 | SOD6 | SM5Z10A |
| ZDW | SG | G1 | SOD6 | SM5Z12A |
| ZDX | SG | G1 | SOD6 | SM5Z13A |
| ZDY | SG | G1 | SOD6 | SM5Z14A |
| ZDZ | SG | G1 | SOD6 | SM5Z15A |
| ZED | SG | G1 | SOD6 | SM5Z16A |
| ZEF | SG | G1 | SOD6 | SM5Z18A |
| ZEH | SG | G1 | SOD6 | SM5Z20A |
| ZEK | SG | G1 | SOD6 | SM5Z22A |
| ZEL | SG | G1 | SOD6 | SM5Z24A |
| ZEN | SG | G1 | SOD6 | SM5Z27A |
| ZEQ | SG | G1 | SOD6 | SM5Z30A |
| ZER | SG | G1 | SOD6 | SM5Z33A |
| ZES | SG | G1 | SOD6 | SM5Z36A |
| ZET | SG | G1 | SOD6 | SM5Z39A |
| ZEV | SG | G1 | SOD6 | SM5Z47A |
| ZFD | SG | G1 | SOD6 | SM5Z62A |
| ZFG | SG | G1 | SOD6 | SM5Z82A |
| ZFK | SG | G1 | SOD6 | SM5Z91A |
| ZFL | SG | G1 | SOD6 | SM5Z100A |
| ZFM | SG | G1 | SOD6 | SM5Z110A |
| ZFR | SG | G1 | SOD6 | SM5Z150A |
| ZFU | SG | G1 | SOD6 | SM5Z180A |
| ZFW | SG | G1 | SOD6 | SM5Z200A |
| 1GWJ | TO | A16 | DO41S | 1GWJ42 |
| 1JU | TO | A16 | DO41S | 1JU41 |
| 1R5B | TO | B16 | DO15L | 1R5BZ41 |
| 1R5G | TO | B16 | DO15L | 1R5GZ41 |
| 1R5GU | TO | B16 | DO15L | 1R5GU41 |

| Code | | | | Type |
|------|---|----|-----------|------|
| 1R5JU | TO | B16 | DO15L | 1R5JU41 |
| 1R5NH | TO | B16 | DO15L | 1R5NH41 |
| 2B | TO | O2 | | 2B4B41 |
| 2G | TO | O2 | | 2G4B41 |
| 2J | TO | O2 | | 2J4B41 |
| 2Y4 | PH | F6 | SOT89 | BZV49C2V4 |
| 2Y7 | PH | F6 | SOT89 | BZV49C2V7 |
| 3B | TO | O3 | | 3B4B41 |
| 3BH | TO | B10 | DO201AD | 3BH41 |
| 3BZ | TO | B10 | DO201AD | 3BZ41 |
| 3G | TO | O3 | | 3G4B41 |
| 3GH | TO | B10 | DO201AD | 3GH41 |
| 3GU | TO | B10 | DO201AD | 3GU41 |
| 3GWJ | TO | B10 | DO201AD | 3GWJ42 |
| 3GZ | TO | B10 | DO201AD | 3GZ41 |
| 3J | TO | O3 | | 3J4B41 |
| 3JH | TO | B10 | DO201AD | 3JH41 |
| 3JU | TO | B10 | DO201AD | 3JU41 |
| 3JZ | TO | B10 | DO201AD | 3JZ41 |
| 3NH | TO | B10 | DO201AD | 3NH41 |
| 3NZ | TO | B10 | DO201AD | 3NZ41 |
| 3S4 | RD | F11 | D PACK | DE3S4M |
| 3S6 | RD | F11 | D PACK | DE3S6M |
| 3TH | TO | B10 | DO201AD | 3TH41 |
| 3Y0 | PH | F6 | SOT89 | BZV49C3V0 |
| 3Y3 | PH | F6 | SOT89 | BZV49C3V3 |
| 3Y6 | PH | F6 | SOT89 | BZV49C3V6 |
| 3Y9 | PH | F6 | SOT89 | BZV49C3V9 |
| 4Y3 | PH | F6 | SOT89 | BZV49C4V3 |
| 4Y7 | PH | F6 | SOT89 | BZV49C4V7 |
| 5B | TO | F14 | MINIDIP4 | O5B4B48 |
| 5B | TO | F14 | MINIDIP4 | O5G4B48 |
| 5B | TO | F14 | MINIDIP4 | O5J4B48 |
| 5B | TO | F15 | H-FLAT | U05B4B48 |
| 5DL2C | TO | I23 | TO220FL | 5DL2C48A |
| 5DL2C | TO | F9 | TO220SM | U5DL2C48A |
| 5DL2CZ | TO | I22 | TO220(N)IS | 5DL2CZ47A |
| 5FL2C | TO | I23 | TO220FL | 5FL2C48A |
| 5FL2C | TO | F9 | TO220SM | U5FL2C48A |
| 5FL2CZ | TO | I22 | TO220(N)IS | 5FL2CZ47A |

| Code | | | | Type |
|------|---|----|-----------|------|
| 5G | TO | F15 | H-FLAT | U05G4B48 |
| 5GL2CZ | TO | I22 | TO220(N)IS | 5GL2CZ47A |
| 5GWJ2C | TO | I23 | TO220FL | 5GWJ2C48 |
| 5GWJ2C | TO | F9 | TO220SM | U5GWJ2C48 |
| 5GWJ2CZ | TO | I22 | TO220(N)IS | 5GWJ2CZ47 |
| 5J | TO | F15 | H-FLAT | U05J4B48 |
| 5JL2CZ | TO | I22 | TO220(N)IS | 5JL2CZ47 |
| 5JWJ2CZ | TO | I22 | TO220(N)IS | 5JWJ2CZ47 |
| 5MWJ2CZ | TO | I22 | TO220(N)IS | 5MWJ2CZ47 |
| 5S4 | RD | F11 | D PACK | DE5S4M |
| 5S4 | RD | F11 | D PACK | DE5S6M |
| 5Y1 | PH | F6 | SOT89 | BZV49C5V1 |
| 5Y6 | PH | F6 | SOT89 | BZV49C5V6 |
| 6V8A | MO | G2 | SOD15 | 1.5SMC6.8A |
| 6V8A | MO | G1 | SOD6 | P6SMB6.8A |
| 6Y2 | PH | F6 | SOT89 | BZV49C6V2 |
| 6Y8 | PH | F6 | SOT89 | BZV49C6V8 |
| 7V5A | MO | G2 | SOD15 | 1.5SMC7.5A |
| 7V5A | MO | G1 | SOD6 | P6SMB7.5A |
| 7Y5 | PH | F6 | SOT89 | BZV49C7V5 |
| 8A | NS | F1 | SOT23 | MMBZ5226B |
| 8A | MO | F1 | SOT23 | MMBZ226BL |
| 8B | NS | F1 | SOT23 | MMBZ5227B |
| 8B | MO | F1 | SOT23 | MMBZ227BL |
| 8C | NS | F1 | SOT23 | MMBZ5228B |
| 8C | MO | F1 | SOT23 | MMBZ228BL |
| 8D | NS | F1 | SOT23 | MMBZ5229B |
| 8D | MO | F1 | SOT23 | MMBZ229BL |
| 8E | NS | F1 | SOT23 | MMBZ5230B |
| 8E | MO | F1 | SOT23 | MMBZ230BL |
| 8F | NS | F1 | SOT23 | MMBZ5231B |
| 8F | MO | F1 | SOT23 | MMBZ231BL |
| 8G | NS | F1 | SOT23 | MMBZ5232B |
| 8G | MO | F1 | SOT23 | MMBZ232BL |
| 8H | NS | F1 | SOT23 | MMBZ5233B |
| 8H | MO | F1 | SOT23 | MMBZ233BL |
| 8J | NS | F1 | SOT23 | MMBZ5234B |
| 8J | MO | F1 | SOT23 | MMBZ234BL |
| 8K | NS | F1 | SOT23 | MMBZ5235B |
| 8K | MO | F1 | SOT23 | MMBZ235BL |

| Code | Mfr | Pkg | Type |
|---|---|---|---|
| 8L | NS | F1 SOT23 | MMBZ5236B |
| 8L | MO | F1 SOT23 | MMBZ236BL |
| 8M | NS | F1 SOT23 | MMBZ5237B |
| 8M | MO | F1 SOT23 | MMBZ237BL |
| 8N | NS | F1 SOT23 | MMBZ5238B |
| 8N | MO | F1 SOT23 | MMBZ238BL |
| 8P | NS | F1 SOT23 | MMBZ5239B |
| 8P | MO | F1 SOT23 | MMBZ239BL |
| 8Q | NS | F1 SOT23 | MMBZ5240B |
| 8Q | MO | F1 SOT23 | MMBZ240BL |
| 8R | NS | F1 SOT23 | MMBZ5241B |
| 8R | MO | F1 SOT23 | MMBZ241BL |
| 8S | NS | F1 SOT23 | MMBZ5242B |
| 8S | MO | F1 SOT23 | MMBZ242BL |
| 8T | NS | F1 SOT23 | MMBZ5243B |
| 8T | MO | F1 SOT23 | MMBZ243BL |
| 8U | NS | F1 SOT23 | MMBZ5244B |
| 8U | MO | F1 SOT23 | MMBZ244BL |
| 8V | NS | F1 SOT23 | MMBZ5245B |
| 8V | MO | F1 SOT23 | MMBZ245BL |
| 8V2A | MO | G2 SOD15 | 1.5SMC8.2A |
| 8V2A | MO | G1 SOD6 | P6SMB8.2A |
| 8W | NS | F1 SOT23 | MMBZ5246B |
| 8W | MO | F1 SOT23 | MMBZ246BL |
| 8X | NS | F1 SOT23 | MMBZ5247B |
| 8X | MO | F1 SOT23 | MMBZ247BL |
| 8Y | NS | F1 SOT23 | MMBZ5248B |
| 8Y | MO | F1 SOT23 | MMBZ248BL |
| 8Y2 | PH | F6 SOT89 | BZV49C8V2 |
| 8Z | NS | F1 SOT23 | MMBZ5249B |
| 8Z | MO | F1 SOT23 | MMBZ249BL |
| 9V1A | MO | G2 SOD15 | 1.5SMC9.1A |
| 9V1A | MO | G1 SOD6 | P6SMB9.1A |
| 9Y1 | PH | F6 SOT89 | BZV49C9V1 |
| 10A | MO | G2 SOD15 | 1.5SMC10A |
| 10A | MO | G1 SOD6 | P6SMB10A |
| 10DL2C | TO | I23 TO220FL | 10DL2C48A |
| 10DL2C | TO | I23 TO220FL | U10DL2C48A |
| 10DL2CZ | TO | I22 TO220(N)IS | 10DL2CZ47A |
| 10DL2CZ | TO | I22 TO220(N)IS | 10FL2CZ47A |

| Code | Mfr | Pkg | Type |
|---|---|---|---|
| 10DL2CZ | TO | I22 TO220(N)IS | 10GL2CZ47A |
| 10FL2C | TO | I23 TO220FL | 10FL2C48A |
| 10FL2C | TO | I23 TO220FL | U10FL2C48A |
| 10GWJ2C | TO | I23 TO220FL | 10GWJ2C48 |
| 10GWJ2C | TO | F9 TO220SM | U10GWJ2C48 |
| 10GWJ2CZ | TO | I22 TO220(N)IS | 10GWJ2CZ47 |
| 10JL2CZ | TO | I22 TO220(N)IS | 10JL2CZ47 |
| 10JWJ2CZ | TO | I22 TO220(N)IS | 10JWJ2CZ47 |
| 10MWJ2CZ | TO | I22 TO220(N)IS | 10MWJ2CZ47 |
| 10Y | PH | F6 SOT89 | BZV49C10 |
| 11A | MO | G2 SOD15 | 1.5SMC11A |
| 11A | NS | F1 SOT23 | MMBD1201 |
| 11A | NS | F1 SOT23 | MMBD1501A |
| 11A | MO | G1 SOD6 | P6SMB11A |
| 11Y | PH | F6 SOT89 | BZV49C11 |
| 12 | TO | G5 DO214AC | U1ZB12 |
| 12A | MO | G2 SOD15 | 1.5SMC12A |
| 12A | NS | F1 SOT23 | MMBD1502A |
| 12A | NS | F1 SOT23 | MMBD1503A |
| 12A | NS | F1 SOT23 | MMBD1504A |
| 12A | NS | F1 SOT23 | MMBD1505A |
| 12A | MO | G1 SOD6 | P6SMB12A |
| 12Y | PH | F6 SOT89 | BZV49C12 |
| 13 | TO | G5 DO214AC | U1ZB13 |
| 13A | MO | G2 SOD15 | 1.5SMC13A |
| 13A | MO | G1 SOD6 | P6SMB13A |
| 13Y | PH | F6 SOT89 | BZV49C13 |
| 15 | TO | G5 DO214AC | U1ZB15 |
| 15A | MO | G2 SOD15 | 1.5SMC15A |
| 15A | MO | G1 SOD6 | P6SMB15A |
| 15Y | PH | F6 SOT89 | BZV49C15 |
| 16 | TO | G5 DO214AC | U1ZB16 |
| 16A | MO | G2 SOD15 | 1.5SMC16A |
| 16A | MO | G1 SOD6 | P6SMB16A |
| 16DL2CZ | TO | I22 TO220(N)IS | 16DL2CZ47A |
| 16DL2CZ | TO | I22 TO220(N)IS | 16FL2CZ47A |
| 16GWJ2CZ | TO | I22 TO220(N)IS | 16GWJ2CZ47 |
| 16Y | PH | F6 SOT89 | BZV49C16 |
| 18 | TO | G5 DO214AC | U1ZB18 |
| 18A | MO | G2 SOD15 | 1.5SMC18A |

| Code | Mfr | Pkg | Type |
|---|---|---|---|
| 18A | MO | F1 SOT23 | MMBZ221BL |
| 18A | MO | G1 SOD6 | P6SMB18A |
| 18B | MO | F1 SOT23 | MMBZ222BL |
| 18C | MO | F1 SOT23 | MMBZ223BL |
| 18D | MO | F1 SOT23 | MMBZ224BL |
| 18E | MO | F1 SOT23 | MMBZ225BL |
| 18F | MO | F1 SOT23 | MMBZ260BL |
| 18G | MO | F1 SOT23 | MMBZ261BL |
| 18H | MO | F1 SOT23 | MMBZ265BL |
| 18J | MO | F1 SOT23 | MMBZ267BL |
| 18K | MO | F1 SOT23 | MMBZ268BL |
| 18L | MO | F1 SOT23 | MMBZ269BL |
| 18Y | PH | F6 SOT89 | BZV49C18 |
| 20 | TO | G5 DO214AC | U1ZB20 |
| 20A | MO | G2 SOD15 | 1.5SMC20A |
| 20A | MO | G1 SOD6 | P6SMB20A |
| 20DL2C | TO | J13 TO3P(N) | 20DL2C41A |
| 20DL2C | TO | F9 TO220SM | 20DL2C48A |
| 20DL2C | TO | I23 TO220FL | 20FL2C48A |
| 20DL2C | TO | J13 TO3P(N) | 20JL2C41A |
| 20DL2C | TO | F9 TO220SM | U20DL2C48A |
| 20DL2C | TO | F9 TO220SM | U20FL2C48A |
| 20DL2CZ | TO | I22 TO220(N)IS | 20DL2CZ47A |
| 20DL2CZ | TO | I22 TO220(N)IS | 20FL2CZ47A |
| 20DL2CZ | TO | J14 TO3P(N)IS | 20DL2CZ51A |
| 20DL2CZ | TO | J14 TO3P(N)IS | 20FL2CZ51A |
| 20FL2C | TO | J13 TO3P(N) | 20FL2C41A |
| 20GL2C | TO | J13 TO3P(N) | 20GL2C41A |
| 20Y | PH | F6 SOT89 | BZV49C20 |
| 22 | TO | G5 DO214AC | U1ZB22 |
| 22A | MO | G2 SOD15 | 1.5SMC22A |
| 22A | MO | G1 SOD6 | P6SMB22A |
| 22Y | PH | F6 SOT89 | BZV49C22 |
| 24 | TO | G5 DO214AC | U1ZB24 |
| 24A | MO | G2 SOD15 | 1.5SMC24A |
| 24A | MO | G1 SOD6 | P6SMB24A |
| 24Y | PH | F6 SOT89 | BZV49C24 |
| 25 | NS | F1 SOT23 | MMBD1202 |
| 26 | NS | F1 SOT23 | MMBD1203 |
| 27 | NS | F1 SOT23 | MMBD1204 |

| Code | 🏭 | ⧫ | | Type |
|------|-----|-----|------|------|
| 27 | TO | G5 | DO214AC | U1ZB27 |
| 27A | MO | G2 | SOD15 | 1.5SMC27A |
| 27A | MO | G1 | SOD6 | P6SMB27A |
| 27Y | PH | F6 | SOT89 | BZV49C27 |
| 28 | NS | F1 | SOT23 | MMBD1205 |
| 29 | NS | F1 | SOT23 | MMBD1401 |
| 30 | TO | B1 | DO15 | 1S1830 |
| 30 | TO | G5 | DO214AC | U1ZB30 |
| 30A | MO | G2 | SOD15 | 1.5SMC30A |
| 30A | MO | G1 | SOD6 | P6SMB30A |
| 30DL2C | TO | J13 | TO3P(N) | 30JL2C41 |
| 30GWJ2C | TO | I23 | TO220FL | 30GWJ2C48 |
| 30GWJ2C | TO | F9 | TO220SM | U30GWJ2C48 |
| 30JWJ2C | TO | I23 | TO220FL | 30JWJ2C48 |
| 30JWJ2C | TO | F9 | TO220SM | G30JWJ2C48 |
| 30Y | PH | F6 | SOT89 | BZV49C30 |
| 31 | NS | F1 | SOT23 | MMBD1402 |
| 32 | NS | F1 | SOT23 | MMBD1403 |
| 33 | NS | F1 | SOT23 | MMBD1404 |
| 33 | TO | G5 | DO214AC | U1ZB33 |
| 33A | MO | G2 | SOD15 | 1.5SMC33A |
| 33A | MO | G1 | SOD6 | P6SMB33A |
| 33Y | PH | F6 | SOT89 | BZV49C33 |
| 34 | NS | F1 | SOT23 | MMBD1405 |
| 36 | TO | G5 | DO214AC | U1ZB36 |
| 36A | MO | G2 | SOD15 | 1.5SMC36A |
| 36A | MO | G1 | SOD6 | P6SMB36A |
| 36Y | PH | F6 | SOT89 | BZV49C36 |
| 39A | MO | G2 | SOD15 | 1.5SMC39A |
| 39A | MO | G1 | SOD6 | P6SMB39A |
| 39Y | PH | F6 | SOT89 | BZV49C39 |
| 43 | TO | G5 | DO214AC | U1ZB43 |
| 43A | MO | G2 | SOD15 | 1.5SMC43A |
| 43A | MO | G1 | SOD6 | P6SMB43A |
| 43Y | PH | F6 | SOT89 | BZV49C43 |
| 47 | TO | G5 | DO214AC | U1ZB47 |
| 47A | MO | G2 | SOD15 | 1.5SMC47A |
| 47A | MO | G1 | SOD6 | P6SMB47A |
| 47Y | PH | F6 | SOT89 | BZV49C47 |
| 51 | TO | G5 | DO214AC | U1ZB51 |

| Code | 🏭 | ⧫ | | Type |
|------|-----|-----|------|------|
| 51A | MO | G2 | SOD15 | 1.5SMC51A |
| 51A | MO | G1 | SOD6 | P6SMB51A |
| 51Y | PH | F6 | SOT89 | BZV49C51 |
| 56A | MO | G2 | SOD15 | 1.5SMC56A |
| 56A | MO | G1 | SOD6 | P6SMB56A |
| 56Y | PH | F6 | SOT89 | BZV49C56 |
| 62A | MO | G2 | SOD15 | 1.5SMC62A |
| 62A | MO | G1 | SOD6 | P6SMB62A |
| 62Y | PH | F6 | SOT89 | BZV49C62 |
| 68 | TO | G5 | DO214AC | U1ZB68 |
| 68A | MO | G2 | SOD15 | 1.5SMC68A |
| 68A | MO | G1 | SOD6 | P6SMB68A |
| 68Y | PH | F6 | SOT89 | BZV49C68 |
| 75 | TO | G5 | DO214AC | U1ZB75 |
| 75A | MO | G2 | SOD15 | 1.5SMC75A |
| 75A | MO | G1 | SOD6 | P6SMB75A |
| 75Y | PH | F6 | SOT89 | BZV49C75 |
| 77/blu | TO | A3 | DO41 | S5277G |
| 77/gre | TO | A3 | DO41 | S5277N |
| 77/whi | TO | A3 | DO41 | S5277B |
| 77/yel | TO | A3 | DO41 | S5277J |
| 81A | NS | F1 | SOT23 | MMBZ5250B |
| 81A | MO | F1 | SOT23 | MMBZ250BL |
| 81A | PH | F1 | SOT23 | PMBZ5250B |
| 81B | NS | F1 | SOT23 | MMBZ5251B |
| 81B | MO | F1 | SOT23 | MMBZ251BL |
| 81B | PH | F1 | SOT23 | PMBZ5251B |
| 81C | NS | F1 | SOT23 | MMBZ5252B |
| 81C | MO | F1 | SOT23 | MMBZ252BL |
| 81C | PH | F1 | SOT23 | PMBZ5252B |
| 81D | NS | F1 | SOT23 | MMBZ5253B |
| 81D | MO | F1 | SOT23 | MMBZ253BL |
| 81D | PH | F1 | SOT23 | PMBZ5253B |
| 81E | NS | F1 | SOT23 | MMBZ5254B |
| 81E | MO | F1 | SOT23 | MMBZ254BL |
| 81E | PH | F1 | SOT23 | PMBZ5254B |
| 81F | NS | F1 | SOT23 | MMBZ5255B |
| 81F | MO | F1 | SOT23 | MMBZ255BL |
| 81F | PH | F1 | SOT23 | PMBZ5255B |
| 81G | NS | F1 | SOT23 | MMBZ5256B |

| Code | 🏭 | ⧫ | | Type |
|------|-----|-----|------|------|
| 81G | MO | F1 | SOT23 | MMBZ256BL |
| 81G | PH | F1 | SOT23 | PMBZ5256B |
| 81H | NS | F1 | SOT23 | MMBZ5257B |
| 81H | MO | F1 | SOT23 | MMBZ257BL |
| 81H | PH | F1 | SOT23 | PMBZ5257B |
| 81J | MO | F1 | SOT23 | MMBZ258BL |
| 81K | MO | F1 | SOT23 | MMBZ259BL |
| 81L | MO | F1 | SOT23 | MMBZ262BL |
| 81M | MO | F1 | SOT23 | MMBZ263BL |
| 81N | MO | F1 | SOT23 | MMBZ264BL |
| 81P | MO | F1 | SOT23 | MMBZ266BL |
| 81Q | MO | F1 | SOT23 | MMBZ270BL |
| 82 | TO | G5 | DO214AC | U1ZB82 |
| 82A | MO | G2 | SOD15 | 1.5SMC82A |
| 82A | MO | G1 | SOD6 | P6SMB82A |
| 85 | TO | B1 | DO15 | 1S1885 |
| 85 | NS | F1 | SOT23 | MMBD1701 |
| 85A | TO | B1 | DO15 | 1S1885A |
| 86 | NS | F1 | SOT23 | MMBD1702 |
| 87 | TO | B1 | DO15 | 1S1887 |
| 87 | NS | F1 | SOT23 | MMBD1703 |
| 87A | TO | B1 | DO15 | 1S1887A |
| 87A | TO | B1 | DO15 | 1S1888A |
| 88 | TO | B1 | DO15 | 1S1888 |
| 88 | NS | F1 | SOT23 | MMBD1704 |
| 89 | NS | F1 | SOT23 | MMBD1705 |
| 91 | MO | G2 | SOD15 | 1.5SMC91A |
| 91A | MO | G1 | SOD6 | P6SMB91A |
| 95b | TO | A3 | DO41 | S5295B |
| 95g | TO | A3 | DO41 | S5295G |
| 95j | TO | A3 | DO41 | S5295J |
| 100 | TO | G5 | DO214AC | U1ZB100 |
| 100A | MO | G1 | SOD6 | P6SMB100A |
| 110 | TO | G5 | DO214AC | U1ZB110 |
| 110A | MO | G1 | SOD6 | P6SMB110A |
| 120A | MO | G1 | SOD6 | P6SMB120A |
| 130A | MO | G1 | SOD6 | P6SMB130A |
| 150 | TO | G5 | DO214AC | U1ZB150 |
| 150A | MO | G1 | SOD6 | P6SMB150A |
| 160A | MO | G1 | SOD6 | P6SMB160A |

| Code | 🏭 | 🔌 | | Type |
|------|-----|-----|-----|------|
| 170A | MO | G1 | SOD6 | P6SMB170A |
| 180 | TO | G5 | DO214AC | U1ZB180 |
| 180A | MO | G1 | SOD6 | P6SMB180A |
| 200 | TO | G5 | DO214AC | U1ZB200 |
| 200 | TO | G5 | DO214AC | U1ZB200-Y |
| 200 | TO | G5 | DO214AC | U1ZB200-Z |
| 200A | MO | G1 | SOD6 | P6SMB200A |
| 220 | TO | G5 | DO214AC | U1ZB220 |
| 220 | TO | G5 | DO214AC | U1ZB220-Y |
| 220 | TO | G5 | DO214AC | U1ZB220-Z |
| 240 | TO | G5 | DO214AC | U1ZB240 |
| 240 | TO | G5 | DO214AC | U1ZB240-Y |
| 240 | TO | G5 | DO214AC | U1ZB240-Z |
| 270 | TO | G5 | DO214AC | U1ZB270 |
| 270 | TO | G5 | DO214AC | U1ZB270-X |
| 270 | TO | G5 | DO214AC | U1ZB270-Y |
| 270 | TO | G5 | DO214AC | U1ZB270-Z |
| 300 | TO | G5 | DO214AC | U1ZB300 |
| 300 | TO | G5 | DO214AC | U1ZB300-X |
| 300 | TO | G5 | DO214AC | U1ZB300-Y |
| 300 | TO | G5 | DO214AC | U1ZB300-Z |
| 330 | TO | G5 | DO214AC | U1ZB330 |
| 330 | TO | G5 | DO214AC | U1ZB330-X |
| 330 | TO | G5 | DO214AC | U1ZB330-Y |
| 330 | TO | G5 | DO214AC | U1ZB330-Z |
| 390 | TO | G5 | DO214AC | U1ZB390 |
| 450APH | PH | A1 | DO35 | PLVA450A |
| 453APH | PH | A1 | DO35 | PLVA453A |
| 456APH | PH | A1 | DO35 | PLVA456A |
| 459APH | PH | A1 | DO35 | PLVA459A |
| 462APH | PH | A1 | DO35 | PLVA462A |
| 465APH | PH | A1 | DO35 | PLVA465A |
| 468APH | PH | A1 | DO35 | PLVA468A |
| 913B | MO | G1 | SOD6 | 1SMB5913BT3 |
| 914B | MO | G1 | SOD6 | 1SMB5914BT3 |
| 915B | MO | G1 | SOD6 | 1SMB5915BT3 |
| 916B | MO | G1 | SOD6 | 1SMB5916BT3 |
| 917B | MO | G1 | SOD6 | 1SMB5917BT3 |
| 918B | MO | G1 | SOD6 | 1SMB5918BT3 |
| 919B | MO | G1 | SOD6 | 1SMB5919BT3 |

| Code | 🏭 | 🔌 | | Type |
|------|-----|-----|-----|------|
| 920B | MO | G1 | SOD6 | 1SMB5920BT3 |
| 921B | MO | G1 | SOD6 | 1SMB5921BT3 |
| 922B | MO | G1 | SOD6 | 1SMB5922BT3 |
| 923B | MO | G1 | SOD6 | 1SMB5923BT3 |
| 924B | MO | G1 | SOD6 | 1SMB5924BT3 |
| 925B | MO | G1 | SOD6 | 1SMB5925BT3 |
| 926B | MO | G1 | SOD6 | 1SMB5926BT3 |
| 927B | MO | G1 | SOD6 | 1SMB5927BT3 |
| 928B | MO | G1 | SOD6 | 1SMB5928BT3 |
| 929B | MO | G1 | SOD6 | 1SMB5929BT3 |
| 930B | MO | G1 | SOD6 | 1SMB5930BT3 |
| 931B | MO | G1 | SOD6 | 1SMB5931BT3 |
| 932B | MO | G1 | SOD6 | 1SMB5932BT3 |
| 933B | MO | G1 | SOD6 | 1SMB5933BT3 |
| 934B | MO | G1 | SOD6 | 1SMB5934BT3 |
| 935B | MO | G1 | SOD6 | 1SMB5935BT3 |
| 936B | MO | G1 | SOD6 | 1SMB5936BT3 |
| 937B | MO | G1 | SOD6 | 1SMB5937BT3 |
| 938B | MO | G1 | SOD6 | 1SMB5938BT3 |
| 939B | MO | G1 | SOD6 | 1SMB5939BT3 |
| 940B | MO | G1 | SOD6 | 1SMB5940BT3 |
| 941B | MO | G1 | SOD6 | 1SMB5941BT3 |
| 942B | MO | G1 | SOD6 | 1SMB5942BT3 |
| 943B | MO | G1 | SOD6 | 1SMB5943BT3 |
| 944B | MO | G1 | SOD6 | 1SMB5944BT3 |
| 945B | MO | G1 | SOD6 | 1SMB5945BT3 |
| 946B | MO | G1 | SOD6 | 1SMB5946BT3 |
| 947B | MO | G1 | SOD6 | 1SMB5947BT3 |
| 948B | MO | G1 | SOD6 | 1SMB5948BT3 |
| 949B | MO | G1 | SOD6 | 1SMB5949BT3 |
| 950B | MO | G1 | SOD6 | 1SMB5950BT3 |
| 951B | MO | G1 | SOD6 | 1SMB5951BT3 |
| 952B | MO | G1 | SOD6 | 1SMB5952BT3 |
| 953B | MO | G1 | SOD6 | 1SMB5953BT3 |
| 954B | MO | G1 | SOD6 | 1SMB5954BT3 |
| 955B | MO | G1 | SOD6 | 1SMB5955BT3 |
| 956B | MO | G1 | SOD6 | 1SMB5956BT3 |

| Code | 🏭 | 🔌 | | Type |
|------|-----|-----|-----|------|

# Chapter 4
# Kapitel 4
# Chapitre 4
# Capitulo 4

**Case Outline Drawings**

**Gehäusezeichnungen**

**Plan de masse des boîtiers**

**Planos de los encapsulados**

# Case Outline Drawings
# Gehäusezeichnungen

# Plan de masse des boîtiers
# Planos de los encapsulados

As measurement in different sources vary (even for same case type), case outline drawings in this book are to be understood as samples only. Not all of the drawings are in accurate scale. For reasons of space efficiency, different manufacturers cases that are comparable in shape and size, are put together. Where possible case names are stated in accordance to JEDEC.

Die Gehäusezeichnungen sind als Prinzipzeichnungen zu verstehen, da die Maßangaben verschiedener Quellen trotz gleicher Bezeichnung differieren. Sie sind nicht in jedem Fall maßstabgerecht. Insbesondere sind aus Platzgründen ähnliche Gehäuse verschiedener Hersteller und solche, deren Abmessungen innerhalb der Toleranzen liegen, zusammengefaßt. Wenn möglich wurde die Gehäusekennzeichnung nach JEDEC berücksichtigt.

Les schémas de boîtiers ne sont que des schémas de principe, à cause des différences qui peuvent exister, malgré la même appellation, entre les différentes sources utilisées. Ils ne sont pas toujours véritablement à l'échelle non plus. En particulier, pour des raisons d'encombrement, des boîtiers semblables par la taille ou la forme, même s'ils sont produits par des fabricants différents, ont été regroupés. Lorsque cela est possible, les boîtiers sont identifiés conformément au système JEDEC.

Los planos de los encapsulados muestran de modo global el aspecto externo del dispositivo, ya que diversas fuentes daban diferentes indicaciones de medidas, a pesar de una común denominación del dispositivo. En cualquier caso, no son planos a escala. Por motivos de espacio, se han resumido encapsulados de tipo parecido de diferentes fabricantes con aquellos de dimensiones similares. En caso de ser posible, se ha mantenido la denominación del encapsulado según JEDEC.

# Case Outline Drawings
# Gehäusezeichnungen

G

25.4 / 27.5
1.53 / 2.00
3.05 / 4.50
25.4 / 27.5
0.46 / 0.56

**DO35**
**SOD27**     A1

---

G

16.0 / 27.5
1.25 / 1.6
2.7 / 3.05
16.0 / 27.5
0.42 / 0.56

**DO34**
**SOD68**     A2

---

G

27.9 / 30.5
2.28 / 2.54
3.94 / 4.4
27.9 / 30.5
0.73 / 0.86

**DO41**     A3

---

G

26.0 min
2.8 / 3.8
4.20 / 4.57
26.0 min
0.85 max

**SOD57**     A4

---

G

26.0 min
3.6 / 4.5
4.2 / 5.0
26.0 min
1.35 max

**SOD64**     A5

---

G

28.0 min
3.15 max
4.3 max
5.0 max
28.0 min
0.81 max

**SOD84**     A6

---

G

29.0 min
1.7 max
3.0 max
3.5 max
29.0 min
0.55 max

**SOD91**     A7

---

G

28.0 min
2.15 max
4.3 max
5.0 max
28.0 min
0.81 max

**SOD81**     A8

# Case Outline Drawings
## Gehäusezeichnungen

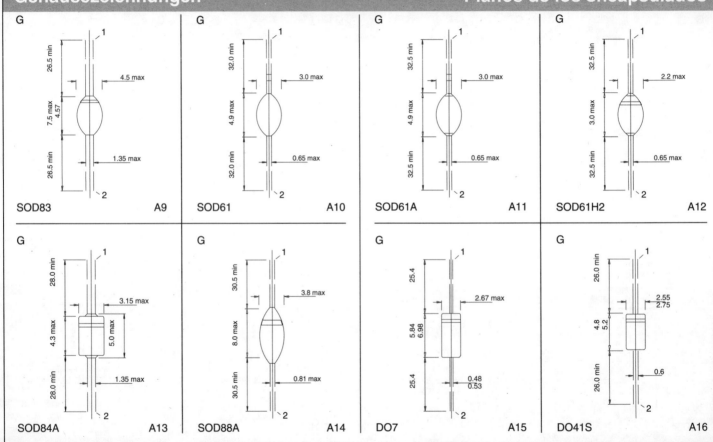

| | |
|---|---|
| SOD83     A9 | SOD61     A10 |
| SOD61A     A11 | SOD61H2     A12 |
| SOD84A     A13 | SOD88A     A14 |
| DO7     A15 | DO41S     A16 |

G

26.0 min · 2.5 · 2.8 / 3.2 · 26.0 min · 0.6

DO41SS      A17

G

27.6-0.7 · 2.5 / 2.9 · 4.8 / 5.2 · 27.6-0.7 · 0.55 / 0.65

A18

G

23.5 · 2.3 / 2.5 · 2.8 / 3.0 · 23.5 · 0.55 / 0.59

A19

G

17.0 min · 1.8 / 2.2 · 3.5 / 2.5 · 17.0 min · 0.5

A20

G

23.5 · 2.3 / 2.7 · 1.0 · 23.5 · 0.5

A21

G

27.0 min · 2.8 / 3.2 · 2.0 · 27.0 min · 0.6

A22

G

27.0 min · 2.8 / 3.2 · 3.0 · 27.0 min · 0.6

A23

P

26.0 / 28.0 · 2.8 / 3.4 · 5.9 / 6.5 · 26.0 / 28.0 · 0.6 / 0.8

DO15
(SOD40)      B1

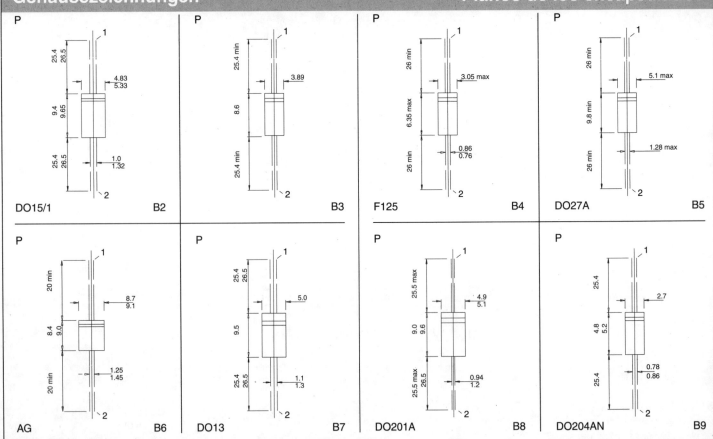

DO15/1    B2

B3

F125    B4

DO27A    B5

AG    B6

DO13    B7

DO201A    B8

DO204AN    B9

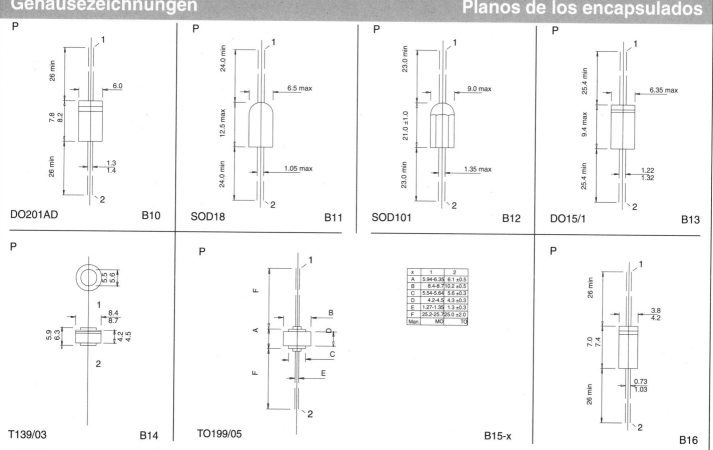

P

26 min
6.0
7.8
8.2
26 min
1.3
1.4

1

2

DO201AD    B10

P

24.0 min
6.5 max
12.5 max
24.0 min
1.05 max

1

2

SOD18    B11

P

23.0 min
9.0 max
21.0 ±1.0
23.0 min
1.35 max

1

2

SOD101    B12

P

25.4 min
6.35 max
9.4 max
25.4 min
1.22
1.32

1

2

DO15/1    B13

P

5.5
5.6
1
8.4
8.7
5.9
6.3
4.2
4.5
2

T139/03    B14

P

1
F
B
A
D
C
F
E
2

TO199/05

| x | 1 | 2 |
|------|-----------|----------|
| A | 5.94-6.35 | 6.1 ±0.5 |
| B | 8.4-8.7 | 10.2 ±0.5 |
| C | 5.54-5.64 | 5.6 ±0.3 |
| D | 4.2-4.5 | 4.3 ±0.3 |
| E | 1.27-1.35 | 1.3 ±0.3 |
| F | 25.2-25.7 | 25.0 ±2.0 |
| Man. | MO | TO |

B15-x

P

26 min
3.8
4.2
7.0
7.4
26 min
0.73
1.03

1

2

B16

# Case Outline Drawings
# Gehäusezeichnungen
# Plan de masse des boîtiers
# Planos de los encapsulados

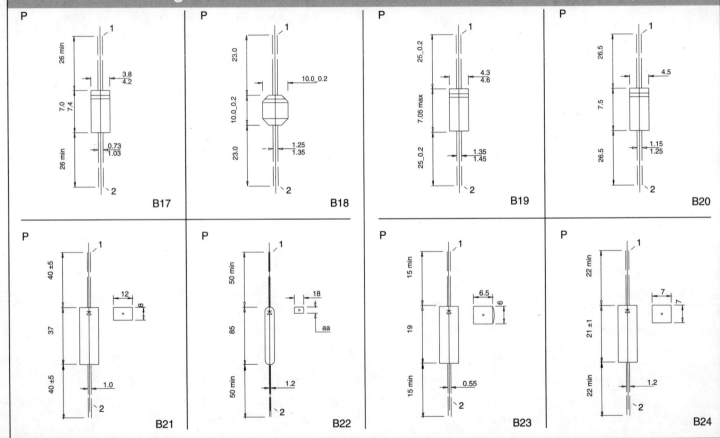

B17

B18

B19

B20

B21

B22

B23

B24

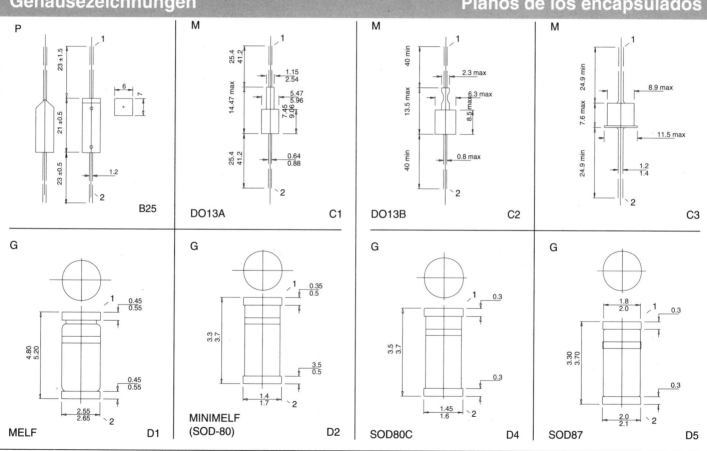

P

B25

M

DO13A  C1

M

DO13B  C2

M

C3

G

MELF  D1

G

MINIMELF
(SOD-80)  D2

G

SOD80C  D4

G

SOD87  D5

**M**

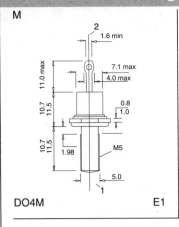

DO4M     E1

**M**

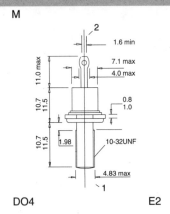

DO4     E2

**M**

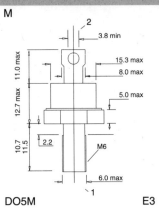

DO5M     E3

**M**

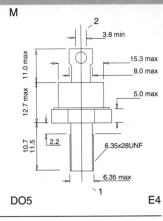

DO5     E4

**P**

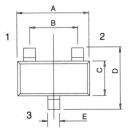

| x | 1 | 2 | 3 | 4 | 5 | 6 |
|---|---|---|---|---|---|---|
| A | 2.9 ±0.1 | 2.9 ±0.2 | 2.9 ±0.2 | 2.9 ±0.1 | 2.9 ±0.1 | 2.9 ±0.1 |
| B | 1.9 | 1.9 ±0.2 | 1.9 ±0.15 | 1.8-2.0 | 1.9 ±0.1 | 1.9-2.05 |
| C | 1.3 ±0.1 | 1.6 ±0.2 | 1.3 ±0.1 | 1.2-1.4 | 1.3 ±0.1 | 1.3 ±0.1 |
| D | 2.5 max | 2.8 ±0.2 | 2.35 ±0.25 | 2.1-2.5 | 2.5 max | 2.1-2.5 |
| E | 0.48 ±0.1 | 0.4 ±0.1 | 0.4 ±0.1 | 0.38-0.46 | 0.35-0.48 | 0.37-0.48 |
| Man. | PH,RD | RO | MO,IT | NS | TE | SG |

| x | 7 |
|---|---|
| A | 2.9 ±0.2 |
| B | 1.9 |
| C | 1.35-1.75 |
| D | 2.2-3.0 |
| E | 0.35-0.5 |
| Man. | TO |

SOT23
TO236     F1-x

**P**

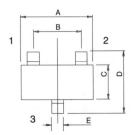

| x | 1 | 2 |
|---|---|---|
| A | 2.0 ±0.2 | 1.6 ±0.1 |
| B | 1.3 ±0.1 | 1.0 ±0.1 |
| C | 1.25 ±0.1 | 0.8 ±0.1 |
| D | 2.1 ±0.1 | 1.6 ±0.2 |
| E | 0.3 ±0.1 | 0.3 ±0.1 |
| Man. | RO | RO |

F2-x

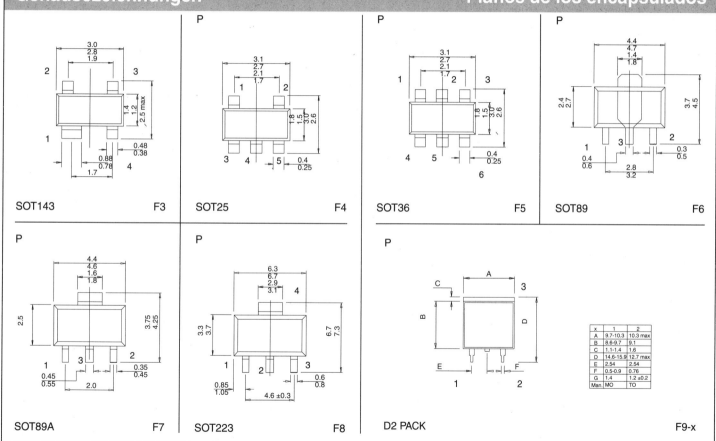

SOT143     F3

SOT25     F4

SOT36     F5

SOT89     F6

SOT89A     F7

SOT223     F8

D2 PACK     F9-x

| x | 1 | 2 |
|---|---|---|
| A | 9.7-10.3 | 10.3 max |
| B | 8.6-9.7 | 9.1 |
| C | 1.1-1.4 | 1.6 |
| D | 14.6-15.9 | 12.7 max |
| E | 2.54 | 2.54 |
| F | 0.5-0.9 | 0.76 |
| G | 1.4 | 1.2 ±0.2 |
| Man. | MO | TO |

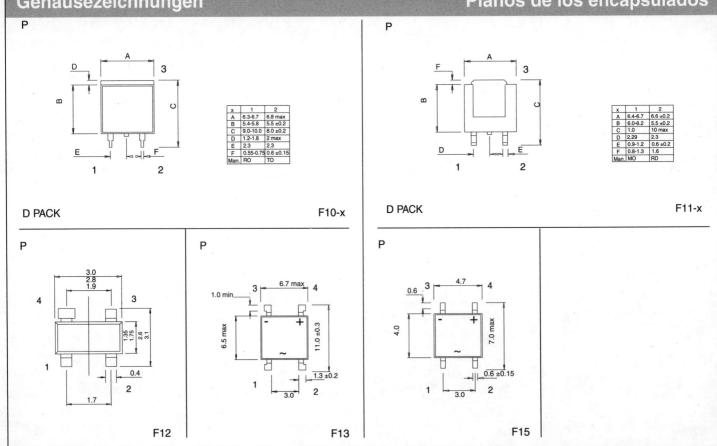

| x | 1 | 2 |
|---|---|---|
| A | 6.3-6.7 | 6.8 max |
| B | 5.4-5.8 | 5.5 ±0.2 |
| C | 9.0-10.0 | 8.0 ±0.2 |
| D | 1.2-1.8 | 2 max |
| E | 2.3 | 2.3 |
| F | 0.55-0.75 | 0.6 ±0.15 |
| Man. | RO | TO |

D PACK                          F10-x

| x | 1 | 2 |
|---|---|---|
| A | 6.4-6.7 | 6.6 ±0.2 |
| B | 6.0-6.2 | 5.5 ±0.2 |
| C | 1.0 | 10 max |
| D | 2.29 | 2.3 |
| E | 0.9-1.2 | 0.6 ±0.2 |
| F | 0.8-1.3 | 1.6 |
| Man. | MO | RD |

D PACK                          F11-x

F12                   F13

F15

# Case Outline Drawings
## Gehäusezeichnungen

P

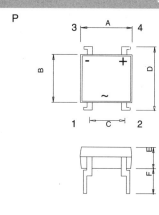

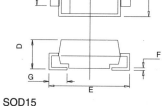

| x | 1 | 2 |
|---|---|---|
| A | 6.7 max | 6.8 ±0.2 |
| B | 6.5 max | 6.5 ±0.2 |
| C | 5.0 ±0.2 | 5.0 ±0.2 |
| D | 7.62/8.8 | 7.62 |
| E | 2.5 | 2.6 ±0.2 |
| F | 4.0 | 4.4 ±0.2 |
| Man. | TO | RD |

**F16-x**

P

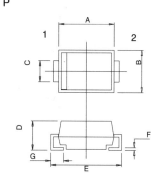

| x | 1 | 2 | 3 | 4 | 5 |
|---|---|---|---|---|---|
| A | 4.9 ±0.2 | 4.5 ±0.3 | 4.5 ±0.2 | | 4.3 ±0.25 |
| B | 4.0 ±0.2 | 2.4 ±0.3 | 2.6 ±0.2 | 1.5 ±0.2 | 3.55 ±0.25 |
| C | 2.2 ±0.1 | 1.4 ±0.2 | 1.5 ±0.1 | 2.2 ±0.1 | 2.0 ±0.1 |
| D | 2.8 ±0.3 | 2.0 ±0.3 | 2.05 ±0.2 | 2.0 ±0.3 | 2.15 ±0.25 |
| E | 6.2 ±0.2 | 4.7 ±0.3 | 5.1 ±0.1 | 5.0 ±0.3 | 5.3 ±0.2 |
| F | 0.3 ±0.02 | 0.2 | 0.2 | 0.2 | 0.22 ±0.08 |
| G | 1.1 ±0.2 | 1.2 ±0.3 | 1.35 ±0.4 | 1.2 ±0.3 | 1.0 ±0.25 |
| Man. | SG | RD | RD | RD | MO |

Cathode marked by band, logo or other marks

**SOD6**

**G1-x**

P

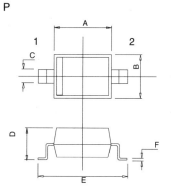

| x | 1 | 2 |
|---|---|---|
| A | 6.45 ±0.15 | 6.85 ±0.25 |
| B | 5.0 ±0.2 | 5.85 ±0.25 |
| C | 3.0 ±0.1 | 3.0 ±0.08 |
| D | 2.8 ±0.3 | 2.15 ±0.25 |
| E | 7.8 ±0.2 | 7.95 ±0.2 |
| F | 0.3 ±0.02 | 0.2 |
| G | 1.5 ±0.2 | 1.0 ±0.25 |
| Man. | SG | MO |

Cathode marked by band, logo or other marks

**SOD15**

**G2-x**

P

| x | 1 |
|---|---|
| A | 1.6-1.8 |
| B | 1.15-1.35 |
| C | 0.25-0.40 |
| D | 1.0 max |
| E | 2.3-2.7 |
| F | 0.1-0.25 |
| Man. | PH |

Cathode marked by band, logo or other marks

**SOD323**

**G3-x**

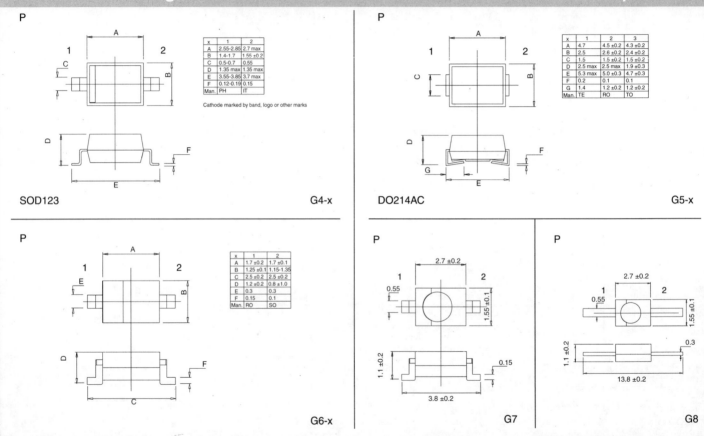

P

| x | 1 | 2 |
|---|---|---|
| A | 2.55-2.85 | 2.7 max |
| B | 1.4-1.7 | 1.55 ±0.2 |
| C | 0.5-0.7 | 0.55 |
| D | 1.35 max | 1.35 max |
| E | 3.55-3.85 | 3.7 max |
| F | 0.12-0.19 | 0.15 |
| Man. | PH | IT |

Cathode marked by band, logo or other marks

SOD123     G4-x

P

| x | 1 | 2 | 3 |
|---|---|---|---|
| A | 4.7 | 4.5 ±0.2 | 4.3 ±0.2 |
| B | 2.5 | 2.6 ±0.2 | 2.4 ±0.2 |
| C | 1.5 | 1.5 ±0.2 | 1.5 ±0.2 |
| D | 2.5 max | 2.5 max | 1.9 ±0.3 |
| E | 5.3 max | 5.0 ±0.3 | 4.7 ±0.3 |
| F | 0.2 | 0.1 | 0.1 |
| G | 1.4 | 1.2 ±0.2 | 1.2 ±0.2 |
| Man. | TE | RO | TO |

DO214AC     G5-x

P

| x | 1 | 2 |
|---|---|---|
| A | 1.7 ±0.2 | 1.7 ±0.1 |
| B | 1.25 ±0.1 | 1.15-1.35 |
| C | 2.5 ±0.2 | 2.5 ±0.2 |
| D | 1.2 ±0.2 | 0.8 ±1.0 |
| E | 0.3 | 0.3 |
| F | 0.15 | 0.1 |
| Man. | RO | SO |

G6-x

P

G7

P

G8

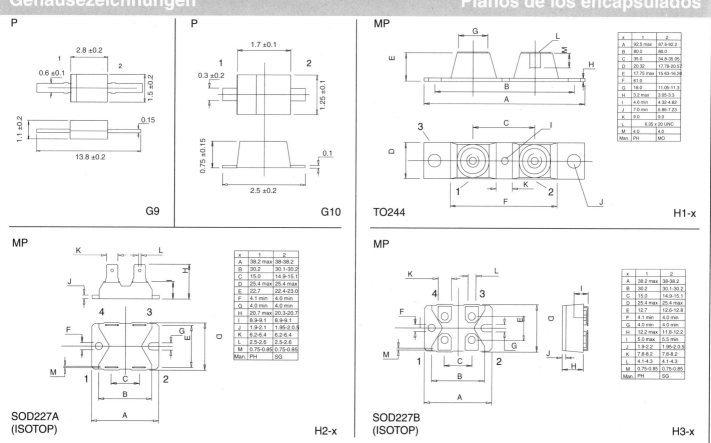

**P** — G9

**P** — G10

**MP** — TO244 — H1-x

| x | 1 | 2 |
|---|---|---|
| A | 92.5 max | 87.6-92.2 |
| B | 80.0 | 80.0 |
| C | 35.0 | 34.8-35.05 |
| D | 20.32 | 17.78-20.57 |
| E | 17.75 max | 15.63-16.26 |
| F | 61.0 | |
| G | 18.0 | 11.05-11.3 |
| H | 3.2 max | 3.05-3.3 |
| I | 4.6 min | 4.32-4.82 |
| J | 7.0 min | 6.86-7.23 |
| K | 9.0 | 9.0 |
| L | 6.35 x 20 UNC | |
| M | 4.0 | 4.0 |
| Man. | PH | MO |

**MP** — SOD227A (ISOTOP) — H2-x

| x | 1 | 2 |
|---|---|---|
| A | 38.2 max | 38-38.2 |
| B | 30.2 | 30.1-30.2 |
| C | 15.0 | 14.9-15.1 |
| D | 25.4 max | 25.4 max |
| E | 22.7 | 22.4-23.0 |
| F | 4.1 min | 4.0 min |
| G | 4.0 min | 4.0 min |
| H | 20.7 max | 20.3-20.7 |
| I | 8.9-9.1 | 8.9-9.1 |
| J | 1.9-2.1 | 1.95-2.0.5 |
| K | 6.2-6.4 | 6.2-6.4 |
| L | 2.5-2.6 | 2.5-2.6 |
| M | 0.75-0.85 | 0.75-0.85 |
| Man. | PH | SG |

**MP** — SOD227B (ISOTOP) — H3-x

| x | 1 | 2 |
|---|---|---|
| A | 38.2 max | 38-38.2 |
| B | 30.2 | 30.1-30.2 |
| C | 15.0 | 14.9-15.1 |
| D | 25.4 max | 25.4 max |
| E | 12.7 | 12.6-12.8 |
| F | 4.1 min | 4.0 min |
| G | 4.0 min | 4.0 min |
| H | 12.2 max | 11.8-12.2 |
| I | 5.0 max | 5.5 min |
| J | 1.9-2.2 | 1.95-2.0.5 |
| K | 7.8-8.2 | 7.8-8.2 |
| L | 4.1-4.3 | 4.1-4.3 |
| M | 0.75-0.85 | 0.75-0.85 |
| Man. | PH | SG |

MP

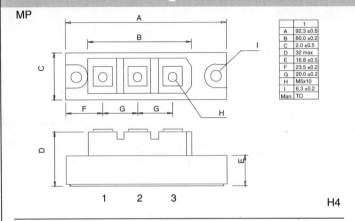

| | 1 |
|---|---|
| A | 92.3 ±0.5 |
| B | 80.0 ±0.2 |
| C | 2.0 ±0.5 |
| D | 32 max |
| E | 16.8 ±0.5 |
| F | 23.5 ±0.2 |
| G | 20.0 ±0.2 |
| H | M5x10 |
| I | 6.3 ±0.2 |
| Man. | TO |

H4

MP

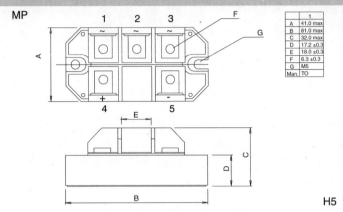

| | 1 |
|---|---|
| A | 41.0 max |
| B | 81.0 max |
| C | 32.0 max |
| D | 17.2 ±0.3 |
| E | 18.0 ±0.3 |
| F | 6.3 ±0.3 |
| G | M5 |
| Man. | TO |

H5

P

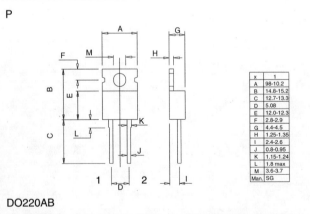

| x | 1 |
|---|---|
| A | 98-10.2 |
| B | 14.8-15.2 |
| C | 12.7-13.3 |
| D | 5.08 |
| E | 12.0-12.3 |
| F | 2.8-2.9 |
| G | 4.4-4.5 |
| H | 1.25-1.35 |
| I | 2.4-2.6 |
| J | 0.8-0.95 |
| K | 1.15-1.24 |
| L | 1.8 max |
| M | 3.6-3.7 |
| Man. | SG |

DO220AB

I1

P

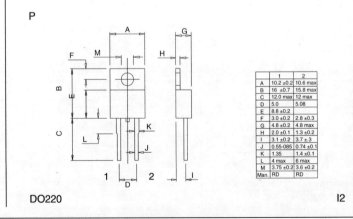

| | 1 | 2 |
|---|---|---|
| A | 10.2 ±0.2 | 10.6 max |
| B | 16 ±0.7 | 15.8 max |
| C | 12.0 max | 12 max |
| D | 5.0 | 5.08 |
| E | 8.8 ±0.2 | |
| F | 3.0 ±0.2 | 2.8 ±0.3 |
| G | 4.8 ±0.2 | 4.8 max |
| H | 2.0 ±0.1 | 1.3 ±0.2 |
| I | 3.1 ±0.2 | 3.7 ±3 |
| J | 0.55-085 | 0.74 ±0.1 |
| K | 1.35 | 1.4 ±0.1 |
| L | 4 max | 6 max |
| M | 3.75 ±0.2 | 3.6 ±0.2 |
| Man. | RD | RD |

DO220

I2

P

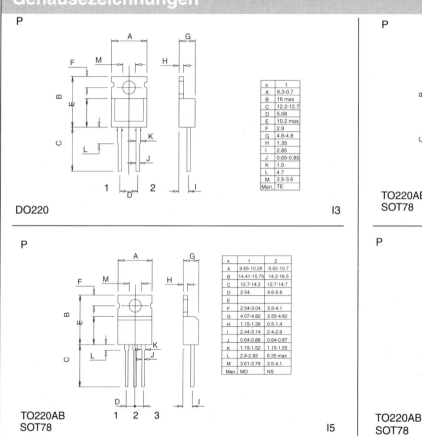

DO220

| x | 1 |
|---|---|
| A | 9.3-0.7 |
| B | 16 max |
| C | 12.2-12.7 |
| D | 5.08 |
| E | 10.2 max |
| F | 2.9 |
| G | 4.6-4.8 |
| H | 1.35 |
| I | 2.85 |
| J | 0.65-0.85 |
| K | 1.0 |
| L | 4.7 |
| M | 3.5-3.6 |
| Man. | TE |

I3

P

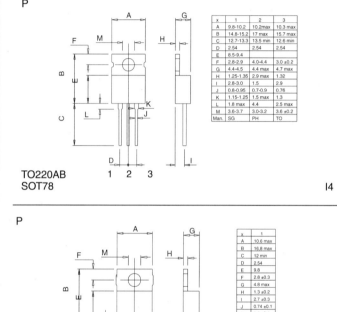

TO220AB
SOT78

| x | 1 | 2 | 3 |
|---|---|---|---|
| A | 9.8-10.2 | 10.2max | 10.3 max |
| B | 14.8-15.2 | 17 max | 15.7 max |
| C | 12.7-13.3 | 13.5 min | 12.6 min |
| D | 2.54 | 2.54 | 2.54 |
| E | 8.5-9.4 | | |
| F | 2.8-2.9 | 4.0-4.4 | 3.0 ±0.2 |
| G | 4.4-4.5 | 4.4 max | 4.7 max |
| H | 1.25-1.35 | 2.9 max | 1.32 |
| I | 2.8-3.0 | 1.5 | 2.9 |
| J | 0.8-0.95 | 0.7-0.9 | 0.76 |
| K | 1.15-1.25 | 1.5 max | 1.3 |
| L | 1.8 max | 4.4 | 2.5 max |
| M | 3.6-3.7 | 3.0-3.2 | 3.6 ±0.2 |
| Man. | SG | PH | TO |

I4

P

TO220AB
SOT78

| x | 1 | 2 |
|---|---|---|
| A | 9.65-10.28 | 9.65-10.7 |
| B | 14.41-15.75 | 14.2-16.5 |
| C | 12.7-14.2 | 12.7-14.7 |
| D | 2.54 | 4.6-5.6 |
| E | | |
| F | 2.54-3.04 | 3.5-4.1 |
| G | 4.07-4.82 | 3.55-4.82 |
| H | 1.15-1.39 | 0.5-1.4 |
| I | 2.44-3.14 | 2.4-2.9 |
| J | 0.64-0.88 | 0.64-0.87 |
| K | 1.15-1.52 | 1.15-1.55 |
| L | 2.8-2.93 | 6.35 max |
| M | 3.61-3.79 | 3.5-4.1 |
| Man. | MO | NS |

I5

P

TO220AB
SOT78

| x | 1 |
|---|---|
| A | 10.6 max |
| B | 16.8 max |
| C | 12 min |
| D | 2.54 |
| E | 9.8 |
| F | 2.8 ±0.3 |
| G | 4.8 max |
| H | 1.3 ±0.2 |
| I | 2.7 ±0.3 |
| J | 0.74 ±0.1 |
| K | 1.4 ±0.1 |
| L | 6 max |
| M | 3.6-3.65 |
| Man. | RD |

I6

P

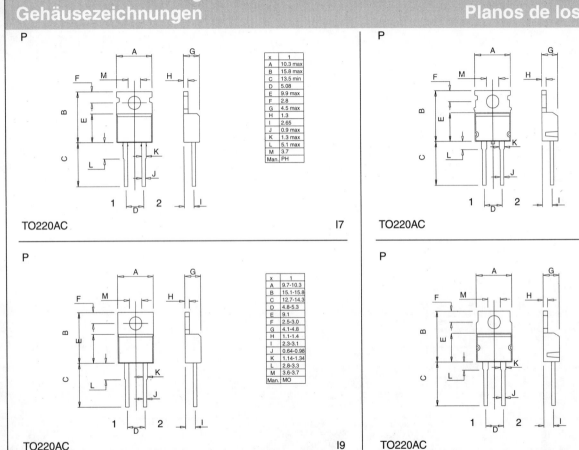

| x | 1 |
|---|---|
| A | 10.3 max |
| B | 15.8 max |
| C | 13.5 min |
| D | 5.08 |
| E | 9.9 max |
| F | 2.8 |
| G | 4.5 max |
| H | 1.3 |
| I | 2.65 |
| J | 0.9 max |
| K | 1.3 max |
| L | 5.1 max |
| M | 3.7 |
| Man. | PH |

TO220AC                                     I7

P

| x | 1 |
|---|---|
| A | 9.7-10.6 |
| B | 14.2-16.5 |
| C | 12.7-14.7 |
| D | 4.6-5.6 |
| E | 8.4 |
| F | 3.5-4.1 |
| G | 3.6-4.8 |
| H | 0.5-1.4 |
| I | 2.6-3.1 |
| J | 0.41-0.51 |
| K | 1.14-1.55 |
| L | 6.4 max |
| M | 3.5-4.1 |
| Man. | NS |

TO220AC                                     I8

P

| x | 1 |
|---|---|
| A | 9.7-10.3 |
| B | 15.1-15.8 |
| C | 12.7-14.3 |
| D | 4.8-5.3 |
| E | 9.1 |
| F | 2.5-3.0 |
| G | 4.1-4.8 |
| H | 1.1-1.4 |
| I | 2.3-3.1 |
| J | 0.64-0.98 |
| K | 1.14-1.34 |
| L | 2.8-3.3 |
| M | 3.6-3.7 |
| Man. | MO |

TO220AC                                     I9

P

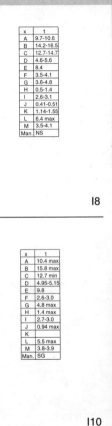

| x | 1 |
|---|---|
| A | 10.4 max |
| B | 15.8 max |
| C | 12.7 min |
| D | 4.95-5.15 |
| E | 9.8 |
| F | 2.6-3.0 |
| G | 4.8 max |
| H | 1.4 max |
| I | 2.7-3.0 |
| J | 0.94 max |
| K |  |
| L | 5.5 max |
| M | 3.8-3.9 |
| Man. | SG |

TO220AC                                     I10

P

| x | 1 |
|---|---|
| A | 10.2 ±0. |
| B | 16,0 ±0.2 |
| C | 12 max |
| D | 2.54 |
| E | 6.8 ±0.2 |
| F | 3.0 ±0.2 |
| G | 4.8 ±0.2 |
| H | 2.0 ±0.1 |
| I | .1 |
| J | 0.55-0.85 |
| K | 1.35 |
| L | 3.5-3.9 |
| M | 3.6-3.65 |
| Man. | RD |

**TO220AB**
**SOT78**

I11

P

| x | 1 |
|---|---|
| A | 10.4 max |
| B | 15.8 max |
| C | 12.7 min |
| D | 5.05 ±0.1 |
| E | 9.8 |
| F | 2.6-3.0 |
| G | 4.8 max |
| H | 1.4 max |
| I | 2.7-3.0 |
| J | 0.94 max |
| K | |
| L | 5.5 max |
| M | 3.8-3.9 |
| Man. | SG |

**TO220AB**

I12

P

| x | 1 |
|---|---|
| A | 10.3 ±0.3 |
| B | 14.2-15.9 |
| C | 12.7-14.7 |
| D | 5.08 ±0.5 |
| E | 8.9 |
| F | 2.5-3.0 |
| G | 4.7 ±0.2 |
| H | 1.26 ±0.1 |
| I | 2.7 ±0.3 |
| J | 0.6 ±0.16 |
| K | 1.35 |
| L | 4.5 max |
| Man. | SG |

**DO220(I)**

I13

P

| | 1 |
|---|---|
| A | 15.2-15.4 |
| B | 20.7-21.1 |
| C | 15-15.0 |
| D | 11.0 |
| E | 3.4 min |
| F | 1.2-1.4 |
| G | 4.1-4.2 |
| H | 1.45-1.55 |
| I | 4.4-4.5 |
| J | 2.7-2.9 |
| Man. | SG |

**DOP3**

I14

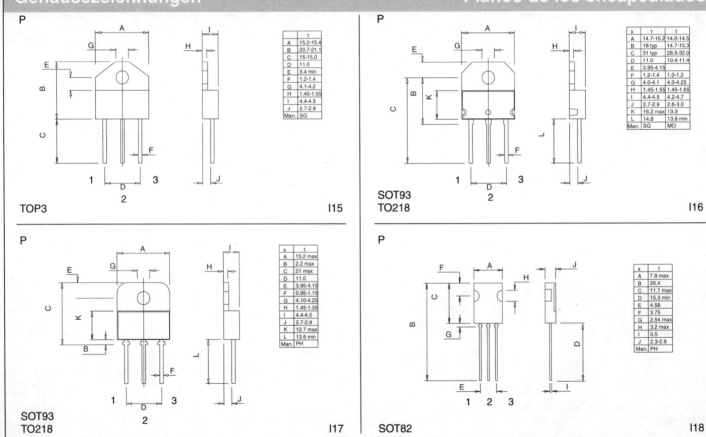

P

| | 1 |
|---|---|
| A | 15.2-15.4 |
| B | 20.7-21.1 |
| C | 15-15.0 |
| D | 11.0 |
| E | 3.4 min |
| F | 1.2-1.4 |
| G | 4.1-4.2 |
| H | 1.45-1.55 |
| I | 4.4-4.5 |
| J | 2.7-2.9 |
| Man. | SG |

TOP3                                                                     I15

P

| x | 1 | 1 |
|---|---|---|
| A | 14.7-15.2 | 14.0-14.5 |
| B | 18 typ | 14.7-15.3 |
| C | 31 typ | 28.5-32.0 |
| D | 11.0 | 10.4-11.4 |
| E | 3.95-4.15 | |
| F | 1.2-1.4 | 1.0-1.2 |
| G | 4.0-4.1 | 4.0-4.25 |
| H | 1.45-1.55 | 1.45-1.65 |
| I | 4.4-4.5 | 4.2-4.7 |
| J | 2.7-2.9 | 2.6-3.0 |
| K | 16.2 max | 13.3 |
| L | 14.8 | 13.8 min |
| Man. | SG | MO |

SOT93
TO218                                                                    I16

P

| x | 1 |
|---|---|
| A | 15.2 max |
| B | 2.2 max |
| C | 21 max |
| D | 11.0 |
| E | 3.95-4.15 |
| F | 0.95-1.15 |
| G | 4.10-4.25 |
| H | 1.45-1.55 |
| I | 4.4-4.5 |
| J | 2.7-2.9 |
| K | 12.7 max |
| L | 13.6 min |
| Man. | PH |

SOT93
TO218                                                                    I17

P

| x | 1 |
|---|---|
| A | 7.8 max |
| B | 26.4 |
| C | 11.1 max |
| D | 15.3 min |
| E | 4.58 |
| F | 3.75 |
| G | 2.54 max |
| H | 3.2 max |
| I | 0.5 |
| J | 2.3-2.8 |
| Man. | PH |

SOT82                                                                    I18

# Case Outline Drawings
# Gehäusezeichnungen

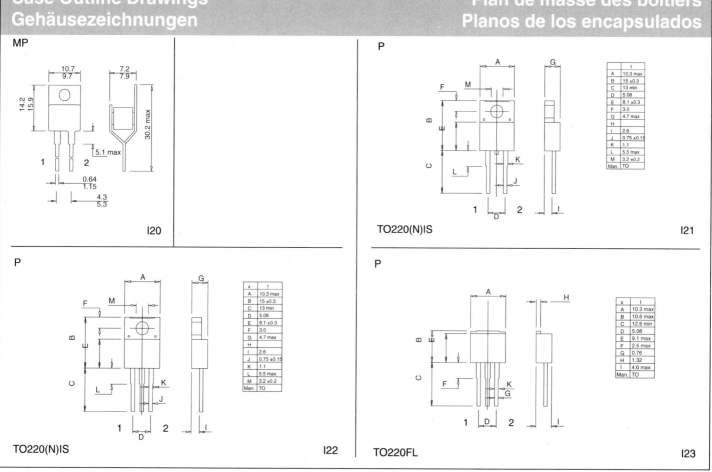

**MP**

I20

**P**

TO220(N)IS

| | 1 |
|---|---|
| A | 10.3 max |
| B | 15 ±0.3 |
| C | 13 min |
| D | 5.08 |
| E | 8.1 ±0.3 |
| F | 3.0 |
| G | 4.7 max |
| H | |
| I | 2.6 |
| J | 0.75 ±0.15 |
| K | 1.1 |
| L | 5.5 max |
| M | 3.2 ±0.2 |
| Man. | TO |

I21

**P**

TO220(N)IS

| x | 1 |
|---|---|
| A | 10.3 max |
| B | 15 ±0.3 |
| C | 13 min |
| D | 5.08 |
| E | 8.1 ±0.3 |
| F | 3.0 |
| G | 4.7 max |
| H | |
| I | 2.6 |
| J | 0.75 ±0.15 |
| K | 1.1 |
| L | 5.5 max |
| M | 3.2 ±0.2 |
| Man. | TO |

I22

**P**

TO220FL

| x | 1 |
|---|---|
| A | 10.3 max |
| B | 10.6 max |
| C | 12.6 min |
| D | 5.08 |
| E | 9.1 max |
| F | 2.5 max |
| G | 0.76 |
| H | 1.32 |
| I | 4.0 max |
| Man. | TO |

I23

P

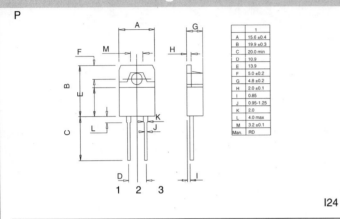

| | 1 |
|---|---|
| A | 15.6 ±0.4 |
| B | 19.9 ±0.3 |
| C | 20.0 min |
| D | 10.9 |
| E | 13.9 |
| F | 5.0 ±0.2 |
| G | 4.8 ±0.2 |
| H | 2.0 ±0.1 |
| I | 0.85 |
| J | 0.95-1.25 |
| K | 2.0 |
| L | 4.0 max |
| M | 3.2 ±0.1 |
| Man. | RD |

I24

P

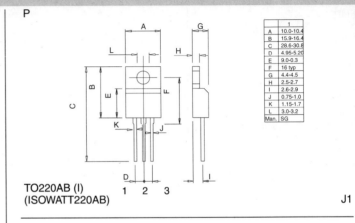

| | 1 |
|---|---|
| A | 10.0-10.4 |
| B | 15.9-16.4 |
| C | 28.6-30.8 |
| D | 4.95-5.20 |
| E | 9.0-0.3 |
| F | 16 typ |
| G | 4.4-4.5 |
| H | 2.5-2.7 |
| I | 2.6-2.9 |
| J | 0.75-1.0 |
| K | 1.15-1.7 |
| L | 3.0-3.2 |
| Man. | SG |

TO220AB (I)
(ISOWATT220AB)

J1

P

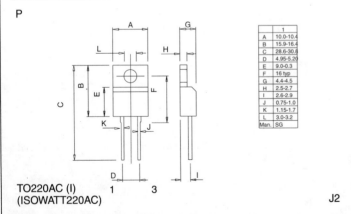

| | 1 |
|---|---|
| A | 10.0-10.4 |
| B | 15.9-16.4 |
| C | 28.6-30.8 |
| D | 4.95-5.20 |
| E | 9.0-0.3 |
| F | 16 typ |
| G | 4.4-4.5 |
| H | 2.5-2.7 |
| I | 2.6-2.9 |
| J | 0.75-1.0 |
| K | 1.15-1.7 |
| L | 3.0-3.2 |
| Man. | SG |

TO220AC (I)
(ISOWATT220AC)

J2

P

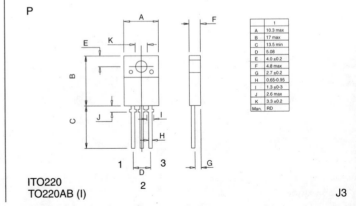

| | 1 |
|---|---|
| A | 10.3 max |
| B | 17 max |
| C | 13.5 min |
| D | 5.08 |
| E | 4.0 ±0.2 |
| F | 4.8 max |
| G | 2.7 ±0.2 |
| H | 0.65-0.95 |
| I | 1.3 ±0-3 |
| J | 2.6 max |
| K | 3.3 ±0.2 |
| Man. | RD |

ITO220
TO220AB (I)

J3

P

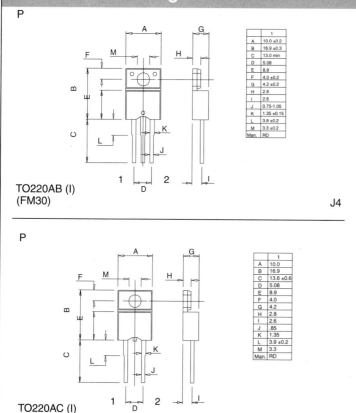

TO220AB (I)
(FM30)

| | 1 |
|---|---|
| A | 10.0 ±0.2 |
| B | 16.9 ±0.3 |
| C | 13.0 min |
| D | 5.08 |
| E | 8.9 |
| F | 4.0 ±0.2 |
| G | 4.2 ±0.2 |
| H | 2.8 |
| I | 2.6 |
| J | 0.75-1.05 |
| K | 1.35 ±0.15 |
| L | 3.9 ±0.2 |
| M | 3.3 ±0.2 |
| Man. | RD |

J4

P

TO220AC (I)
(FM20)

| | 1 |
|---|---|
| A | 10.0 |
| B | 16.9 |
| C | 13.6 ±0.6 |
| D | 5.08 |
| E | 8.9 |
| F | 4.0 |
| G | 4.2 |
| H | 2.8 |
| I | 2.6 |
| J | .85 |
| K | 1.35 |
| L | 3.9 ±0.2 |
| M | 3.3 |
| Man. | RD |

J6

P

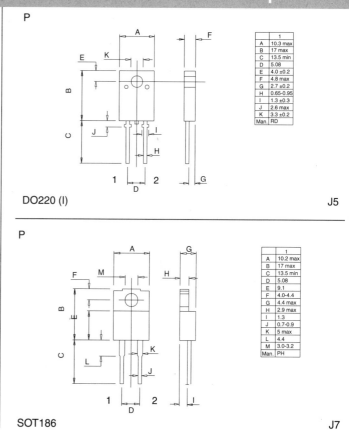

DO220 (I)

| | 1 |
|---|---|
| A | 10.3 max |
| B | 17 max |
| C | 13.5 min |
| D | 5.08 |
| E | 4.0 ±0.2 |
| F | 4.8 max |
| G | 2.7 ±0.2 |
| H | 0.65-0.95 |
| I | 1.3 ±0.3 |
| J | 2.6 max |
| K | 3.3 ±0.2 |
| Man. | RD |

J5

P

SOT186

| | 1 |
|---|---|
| A | 10.2 max |
| B | 17 max |
| C | 13.5 min |
| D | 5.08 |
| E | 9.1 |
| F | 4.0-4.4 |
| G | 4.4 max |
| H | 2.9 max |
| I | 1.3 |
| J | 0.7-0.9 |
| K | 5 max |
| L | 4.4 |
| M | 3.0-3.2 |
| Man. | PH |

J7

P

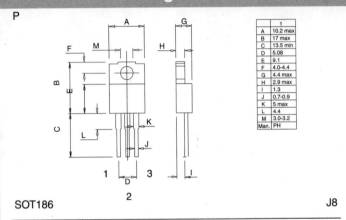

| | 1 |
|---|---|
| A | 10.2 max |
| B | 17 max |
| C | 13.5 min |
| D | 5.08 |
| E | 9.1 |
| F | 4.0-4.4 |
| G | 4.4 max |
| H | 2.9 max |
| I | 1.3 |
| J | 0.7-0.9 |
| K | 5 max |
| L | 4.4 |
| M | 3.0-3.2 |
| Man. | PH |

SOT186　　　　　　　　　　　　　J8

P

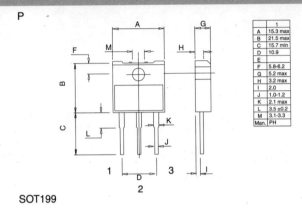

| | 1 |
|---|---|
| A | 15.3 max |
| B | 21.5 max |
| C | 15.7 min |
| D | 10.9 |
| E | |
| F | 5.8-6.2 |
| G | 5.2 max |
| H | 3.2 max |
| I | 2.0 |
| J | 1.0-1.2 |
| K | 2.1 max |
| L | 3.5 ±0.2 |
| M | 3.1-3.3 |
| Man. | PH |

SOT199　　　　　　　　　　　　　J9

P

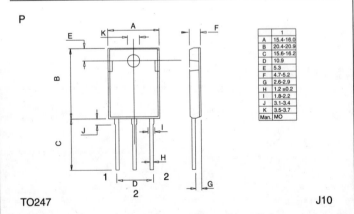

| | 1 |
|---|---|
| A | 15.4-16.0 |
| B | 20.4-20.9 |
| C | 15.6-16.2 |
| D | 10.9 |
| E | 5.3 |
| F | 4.7-5.2 |
| G | 2.6-2.9 |
| H | 1.2 ±0.2 |
| I | 1.8-2.2 |
| J | 3.1-3.4 |
| K | 3.5-3.7 |
| Man. | MO |

TO247　　　　　　　　　　　　　J10

P

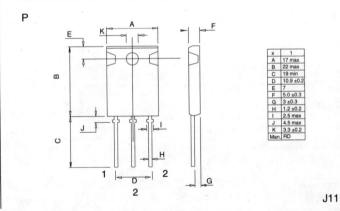

| x | 1 |
|---|---|
| A | 17 max |
| B | 22 max |
| C | 19 min |
| D | 10.9 ±0.2 |
| E | 7 |
| F | 5.0 ±0.3 |
| G | 3 ±0.3 |
| H | 1.2 ±0.2 |
| I | 2.5 max |
| J | 4.5 max |
| K | 3.3 ±0.2 |
| Man. | RD |

J11

P

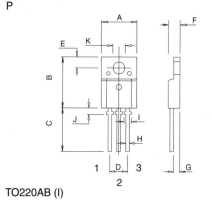

| x | 1 |
|---|---|
| A | 10.0-10.2 |
| B | 15.8-16.0 |
| C | 12.7-14.3 |
| D | 5.08 |
| E | 3.2-3.4 |
| F | 4.6-4.8 |
| G | 2.7-2.8 |
| H | 0.67-0.86 |
| I | 1.14-1.52 |
| J | 3.3-3.3 |
| K | 3.1-3.3 |
| Man. | MO |

TO220AB (I)                                    J12

P

| | 1 |
|---|---|
| A | 15.0 max |
| B | 20 ±0.3 |
| C | 20.5 ±0.5 |
| D | 10.9 ±0.2 |
| E | 2.0 |
| F | 4.8 max |
| G | 2.8 max |
| H | 0.75-1.3 |
| I | 2.0 ±0.3 |
| J | 3.3 max |
| K | 3.2 ±0.2 |
| Man. | TO |

TO3P(N)                                        J13

P

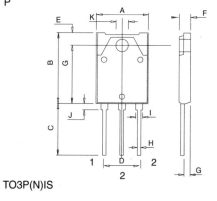

| | 1 |
|---|---|
| A | 15.8 ±0.5 |
| B | 21 ±0.5 |
| C | 19.4 min |
| D | 10.9 ±0.2 |
| E | 5.5 |
| F | 5.3 ±0.3 |
| G | 15.5 |
| H | 0.75-1.15 |
| I | 2.0 ±0.25 |
| J | 3.6 max |
| K | 3.6 ±0.2 |
| Man. | TO |

TO3P(N)IS                                      J14

P

| | 1 |
|---|---|
| A | 15.5 ±0.5 |
| B | 26.5 ±0.5 |
| C | 16.4 min |
| D | 10.9 |
| E | 15.1 |
| F | 4.5 |
| G | 5.5 ±0.3 |
| H | 3.0 ±0.3 |
| I | 3.3 |
| J | 0.95 max |
| K | 2.0 |
| L | 4.5 |
| M | 3.6 ±0.3 |
| Man. | TO |

DO3P(H)IS                                      J15

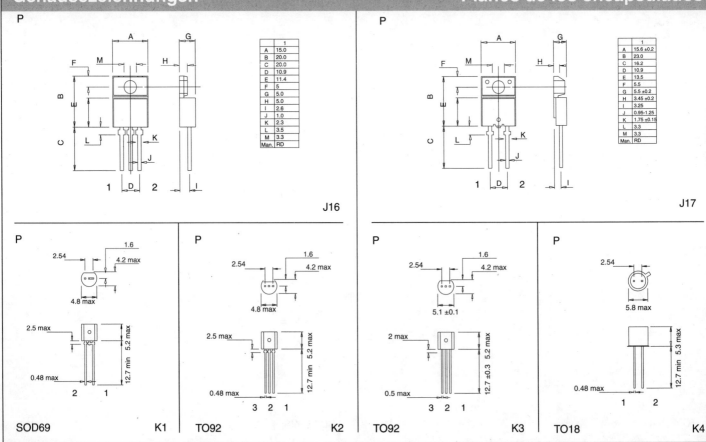

**P**

| | 1 |
|---|---|
| A | 15.0 |
| B | 20.0 |
| C | 20.0 |
| D | 10.9 |
| E | 11.4 |
| F | 5 |
| G | 5.0 |
| H | 5.0 |
| I | 2.6 |
| J | 1.0 |
| K | 2.3 |
| L | 3.5 |
| M | 3.3 |
| Man. | RD |

J16

**P**

| | 1 |
|---|---|
| A | 15.6 ±0.2 |
| B | 23.0 |
| C | 16.2 |
| D | 10.9 |
| E | 13.5 |
| F | 5.5 |
| G | 5.5 ±0.2 |
| H | 3.45 ±0.2 |
| I | 3.25 |
| J | 0.95-1.25 |
| K | 1.75 ±0.15 |
| L | 3.3 |
| M | 3.3 |
| Man. | RD |

J17

SOD69     K1

TO92     K2

TO92     K3

TO18     K4

M

| | 1 |
|---|---|
| A | 39.4 max |
| B | 30.2 |
| C | 21.1 max |
| D | 26.7 max |
| E | 10.9 |
| F | 16.9 |
| G | 3.85-4.1 |
| H | 3.4 |
| I | 6.4-11.4 |
| J | 1.0-1.1 |
| Man. | MO |

TO204AA                                    L1

M

| | 1 |
|---|---|
| A | 39.4 max |
| B | 30.2 |
| C | 21.1 max |
| D | 26.7 max |
| E | 10.9 |
| F | 16.9 |
| G | 3.85-4.1 |
| H | 3.4 |
| I | 6.4-11.4 |
| J | 1.0-1.1 |
| Man. | MO |

TO204AA                                    L2

P

TO1                          M1

P

N1

P

SOD28                        N2

P

SOD28                        N3

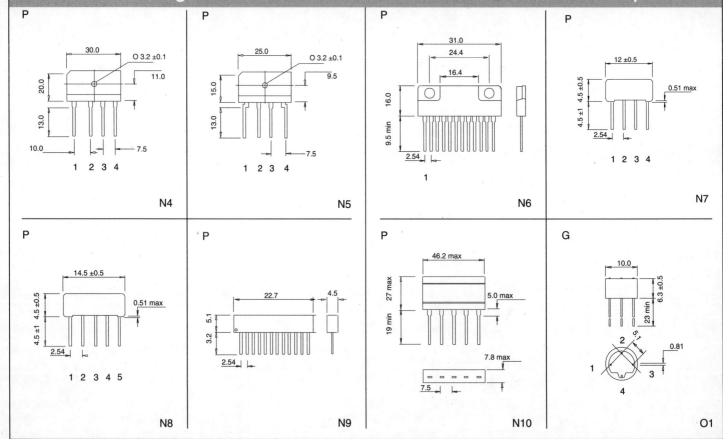

N4

N5

N6

N7

N8

N9

N10

O1

P

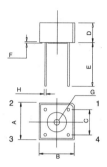

| x | 1 |
|---|---|
| A | 13 max |
| B | 13 max |
| C | 7.5 ±0.5 |
| D | 7 max |
| E | 16 min |
| F | 0.5 |
| G | 3.2 |
| H | 0.8 |
| Man. | TO |

O2

P

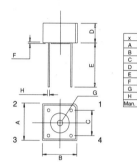

| x | 1 |
|---|---|
| A | 15.5 max |
| B | 15.5 max |
| C | 10 ±1 |
| D | 7 max |
| E | 16 min |
| F | 0.2 |
| G | 3.2 |
| H | 1.0 |
| Man. | TO |

O3

P

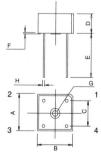

| x | 1 | 2 |
|---|---|---|
| A | 17.5 max | 17 max |
| B | 17.5 max | 17 max |
| C | 10 ±0.5 | 10 |
| D | 7 ±0.5 | 7.5 max |
| E | 11 min | 25 min |
| F | 0.5 | |
| G | 3.2 | 6 max |
| H | 1.5 | 1.4 ±0.1 |
| Man. | TO | RD |

O4

P

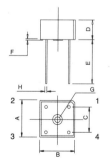

| | 1 | 2 |
|---|---|---|
| A | 25 max | 25 max |
| B | 25 max | 25 max |
| C | 15 ±0.5 | 15 |
| D | 8 ±0.5 | 7.5 max |
| E | 17 min | 25 min |
| F | 0.5 | |
| G | 3.2 | 7 max |
| H | 1.5 | 1.4 ±0.1 |
| Man. | TO | RD |

O5

P

|     | 1 | 2 |
|-----|-----------|-----------|
| A | 25.5 max | 25.5 max |
| B | 25.5 max | 25.5 max |
| C | 18 | 19 |
| D | 8.0 | 11.0 |
| E | 14 max | 14 max |
| F | 9 | 9 max |
| G | 4.5 | 4.5 |
| H | 6.35 | 6.35 |
| Man. | TO | RD |

O6

P

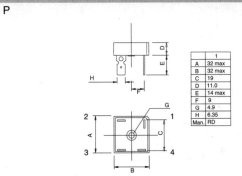

|     | 1 |
|-----|---------|
| A | 32 max |
| B | 32 max |
| C | 19 |
| D | 11.0 |
| E | 14 max |
| F | 9 |
| G | 4.9 |
| H | 6.35 |
| Man. | RD |

O7

P

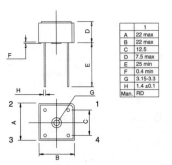

|     | 1 |
|-----|---------|
| A | 22 max |
| B | 22 max |
| C | 12.5 |
| D | 7.5 max |
| E | 25 min |
| F | 0.4 min |
| G | 3.15-3.3 |
| H | 1.4 ±0.1 |
| Man. | RD |

O8

P

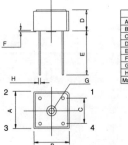

|     | 1 |
|-----|---------|
| A | 26.5 max |
| B | 26.5 max |
| C | 15 |
| D | 7.5 max |
| E | 25 min |
| F | 0.4 min |
| G | 4.5 |
| H | 1.6 |
| Man. | RD |

O9

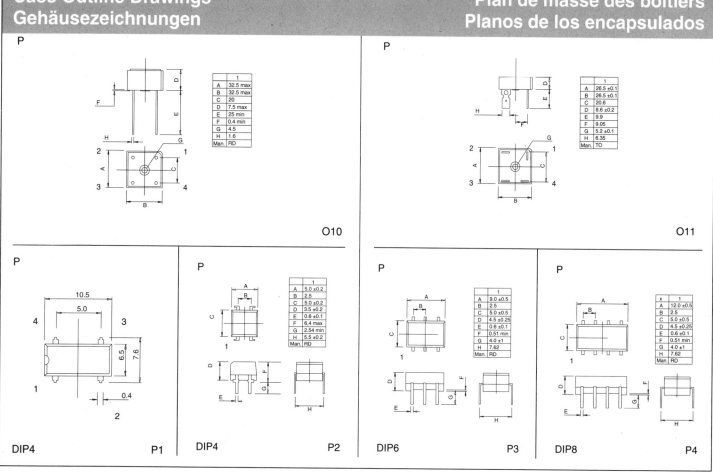

P

|      | 1        |
|------|----------|
| A    | 32.5 max |
| B    | 32.5 max |
| C    | 20       |
| D    | 7.5 max  |
| E    | 25 min   |
| F    | 0.4 min  |
| G    | 4.5      |
| H    | 1.6      |
| Man. | RD       |

O10

P

|      | 1        |
|------|----------|
| A    | 26.5 ±0.1 |
| B    | 26.5 ±0.1 |
| C    | 20.6     |
| D    | 8.6 ±0.2 |
| E    | 9.9      |
| F    | 9.05     |
| G    | 5.2 ±0.1 |
| H    | 6.35     |
| Man. | TO       |

O11

P

DIP4                 P1

P

|      | 1        |
|------|----------|
| A    | 5.0 ±0.2 |
| B    | 2.5      |
| C    | 5.0 ±0.2 |
| D    | 3.5 ±0.2 |
| E    | 0.6 ±0.1 |
| F    | 6,4 max  |
| G    | 2.54 min |
| H    | 5.5 ±0.2 |
| Man. | RD       |

DIP4                 P2

P

|      | 1        |
|------|----------|
| A    | 9.0 ±0.5 |
| B    | 2.5      |
| C    | 5.0 ±0.5 |
| D    | 4.5 ±0.25 |
| E    | 0.6 ±0.1 |
| F    | 0.51 min |
| G    | 4.0 ±1   |
| H    | 7.62     |
| Man. | RD       |

DIP6                 P3

P

|      | x        | 1        |
|------|----------|----------|
| A    |          | 12.0 ±0.5 |
| B    |          | 2.5      |
| C    |          | 5.0 ±0.5 |
| D    |          | 4.5 ±0.25 |
| E    |          | 0.6 ±0.1 |
| F    |          | 0.51 min |
| G    |          | 4.0 ±1   |
| H    |          | 7.62     |
| Man. |          | RD       |

DIP8                 P4

IWT
SEMICONDUCTOR
REFERENCE

● Parametric search
● More than 20 000
  up-to-date devices
● Data export to other
  applications

iWT
INTERNATIONAL
THOMSON PUBLISHING

Diodes & Logic Devices

English, Deutsch, Français, Espãnol

Auswählen von Halbleiter-Bau-elementen in Sekunden-schnelle mit der iwt semiconductor reference: Per Mausklick kann der Anwender auf über 7000 verschiedene Diodentypen sowie über 700 Logikchips mit mehr als 20.000 Vergleichstypen zugreifen. Jeder Typ ist mit seinen wichtigsten Kenndaten und anwendungsrelevanten Eigenschaften beschrieben. Über 2000 Vektorgraphiken zeigen Gehäuseform/ -bemaßung, Anschlußbilder,

Funktionstabellen, Logiksymbole und Schaltzeichen. Funktionen wie parametrische Suche ermöglichen es, eine Auswahl nach vorzugebenden Grenz- bzw. Kenndaten zu treffen. Mit der integrierten Exportfunktion kann der Anwender Gehäusezeichnungen oder Bauteilelisten via Clipboard in andere Anwendungen übernehmen.

**Behandelte Dioden:**
Kleinsignal- und Gleichrichterdioden, Z-Dioden, C-Dioden, Suppressordioden, Diodenpaare, Gleichrichterbrücken

**Behandelte Logikbausteine:**
4000- / 74HC4000-CMOS-Serie mit HL-, LV- und SSMD-Typen, 7400 CMOS- & TTL-Serie mit SN-, LS-, HC- und ACT-Typen.

iWT
INTERNATIONAL
THOMSON PUBLISHING

**IWT-Verlag GmbH**

Königswinterer Straße 418
53 227 Bonn
Tel.: 0228 / 97 02 4-0
Fax.: 0228 /44 13 42

CD-ROM mit Handbuch,
erscheint ca. 2. Quartal 1995,
ca. 198.- DM (unverbindliche Preisempfehlung)
ISBN 3-88322-2616-8